Audiovisual Speech Processing

When we speak, we configure the vocal tract which shapes the visible motions of the face and the patterning of the audible speech acoustics. Similarly, we use these visible and audible behaviors to perceive speech. This book showcases a broad range of research investigating how these two types of signals are used in spoken communication, how they interact, and how they can be used to enhance the realistic synthesis and recognition of audible and visible speech. The volume begins by addressing two important questions about human audiovisual performance: how auditory and visual signals combine to access the mental lexicon, and where in the brain this and related processes take place. It then turns to the production and perception of multimodal speech, and how structures are coordinated within and across the two modalities. Finally, the book presents overviews and recent developments in machine-based speech recognition and synthesis of AV speech.

GÉRARD BAILLY is a senior CNRS Research Director at the Speech and Cognition Department, GIPSA-Lab, University of Grenoble where he is now Head of Department.

PASCAL PERRIER is a professor in the GIPSA-Lab at the University of Grenoble.

ERIC VATIKIOTIS-BATESON is Professor in the Department of Linguistics and Director of the Cognitive Systems program at the University of British Colombia.

Audiovisual Speech Processing

Edited by
Gérard Bailly, Pascal Perrier, and Eric Vatikiotis-Bateson

CAMBRIDGE
UNIVERSITY PRESS

CAMBRIDGE UNIVERSITY PRESS
Cambridge, New York, Melbourne, Madrid, Cape Town,
Singapore, São Paulo, Delhi, Mexico City

Cambridge University Press
The Edinburgh Building, Cambridge CB2 8RU, UK

Published in the United States of America by Cambridge University Press, New York

www.cambridge.org
Information on this title: www.cambridge.org/9781107006829

First published 2012

Printed in the United Kingdom at the University Press, Cambridge

A catalog record for this publication is available from the British Library

Library of Congress Cataloging in Publication data
Audiovisual speech processing / [edited by] G. Bailly, P. Perrier,
and E. Vatikiotis-Bateson.
p. ; cm.
Includes bibliographical references and index.
ISBN 978-1-107-00682-9 (hardback)
I. Bailly, G. (Gérard) II. Perrier, Pascal. III. Vatikiotis-Bateson, Eric.
[DNLM: 1. Speech Perception. 2. Lipreading. 3. Phonetics.
4. Speech – physiology. 5. Visual Perception. WV 272]
616.85′5–dc23

2011053319

ISBN 978-1-107-00682-9 Hardback

Dedicated to Christian Benoît (1956–1998)

Contents

Figures

Tables

Contributors

VIRGINIE ATTINA MARCS Auditory Laboratories, University of Western Sydney – Australia. Dr. Virginie Attina did her doctoral research on the production and perception of Cued Speech at GIPSA-Lab, Grenoble, France. She then worked on the phonology of the deaf exposed to Cued Speech at the University of La Laguna, Spain. In 2007, she joined the Brain Dynamics and Cognition lab (U821, INSERM, Bron, France) to work on new interfaces in the study of cerebral activity. She is now a postdoctoral research fellow at MARCS Auditory Laboratories (UWS, Australia) working on tone languages with Professor D. Burnham. She is more generally interested in multimodal speech production, perception, and integration using a wide range of techniques (motion capture, eyetracking, and electrophysiology).

PIERRE BADIN Speech and Cognition Department, GIPSA-Lab, CNRS & Grenoble University – France. Pierre Badin is a senior CNRS Research Director at the Speech and Cognition Department, GIPSA-lab, Grenoble. Head of the "Vocal Tract Acoustics" team from 1990 to 2002, Associate Director of the Grenoble ICP from 2003 to 2006, he has been Deputy Head of the department since 2007. He has worked in the field of speech communication for more than thirty years. He gained international experience through extended research periods in Sweden, Japan, and UK, and is involved in a number of national and international projects. He is associate editor for speech at *Acta Acustica*, and a reviewer for many international journals. His current interest is speech production and articulatory modeling, with an emphasis on data acquisition, development of virtual talking heads for augmented speech, and speech inversion.

GÉRARD BAILLY Speech and Cognition Department, GIPSA-Lab, CNRS & Grenoble University – France. Gérard Bailly is a senior CNRS Research Director at the Speech and Cognition Department, GIPSA-lab, Grenoble where he is now Head of Department. He has worked in the field of speech communication for more than twenty-five years. He has supervised 20 PhD

Theses and authored 32 journal papers and over 200 book chapters and papers in major international conferences. He coedited *Talking Machines: Theories, Models and Designs* (1992) and *Improvements in Speech Synthesis* (2002). He is associate editor for the *Journal of Acoustics, Speech & Music Processing*, the *Journal of Multimodal User Interfaces* and a reviewer for many international journals. He is a founder member of the ISCA SynSIG and SproSIG special-interest groups. His current interest is multimodal and situated interaction with conversational agents using speech, facial expressions, head movements, and eye gaze.

DENIS BEAUTEMPS Speech and Cognition Department, GIPSA-Lab, CNRS & Grenoble University – France. Denis Beautemps is a CNRS Researcher at the Speech and Cognition Department, GIPSA-lab, Grenoble. He has worked in the field of speech communication for more than ten years. He is now the head of the "Talking Machines, Conversational Agents, Face-to-Face interaction" team. His current interest is multimodal and supplemented speech, fusion of multimodal components. He is particularly studying the perception, production, and automatic processing of Cued Speech.

ATEF BEN YOUSSEF Speech and Cognition Department, GIPSA-Lab, CNRS & Grenoble University – France. Atef Ben Youssef is a PhD student in signal, image, speech, and telecoms at Polytechnic Institute of Grenoble, France. He has an MSc from Grenoble University III, France and Monastir University, Tunisia. He joined GIPSA-Lab in 2008. His thesis focused on talking heads for augmented speech communication and his research interests are in the area of speech analysis and include speech production, synthesis, recognition, and multimodal processing. He works on acoustic-to-articulatory speech inversion using statistical methods, e.g. acoustic phone recognition, articulatory phone synthesis.

LYNNE BERNSTEIN Department of Speech and Hearing Sciences, George Washington University – USA. Lynne E. Bernstein is a Professor in the Speech and Hearing Sciences Department of the George Washington University, Washington, DC. There, she leads the Communication Neuroscience Laboratory. She is also the Program Director for the Cognitive Neuroscience Program of the US National Science Foundation. For almost fifteen years, until the past year, her laboratory was located at the House Ear Institute in Los Angeles, California. Her research has focused on speech perception, lipreading, and multisensory integration in hearing and deaf adults.

JONAS BESKOW Centre for Speech Technology, KTH, Stockholm – Sweden Jonas Beskow is Associate Professor at the KTH Centre for Speech

Technology (Stockholm, Sweden). His research interests are in the areas of visual and acoustic speech processing and synthesis and embodied conversational agents, and application of audiovisual speech technology to facilitation of human communication. One example of this is the SynFace system for real-time lipreading support for hard-of-hearing persons. Jonas has also had a key role in the development of WaveSurfer, an open-source application used by speech and audio researchers worldwide. In 1998–1999 Jonas spent eighteen months at the Perceptual Science Lab at University of California Santa Cruz supported by a Fulbright grant. In 2006 he received the Chester Carlson Award from Xerox and the Royal Swedish Academy of Engineering Science.

CHRISTOPH BREGLER Vision Learning Graphics (VLG) Group, Courant Institute, New York University – USA Chris Bregler is an Associate Professor of Computer Science at NYU's Courant Institute. He received his MS and PhD in Computer Science from UC Berkeley in 1995 and 1998 and his Diplom from Karlsruhe University in 1993. Prior to NYU he was on the faculty at Stanford University and worked for several companies including Hewlett Packard, Interval, Disney Feature Animation, and LucasFilm's ILM. He founded the Stanford Movement Group and the NYU Movement Group, which does research in vision and graphics with a focus on motion capture, animation, interactive media, and applications to entertainment, art, and medicine. This resulted in numerous publications, patents, and awards from the National Science Foundation, Sloan Foundation, Packard Foundation, Office of Naval Research, Electronic Arts, Microsoft, and other sources. He was named Stanford Joyce Faculty Fellow and Terman Fellow in 1999. He received the Olympus Prize for achievements in computer vision and AI in 2002, and was named a Sloan Research Fellow in 2003. He was the chair for the SIGGRAPH 2004 Electronic Theater and Computer Animation Festival. At CVPR 2008 he was awarded the IEEE Longuet-Higgins Prize for "Fundamental Contributions in Computer Vision that have withstood the test of time."

N. MICHAEL BROOKE Lately with Department of Computer Science, University of Bath, Bath – UK. Lately Reader in Computing at the University of Bath and active in the field of audiovisual speech processing since 1978, N. Michael Brooke has been a visiting scientist at the MRC Institute of Hearing Research in Nottingham, at AT&T Bell Laboratories, Murray Hill, NJ, and at the Speech Unit of DRA Malvern. He was, with C. Benoît, a Co-Director of the NATO Advanced Study Institute meeting on Speech reading held at Bonas in 1995. He has lectured widely in the USA and Europe and has also been secretary, then chairman, of the Speech Group of the UK Institute of Acoustics. He retired in 1999.

VICKI BRUCE School of Psychology, Newcastle University, Newcastle upon Tyne – UK. Vicki Bruce graduated from Newnham College, University of Cambridge in 1974 with a BA in Natural Sciences and completed her PhD "Processing and remembering pictorial information" in 1977 at the MRC Applied Psychology Unit, supervised by Alan Baddeley. Bruce worked briefly as a demonstrator at Newcastle University before moving to the University of Nottingham as a Lecturer in 1978, where she was promoted to Reader in 1988 and Professor in 1990. In 1992 she moved to University of Stirling, where she was Deputy Principal for Research from 1995 until 2002. From 2002 to 2008 she was Vice Principal and Head of the College of Humanities and Social Science at the University of Edinburgh. In 2008 she became Head of the School of Psychology at Newcastle University. She is known for her work on human face perception and person memory, including face recognition and recall by eye-witnesses and gaze and other aspects of social cognition. She is also interested in visual cognition more generally.

DENIS BURNHAM MARCS Institute, University of Western Sydney – Australia. Following an honours degree (University of New England, Australia, 1974), and PhD (Monash University, 1980), Burnham was in the School of Psychology at the University of NSW for eighteen years before taking up the position of Inaugural Director of MARCS Auditory Laboratories, Sydney, Australia. MARCS Labs has over sixty members and specializes in speech and music research. Burnham's own research concerns five areas of speech perception and production: *Ontogenetic* studies of infants' and children's speech perception development; phonetic, attentional, and emotional aspects of *Special Speech Registers* to infants, foreigners, pets, lovers, and computers; *Cross-Language* studies on the relationship between speech perception and vocabulary, reading, and second language learning; *Auditory-Visual* speech perception studies with infants, children, and adults within and across languages; and *Lexical Tone*, an understudied but prevalent speech feature affording investigations of speech-music, and segmental-suprasegmental relationships. Burnham is President, Australasian Speech Science and Technology Association (ASSTA); Executive member, ARC Research Network on Human Communication Science (HCSNet); member of the International Advisory Council (IAC) and Interspeech Steering Committee (ISC) of the International Speech Communication Association (ISCA); and Co-founder/Vice-Chair, Auditory-Visual Speech Perception Association (AVISA). Burnham has been funded continuously by the Australian Research Council (ARC) and other grant bodies for the past twenty-six years, and has directed various large inter-disciplinary and international research projects. Currently he is lead

Chief Investigator (CI) on an ARC Discovery grant on tone perception (2009–2012); lead CI of an ARC and National Health and Medical Research Council Special Initiative, the $3.4M Thinking Head project (2005–2011) encompassing Embodied Conversational Agents and Human-Robot Interaction; and lead CI of the $1M ARC infrastructure project, the Big Australian Speech Corpus (Big ASC, 2010), in which 3 hours of speech data from 1000 people all around Australia are being collected.

RUTH CAMPBELL Deafness Cognition and Language (DCAL) Research Centre, UCL – UK. Ruth Campbell retired from University College London, where she was Professor of Communication Disorder from 1996 to 2008. Her previous appointments were at Goldsmiths College, University of London, and Oxford University. She trained as a cognitive psychologist and neuropsychologist and has had interests in the processes underlying speechreading for thirty years.

MARIE-AGNÈS CATHIARD Center for Research on the Imaginary (CRI), Grenoble University – France. Marie-Agnès Cathiard, Doctor in Cognitive Psychology of Mendès-France University (Grenoble), is Maître de Conférences in Phonetics and Cognition at Stendhal University (Grenoble). Her main interests are in visual and audiovisual speech perception and in the production and perception of French Cued Speech. Her recent projects at the Center for Research on the Imaginary (CRI Stendhal) deal with body-part illusions in speech (face and hand), within the cognitive framework concerned with limb and body phantom phenomena. International publications in: *Speech Communication* (Ed.), *Revue Parole*, *AMSE-Journals*, *Behavioral and Brain Sciences*, *NeuroImage*, *Perception & Psychophysics*; and in books: *Phonetics, Phonology, and Cognition* (2002); *Lecture Notes in Artificial Intelligence* (2006); *Emergence of Linguistic Abilities* (Cambridge, 2008); *Speech Motor Control* (2010); *Cued Speech* (2010).

RASHID CLARK Rashid Clark is currently an independent contractor, and was a part of the Perceptual Science Laboratory at the University of California, Santa Cruz from 1998–2002, contributing as a tools developer. He currently works in the gaming industry as a software engineer. His more general interests include merging the technical and the aesthetic, and currently develops the internet cartoon series, *The Cosmospolitans*. Rashid received his BA in Cybernetics from the University of California, Los Angeles in 1995.

MICHAEL M. COHEN Michael M. Cohen is a Principal Investigator on a SBIR research grant iGlasses: an automatic wearable speech supplement in face-to-face communication and classroom situations, awarded to Animated Speech Corporation, now TeachTown. He was previously a research associate in the Program in Experimental Psychology at the University of California – Santa Cruz. His research interests include speech perception and production, speechreading, information integration, learning, and computer facial animation. He received a BS in Computer Science and Psychology (1975) and an MS in Psychology (1979) from UW-Madison, and a PhD in Experimental Psychology (1984) from UC-Santa Cruz.

TONY EZZAT MIT – CBCL, McGovern Institute – USA. Tony Ezzat is a Research Affiliate at the Center for Biological and Computational Learning at MIT, as well as a Principal Scientist at Kayak.com. His research interests span a wide variety of topics including speech processing, auditory neuroscience, computer vision, computer graphics, and machine learning. His Thesis work on audiovisual speech synthesis received the Christian Benoit Prize in 2002.

GADI GEIGER MIT – CBCL, McGovern Institute – USA. Gadi Geiger is a Research Scientist at the Center for Biological and Computational Learning at MIT. His research is on visual and auditory perception. Over the last two decades his research has focused on visual and auditory perceptual aspects in dyslexia.

RAFAËL LABOISSIÈRE Space and Action, U864, INSERM/Claude Bernard University, Lyon 1 – France. Dr Rafael Laboissière was awarded his PhD by the Institut National Polytechnique de Grenoble in 1992 since when he has been a CNRS researcher in France. He worked on biomechanical and neurophysiological models of speech production at the Institut de la Communication Parlée, Grenoble till 2001. Between 2001 and 2005 he was the head of the Sensorimotor Coordination team at the Max Planck Institute for Human Cognitive and Brain Sciences in Munich, Germany. His current research interests involve human motor control and multisensory integration.

KAREN LANDER Department of Psychology, University of Manchester – UK. Dr. Karen Lander received her PhD from the University of Stirling in 1999. She then worked as a Research Fellow for one year, at the University of Stirling, on an ESRC grant awarded to Professor Vicki Bruce and herself. She has been a lecturer at the Department of Psychology, University of Manchester, since January 2001. She was promoted to Senior Lecturer in 2008, and has worked extensively on the role of movement in the recognition and learning of faces and more generally in face perception.

HÉLÈNE LOEVENBRÜCK Speech and Cognition Department, GIPSA-Lab, CNRS & Grenoble University – France. Hélène Loevenbruck is currently CNRS Research Associate at the Speech and Cognition Department of GIPSA-Lab. She received an engineering training in electronics, signal processing, and computer science and obtained an MSc in cognitive sciences in 1992. After her PhD at the former Institut de la Communication Parlée on articulatory control, she was assistant lecturer in computer science and obtained a second MSc in phonetics. In 1997–98 she spent a post-doctoral year at the Department of Linguistics of the Ohio State University in the United States. She was awarded a bronze medal from the CNRS in 2006 for her works on the neural correlates of vocal pointing. Her research areas include (i) the acoustic, articulatory, perceptual, and neural correlates of prosody, (ii) language development (prosody, phonology, crosslinguistic differences), (iii) auditory verbal hallucination in schizophrenia (EMG and fMRI), (iv) murmured, silent, and inner speech (NAM, EMG, ultrasound), (v) self/other speech perception.

JUERGEN LUETTIN Robert Bosch GmbH, Corporate Research (CR/AEA5) – Germany. Dr. Juergen Luettin was awarded his PhD by the University of Sheffield, UK in 1997. From 1997 to 2000 he headed the computer vision group at IDIAP (Dalle Molle Institute for Perceptual Artificial Intelligence), Switzerland, acquired several EU and national research projects in speech and image processing and has been an invited scientist at Johns Hopkins University, USA. From 2000 to 2002 he headed the pattern recognition group at Ascom AG, Switzerland and was responsible for research and development in video surveillance products. In 2002 he joined the video-based driver assistance systems division at Robert Bosch GmbH, Stuttgart. His current work is on electromobility and system development and he is also a consultant and instructor for systems and requirements engineering. Dr. Luettin has published over forty scientific articles.

MAIRÉAD MACSWEENEY Institute of Cognitive Neuroscience, University College London – UK. Dr. Mairéad MacSweeney is Wellcome Trust Career Development Research Fellow, based at the Institute of Cognitive Neuroscience, University College London. She trained as a psychologist and has a particular interest in the neurobiological basis of language processing in people born profoundly deaf. This includes sign language processing, reading, and speechreading.

DOMINIC W. MASSARO Department of Psychology, University of California – USA. Dominic W. Massaro is Professor of Psychology and Computer Engineering at the University of California, Santa Cruz. He is best known for his fuzzy logical model of perception, and more recently, for his development of the computer-animated talking head Baldi. Massaro is Director of the Perceptual Science Laboratory, past president of the Society for Computers in Psychology, book review editor for the *American Journal of Psychology*, founding Chair of UCSC's Digital Arts and New Media program, and was founding co-editor of the interdisciplinary journal *Interpreting*. He has been a Guggenheim Fellow, a University of Wisconsin Romnes Fellow, a James McKeen Cattell Fellow, an NIMH Fellow, and in 2006 was recognized as a Tech Museum Award Laureate. Massaro received his BA in Psychology from the University of California, Los Angeles in 1965, and completed his PhD in Mathematical Psychology at the University of Massachusetts, Amherst in 1968. After his postdoctoral work at the University of California, San Diego, he was Professor of Psychology at the University of Wisconsin, Madison from 1970 to 1979, before moving to UCSC where he has remained since. Massaro's research focuses on applying an information processing approach to the study of language, perception, memory, cognition, and decision making. In collaboration with Gregg Oden, he developed the fuzzy logical model of perception, which stresses the integration of multiple sources of information when modeling perception. Stemming from this early work, Massaro established a research program demonstrating the importance of information from the face in speech perception. As part of this program, Massaro, along with researcher Michael Cohen, developed the computer-animated talking head known as Baldi. The Baldi technology is special in its extraordinary accuracy, and has been expanded to speak in numerous languages. In recent years, Massaro has become more involved with applied research, using his talking head technology to benefit language learners, including those facing learning challenges such as deafness and autism. For this work, he was named a 2006 Tech Microsoft Education Award Laureate by the Tech Museum of Innovation.

IAIN MATTHEWS Disney Research, Pittsburgh – USA. Iain Matthews is a Senior Research Scientist at Disney Research, Pittsburgh, where he leads the computer vision group. He also holds an adjunct appointment at The Robotics Institute, Carnegie Mellon University. Prior to joining Disney he spent two years at Weta Digital working on the facial motion capture system for James Cameron's *Avatar*, and the upcoming Spielberg/Jackson movie *Tin Tin*. Between 1999–2007 he was post-doc then systems faculty at Carnegie Mellon University, working on real-time, high fidelity, non-rigid face tracking. He obtained his PhD in Audio-Visual Speech Recognition from the University of East Anglia in 1998.

KEVIN MUNHALL Departments of Psychology and Otolaryngology, Queen's University, Kingston, Canada Kevin Munhall is the director of the Queen's

Biological Communication Centre. He did his undergraduate studies at the University of Waterloo and his graduate work at McGill University under the supervision of David Ostry. He was a post-doctoral fellow at Haskins Laboratories from 1984–86 and following that he was a Research Scientist at Haskins. Munhall taught at York University in Toronto and the University of Western Ontario before taking up a position at Queen's University in 1990. His research has focused on coordination in articulation, auditory feedback in speech production and audiovisual speech communication.

CHALAPATHY NETI Human Language Technologies Department, IBM Thomas J. Watson, Research Center – USA. Chalapathy Neti is currently the Associate Director and Global Leader, Healthcare Transformation, at IBM Research. Previous to this, he was an Executive Architect in the Information Agenda organization, IBM Software Group where he consulted with healthcare institutions to develop an information management strategy for improved outcomes and efficiency. Prior to his assignment in Software Group, Chalapathy Neti was a Senior Manager for Information Analysis and Interaction technologies at IBM Research. In this role, he managed several research groups involved in developing text, image, and video analysis technologies and its application to bio-medical informatics, medical imaging, and real-time decision intelligence (e.g. customer intelligence, fraud detection, and video surveillance. Before taking on the senior management role, he held various senior technical and management positions including the CTO of IBM's Digital Media business, manager of audiovisual speech technologies and technical roles in rich media analysis (speech, audio, and video) and mining. He has been with IBM since 1990. Chalapathy Neti received his PhD degree in Biomedical Engineering from the Johns Hopkins University (1990), and BS degree from Indian Institute of Technology, Kanpur (1980). He has more than twenty years of advanced R&D experience and has authored over fifty articles (conference and journal) in various fields related to bio-medical informatics, medical imaging, speech and video analysis, computational neuroscience and VLSI design. He has sixteen patents and several pending. He is an active member of IEEE, a former member of IEEE Multimedia Signal Processing technical committee (2001–2004), an associate editor of *IEEE transactions on Multimedia* (2002–2005) and a guest editor for the *IBM Systems Journal*. He is currently a member of the Executive Review Board of MI3C (Medical Imaging Informatics Innovation Center – a collaboration between IBM and Mayo Clinic).

PASCAL PERRIER Speech and Cognition Department, GIPSA-Lab, CNRS & Grenoble University – France. Pascal Perrier was awarded a PhD in Electronic Systems by the Institut National Polytechnique de Grenoble in

1982 and an HDR (Accreditation in Research Supervision) in Speech Communication in 1990. He is currently a Professor at Grenoble INP, where he teaches digital signal processing, digital communication, and speech processing. He is a member of the research laboratory GIPSA-Lab, where he was the head of the research group on Acoustics Aeroacoustics, Biomechanics and Control from 2005 to 2009. He co-authored 50 peer-reviewed international journal articles or book chapters, and around 100 papers in international conference proceedings. He is co-editor of the book *Some Aspects of Speech and the Brain* published in 2009. He has established collaborative projects with labs in different parts of the world, in particular the Centre for General Linguistics (ZAS) in Berlin, the Speech Communication group at MIT in Cambridge, USA, the Phonetic Laboratory at UQAM in Montréal, Canada, the JAIST in Ishikawa, Japan, and the MAGIC lab at UBC in Vancouver, Canada. He was Chair of AFCP (Association Francophone de la Communication Parlée), Special Interest Group of ISCA, from 2005 to 2006. His research interests include speech motor control, biomechanical modeling of speech articulators, and the interaction between physical and linguistic constraints in speech production.

TOMASO A. POGGIO Massachusetts Institute of Technology, McGovern Institute for Brain Research, Brain and Cognitive Sciences Department – USA. Tomaso A. Poggio is the Eugene McDermott Professor at the Department of Brain and Cognitive Sciences; Co-Director, Center for Biological and Computational Learning (CBCL); member of the Computer Science and Artificial Intelligence Laboratory (CSAIL) at MIT; and a member of the faculty of the McGovern Institute for Brain Research at MIT. Previous to his appointments at MIT, he spent ten years at the Max Planck Institut für Biologische Kybernetik, Tübingen, Germany. Professor Poggio's current research focuses on mathematical theories of learning and on computational models of brain function with the goal to understand human intelligence and to build intelligent machines that can mimic human performance. Professor Poggio is a Founding Fellow of AAAI, a Foreign Member of the Italian Academy of Sciences, a Fellow of the American Academy of Arts and Sciences and a member of the American Association for the Advancement of Science (AAAS). He was awarded the Otto-Hahn-Medaille Award of the Max-Planck-Society, the Max Planck Research Award (with M. Fahle), from the Alexander von Humboldt Foundation, the MIT 50K Entrepreneurship Competition Award, the Laurea Honoris Causa from the University of Pavia in 2000 (Volta Bicentennial), the 2003 Gabor Award, and the 2009 Okawa Prize.

GERASIMOS POTAMIANOS Institute of Informatics and Telecommunications, NCSR "Demokritos" – Greece. Dr. Gerasimos Potamianos was awarded his

PhD in Electrical and Computer Engineering from Johns Hopkins University, in Baltimore, Maryland in 1994. Since then, he has worked in the US at the Center for Language and Speech Processing at Johns Hopkins, at AT&T Labs – Research, and at the IBM T. J. Watson Research Center, and in Greece at the Institute of Computer Science (ICS) at FORTH, Crete. He is currently Research Director at the National Center for Scientific Research, "Demokritos" in Athens, Greece. His interests span the areas of multimodal speech processing with applications to human–computer interaction and ambient intelligence, with particular emphasis on audiovisual speech processing, automatic speech recognition, multimedia signal processing and fusion, as well as multimodal scene analysis. He has published over ninety articles in these areas and holds seven patents.

ROBERT E. REMEZ Department of Psychology, Barnard College, Columbia University – USA. Robert E. Remez is Professor of Psychology at Barnard College of Columbia University. He is Chair of the Columbia University Seminar on Language & Cognition. He has been an Associate Editor of the journals *Perception & Psychophysics* and *Journal of Experimental Psychology: Human Perception and Performance*, and he is co-editor, with David Pisoni, of the *Handbook of Speech Perception*. A Fellow of the Acoustical Society of America, the Association for Psychological Science, the American Association for the Advancement of Science, and the American Psychological Association, his research reports have appeared in the *American Psychologist*, *Developmental Psychology*, *Ear & Hearing*, *Journal of Experimental Psychology*, *Journal of Phonetics*, *Journal of the Acoustical Society*, *Memory & Cognition*, *Attention*, *Perception & Psychophysics*, *Psychological Review*, *Psychological Science*, *Psychonomic Bulletin & Review*, *Scandinavian Journal of Psychology*, *Science*, and *Speech Communication*.

LIONEL REVÉRET Jean Kuntzman Laboratory (LJK), INRIA – Grenoble University – France. Lionel Revéret is an INRIA researcher. He is with the EVASION project (formerly iMAGIS), in the Rhone-Alpes Research Unit of the INRIA located near Grenoble. He was awarded his PhD by the Institute of Spoken Communication (ICP) of the INPG University in Grenoble in 1999. His doctoral thesis dealt with issues in analysis and synthesis of lip motion during speech production, combining video tracking, and 3D modeling. Part of this doctoral research was spent as a visiting scholar at the ATR-HIP laboratories in Japan. He has since been involved in a France Télécom research project to extend visual speech analysis and synthesis to the whole face, using 3D textured model of the head and articulatory control (project MOTHER). From July 2000 to September 2001 as a Post-Doctoral Researcher at the Computational Perception Laboratory (CPL) at

GeorgiaTech he worked with Professor Irfan Essa on combining studies on visual speech and facial expressions. He is currently working on video-based motion capture, in particular in the measurement of animal motion and plant motion under wind effect.

CHRISTOPHE SAVARIAUX Speech and Cognition Department, GIPSA-Lab, CNRS & Grenoble University – France. Christophe Savariaux is a CNRS research engineer in charge of the Stendhal experimentation platform. This platform is dedicated to the acquisition of multimodal speech data using different techniques, such as multiple cameras, electromagnetic articulography, and aerodynamic/physiologic sensors. Christophe Savariaux works in collaboration with the teams of the Speech and Cognition Department for which he has developed different software toolkits for data visualization and analysis. His current interest is speech production, in particular the recovery of phonetic contrasts after temporary or permanent impairment of speech articulators.

JEAN-LUC SCHWARTZ Speech and Cognition Department, GIPSA-Lab, CNRS & Grenoble University – France. Dr. Jean-Luc Schwartz is a senior CNRS Research Director at the Speech and Cognition Department, GIPSA-Lab, Grenoble. He was in charge of ICP (Institut de la Communication Parlée) from 2003 to 2006. His main areas of research involve speech and cognition, and more precisely auditory modeling, audiovisual speech perception, perceptuo-motor interactions, speech robotics, and the emergence of language. He has been involved in many national and European projects, and responsible for a number of them (for example, within the CNRS program ROBEA, within the "Complex Systems in Human and Social Sciences" program, and within the European Science Foundation "Origin of Man, Language and Languages" program). He has coordinated a number of special issues of journals such as *Speech Communication*, *Interaction Studies* and *Primatologie*, and organized several international workshops on Audiovisual Speech Processing, Language Emergence, or Face to Face Communication. He has authored or co-authored more than fifty publications in international journals (including *JASA*, *Speech Communication*, *Computer Speech and Language*, *IEEE Transactions on Speech and Audio Processing*, *Interaction Studies*, *Journal of Phonetics*, *Behavioural and Brain Research*, *Perception and Psychophysics*, *Cognition*, *NeuroImage*), and about thirty book chapters.

SIMON D. SCOTT Centre of Innovation & Technology (CTI), Asia Pacific University College of Innovation & Technology – Malaysia. Professor Dr Simon David Scott is the Chief Technologist of the Centre of Innovation & Technology (CTI), Asia Pacific University College of Innovation &

Technology. Under his direction, CTI (www.cti.my) has been awarded over RM4 million in research funding from the Malaysian Ministry of Science, Technology and Innovation and has produced numerous commercial products, winning various national and international awards including eight APICTA and two PIKOM Product of the Year awards. Previous positions include CTO of Guardware Ltd., Visiting Research Fellow at British Telecom's BTexact Asian Research Centre, and Research Officer at the University of Bath, UK.

KAORU SEKIYAMA Faculty of Letters, Kumamoto University – Japan. Kaoru Sekiyama was awarded her PhD by Osaka City University, Osaka, Japan. She spent some time at the City University of New York and Massachusetts Institute of Technology to collect data for her cross-linguistic studies while she was an assistant professor at Kanazawa University (Kanazawa, Japan). After working at Future University (Hakodate, Japan), she has been Professor of Cognitive Psychology at Kumamoto University (Kumamoto, Japan), since 2006. Her research interests include auditory-visual speech perception, experience-based modification of cognition, development, aging, brain plasticity, adaptation to reversed vision, body schema, visuomotor coordination, and crossmodal perception. Concerning speech perception, she has studied developmental and cross-linguistic examinations of auditory-visual speech perception with behavioral and neural measures.

MALCOM SLANEY Yahoo! Research, Santa Clara, USA. Malcolm Slaney is a principal scientist at Yahoo! Research Laboratory working on all types of multimedia data. He received his PhD from Purdue University for his work on computed imaging. He is a co-author, with A. C. Kak, of the IEEE book *Principles of Computerized Tomographic Imaging*. This book was republished by SIAM in their "Classics in Applied Mathematics" series. He is co-editor, with Steven Greenberg, of the book *Computational Models of Auditory Function*. Before Yahoo!, Dr. Slaney worked at Bell Laboratory, Schlumberger Palo Alto Research, Apple Computer, Interval Research, and IBM's Almaden Research Center. He is also a (consulting) Professor at Stanford's CCRMA where he organizes and teaches the Hearing Seminar. His research interests include auditory modeling and perception, multimedia analysis and synthesis, compressed-domain processing, similarity and search, and machine learning. For the last several years he has led the auditory group at the Telluride Neuromorphic Workshop. He is a Fellow of the IEEE.

MARIJA TABAIN Linguistics Program, La Trobe University, Melbourne – Australia. Marija Tabain is senior lecturer in phonetics at La Trobe

University in Melbourne. Following undergraduate degrees in music, modern languages and linguistics (at the University of Melbourne) and postgraduate study in phonetics (at Macquarie University, Sydney), she held postdoctoral positions in electrical engineering (at the Institut National Polytechnique de Grenoble in France) and psychology (at the University of California, Santa Cruz; at Macquarie University; and at the University of Western Sydney). She is active in the field of speech production research, in particular using electro-palatography and electro-magnetic articulography. Her research has focused on many different languages, including English, French, and Russian; and the Australian languages Arrernte, Pitjantjatjara, Warlpiri, Yanyuwa, and Yindjibarndi. Her work has been published in the *Journal of the Acoustical Society of America*, the *Journal of the International Phonetic Association*, the *Journal of Phonetics*, *Phonetica*, and *Language and Speech*. She is also co-editor, with Jonathan Harrington, of *Speech Production: Models, Phonetic Processes and Techniques*.

ERIC VATIKIOTIS-BATESON Department of Linguistics, University of British Colombia, Vancouver – Canada. Eric Vatikiotis-Bateson received a Bachelor's degree in philosophy and physics from St. John's College, Maryland, in 1974, a certificate in ethnographic film making in 1976, and an MA in Linguistics from Indiana University in 1978. From 1982–1987 he was an NIH pre-doctoral fellow at Haskins Laboratories (Connecticut) investigating 'the organization and control of speech production'. After receiving a PhD in Linguistics from Indiana University in 1987 he was appointed staff scientist at Haskins Labs. From 1990 to 2003 he was at ATR International in Japan. During this time, he and his collaborators examined the production, perception, and associated brain functions of multimodal communication in complex environments, especially spoken language processing, generating more than 150 technical papers and journal articles and several patents on multimodal signal coding and decoding. From 2000 to 2003, he headed the Communication Dynamics Project in the ATR Human Information Science Lab. Since 2003, Vatikiotis-Bateson has held a Canada Research Chair (NSERC, Tier 1) in Linguistics and Cognitive Science and is Director of the Cognitive Systems Program at the University of British Columbia in Vancouver, Canada.

ANNE VILAIN Speech and Cognition Department, GIPSA-Lab, CNRS & Grenoble University – France. Anne Vilain is an Associate Professor in Phonetics at the Université Stendhal, Grenoble (since 2001). She is a researcher at the Speech and Cognition Department of GIPSA-Lab (UMR CNRS 5216), in the Speech, Brain, Multimodality and Development research group. Her main research areas are: (i) the emergence of phonology, through the development of speech motor control from babbling to first words, (ii) gesture/speech interaction in language evolution, language development, and in adult language production, and (iii) phonetic and phonological language description and documentation. She is the co-author of several book chapters, co-editor of journal issues and books, and co-organizer of international conferences. She also teaches articulatory, acoustic, and experimental phonetics, phonology, speech acquisition, language morphogenesis in ontogeny and phylogeny.

Preface

Christian was our friend, a much loved friend with whom we shared everything: our hopes, projects, discussions, experiences, discoveries . . . He loved life, he loved humanity, and he loved being surrounded by people and communicating with them. More than ten years after he abruptly passed away, dancing and singing, we dedicate this book to him as a way to keep him and his spirit alive within our scientific community.

Christian specifically liked to read three kinds of publication. First was the French newspaper *Libération*, which was founded during Christian's adolescence when he discovered political commitment. Christian never forgot to buy his copy each morning. Second was the *Bandes Dessinées*, the French version of the north American comics. He owned a marvelous collection of these that amused every visitor to his home. Finally, he loved and published works about speech science. He contributed as an author or as an editor to a number of such works. Although proud of each contribution, for him the most important was certainly the 1992 edition of the proceedings of the *First ESCA Workshop on Speech Synthesis*, produced in collaboration with Gérard Bailly and Tom Sawallis. He was very excited by this task, and worked hard on it for many months to make sure that it would make an interesting and lasting contribution to the field, which it has. Having a strong sense of humor, Christian also wanted the book to be fun. Coupling this with his constant desire to see as much interaction as possible between apparently disparate people and endeavors, he commissioned a Bandes Dessinées cartoonist to draw a picture for the cover page. The cartoon, reproduced here, shows a grandmother robot sitting on an armchair just beginning to tell two children a story: Il était une fois . . . – "Once upon a time . . ." This wonderfully captures Christian's concept of research in speech communication: a domain where scientists have fun working hard to increase human understanding and the quality of life.

In close collaboration with Christian Abry and Tahar Lallouache, and with his students Oscar Angola, Tayeb Mohamadi, Thierry Guiard-Marigny, Ali Adjoudani, Bertrand LeGoff, and Lionel Revéret, Christian was a pioneer in the synthesis and recognition of audiovisual speech. His dedication and enthusiasm for the endeavor influenced academic and industrial researchers

throughout Europe, the Americas, Asia, and Australia. He established strong and fruitful international collaborations, principally with Dominic Massaro and Michael Cohen from the University of California in Santa Cruz, where he spent a sabbatical leave in 1993, and with Eric Vatikiotis-Bateson at ATR in Kyoto, which he visited many times. These are but a few of the collaborations that had begun to burgeon. At the time of his death in April, 1998, he was already a key member in a number of French and European projects; indeed, he and his research team were recognized as a most welcome addition to any research project.

Alongside his dedication to having fun with science, Christian was also quite serious about using his prodigious social and communicative talents to foster institutional structures aimed at facilitating the growth and development of speech science as a multi-faceted discipline that, especially within Europe, would break down the barriers imposed by competition and prejudice, be they institutional, national, international, or inter-continental. The vehicle for his dream of a barrier-free venue for the exchange of research ideas was the European Speech Communication Association (ESCA) which sponsors full-scale conferences where academic and industrial researchers convene annually and numerous topical and training workshops. Christian was Secretary of ESCA from 1993, but died before realizing his dream of globalizing the society by getting rid of the reference to Europe in its name. Soon after his death, ESCA was renamed ISCA (the International . . .).

Among his very creative initiatives, we will briefly mention two that illustrate his interest in stimulating scientific research and education. Along with David Stork and N. Michael Brooke, Christian co-organized a NATO Advanced Study Institute (ASI) workshop in 1995 entitled, "Speechreading by Man and Machine: Models, Systems and Applications." This workshop brought together for the first time engineers, primarily from industry, and psychologists, hearing specialists, and others from academia and public health to consider issues of common interest in auditory and visual speech processing (AVSP). Christian's involvement with the NATO-ASI and his quick-witted decision to follow through with subsequent AVSP workshops (Philadelphia 1996; Rhodes 1997; Terrigal 1998; Santa Cruz 1999; Scheelsminde 2001; St-Jorioz 2003; Vancouver 2005; Hilvarenbeek 2007; Moreton Island 2008; Norwich 2009) gave coherence to this new sub-discipline of speech science. Christian then wisely sought and received recognition and sponsorship for this new area of inquiry from ESCA, by advocating the importance of special interest groups (SIG) for addressing new areas of interest without interrupting the main stream of the professional society. The day he died he had just drafted the details of what would have been the first of these within ESCA/ISCA, now known as AVISA (the Auditory-Visual Speech Association). The year 1998 saw also the creation of SynSIG (the Speech Synthesis Special Interest Group), that together with AVISA cover Christian's research themes.

The Christian Benoît association was created on April 26, 1999. Founded by personal donations, the ICP and ISCA, its scientific committee biannually awards the "Christian Benoît" prize to a young researcher in order to help him or her develop a multimedia project. The first laureates are Tony Ezzat (from Medialab, MIT, USA, see his contribution in this volume) and Johanna Barry (from Bionic Ear Institute, University of Melbourne, Australia), Olov Engwal (from Department of Speech, Music and Hearing , KTH, Stockholm, Sweden), Susanne Fuchs (from Center of General Linguistics in Berlin, Germany) and Sascha Fagel (from Department for Language and Communication of the Berlin Institute of Technology, Germany).

At the ICP, thanks to Christian's pioneering efforts, a large number of projects have been developed in auditory and visual speech processing, the branch of spoken communication research that he was so instrumental in establishing. Some of these projects extend and improve upon Christian's work. Gérard Bailly, Pierre Badin, Frédéric Elisei, and Matthias Odisio extended his pioneer work on lips towards a data-driven talking head that drives not only the visible movements of the entire face but also pilots the underlying speech articulator: the jaw, the tongue and more recently the velum. Virginie Attina, Gérard Bailly, Denis Beautemps, Marie Cathiard, and Guillaume Gibert are developing a system for synthesizing cued-speech, the use of synchronized hand motions to facilitate communication for hearing-impaired people. Christian was passionately involved with cued-speech research during the last weeks of his life.

Christian would probably have liked to be one of the editors of this book. He knew all the contributors personally and he would have enjoyed reading their papers, arguing and joking with them, and simply being part of a communicative process he understood so well.

This book is "absolutely" dedicated to him!

Acknowledgments

We would like to express our gratitude to all contributors and reviewers (a special thanks to Denis Burnham and Caroline Jones for correcting our numerous French tweaks), and to our partners at Cambridge University Press, in particular our commissioning editor Helen Barton, whose unrelenting efforts made this book possible.

Introduction

The books *Hearing By Eye* (Dodd and Campbell 1987) and *Speech Perception by Ear and Eye* (Massaro 1987) were the first volumes that considered speech-reading as a psychological process of interest beyond its direct applications in hearing loss and deafness (see for example, Jeffers and Barley 1971). Eight years later, David G. Stork, Christian Benoît, and N. Michael Brooke organized the landmark NATO workshop "Speechreading by Man and Machine: Models, Systems and Applications." The workshop was "the first forum on the inter-disciplinary study of speechreading (lipreading) – production, perception and learning by both humans and machines." This workshop was followed by several volumes (Stork and Hennecke 1996; Campbell *et al.* 1998; Massaro 1998b) and was undoubtedly a major step towards the design of an audiovisual (AV) speech processing community: you will find in this volume numerous references to the series of subsequent AVSP workshops (Rhodes 1997; Terrigal 1998; Santa Cruz 1999; Scheelsminde 2001; St-Jorioz 2003; Vancouver 2005; Hilvarenbeek 2007; Tangalooma 2008; Norwich 2009; Hakone 2010) sponsored first by the European Speech Communication Association then by the AVSP Special Interest Group of the International Speech Communication Association, both bodies in which Christian Benoît was constantly promoting AV speech processing. These workshops together with dedicated workshops (see for example the AV speech recognition workshop organized in 2000 by Chalapathy *et al.*) and special sessions in international conferences have fostered the development of innumerable lines of AV speech research.

The book is divided into four main parts although most chapters address most of the questions.

The first part of the book is largely devoted to AV speech perception and to two main questions concerning human AV performance: how and where (in the brain) auditory (A) and visual (V) signals combine to access the mental lexicon. Although speech can be perceived by vision alone (i.e., via lipreading/speech-reading) and visual speech perception (Bernstein) can provide sufficient phonetic information to access the mental lexicon, talking faces constitute a major part of an infant's perceptual experience: through the process of watching and listening while people talk to them and point out objects of the world, infants have the opportunity to attribute semantics to the sounds they hear. Developmental studies (Burnham and Sekiyama) can thus contribute to explaining how auditory and visual information combine. Idiosyncrasies of human brain circuitry also hold clues to the evolution and development of human language, and its accessibility by eye and ear (Campbell and MacSweeney). One commonly accepted term of this intersensory integration is that the two signals carry both complementary and redundant information on the phonetic properties of the original message. The striking observation is however that the integration is something more than taking the best of both worlds and that AV perception is able to perceive properties that are carried by neither modality alone (Remez). Some answers to this puzzle could be found in a more intimate intersensory integration at the signal level, notably that which comprises the dynamic aspects of both signals (Lander and Bruce) which are in fact audible and visible traces of the same articulatory gestures.

The second part of the book is dedicated to the production and perception of visible speech i.e. speech movements. We have access to dynamic AV information (Lander and Bruce) as consequences of the acoustic and aerodynamic consequences of the motion of speech articulators. A production-aware "grounded" perception can benefit from the availability of sensorimotor maps (which may or may not include dynamic representations) whose existence has been proved to be useful for the control of most biological movements. This intersensory integration is not only necessary for perception (and therefore comprehension) but also for movement learning and control (Cathiard *et al.*) Accurate descriptions and models of coordinate structures linking activations of the different speech segments are thereby necessary: for instance Beautemps, Cathiard *et al.* describe coordination between hand and vocal tract motions in manual cued speech.

The third part of the book presents some of the latest developments in AV speech processing by machines, particularly in AV speech recognition and synthesis (Brooke and Scott). In parallel with the development of AV research, computer-generated facial animation (Parke and Waters 1996) has attracted considerable attention and progress. Areas of application have set aside the traditional field of the animation and games industry to address more challenging applications where the metaphor of face-to-face conversation is applied to human–computer interfaces (Cassell *et al.* 2000). Of course, we are still a long way from building a computer which can carry on a face-to-face conversation with a human and which can pass a face-to-face Turing test, i.e. one whose computed behavior cannot be detected from natural human interaction. However, noticeable progress has been made in giving computers the "gift" of AV speech (Brooke and Scott). AV speech recognition outperforms acoustic-only speech recognition especially for degraded speech (Potamianos, Chapalatti *et al.*) while the realism of facial animation has been drastically improved by image-based speech synthesis (Ezzat *et al*; Slaney and Bregler). The chapter by Massaro *et al.* on the Baldi talking head and its further developments for virtual speech tutoring concludes this part by reporting experimental work on augmented communication.

The fourth part focuses on the nature of the information related to oro-facial gestures (head, vocal tract, and face movements), which is necessary to enable an efficient contribution of the visual component in the audiovisual processing of speech. Bateson and Munhall's approach is based on experimental studies of the perception of multimodal natural and synthetic stimuli in which various characteristics are either degraded or carefully preserved. Bailly, Badin *et al.* use a modeling approach based on a careful analysis of real speakers' data to study the main degrees of freedom of the speech production system and their impact on the audiovisual perception of speech.

This work has been accomplished because a body of researchers is now working on the various aspects of audiovisual speech processing. Most of this synergy is due to the research field itself where the majority of the paradigms of unimodal speech research have been renewed and questioned. Part of this synergy is also due to the communicative enthusiasm of researchers such as Christian Benoît.

Scientific outcomes of multimodal speech communication studies are numerous and they cover a broad scope. We acknowledge that little is said in this book about them. Indeed, it was our decision to focus mainly on basics. However, we would like to mention one of the most exciting current outcomes: Face-to-Face speech communication. Interaction loops between production and perception of speech and gestures are at the core of this aspect of human communication, transmitting via multimodal signals parallel information about what the interlocutors say, think about what they say and how they feel when they say it. Convergence or imitation phenomena, which are at the core of L1 and L2 learning process in babies and adults, result from this interaction. Face-to-face communication studies require the integration of all the mechanisms of embodied speech production and audiovisual speech communication, and combining them with social and physical interactions between humans and between humans and their environment (see notably extended papers of presentations dicussed at two workshops organized in Grenoble: Abry *et al.* 2009; Dohen *et al.* 2010). The quest for neurophysiological and behavioral correlates of these sensorimotor loops constitute an exciting research program that would certainly have attracted Christian Benoît's attention and titillated his insatiable curiosity.

1 Three puzzles of multimodal speech perception

R. E. Remez

1.1 Introduction

Why look at the talker when you listen? This question is the straightforward practical topic of a research report at the origin of studies of multimodal speech perception (Sumby and Pollack 1954). A crucial part of the answer is furnished in this early report: Looking boosts intelligibility throughout a range of listening conditions. But despite the longstanding acknowledgment of the potential of vision in speech perception, multimodal speech perception remains a test of our theories today. The benefit of watching the talker while listening is neither well described nor well understood; this predicament is a natural consequence of a unimodal research strategy that has largely followed articulated sound into the ear. This practice has spawned a range of theoretical descriptions of the perception of speech, although it is fair to say that every account feels the weight of the multimodal problem. No hypothesis about speech perception is immune to the test, and it is a severe challenge.

Technical attention to multimodal speech perception has added to the inventory of types of multimodal integration, and the accumulated new cases are no easier to accommodate than Sumby and Pollack's original benchmarks. This essay reviews three multimodal challenges to our understanding of speech perception, with the goal of sketching the boundaries of a unified account. The approach taken here is perceptual and general in emphasis, rather than specifically phonetic or psycholinguistic. This conceptual gambit affords an opportunity to compare speech perception to other perceptual functions, in an effort to situate speech perception as a particular functional allocation of resources drawn from a common perceptual stock. As intellectual strategy, it admits the influence of Stein and Meredith (1993), whose physiological studies of living species nonetheless describe the ancient phylogeny of multisensory unity. Of course, speech is young, certainly compared to structures of the vertebrate brainstem that compose a crucial neural constituent of multisensory convergence. It will be instructive to see how the perceptual functions accommodating speech fit within this scheme, and in order to take up the challenge, three puzzles to consider are: (1) Organization, (2) Event Perception, and (3) Experience.

1.2 Organization

To apprehend an utterance, a perceiver finds the effects of speech amid ongoing sensory flux and, informed by experience with language, resolves the linguistic message. The self-evident sufficiency of listening as a means to perceiving and understanding encourages an auditory bias in explaining perception, and from that perspective the original finding of Sumby and Pollack (1954) was unprecedented.

1.2.1 Assessing audiovisual speech transmission

Sumby and Pollack had aimed to calibrate the usefulness of viewing a talker while listening, motivated by the practical aim of devising improvements in spoken exchanges within a noisy workplace. In their test, talker and perceiver sat five feet apart, on each trial the talker producing an English spondee (for example, "cupcake," "baseball") chosen from a fixed list of words. The perceiver wore a headphone set through which the acoustic test items were delivered. The subject also held a copy of the word list and was asked to indicate the spoken item on each trial. Three factors were manipulated to assess the contribution of vision to speech perception. First, to estimate the baseline performance for listening, a group of participants was tested who did not look at the talker. Their performance was compared to an audiovisual condition, in which the perceivers faced the live talker, looking while listening. Second, to measure visual influence as a function of auditory resolution, the level of speech relative to noise was varied in 6 dB steps from –30 dB to 0 dB, with an additional condition in which speech was presented in the clear. Third, to estimate the effect of uncertainty, the size of the set of words from which each item was drawn was also varied, from a set of eight at the smallest to 256 at the greatest. The family of curves of the results of these tests is a thing of beauty.

Some aspects of the outcome were expectable, namely, that identification performance varied inversely with the acoustic signal-to-noise ratio (S/N) both when listening alone and when listening and looking, and, that performance was poorer the larger the set of words from which the item on each trial was chosen, true no less of the listener as of the audiovisual perceiver. The greatest contribution of vision to word identification occurred with the smallest lexical set at the lowest acoustic S/N, or, as Sumby and Pollack state it, the visual contribution to speech intelligibility increases as the speech-to-noise ratio decreases. To a first approximation, the finding is coincident with common sense, namely, that listening is ordinarily sufficient, and its insufficiency for whatever cause promotes a shift in attention to include the visual supplement, even presuming that an optic-to-phonetic projection differs hugely in dynamic from an acoustic-to-phonetic projection (Auer *et al.* 1997). However, a crucial analysis performed by Sumby and Pollack shows a rather different characterization of the interplay

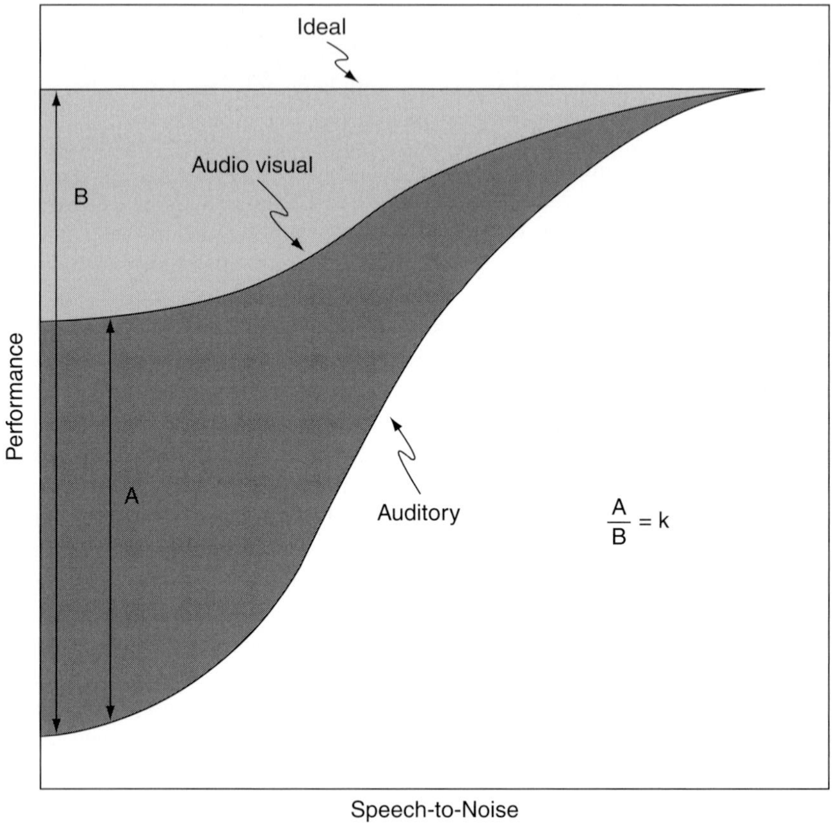

Figure 1.1 The relation between auditory and visual speech perception in a classic study by Sumby and Pollack (1954).

of visual and auditory contributions. Although the absolute visual contribution to audiovisual speech perception was greatest when the S/N was smallest, the relative contribution of vision was actually constant across a wide range of S/N. To assess this, Sumby and Pollack estimated the potential contribution of vision and the actual contribution, finding the ratio of these two estimates at each S/N. Remarkably, the constancy of the ratio shows that the relative information supplied by visual observation of the talker's face is independent of the S/N. Their schematic illustration of this assessment of the visual contribution is shown in Figure 1.1.

If the greatest absolute benefit of audiovisual speech perception occurs when the auditory component is compromised, the findings also indicate that there is benefit of vision to intelligibility regardless of the auditory baseline. This shows that the perceptual disposition to combine the two sensory streams is robust, and provides a glimpse of the principles of the perceptual organization of speech apprehended audiovisually. To unpack the surprise in this early study, consider the conditional dependence on vision that Sumby and Pollack imply as a default hypothesis. If speech perception relied on auditory inflow only when it yielded adequate intelligibility, visual attention to a talker would be conditional on the degree of auditory failure. Instead, the finding that visual attention persists, and contributes to speech perception over wide ranges of variation in auditory success exposes two aspects of perceptual organization.

First, audiovisual attention to a talker is primary, perhaps reflecting a natural mode of attention. Second, audiovisual attention is independent of the symbolic process that projects auditory forms into phonetic attributes. The combination of visual and auditory streams occurred regardless of the degree of success or failure in lexical identification. Two ensuing projects show that this early finding of Sumby and Pollack was genuine. They conclude that beyond the propensity of a perceiver to treat visual and auditory samples of speech as combinable by default, the audiovisual dynamic is remarkably indifferent to superordinate linguistic or symbolic properties (Remez *et al.* 1994).

1.2.2 The autonomy of audiovisual coherence

The audiovisual speech perception study of McGurk and MacDonald (1976) is now well known. In their project, a perceiver reported the syllable pair spoken on each trial by a recorded female talker, with auditory or auditory-visual exposure. Although the auditory contribution to perception was unequivocal when it was the sole basis for consonant identification, in combination with vision it did not dominate. Instead, subjects reported a variety of compromises or fusions between the auditory and visual streams. For understanding perceptual organization, the crucial evidence was provided by specific compromises. For example, in the instance in which the audible display conveyed [pɑ] and the visible display conveyed [kɑ], a plausible audiovisual compromise is [tɑ], preserving the audible and visible stop manner, and the audible voicelessness, and compromising on consonantal articulatory place.

Although such instances of fusion of the audible and visible consonants were disclosed by each group of subjects, listeners also reported combinations that, remarkably, were not consistent with English phonotactics. The oddity of the audiovisual combination /bdɑ/ and /bgɑ/, for instance, is its atypicality (or, perhaps, its illegality given English sonorance) in words. These reports express speech perception unbiased by its service to lexical identification and released from experience of the likely sequence of phonemes in English syllables. Once the organization of the multisensory samples of speech is determined, the functions of phonetic perception yield segmental values bound to the sensory patterns, even sequences that are inconceivable given the regular properties of the language. It is not unreasonable to take such findings as critical counter-evidence to accounts of speech perception appealing to simple interactive activation (McClelland and Elman 1986) because this phenomenon, while exhibiting interaction of sensory modalities, denies interaction of lexical knowledge and sensory resolution in the identification of segments.

1.2.3 A unimodal parallel

We found a similar function operating in perceptual organization at a fundamental level in a unimodal case. In explaining the means by which a listener finds and follows a speech signal, whether a single talker speaks in the clear or a group of talkers yak away in a cocktail party and the listener tries to pick one out of the din, the commonplace account had been Auditory Scene Analysis (Bregman 1990). This model added a well-grounded empirical base to the proposal of Wertheimer (1938), that the starting point for the perception of objects and events, whether visible or audible, was an organized sensory field, and not simply an unaltered summary of receptor activity. Through clever tests that extrapolated Wertheimer's principles of grouping by likeness, the auditory evidence seemed to warrant an account of perceptual organization in which elements were grouped according to their similarity, or continuity, or proximity, or their temporal coincidence. Given a welter of auditory elements in sensory flux, this account described the creation of segregated perceptual streams of like elements, binding them in a domain over which perceptual analysis then occurred (cf. Triesman 1993).

In contrast to the ideal test cases that provided empirical motivation for Auditory Scene Analysis, speech posed a recalcitrant instance with its acoustically heterogeneous signal and its extremely brief elements that fade without a trace in auditory memory within 100 ms of transduction. A perceiver who sorted a speech stream into its like elements would bind the clicks together, the whistles together, the hisses together, the buzzes together, and the hums together, losing the natural intercalation of the acoustic elements and sacrificing the precise temporal grain of the multiple acoustic correlates of phonetic expression that arguably confers perceptual robustness (Liberman and Cooper 1972). We proposed (Remez *et al.* 1994) that perceptual organization of speech must, instead, be keyed to coarse-grain modulation of the spectrum, but indifferent to the short-term acoustic elements composing the stream. The constituents of a speech signal would cohere in a perceptual stream, we claimed, when a physical acoustic pattern consistent with phonologically governed articulation can be sampled by a listener despite the dissimilarities among the acoustic constituents. Clearly, the key to this kind of perceptual organization is a perceptual susceptibility to the characteristic modulations imposed by articulation on an acoustic carrier (see also Smith *et al.* 2002; Elliott and Theunissen 2009).

Our experiments aimed to test this conjecture by attempting to disrupt perceptual organization, in order to deduce the principle of organization from the conditions in which interference succeeded or failed. After Sumby and Pollack, and after McGurk and MacDonald, we suspected that perceptual organization was certainly subphonemic, not dependent on a lexical process, and possibly subphonetic, not dependent on segment identification. In establishing the sensory integrity of speech, listeners were acutely sensitive to the pattern of frequency variation of acoustic patterns, we found. We presented a sinewave replica of a sentence with a supernumerary tone in the frequency range of the second formant. If this tone varied over a natural extent in a natural manner it impeded the integration of the elements of a speech signal, similarly replicated in tone analogs. But, perceptual organization was not impaired by an extraneous tone when it exhibited an arbitrary pattern of variation inconsistent with vocal resonance changes (also, Roberts *et al.* 2010).

Whether the supernumerary tone interfered or not, our control tests showed that it did not evoke phonetic impressions, a crucial bit of evidence that it was interfering with the step at which the auditory flux is resolved into streams of common origin, rather than the step at which segmental phonetic attributes are resolved. Although this finding is incompatible with a version of pandemonium proposed in a peremptory account by Liberman (1979), as an instance of perceptual verticality, Liberman (1996) conceded that it is a legitimate alternative to Auditory Scene Analysis.

1.2.4 The puzzle

Together, these projects allow a sketch of the characteristics of audiovisual perceptual organization preliminary to new research. For one, audiovisual attention to speech is ineluctable, as Sumby and Pollack showed, and perceivers combine visible and audible samples of speech naturally. For another, intersensory integration in perceiving speech is fundamental to success in extracting the linguistic message, but it is not contingent on the likely or regular properties. An organized stream of visible and audible samples, once formed, is analyzed as if its sensory pattern is projected into a phonetic sequence without the influence of the lexical or indeed the phonemic experience of the perceiver. By this assumption we can reconcile the reports of McGurk and MacDonald with those of Sumby and Pollack. Last, our studies with sinewave replicas of speech show that even within the auditory modality a listener does not find the speech signal by applying a standard of similarity to the variety of auditory impressions in any moment or brief temporal span. Instead, a rather abstract sensitivity to vocal modulation, independent of the elements, appears to do the trick, and such sensitivity surely applies to the intermodal circumstance. Perhaps a voiced stop hold, a release burst, and a voiced oral resonance are less dissimilar to one another than any of these is to a 2½ -D sketch of the vermilion border of the lips. But, the principle that this research defends is that of organization by sensitivity to characteristic change, rather than to characteristic elements, and is a candidate for evaluation as a principle of multimodal organization in speech perception, not just within the auditory modality.

1.3 Event perception and speech perception

A second puzzle about multimodal speech perception stems from the rather different ontology that results from introducing the visual modality to the description. As long as the theoretician's goal is restricted to explaining the speech chain in auditory terms, the present simplifying assumptions typical of our field can endure. Specifically, the perceiver can be characterized as a listener to language, as if the expression of speech were brought about by linguistic plans alone. Similarly, the precise situation of speech within the plenum of events that engages a perceiver need not be specified. It is enough to conceptualize the listener identifying the next item in a list of syllables or words or sentences, and distinguishing the present one from all other possibilities that a vocal tract produces. In this constrained world, speech originates in no particular place, and the talker remains occult, literally, though the effects of speech are detectable by ear. The circumstances differ in an audiovisual setting.

The events of audiovisual speech perception, while arrayed through the artifice of video technology, are less readily subject to the common explanatory idealizations of auditory non-linearity or vocal tract gestures. A specific talker is finally visible, and many of the depicted characteristics are unassailable. Clearly, the theoretical burden alters, for the visible and audible talker is encountered within an ongoing scene in which durable objects and events, albeit non-distinctive linguistically, are concurrent with the acts of language production. The coalescence of event perception and speech perception is a fundamental topic of investigation now, and the basic problems are beginning to take shape. Specifically, the perception of speech appears to use different criteria, and possibly a different grain of sensitivity than the perception of events more generally.

1.3.1 Temporal coincidence and phonetic perception

Is it tautology to assert that the perceiver registers that an event includes speech, and therefore, when it is possible, perceives the linguistic properties of the speech? In a vulgar ecology of language, it must be true that the distribution of phonetic properties lies within the distribution of vocally produced sound, and it is reasonable to suppose that the perception of speech is contingent on the perception of vocalization. The relation of the two distributions is that of subset and superset, for we must include paralinguistic sound as well as the non-linguistic acoustic effects of respiration and deglutition, originating from the same bodily parts under different organization in this ecological miniature. The logic of this nesting is the key to the surprise in some studies that revealed an odd relation between event perception and phonetic perception.

In movie houses, temporal misalignment of the visible action and the soundtrack used to be common not long ago, although the present generation of technology prevents this from happening under ordinary circumstances. Because of the hazard for slack in the film path through the projector, the moving picture would occasionally lead the sound by as much as a third of a second. It was noticeable. The benchmark for distinguishing coincidence from temporal discrepancy is 20 ms, according to Hirsh and Sherrick (1961). But, the matter of fixing a corresponding threshold for audiovisual speech perception is a technical problem. Perceivers notice discrepancy in sight and sound though audiovisual integration is not blocked over a wide range of divergence.

With discrepancy up to 80 ms in audiovisual presentation of sentences, McGrath and Summerfield (1983) reported little deterioration in transcription performance. We can safely conclude that perceivers were aware of the audiovisual misalignment in such presentation, and therefore that there are two perceptual states accompanying a spoken event in such a circumstance. In one, the perception of the speaker is registered as an artifact in which visual appearance and auditory experience are discrepant. In the other, the visual appearance and auditory experience remain coherent phonetically, jointly promoting the perception of the linguistic message. This paradoxical phenomenon was the topic of a study by Munhall *et al.* (1996), who used temporal misalignment and the audiovisual perceptual integration discovered by McGurk and MacDonald to calibrate the relation of event perception and phonetic perception.

In their procedure, Munhall *et al.* asked perceivers to report the intervocalic consonant in an audiovisual presentation of vowel-consonant-vowel (VCV) syllables. The visible face said either [ɑgɑ] or [igi] and the audible speech said [ɑbɑ]. Temporal coincidence evoked reports of an intervocalic [d], a blend typical of the original phenomenon reported by McGurk and MacDonald. Temporal discrepancy was manipulated in 60 ms steps over a range of 360 ms of acoustic lead to 360 ms of acoustic lag. Naturally, at the extreme divergence, the participants reported [b] as the intervocalic consonant, an indication that the effect of the visible articulation no longer combined with the audible speech. However, even at values of discrepancy as great as 180 ms, at which the temporal misalignment was unmistakable, viewers continued to report [d], reflecting the place feature blend brought about by audiovisual integration. The terrifying conclusion of this study, since replicated by Bertelson *et al.* (1997), is that the perceptual criteria for intersensory combination in speech perception do not derive from the threshold for the detection of coincidence in event perception. The simple distinction between one and two, so to speak, is expressed differently if the perceiver is appraising the phonetic series or the event of vocalization. Perhaps no less troubling for a general account is the report by Brancazio and Miller (2005) that the distribution of conditions in which a McGurk effect occurs actually underestimates the range in which audiovisual integration affects phonetic perception.

1.3.2 Whose face, whose voice?

In addition to temporal misalignment, the audiovisual study of speech permits the assessment of other factors in perception. It seems that perceivers are extremely forgiving of acoustic speech samples presented with video samples of speech of an obviously different talker. This flexibility expresses the versatility inherent in speech perception, we should conclude, and is akin to the tolerance for speech produced under all sorts of distorting conditions: with a cold, over a battlefield telephone, with a diplophonic larynx, with a dental appliance, with a sabre wound of the cheek, with a walkie-talkie, with a partial glossectomy, with a bolus of food in the mouth, with a pipe clenched between the teeth, with a decorative stud worn in the tongue. However, perceivers are not indefinitely plastic.

If acoustic speech samples are presented with video displays of an articulating face, it seems to matter perceptually if the talker is familiar to the perceiver. Again exploiting the propensity of perceivers to blend visible and audible features of speech, *d'après* McGurk and MacDonald, the incidence of instances of blending was used by Walker *et al.* (1995) to assay the effect of familiarity on intersensory integration. A set of audiovisual samples was created in which half of the trials exhibited mismatched faces and voices. The same test materials were used with two groups of subjects, one who knew the talkers and one who knew none of them. The critical performance measure was the perception of consonant place reflecting audiovisual blending. Remarkably, the listeners who were not familiar with the talkers did not seem to mind the mismatches, even those in which a male face and a female voice or a female face and a male voice were paired, although the rude power of discernment would have been enough to determine that a discrepant event was unfolding. This instance parallels the case of temporal misalignment, in which the conditions sufficient to detect discrepancy did not impair multimodal integration of speech perception. There is more to this story, of course. The eventual solution to this puzzle appears to lie in the effects of perceptual familiarity with the articulatory habits of specific individuals (cf. Remez *et al.* 1997). For those perceivers who knew the talkers in Walker's project, a tendency towards diminished fusion was observed, although familiarity did not cause a complete blockade on intermodal integration.

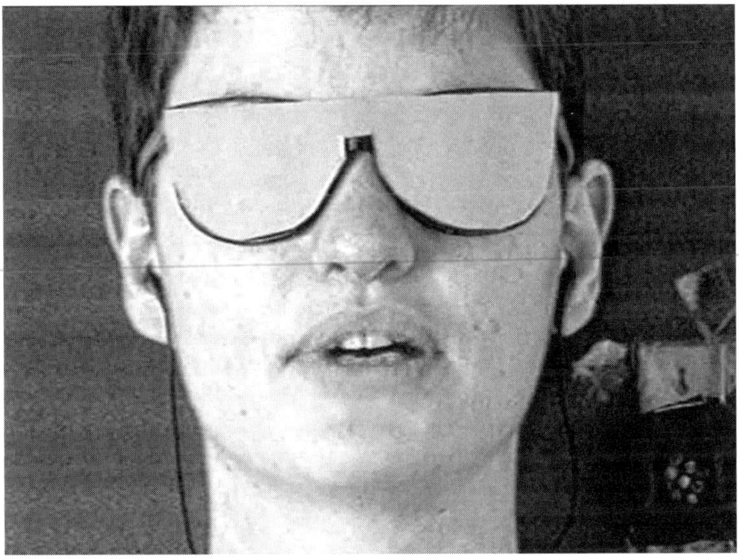

Figure 1.2 A video frame of the gamine used in a study of audiovisual intelligibility by Schwippert and Benoît (1997).

The extent of the puzzle, too, can be appreciated from an ingenious study in this genre by Schwippert and Benoît (1997). Their method also imposed a mismatch between visible and audible speech samples. A male and a female talker spoke a carrier sentence with a three-syllable nonsense word (a VCVCV) in sentence-final position. These acoustic samples were mixed with noise at −6 or −12 dB S/N, and synchronized to a video sample of the female talker outfitted in the manner of a gamine, with short hair, wearing neither jewelry nor make-up, and whose goggles concealed her eyes (see Figure 1.2). Here, familiarity with the female talker led to greater intelligibility across the conditions, even those in which acoustic samples of a male talker were used. And, in a revealing (and wild) finding that deserves renewed attention, subjects of the study were misled by the experimenters' ruse in unimodal presentation but not in the audiovisual presentation. Specifically, when the female speech samples were presented unimodally in noise at −12 dB, 82 percent of listeners believed that the talker was male. When the video presentation of the articulating face was shown unimodally to naive observers, 68 percent of them believed that the gamine was a gamin. But, in the audiovisual conditions, 75 percent of naive observers reported that the talker was female. This study suggests that the ability to notice an audiovisual discrepancy in the event within which the speech occurs is potentially subordinate to the appropriation of multimodal streams for speech perception. It should go without saying that this ordering of the nesting of events is exactly inverted from common sense, in which speech takes its context from preceding and following social events. At the perceptual level, this is an instance in which the perception of the talker (man or woman) is contingent on the audiovisual combination that specifically promotes the perception of the linguistic attributes. It is a provocative observation.

1.3.3 Whose vowels?

A related approach to this method was applied in a study of talker attributes by Johnson *et al.* (1999). The general question was motivated by classic considerations of normalization, otherwise understood as the perceptual accommodation of differences in acoustic-phonetic expression that are consistent within the utterances of a talker but that vary between talkers. A synthesized set of acoustic syllables was used spanning the vowels /ʊ/ and /ʌ/, each realized in an /hVd/ frame. When this series of HOOD to HUD was synthesized with a low fundamental, it was considered to be robustly male in quality, and with a higher fundamental frequency and breathy source it was considered to be robustly female.

Video samples were also prepared of two talkers pronouncing HUD, each of whom had won a laboratory pageant as "most male looking" or "most female looking," the complementary conditions to the androgyne of Schwippert and Benoît. When the male or female acoustic series was presented with the male or female visual samples, the category boundary between /ʊ/ and /ʌ/ changed accordingly, as if the depiction of a male talker drew the category crossover toward a lower frequency of the first formant, all other things being equal, and the depiction of the female talker drew the crossover toward a higher frequency first formant. Consistent with the relation that we have seen between event perception and speech perception, an effect of sex typicality of the acoustic samples was also observed independently of the visually depicted sex of the talker. This circumstance is familiar from the brief review of selected cases here, and indicates the difficulty of reconciling the perception of speech with general perceptual focus on the attributes of events.

1.3.4 The puzzle

Bringing speech perception into a multimodal framework seemed initially to be one way to rescue phonetic perception from the historical dispute between proponents of general auditory mechanisms and special phonetic sensitivity (cf. Remez 1996; Trout 2001). It is not too inaccurate to propose that an emphasis on intersensory coalescence placed a premium on identifying the useful samples delivered by each of the senses, admitting that the phonetic categories of experience held intrinsic linguistic standing.

The experiments that we reviewed here show how difficult it will be to place speech perception neatly within a general account of event perception. The perceivers in each of these studies readily tolerated huge discrepancies in the event structure without losing the thread of the phonetic structure. This confounds common sense by suggesting that the obvious nesting of speech perception within the perception of events cannot be simply true. Although it would be logical for the global parameters of events to be registered by general perceptual faculties that passed the values to specific phonetic functions, it seems as if nothing so elegant occurs. Instead, the perceiver is built to sustain two incompatible states, one responsive to subtle incongruities and misalignments in the structure of events, and the other determined to resolve the phonetic segments despite the appearance of disorder in the event. And, in at least one provocative instance the perception of the event depends on the integration of sensory samples of speech, reversing the causal chain that ordinary impressions recommend. This is a puzzle that promises to expose the relation of speech to other concurrent perceptual capabilities, and should provide the vehicle to take our accounts far from the old debate between auditory or gestural form.

1.4 Experience

The infinite use of finite means is a clear characterization of the relation between the fixed stock of linguistic objects and the expressions that they compose without limit. A perceiver, aware of the finite means through personal experience, must resolve them from the states that they induce in the sensorium, and to declare that sensory variation is infinite hardly stretches the point. Although the perceiver of English can be confident that at any moment speech is likely to contain an orderly progression of segments drawn from a set of no more than three dozen, the sensory manifestations of this small set are indefinitely graded. The signature problem of speech perception is an account of the perceiver's accommodation to variation in sensory form of the phoneme, and this problem recurs in the multimodal circumstance. The complete measure of this problem has not yet been taken. Audiovisual speech perception studies presently focus on citation forms, with a well-lighted face presented without shadow or blemish, head-on. The rare study examines the perceptual effect of oblique views of the face (for example, Jordan and Thomas 2001), a rather commonplace circumstance in which speech is encountered multimodally. To acknowledge that things stand at the very beginning in the study of multimodal speech perception is not to deny that we still have far to go to gauge the natural variation that perceivers contend with on the acoustic side of things, too. In aiming to create a descriptively adequate account it will be productive to keep in mind that the search for the distinctive acoustic correlates of the phonetic distinctive features (Delattre *et al.* 1955) falsely presumed that the sensory effects of speech would be no more varied than the finite set of features. Of course, the limits on the sensory tolerance for multimodal integration remain to be found, but there are several studies that indicate that the perceiver is likely to be no less tolerant of variation multimodally than unimodally.

1.4.1 Perceptual tuning to a talker

In perceiving speech, the acoustic variation attributable to talker differences has several causes. Talkers differ in scale, some larger, some smaller, and this affects the overall range and central tendency over which vocal sound production occurs. In addition to this physical difference, talkers express the dialectal characteristics of the local language community in habits of articulation and style. The implementation of phoneme contrasts in a set of phonetic forms typical of a community does not yet exhaust the variation, for individuals express personal style within a dialect, and this also colors utterances. If some of this style is phonetic, the balance is paralinguistic, and affective expression that rides along on the stream of language also perturbs the consistency in the relation of contrastive phoneme and phonetic expression. A perceiver who identifies the message of a talker negotiates these confluent causes that drive the phonetic realization to vary, and because the variation is phonetic, and not simply a matter of physical scale, the attributes of talker differences derived from consideration of auditory samples apply with equal force to visual samples. To accommodate this variation in perception takes resources (Pardo and Remez 2006).

The effect of perceptual tuning to the characteristics of a visible talker was reported by Yakel *et al.* (2000). This was a unimodal visual project, but it is useful to consider in this context because it assesses the potential contribution in the multimodal case. In this straightforward project, a normal-hearing volunteer was asked to speechread a list of 100 sentences. Two presentation procedures were used. In one, the same talker was shown producing all of the sentences. In another, ten different talkers, five men and five women, were sampled to compose the video corpora and sentences were ordered to assign a different talker to consecutive trials. Using a measure of intelligibility, Yakel found that subjects who attended to the visible speech of a single talker fared better in transcription than those who attended to a different talker on each trial. The resources required for normalization of talker differences were applied in the condition of multiple talker presentation, leaving less available for visual speech perception, but this demand occurred far less consistently or not at all in the condition of single talker presentation. The authors conclude that the normalization of talkers perceived visually is similar to that which had been observed in auditory unimodal instances. It is important to note that the specific problem of non-uniform vocal tract scaling that has characterized this technical problem since Fant (1966) really does not apply in the silent speechreading circumstance. The scale variation observed among fronto-parallel projections of articulating faces lacks an isomorphism with the acoustic version, because the visible features of a face do not match the audible structures of the supralaryngeal vocal tract.

Are there properties common to the visual and auditory normalization of talker differences? Our own project in the perception of individual talker characteristics determined that perceivers notice and remember personal attributes of talkers far more detailed and extensive than vocal quality (Remez *et al.* 1997). Indeed, the precise habits of articulation that express the phonetic variety of dialect and idiolect are useful for recognizing familiar talkers from their speech and for learning to identify new talkers (Sheffert *et al.* 2002). When a new talker is encountered multimodally, it is easy to imagine a perceiver taking an inventory of the excursion of the landmarks of a talker's face, especially in view of the prospect of gleaning phonetic attributes from the movement of facial features other than the oral articulators when they are correlated with the message (Vatikiotis-Bateson *et al.* 1998). The attunement of perception to a talker's characteristics apparently occurs early in development, and there may be no time in life during which such attention is learned from rudiments. Nonetheless, some studies with subjects who use sensory prostheses illustrate the nature of experience that promotes intersensory coherence.

1.4.2 Sensory substitution

What kind of experience is useful in promoting intermodal integration and the resolution of linguistic attributes from sensory combination? In the broadest setting of this problem, it is important to note that speech is multisensory in nature, and not just audiovisual. Of course it is auditory, and a primary experience of speech is that of the listener. Another sort of auditory function, though, is reafference, when the sound of one's own production is used to control coordinated action. Speech is also visual, both when viewing a talker and when viewing the self, which mirrors and other technology permit. With the exception of Tadoma, speech is not haptic in the ordinary sense, but production of speech elicits reafferent orofacial somatosensory impressions, and a kind of haptic experience of effort and placement that is not simply kinesthetic. This sensory mix is useful in self-regulation and in perception, as a study by Lachs *et al.* (2001) showed. This study is a variant of Sumby and Pollack, in which Lachs aimed to determine the conditions in which a cochlear implant delivered successful sensory inflow for speech perception.

The children examined by Lachs had all used electrocochlear substitution for audition for two years, and had developed language after being implanted at the average age of four-and-a-half years. These youngsters, almost seven years old at the time of testing, were assayed with a variety of speech perception instruments under auditory, visual, and combined audiovisual presentation. A test of common phrases was the main dependent measure, obtained with several other measures of the identification of isolated words, and of the intelligibility of speech produced by each child. Most generally, this investigation found that a child's ability to perceive words in unimodal auditory conditions predicted the ability to integrate auditory and visual sensory streams multimodally. This corroborates Sumby and Pollack, specifically, that the integration of vision and hearing in service of speech perception is a natural mode of attention, and that the implanted children who resolved auditory information about words with the greatest proficiency were also the most adept at detecting the coherent properties of a visible face. Moreover, the same children who were proficient in multimodal speech understanding were also the sources of the most intelligible speech among the subjects.

It would be difficult to ascribe productive differences in speaking to the duration in which the cochlear implant had been in use, for the subjects were nearly uniform in this regard. Although experience with the sensory effects of speech did not distinguish the subjects from one another, susceptibility to symbolic processes predicted better articulation and receptive language, both uni- and multimodally. This is an unfortunate outcome for a sensory-based premise for speech perception, for it looks as though the children were matched on the distribution of sensory effects yet differed nonetheless in their linguistic facility. Evidently, there is a complex interchange between the reafferent sensory function of hearing, even prosthetically, and the perception of spoken words, suggesting at coarsest grain that experience producing language makes the greatest difference in multimodal speech perception, rather than experience with a specific form of incident sensory effects. In a theoretical note, Lachs *et al.* argue this point without disputing the historical resonance of the motor theory and efferent readiness in the account.

1.4.3 Natural quality

How important is naturalness? We have presented a case report of an adventitiously deafened adult, Mr. S, who had become an expert speechreader by the time he was implanted with an electrocochlear auditory prosthesis (Goh *et al.* 2001). Although the cochlear implant provides auditory samples of the incident speech, the device does not evoke natural vocal qualities. The rasping, noisy character of sound delivered by the implant contrasts with the melodiousness of the voice, yet the modulation of this anomalous sounding carrier is effective in sustaining speech perception. In the case of Mr. S, we sought to determine whether his lifelong experience with natural speech conveyed auditorily would inhibit his ability to derive linguistic attributes from multimodal settings. And, just to guarantee that the auditory properties he experienced would differ from natural vocal qualities, we used sinewave replicas of speech as the auditory driver.

We tested Mr. S's speech perception when he saw the talker but could not hear her, or when he heard her but could not see her, and in the multimodal setting. We compared his scores to group data from normal hearing adults evaluated under the same test conditions (Remez *et al.* 1998). It was hardly a surprise that this expert speechreader excelled in the visual presentation of speech, nor that his performance level surpassed the normal hearing adults. In the auditory presentation, the normal hearing subjects fared slightly better than Mr. S, indicating that experience with the natural auditory qualities of speech did not impair the use of anomalous signals in apprehending phonetic properties. Most surprising, though, was the special ability of Mr. S to function in the multimodal case, in which the gain available from sensory combination exceeded the performance of normal hearing subjects by almost 30 percent. Although this subject's excellent skill in speechreading was evident in the unimodal conditions, his facility with visual presentation allowed him to extract more useful value from the auditory stream than normal subjects did, despite the absence of speech-like auditory qualities delivered over the implant.

1.4.4 The puzzle

This finding of greater auditory benefit due to experience with a visible face is a bit confounding, because it suggests that the coalescence of sensory streams is susceptible to the education of attention acting transmodally. It highlights an aspect of audiovisual speech perception that warrants adequate description, namely, that there is potential for superadditivity in combining vision and audition. In this respect, the reliance of the field on the paradigm of McGurk and MacDonald has been limiting though extremely useful (and see Brancazio and Miller 2005). Specifically, the circumstance of multimodal rivalry and the reconciliation of conflict presupposes that the eye and the ear each capture a phoneme sequence to contribute to a common sensory metric. Our study with Mr. S revealed that he and the normal hearing listeners alike were able to resolve phonetic properties multimodally that were unavailable unimodally. Although it is possible that such perceptual prowess inheres in facile comparison of a new circumstance to a remembered sensory experience of speech, this seems to be an unlikely role of experience in multimodal speech perception. Instead, it seems as though the experience of linguistic properties however they are expressed promotes the ability to transpose the perceptual standards across modalities. This perceptual ability lies well beyond the versatility that we are used to considering when we describe perception.

1.5 A conclusion

In some opinion, research on audiovisual speech perception holds the force to break the cherished theoretical stalemates of our community, and to dislodge even the most durable accounts of speech perception. However, the fifty years since Sumby and Pollack's report evidently has not given us long enough to take the conceptual plunge, although a glance at contemporary research shows that we are in a phase right now during which we are looking before we leap. This conservatism is justified, for few research problems in perception match the complexity of intermodal correspondence, audiovisual integration, and multisensory perceptual organization. Within the audiovisual speech perception community it has been possible to escape the feeling of déjà vu, although the penalty for seeking this excitement has been uncertainty about the useful or applicable theoretical devices. There are a few ways that contemporary studies try to reconcile multimodal speech perception with the rest of speech perception, and, indeed, with the rest of perception. To scope the range of conservative accommodations to multimodal speech perception, at one end of the distribution we are asked to imagine the nature of phonology had Trubetzkoi been deaf; in another, we are asked to favor the agency of the productive phonetic homunculus whichever lemniscus its effects excite; in yet another, we are asked to remain calm about the pathways of sensory inflow because it all winds up in the same place, anyway. In this brief and selective review of research on multimodal speech perception, a set of three puzzles is offered that holds the promise to push the field forward. At the same time that basic research on audiovisual speech perception uncovers new phenomena that warrant explanation, the findings of intersensory combination provoke attention to unnoticed aspects of speech in a traditional tract-to-ear chain. The benefits anticipated of the campaign, therefore, are salutary for the traditionalists and the pioneers alike.

1.6 Acknowledgments

The author is grateful to Rebecca Piorkowski for weighing the arguments while they took shape, and for advice and counsel in the preparation of Figure 1.1. For help with Figure 1.2, the author acknowledges the generosity of Lionel Revéret and Cynthia Yang. For incisive comments on this manuscript, the author thanks Eric Vatikiotis-Bateson. This research was supported by an award to Barnard College from the National Institute on Deafness and Other Communication Disorders (DC00308).

2 Visual speech perception

L. E. Bernstein

2.1 Introduction

Phonetic perception is the perception of the linguistically relevant attributes of physical speech signals. In the mid twentieth century, phonetic perception research was almost exclusively on auditory phonetic perception. By the end of the century, significant research effort had shifted to audiovisual and visual-only phonetic perception. The shift took place following discovery of the so-called *McGurk effect* (McGurk and MacDonald 1976), which is brought about when visual speech information that conflicts with auditory speech information influences auditory perception. Before the discovery of the McGurk effect, researchers had reported that under noisy conditions, enhancements to auditory speech intelligibility and language comprehension occur when the listener can also view the talker (e.g., Sumby and Pollack 1954); but the significance of those reports in showing visual influences on auditory speech perception was not particularly well-appreciated until after the McGurk effect was reported.

The McGurk effect focused attention on phonetic perception, because the stimuli were nonsense syllables as opposed to words, and the effect was at the level of phonetic perception. But the McGurk effect drew attention primarily to audiovisual integration of speech and not to visual phonetic perception. Visual speech perception still is viewed primarily as an influence on auditory speech perception (Schroeder *et al.* 2008). However, the literature in audiology and deaf education offers studies on speech perceived by vision alone (via lipreading/speechreading) (see for an early review, Jeffers and Barley 1971). In addition, experimental studies have been published on visual speech perception (e.g., Summerfield 1991; Dodd *et al.* 1998; Bernstein *et al.* 2000b; Mohammed *et al.* 2005; Auer and Bernstein 2007).

This chapter discusses research on visual phonetic perception and spoken word recognition. Experiments are described that are consistent with the view that visual speech stimuli are phonetically impoverished, but that the phonetic information is not so reduced that accurate visual spoken word recognition is impossible. Spoken word recognition involves the projection of visual phonetic information to the mental lexicon, whose structure supports word recognition, even when only incomplete visual phonetic information is available (Auer 2000; Mattys *et al.* 2002). A spoken word can be recognized despite phonetic impoverishment, if it is sufficiently distinct from other words in the mental lexicon; and visual phonetic information can be sufficiently distinct. Furthermore, the research presented here is consistent with the hypothesis that word distinctiveness is modality-dependent: Visual phonetic perceptual patterns of segmental similarity predict word distinctiveness for lipreading words better than do auditory phonetic perception patterns (Auer 2002). In emphasizing the role that visual phonetic perception plays in visual spoken word recognition, the chapter departs from treatments of visual speech perception that focus on either phoneme identification or sentence lipreading.

Although the view that speech perception is a specialized function of the auditory system (e.g., Liberman 1982) has yielded (e.g., Liberman and Mattingly 1985) in response to multiple demonstrations of visual influences on speech perception, knowledge about visual phonetic perception lags far behind knowledge about auditory phonetic perception. For over sixty years, studies of auditory phonetic perception detailed the acoustic characteristics of natural and synthesized speech signals and their effects on perceptual discrimination and identification. Hand in hand with studies of acoustic speech signals has gone the development of a range of theoretical explanations for auditory speech perception (e.g., Fowler 1986; Remez 1994; Nearey 1997; Liberman and Whalen 2000; Pisoni and Remez 2004). In contrast, relatively little is known about visual speech perception, particularly, visual phonetic perception and visual speech signals (c.f., Benguerel and Pichora-Fuller 1982; Montgomery and Jackson 1983; Montgomery *et al.* 1987; Jiang *et al.* 2007).

Specifically, knowledge is lacking about visual speech signal characteristics and their relationships to visual speech perception. There are various impediments to acquiring such knowledge. There are difficulties in measuring and manipulating visual speech stimuli. There is a longstanding view that visual speech information is so impoverished that there is not much to see in the stimulus (e.g., Kuhl and Meltzoff 1988). In addition, the visual system and visual perception have been entirely separate scientific domains from auditory speech perception. Thus, the vast literature on low- and high-level human visual processing has for the most part not influenced thinking about visual speech perception (c.f., Jordan *et al.* 2000; Thomas and Jordan 2004). This chapter includes suggestions for research strategies for visual phonetic perception that draw on knowledge from visual perception.

Understanding of visual speech processing can be accelerated by investigating perception in congenitally deaf[1] perceivers. Individuals with visual perception of speech but without auditory experience, or with only highly degraded auditory experience, afford the opportunity to inquire about the extent to which the visual system by itself can support the operations involved in acquiring and using a spoken language. In this chapter, the experiments that are described in detail involved participation by both deaf and hearing adults.

2.1.1 *Visual speech perception and visual speech signals*

Phonetic attributes of speech stimuli are the linguistically relevant, physical (measurable) attributes of speech signals. The face reveals less phonetic information than does the voice. The impoverishment of optical phonetic signals relative to acoustic phonetic signals is simply explained. The vocal organs (Catford 1977) – nasal cavity, oral cavity, velum, tongue, pharynx, larynx, glottis, trachea, and lungs – are mostly hidden from the eye, although their activities and dimensions are the distal cause of the acoustic signals to the ear (Stevens 1998). That is, information about the linguistically relevant state of all of the vocal organs is present in acoustic signals. In contrast, the visual perceiver can obtain direct information about the vocal organs only from the lips and intermittently the interior of the oral cavity with views of the tongue. However, vocal activities have effects on other visible face parts such as the jaw and the skin tissue of the lower face and cheeks. The jaw and cheeks are not considered to be vocal organs (Catford 1977), but the activities of the vocal organs have direct effects on them.

Movements of labeled points on the skin surface of the cheeks and jaw have been shown to be highly correlated with both tongue motion and acoustic characteristics (Yehia *et al.* 1998; Jiang *et al.* 2000). Perceptual studies confirm that perceivers use the information from the jaw and cheeks, in addition to the mouth and view into the oral cavity (Benoît *et al.* 1995b; Preminger *et al.* 1998). But all these sources of visual phonetic information are limited in comparison with auditory phonetic information, which can be available whether the mouth is open or not and is available for the activity of vocal organs that have minimal, if any, effect on visible structures: The state of the velum, related to nasality, and the state of the larynx, related to voice fundamental frequency are not available to the visual perceiver.

As a result of the impoverishment of visual phonetic information, visual speech perception and spoken word recognition performed by *even* the upper quartile of *hearing* lipreaders is similar in accuracy to listening to speech under difficult to somewhat difficult conditions (at the level of approximately 27–69 percent words correct in sentences) (Bernstein *et al.* 2000a; Auer and Bernstein 2007). Accuracy achieved by the upper quartile of *deaf* lipreaders (at the level of approximately 48–85 percent words correct in sentences) is similar to listening under somewhat difficult to somewhat favorable conditions.

2.1.2 Phonetic impoverishment in relationship to words

A fundamental question is the extent to which the phonetic impoverishment of visual speech stimuli results in too little phonetic information to preserve the distinctiveness of the forms of different morphemes or words (c.f. Jakobson *et al.* 1969). Typically, lexical or morphological distinctiveness is described in terms of constituent phonemes. Phonemes are not sound units but rather distinctions at the segmental level of language. Phonemes are phonemes, because they differentiate morphemes or words and are identified within a language by conducting an inventory of the distinct lexical forms in that language (Gleason 1961). That is, phonemes are the phonological units of a language that comprise the different lexical forms in that language. Particular phonemes are instantiated on the basis of many phonetic characteristics that typically vary across phonetic contexts (e.g. Lisker 1978; Liberman 1982). However, as Liberman and Mattingly (1985) point out, "while each [acoustic phonetic] cue is, by definition more or less sufficient, none is truly necessary. The absence of any single cue, no matter how seemingly characteristic of the phonetic category, can be compensated for by others, not without some cost to naturalness or even intelligibility, perhaps, but still to such an extent that the intended category is, in fact, perceived" (pp. 11–12). That speech perception is resistant to loss of phonetic information is demonstrated, for example, by perception of sinewave speech, for which the formants are replaced by single sinusoidal components at the formant center frequencies (Remez *et al.* 1981). These stimuli do not have fundamental frequencies, frication, aspiration, or harmonic spacing – all of which are phonetic attributes – but listeners can frequently recover their linguistic content.

Estimation of the phonetic information in visible speech has almost invariably involved asking perceivers to identify nonsense syllables under forced-choice laboratory conditions (c.f., Bernstein *et al.* 2000b). Phoneme identification rates for nonsense syllable stimuli, depending on phonetic context, have been reported to be below 50 percent correct (Fisher 1968; Wozniak and Jackson 1979; Lesner and Kricos 1981; Walden *et al.* 1981; and rates range between 19 percent and 46 percent in Owens and Blazek 1985, and between 21 and 43 percent in Auer *et al.* 1997). Percent correct identification of vowels in /h/V/g/ (where V = vowel) stimuli by adults with normal hearing in a study by Montgomery and Jackson (1983) varied between 42 percent and 59 percent. However, Auer *et al.* (1997) reported 75 percent correct vowel identification for 19 vowels, including r-colored vowels across four phonetic contexts. Visual phonetic stimuli are impoverished, but phoneme identification scores are not a complete answer to the question of whether or not the information afforded visually to recognize words is adequate. In order to answer that question, other factors need to be known, such as the confusion patterns among phonemes and their effects on word distinctiveness.

Visemes Investigation of the information in visible speech has typically involved, in addition to the collection of percent correct scores, the examination of correct and incorrect response patterns. Fairly systematic, although far from invariant (cf., Owens and Blazek 1985), clusters of confusions among phonemes have been observed. For example, /m b p/ are typically highly confused by perceivers. These clusters have come to be regarded as perceptual categories referred to as *visemes* (e.g., Massaro 1998b).

Fisher (1968) coined the term *viseme* as shorthand for *visual phoneme* and defined the *viseme* to be the visible analogue to the phoneme. That is, Fisher equated phonemes with sound units and then equated phonemes to visemes. However, as explained earlier, phonemes are not sound units but rather distinctive units at the segmental (phonological) level of language. Phonemes are phonemes, because they differentiate words or morphemes. Phonemes are phonological units. In contrast, visemes are visemes, because the phonemes they comprise are phonetically impoverished, and their ability to differentiate words is reduced. In his experiment on visemes, Fisher asked participants to identify the initial or final phoneme of a word. However, the forced-choice identification options given the participants did not include the phoneme that the talker had actually spoken. That is, Fisher assumed that the stimulus phoneme was ambiguous with at least one other phoneme.

This assumption was probably based on results in Woodward and Barber (1960), cited in Fisher (1968). Woodward and Barber had sought to discover the minimal perceptual units of lipreading. They conducted a discrimination experiment with CV (consonant-vowel) nonsense syllables. They did not test every phonemic contrast in English but rather based selection of stimulus pairs on feature analysis and a theoretical scale of perceptual dissimilarity. They calculated a discrimination value for each of their stimulus pairs by subtracting the percentage of *same* responses from *different* responses for each order of stimuli and adding the results. They then divided the range of obtained values into phoneme pairs that were considered to be *contrastive*, *similar*, or *equivalent*. Although they had quantified a dissimilarity scale, they concluded that almost all the articulatory features of English were neutralized for the lipreader. Only four sets of English consonants were classified as visually contrastive: /t, d, n, l, θ, ð, s, z, tʃ, dʒ, ʃ, ʒ, j, k, g, h/, /p, b, m/, /f, v/, and /hw, w, r/. They concluded that the derived groupings were perceptual units, and that further differentiation within groups required information from grammar, the lexicon, and/or phonological context. Fisher adopted the suggestion that phonemes that were grouped together according to such criteria were perceptual categories, and his research methodology did not have the potential to disconfirm the suggestion.

Subsequently, Walden, Prosek, Montgomery, Scherr, and Jones (1977) developed a methodology for defining visemes based on nonsense syllable confusion matrices obtained in identification studies. The responses in the confusion matrices were submitted to cluster analysis. Phonemes were assigned to viseme groups when a cluster represented at least 75 percent of responses to the phonemes in that cluster. This method has become standard for reducing confusion data to visemes (e.g., Owens and Blazek 1985). Interestingly, the cluster analysis method implies that perception is not as categorical as the viseme notion implies. Were visemes discrete perceptual categories, confusion matrices would have only responses within the clusters, and the hierarchical cluster analysis methodology would not be needed to assign phonemes to visemes. In fact, confusion matrices are usually quite noisy, therefore requiring an operational approach to assigning viseme clusters. Despite this problem, as suggested earlier, the perceptual category status of visemes has become accepted (e.g., Massaro 1998b).

Homophenous words Words comprising visemes are said to be *homophenous*, different-sounding but like-appearing to the lipreader (Nitchie 1916; Berger 1972). For example, / p, b, m / are considered to be a viseme, and therefore, the words *bat*, *mat*, and *pat* are predicted to be homophenous. Berger (1972) and Nitchie (1916) suggested that approximately 50–60 percent of the words in English are homophenous. The notions of the viseme and of homophenу are consistent. They have both been invoked to explain the difficulty of lipreading. Low mean lipreading scores for word stimuli reported in the literature (e.g., Rönnberg 1995; Rönnberg *et al.* 1998) are consistent with the prediction that phonetic information is inadequate to maintain lexical distinctiveness. But mean scores fail to disclose wide performance ranges across individuals, including perceivers who are highly effective in identifying spoken words visually (Bernstein *et al.* 2000a; Mohammed *et al.* 2005; Auer and Bernstein 2007). So mean word lipreading scores do not answer the question about the extent to which adequate phonetic information is afforded in visual speech signals. Also, as discussed below, word recognition is not completely explained in terms of phonetic perception.

2.1.3 Spoken word recognition

During the bottom-up, auditory perceptual processing of spoken words, phonetic information is thought to activate word forms stored in lexical memory. Word recognition is described as selection of (or discrimination of) a word form from among other stored word forms (e.g. Luce 1986; McClelland and Elman 1986; Luce and Pisoni 1998). Lexical access follows recognition, making information such as the word's meaning available to yet higher-level psycholinguistic processes (Tyler and Frauenfelder 1978). The generally accepted view is that spoken word recognition involves both activation and competition among stored word forms during the temporal processing of speech information

(Forster 1979; Morton 1979; McClelland and Rumelhart 1981; Marslen-Wilson 1987; Marslen-Wilson 1989; Marslen-Wilson 1993; Norris 1994). The similarity between the stimulus input representation and the stored word forms is what drives activation levels of the stored word forms. Activation is a continuous temporal function that is sensitive to phonetic information (e.g., Andruski *et al.* 1994; Connine *et al.* 1994; Marslen-Wilson and Warren 1994; Luce and Pisoni 1998). That is, form-based similarity is a function of phonetic or segmental similarity between the input representation and the stored word forms over time. Given that form-based activation spreads among stored word forms as a function of their similarity to the input representation, word recognition theories have incorporated mechanisms to explain competition, and how it is resolved (e.g., TRACE McClelland and Elman 1986; Marslen-Wilson 1987; Marslen-Wilson 1990; SHORTLIST Norris 1994; PARSYN Luce, Goldinger *et al.* 2000).

If visual phonetic stimuli lack *most* of the information for distinguishing among words, then the problem of selecting words in memory based on bottom-up stimulus information is indeed severe, if not virtually impossible. A highly impoverished visual spoken word stimulus would be predicted to afford too little information to select a single word stored in memory. Instead it would be predicted to result in a low level of activation for a large set of competing word candidates, and threshold for recognition would be predicted to be insufficient for recognition.

Several relevant empirical issues arise from the foregoing discussion. How impoverished are visual phonetic signals? Is visual speech perception the perception of a small set of segmental categories? Are visual spoken word stimuli processed relationally at the level of the lexicon in terms of their visual phonetic distinctiveness? Or is visual spoken word recognition achieved by some type of transformation to the form-based representations that auditory processes ordinarily output? Does our understanding of visual speech perception depend on the characteristics of the perceiver? The studies discussed below addressed these questions.

2.2 Evaluation of visemes and word homopheny

Some investigators have noted that viseme clusters vary across talkers and phonetic contexts (e.g., Owens and Blazek 1985), suggesting that the viseme can only loosely be interpreted as a perceptual category. An experiment was carried out based on the question whether words that comprise visemes are actually homophenous. The *phoneme equivalence class* (PEC), the generalization of the viseme, was defined as a set of phonemes that are grouped together due to their perceptual similarity (Auer and Bernstein 1997). The *lexical equivalence class* (LEC) was defined as the set of words rendered notationally identical by re-transcribing words in a lexicon in terms of a set of PECs (Auer and Bernstein 1997). For example, if / b p m / are a PEC, *B* = {b, p, m}. In addition, if *T* = {t, s, z} and *A* = {i, ɪ, ɛ, a^{i}, e, æ, ʌ}, then *bat*, *mat*, and *pat*, would be in the same LEC, *BAT* = {bat, mat, pat, mass, miss, bate, . . . }.

The notation "{}" is used to define a set. The use of the term *equivalence class* to define the PEC and the LEC is not intended to imply stimulus equivalence. The formation of phoneme equivalence classes is an operation on confusion matrices that involves groupings that represent levels of perceptual similarity. For any sets of PECs and associated LECs, it is an empirical question to what extent the members of the class are perceptually equivalent to each other.

Bernstein *et al.* (1997) conducted an experiment with hearing adults to examine whether words predicted to be in the same LEC under several different definitions of PECs were in fact visually distinguishable. Their results are summarized below. In addition, two groups of participants (deaf and hearing) with above-average lipreading were tested, and their results are also reported here. The stimuli used in both studies were video recorded spoken monosyllabic words (Bernstein and Eberhardt 1986a). Participants performed a target identification task: On each trial, they were presented with an orthographic word (the target word), followed by a spoken target-distracter word pair, with the order of the spoken words counterbalanced and the sets of target–distracter pairs pseudo-randomized for each participant. Participants were directed to indicate which of the spoken words matched the orthographic target. Feedback was given during practice but not during experimental trials. Chance performance would suggest that target-distracter word pairs were homophonous.

The target identification task required both discrimination between target and distracter and target identification. That is, to be successful, participants had to discriminate between the two stimuli in a pair, and they had to identify which of the two stimuli was the target. Had the task been simply AX (same–different) discrimination, participants could have detected non-linguistic differences in the naturally spoken words and used those differences in generating their response. By requiring a linguistic identification, uncontrollable non-linguistic stimulus differences did not compromise the experiment.

2.2.1 Experimental method

For each target identification trial, the distracter was a word that, given a particular criterion for PECs, was predicted to be perceptually indiscriminable from its corresponding target word. The procedure for selecting target–distracter pairs comprised multiple steps. Briefly stated, they included (1) collection of stimulus–response confusion matrices for phoneme identification in nonsense syllables (spoken by the same talker who spoke the words in the target identification trials), (2) hierarchical cluster analysis of stimulus–response phoneme confusion matrices, (3) generation of PECs from the hierarchical cluster analyses, and finally (4) selection of target–distracter word pairs from groups of words within the same LECs.

Target–distracter pairs were selected using three different PEC criteria, *difficult*, *standard*, and *easy*. The *standard* (viseme) level[2] PECs were defined as the lowest level in the hierarchical cluster analysis solution (an inverted tree structure) for the phoneme identifications at which at least 75 percent of all responses were within one of the clusters. (The levels from low to high being, respectively, the level at which no phonemes are grouped together *versus* the level at which all phonemes are grouped together.) The *difficult* equivalence class level was defined as the level in the hierarchical cluster analysis halfway between the *standard* level and the lowest level in the hierarchical cluster analysis. At intervening levels in the hierarchy, classes were based on the frequency of phoneme confusions; phonemes joined classes at low levels if they were often confused and joined at higher levels, if they were rarely or never confused. Therefore, in order for phonemes to be in PECs at the *difficult* level, they had to be frequently confused. The *easy* equivalence class level was defined as the level in the hierarchical cluster analysis halfway between the *standard* level and the highest level in the hierarchical cluster analysis. PECs at the *easy* level included phonemes that were infrequently confused with each other.

The phoneme equivalence classes are listed in Table 2.1. The hierarchical relationship between levels can be observed in the tabled PECs. The table also lists percent correct phonemes from the identification experiments used to generate the confusions (Bernstein *et al.* 1993; Iverson *et al.* 1998). Due to the hierarchical relationship among PECs, words that were members of the *standard* LECs could inadvertently have been target–distracter pairs at the *difficult* equivalence class level. Likewise, words that were members of *easy*

Table 2.1 *Phoneme equivalence classes.*

Correct	%	Level	Phoneme Equivalence Classes
Consonants Vowels	47.8 51.3	Difficult	{p} {b m} {f v} {θ ð} {w} {r} {tʃ dʒ ʃʒ} {t} {d} {s z} {k} {g} {n} {l} {h} {i ɪ} {ɛ e æ} {a^{i}} {ə} {a ɔ} {o} {a^{u}} {o^{i}} {ʌ} {ʊ u}
		Standard	{p b m} {f v} {θ ð} {w} {r} {tʃ dʒ ʃʒ d} {t s z} {k g h} {n l} {i ɪ ɛ a^{i} e æ ʌ} {ə o o^{i} ʊ u} {a ɔ} {a^{u}}
		Easy	{p b m w} {f v} {θ ð t s z} {r tʃ dʒ ʃʒ d} {k g n l h} {i ɪ ɛ a^{i} e æ a ɔ a^{u} ʌ} {ə o o^{i} ʊ u}

lexical equivalence classes could inadvertently have been members of LECs at the two lower levels. For this reason, target–distracter pairs were selected only if they *did not* also qualify at a more difficult level.

During experimental trials, every participant received every target word and an equal number of distracters for each phoneme equivalence class level. However, the distracters were counterbalanced across participants so that each received only one of the potential distracters for each target. For example, for the target word *pane*, one third of participants received the *difficult* level distracter word *pan*, one third received the *standard* level distracter word *peal*, and one third received the *easy* level distracter word *puck*. Fifteen target words were presented twice in each trial order (the target was either the first or second spoken word), for a total of sixty trials. Forty-six hearing adults, who were not screened for lipreading ability, were tested.

2.2.2 Results

Figure 2.1 shows the results for this experiment (results labeled *unscreened hearing* in the figure) and its companion reported further below. Scores at the standard level showed performance to be significantly above chance [t (45) = 13.603, p = .000; where chance = .50]. Inspection of individual participants' scores revealed that six participants obtained at least .90 proportion correct at the *standard* level. Performance at the *difficult* level was also above chance [t (45) = 7.199, p = .000]. Thus, this experiment showed that the standard

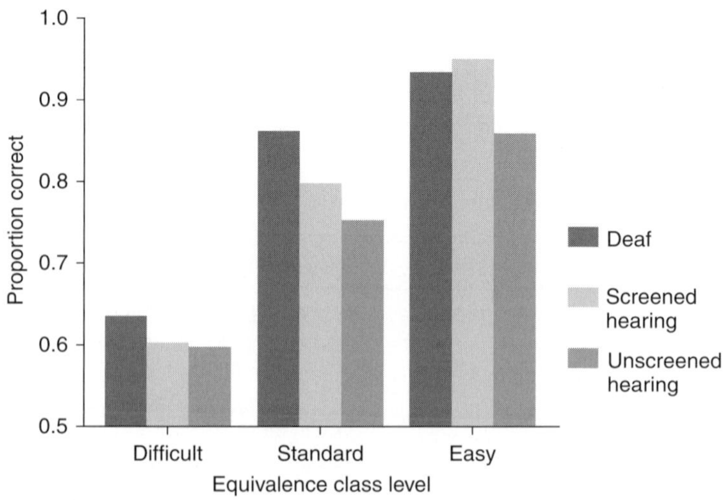

Figure 2.1 Results from the target identification task.

(viseme) level of phoneme groupings resulted in discriminable and identifiable words. Even at the *difficult* level, performance was above chance. The results suggested that participants processed sub-PEC phonetic information, even at the *difficult* level.

Word pairs were selected according to criteria that had predicted progressively better performance from *difficult*, to *standard*, to *easy* levels. Repeated measures analyses of variance were conducted with level as the repeated factor.[3] Level was a significant main effect [F (2, 90) = 68.745, p =.000]. Contrasts showed that each level was significantly different from the next [*difficult* to *standard*, F (1, 45) = 42.970, p = .000; *standard* to *easy*, F (1, 45) = 32.277, p = .000]. These results showed that although none of the levels corresponded to homopheny, they did result in graded differences.

In a subsequent experiment, deaf and hearing participants with above-average lipreading screening scores were tested. Nine hearing young adults and nine deaf college students, who all scored above the passing score on a lipreading screening test (normed separately for deaf vs. hearing adults) (Auer and Bernstein 2007), were recruited. Thirty-seven out of 257 words was the minimum score for hearing participants and 86 out of 257 was the minimum for deaf participants. Obtained scores for the hearing participants ranged between 46 and 166 words correct (mean 101). Scores for the deaf participants ranged between 104 and 168 words correct (mean 126). There was not a statistically significant difference between group means. All of the deaf participants had a pre-lingual hearing impairment of at least 85 dB HL pure tone average bilaterally. Better ear pure tone averages ranged between 85 dB HL and 120 dB HL. Eight out of nine deaf participants reported birth as the age of hearing impairment onset. All of the deaf participants reported having been educated for eight or more years in an environment in which English (either spoken or in a signed form) was the language of instruction.

Figure 2.1 shows the mean scores for the screened deaf and hearing participants. Across all participants, scores for the *standard* pairs were above chance [t (17) = 10.72, p = .000]. At the *difficult* level, performance was also above chance [t (17) = 5.10, p = .000]. Inspection of individual participants' scores revealed that five deaf participants obtained scores in the range .65 to .75 correct at the *difficult* level. Three hearing participants obtained scores in the range of .65 to .80 at the *difficult* level. Six deaf participants obtained scores of .80 to 1.0 at the *standard* (viseme) level. Seven hearing participants obtained scores in the range of .85 to .90 at the *standard* level.

In a repeated measures analysis of variance with the between factor group (deaf vs. hearing), group was not a significant factor (p = .454). Level was a significant factor [F (2, 32) = 46.757, p = .000]. Contrast tests showed each level was significantly different from the next [*standard* versus *difficult* F (1, 16) = 31.569, p = .000, and *easy* versus *standard* F (1, 16) = 15.475, p = .001].

2.2.3 *Summary*

The experiments reported above show that phonetic information available to lipreaders is not so impoverished that words comprising PECs (even at the *difficult* level) cannot be discriminated and identified. When given a choice between two words that were homophenous according to the definition for standard viseme groupings, perceivers were very accurate at selecting the correct spoken target word. This supports the conclusion that loss of phonetic information is not equivalent to creation of a small set of segmental perceptual categories as implied by the notion of the viseme. One argument in support of the viseme could be that the concept is correct, but the grouping procedures to generate PECs should comprise only more similar members. However, in the experiments above, the *difficult* level used twelve distinctions more than did the *standard* level, and yet performance was above chance. So, the concept of the viseme could be retained by generating a still more difficult set of PECs, that is, ones that resulted in greater similarity of words within LECs; but the general notion that phonetic information is so impoverished that only a few broad categories are perceived would seem to be discredited. In addition, the study demonstrated that segmental similarity estimated with nonsense syllable identification was able to predict the similarity of whole words. This is evidence that the phonetic information is relevant at the level of word recognition. Although the results imply that above-average deaf and hearing lipreaders are not different from each other, other results suggest that overall, the best lipreaders are individuals with prelingual deafness and reliance on spoken language (Bernstein *et al.* 2000b; Mohammed *et al.* 2005; Auer and Bernstein 2007).

2.3 Phonetic distinctiveness of English words

In the experiments described above, participants demonstrated accuracy in their judgments of the target word under forced choice conditions. Speech communication does not typically afford such a restricted range of words to be recognized. As discussed earlier, during the bottom up, auditory perceptual processing of spoken words, phonetic information is thought to activate memory of word forms. Word recognition is the process of selection of (or discrimination of) a word form from among other stored word forms. The experiments described in the previous section showed that more phonetic information was available for word recognition than implied by the viseme notion. Nevertheless, the fundamental question remains how, under open set conditions, the impoverished visual phonetic word stimulus is recognized from among other similar word forms stored in memory.

Some insights into the magnitude of the open set word recognition problem have been achieved by conducting computational modeling studies of the effects of phonetic impoverishment on the form-based distinctiveness of words. Auer and Bernstein (1997) investigated the effects of visual phonetic impoverishment on phonemically transcribed words in the PhLex database (Seitz *et al.* 1995). The modeling method involved the following steps:

1. Rules were developed to re-transcribe words so that their transcriptions comprised only the single-character expressions standing for PECs at a particular level of phoneme confusability.
2. Re-transcription rules were applied to the words in a phonemically transcribed, computer-readable lexicon.
3. The re-transcribed words were sorted so that words rendered identical (no longer notationally distinct) were placed in the same lexical equivalence classes (LECs).
4. Quantitative measures were applied to estimate the effects of the re-transcription on the lexicon and on word recognition.

Application of this method to the 32 377-word PhLex database (Seitz *et al.* 1995) showed that when only 12 PECs were used – {u ʊ ər}, {o aʊ}, {i ɪ ɛ e æ}, {ɔi}, {ɔ ai ə ɑ ʌ j}, {p b m}, {f v}, {l n k ŋ g h}, {d t s z}, {w r}, {θ ð} and {tʃ dʒ ʃ ʒ} – 54 percent of words (frequency weighted) were notationally distinct. When 19 PECs were used – {u ʊ ər}, {o aʊ}, {i ɪ}, {ɛ e}, {æ}, {ɔi}, {ɔ}, {ai ə ɑ ʌ j}, {p b m}, {f v}, {l}, {n k}, {ŋ g}, {h}, {d}, {t s z}, {w r}, {θ ð} and {tʃ dʒ ʃ ʒ} – 76 percent of words (frequency weighted) were distinct. These results showed that when the lexicon as a whole is considered, relatively small improvements in segmental distinctiveness (fewer phonemes within PECs) resulted in large increases in word distinctiveness. This result is consistent with the target identification results above in that both suggest that lexical distinctiveness is a function of available phonetic information.

Iverson, Bernstein, and Auer (1998) applied the same type of analyses but used 13 PECs – {p b m}, {f v}, {θ ð}, {tʃ dʒ ʃ ʒ d}, {t s z}, {l n}, {j k ŋ g h}, {w}, {r}, {i ɪ ei ai ɛ æ ʌ ə}, {ər o ɔi u ʊ}, {aʊ} and {ɔ ɑ} – and also analyzed monosyllabic separately from multisyllabic words: 31 075 words in the PhLex database were found to comprise 5 073 monosyllabic and 26 002 di- and multisyllabic words. Few monosyllabic words were distinct on this re-coding, 15 percent (12 percent frequency weighted). But most di- and multisyllabic words were distinct, 78 percent (74 percent frequency weighted).

In the context of attempting to understand the implications of phonetic impoverishment on word recognition, it is important in addition to consider not just the number but also the size of LECs under a particular set of PEC re-transcription rules. In Iverson *et al.*, it was found that the expected class size for monosyllabic words was 9.2 (9.8 frequency weighted), and the expected class size for di- and multisyllabic words combined was 1.7 (1.8 frequency weighted). That is, on average, monosyllabic words become similar to 8.2 other words under the PECs that were used there to re-transcribe the lexicon, but di- and multisyllabic become similar to fewer than one word. Given that the PECs in that study represented a very conservative estimate of available phonetic information (the standard level), the results suggested that the structure of the lexicon is very favorable to relatively high levels of accurate visual spoken word recognition under conditions of good phonetic perception (i.e., proficient lipreading).

2.3.1 Predictability of visual spoken word recognition

If spoken word recognition is a process of selecting within the mental lexicon a single word candidate most similar to the input phonetic stimulus, then with modeling methods of the type described above, it should be possible to predict relative visual spoken word recognition accuracy. As a corollary, if similarity is modality-specific, predictions based on visual phoneme identification should be more accurate than ones based on auditory perception.

The first prediction was investigated by Mattys, Bernstein, and Auer (2002) who conducted a study in which eight deaf and eight hearing adult participants performed open set identification for words that varied in word frequency of occurrence (high vs. low) and size of the LEC (UNIQUE, MEDIUM, LARGE) in which they were grouped. The PECs used to re-transcribe the lexicon in order to generate the stimulus word lists were based on the standard level of phoneme clustering and confusion data obtained from a very large phoneme identification study (Auer *et al.* 1997). Words in UNIQUE size LECs were predicted to be visually distinct and most intelligible. Stimulus words from MEDIUM LECs had 1–5 possible words that were highly similar to the stimulus word, and therefore predicted to be less intelligible. Words from LARGE LECs had 9–59 possible words that were highly similar to the stimulus word, and therefore predicted to be least intelligible. In addition, for each combination of frequency and LEC size, words were selected that were monosyllables or disyllables.

All the participants in the study were screened for better-than-average lipreading accuracy, because a goal of the study was to test the prediction method. Random selection of participants would virtually have guaranteed that some individuals would perform at low levels of accuracy, and therefore increased the variance in the estimated effects. The participants' task was to view 150 isolated monosyllabic and 130 isolated disyllabic spoken words presented pseudorandomly within length groupings, and after each word, type at a computer terminal their identification response. Responses were scored in terms of whole words correct and the number of phonemes correct.

Statistical analyses showed significant effects of LEC size, word frequency of occurrence, and word length. Whole words were identified more accurately when their LEC size was low, when their frequency of occurrence was high, and when they were monosyllables. Mattys *et al.* interpreted their results as a clear indication that visual spoken word recognition is strongly influenced by the number of visually similar words in the lexicon and by the frequency of occurrence of the test words. When responses were scored in terms of phonemes correct, statistical analysis showed that deaf participants were more accurate than hearing participants (63 percent vs. 57 percent, respectively, phonemes correct across all words). The highest accuracy was obtained for UNIQUE words, for which deaf participants' mean was 82 percent, with a maximum of 93 percent for one individual.

Mattys *et al.* performed various analyses of the word and phoneme errors in the responses. They found that when participants incorrectly identified a stimulus word, they chose a word within the same LEC as their response far more often than would be predicted by chance. Furthermore, they found that the proportion of those within-LEC errors was higher among deaf than among hearing participants. Thus, deaf participants were more accurate in two respects, the proportion of their phonemes correct and the proportion of their within-class, although incorrect, word responses.

The second prediction suggested earlier was investigated in a related study. Auer (2000) investigated, in screened deaf and hearing adults, spoken word identification accuracy for isolated monosyllabic words selected either to control for segmental intelligibility or to control for similarity to other words. Similarity to other words was computed using the Neighborhood Activation Model (NAM by Luce and Pisoni 1998). Auer showed that when predicted stimulus segmental intelligibility was controlled, words with fewer neighbors were easier to identify than words with many neighbors, consistent with the findings of Mattys *et al.* (2002), using the LEC modeling. Furthermore, Auer examined the effect of computing neighborhood estimates using results from auditory speech in noise. That is, he substituted auditory segmental confusion data for visual segmental confusion data in the NAM computations. This substitution drastically reduced the predictability of visual word identification based on computed NAM values. Both participant groups showed that visual phonetic similarity was a better predictor of visual spoken word recognition than auditory phonetic similarity. This result supports the hypothesis that form-based similarity at the level of the lexicon is modality-specific. That is, visual phonetic information is relevant at the level of the mental lexicon. In addition, the fact that results with hearing adults were similar to ones with prelingually deaf adults suggested that the stimuli were perceived similarly across the two groups. Of course, the prelingually deaf adults had little if any auditory phonetic experience. So the similarity across groups in their performance supports a visual basis for perception, independent of auditory speech experience.

2.3.2 Summary

Current theories of spoken word recognition predict that reduced phonetic information should reduce word recognition accuracy. Furthermore, given that words are recognized in relation to other words, the extent to which any particular word becomes similar to other words should have a predictable effect on the accuracy with which it is recognized. This was confirmed by the open set word identification experiments (Auer 2000; Mattys *et al.* 2002). Importantly, the evidence supports the hypothesis that word distinctiveness is modality-dependent (Auer 2000). That is, confusability (similarity) for visually presented nonsense syllables more adequately accounted for visual spoken word recognition than did confusability for auditorily presented nonsense syllables.

2.4 Research strategies

The visual speech stimulus is complex. In addition, the face can convey the talker's identity, gender, state of arousal, and emotion, among other perceptible characteristics. As a visual stimulus, speech might, for example, comprise edges, directions of motion, kinematics, shapes, and/or configurations. These features might map directly to linguistically relevant internal phonetic representations. But many other features or combinations of features might be the ones that map to internal representations.

Our current understanding of visual speech perception is limited by our current understanding of the visual speech stimulus. One approach to a theory of the visual speech stimulus is suggested by Stevens' (1981) approach to research on auditory phonetic features. He considered whether the auditory system imposes a linguistically useful classificatory structure on the sounds of language. He hypothesized that this psychoacoustic classificatory structure projects onto distinctive phonological features. If this is true, the mapping from psychoacoustics to distinctive features is essentially transparent. Stevens (1989b) presented a set of distinctive features (such as vocalic – high, low, back, round, etc. – nonvocalic, sonorant, continuant, coronal, etc.) and suggested that "the perceptual correlate of each of the features can be described in terms of a threshold phenomenon . . ., and that the human perceptual system is equipped with fifteen to twenty of these threshold processes corresponding to features" (pp. 84–85).

For example, the auditory system is sensitive to the contrast between rapid *versus* slow spectral changes. Rapid spectral change occurs when there are articulatory transitions between relatively constricted (consonantal) and relatively unconstricted (vocalic) vocal tract configurations. The visual analogue for this contrast must also be rapid movements from or to relatively open mouth positions. Other auditory contrasts include rapid *versus* slow amplitude change, place of articulation of stop consonants, and vowel features (such as high-low, and front-back), all of which have visual manifestations (Montgomery and Jackson 1983; Abry and Boë 1986; Finn 1986). Open *versus* closed mouth corresponds approximately to high *versus* low amplitude acoustic signals. Problematic for the visual system are contrasts such as nasal *versus* non-nasal, and voiced *versus* voiceless, because these distinctions originate in part at invisible structures (that is, the velum and the glottis). For voicing, it is likely, however, that other phonetic attributes, such as vowel duration for post-vocalic stop consonants (Raphael 1971), can in part overcome the deficit in information about the state of the glottis. From the perspective of this chapter, which emphasizes that distinctive information is needed for spoken word recognition, the analysis of such distinctions afforded by the visual stimulus is highly attractive.

The foregoing suggests that there are visible articulatory motions that are strongly correlated with acoustic phonetic characteristics. In fact, this has been demonstrated by researchers such as Jiang *et al.* (2000) and Yehia *et al.* (1998). However, auditory-to-visual correlations are not what are needed for an explanation of visual phonetic perception. Stevens' type of project applied to visual phonetic perception would ask what classificatory structure is imposed by visual psychophysics. Rather than pointing to the visible analogue of audible articulatory effects, a visual explanation for speech perception would be in terms of visual features. But that route requires a deep understanding of high-level vision from the perspective of vision scientists. That avenue of research remains, for the most part, to be explored.

A different approach, which was taken by Bernstein and colleagues (Bernstein *et al.* 2001; Jiang *et al.* 2007), sought not the features of speech but the dissimilarity relationships among speech segments. This approach follows from an observation in Shepard and Chipman (1970). They noted that internal representations of perceptual objects are unlikely to be structurally isomorphic with stimuli, in the sense that the internal representation of a square is not likely to be square. In order to approach the problem of establishing relationships between complex stimuli and internal perceptual representations, they argued that an "isomorphism should be sought – not in the first-order relation between (a) an individual object, and (b) its corresponding internal representation – but in the second-order relation between (a) the relations among alternative external objects, and (b) the relations among their corresponding internal representations. Thus, although the internal representation for a square need not itself be square, it should (whatever it is) at least have a closer functional relation to the internal representation for a rectangle than to that, say, for a green flash or the taste of a persimmon" (p. 2). Shepard and Chipman suggest that seeking first-order relationships between, for example, linguistically relevant features, might follow from seeking the relationship between the dissimilarity of the physical speech segments and their perceptual dissimilarity.

To operationalize this suggestion, Bernstein and colleagues (Bernstein *et al.* 2001; Jiang *et al.* 2007) used a three-dimensional optical recording system and a video camera to record talkers saying consonant-vowel nonsense syllables. Participants perceptually identified the talkers' utterances in a forced-choice identification task. Then, perceptual confusion matrices were analyzed using multidimensional scaling. Euclidean distances were calculated between the positions of the category identifications in multidimensional space. The physical distances among the stimuli were also calculated using the three-dimensional optical recordings. Multilinear regression techniques were used to generate a prediction of the perceptual distances based on the optical recordings. With weighting and the full set of 3D optical data, the variance accounted for in the perceptual data on consonants ranged between 46% and 66% across talkers, and between 49% and 64% across vowels. Thus, the physical phonetic dissimilarity of visual speech stimuli was linearly related to their perceptual dissimilarity. Knowledge of these dissimilarity relationships can now be used in other experiments on the perceptual and neural underpinnings of visual phonetic perception.

In auditory phonetic perception, the goal of mapping psychoacoustic properties to phonetic classes historically followed in part from the view that articulatory events are optimized for auditory perception (Stevens 1981; Ohala 1992). That this might be true – but only for auditory perception – is a possibility. It is easy to imagine optical phonetic cues that could contribute to a more highly informational optical phonetics, yet do not occur. Nose wrinkling, head tilting, cheek puffing, and brow furling are among possible facial maneuvers that are not used for speech segment production but do occur in American Sign Language (Valli and Lucas 1992). Furthermore, research on Cued Speech, a manual code to augment lipreading (Cornett 1967; Charlier and Leybaert 2000), suggests that informational distinctiveness comparable to auditory speech stimuli can be achieved visually, even though natural language appears not to have opted for that possibility. Thus, while the possibility that speech is optimized for the auditory system is plausible, the possibility that it is optimized for the visual system seems remote. However, the extent to which optical speech signals conform to the processing demands of the visual system and the extent to which visual system processes impose classificatory structure on visual speech stimuli are important empirical questions that need to be answered for a theory of the visual speech stimulus and visual phonetic perception.

2.4.1 Summary

A detailed account of the visual phonetic stimulus is needed. It will require knowledge of visual system processing and knowledge of the linguistically relevant visual information in speech signals. A theory of the visual phonetic stimulus could involve first-order relationships between the stimuli and perception. That is, it could involve hypothesized visual speech features. Alternatively, a theory of the visual phonetic stimulus could involve second-order relationships between the dissimilarities among the phonetic stimuli and the dissimilarities in perceptual structure.

2.5 General conclusions

A complete explanation for visual speech perception will require an account of phonetic perception and the projection of information from that level of processing onto stored word forms in the mental lexicon. Initial studies support the view that visual spoken word recognition crucially depends on the visual phonetic distinctiveness of segmental information. Such information is afforded by the talking face, although less so than by the voice. For some individuals, in a manner that is not yet understood, the necessity of relying on visual phonetic information for communication due to deafness results in enhanced visual speech perceptual processing. Whether this involves specialized visual phonetic processes that occur also in perceivers with normal hearing is an empirical question. However, the current technologies for research on phonetic perception, including brain and behavioral methods, have the potential to help disclose answers to such questions.

For over fifty years of the twentieth century, the study of speech perception was mostly the study of auditory speech perception. Speech perception was often viewed as either a specialization of the auditory system or the result of acoustic signals specialized for the auditory system. We now know that the visual system can be a full-fledged player in the speech perception game, but much remains to be learned about how the game is played.

2.6 Acknowledgments

This chapter was written with the support of grants from the NIH/NIDCD (DC02107, DC008583). Also, this chapter was written with the support of the National Science Foundation. The views expressed here are those of the author and do not necessarily represent those of the National Science Foundation.

3 Dynamic information for face perception

K. Lander and V. Bruce

3.1 Introduction

All faces share the same spatial configuration – eyes above nose above mouth. Yet, when we look at a face, even briefly, we not only classify the face as a face, but we also notice its individual uniqueness. The human face provides a wide range of social signals to the perceiver. It tells us about gender, intention, health, and approximate age. The relative shapes and postures of the facial features help to specify the emotional state of the person (Ekman 1982), and movements of the lips and tongue help us to distinguish different speech sounds (for example see Campbell 1986). Direction of eye gaze often signals the focus of our attention (Kleinke 1986), and aids turn-taking during conversation (Kendon 1967). In addition to these kinds of information, the face provides a particularly accessible and salient cue to identity, although people can of course be identified by means other than the face. Voice, body shape, and clothing may all act as cues to identity, in circumstances where facial detail is not available.

Face research has been criticized for its reliance on static photographs of faces (Bruce 1994), which may be processed in a different manner to real faces (Pike *et al.* 1997). One obvious difference between a photograph of a face and the real thing is that the latter moves. Indeed, the preponderance of our experience with faces is not with static images, but with live moving faces. At a simplistic level, information from the face can be thought of in two distinct ways – that based on static-based parameters (time-independent), and that based on dynamic[1] (time-varying) parameters. Dynamic information arises because the face moves in a variety of ways, some to do with its signal-sending functions (smiling, nodding, speaking) and some to do with other functions (looking, chewing). When we yawn, when we laugh, when we talk, and when we smile, our face moves in a complex manner. Faces move in both rigid and non-rigid ways. During rigid motion, the face maintains its three-dimensional form, while the whole head changes its relative position and/or orientation. In non-rigid motion, individual parts of the face move in relation to one other, as during the formation of expressions or the articulation of speech. Typically, a complex combination of both rigid and non-rigid motion is required for everyday interaction, with head and face movements superimposed onto larger body movements (Munhall and Vatikiotis-Bateson 1998). In this chapter we examine the usefulness of facial motion for a variety of face perception tasks.

One way to illustrate the importance of information conveyed by motion is to present displays in which motion is just about the only source of information available. In the classic experiment of this kind, Johansson (1973) attached small lights to the major joints of an actor's body, videotaped in the dark performing a range of activities. When the tape was played the contrast was adjusted, so that just the movements of the 'point-lights' were visible. Importantly, when static the point-lights appeared as a random distribution to the viewer, and it was only when the video was played that the prevailing structure of a moving person became apparent. Work using this point-light technique has shown that isolated dynamic information can convey useful information about the gender of the actor (Kozlowski and Cutting 1977), the approximate amount of weight lifted (Runeson and Frykholm 1981; Bingham 1987), and emotion displayed during a dance routine (Dittrich *et al.* 1996).

A similar point-light technique has also been applied to human faces. Bassili (1978) attached a large number of bright dots to the surface of the face, which was then filmed carrying out a series of different expressions. Results indicated that when the point-light display was shown moving, participants were highly accurate at determining which expression was shown. In a follow-up experiment, Bruce and Valentine (1988) created point-light displays of a number of personally familiar colleagues, and asked other members of the department to act as participants. Results concurred with Bassili (1978), indicating that decisions such as identifying a face as a face, and discriminating between different facial expressions, could be made much more accurately from moving point-light displays, compared to static displays. Bruce and Valentine (1988) also asked participants to try and decide the sex of each face as well as identifying the person viewed. Participants' abilities to categorize gender and to identify which person (from the six familiar faces captured) appeared in each clip was significantly better when the displays were seen moving, compared to when static, though overall performance was very poor. Even though performance in this 'identity' task was highly inaccurate, this study does provide us with limited evidence that isolated dynamic information is also helpful for within-category discriminations, of the type involved in recognizing an individual's face.

Thus, initial evidence indicates an important role for dynamic information in categorizing faces in various ways. The following sections review further evidence to support this claim, focusing on the role that dynamic information plays in categorizing facial expressions and processing visual speech. We then address in more detail whether the additional information afforded by motion is also useful during identity processing. Here we describe some of our own work which suggests that dynamic information does indeed act as a useful cue when recognizing familiar faces, particularly when recognition is problematic from static form alone. However, the role of motion in recognition memory for relatively unfamiliar faces is much less clear from current evidence. Finally, we evaluate the importance of these findings from both a practical and theoretical perspective.

3.2 Motion information for expression perception

Much past research on facial expression processing has utilized static facial images, devoid of motion. Bruner and Taguiri (1954) state that 'historically speaking, we may have been done a disservice by the pioneering efforts of those, who, like Darwin, took the human face in a state of arrested animation as an adequate stimulus situation for studying how well we recognize human emotion'. Indeed, while it is clear that judgements of emotion from static images can be very accurate (see Ekman 1982), ordinarily when we assess an individual's emotion we have a wealth of cues in addition to a fixed facial expression. The patterning of the facial expression from onset to offset provides dynamic cues, often accompanied by larger body movements. These cues, in turn, are supplemented by our knowledge of the context of the emotional response, and sometimes, by knowledge of the individual exhibiting the expression.

Although most past research has utilized static images of faces, it seems unlikely that the information provided by motion is redundant. Edwards (1998) suggests that humans are attuned to the dynamic aspects of facial expressions of emotion. He presented participants with a number of photographs, each of which depicted a 'snapshot' of the same expression, taken at intervals of 67 ms in real time. Participants were asked to reproduce the progression of the spontaneous expression (from onset to offset), from the scrambled series of photographs. Results indicated that participants were able to utilize extremely subtle dynamic cues between the expression photographs, to reproduce the correct temporal progression of the display, at above-chance accuracy.

Dynamic aspects (e.g. speed of onset and offset, degree of irregularity) of facial movement also appear to distinguish genuine from posed emotional facial expressions (see Duchenne 1990). During the 1970s, Ekman and Friesen (1978) developed a 'Facial Action Coding System', or FACS. This system allows a researcher to precisely catalogue the movement of different groups of facial muscles over the time course of an expression. Using this system Ekman and his colleagues claim that it is possible to distinguish between 7000 different facial expressions (including 19 different types of smiles). Often differences between expressions are reflected in their temporal dynamic properties. For example, Ekman, Friesen, and Simons (1985) found that the onset of a posed 'startle' expression was 100 msecs later than a spontaneous 'startle' expression. Ekman and Friesen (1982) speculated that false (deceptive) expressions tend to have very short onset and offset times, and are typically over-long or unusually short. In line with this suggestion, Weiss, Blum, and Gleberman (1987) found that deliberate facial expressions had shorter onset times and more irregularities (pauses and stepwise intensity changes). Hess and Kleck (1990) found these differences were most marked when the deception involved the concealment of a different emotion (for example, smiling while watching a disgusting episode). However, later work by Hess and Kleck (1994) suggested that participants were relatively poor at using these cues to differentiate between genuine and posed expressions.

Further evidence for the importance of dynamic information during expression decoding has been found from experimental studies, studies of the patterns of impairments found in brain-injured patients, and more recent work using brain imaging techniques.

Matsuzaki and Sato (2008) examined the contribution of motion information to facial expression perception using point-light displays of faces. In the motion condition, apparent motion was induced by displaying a neutral expression followed by an emotional face image. In the repetition condition, the same emotional face image was presented twice. Results indicated that correct expression perception was higher in the motion than the repetition condition, and that this advantage was reduced when a white blank field was inserted between the neutral and emotional expression. Thus, even viewing a simplistic induced motion display served to increase expression recognition.

Interestingly, Kamachi *et al.* (2001) found that the precise dynamic characteristics of the observed motion affected how well different expressions could be recognized. In this study, dynamic expressions were created by displaying morph sequences, morphing between a neutral and a peak expression. Adding different numbers of intervening frames to the sequence, fast (6 frames), medium (26 frames), and slow (101 frames) changed the speed of the motion. In a free description task participants were asked to describe the emotion viewed. Results suggested that sadness was most accurately identified from slow sequences, with happiness, and, to a lesser extent surprise, most accurately from fast sequences. Angry expressions were best recognized from medium speed sequences. A second experiment confirmed that this result was not simply due to differences in the total time of the display, but rather reflected differences in the dynamic properties of the observed motion. Later work by Pollick, Hill, Calder, and Paterson (2003) found that changing the duration of an expression had a small effect on ratings of emotional intensity, with a trend for expressions with shorter durations to have lower ratings of intensity.

Finally, in terms of experimental work, Bould, Morris, and Wink (2008) investigated the importance of dynamic temporal characteristic information in facilitating the recognition of subtle expressions of emotion. In Experiment 1 there were three conditions, dynamic moving sequences that showed the expression emerging from neutral to a subtle emotion, a dynamic presentation containing nine static stills from the dynamic moving sequences (ran together to encapsulate a moving sequence) and a First-Last condition containing only the first (neutral) and last (subtle emotion) stills. The results showed recognition was significantly better for the dynamic moving sequences than both the Dynamic-9 and First-Last conditions. Further experiments changed the dynamics of the moving sequences by speeding up, slowing down, or disrupting the rhythm of the motion sequences. These manipulations significantly reduced recognition, and it was concluded that in addition to the perception of change, recognition is facilitated by the characteristic muscular movements associated with the portrayal of each emotion.

In terms of patient work, Humphreys, Donnelly, and Riddoch (1993) report the case study of a brain-injured patient, with severe face processing impairments. Patient HJA is markedly impaired at recognizing the identity of familiar faces, and is poor at making gender and emotional expression judgements from static photographs. In contrast, when asked to make judgements of expression or gender from moving point-light displays, he performs normally. It seems that with expressions, this patient is able to use movement but not static form information. This pattern of deficits supports not only the idea that identity and expression processing fractionate (see later in this chapter), but that expression processing itself can be separated according to whether expression is conveyed through static form or motion information.

Recent work by Trautmann, Fehr, and Herrmann (2009) used an fMRI study to examine the neural networks involved in the emotion perception of static and dynamic facial stimuli separately (neutral, happy, and disgusted expressions). Dynamic faces indicated enhanced emotion-specific brain activation patterns in the parahippocampal gyrus (PHG), including the amygdala (AMG), fusiform gyrus (FG), superior temporal gyrus (STG), inferior frontal gyrus (IFG), and occipital and orbitofrontal cortex (OFC). Post hoc ratings of the dynamic stimuli revealed a better recognizability in comparison to the static stimuli.

In conclusion, while most work by psychologists interested in emotional expressions has used static displays of posed expressions it seems likely that motion information provides an important dimension of emotional processing in everyday interpersonal interactions. Dynamic facial expressions might provide a more appropriate approach to examine the processing of emotional face perception than static stimuli.

3.3 Motion information for visual speech perception

It has been well documented that visual information from a talker's mouth and face plays an important role in the perception and understanding of spoken language (see Massaro 1987 for an early review, and contributions to this volume). Under noisy conditions, viewing the talking face supplements the auditory signal, increasing perceptual accuracy (e.g. Sumby and Pollack 1954; Walden *et al.* 1977). We make use of visual information from the face even during the understanding of clear and unambiguous speech (see Reisberg *et al.* 1987; Vitkovich and Barber 1994). The classic demonstration that we use visual information when perceiving speech is 'the McGurk effect' where visual and auditory speech signals are combined in a way which can give rise to illusory percepts of phonemes which do not correspond to what was seen or heard (e.g. auditory 'ba' plus visual 'ga' often results in observers hearing 'da') (McGurk and MacDonald 1976).

Most current descriptions of visual speech information are based on static parameters, such as lip shape, tongue height, place of cavity constriction, and amount of visible teeth (Montgomery and Jackson 1983; Summerfield and McGrath 1984). Indeed, there is much evidence to support the fact that static-based parameters can convey some visual speech information. For example, Campbell (1986) showed that participants could readily distinguish between point vowels, such as 'ee' and 'oo' from photographs of faces posturing articulatory positions. However, just because we can make use of static-based information for visual speech, does not preclude the use of the dynamic information afforded by a moving speaking face.

Evidence demonstrating the salience of isolated dynamic information for visual speech processing comes from studies carried out using point-light displays. In early work, Summerfield (1979) used simplistic point-light displays (four 'points' placed on lips) to determine if visible lip motion could help listeners process heard speech, played against a background of interfering prose. Although listeners were able to identify the visual displays as moving lips, comprehension of speech was only marginally improved. However, a follow-up study by Rosenblum, Johnson and Saldaña (1996) found that moving point-light configurations could indeed enhance the perception of speech, embedded in white noise. No such advantage was found with static point-light displays.

Additional evidence for the salience of dynamic information in visual speech processing comes from Rosenblum and Saldaña (1996), who found that point-light displays could generate audiovisual fusion illusions (McGurk and MacDonald 1976). For example, when a moving point-light display of a face saying /va/ was paired with an auditory /ba/, participants often experienced that /fa/ was spoken. No such fusions, between what was seen and what was heard, were found when the visual display was a static image of a face mouthing /va/ (but see Benoît *et al.* 1995). The fact that static facial speech does not integrate strongly with auditory speech, led Rosenblum and Saldaña (1998) to suggest 'that time-varying (dynamic) dimensions of visible speech should be given serious consideration as the most salient informational form'.

Other evidence for the primacy of dynamic information in visual speech comes from Vitkovitch and Barber (1994), who investigated the effect of frame rate on speechreading ability. Results indicated that faster frame rates (16.5 Hz to 30 Hz) were much better at conveying visual speech, than images presented at a slower rate (8.3 Hz to 12.5 Hz). Vitkovitch and Barber (1994) concluded that this increase must be due to additional information becoming available to the viewer as the frame rate is increased. The most likely source of this information is from dynamic parameters.[2]

It is clear then that dynamic information has an important role to play in the processing of visual speech, although it is difficult, based on the research outlined so far, to assess its relative importance compared with information based on static parameters. One interesting way to explore this issue involves the testing of brain-injured patients, who have established problems with the perception of visual motion (e.g. McLeod *et al.* 1996). Here, it is possible to directly clarify the importance of dynamic facial information for speech-reading, as dynamic information is not available to these patients. Campbell and colleagues (1997) reported the speechreading ability of one such patient (LM). While LM's reading of natural speech was severely impaired, she was able to recognize speech patterns from face photographs and provide reasonable speechreading of monosyllables produced in isolation. As with other visual events (for example, tracking the direction of gaze) the rate of presentation was critical to her performance. She was able to report events during slow presentation (~ one event/2 seconds), but was poor at distinguishing between normal, fast (double-speed), or slow (half-speed) seen speech. Campbell *et al.* (1997) concluded that visible speech perception cannot be based solely on dynamic properties of speech, otherwise LM should have lost the ability to perform any speechreading task (from either static or moving displays). Instead, Campbell *et al.* (1997) suggest that both static and dynamic information is required for effective speechreading of natural speech. However, Rosenblum and Saldaña (1998) emphasize that data from brain-injured patients should be cautiously interpreted, since speech-reading ability varies considerably between individuals (Demorest *et al.* 1996) and the speechreading ability of these patients prior to their lesions is not known.

In summary, much research has emphasized the importance of dynamic information for visual speech processing. This observation, alongside the previous discussion of expression processing, leads naturally to the question of whether dynamic information, which is available from a moving face and clearly used in at least some processing tasks, might also provide information useful for the recognition of identity. Next, we report a series of experiments that compare recognition performance from moving and static faces, to answer this question.

3.4 Dynamic information for familiar face recognition

The majority of research on face recognition has been concerned with how static faces are recognized, and static form-based information has – implicitly or explicitly – been emphasized in most theoretical accounts of face recognition. It has long been known that static-based information, about the shape and configuration of individual features (for example, see Tanaka and Farah 1993) and the overall shape and pigmentation of the skin, is utilized in the recognition of identity (see Bruce and Langton 1994; Kemp *et al.* 1996). This information can, of course, be as easily extracted from a static face image as a moving one.

Given that our recognition of known people from photographs or pictures is typically so good (see Burton *et al.* 1999), it has often been assumed that 'motion is little used for face identification' (Humphreys *et al.* 1993). However this conclusion seems premature, considering that dynamic information seems to be particularly salient for both expression processing and visual speech processing. Indeed, seeing a face move undoubtedly adds additional information for the viewer, unavailable from a static image. The key question, then, involves determining the nature and role this additional information afforded by motion plays in identity processing. It is important to investigate this issue not only to advance our theoretical understanding of the processes involved in face recognition, but also to determine whether static images are an adequate way to represent faces in studies of this kind.

Initial findings by Bruce and Valentine (1988), using point-light displays, suggested that isolated dynamic information may act as a cue to identity when static cues are impoverished. More convincing evidence that movement is important in the recognition of individual faces comes from Knight and Johnston (1997). Knight and Johnston (1997) presented famous faces either in a negative (contrast-reversed) format or upside down, and compared recognition performance from moving and static sequences. In experiments of this kind it is usually necessary to degrade spatial cues to reduce recognition performance away from ceiling. Results indicated that moving famous faces were recognized significantly more accurately than static ones, but only when these were shown as upright-negative images. Knight and Johnston (1997) proposed that seeing the face move may provide evidence about its three-dimensional structure, compensating for the degraded depth cues available within a negative image (see Bruce and Langton 1994). Alternatively, they suggest that known faces may have characteristic facial gestures, idiosyncratic to the individual viewed.

Our follow-up research (see Lander *et al.* 1999; Lander *et al.* 2001) showed that the recognition advantage for moving faces is not specific to upright-negated images. Instead motion confers benefits through a range of image manipulations, including thresholding (where a multiple grey-level image is converted to a one-bit per pixel black-and-white image), pixelation, and Gaussian blurring. In these studies what seems important for the demonstration of a motion recognition advantage is not the nature of the image manipulation but rather that recognition performance is below ceiling, allowing higher recognition rates to be found. Our moving sequences show famous faces, pictured from the shoulders up, talking and expressing. Thus, these experiments clearly demonstrate that non-rigid movement adds useful information when recognizing the identity of famous faces shown in difficult viewing conditions. It is important to note at this point that the motion recognition advantage is not simply due to the increased number of static images shown when the face is in motion (25 frames per second in UK). Indeed when the number of images is equated across static and moving presentation conditions (Lander and Bruce 2001) there was still an advantage for viewing the face in motion.

Furthermore, the viewing conditions in which facial motion is observed have been shown to affect the extent to which motion aids recognition. Research indicates that disruptions to the natural movement of the face can influence the size of the motion advantage in facial recognition. Lander *et al.* (1999) and Lander and Bruce (2001) found lower recognition rates of famous faces when the motion was slowed down, speeded up, reversed or rhythmically disrupted. Thus, seeing the precise dynamic characteristics of the face in motion provides the greatest advantage for facial recognition. A further demonstration of this point comes from research using both natural and artificially created (morphed) smiling stimuli (Lander *et al.* 2006). In order to create an artificially moving sequence, Lander *et al.* (2006) used a morphing technique to create intermediate face images between the first and last frames of a natural smile. When shown in sequence, these images were used to create an artificially moving smile that lasted the same amount of time, and had the same start and end point as the natural smile for that individual. Results found that familiar faces were recognized significantly better when shown naturally smiling compared with a static neutral face, a static smiling face, or a morphed smiling sequence. This further demonstrates the necessity for motion to be natural in order to facilitate the motion advantage.

Lander *et al.* (2006) whilst investigating the effects of natural vs morphed motion found a main effect of familiarity, revealing that the nature of the to-be-recognized face can also mediate what effect motion has on facial recognition. It is posited that the more familiar a person's face is, the more we may be able to utilize the movement of their face as a cue to identity. Indeed, characteristic motion patterns may become a more accessible cue to identity as a face becomes increasingly familiar. Indeed, in recent work, Butcher (2009) found a significant positive correlation between rated face familiarity and the recognition advantage for moving compared with static faces. This research was conducted using famous faces and found that the more familiar the famous face was rated to be, the larger the recognition advantage for viewing that face in motion.

Another factor of the to-be-recognized face that has been shown to be important in understanding what mediates the motion advantage is distinctiveness. Facial recognition research has demonstrated a clear benefit for faces that are thought to be spatially distinctive, as findings indicate that distinctive faces are better recognized than faces that are rated as being 'typical' (Light *et al.* 1979; Bartlett *et al.* 1984; Valentine and Bruce 1986; Valentine and Ferrara 1991; Vokey and Read 1992). It has also been established that a larger motion recognition advantage is attained from distinctive motion than typical motion (Lander and Chuang 2005; Butcher 2009). Lander and Chuang (2005) found that the more distinctive or characteristic a person's motion was rated to be, the more useful a cue to recognition it was. This finding can be considered within Valentine's (1991) multi dimensional face space model of facial recognition, which is often used to provide an explanation for the spatial distinctiveness effect. This model posits that faces similar to a prototype or 'typical' face are clustered closer together in face space making them harder to differentiate from each other, leading to distinctive faces that are positioned away from this cluster, to be easily recognized. Due to the homogeneous nature of faces on the whole, many faces are perceived as similar to the prototype so their representations in face space cluster close to the prototype representation, leading to distinction between these faces being more difficult.

A similar theoretical explanation could be applied to moving faces, whereby faces in the centre of the space move in a typical manner. Consequently, faces that exhibit distinctive facial motions could be located away from the centre of the space, making them easier to recognize than faces displaying typical motion. It is important here to consider that distinctiveness in facial motion may refer to (1) a motion characteristic or typical of a particular individual; (2) an odd motion for a particular individual to produce or; (3) a generally odd or unusual motion. Also, it may be that spatial and temporal distinctiveness of faces are in some way related. For instance, spatially distinctive faces might naturally have more distinctive movements, a notion that should itself be addressed in future research.

Having clearly demonstrated a moving recognition advantage it is important to investigate the theoretical basis of this effect. Two theories have been proposed by O'Toole, Roark, and Abdi (2002), namely the representation enhancement hypothesis and the supplemental information hypothesis. The representation enhancement hypothesis (O'Toole *et al.* 2002) suggests that facial motion aids recognition by facilitating the perception of the three-dimensional structure of the face. It posits that the quality of the structural information available from a human face is enhanced by facial motion, and this benefit surpasses the benefit provided by merely seeing the face from many static viewpoints

(Pike *et al.* 1997; Christie and Bruce 1998; Lander *et al.* 1999). As this mechanism is not dependent on any previous experience with an individual face it seems to predict that motion should aid recognition of previously unfamiliar faces, a notion discussed later in this chapter.

In contrast, the supplemental information hypothesis (O'Toole *et al.* 2002) assumes that we represent the characteristic facial motions of an individual's face as part of our stored facial representation for that individual. For the particular individual's characteristic facial motions to be learnt, experience with that face is needed – the face must be familiar. 'Characteristic motion signatures' are learnt over time, allowing a memory of what facial motions a person typically exhibits to be stored as part of their facial representation. Therefore when motion information for an individual has been integrated into the representation of their face, this information can be retrieved and used to aid recognition of that face.

When considering the theoretical basis of the motion recognition advantage from a cognitive and representational perspective, a number of studies have provided support for the idea that facial motion becomes intrinsic to a familiar individual's face representation. For example, Knappmeyer, Thornton, and Bülthoff (2003) used two synthetic heads, each animated by the movement of a different volunteer. Participants viewed and thus became familiar with either head A with motion from volunteer A, or head B with motion from volunteer B. In the test phase an animated head constructed from the morph of the two synthetic heads (A and B) was produced. Participants were asked to identify whose head was shown. It was found that participants' identity judgements were biased by the motion they had originally learnt from head A or B, demonstrating that representations of an individual's characteristic facial motions are learnt and are inherent to that individual's face representation.

Repetition priming studies (Lander and Bruce 2004; also see Lander *et al.* 2009) have also found evidence that is consistent with the view that dynamic (motion) information is inherent to the face representation of a particular individual. Repetition priming is the facilitation demonstrated at test when the to-be-recognized item (here a face) has previously been encountered at some point prior to the test (Lewis and Ellis 1999). Such priming effects have previously been demonstrated for words (Jackson and Morton 1984) and objects (Warren and Morton 1982; Bruce *et al.* 2000) as well for familiar faces (Bruce and Valentine 1985). Repetition priming has been used to probe the nature of the representations underlying recognition of faces (e.g. Ellis *et al.* 1996; Ellis *et al.* 1997). It is proposed that when priming is sensitive to some change in the form of the faces between study and test, this parameter may be intrinsic to the representations that mediate face recognition. In the prime phase of Lander and Bruce's (2004) experiments, participants were presented with a series of famous faces and asked to name or provide some semantic information about the person presented. Half of the faces were presented in static form and half in motion. In the test phase participants were presented with a series of faces and asked to make familiarity judgements about them, indicating whether each face was familiar or unfamiliar. Lander and Bruce (2004) found that, even when the same static image was shown in the prime and the test phases, a moving image primed more effectively than a static image (Experiment 1). This finding was extended (Experiment 2) to reveal that a moving image remains the most effective prime, compared to a static image prime, when moving images are used in the test phase. Significantly, providing support for the notion of 'characteristic motion signatures' inherent to a person's face representation, Lander and Bruce (2004) also found that the largest priming advantage was found with naturally moving faces, rather than with those shown in slow motion (Experiment 3). However, it was also observed that viewing the same moving facial sequence at prime as at test produced more priming than using differing moving images (Experiment 4).

3.5 Dynamic information for unfamiliar face learning

O'Toole *et al.*'s (2002) first explanation of the advantages of dynamic presentation of faces should predict benefits for unfamiliar face recognition too. However, in contrast to these intriguing effects on the identification of familiar faces, the effect of motion on the learning of unfamiliar faces is much less clear. Early work conducted by Christie and Bruce (1998) found no advantage for either rigid or non-rigid motion in face learning. In this incidental learning task, participants were shown faces either as a moving computer-animated display or as a series of static images, and were asked to decide whether they thought each person shown studied arts or science subjects at university. The number of frames in the moving and static conditions was equated in the learning phase. The motion involved was either non-rigid (expression changes) or rigid (head nodding or shaking). At test, participants either saw moving sequences or a single static image (so the number of frames was not equated at test) and were asked which were the faces of people seen earlier in the arts/science task. Results indicated there was no benefit for studying faces in motion on the subsequent recognition task. However, there was a slight benefit for testing faces in (rigid) motion, compared to static images. In line with this finding, Schiff, Banka, and De Bordes Galdi (1986) found an advantage for testing recognition memory for unfamiliar faces using a moving sequence rather than a static 'mug-shot' photograph. These findings can be compared with those using familiar faces (Knight and Johnston 1997; Lander *et al.* 1999; Lander *et al.* 2001) who also found a beneficial effect of motion at test.

Despite this early work a number of studies have found an advantage for learning faces from moving sequences. For example, Pike, Kemp, Towell, and

Phillips (1997) filmed actors rotating on a motorized chair, which was illuminated from a single light source. In the learning phase, participants were asked to try and learn the identity of previously unfamiliar faces from either dynamic sequences (10-second clip), multiple static images (5 images selected from the moving sequence, each presented for 2 seconds) or a single static image (single image presented for 10-seconds). The dynamic sequence showed the target initially facing the video camera, and then undergoing a full 360-degree rotation of the chair. At test, participants viewed a single (full-face) static image, different from any shown in the learning phase. They were asked to decide if the face shown had been present in the earlier learning phase. Results indicated that there was a significant advantage for faces learned via a coherent moving sequence. Bruce and Valentine (1988) reported a similar trend in an experiment which compared learning from video sequences of the target faces speaking, nodding etc. to sequences of single static images. Again, test images were single images taken from a different viewpoint, on a different occasion. In this experiment performance was best when the faces were learned via a moving sequence, although the difference between the moving and static condition failed to reach significance. The failure to reach significance was explained by the authors in terms of the variability of performance, for this task, across the participant population.

In later follow-up work, Lander and Bruce (2003) conducted four experiments that aimed to investigate the usefulness of rigid (head nodding, shaking) and non-rigid (talking, expressions) motion for establishing new face representations of previously unfamiliar faces. Results showed that viewing a face in motion leads to more accurate face learning, compared with viewing a single static image (Experiment 1). The advantage for viewing the face moving rigidly seemed to be due to the different angles of view contained in these sequences (Experiment 2). However, the advantage for non-rigid motion was not simply due to multiple images (Experiment 3) and was not specifically linked to forwards motion but also extended to reversed sequences (Experiment 4). Thus, although there seems to be clear beneficial effects of motion for face learning, they do not seem to be due to the specific dynamic properties of the sequences shown. Instead, the advantage for non-rigid motion may reflect increased attention to faces moving in a socially important manner.

Finally, Lander and Davies (2007) investigated the impact of facial motion as a previously unfamiliar face becomes known. We presented participants with a series of faces each preceded by a name, and asked participants to try to learn the names for the faces. When the participants felt they had learnt the names correctly they continued onto the recognition phase in which they were presented with the same faces (same presentation method as in learning phase), and asked to name the individual. The learning phase was repeated and the participant was asked to try and learn the names of the faces again if any of the names were incorrectly recalled, after which they took the recognition test again. This procedure was replicated until the participant correctly named all 12 faces shown. In the test phase, participants were presented with 48 degraded faces; 24 as single static images and 24 moving. In the moving condition the faces were each presented for 5 seconds. Participants were informed that some would be learnt faces and some would be 'new' faces, for which they had not learnt names. Participants were asked to name the face or respond 'new' and to provide a response for every trial. Results suggested that facial motion learning was rapid, and as such the beneficial effect of motion was not highly dependent on the amount of time the face was seen for. Rather there was support for the idea of rapidly learnt characteristic facial motion patterns, with results only revealing an advantage for recognizing a face in motion (at test) when the face had been learnt moving. Conversely, when the face was learnt as a static image, there was no advantage for recognizing moving faces compared with a static image. Indeed, it seems that participants were able to extract and encode dynamic information even when viewing very short moving clips of 5 seconds. Furthermore, the beneficial effect of motion was shown to remain stable despite prolonged viewing and learning of the face identity in Experiment 2. In this experiment, participants were assigned to one of four experimental groups. Group 1 viewed episode 1 of a TV drama before the test phase, group 2 viewed episodes 1 and 2, group 3 episodes 1 to 3 and group 4 episodes 1 to 4. Each episode was 30 minutes in length. In the test phase, participants viewed moving and static degraded images of the characters and were asked to try and identify them by character name or other unambiguous semantic information. The results revealed that, although better recognition of characters from the TV drama was seen as the number of episodes viewed increased, the relative importance of motion information did not increase with a viewer's experience with the face (O'Toole *et al.* 2002). The size of the beneficial effect remained relatively stable across time demonstrating how rapidly motion information, through familiarization with the to-be-recognized face, can be integrated into a face representation and utilized at recognition.

To summarize, the role of movement in building face representations is somewhat unclear. Christie and Bruce (1998) found no benefit for learning faces that were moving either non-rigidly or rigidly. In contrast Pike *et al.* (1997) and Lander and Bruce (2003) found that learning faces in rigid motion did subsequently help participants recognize the faces more accurately, compared with when they were originally presented as a single static image or as a series of statics. It is clear, however, that as a face moves from being unfamiliar to familiar that motion information becomes an important cue to identity (Lander and Davies 2007), however it is unknown how this process is undertaken. Further work is needed to investigate the familiarization process, and to evaluate the role of motion in building face representations.

3.6 Practical considerations

The effects we have reviewed have practical as well as theoretical implications. It has become increasingly important to gain an understanding of how human observers process moving faces, from an applied perspective. In terms of application, facial 'animation' has become a developing computer technology, highly important in the entertainment industry (for example Parke and Waters 1996). Animation techniques also have wider impact, for example allowing the construction of realistic dynamic faces useful in the planning of reconstructive facial surgery and forensic medicine (Alley 1999). A better understanding of how dynamic information is processed by the human observer should help the development of face animation systems, as well as giving a practical estimate of when (and why) seeing a face move can aid the recognition of identity.

With the use of Closed Circuit Television (CCTV) surveillance systems now commonplace in the UK, moving video footage is often used as a source of evidence in the criminal justice process. Often the video footage captured is of poor 'grainy' quality with additional image size, lighting, and focus problems (Aldridge and Knupfer 1994). Typically the role of the police, witnesses, and jurors alike is either to identify the (familiar) target from the footage or to 'match' the viewed person to a (captured) suspect. Experiments described in this chapter suggest that the recognition of known faces from degraded video footage is significantly better when the image is viewed moving rather than static. It seems likely that viewing moving CCTV footage will help to maximize the chances of an observer recognizing a known person. This suggestion also has implications for the design and installation of CCTV systems, as many current systems do not capture continuous motion, but rather operate on a time lapse basis. There may be some very real benefits to be gained from the installation of 'continuous' motion systems, although further work is needed to investigate the extent of this potential beneficial effect under these circumstances.

While often it is important to reveal the identity of people shown in video sequences, sometimes attempts must be made to conceal this. In the UK, for example, documentary programmes often show people who for various legal or security reasons should not be identifiable to viewers of the programme. Sometimes faces are concealed by pixellating the face area – presenting the face as a small number of square pixels whose grey levels flicker as the image moves on the screen. More recently some television companies have been using blurring rather than pixellation to conceal identity. While these effects on the surface appear to disguise information which could specify individual identity, our research has shown that familiar faces can quite often be recognized from such image sequences, with moving sequences giving very much higher recognition than static ones (Lander *et al.* 2001). It may be extremely difficult for a film editor unfamiliar with a person shown on the film to judge appropriate levels of image degradation to protect a person from recognition by someone who knows them well. We recommend that the only certain way to conceal identities of faces in moving sequences is to cover them completely with an opaque block.

3.7 Theoretical interpretations

So, it seems that non-rigid movement patterns – either of faces generally, or of specific faces, aid the recognition of identity. How might this 'dynamic' information be stored in memory? One possibility is that the motion trace is quite distinct from the static form-based representation. If this were the case then dynamic information may feed into the face identity system either directly or via other aspects of face processing, where dynamic information is known to be important, for example via expression and/or visual speech processing. However, it is difficult to conceptualize how dynamic information from expression processing and/or visual speech processing could play a role in identity processing, in terms of our current understanding of face processing, as we now explain in a little more detail.

Bruce and Young (1986) proposed that expression and visual speech processing operate independently of each other and of face identification, and all are processed in parallel from a viewed face (see Figure 3.1). There is a considerable body of converging evidence to support this suggestion of independence.

Firstly, between expression processing and identity processing, evidence comes from prosopagnosic patients who are unable to recognize familiar faces, instead typically identifying the person from their voice or gait (Damasio *et al.* 1990). Bruyer *et al.* (1983) reported the case of 'Mr W', who could accurately perceive and interpret expressions, but was unable to accurately recognize familiar faces (also see Shuttleworth *et al.* 1982; Schweinberger *et al.* 1995). Conversely, a number of non-prosopagnosic patients have been found who are impaired at facial expression judgements, but have no problems identifying familiar people (Kurucz *et al.* 1979; Etcoff 1984; Parry *et al.* 1991; Humphreys *et al.* 1993; Young *et al.* 1993). It seems that there is a double dissociation between facial expression processing and identity processing, supporting the notion of independence. Further support for this dissociation comes from Young, McWeeny, Hay, and Ellis (1986) who did a matching task with 'normal' participants. Participants were required to decide as quickly as possible whether two faces presented simultaneously belonged to the same person (identity matching) or showed the same expression (expression matching). Half of the stimuli faces were familiar to the participants and half were unfamiliar. For the identity matching task, reaction times were significantly faster with familiar faces, but there was no difference across familiarity in the expression matching task. Results clearly support the view, proposed by

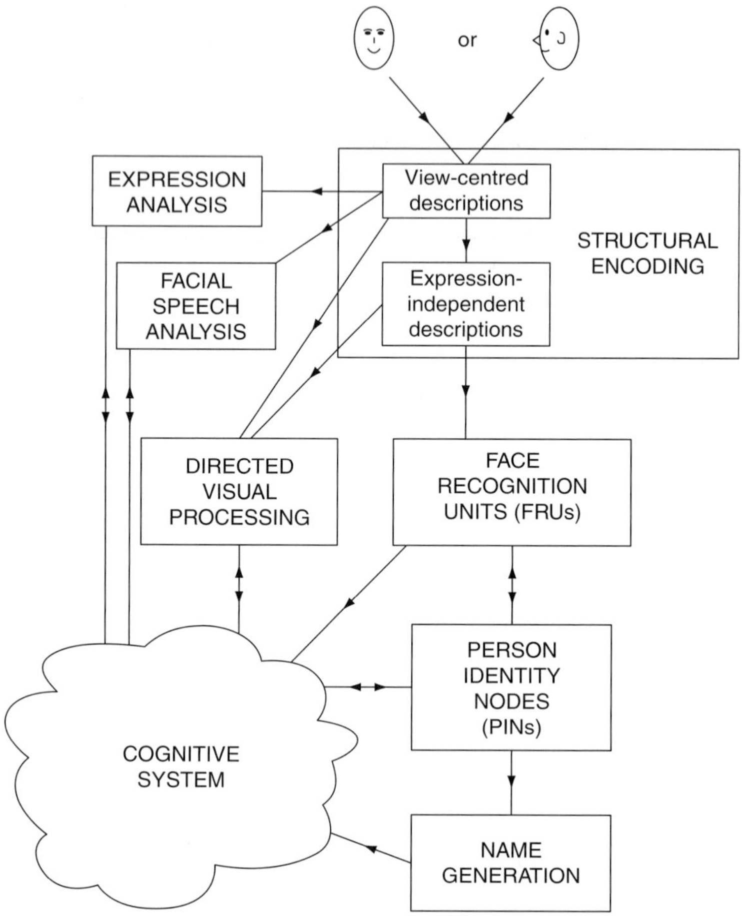

Figure 3.1 A functional model for face recognition (Bruce and Young 1986)

Bruce and Young (1986), that expression processing and identity are carried out independently.

Secondly, support for independence between visual speech processing and identity processing comes from a study by Campbell, Landis, and Regard (1986). They reported the case of a prosopagnosic patient, 'Mrs D', who despite being severely impaired at identifying familiar faces, performed entirely normally on all visual speech processing tasks. In contrast, another patient, 'Mrs T', was unable to perform these speechreading tasks but was unimpaired at recognizing faces or expressions. This pattern of impairments indicates that there is a double dissociation between visual speech processing and identity processing.

Campbell, Brooks, De Haan, and Roberts (1996) also found that while matching judgements based on identity were significantly affected by familiarity (reaction times to familiar faces were significantly faster than to unfamiliar faces), no such effect of familiarity was found when the matching task involved decisions about visual speech (Experiment 1). Results again confirm that visual speech decisions are relatively insensitive to face familiarity.

In summary then, there is considerable evidence to support the notion that both expression processing and visual speech processing operate independently to identity processing. However, most of the studies supporting independence have used static images of faces as stimuli. Here, we are concerned with the importance of dynamic information, provided by expression and/or visual speech processing, for identity processing. It is difficult to address this issue using static stimuli, instead dynamic faces should be used. Indeed, a number of recent studies, using dynamic stimuli, have indicated that there may be some subtle links between these different types of processing. For example, Walker, Bruce, and O'Malley (1995) utilized the McGurk effect to examine the claims of independence between identity and facial speech processing. The issue of familiarity and speechreading was studied by manipulating the familiarity of the faces used to create the McGurk stimuli, in that participants were either familiar or unfamiliar with the people 'speaking' the syllables. Also the faces and voices used were either congruent (they were from the same person) or incongruent (from different people, some gender matched, some not). Results showed that participants who were familiar with the people reported significantly less expected combination responses, compared to those participants who were unfamiliar with the seen face (regardless of the whether the face and voice were congruent or incongruent). A similar familiarity effect was reported for the expected blend responses when the seen face and heard voice were incongruent (from different people). So, when the face and voice came from different but familiar people, participants rarely reported McGurk blend illusions (perceived 'da' following seen 'ga' with auditory 'ba'), but when the same materials were shown to participants unfamiliar with the faces then McGurk blend illusions were common even when face and voice were of people of different genders. These results do not support the dissociation between facial identity and facial speech processing found previously using static stimuli (see Campbell *et al.* 1986; de Gelder *et al.* 1991 outlined earlier in this chapter) but show instead that audiovisual speech integration can be influenced by signals from the identity system.

It is clear that speakers show systematic individual variations in the articulation of phonemes. These idiosyncrasies are evident in facial speech as well as auditory speech (see Montgomery and Jackson 1983). Evidence has suggested that speech perception is affected by familiarity with a speaker's voice (Nygaard *et al.* 1994). Similarly Lander and Davies (2008) found that speechreading performance is influenced by face familiarity. In this experiment, we first measured the baseline speechreading performance of participants, from unfamiliar faces. Next, participants were familiarized with the face and voice of either the same or a different speaker, or were asked to take part in a word puzzle instead. Speechreading performance was measured again, before participants completed a further period of familiarization (or puzzle completion) and a final speechreading performance task. Results showed that speechreading performance increased overall with practice but that performance increased significantly more as participants became increasingly familiar with the same speaker. Our findings demonstrate the importance of talker-specific variations or other instance-based characteristics and suggest that these are a useful source of information for speechreading.

Recently there have also been demonstrations that identity can influence facial expression processing as well as facial speech processing. Schweinberger and Soukup (1998) used a Garner (1974) interference paradigm to test the independence between face identification and facial speech processing, and face identification and expression analysis. Consistent with the Bruce and Young framework, they observed that responses based upon facial identities were unaffected by variation in expressions, or by facial speech; however, responses based upon facial expressions and facial speech were affected by variations in identity – suggesting that the identity of a face can influence the analysis conducted within these other routes. This asymmetric interference of identities onto expressions, but not expressions onto identities, was replicated by Schweinberger, Burton, and Kelly (1999).

These recent findings suggest that there may be some moderation of the facial expression routes and the facial speech analysis routes on the basis of facial identity (see also Baudouin *et al.* 2000). Importantly, though, the facial identification route itself appears uninfluenced by variations in expression or speech. This affirms the position of Bruce and Young (1986) that the task of face recognition is logically and functionally independent of other uses made of facial information which has consequences for the ways in which face recognition can be studied and explained. Importantly for our purposes here, however, it makes it appear unlikely that the source of the effects of dynamic information on identification lies within the expression and facial speech systems, since there is no evidence that these feed into the person identification pathway.

Instead it seems that dynamic information may in some way be represented within the identification system itself. The Bruce and Young (1986) model and more recent developments of it (Burton *et al.* 1990; Burton *et al.* 1999) have assumed that the face is one of a number of means by which more abstract person identities can be established. Voices and written names are the most frequently mentioned examples of other access routes, but occasionally it has been suggested that 'gait' forms a further means of access (though gait patterns alone seem to be relatively poor cues to identity – see Burton *et al.* 1999). It is possible that the dynamic information associated with a person's expressive and speech movements is part of some more general memory of the way people move. Such a view would see facial dynamics as a discrete source of information about personal identity, like voices and written names, but not incorporated within the face representation system itself. Alternatively if dynamic information is stored within the face identity system then it may be linked to the *static* form-based face representations, or, may be intrinsically incorporated into the representations themselves (cf. dynamic representations in Freyd 1987; 1993). If the representations mediating face recognition are dynamic (whereby the temporal dimension is inextricably embedded in the representation, see Freyd and Pantzer 1995) then recognition from a static image should be thought of as a 'snapshot' within an essentially dynamic process.

Finally, when considering the underpinning theoretical basis for the moving recognition advantage, it is interesting to note that a possible dissociation has been revealed between the ability to recognize a face from the motion it produces, and the ability to recognize it from a static image. In this work, Steede, Tree, and Hole (2007) reported the case study of a developmental prosopagnosic patient, CS. Despite CS being impaired at recognizing static faces, he was able to effectively discriminate between different dynamic identities, and demonstrated the ability to learn the names of individuals on the basis of their facial movement information (at levels equivalent to control subjects). This case study indicates a possible dissociation between the cognitive mechanisms involved in the processes of recognizing a static face and those involved in recognizing a dynamic face. This research is supported by neuroimaging studies that have demonstrated functional separation of motion and structural aspects of face perception in humans (Haxby *et al.* 2002). Haxby *et al.* (2002) found that facial movements activated the superior temporal sulcus (STS) area while the more shape-based aspects of the face activated the fusiform gyrus. Further neuropsychological studies have revealed differential activations for processing motion and static face information (Schultz and Pilz 2009). Based on such neuroimaging studies O'Toole *et al.* (2002) proposed a 'two-route' model of face recognition that could explain why facial motion information aids recognition when other stimulus cues, e.g. spatial information and pigmentation, are absent. O'Toole *et al.* (2002) argued that the moving aspects of a face may be encoded and represented separately from static-based aspects of the face. However, Schultz and Pilz (2009) have provided evidence to suggest that spatial and temporal aspects of a face are processed in an integrative manner. Schultz and Pilz (2009) found that for most of the classic face-sensitive areas (bilateral fusiform gyrus, left inferior occipital gyrus and the right superior temporal sulcus [STS]) the response to dynamic faces was higher than to static faces, with the STS revealed as the region most sensitive to moving faces. Thus, there is evidence that both motion and form related areas participate in the processing of moving faces, with higher brain activation for moving than static faces.

Despite support for a potential dissociation between the processing of static and moving faces, research findings are mixed. Steede *et al.* (2007) suggested that CS could use motion as a cue to identity, even when impaired at static face recognition. However, Lander, Humphreys and Bruce (2004) found that an acquired prosopagnosic patient HJA was not able to overtly or covertly use motion as a cue to facial identity. In Experiment 1, HJA attempted to recognize the identity of dynamic and static famous faces. HJA was found to be severely impaired in his ability to recognize identity, and was not significantly better at recognizing moving faces compared with static ones. In order to test HJA's ability to learn face–name pairings a second experiment was conducted using an implicit face recognition task. In this experiment HJA was asked to try and learn true and untrue names for famous faces, which were shown in either a moving clip or a static image. HJA found this a difficult task and was no better with moving faces or true face–name pairings. Some prosopagnosic patients have previously found it easier to learn true face–name pairings more accurately and efficiently than untrue ones (covert recognition by de Haan *et al.* 1987). A final experiment demonstrated that HJA was able to decide whether two sequentially presented dynamic unfamiliar faces had the same or differing identities. HJA was found to be better at doing this task with moving rather than static images and performance with moving stimuli was found to be comparable to the performance of control participants. His good performance on this matching task demonstrates that HJA retains good enough motion-processing abilities to enable him to match dynamic facial signatures, yet insufficient abilities to allow him to store, recognize, or learn facial identity on the basis of facial movements.

3.8 Future research and conclusions

Our current and future programme of research is aimed at trying to tease apart different theoretical interpretations of the effects of dynamic information on face recognition.

Some questions could be answered making use of the kind of synthetic animated face displays that Christian Benoît was developing at the time of his death (e.g. Le Goff and Benoît 1997 – see also several contributions to this volume). For example, what would happen if we showed one face displaying someone else's movements? Would Al Gore's face be easier to recognize if animated with movements derived from Bill Clinton's face? Here static-based and dynamic cues to identity would be in conflict, allowing us to investigate the relative importance of static and dynamic cues to identity. Using high-quality three-dimensional models of faces derived from cyberware scanners and animated using sophisticated models of expressive and speech movements it should be possible to ask such questions. Using animated head models we should also be able to investigate whether benefits of movement for face identification depend upon the face having been learned in movement. Most of us are familiar with famous faces from past centuries that we have seen only in portraits or photographs. Would Abraham Lincoln be easier to recognize if shown as an animated model than in conventional portrait form? If no effects are found, then this further supports the idea that dynamic benefits do not arise from a very general facilitation of the identification system from patterns of natural movement, but rather reflect specific knowledge about characteristic individual facial gestures. Such experiments in the future could help us to understand the ways in which patterns of movement in facial expressions and facial speech help us to retrieve the identities of faces.

To conclude, while faces are complex, mobile surfaces which change both rigidly and non-rigidly when gesturing, expressing, and talking, much past research on face perception has ignored this mobility, and considered information to be derived from static snap shots of the facial form. Here we have reviewed evidence suggesting that dynamic information provides an important source of information for expression processing, speech perception, and for identification of faces. Future research will help us to understand the way in which dynamic information from the face is represented in memory and the precise mechanism by which it facilitates the retrieval of other information about personal identity.

4 Investigating auditory-visual speech perception development

D. Burnham and K. Sekiyama

4.1 Speech perception is auditory-visual

Optical information from facial movements of a talker contributes to speech perception not only when acoustic information is degraded (Sumby and Pollack 1954) or when the listener is hearing-impaired, but also when the acoustic information is clearly audible. This is most clearly shown in the classic *McGurk effect* or *fusion illusion*, in which dubbing the auditory speech syllable /ba/ onto the lip movements for /ga/ results in the emergent perception of 'da' or 'tha'. This occurs both when the observer is aware, and when the observer is unaware of the conflicting sources of information (McGurk and MacDonald 1976; McDonald and McGurk 1978). The beauty of this effect is not the fact that it results in an illusion, but that it unequivocally shows that visual information is used in speech perception even when auditory information is clear and undegraded.

Thus speech perception is a multisensory event, and as such it is an exemplar of humans' and other animals' ubiquitous propensity for multisensory perception. Multisensory perception occurs across various modalities, e.g., across vision and touch, both in human adults (Singer and Day 1969; Calvert *et al.* 2004), and infants (Rose *et al.* 1981). In the auditory-visual realm, there is some evidence that auditory-visual speech perception is a phenomenon that stands apart from non-linguistic auditory-visual perception of events (Saldaña and Rosenblum 1993; Saldaña and Rosenblum 1994; Sekular *et al.* 1997; Shams *et al.* 2000). Be that as it may, here only the development of auditory-visual *speech* perception is discussed (for an excellent review and theoretical proposal regarding the development of auditory-visual perception in general, see Lewkowicz 2000).

Given that speech perception is an auditory-visual phenomenon, two intriguing questions arise:

- By what process does auditory-visual speech perception occur?
- What is the developmental course of auditory-visual speech perception; how does auditory-visual speech perception change as a function of age and type of experience?

This chapter addresses these two questions, with due consideration of the appropriate research methods to be used for their resolution. The chapter concludes with a discussion of the implications of this work for automatic speech recognition.

4.2 Auditory-visual speech perception

How does auditory-visual speech perception occur? One of the most persistent models of auditory-visual speech processing is the Fuzzy Logical Model of Perception (FLMP – Massaro 1987; Massaro and Stork 1998), which is a late integration, prototype model. The model operates in three stages. First, incoming information from various sources, including auditory, visual, and top-down sources, is *evaluated* in parallel, and fuzzy truth values are independently assigned for the features in each source. Second, information from the various sources is *integrated*, with the least ambiguous carrying the most weight. (As this is the point at which the fuzzy truth values from different modalities are integrated, it is here that auditory-visual integration could be said to occur.) Finally, the result is *compared* with all relevant phoneme prototypes so that a decision can be made about the identity of the incoming phoneme.

Another major class of theory holds that speech perception is a multimodal perceptual event and, as for any other event, auditory and visual speech information are perceived early and directly, without the need for learned associations or phonological prototypes. Such early integration models involve the (re)presentation of auditory and visual speech information in a common metric, which may be auditory (Summerfield 1987), gestural or articulatory (Summerfield 1979; McGurk and Buchanan 1981; Liberman and Mattingly 1985; Liberman and Mattingly 1989), amodal (Kuhl and Meltzoff 1984; Studdert-Kennedy 1986; Kuhl and Meltzoff 1988) or phonetic (Green *et al.* 1991; Burnham and Dodd 1996; Burnham 1998; Green 1998). Thus in these models multimodal information is perceived *before* auditory and visual speech information are processed unimodally. As speech information could be considered to be fully processed once language-specific phonemes are identified, then in these early integration models, speech should be represented in a common metric at a sensory or phonetic level of speech processing, i.e., *before* language-specific phonemic processing is engaged (Burnham 2000; Burnham *et al.* 2002). In contrast, in the FLMP, as prototypes are learned on the basis of specific linguistic input, and as their resolution improves with experience, the common metric is engaged at or beyond the phonemic level of processing, i.e., *at or after* when language-specific speech processing comes into play.

The issue of the processing level at which auditory-visual speech perception occurs intersects with the issue of speech perception development. If auditory-visual speech perception were to be present at or soon after birth, then auditory-visual speech perception processes must necessarily be relatively low level, and/or unencumbered by experience. If, on the other hand, auditory-visual speech perception did not appear until a certain age or until after certain critical experiences, then this would imply that auditory-visual speech perception processes involve higher mental processes and/or that they are established as a function of experience.

Where and when a common representation of auditory and visual speech information occurs is of course an empirical question, and developmental studies are crucial for resolving this issue. Developmental studies are also crucial for determining whether and to what extent perceptual, linguistic, or cultural experience on the one hand, and cognitive processing capacity on the other, affect auditory-visual speech processing. The results of developmental studies will also be of interest with respect to theoretical formulations of speech perception, and applications of auditory-visual speech processing, such as ASR (automatic speech recognition). These various developmental issues drive the content of this chapter.

4.3 Methods for investigating development

The two main methods for investigating human development are set out below.

- **The Ontogenetic (*Amount*) Method** involves comparing the abilities of individuals of different ages brought up in functionally identical environments on a common task. By such means the effect that *amount* of experience (perceptual, linguistic, cultural etc.), and *amount* of maturation (such as cognitive processing capacity) may have on development can be determined.
- **The Differential Experience (*Type*) Method** involves comparing the ability of individuals of the same age brought up in functionally different environments on a common task. By such means the effect that the *type* of exposure or experience (for example, perceptual, linguistic, cultural) may have on development can be determined.

When speech and language are involved, these methods take on interesting characteristics. In the *ontogenetic method* there are various developmental milestones which may affect language processing – the increased attention to language-specific phonemes around 6 to 12 months of age (see Werker and Tees 1984a; Werker and Tees 1999), the attachment of meaning to sounds and the onset of speech production in the second year (Stager and Werker 1997; Stager and Werker 1998), the incredible exponential expansion of vocabulary, syntax, and semantics from 2 to 5 years, and the onset of reading instruction around age 6 years (Burnham 1986; Burnham 2000; Burnham 2003; Horlyck *et al.* 2010).

In the *differential experience method* the fact that human civilizations developed in valleys and over seas means that well before the first scientist strode the earth and wondered why, mini-speech-perception laboratories – that

Table 4.1 *Ontogenetic (amount) and cross-language (type) methods for investigating linguistic development.*

Ontogenetic (amount)	Cross-language (type)	Ontogenetic and cross-language (amount and type)
By judicious choice of ages, the effect of linguistic experience and maturation on development can be evaluated.	By judicious choice of languages, the effect of particular linguistic structures on development can be evaluated.	By judicious choice of ages and languages, the effect of linguistic experience, maturation, and linguistic structures on development can be evaluated.

is, languages – evolved. Languages differ in many ways, so by judicious cross-language comparisons, researchers can investigate the effect of the presence, absence, or degree of certain syntactic, semantic, pragmatic, or phonological devices. To take the case of phonology, languages differ in the number and types of consonants and vowels they employ, the particular consonant and vowel oppositions, and whether pitch information is used just in prosody or whether it is also employed as lexicalized tone. These differences give rise to cross-language differences in speech perception abilities. For example, we have found that adult speakers of English (a language which does not have lexicalized tone), perceive pitch differences carried on speech syllables rather poorly, but perceive the same pitch differences much better when they are presented as hums or violin sounds. On the other hand, tonal and pitch-accented-language speakers (Thai, Cantonese, Swedish) perceive pitch well under all three conditions (Burnham *et al.* 1996). Thus experience with particular language structures modifies the manner in which speech is processed.

To return to the two types of developmental methods of study, their separate and combined attributes are summarized in Table 4.1.

4.4 The ontogenetic development method

4.4.1 Auditory-visual speech perception in infants

To evaluate the role of the *amount* of experience on development, it is first necessary to know the initial state of the system. It is well established that speech perception is sophisticated and universal at birth: newborns, irrespective of their language environment, perceive just about any speech contrast researchers like to test them on. Then as a function of phonemic experience their speech perception is reorganized such that the phones phonemically relevant in the ambient language continue to be perceived (Pegg and Walker 1997), while phonemically irrelevant phones tend to be disregarded (Werker and Tees 1999). Nevertheless, such disregarded sounds can still be perceived under certain conditions, e.g., following extensive training, or in discrimination tasks with short inter-stimulus intervals (Werker and Tees 1984b; Werker and Logan 1985) (for reviews see Werker and Tees 1999; Burnham *et al.* 2002; Burnham and Mattock 2010). Thus infants' perception of the wide range of speech sounds remains intact (there is no sensorineural loss), but the way in which they perform in discrimination tasks changes – the more relevant native speech sounds have precedence over non-native sounds.[1]

The status of auditory-*visual* speech perception *at* birth is not explicitly known, though there is evidence for auditory-visual speech perception abilities shortly *after* birth. Infants match faces and voices on the basis of whether face and voice are in or out of synchrony by two months of age (Dodd 1979; Burnham and Dodd 1998); on the basis of the gender of face and voice by six months of age (Francis and McCroy 1983; Walker-Andrews *et al.* 1991); and on the basis of vowel colour (Kuhl and Meltzoff 1982; Kuhl and Meltzoff 1984; Kuhl and Meltzoff 1988; Patterson and Werker 1999) and consonant–vowel combinations (MacKain *et al.* 1983) by four and six months respectively. Interestingly, matching face and voice on the basis of vowel colour, precedes matching on the basis of gender: 2-month-old (Patterson and Werker 2003) and 4.5-month-old (Patterson and Werker 1999) infants match for vowel colour but not gender, and 8-month-olds match on the basis of both (Patterson and Werker 2002). Thus it appears that matching on the basis of gender requires more culturally specific learning than does matching on the basis of linguistic features, at least when considered at the behavioural level. At the neural level, however, it may be the case that gender matching emerges as early as lip–voice matching (Bristow *et al.* 2008). The question thus arises whether linguistic matching skills are affected by specific language experience. It appears so, at least in early infancy. Studying language specificity in lip–voice matching, Dodd and Burnham (1988) found that when 4.5-month-old English language infants are presented with two people side-by-side, one speaking English, and the other speaking Greek, infants match the appropriate face with a centrally located voice, but only when the voice is speaking English. Younger infants of 2.5 months, did not show this effect. This is consistent with a recent finding on the development of visual language discrimination – 4- to 6-month-old English learning infants have been shown to discriminate silent movie clips of English from those of French (Weikum, *et al.* 2007).

These results generally show that infants perceive structural correspondences between seen and heard speech, and match visual and auditory speech by at least three months. Auditory-visual speech matching appears to precede other auditory-visual matching skills and appears to be first and most evident in infants' native language. However, these matching studies cannot distinguish between two possible mechanisms that might be invoked to explain their results: (a) that infants perceive speech as an integrated auditory-visual event, or (b) that infants match the characteristics of one modality with those of the other. Investigations require infants to integrate rather than just match auditory and visual components. If infants were found to perceive an emergent percept in the McGurk effect paradigm, then it could be more confidently claimed that the first alternative is the case.

There is now good evidence that infants integrate auditory and visual information in their perception of speech. A study by Rosenblum and colleagues (Johnson *et al.* 1995; Rosenblum *et al.* 1997) rests on the observation that adults perceive auditory /ba/, visual /va/ as 'va', but auditory /da/, visual /va/ as 'da'. They habituated 5-month-old infants' visual fixation to auditory-visual /va/ and then tested them on different auditory-visual combinations. There was generalization of habituation to an auditory /ba/, visual /va/ presentation, showing that infants perceived this to be the same as, or at least similar to, auditory-visual /va/. However, habituation did *not* generalize to an auditory /da/, visual /va/ presentation, showing that infants perceived this to be different from auditory-visual /va/. These results show that 5-month-old infants appear to perceive auditory /ba/, visual /va/ as 'va', whereas auditory /da/, visual /va/ is not perceived as 'va', but possibly as 'da'. Thus in one combination the auditory information is dominant, and in the other the visual information is dominant, just as is the case with adults. Secondly, in a similar study Desjardins and Werker (1996, 2004) found that 4-month-old infants habituated to auditory-visual /vi/ showed no recovery of visual fixation (i.e., no novelty response) when presented with auditory /bi/, visual /vi/, but that infants habituated to auditory-visual /bi/ *did* show recovery of visual fixation to auditory /bi/, visual /vi/ (although this was the case only for female infants). These results support Rosenblum's (Johnson *et al.* 1995; Rosenblum, Schmuckler *et al.* 1997) conclusion that infants perceive auditory /b/, visual /v/ as 'v', and like Rosenblum, that there is a visual influence in speech perception by infants (Kushnerenko *et al.* 2010).

Using the traditional McGurk effect, Burnham and Dodd (1996; 1998; 2004) tested whether 4.5-month-old infants perceive an emergent percept, /da/ or /ða/, when presented with auditory /ba/, visual /ga/, just as children and adults do. Infants habituated to auditory /ba/, visual /ga/ had greater test trial fixations to hear /da/ or /ða/ than /ba/, whereas infants habituated to matching auditory-visual /ba/, showed no such preference. (In auditory-visual speech perception studies, familiarity preferences are often found – see Burnham and Dodd 2004). This study provides strong evidence that infants of this age perceive auditory /ba/, visual /ga/ as /da/ or /ða/. So, it appears that, over and above the differential auditory and visual *dominance* under certain auditory-visual stimulus conditions (Johnson *et al.* 1995; Desjardins and Werker 1996; Rosenblum *et al.* 1997;

Desjardins and Werker 2004) there is an emergent or fusion percept in infancy, evidence for auditory-visual *integration* of speech by at least 4.5 months of age. Together these studies from three separate laboratories provide strong evidence that (a) infants use both auditory and visual information in their speech perception, (b) infants perceive auditory and visual information in a common metric, and (c) as they do so at an age which is presumably prior to full language-specific phonemic processing, this common metric is possibly phonetic in nature.

Recently, neural correlates of the McGurk effect have been reported in 5-month-old infants (Kushnerenko *et al.* 2008). In this study, event-related brain potentials (ERPs) were measured during presentations of audiovisual speech stimuli: congruent auditory-visual /ba/ and auditory-visual /ga/, a fusion pair (auditory /ba/, visual /ga/), and a combination pair (auditory /ga/, visual /ba/). In the resultant ERP, the waveforms for these four types of stimuli were different. In the occipital cortex, waveforms of early components (190~290 ms) were the same irrespective of the auditory component, but were different depending on the visual component, indicating discrimination of visual /ba/ from visual /ga/. In the frontal and temporal cortices, only the combination pair showed a different waveform compared with the other stimuli in late components (290~590 ms), perhaps due to the detected incongruence. These results indicate that the fusion pair was perceived as if it were a congruent stimulus. They are further investigating whether or not this means integrated auditory-visual perception for the fusion pair (Kushnerenko *et al.* 2010).

Finally, the development of auditory-visual speech perception in infancy may be affected by the nature of the linguistic environment. Testing Japanese infants, Mugitani *et al.* (2008) found that development of lip–voice vowel matching in Japanese-learning infants is slower (8 to 11 months) compared with reported data in English (2 to 4 months, see above in this section).

4.4.2 The development of auditory-visual speech perception

The original report of the McGurk effect included ontogenetic development data (McGurk and MacDonald 1976) with pre-schoolers (3 to 5 years), school children (7 to 8 years), and adults (18 to 40 years). Participants were tested with auditory /ba/, /ga/, /pa/, and /ka/, each of which was combined with an incompatible visual syllable. For these incongruent auditory-visual stimuli, for example, auditory /ba/ paired with visual /ga/, participants reported hearing 'da' (*fused* response) 'ga' (*visual* response), or 'ba' (*auditory* response). In other cases, for example, auditory /ga/ paired with visual /ba/, 'combined' 'bga' responses were observed. All non-auditory (fused, combined, and visual) responses can be regarded as being visually influenced. Mean visually influenced responses were 59%, 52%, and 92% for pre-schoolers, school children, and adults respectively, in spite of the fact that the three groups identified the auditory-only stimuli equally accurately (91%,

97%, and 99%). Thus, younger children showed a much weaker visual influence, about half that of the adults.

Massaro *et al.* (1986) reported similar results using ambiguous speech sounds. They tested children (4 to 6 years) and adults, with synthesized speech sounds ranging from /ba/ to /da/ in five steps. Each of these was combined with a face articulating /ba/ or /da/. In the visual-only condition speechreading performance was poorer in children (79% correct) than adults (96%). For the auditory-visual stimuli, similar age differences were observed: there was more visual influence for the adults than for the children for each of the stimuli. The authors suggested that the weaker visual influence for the children is possibly due to their poorer speechreading ability.

Hockley and Polka (1994) also reported a developmental increase in visual influence, this time between 5 and 11 years of age. They tested five age groups (5-, 7-, 9-, 11-year-olds, and adults) using /ba/, /va/, /ða/, /da/, and /ga/ articulated by a male talker. Similar to the earlier research, the results showed an increase across ages in speechreading ability and in the degree of visual influence as a function of increasing age.

The developmental increase in visual influence in these three studies is possibly related to experience in articulating speech sounds. Desjardins *et al.* (1997) showed that preschool children who make articulation errors are less influenced by visual cues than are children who can correctly produce consonants. Based on an articulation test they divided preschoolers (3 to 5 years of age) into two groups: those who made substitution errors and those who did not. Subsequent perception tests revealed that the substituter children were the poorest at speechreading, and had the lowest degree of visual influence in auditory-visual speech perception, followed by the non-substituter children and then the adults. The three groups did not differ, however, in auditory-only speech perception. The authors concluded that experience in correctly producing consonants impacts upon the representation of visible speech. It is, of course, possible that the opposite causal effect is the case, namely, that poor speechreading impacts upon articulation ability. However, Siva and colleagues (Siva 1995; Siva *et al.* 1995) have shown that cerebral-palsied adults, lacking in experience of normal speech production, tend to show less visual influence in speech perception under some conditions than non-impaired adults. Thus, it appears that articulation experience affects speechreading, rather than the other way around.

4.5 The cross-language development method

In an attempt to replicate the original McGurk effect results, we tested native speakers of Japanese with speech stimuli, /ba/, /da/, /ga/, /pa/, /ta/, /ka/, /ma/, /na/, /ra/, and /wa/, articulated by a native Japanese talker (Sekiyama and Tohkura 1991). In a pilot experiment, the evidence of the McGurk effect was very weak. So we set up two conditions. In the noise-added condition, white noise was added to the auditory component of the stimuli. In the quiet condition, no noise was added. The Japanese participants reported a weak McGurk effect in the quiet condition, but a strong effect in the noise-added condition. It was as if the native Japanese talkers used visual information in speech perception only when the auditory component of the stimuli was not perfectly intelligible (but see Massaro *et al.* 1993). Although the cause of this weak visual influence is not clear, it may be related to the Japanese cultural habit of avoiding staring at the person to whom one is talking. (Note that this cultural habit seems to be diminishing as younger generations of Japanese become more westernized.)

Subsequently, we conducted cross-language comparisons (Sekiyama and Tohkura 1993) with two sets of stimuli. One set was Japanese (identical to the stimuli in the above study), and the other English (stimuli articulated by a native English talker). The two sets of stimuli were presented to two language groups, native speakers of Japanese and of American English. On average the Japanese participants showed a weaker McGurk effect than did the Americans. So again a language-influenced McGurk effect was found. Nevertheless, the Japanese reported a stronger McGurk effect with the non-native (English) speech stimuli than with the native (Japanese) stimuli. Intriguingly, a similar foreign talker effect was found for the American participants: the Americans showed a stronger McGurk effect for the (foreign) Japanese than for the (native) English stimuli. The generality of this foreign talker effect is supported by subsequent studies. The effect for American English and Japanese talkers and perceivers has also been found by Kuhl and her colleagues (Kuhl *et al.* 1994). In other languages, the foreign talker effect has been found with Austrian and Hungarian participants presented with an Austrian talker (Grassegger 1995), Dutch and Cantonese language participants listening to a Dutch talker (de Gelder *et al.* 1995), and German and Spanish participants listening to German and Spanish talkers (Fuster-Duran 1996). The exact nature of this foreign speaker effect is not yet known, although it appears that there may be some element of expectancy involved: a study by Burnham and Lau (1999) suggests that when perceivers expected to see a foreign face there were greater foreign speaker effects than when they did not expect to see a foreign speaker. Thus one reason for the weak Japanese McGurk effect may be the lack of expectancy for foreign speakers in everyday situations, due to the homogeneity of race and language and the relatively isolated habitation on the islands of Japan.

To return to the language-influenced McGurk effect, one might think that the Japanese adult perceivers are poor speechreaders like young English-speaking children (Massaro *et al.* 1986; Hockley and Polka 1994; Desjardins *et al.* 1997). However, this is unlikely because the Japanese adults *did* use visual information in the noise-added condition. Thus, in the quiet condition they must also have perceived visual information, but did not make use of it. In fact, Sekiyama (1994) showed that the Japanese perceivers more frequently noticed the incompatibility between auditory and visual cues in the McGurk-type stimuli than did the American perceivers. This implies that the cultural habit explanation put forward above for the weak visual influence for Japanese perceivers is incorrect. It seems that the Japanese are subject to auditory capture *in spite of* perceiving visual cues.

Further data were obtained from native speakers of Chinese (Sekiyama 1997). The same Japanese and English stimuli were used as in the above study, thus both stimulus sets were non-native for the perceivers. The Chinese participants showed a weak McGurk effect for both Japanese and English stimuli (this is consistent with results of a study by de Gelder and Vroomen 1992; but may be inconsistent with Chen and Massaro 2004). Comparison of these results with Sekiyama's Japanese and American results (Sekiyama and Tohkura 1993; Sekiyama 1994) revealed that the McGurk effect was weakest in the Chinese, intermediate in the Japanese, and strongest in the Americans. This suggests another explanation of the language-influenced McGurk effect, other than the cultural habit explanation given above. It may be that the degree of visual influence in the McGurk effect is inversely proportional to the use of tonal information in the perceivers' native language. Consider the following. In Chinese the meanings of spoken words are determined not only by vowel and consonant combinations, but also by the pitch pattern (tone) of the word. A similar device, pitch-accent, operates in Japanese on multisyllabic words. Now, while it has recently been found that there is some reliable visual information for tone (Burnham and Lau 1998; Burnham *et al.* 2000; Burnham *et al.* 2001), it may reasonably be assumed that tone and pitch-accent are most strongly carried by the auditory modality. If so, then auditory information should be weighted more strongly and visual information less strongly in tonal languages. This proposal is consistent with the observed results: auditory information is used less (and visual more) in English (no tones), than in Japanese (two pitch-accents), and in turn than Chinese (four tones in Mandarin, and six tones in Cantonese).

Finally, using ERP, we examined neural processes in auditory-visual speech perception in adult native speakers of Japanese and English. With auditory-visual congruent syllables and auditory-only syllables as stimuli, Hisanaga *et al.* (2009) found that a visual facilitation (i.e., a reduction in latency due to additional visual speech) for the Japanese speakers was not observed at P2, but limited to N1, whereas the English speakers showed a reduction in latencies at both N1 and P2 as reported by van Wassenhove *et al.* (2005). These results indicate that the visual influence for the Japanese speakers is only at the sensory and not at the perceptual (integration) level.

4.6 Combined methods

From the ontogenetic studies we have found that the sheer *amount* of experience affects both auditory-visual speech perception and speechreading. From the differential experience cross-language studies we have found (a) that the McGurk effect is influenced by language background (it is stronger in English than in Japanese language perceivers); and (b) that the McGurk effect is stronger when viewing a foreign language speaker.

Thus, both the ontogenetic and the differential experience methods provide valuable information about auditory-visual speech perception development. Both the *amount* and the *type* of language experience affect auditory-visual speech perception. To obtain a full picture of auditory-visual speech perception development, a combined amount–type study is required. We (Sekiyama and Burnham 2008) conducted a series of experiments combining the ontogenetic and differential experience methods in order to examine how the amount and type of language experience may affect the ontogenetic source and course of cross-language differences in auditory-visual speech perception.

In the first study native Japanese and native Australian English language adults were tested; in the second their results were compared with native Japanese and native Australian English language children (6-, 8-, and 11-year olds). To control for the foreign/native language talker effect, we used both English and Japanese syllables (congruent auditory-visual combinations and McGurk-style mismatches) articulated by two English and two Japanese talkers. The first experiment showed the expected greater use of visual information by the English than the Japanese adults. The inclusion of reaction time (RT) measures allows information to be garnered regarding a possible sensory-bias basis of this result: while Japanese adults reacted more quickly to auditory-only (AO) stimuli than did English-language adults, English language adults were relatively much faster in the visually-only (VO) than in the AO condition. In the second experiment at 6 years Japanese- and English-language children demonstrated an equivalent level of visual influence in auditory-visual speech perception. However, between 6 and 8 years the amount of visual influence increased significantly and dramatically for the English- but not the Japanese-language children. Thereafter, 8-, 11-years, and adulthood, the level of visual influence remained at this elevated level for English-language participants, and remained at the same lower level across age for the four Japanese groups – 6-, 8-, 11-year-olds, and adults. An additional result that may help explain this effect is that at 6 years Japanese participants were more accurate with auditory-only stimuli than the English language participants, though this difference disappeared at later stages. Such an early auditory superiority in Japanese children may render visual supplementation redundant and the fact that Japanese adults have lower RTs to auditory information than English language adults may be a consequence of this early auditory proficiency.

Thus the onset of the difference in auditory-visual speech perception between Japanese and English speakers has been localized between 6 and 8 years using this combined ontogenetic/differential experience method. Nevertheless, the exact cause of this effect is yet unknown. Sekiyama and Burnham (2008) speculate that due to the very crowded vowel space in English and its predominance of consonant clusters, visual information is more important for English-language children as they begin to learn to read than for Japanese children who have a phonologically less crowded 5-vowel language with few if any clusters. (Indeed a follow-up study by Erdener and Burnham (under review) suggests that English-language children's relative use of visual speech information is related to their language-specific speech perception, their ability to attend to native and disregard non-native speech sounds as they begin to learn to read.) This study (Sekiyama and Burnham 2008) shows the power of the combined ontogenetic/differential experience method and paves the way for further in-depth studies of auditory-visual speech perception.

4.7 Conclusions and an application: automatic speech recognition

There are now very good reasons to move away from considering speech perception as purely auditory to considering it to be auditory-visual. This is evident in three areas: experimental studies, theories, and applications such as automatic speech recognition (ASR). Early *experimental studies* of speech and speech perception were concerned only with auditory speech. As we have shown in this chapter, it is now well established that speech perception is a multisensory event, and that human speech perception both uses and benefits from visual information when it is available (see, for example, Benoît 2000). Similarly, *speech perception theories* have mostly concerned auditorily presented phonemes (Nygaard and Pisoni 1995), but have now been elaborated to cover auditory-visual speech perception (Massaro 1987; Burnham 1998; Green 1998; Massaro 1998b). Finally *automatic speech recognition (ASR)* systems and speech synthesis systems first contented themselves with recognition and manufacture of auditory phonemes. Now ASR and synthesis systems based on auditory-*visual* information are becoming evident, and the use of visual in conjunction with auditory speech information significantly improves the performance of such systems (Cohen and Massaro 1990; Benoît and Pols 1992; Brooke and Scott 1998b).

One of the main drawbacks of ASR at the moment is that it requires extensive training on any particular voice (and face) before anywhere near adequate accuracy is attained. This is not the case in human speech perception (Rosner and Pickering 1994), and so some understanding of how human speech perception has become so efficient would be very useful. Human learning about speech (at least auditory speech) proceeds in what might be considered a perverse manner; human infants perceive just about all speech sounds at birth, and then learn to ignore just those sounds that are not useful to them in their native language environment. However, the ability to perceive these sounds is not lost; with some training adults can discriminate non-native speech sounds separated by a short inter-stimulus interval (Werker and Tees 1984b; Werker and Logan 1985). Thus humans learn to attend to the critical aspects of speech, and perhaps learn to attend to higher-order invariant speech characteristics that remain unchanged across speakers and situations.

We believe that the next step in ASR development, following the inclusion of visual information, is to incorporate knowledge about the development of the perception of both auditory and visual speech. As visual information has been found to augment ASR systems, we feel that so will also be the addition of developmental information. For example, the language-specific manner in which a particular language is processed is the result of a developmental process in which infants resonate to and learn about the regularities of that language. This happens at both the phone and word level. At the phone level, infants pick up what phonetic variations are and are not important in their native language, and respond preferentially to distinctions that are phonemically relevant in their native language (Werker and Tees 1999). At the word level it has been shown that infants take into account the statistical regularities of phoneme strings in the language they hear about them, and use this information in parsing the speech stream (Saffran *et al.* 1996). Developmental processes of auditory-visual speech perception both within and between languages, will also inform ASR techniques. Why do humans use visual information more when they observe a foreign talker? When do they start to do this and how? What phonetic or cultural factors cause Cantonese language users to use visual information less than their Japanese language counterparts and they less, in turn, than their English language counterparts? When and how do infants or children in these language environments learn to use visual information more or less? How does speechreading ability and its development relate to auditory-visual speech perception ability? Answers to these questions will assist in the development of theories of auditory-visual speech perception development, and the development of ASR systems. One obvious implication is that auditory-visual ASR algorithms should allow multiple determinants (accents, allophones, auditory information and visual information) of relevant phonemes and words, and constrain these multiple inputs to meaningful distinctions, while still registering the variations. On the basis of our knowledge of infant speech perception development such exposure to a range of auditory-visual information in speech in a particular language may result in better recognition rates, but only if there are subtle shifts in the way in which speech corpora and accompanying acoustic models and language models are used by ASR systems.

It is clear that speech is a rich, over-specified stimulus. We humans are extremely good at learning very quickly to use just that speech information that is useful to us in a specific language or situation. Only if we can discover how we learn to do this can we then teach machines to do the same.

4.8 Acknowledgments

Writing this chapter and some of the research reported herein was supported by an Australian Research Council (ARC) Large grant, A00001283, to the first author, and ARC Discovery grants to both authors (DP0211947, DP0558698); by a research grant from Hayao Nakayama Foundation, and a Grant-in-Aid for Scientific Research from the Japanese Ministry of Education, Science, and Culture, 10610070 and 21243040 to the second author, and by funding from the University of Western Sydney to MARCS Institute. The assistance of the NSW Department of Education and Training in allowing us to test primary school children is gratefully acknowledged. The helpful comments of Ms Helen Tam, and Mr Doğu Erdener on an earlier draft are greatly appreciated.

5 Brain bases for seeing speech: fMRI studies of speechreading

R. Campbell and M. MacSweeney

5.1 Introduction

This volume confirms that the ability to extract linguistic information from viewing the talker's face is a fundamental aspect of speech processing. In this chapter we explore the cortical substrates that support these processes. There are a number of reasons why the identification of these visual speech circuits in the brain is important. One practical one is that it may help determine suitability for hearing aids, especially cochlear implants (Okazawa *et al.* 1996; Giraud and Truy 2002; Lazard *et al.* 2010). Another is that there are brain correlates of good or poorer speechreading which may offer insights into individual differences in speechreading ability (see Ludman *et al.* 2000). There are also theoretical reasons to explore these brain bases. Cortical architecture reflects our evolutionary inheritance: Ape brains resemble human ones in very many respects, including the cortical organization of acoustic and visual sensation. Neurophysiological responses in macaque cortex show mutual modulation of vision and audition within key temporal regions formerly thought to be "purely" auditory. In turn, this suggests a broad-based, multimodal processing capacity for communication within lateral temporal regions, which could be the bedrock upon which a dedicated human speech processing system has evolved (see Ghazanfar *et al.* 2005; Ghazanfar and Schroeder 2006; Ghazanfar 2009).

However, our interest was initially driven by other concerns. There had been suggestive evidence from patients with discrete lesions of the brain that watching faces speaking might call on distinct brain mechanisms, and that these could be different from those used for identifying other facial actions, such as facial expressions (see Campbell 1996). Nevertheless little was known about the precise brain networks involved in speechreading. Watching speech was known to be more similar to hearing speech than to reading written words; for example, in terms of its representations in immediate memory (Campbell and Dodd 1980). But did this extend to cortical circuits? In our first studies, we wanted to know to what extent speech that is seen but not heard might engage the networks used for hearing speech, and which other brain networks might be engaged. These questions are related to further issues. How do the circuits for audiovisual speech relate to those for visual or auditory speech alone? How might the cortical bases for silent speechreading reflect the individual's experience with heard language? That is, do people who are born deaf show similar or different patterns of activation than hearing people when (silently) speechreading? The technique that we have exploited to address these questions is functional magnetic resonance imaging (fMRI). This brain mapping technique is non-invasive, unlike positron emission tomography (PET), which requires the participant to ingest small amounts of radioactive substances.[1] fMRI offers reasonably high spatial resolution (i.e., on the order of millimeters) of most brain regions. It can give a "cumulative snapshot" of those areas that are active during the period of scanning (typically several seconds). It does not lend itself to showing the discrete temporal sequence of brain events that are set in train when viewing a speaking face, although recent developments in analytic methods can model the fMRI data with respect to stages of information flow (e.g. von Kriegstein *et al.* 2008). For good temporal resolution, dynamic techniques, using, for example, scalp measurements of electrochemical brain potentials (event-related potentials, ERPs; see e.g. Callan *et al.* 2001; Allison *et al.* 2000), or magnetoencephalography (MEG Ð see Levänen 1999) are preferred, although spatial resolution is less good using these techniques. One compelling strategy is to combine inferences from spatial analysis using fMRI or PET, alongside analysis of the fine-grain temporal sequences of brain events using MEG or scalp electroencephalography (EEG), and this is where much current research activity is focused (e.g. Calvert and Thesen 2004; Hertrich *et al.* 2007; Hertrich *et al.* 2009; Arnal *et al.* 2009; Hertrich *et al.* 2010). A further imaging technique which has been used to explore audiovisual speech processing is TMS – transcranial magnetic stimulation. To date, this has been used to explore contributions of primary motor cortex (M1 – see below) to audiovisual speech processing (Watkins *et al.* 2003; Sato *et al.* 2010).

5.2 Route maps and guidelines

5.2.1 Brain regions

The cerebral cortex shows local specialization. The visual areas of the human brain are located at the back of the brain in the occipital lobes. Acoustic sensation is processed initially just behind the ears, in the left and right temporal lobe, within Heschl's gyrus on the temporal plane (*planum temporale*) below the lateral surface of the temporal lobe (see Figure 5.1 to Figure 5.4 for these locations).

The left temporal lobe is preferentially involved in understanding language, and the superior part of the left temporal lobe is named Wernicke's region, after

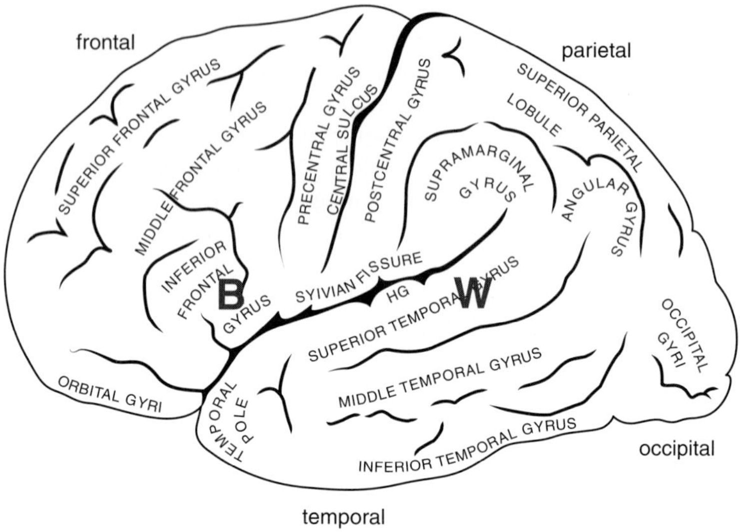

Figure 5.1 A schematic view of the left hemisphere, showing its major folds (sulci) and convolutions (gyri). Two language areas are also shown: "B" is Broca's area; "W" is Wernicke's area. These are general (functional) regions, not specific cortical locales (adapted from Damasio and Damasio 1989).

the nineteenth-century neurologist and psychiatrist Karl Wernicke, who has been credited with the suggestion that these regions support language comprehension. Another important brain region for language is in the inferior part of the left prefrontal lobe. Here lies Broca's area, named after the French clinician Paul Broca who first described a case with damage in just this region in 1847. Patients with lesions in Broca's area have difficulty in verbal production. The region is also implicated in syntactic processing, especially function words and verbs, and in processing inflectional morphology.

One mode of understanding cortical organization that has stood the test of time was indicated by the Russian neurologist, A. R. Luria (1973). He suggested a three-part functional hierarchy reflected in brain topography. **Primary** regions are where sensation and action are implemented at the most fine-grained level. For sensation, these regions are those that receive projections from the afferent sensory neurons via subcortical relays. For action, they are the regions that project to the efferent neural system, also via subcortical structures. For vision, this means that primary cortex in the calcarine fissure of the occipital lobes (visual areas V1, V2) is organized so that the visual features and spatial organization of the visual field are retained in the organization of cortical cell responses. Because of this, damage to parts of the occipital lobe leads to

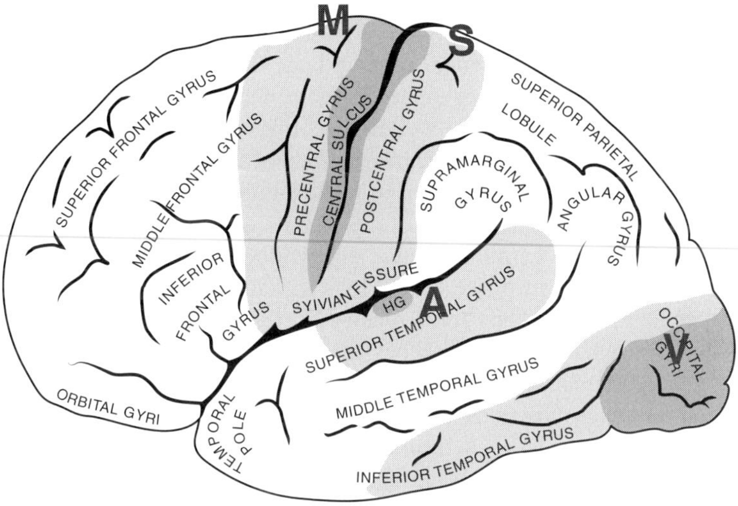

Figure 5.2 Functional organization of the cortex, lateral view, adapted from Luria (1973). Primary regions are shaded darker, secondary areas are shaded lighter. Unshaded regions can be considered tertiary. V=vision, A=audition, S = somatosensory, M = motor.

blindness as dense and as localized to specific parts of the visual field as that caused by retinal damage.

As for perception, so too for action. The primary motor region, which lies on the anterior surface of the central sulcus, maps the human body topographically (somatotopic organization). If there is damage to the motor strip, immobility will be as acute as that suffered if the spinal nerve to that set of muscles is severed, and as specific to those muscle groups.

So, to summarize, in addition to a primary motor area, at least three discrete and cortically widely separated primary sensory regions can be identified: (1) vision in occipital regions (V1/2), (2) audition in Heschl's gyrus, a deep "fold" in the superior lateral temporal surface (A1), (3) somatosensory perception in the sensory strip on the posterior surface of the central sulcus (S1). These locations are indicated in Figure 5.2. They are, by definition, modality-specific.

Regions proximate to these primary sites show higher-level organization with less strict "point-for-point" organization. Such **secondary** areas for vision, for example, include V5/MT, a visual motion sensitive region, as well as some parts of the inferior temporal lobe that specialize for face or written-word or object processing. Within the parietal lobes, various spatial coding relations are mapped, so that cells here may be sensitive to spatial location but relatively indifferent to the type of object in view.

Finally, Luria suggested that **tertiary** areas are multimodal in their sensitivity and can support abstract representations. The tertiary zones are proximate to the secondary ones, but are distant from the primary ones. One good example of this is in the frontal lobe. The tertiary region here is the most anterior, prefrontal part. This is concerned with the highest level of executive function: general plans, monitoring long-term outcomes. This can be thought of as the strategic centre of the brain, involved in planning ("I want to make a cup of tea"). Moving in a posterior direction, the secondary motor areas effect more tactical aspects of action preparation ("I need to find the kettle, fill it with water and set it to boil"), while the most posterior part of the frontal lobe includes M1 where voluntary actions of specific muscle groups are initiated (Figure 5.2).

This general organizational landscape suggests that Broca's area, lying within secondary (motor) regions has become specialized for the realization of specialized language functions including speech planning and (relatively abstract) aspects of production. A recent perspective emphasizes the role of Broca's area in the *selection* of word and action (Thompson-Schill 2005). Wernicke's area, on one account, specializes in processing speech-like and language-like features of the auditory input signal (Wise *et al.* 2001), but the role of these regions in relation to visible speech and audiovisual speech processing had not been addressed.

5.2.2 Networks and connections

The organization of cortical grey matter, as sketched here, is not the only aspect of brain organization that should guide us. The brain is a dynamic system across which neural events unfold that support the various functional analyses and action plans that comprise behavior. In addition to connections between neighboring neurons that allow the development of functionally distinct cortical regions to emerge as sketched above, long fiber tracts (white matter) connect posterior and anterior regions (uncinate and arcuate tracts), as well as homologous regions in each hemisphere (commissural tracts). White matter tracts are now imageable, using diffusion tensor techniques (DTI, see Appendix). The neural pathways for the analysis of the signal from its registration in primary sensory regions for vision and audition right up to the conscious awareness and representation of a speech act require many different levels of analysis, supported by multiple neural connections, including white matter connections between different brain regions. These levels of analysis can be described in terms of different information processing stages, with bi-directional qualities. That is, the direction of information flow can be top-down, as well as bottom-up. Thus, a *network* approach can be used to describe how different functional processes may be supported by multiple, interrelated patterns of activation across discrete brain regions.

5.2.3 *Processing streams*

The acoustic qualities of the auditory signal are processed hierarchically according to spectrographic characteristics within Heschl's gyrus and surrounding auditory belt (roughly Brodmann area 41) and parabelt (including Brodmann area 42) regions of the *planum temporale* and very superior parts of the lateral surface of the temporal lobes (Binder *et al.* 2000; Hackett 2003; Binder *et al.* 2004). From these sites, which constitute, essentially, primary auditory cortex in Luria's terms (A1), emerge two distinct processing streams, first identified in animal models (for a review, see Scott and Johnsrude 2003; Rauschecker and Scott 2009; Hickok and Poeppel 2004; Hickok and Poeppel 2007). One, the postero-dorsal stream, projecting to the temporo-parietal junction, on to inferior parietal sites, thence to dorsolateral pre-frontal cortex (DLPFC) supports the localization of sounds. This is conceptualized as a "where" stream (Scott and Johnsrude 2003). The other, the "what" stream, comprises an anterior projection along the superior temporal gyrus towards the temporal pole, and thence via uncinate tracts to ventrolateral prefrontal cortex including Broca's area (Scott and Johnsrude 2003; Hickok and Poeppel 2004). This route allows the identification of discrete sounds as events/objects, and also supports the identification of individual voices (Warren *et al.* 2006). Figure 5.3 shows the approximate directions of these streams, overlaid on a schematic of the "opened" superior temporal regions.

Can this model, based originally on animal data, accommodate speech processing? PET studies using systematically degraded speech signals show a gradient of activation reflecting the intelligibility of the sound signal. Higher intelligibility correlates with more anterior superior temporal activation, irrespective of the complexity of the speech sound (Scott *et al.* 2006). Lesions of anterior temporal regions lead to impaired comprehension of speech (Scott and Johnsrude 2003; Hickok and Poeppel 2004; Hickok and Poeppel 2007). The anterior stream appears to constitute a "what" stream, supporting the progressive identification of phonological, lexical, and semantic features of the auditory signal. What, then, is the role of the posterior stream in speech processing? One compelling suggestion is that this constitutes a "how" pathway for speech, integrating articulatory and acoustic plans online, to enable not only fluent speech production, but also its accurate perception in terms of the intended speech act. The sensorimotor characteristics of speech may be better captured by this stream (Scott and Johnsrude 2003; Rauschecker and Scott 2009). Hickok and Poeppel (2007) suggest that it is this dorsal route that shows very strong (left-) lateralization, in contrast to the ventral stream which may involve a greater degree of bilateral processing of the speech signal.

Why should the speech processing system require the "belt-and-braces" of two speech processing streams? One reason is in the variability of speech. We

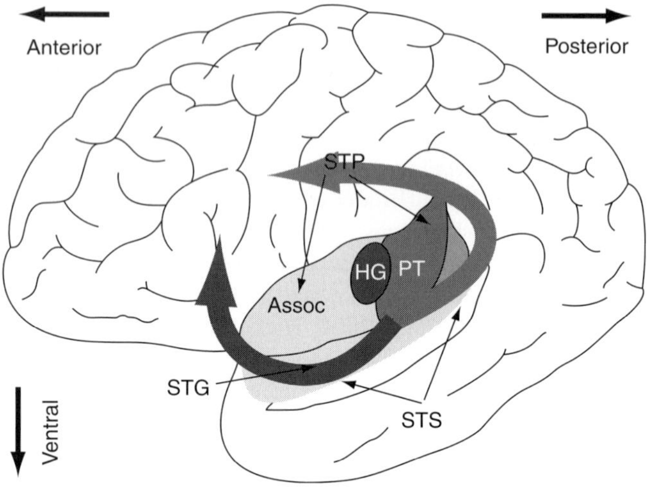

Figure 5.3 This schematic view "opens out" the superior surface of the temporal lobe, as if the frontal lobe has been drawn away from the temporal lobe on which it normally lies. This reveals the superior temporal plane (STP) including the *planum temporale* (PT), and Heschl's gyrus (HG). Within this extensive region are critical sites for acoustic analysis. Primary auditory cortex (A1) occupies HG. On the lateral surface of the temporal lobe, and visible in lateral view, the uppermost gyrus is the superior temporal gyrus (STG), with the superior temporal sulcus (STS) along its ventral parts (after Wise *et al.* 2001). This comprises region A2. The lower shaded arrow shows the approximate direction of forward flow of the anterior, ventral auditory stream ("what"); the upper shaded arrow shows the posterior, dorsal ("where/how") stream.

are surprisingly good at identifying an utterance whether it is spoken by a man or child, slowly or quickly, over a poor phone line or by a casual speaker. Speech processing takes account of coarticulatory processes used by the talker. It manages wide variation in talker style (accent, register). All of these affect the acoustic properties of the signal in such varied ways that there are rarely observable regularities in the spectrographic record. Speech constancy is a non-trivial issue for speech perception. This was recognized by motor theorists of speech perception, who proposed a critical role for the activation of articulatory representations in the *listener* in order for speech to be effectively heard and understood (Liberman and Mattingly 1985; Liberman and Whalen 2000). Recent models of sensorimotor control offer more detailed outlines of how motor representations and sensory inputs may interact dynamically to shape ongoing perceptual processes as speech is perceived (Rauschecker and Scott 2009). Hickok and Poeppel (2007) suggest tasks that require the *recognition* of a spoken utterance may rely more on the ventral stream, while *speech perception* itself makes more use of the dorsal stream.

Finally, it would be a mistake to conceive of these streams as solely forward-flowing. Neuroanatomical studies suggest that there can be modulation of "earlier" regions by "later" processing stages. That is, information could, for some processing, flow "back" to primary sensory regions as well as "forward" to tertiary sites. This is discussed in more detail below. For the dorsal stream, especially, it seems necessary to invoke both forward and inverse models to match the action plan for a speech gesture (frontal, fronto-parietal), with the acoustic properties of its realization (temporal, temporo-parietal).

5.2.4 Implications for speechreading and audiovisual speech

We have provided a broad brushstroke picture of the brain areas implicated in cognitive function, and of speech processing cortex in particular. We have outlined the characteristics of the cortical flow of the auditory speech stream(s) from primary auditory regions within Heschl's gyrus, through secondary, neighboring regions in the *planum temporale* and on the lateral surface of the mid-superior temporal gyrus, firstly, to tertiary regions in anterior parts of the superior temporal lobe ("what" – a "ventral route") and, secondly, to posterior, temporo-parietal regions ("how" – a dorsal route), with each stream involving frontal activation as a putative processing "endpoint" of forward information flow from the sensorium. This was clarified in order to set the groundwork for analyzing speechreading, since speechreading by eye must lead to a representation that is speech-based (Campbell 2011). We are now in a better position to pose specific questions about speechreading in terms of cortical activation. To what extent will watching silent speech activate well-established hearing and speech regions including Wernicke's and Broca's areas? How are primary and secondary auditory areas implicated? Does seen speech impact more on the dorsal than the ventral stream, or vice versa? Are there indications of distinct processing streams for seen silent speech, echoing those that have been demonstrated for heard speech? Most importantly, how might circuits specialized for visual processing interact with those that engage the language and hearing regions?

5.3 Silent speechreading and auditory cortex

Our initial study (Calvert *et al.* 1997) asked to what extent do listening to and viewing the same speech event activate similar brain regions. We used a videotape of a speaker speaking numbers, and in order to be sure that the participant actually speechread the material we asked them to 'mentally (silently) rehearse' the lipread numbers in the scanner. The results are summarized, schematically, in Figure 5.4, which is based on Calvert *et al.*'s (1997) findings.

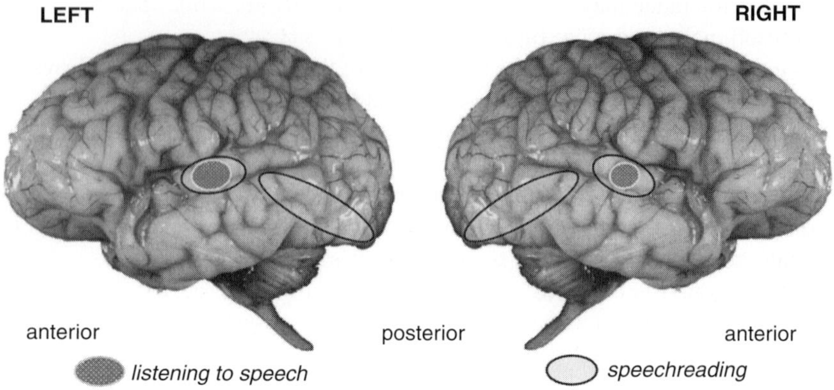

Figure 5.4 Lateral views of the left and right hemispheres, with areas of activation indicated schematically as bounded ellipses. Speechreading and hearing activate primary and secondary auditory cortex (small grey textured ellipse, white border). Speechreading alone (open ellipses, black border) activates other lateral temporal and posterior, visual processing regions. The ellipses correspond approximately to the regions illustrated in figure 1 of Calvert *et al.* (1997).

In our study, as in many others, auditory speech activation was confined to temporal regions, and was focused on Heschl's gyrus (HG) extending throughout much of the superior temporal gyrus (STG). These areas are indicated in Figure 5.4. Watching silent speech activated visual regions in posterior temporo-occipital cortex. Many of these had been identified by other studies as active when watching any sort of moving event. More interestingly, we found that in some regions, the activation pattern for heard and for seen speech was co-incident. These included the lateral parts of Heschl's gyrus (primary auditory cortex (A1)), and secondary auditory cortex in superior temporal regions (A2) bilaterally. Previous studies had suggested that *only* acoustic stimuli activated these regions; they were believed to be dedicated solely to auditory sensory processing.

The fact that seeing speech could generate activation in acoustically specialized regions immediately suggested further questions: Was seen speech the only type of visual event that could activate these auditory sites? What caused this pattern? Would we see it in deaf people?

5.3.1 How specific is the activation?

In one of Calvert *et al.*'s 1997 experiments (Experiment 3) we attempted to see if all face actions generated similar activation patterns. In the scanner, participants counted closed mouth twitching gestures (gurns) that could not be interpreted as speech. The patterns of activation for watching speech and for watching gurning actions were then compared. Speechreading activated lateral superior temporal regions, including auditory cortex, to a greater extent than counting the number of closed-mouth facial actions (gurning). This suggested that speechreading, rather than other forms of facial action, "reached the part others could not reach," namely auditory cortex. However, this may have been a premature conclusion. Because speechreading and gurning were contrasted directly, rather than in relation to a control (baseline) condition, we could not determine what the common regions of activation were. The contrast analysis only allowed us to conclude that there were differences between the conditions.

We therefore returned to this question, incorporating appropriate baseline conditions and more powerful image acquisition techniques. Our volunteers this time were a new population of fourteen right-handed English speakers (Campbell *et al.* 2001). We replicated the original findings (see below), but additionally were able to specify those areas activated by watching gurns and those activated by seeing speech, when both these face action conditions were contrasted with watching a still face.

Watching gurns activated visual movement cortex (V5/MT) – a posterior (occipito-temporal) region activated by any kind of visual movement. But activation extended beyond V5/MT into the temporal lobes, including the temporal gyri on the lateral surface of the temporal lobe (inferior, middle, and superior). Activation tended to be right-sided. The peak activation locus was in inferior-middle temporal regions, extending into superior temporal gyrus. However activation did not extend into primary/secondary auditory cortex (A1/A2).

Compared with watching a still face, watching speech also generated activation in lateral posterior regions including V5/MT. However, the speech task generated activation that showed a peak within the superior temporal gyrus, bilaterally. Thus the sites that were activated *both* by watching speech and by watching gurning movements included areas specialized for visual movement processing of any sort (V5/MT), parts of inferior temporal lobes and (posterior parts of) the superior temporal gyrus. When the gurn and speechreading conditions were contrasted directly, the pattern is as appears in Figure 5.5, and closely replicated the original findings.

This study confirmed that watching speech – not watching gurns –activates auditory cortex, where we define auditory cortex as those regions hitherto shown to be specific for the processing of acoustic input (Heschl's gyrus at its lateral junction with superior temporal gyrus). Speech was more left-lateralized than gurn watching. More recent results from our own labs (e.g. Calvert and Campbell 2003; Capek *et al.* 2008b; Capek *et al.* 2008a), and from others (e.g. Sadato *et al.* 2005; Paulesu *et al.* 2003), confirm this general picture.

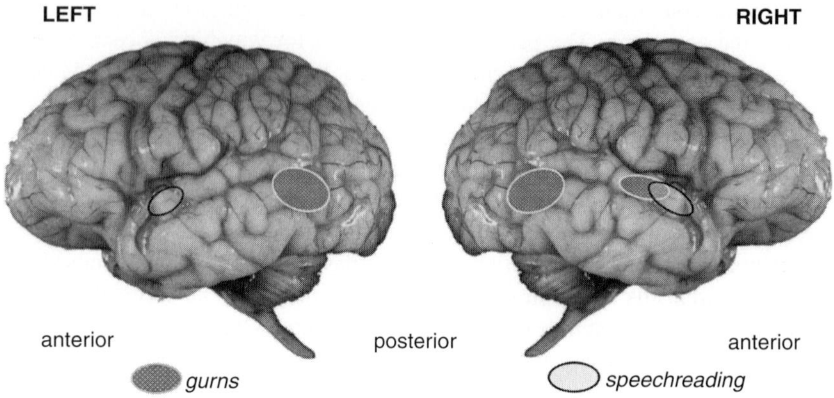

Figure 5.5 Schematic showing differential activation in the lateral temporal lobes when watching non-speech actions (white-bordered grey ellipse) and watching speech (black-bordered ellipse). Renderings based on data from Campbell *et al.* (2001). A peak activation site in right STS is activated by both types of face action. Speech, but not gurn observation extended into auditory cortex.

5.3.2 *Controversy: which parts of auditory cortex are activated by silent seen speech in hearing people?*

That seeing speech could activate auditory cortex in hearing people has been a controversial finding, since it implies that dedicated acoustic processing regions may be accessible by a specific form of visual stimulation. One possibility was that the concurrent noise of the scanner may have contributed to auditory cortex activation when viewers observed silent speech, by giving an illusion of (heard) speech in noise. In the gurn condition, the "listener" would be unlikely to be subject to such an illusion. We were able to test this by taking advantage of one of the principles of functional magnetic resonance imaging. fMRI gives an indirect measure of blood flow in brain regions. Blood flow lags the electrophysiological event by several seconds. Peak dynamic blood flow changes, measured by the scanner, can occur three to eight seconds after the stimulus event and its immediate neurochemical localized response. The scanner is noisy only during the period when the brain activation pattern is being measured ("image collection"). By presenting a silent speechreading task, and then waiting for five seconds before image collection, it was possible to measure the activation generated by the single, silent speechreading event. Under these sparse-scanning conditions, where noise during speechreading was absent, we still found activation in auditory cortex in the lateral parts of Heschl's gyrus (A1), and its junction with the superior temporal gyrus – BA 41, 42 (MacSweeney *et al.* 2000).

Nevertheless, not all investigators find activation in these regions when people are speechreading. In particular, Bernstein *et al.* (2002) claim that auditory cortex is not activated by silent speechreading. Their studies required participants to match speechread words presented in sequence (a recognition task) in one condition, while in another they measured activation induced by hearing words. They then mapped the two activation patterns, seeking the regions of overlap on a person-by-person basis. They found activation by the seen-speech matching task in superior temporal gyri, including STS, but they report no activation in primary auditory cortex as such. By contrast, in our studies, participants were required to generate a language-level representation of the lipread stimulus by covert rehearsal. A further, independent study by Sadato *et al.* (2005) used yet another task. They required respondents to match the first and last of a series of four images of vowel actions, where the mouth patterns were selected from four point vowel mouthshapes. For a group of nineteen hearing respondents, they reported activation within the *planum temporale* for this task, compared to a similar task requiring matching closed (gurning) mouths. In a further study specifically designed to address the issue of whether primary auditory cortex is activated during silent speech perception, Pekkola *et al.* (2005), using more powerful fMRI (3T) scanning procedures, found clear evidence, on a person-by-person basis, for activation in A1 by seen vowel actions in six out of nine participants.

It is possible that A1 activation by visible speech is task-specific. Speech imagery may be critical. Speech imagery appears to be an important aspect of the degree of activation in Heschl's gyrus when other visual material, such as written words, is presented (Haist *et al.* 2001). A dual processing stream account could be invoked to address these discrepant findings across different processing tasks and individuals. Activation within A1 may be more likely when the dorsal stream is involved, since this involves sensorimotor aspects of processing, where the viewer is engaged in active auditory speech imagery.

5.3.3 Still and moving speech: dual routes for silent speechreading?

Visible speech has some unique characteristics as a visual information source. While it is dynamic, and the temporally varying trace of the visible actions of the face corresponds closely to a range of acoustic parameters of speech (Yehia *et al.* 2002; Munhall and Vatikiotis-Bateson 1998; Jiang *et al.* 2002; Jiang et al. 2007; Chandrasekaran *et al.* 2009), the stilled facial image itself can afford some speech information. For instance the shape of an open mouth can (to some extent) indicate vowel identity (compare "ee", "ah", and "oo"). Sight of tongue between teeth ("th") or top teeth on lower lip ("ff") is also indicative of a speech gesture (a dental or labiodental "sound"). Lesion studies suggest that speech seen as a still image and speech seen in natural movement can dissociate.

A neuropsychological patient has been described who accurately reported the speech sound visible from a still photograph, but not from a movie clip of speech (Campbell *et al.* 1997). Other patients show the opposite dissociation (Campbell 1996; Munhall *et al.* 2002). Do these doubly dissociable characteristics of seen speech have implications for the neural networks that support speechreading in normal hearing populations?

Calvert and Campbell (2003) compared fMRI activation in response to natural visible (silent) speech and to a visual display comprising sequences of still photo images digitally captured from the natural speech sequence. Spoken disyllables (vowel-consonant-vowel) were seen. The still images were captured at the apex of the gesture – so for 'th', the image clearly showed the tongue between the teeth, and for the vowels, the image captured was that which best showed the vowel's identity in terms of mouth shape. The series of stills thus comprised just three images: vowel, consonant, and vowel again. However, the video sequence was built up so that the natural onset and offset times of the vowel and consonant were preserved (i.e., multiple frames of vowel, then consonant, then vowel again). The overall duration of the still lip series was identical to that for the normal speech sample, and care was taken to avoid illusory movement effects. The visual impression was of a still image of a vowel (about 0.5 s), followed by a consonant (about 0.25 s) followed by a vowel. Participants in the scanner were asked to detect a dental consonantal target ("v") among the disyllables seen. Although the posterior superior temporal sulcus (STSp) was activated in both natural and still conditions, it was activated more strongly by natural movement than by the still image series.

STSp seems particularly sensitive to natural movement in visible speech processing. In a complementary finding, Santi *et al.* (2003) found that pointlight illuminated speaking faces which carried no information about visual form generated activation in STSp. Finally, a recent study (Capek *et al.* 2005; Campbell 2008) used only stilled photo-images of lip actions, each presented for one second, for participants in the scanner to classify as vowels or consonants. Under these conditions, no activation of STSp was detectable. So, images of lips and their possible actions are not always sufficient to generate activation of this region; STSp activation requires either that visual motion be available in the stimulus, or that the task requires access to a dynamic representation of heard or seen speech.

It may be no accident that two routes for speechreading echo those that have been described for acoustic speech processing. Similar principles may underlie each. Thus, the anterior visible speech stream may be essentially associative, reflecting, for example, (learned) co-incidence of a particular speaker's auditory and visual characteristics, and likely to be activated in the context of a task that need not require on line speech processing. By contrast, tasks that recruit more "lifelike" representations may be invoked by natural movement, involving sensorimotor processes within the dorsal stream.

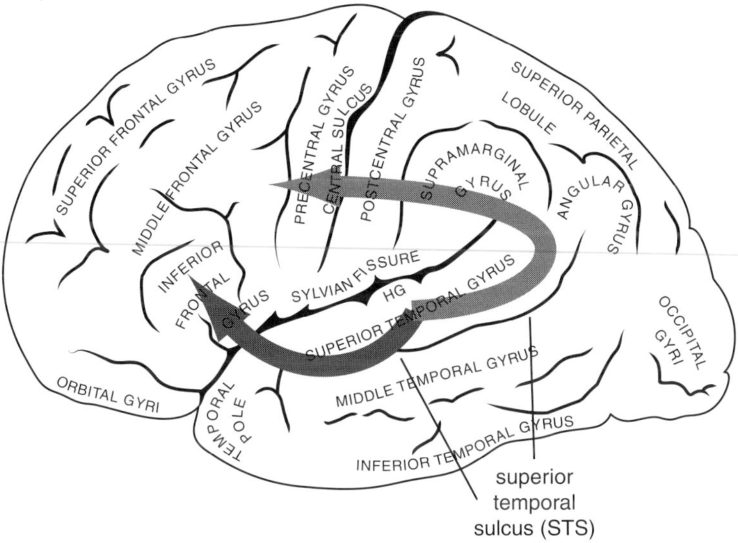

Figure 5.6 Schematic lateral view of left hemisphere highlighting superior temporal regions. Superior temporal sulcus (STS) is the ventral (under-) part of superior temporal gyrus (STG). The directions of the (auditory) ventral, anterior ("what") and dorsal posterior ("how") speech streams are schematically indicated as shaded arrows – the lighter arrow indicates the dorsal stream, the darker arrow the ventral stream.

5.3.4 *The role of the superior temporal sulcus*

The superior temporal gyrus (STG) runs the length of the upper part of the temporal lobe along the superior plane of the sylvian fissure. We have already noted that this structure supports, in its anterior parts, the "what" stream, and, posteriorly, the "how" stream for auditory speech processing. The underside or ventral part of the gyrus is the superior temporal sulcus (STS; see Figure 5.6). Outwith speech processing, neurophysiological studies have long suggested that the posterior half of STS (STSp) appears to be a crucial "hub" region in relation to the processing of communicative acts – whatever their modality. The STSp, extending to the temporoparietal junction at the inferior parietal lobule, is a tertiary region in Luria's terminology. It is highly multimodal, with projections from not only auditory and visual cortex, but also somatosensory cortex. It can be activated by written, heard, or seen language (including sign language – see, for example, Sadato *et al.* 2005; Söderfeldt *et al.* 1997; Pettito *et al.* 2000; MacSweeney *et al.* 2002b; MacSweeney *et al.* 2004; MacSweeney *et al.* 2006; Newman *et al.* 2010). It is also a key region for the perception of socially relevant events and supports theory-of-mind processing (Brothers 1990; Saxe and Kanwisher 2003).

As we have seen, STSp is especially sensitive to mouth movement (see Figure 5.5) as also quoted by other authors (Puce *et al.* 1998; Pelphrey *et al.* 2005). To what extent could its role in speechreading reflect a more profound specialization – that of integrating speech across modalities? How might activation in STSp be related to activation in primary auditory cortex (A1)?

5.3.5 STSp and audiovisual speech: a binding function?

An early indication that lateral superior temporal regions were implicated in seeing speech was the demonstration by Sams and colleagues (Sams *et al.* 1991; Sams and Levänen 1996; Levänen 1999) that a physiological correlate of auditory speech matching could be induced by an audiovisual token. The localization of this function, which used magnetoencephalography (MEG) to measure the response, appeared to be in auditory cortex, extending into superior temporal cortex. However, MEG has relatively poor spatial localization, making it difficult to be certain just which lateral superior temporal regions were differentially activated by audiovisual speech compared with heard speech. Calvert *et al.* (1999; 2000) used fMRI to explore the pattern of activation generated by audiovisual speech in relation to that for heard or seen speech alone. Bimodal speech is much easier to process than speech that is seen silently, because many phonetic contrasts that are hard to distinguish by eye are available readily to the ear. Perhaps less obviously, seeing the speaker improves speech perception even when the acoustic input is sufficient for identification (Reisberg *et al.* 1987). When the acoustic and visual displays are congruent, the integrated percept is more readily identified than would be predicted from a simple additive model based on performance in each modality alone.

Calvert *et al.*'s idea was that this superadditive characteristic of audiovisual speech with respect to the combining modalities might be related to STSp activation. Furthermore, it was predicted that STSp, receiving input from both visual and auditory sensory regions, might then enhance activation in each of the primary sensory regions, by recursive or back-projected neural projections. Activation of both primary visual movement (V5/MT) and primary auditory (A1) regions was compared when the input condition was bimodal compared with each of the unimodal conditions. Under bimodal stimulation, there was greater activation in both V5 and A1. This unimodal enhancement was linked directly to STSp activation, co-occurring with STS activation in the bimodal condition. Moreover, it only occurred when *congruent*, *synchronized* audiovisual stimuli were presented. Thus, STSp appears to offer a cortical mechanism for the modulation of the influence of one speech modality on another, in particular for the superadditive properties of congruent audiovisual speech (see Figure 5.7). Many further independent studies now confirm a special role for STSp in audiovisual speech processing compared with unimodal seen or

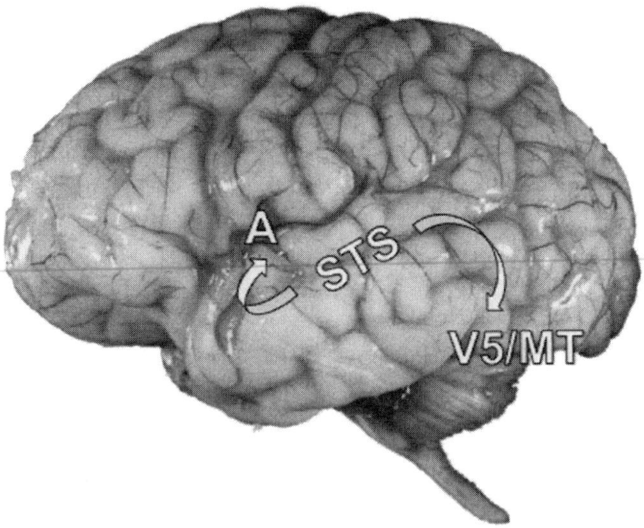

Figure 5.7 Audiovisual binding: A role for STS. Activation in STS (audiovisual speech) can enhance activation in primary auditory sensory cortex (A) and visual movement cortex (V5/MT) (from Calvert *et al.* 2000).

heard speech (e.g. Wright *et al.* 2003; Capek *et al.* 2004; Sekiyama *et al.* 2003; Callan *et al.* 2003; Callan *et al.* 2004; Miller and D'Esposito 2005; Hertrich *et al.* 2010).

The acoustic trace does not need to be well specified for audiovisual integration to occur, and for STSp to be implicated. Thus sinewave speech comprising time-varying pure tone analogues of acoustic speech formants, is typically initially heard as a non-speech sound, such as a series of tweets. However, when synchronized to coherent visible speech, some listeners perceive the signal as speech (Remez *et al.* 1994). Möttönen *et al.* (2006) showed that STSp is specifically activated when sinewave speech is accompanied by coherent natural visible speech – but only when this is "heard" as speech, and not when there is no (integrated) speech perception.[2]

Increasingly sensitive fMRI methods are revealing further organizational principles in relation to STSp function in audiovisual speech. Van Atteveldt *et al.* (2010) used fMRI adaptation to explore the effects of audiovisual speech congruence. Neural populations that are sensitive to a specific signal can adapt readily to repetitions of that signal, and this is detected as a reduction in fMRI activation for repeated compared with single exposures. Adaptation to congruent audiovisual syllables was restricted to regions within STS. It did not extend back to primary cortices. Benoît *et al.* (2010) report similar findings in relation to audiovisual illusory syllables (McGurk stimuli, McGurk and MacDonald, 1976). However, in this case, sensitivity to McGurk illusions correlated with activation in primary cortices, underlining the relationship between primary sensory cortex activation, via binding sites, and perceptual experience of audiovisual congruence.

More direct imaging methods also illustrate the special role of STSp in audiovisual speech integration. Reale *et al.* (2007) made use of a surgical technique to explore the role of STSp in audiovisual speech integration. Ten patients awaiting surgery for intractable epilepsy were implanted with electrode nets inserted subdurally, on the pial covering of the temporo-parietal cortical surface. The patients were then shown auditory, visual, and a variety of audiovisual speech tokens (CV syllables). STSp, and only this region (compared with other lateral temporo-parietal fields covered by the net) showed an evoked auditory response to a spoken syllable that was sensitive to the congruence of a synchronized visual mouth pattern. While this study could not explore further the impact of this activation on primary visual or auditory regions, other electrophysiological studies using scalp and deep electrodes have attempted to do this, and these are discussed further, below.

5.4 Audiovisual integration: timing

We have noted that, in principle, connections within speech processing streams can sometimes allow back as well as forward information flow, and have invoked this as a principle to account for activation in A1 and V5/MT by seen speech, consequent on activation in STSp. In fact, it is likely that such "back-activation" can be even more radical, with the sight of speech or music affecting (subcortical) auditory brainstem responses (Musacchia *et al.* 2006; Musacchia *et al.* 2007). But at what stage in processing do such multisensory interactions occur? Is STSp the *only* brain site that effects cross-talk between input modalities for speech that is seen, heard, and seen-and-heard? In order to explore this, we need a model of the time-course of neural events in audiovisual speech processing.

fMRI is not a sensitive technique to explore *when* in processing the visible and auditory speech signals affect each other. Its temporal resolution cannot track the speed of synaptic transmission to a specific event. For that, an electrophysiological signature of such an event is needed to trace (forward) information flow between different regions. While this review is focused on fMRI work, at this point we should consider how other techniques, especially EEG and MEG, may clarify the time-course and locales of audiovisual speech processing.

Until recently it appeared that a simple sequential analysis model sufficed. This assumed that integration in STSp occurred after the auditory and the visual speech signals had been independently analyzed (e.g. Calvert and Campbell 2003; Colin *et al.* 2002). However, evidence is accumulating that there can be more direct, early influences of vision on auditory speech processing. From scalp EEG studies using natural audiovisual speech, auditory event-related potentials (ERPs), were found to be affected by visual speech cues as early as around 100 msec. from sight of a mouth gesture (the acoustic N1 stage – Besle *et al.* 2004; Möttönen *et al.* 2004; van Wassenhove *et al.* 2005; Pilling 2009). Since visible mouth gestures can precede the acoustic onset of an utterance by up to 100 ms, it would appear that vision can "prime" auditory cortex. Direct pathways from visual to auditory cortex could be implicated, since neural events affecting auditory regions, but originating within STSp (back projection) would generate much longer latencies reflecting the recruitment of "higher-level" functions.

However, such studies give no direct information concerning the location source of the critical events. A deep electrode study with ten patients awaiting surgery for epilepsy (see the description above, on Reale *et al.* 2007), supported the direct cortical activation inference more clearly (Besle *et al.* 2008). Patients were shown audiovisual clips of a single speaker uttering CV syllables ("pi, pa, po, py. . ."), as well as auditory-alone and visual-alone versions, and were asked to respond to a specific target syllable. Electrodes on the brain surface were positioned to track excitation at Heschl's gyrus and other parts of the planum temporale. More electrodes, lying over inferior and middle temporal regions could track neural events in (visual) movement cortex and other visual regions. The recorded EEG events were locked to the onset of both the auditory and the visual signal in natural audiovisual speech tokens. In addition to superior temporal activation indicating late integration, neural events were recorded at both MT/V5 and in A1/2 "well before visual activations in other parts of the brain" (Besle *et al.* 2008). Such feed forward activation need not imply that visual movement cortex analyzes speech qualities exhaustively, but rather that some more general aspect of speech – possibly an alerting signal that a speech sound might occur – allows the visual system to affect processing of the upcoming auditory signal.[3]

Another way to explore such direct feed forward modulation of vision on audition is to combine MEG or EEG with fMRI and behavioral data. A study by Arnal *et al.* (2009) used audiovisually congruent and incongruent syllables as stimulus material. MEG established an early, possibly direct, effect of excitation in V5/MT on A1/2 by coherent audiovisual speech. Here is another piece of evidence that events in relatively low level visual regions can impact quickly on auditory cortex. In an fMRI study, this team then showed that correlations between activation in visual motion regions and auditory regions reflected the extent to which the visual event predicted the auditory stimulus. By contrast, audiovisual congruity (i.e. detecting whether a particular syllable was composed of congruent or incongruent audiovisual tracks) was the factor which characterized connections between STSp and primary regions.

The picture that is emerging from these studies is of at least two mechanisms that support audiovisual speech processing. One involves secondary auditory regions, focused on STSp, which can not only integrate acoustic and visual signals, but coordinate back projections to sensory regions. This route is likely to be implicated in identifying (linguistic) components in the audiovisual speech stream. The other is a fast route that allows visual events to affect an auditory speech response before STSp has been activated. However, the precise functional characteristics of the two routes, and their interactions, await further clarification.

5.5 Speechreading: other cortical regions

The discussion so far has focused on lateral temporal cortical regions and the interaction of auditory and visual signal streams. Yet other cortical regions are strongly implicated in visual and audiovisual speech processing. Activation in insular regions and in frontal (dorsolateral as well as inferior frontal – i.e. Broca's area) is consistent with the dual-path model of speech processing, where pathways extending from posterior to anterior brain regions allow for speech processing to be fully effected. Following the implication that different cortical regions show functional differentiation within the speech streams we should predict different patterns of stimulus sensitivity in frontal ("later") than more posterior ("earlier") processing regions. Skipper *et al* (2007) showed that "illusory" McGurk stimuli ("ta" experienced when seen "ga" and heard "pa" were coincident) more closely resembled auditory "ta" representations within frontal regions, while posterior sensory regions showed more distinctive responses reflecting the characteristics of each sensory modality.

Often, watching speech generates greater frontal activation than observing other actions, or listening to speech (e.g. Campbell *et al.* 2001; Buccino *et al.* 2001; Santi *et al.* 2003; Watkins *et al.* 2003; Callan *et al.* 2003; Callan *et al.* 2004; Skipper *et al.* 2005; Ojanen 2005; Fridriksson *et al.* 2008; Okada and Hickok 2009). This suggests that speechreading can make particular demands on the speech processing system. However, to date there are no clear indications of the extent to which distinctive activation in different frontal regions may relate to the specific speechreading or audiovisual task, or to one or other speech processing stream (but see Skipper *et al.* 2007; Fridriksson *et al.* 2008; Okada and Hickok 2009; Szycik *et al.* 2009, for speculations). Nor is there any compelling evidence for direct, unmoderated connections between frontal and inferior temporal regions – for instance, for visual motion detection. Such a scheme might be implied by strong versions of mirror-neuron theory, which give primacy in neural processing to prefrontal regions that specialize in matching observed actions with those that can be produced by the observer (see Appendix). A study by Sato *et al.* (2010), using single pulse TMS, noted (fast – around 100 ms) changes in excitability in the region of tongue representation in primary motor cortex, M1, consequent on observing audiovisual stimuli that involved bilabial syllables ("ba"). Such studies need to be replicated and extended, since it is not clear to what extent these effects were specific to the observed syllables or even to M1. The tongue and mouth area of primary somatosensory cortex, S1, which is close to the homologous regions in M1, is activated specifically when watching speech compared to listening to it (Möttönen *et al.* 2005).

The coordinated activation of cortical networks that involve frontal systems with multiple sensory systems seems to be a hallmark of visual speech processing, not just of audiovisual speech processing. Both the anterior and the posterior speech stream can be implicated (and see Campbell 2008). The broader picture is of a cortical system that is inherently sensitive to the multimodal correspondence of coherent speech events.

5.6 Speechreading in people born deaf

For many deaf people a spoken language, perceived by watching the speaker's face, is the first language to which they are exposed, since fewer than 5 percent of deaf children are born to deaf, signing parents (Mitchell and Karchmer 2004). Deaf speechreaders often outperform hearing people on tasks of speechreading (Mohammed *et al.* 2006; Rönnberg *et al.* 1999; Andersson and Lidestam 2005) and visual speech discrimination (Bernstein *et al.* 2000b). Skilled deaf speechreaders appear to process seen speech in ways that look very similar to the processes used by hearing people (Woodhouse *et al.* 2009).

The cortical circuits activated when deaf people speechread offer unique insights into how sensory loss, combined with "special" experience, may shape the developing brain. Which brain regions might be activated by speechreading in individuals who have never experienced useable heard speech, but who understand it entirely by eye? If speech processing is inherently multimodal, and seen speech processing in hearing people calls on auditory, somatosensory, and action systems, how do deaf brains become configured to process speech that is not heard? The first question that we asked was would STSp be less – or more – implicated in deaf than hearing speechreading? Thirteen profoundly congenitally deaf volunteers, all of whom were native signers of British Sign Language, and thirteen hearing non-signers were asked to speechread a list of unrelated words (Capek *et al.* 2008a). Their task was to identify the target word 'yes'. Both groups showed extensive bilateral activation of frontotemporal regions for this task. There was significantly greater activation in the deaf than hearing group in the left and right superior temporal cortices. Was this because deaf participants were just better speechreaders? Performance on the Test of Adult Speechreading (TAS: Mohammed *et al.* 2006), performed outside the scanner, showed that the deaf group were superior speechreaders. Moreover, individual TAS scores correlated positively with activation in left STSp. However, when these scores were included as a covariate in the analyses, the left superior temporal region was still the only region showing a significant group difference (deaf > hearing). That is, the activation in this region was not only related to speechreading skill, but also to some other factor distinguishing deaf and hearing participants.[4]

These findings suggest, firstly, that "auditory" cortical regions in deaf-native signers may be relatively more susceptible to activation by a visual language than would be the case for hearing people or for deaf people who do not use a sign language (also see Sadato *et al.* 2005). It's also likely that the word detection task (Capek *et al.* 2008a) may preferentially activate the "how" (dorsal) stream, compared with rehearsal of overlearned (lipread) digit sequences (MacSweeney *et al.*, 2001, 2002b – at least in deaf speechreaders).

But where does this leave the binding hypothesis – that activation in STSp reflects audiovisual experience in which visual and acoustic signals become bound together in a coherent experience of audiovisual speech? While this region is engaged for audiovisual binding in hearing people, its extensive activation in deaf speechreading (Capek *et al.* 2008a) suggests a further functional specialization. The positive correlation of activation of (left) STSp with speechreading skill in both deaf (Capek *et al.* 2008a) and hearing people (Hall *et al.* 2005) indicates that this region is specialized for analyzing speech from facial actions – irrespective of hearing status. However, the further finding, of *greater* activation of this region in deaf people, supports an interpretation in terms of cross-modal plasticity. That is, when auditory input is absent, auditory cortex is relatively more sensitive to projections from other sensory modalities, especially vision (see MacSweeney *et al.* 2002a; MacSweeney *et al.* 2004; Bavelier and Neville 2002; Sadato *et al.* 2005).

How specific is the activation in superior temporal regions in relation to language, speech, and hearing status? Capek *et al* (2010) directly compared deaf people (who knew British Sign Language – BSL), and hearing participants (who did not know BSL). They were scanned in two experimental conditions. In one, they observed lists of signs and were asked to respond when a particular target gesture occurred. This was a task that both deaf and hearing respondents could do readily and accurately. In the other they speechread word lists. Left STSp showed a particular pattern of activation that was sensitive both to task and to group. This region was strongly activated by silent speech in the deaf and the hearing participants. However activation in STSp for sign lists was seen *only* in the deaf group, who knew BSL. We interpreted this pattern as suggesting that

STSp has a specific role in (visible) language processing: both language modes were available to deaf, while only one (speechreading) was accessible to hearing participants. Sadato *et al.* (2005) drew rather different conclusions from their study of deaf and hearing participants performing recognition matching tasks on seen speech and videoclips of Japanese sign language. That study also included a further task of dot detection. Focusing on *planum temporale* rather than STSp[5], they found greater activation in deaf than hearing participants – irrespective of task. Only in the speechreading condition did they observe significant activation in this region in hearing participants. They argue that the involvement of the *planum temporale* in speechreading in deaf participants reflects general colonization of auditory cortex by visual projections, and is specific neither to speech nor language processing. Further studies are needed to probe this issue further.

The long-term experience of deafness may also re-set the relative salience and neural activation patterns of regions other than superior temporal ones in relation to speechreading. For example, in people who had been deaf, but who experienced hearing anew through cochlear implantation, the pattern of audiovisual and visual activation looks different than that observed in people with an uninterrupted developmental history of normal hearing (Giraud and Truy 2002). People with CI can show distinctive activation in (inferior temporal) visual areas when hearing speech through their implants. Since these regions include face processing regions within the fusiform gyrus, it has been suggested that representations based on seen speech are activated when speech is newly heard via an underspecified acoustic signal (Giraud and Truy 2002). Such re-setting of the relative activation of visual and auditory signals in relation to audiovisual exposure can occur on a short time-scale, too. Thus, for people with normal hearing, some short-term exposure to the sight of someone speaking improves later perceptual processing when that talker is heard. Visual face-movement regions were implicated in this skill (von Kriegstein *et al.* 2008; and see Campbell 2011, for further discussion). Similarly, Lee *et al.* (2007) suggest that the (more efficient) specialization of superior temporal regions for speechreading in deaf compared with hearing people may be a relatively fast-acting process: they reported superior temporal activation in a small group of deaf adults which was independent of the duration of their deafness.

Recent MEG studies (Suh *et al.* 2009) show that latency of responses from superior temporal regions varied with the duration of deafness in adults. Two groups were studied: adults who were born deaf, and those who became deaf later. Neural responses were fastest in the late deaf, slowest in people born deaf. People with normal hearing showed intermediate latency for the auditory dipole event. The implications of this study are as yet unclear, since latency of the neural response did not correlate with the amplitude of the response (number of dipoles activated), nor with speechreading skill.

To summarize, recent studies suggest that speechreading engages a fronto-temporal network in born-deaf and in hearing people, alike. However, the extent to which the planum temporale and adjacent STSp play a language-specific role in deaf people, and the impact of early hearing experience in people who become deaf, or of duration of deafness itself, is not yet clear. It is likely that some non-specific activation of putative auditory regions by vision can occur in people born deaf when these regions have not experienced coherent acoustic stimulation, while in people who become deaf, some "resetting" of the activation patterns in different brain regions is likely. Cochlear implantation can "reset" patterns of activation – especially for speech processing. It should also be noted that the resting brain (i.e. when no specific task is performed during neuroimaging) shows a more widespread pattern of activation – including visual regions in the inferior temporal lobe – following CI than before CI (Strelnikov *et al.* 2010).

5.7 Conclusions, directions

The studies reported here cover a relatively short time span of around fifteen years. Yet, in this period, the use of neuroimaging techniques to map brain function has expanded at an enormous rate. The first ten years of human fMRI studies were largely concerned with defining cortical specializations in terms that could relate to lesion studies in neuropsychology, such as those of Luria (1973). That was the direction that we came from, since our earlier work showed how speechreading could be implicated in various ways in people with discrete brain lesions (Campbell 1996). Those studies showed us clearly that watching speech activates auditory speech processing regions, albeit via biological movement signals. In this respect, speechreading may enjoy a special status compared with other types of visual material such as written words, or compared to other types of facial or manual communication (Capek *et al.* 2010). Speechreading may engage multisensory and sensori-motor speech processing mechanisms to a greater degree than simply listening to speech. This is not surprising: speechreading cannot deliver all the acoustically available speech contrasts – it must make do with a systematically degraded signal that may require relatively greater input from "higher" processing stages (Calvert and Campbell 2003; Campbell 2008). In deaf people, speechreading seems to involve similar, primarily superior temporal (i.e. auditory) processing regions as in hearing people – but to a greater extent.

However, these pioneering fMRI studies presented a rather static view of brain function, focusing on specializations as relatively fixed and discrete. More recently, with the technical developments in imaging neural connections and in aligning fMRI with event-locked electrophysiological recordings, as well as with longitudinal and developmental studies, a more dynamic picture of brain function is starting to emerge. Firstly, on the behavioral front, work with atypical populations, such as deaf people, offers unique insights into long-term brain plasticity (see, for instance, Strelnikov *et al.* 2010). We have noted that cross-modal plasticity plays a role in the recruitment of superior temporal regions for non-auditory processing in the brains of people born deaf. Long-term studies with deaf children learning to master visual speech, and ongoing studies with cochlear implant patients should clarify the extent to which (for instance) particular visual regions, especially in V5/MT, may become recruited for speech processing, as well as the role of STSp in moderating such activation, if present. So, too, the involvement of frontal parts of the speech processing system can be addressed in deaf, as in hearing people, to offer insights into the extent to which hearing speech moderates the cortical bases of speech representations and speech processes (MacSweeney *et al.* 2009).

Audiovisual speech processing offers a natural model system for addressing key questions in neural function such as how are sensory events analyzed by dedicated, sensory-specific mechanisms, then "aligned" to deliver multimodal and, indeed, amodal percepts. Do signal characteristics that contribute to the unified percept, based on correspondences between the visual and auditory speech signal play a key role (Bernstein *et al.* 2008; Loh *et al.* 2010)? To date, while two processing mechanisms – a fast forward flow from visual to auditory cortex, and a slow integrative mechanism utilizing STSp – have been described, much work remains to be done to clarify how these systems function and interact.

Despite the many recent advances in neuroimaging methods, lesion studies can still offer important clues to the organization of seen speech. Hamilton *et al.* (2006) describe a patient with parietal damage who lost the ability to experience audiovisual speech coherently, with no apparent difficulty in processing unimodal speech. No such patient had been described before, and no parietal regions (other than inferior parietal regions bordering on STSp) had been implicated in seeing speech. Nowadays, we have tools and techniques that could probe the possible bases for such anomalous perceptions – and relatively well formulated models of signal processing and information flow to guide interpretation. They will lead us in interesting directions.

5.8 Acknowledgments

Both authors are members of the Deafness Cognition and Language Centre (DCAL), established with funding from the ESRC (UK), at University College, London. Mairéad MacSweeney is supported by the Wellcome Trust (UK). The work described here by Campbell, MacSweeney and colleagues was supported by the Medical Research Council, UK ("Functional Cortical Imaging of Language in Deafness", MRC Grant. G702921N) and by the Wellcome Trust

("Imaging the Deaf Brain", see www.ucl.ac.uk/HCS/deafbrain/). We thank all participants and colleagues for their contribution to this work, especially Cheryl Capek, Bencie Woll, Gemma Calvert, Dafydd Waters, Tony David, Phil McGuire, and Mick Brammer.

5.9 Appendix: Glossary of acronyms and terms

5.9.1 Functional imaging techniques (and see Cabeza and Kingstone 2006 for further details)

fMRI – functional Magnetic Resonance Imaging. A brain imaging technique that uses the changes in local electromagnetic fields due to blood-flow changes following neural activity, to map cortical activation. To measure these changes, the participant is placed in a high-intensity magnetic field (1.5 to 4 Tesla), and images are acquired based on computerized tomography. Because it uses a high magnetic field to track brain activation it is currently unsuitable for testing people wearing hearing aids (including cochlear implants). It also requires relatively rigid head position to be maintained throughout scanning. A certain number of repeated scans are not thought to be harmful to health. Spatial resolution is, at best, about five millimeters; temporal resolution half to three-quarters of a second. More recent developments in magnetic resonance imaging include Diffusion Tensor Imaging (DTI) – a technique that enables the measurement of the restricted diffusion of water in tissue in order to produce neural tract (white matter) images as opposed to images based on grey matter regions of activation (Jones in press). This is a form of structural imaging, especially useful for analyzing long-distance connections between brain regions. In order to analyze *functional* connections between brain regions, correlational analysis (principal component analysis – see Friston *et al.* 1993) can be used to explore BOLD signal similarity between a seed region (ROI) and other brain regions.

PET – Positron Emission Tomography. A brain imaging technique that maps activation by tracing changes in cortical metabolism associated with neural activity. These are tracked by scanning for local changes in uptake of radioactive tracer metabolites. Because of the ingestion of radioactive materials, PET scanning should not be undertaken more than once over several years unless clinical conditions dictate it. PET scanning can be used to measure brain activation with relative freedom of movement and can also be used with people wearing hearing aids. Spatial resolution is similar to that for fMRI.

MEG and EEG – magnetoencephalography and electro-encephalography. Both track changes in cortical activity across the brain by mapping changes in scalp fields. These are local magnetic and electrical fields respectively, and can be measured non-invasively. The idea is that these scalp waveforms reflect underlying neural sources. As functional mapping techniques, they tend to use waveform signatures associated with specific cognitive events and explore their distribution in time and space. The most immediate such waveforms are pre-attentive ones such as the visual/auditory evoked responses to a non-specific visual or acoustic event. More high-level cognitive events can include a range of "mismatch" phenomena, when an unexpected cognitive event occurs following a series of expected ones. For example, a semantic mismatch negativity wave may occur when, after listening to spoken examples from one category, a category switch is introduced.

While temporal resolution is extremely fine, spatial localization to the level achieved by fMRI and PET is currently difficult to achieve, since it relies on mathematical modeling of the source electromagnetic properties of deep brain structures as surface (scalp) waveforms. The complexity of these resultant waveforms may set insoluble limits on the precision of localization of some brain structures.

TMS – Transcranial magnetic stimulation offers a form of "reversible brain lesion." The application of localized magnetic induction to particular regions of the scalp can temporarily block neural transmission in the region lying below the induction wand. If used over primary motor cortex (M1), it produces muscle activity which can be recorded as a motor-evoked potential (MEP). The extent to which this is, in turn, disrupted by performing an experimental task can indicate the specialization of that region for the task.

5.9.2 Anatomical regions

STG – superior temporal gyrus. The uppermost of the three gyri (folds) on the lateral surface of each temporal lobe. It extends from the temporal pole (anterior) to the supra marginal gyrus (posterior).

STS – superior temporal sulcus. The ventral (underside) of the superior temporal gyrus. It extends for the length of the gyrus.

HG – Heschl's gyrus. A deep fold within the *Planum Temporale* on the upper (hidden) surface of the temporal lobe. It is the first cortical processing site for acoustic input analysis.

PT – Planum Temporale (temporal plane). The upper or superior surface of the temporal lobe, normally lying under the posterior inferior parts of the frontal lobe. The infold between the two lobes is the *Sylvian fissure*. Most of the PT is associated with acoustic processing.

FG – Fusiform gyrus. A long gyrus which lies within Brodmann area 37, within the inferior temporal lobe. Bordered medially by the collateral sulcus and laterally by the occipitotemporal sulcus, it can be considered a secondary visual region with several "specializations" along its length. In its midregions it is reliably activated in observing faces, including speechreading. Other parts of

FG appear specialized for recognizing written words and word-parts (left hemisphere).

Insular cortex (insula) lies medially between frontal and temporal lobes. The anterior insula, with many connections to the limbic system, is functionally specialized for "own body awareness." It is often implicated in speech processing, both in perception and in production. Insular lesions can give rise to progressive aphasia.

DLPFC – Dorsolateral prefrontal cortex (Brodmann areas 9, 46), can be considered a secondary motor area, responsible for motor planning and organization. It is implicated in working memory and is part of the dorsal speech processing stream.

5.9.3 Functionally defined regions

A1 – primary auditory cortex. Regions within HG, in each temporal lobe, that support a number of basic analyses of acoustic information. It receives major projections from the *inferior colliculus*, a subcortical relay from the auditory nerve. Its internal organization is tonotopic (high spectral frequencies in specific locations, low ones distant from them). Further principles of organization within A1 remain to be determined.

A2 – secondary auditory cortex. Those regions, contiguous to primary auditory cortex, within the PT, that receive most of their input from primary auditory cortex and support higher-order acoustic analyses. A2 extends laterally to the upper part of STG.

V1 – primary visual cortex within the calcarine fissure. The area that receives projections primarily from the subcortical visual relay site, the *lateral geniculate nucleus*. The elements of vision start to be represented and analyzed here (contours, movement).

V2 – secondary visual cortex. Projections from V1 to neighboring regions extending into occipital and inferior temporal regions constitute V2. Functionally, these regions support a range of more complex visual analyses than in V1, including hue-sensitive and motion-direction sets of cells. The columnar organization of cells in this region and in V1 give them both a striped appearance, and these areas are also known as striate visual cortex. Unlike more anterior visual regions (V3,V4), V1 and V2 have small receptive fields, and therefore show fine sensitivity to location.

V5/MT – visual movement cortex. At the boundary between the occipital, parietal, and temporal lobes, and extending into inferior temporal cortex (parts of Brodmann areas 19 and 37), this cortical region supports the processing of visual movement. It receives inputs from the motion-sensitive detectors of V1 and from similar motion-sensitive regions (the thick stripes) of V2.

S1 – primary somatosensory cortex, the first cortical projection site for touch sensation, lies on the most anterior surface of the parietal lobe, reflecting **primary motor cortex (M1)** on the posterior strip of the frontal lobe. Both strips are organized somatotopically, with feet represented at the most superior parts, tongue, lips and teeth at the most inferior, close to STSp.

5.9.4 *Historically defined regions*

Broca's area. A fairly extensive part of the left inferior frontal lobe, including Brodmann's anatomical regions 44 and 45. Traditionally associated with language production.

Wernicke's area A fairly extensive part of the left superior temporal lobe bounded by the supramarginal gyrus posteriorly and the inferior temporal gyrus ventrally (Brodmann areas 22 and 21). It is traditionally associated with language perception.

Mirror neurons First described as a population of neurons in macaque prefrontal cortex that fired when an action was observed, made or planned (Rizzolatti *et al.* 1996a), mirror neuron theory led to the proposal that intentional motor systems were necessarily and inevitably engaged in observing the actions of a conspecific. When applied to speech processing, it implicated ventral prefrontal regions (including Broca's area) as "drivers" of speech perception. The underlying notion is that speech is perceived through simulation of its production (Rizzolatti and Arbib 1998). More recent formulations of mirror neuron theory have retracted from this focus on prefrontal cell populations, towards a network model in which mutually interactive action/perception processing occurs, involving not only frontal but inferior parietal, and especially STSp regions (Rizzolatti and Craighero 2004). In many respects, mirror-neuron theory can now be aligned with dorsal route processing assumptions (Rauschecker and Scott 2009).

6 Temporal organization of Cued Speech production

D. Beautemps, M.-A. Cathiard, V. Attina, and C. Savariaux

6.1 Introduction

Speech communication is multimodal by nature. It is well known that hearing people use both auditory and visual information for speech perception (Reisberg *et al.* 1987).[1] For deaf people, visual speech constitutes the main speech modality. Listeners with hearing loss who have been orally educated typically rely heavily on speechreading based on lips and facial visual information. However lipreading alone is not sufficient due to the similarity in visual lip shapes of speech units. Indeed, even the best speechreaders do not identify more than 50 percent of phonemes in nonsense syllables (Owens and Blazek 1985) or in words or sentences (Bernstein *et al.* 2000).

This chapter deals with Cued Speech, a manual augmentation for lipreading visual information. Our interest in this method was motivated by its effectiveness in allowing access to complete phonological representations of speech for deaf people, from the age of one month, access to language and eventually performance in reading and writing similar to that of hearing people. Finally with the current high level of development of cochlear implants this method helps facilitate access to the auditory modality.

A large amount of work has been devoted to the effectiveness of Cued Speech but none has investigated the motor organization of Cued Speech production, i.e. the coarticulation of Cued Speech articulators. Why might the production of an artificial system as long ago as 1967 be of interest? Apart from the clear evidence that such a coding system helps in acquiring another artificial system such as reading, Cued Speech provides a unique opportunity to study lip–hand coordination at syllable level. This contribution presents a study of the temporal organization of the manual cue in relation to the movement of the lips and the acoustic indices of the corresponding speech sound, in order to characterize the nature of the syllabic structure of Cued Speech with reference to speech coarticulation.

6.2 Overview on manual cueing

6.2.1 Cued Speech system

Cued Speech was designed to complement speechreading. Developed by Cornett (Cornett 1967; Cornett 1982), this system is based on the association of lip shapes with cues formed by the hand. While uttering, the speaker uses one hand to point out specific positions around the mouth, palm towards the speaker so that the speechreader can see the back of the hand simultaneously with the lips. The cues are formed along two parameters: hand placement and hand shape. Placements of the hand code vowels while hand shapes (or configurations) distinguish the consonants. In English, eight hand shapes and four hand placements are used to group phonemes (Figure 6.1). The primary factor in assignment of phonemes to groups associated with a single hand shape or hand placement is the visual contrast at the lips (Woodward and Barber 1960). For example, phonemes [p], [b], and [m], with identical visual shapes, are associated to different hand shapes, while phonemes easily discriminated from the lips alone are grouped in the same configuration. Each group of consonants is assigned to a hand shape. For the highest frequency group the hand shapes that require less energy to execute are chosen. The frequency of appearance of consonant clusters and the difficulties these might present in changing quickly from one hand configuration to another are also taken into account.

Vowel grouping was worked out similarly, high priority being given to the ease of cueing for diphthongs. Vowel positions are indicated with one of the fingers. The middle finger is used for all the consonant cues except those of the [d, p, ʒ], [j, tʃ], and [l, ʃ, w] groups, for which the index finger is used. An exception exists for the [j, tʃ] group: The middle finger is used as the pointer for the mouth position, while the index finger is used for the chin, throat, and side positions.

The information given by the hand is not sufficient for phoneme identification. The visible information of the lips is still essential. The identification by the lips of a group of look-alike consonants and the simultaneous identification of a group of consonants by the hand shape result in the identification of a single consonant. Thus the combination of hand shape and hand location with the information visible on the lips identifies a single consonant-vowel syllable.

The system was based on the CV syllabification of speech. The syllable strings $C(C_n)V(C_m)$, as complex as they can be, are broken down into CVs each CV being coded both by the shape of the hand for the consonant and by the place of the hand on the face side for the vowel. When a syllable consists only of a vowel, this V syllable is coded using hand shape N°5 (Figure 6.1), with the hand at the appropriate position for the vowel. If a consonant cannot be linked to a vowel, as is the case when two consonants follow each other or when a

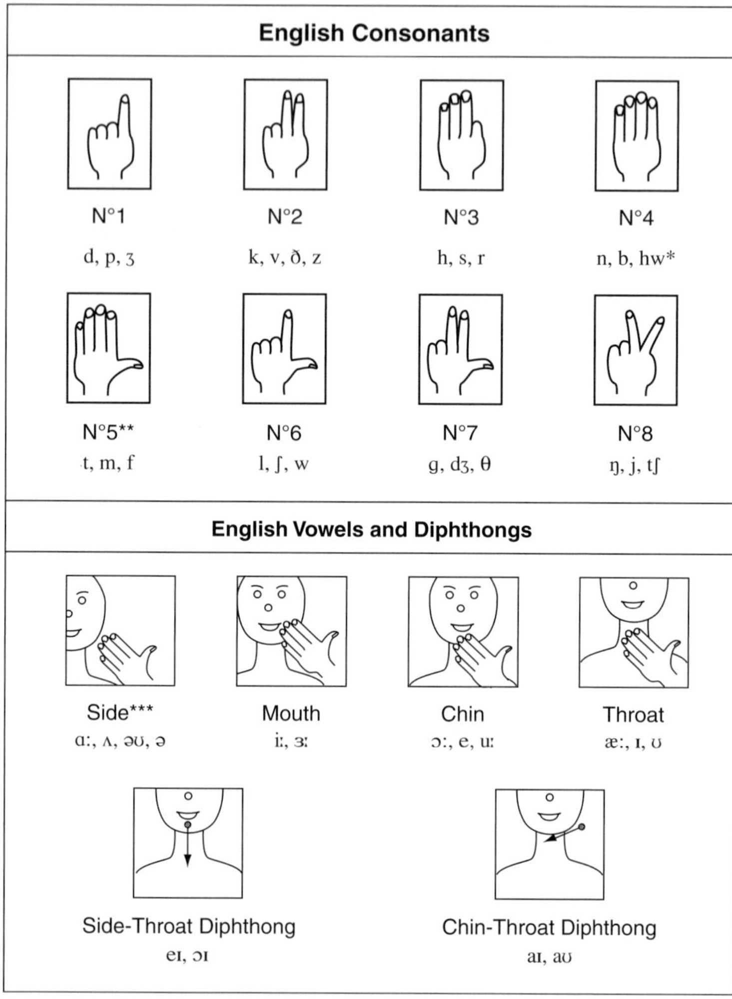

Figure 6.1 Visible cues for English consonants, vowels, and diphthongs (from Cornett 1967)
Notes: * Some teachers of Cued Speech may prefer to cue /hw/ as /h/ plus w; ** This hand shape is also used for a vowel without a preceding consonant; *** The side position is used also when a consonant is cued without a following vowel.

consonant is followed by a schwa, the hand is placed at the side position with the associated consonant hand shape. Diphthongs are considered to be pairs of vowels (VV) and are therefore cued with a shift from the position of the first vowel towards the position of the second vowel (cf. Figure 6.1).

Finally, in the adaptation of Cued Speech to other languages (more than 50 in Cornett 1988), the criterion of compatibility with the English version was given a higher priority than phoneme frequency of the considered language. An additional position next to the cheekbone is needed for coding all vowels used in French, German, Italian, and Spanish. In German, some hand shapes code consonant clusters directly (as it is the case for the frequently encountered [ʃt], [ʃp], [tʃ], and [ʃv] clusters) to avoid affecting speech rhythm, a problem that would occur with frequent consecutive hand shape modifications (Pierre Lutz, personal communication).

6.2.2 *Perceptual effectiveness of manual cueing*

The perceptual effectiveness of Cued Speech has been evaluated in many studies. Nicholls and Ling (1982) presented eighteen profoundly hearing-impaired children with CV or VC syllables made of twenty-eight English consonants combined with the vowels [i, a, u] in seven conditions, with auditory, lipreading and manual cue presentations combined. A similar test was conducted with familiar monosyllabic nouns inserted in sentences. Under audition (A) alone, subjects correctly identified 2.3% syllables, whereas scores in lipreading (L), audition + lipreading (AL), manual cues alone (C) and audition + manual cues (AC) reached 30 to 39% without significant differences. Higher scores were obtained with lipreading + manual cues (LC = 83.5%) and audition + lipreading + manual cues (ALC = 80.4%). This last result was also found for the test sentences where the mean scores for key words reached more than 90% in the LC and ALC conditions.

Uchanski *et al.* (1994) confirmed the effectiveness of Cued Speech for the identification of various conversational materials (sentences with high or low predictability). The highly trained subjects obtained mean scores varying from 78% to 97% with Cued Speech against 21% to 62% with lipreading alone.

For French, Alégria *et al.* (1992) tested deaf children who had been exposed to Cued Speech early (before the age of three) both at home and at school. They compared these early-exposed children with children exposed late from the age of six and only at school. The subjects exposed early and intensively to Cued Speech were better lipreaders and better Cued Speech readers in identifying words and pseudo words. It seems that early exposure to Cued Speech allows children to develop more accurate phonological representations (Leybaert 2000). Thereafter their reading and writing skills progress in a similar way to those of hearing children since Cued Speech early-exposed deaf children can use precise grapheme to phoneme correspondences (Leybaert 1996).

Finally, the studies on working memory of Cued Speech deaf children reveal that they use a phonological loop probably based on the visual components of

Cued Speech: mouth shapes, hand shapes, and hand placements (Leybaert and Lechat 2001).

6.2.3 Phonological representations in Cued Speech

Fleetwood and Metzger (1998, p. 29) proposed the term *cuem*, which 'refers to an articulatory system that employs non-manual signals (NMS) found on the mouth and the hand shapes and hand placements of Cued Speech to produce visibly discrete symbols that represent phonemic (and tonemic) values'. Neither the production nor the reception of acoustic information or of speech is implied in the term '*cuem*'. The authors maintain that Cued Speech can be delivered without production of an acoustic speech signal. This is the usual situation in an interpreting task where the Cued Speech speaker translates silently into cues for deaf people as the hearing speaker is talking. The authors also refer to the studies of Nicholls (1979) and Nicholls and Ling (1982), which claim that the acoustic signal is not necessary in Cued Speech. Nicholls and Ling (1982) found no advantage of audition for syllable identification; the score obtained in the Cued Speech presentation (manual cues alone; C = 36%) was not significantly different from the Audition + Cued Speech score (AC = 39%). Similarly, there was no difference between the lipreading + Cued Speech condition (LC = 83.5%) and audition + lipreading + Cued Speech condition (ALC = 80.4%). The pattern of results was quite different for key words; a better score was recorded for the AC condition (59.2% for low predictability sentences and 68.8% for high predictability) than for the C condition (respectively, 42.9% and 50.0%); in LC and ALC, key word scores were similar, around 96%, revealing a ceiling effect. The advantage of the AC condition for key words in sentences was explained as the use of supra-segmental information. Nicholls and Ling (1982) concluded that speech information in Cued Speech can be perceived through vision alone. Thus Fleetwood and Metzger (1998) proposed that the phonological representations underlying the perception of Cued Speech be defined only by the mouth shapes, hand shapes and hand positions (Fleetwood and Metzger 1998).

However we think this position is perhaps too restrictive. In their taxonomy of tactile speech perception methods, Oerlemans and Blamey (1998) proposed to distinguish between the speech-based and language-based tactile codes. The code was considered speech-based when the user had direct access to the articulatory gestures, as in the Tadoma method (Reed *et al.* 1985), where the blind-deaf user directly touches the vocal tract of the speaker, placing a hand on the talker's face. In contrast, the tactile version of Sign Language was classified as language-based. If the same taxonomy for visual perception is used, speech-based and language-based methods can be distinguished. In our view, Cued Speech is clearly a speech-based code, since the visual lip and mouth information directly results from the articulatory gestures. The fact that the emission of sound is not necessary for the production or reception of Cued Speech does not mean that the code is purely visual.

We maintain that Cued Speech is speech-based in the sense that articulatory gestures are recovered from the visual modality. As we will show, these visual lip cues are highly dependent on the speech flow for their temporal time-course.

6.2.4 *Face and hand coordination for Cued Speech*

The fact that manual cues must be associated with lip shapes to be effective for speech perception reveals a real coordination between hand and mouth. As yet no fundamental study has been devoted to the analysis of the skilled production of Cued Speech gestures, i.e. the temporal organization existing between lip movements and hand gestures in relation to the acoustic realization.[2] Except for a theoretical aside by Cornett pointing out some consonant clusters where speech should be delayed to leave the hand enough time to reach the correct position (Cornett 1967, p. 9), the problems of cue presentation timing are only incidentally touched on in the course of technological investigations.[3]

In the Cornett Autocuer system (Cornett 1988), cues are defined from the sound recognition of the pronounced word and are displayed on one group of LEDs on glasses worn by the speechreader. The whole process involves a delay of 150 to 200 ms for the cue display, compared to the production time of the corresponding sound. This system, designed for isolated words, attained 82% correct identification.

In the system for the automatic generation of Cued Speech developed by Duchnowski *et al.* (2000) for American English the cues are presented with the help of pre-recorded hands, and rules for temporal coordination with sound are proposed. This system uses a phonetic recognizer of audio speech to obtain a list of phones which are then converted to a time-marked stream of cue codes. The appropriate cues are visually displayed by superimposing hand shapes on the video signal of the speaker's face. The display is presented with a delay of two seconds, a delay that is necessary to correctly identify the cue (since the cue can only be determined at the end of each CV syllable). The superimposed hand shapes are always digitized images of a real hand. Scores of correct word identification reached a mean value of 66% and were higher than the 35% obtained with speechreading alone but they were still under the 90% level obtained with Manual Cued Speech. This 66% mean score was obtained for the more efficient display, called 'synchronous', in which 100 ms were allocated to the hand target position and 150 ms to the transition between two positions. In this 'synchronous' display, the time at which cues were displayed was advanced by 100 ms relative to the start time determined by the recognizer; i.e. for stop consonants, the detected instant of acoustic silence (Duchnowski, personal communication). This advance was fixed empirically by the authors.

In these investigations, the time of cue presentation is related only to the corresponding acoustic events: there is no discussion of the relation between cue presentation and lip motion. However it is well known that lip gesture can anticipate acoustic realization (Perkell 1990; Abry *et al.* 1996, for French). In the Autocuer system, the cue presentation is automatically later than lip motion. The impact of this delay was not evaluated and the identification scores were still high for isolated words. On the other hand, the closer timing of the hand to the acoustic realization is a key factor for the improvement of the Duchnowski *et al.* (2000) system. It should be stressed that this latter system functions with continuous speech and uses hand cues; thus it is closer to the natural Cued Speech conditions than the Autocuer.

6.3 First results on Cued Speech production

It has been mentioned that the Cued Speech system is based on CV syllabic organization, the hand giving information on both the consonant and the vowel. The shifting of the hand between two hand positions corresponds to the vocalic transition and the hand shape (or finger configuration) constitutes the consonant information. The main objective of this section is to determine precisely how the hand gesture *co-produces* the consonantal and vocalic information. In short, is the temporal organization of vocalic and consonant hand gestures similar to the organization of speech, as revealed by the classical model of coarticulation (Öhman 1967b)?

To this end we will examine a comparative study of the temporal organization of manual cues with lip and acoustic gestures. The temporal organization of Cued Speech articulators is analysed from a recording of a Cued Speech speaker. The time-course of the lip parameter and the hand x y coordinates are investigated in relation to acoustic events. The occurrence of hand shape formation is measured in relation to hand position.

6.3.1 The Cued Speech speaker

The Cued Speech speaker is a thirty-six-year-old French female who has been using Cued Speech at home with her hearing-impaired child for eight years. She qualified in Cued Speech for French in 1996 and regularly translates into Cued Speech code at school.

6.3.2 Audiovisual data

The different parameters involved in the analysis were derived from the processing of an audiovisual recording of the Cued Speech speaker. The recording was made in a soundproof booth, at 50 frames per second. A first camera in wide focus was used for the hand and the face. A second one in zoom mode dedicated to the lips was synchronized with the first one. The lips were made up in blue. Coloured marks were placed on the hand for tracking hand movement. A second experiment was devoted to the analysis of hand shape formation. In this investigation the Cued Speech speaker was wearing a data glove with two sensors for each of the five fingers covering the first and second articulation with an additional sensor between the fingers. The sensor raw data has a linear relationship to the deviation angle between two segments of a finger articulation. The hand position is located with the use of coloured landmarks placed on the glove. In both experiments, the subject wore opaque goggles to protect her eyes against the halogen spotlight and her head was maintained in a fixed position with a helmet. Blue marks were placed on the speaker's goggles as reference points.

Two Betacam recorders had to be synchronized. At the beginning of the recording session a push button was activated, switching on the set of LEDs (placed in the field of the two cameras) during the first A-frame instant of the video image. This enabled the correspondence between the time codes of the two cameras to be calculated. The audio line was digitized in synchrony with the video image. When the data glove was used a system for synchronization with the audio part was needed. In this system an audio signal was released at the thumb and index finger contact and recorded on the audio line of the video tape. Finger contact resulted in a plateau on the raw data from the glove sensors measuring the movement of the two fingers which allowed synchronization of the data glove with the audio recording. The delay between the time codes of the two cameras was calculated using the first system.

The image processing-based automatic extraction system developed at ICP (Lallouache 1991) provided a set of lip parameters every 20 ms. We chose to explore the temporal evolution of the between-lip area (S), which is a good parameter for characterizing sounds at both the acoustic and articulatory levels. In synchrony with lip area parameter and audio signal, the x and y coordinates of the hand landmark placed near the wrist were extracted. The onset and offset of hand and lip gesture transitions were manually labelled at the acceleration peaks (Schmidt 1988; Perkell 1990).[4] On the audio signal, the onsets and offsets of the acoustic realization for consonants and the vowels were also labelled.

These two experiments had complementary objectives. The first explored the movement of the hand from one hand position to another, i.e. the carrier gesture of Cued Speech. Because the hand shape was fixed, interference with hand shape formation was avoided. The second experiment tested the timing of the production of hand shape formation in relation to hand position.

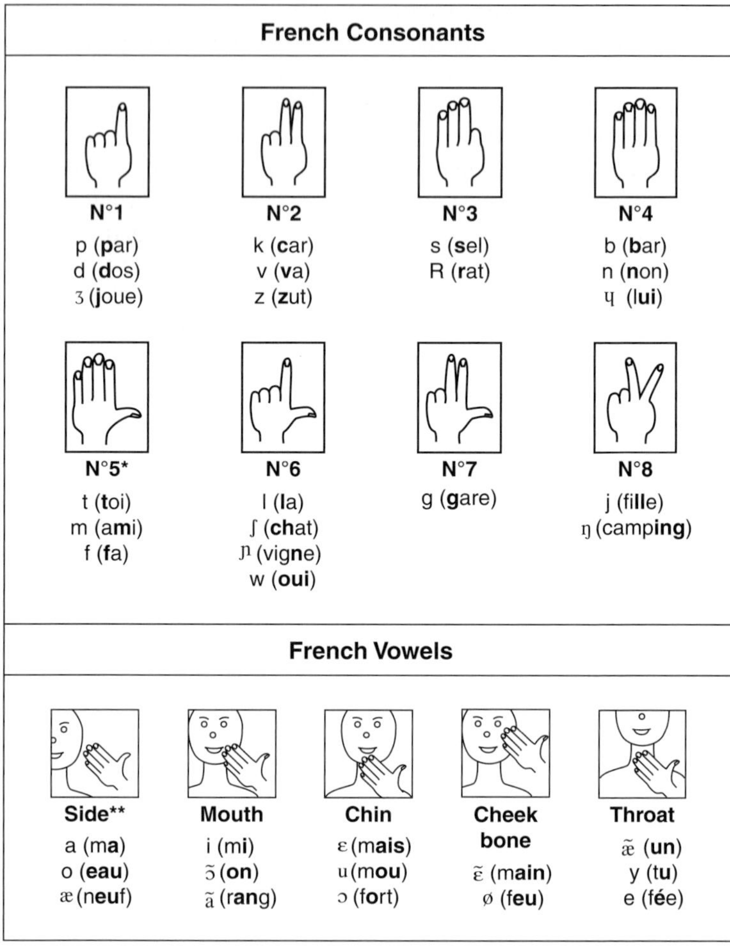

Figure 6.2 Hand placements and hand shapes used in French.
Notes: * This hand shape is also used for a vowel not preceded by a consonant.
** This position is also used when a consonant is isolated or followed by a schwa.

6.3.3 *Experiment 1: Hand displacement*

6.3.3.1 Corpus Displacement of the hand was analysed with [$CaCV_1CV_2CV_1$] sequences made up of [m, p, t] consonants for C combined with the vowels [a, i, u, ø, e] for V_1 and V_2, i.e., the vowel with the best visibility for each of the five hand positions of the French code (Figure 6.2).

The choice of consonants was fixed according to their labial or acoustic characteristics: [m, p] present a typical bilabial occlusion that appears on the lip video signal as a null lip area, and [p, t] are marked by a clear silent period. The hand shape was fixed during the production of the whole sequence: [m] and [t] are coded with the same hand shape as isolated vowels are (hand shape N°5), while [p] is associated with hand shape N°1. The whole corpus contained twenty sequences, such as [mamamima], for each of the three consonants. A control condition with no consonant for the second (S_2) and third (S_3) syllables was also used, i.e., [maV_1V_2mV_1], made up of the vowels [a, i, u, ø, e] for V_1 and V_2 (e.g., [maaima]). We thus obtained twenty additional sequences. For each of the eighty sequences the analysis was carried out on [CV_2] or [V_2] in the absence of a consonant (i.e. on transitions from the S_2 syllable towards S_3 and from S_3 towards S_4), in order to avoid the biases inherent at the beginning of the gesture.

Consider, for example, the [pupøpu] $S_2S_3S_4$ sequence (from the whole [papupøpu] $S_1S_2S_3S_4$ sequence) in Figure 6.3. The following events were determined for the hand trajectory:

- M1 is the beginning of the hand gesture (determined by acceleration peak) towards the position corresponding to S3;
- M2 is the hand position target reached (coding S_3). It is determined by peak deceleration and maintained until M3, the instant of peak acceleration and the time at which the hand begins the gesture towards the following position for S_4 coding;
- M4 corresponds to the S_4 hand target reached. In the case of non-concordance of acceleration events on x and y, the first M1 and M3 and the last M2 and M4 points were considered. The hand target is defined as a time when the hand reaches the target both in x and y, i.e. between the end of the transition and the beginning of the transition towards the following target.
- For lip area, L1 marks the beginning of the vowel gesture. This was easily detectable for sequences with [p] and [m] consonants, since L1 was coincident with the end of the lip closure phase. We used the beginning of the acoustical silence to determine L1 in the case of sequences with [t]. L2 is the lip target instant labelled at the end of the lip transition towards the maximal lip-opening target (in the case of absence of a lip vocalic plateau the acceleration peak coincided with the maximal lip value).
- For the corresponding acoustic signal A1 marks the beginning of the consonant of the S_3 syllable.

6.3.3.2 Results For this analysis we took into account only the transitions from the S_2 syllable towards S_3 and from S_3 towards S_4. In order to evaluate the coordination between lip, hand, and sound, we determined different duration

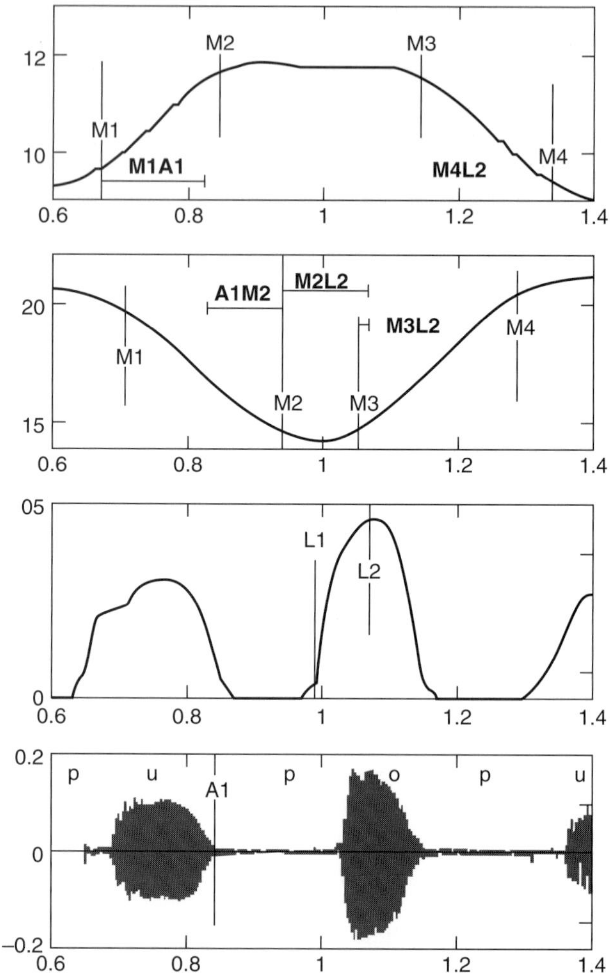

Figure 6.3 Speech vs. lips and hand motion for the [pupøpu] sequence. From top to bottom: horizontal x (cm) and vertical y (cm) hand motion paths are shown in the top two panes (an increase in x means that the hand moves from the face to the right side, an increase in y means the hand moves towards the bottom of the face); the two bottom panes contain the lip area (cm^2) time-course and the corresponding audio signal.

intervals. From the events labelled on each signal, we located the following intervals:

- M1A1 corresponds to the interval between the beginning of the manual gesture for S_3 and the acoustic consonant closure;

- A1M2 is the interval between the acoustic consonant closure and the onset of the hand target;
- M2L2 is the interval between the onset of the hand target and the onset of the lip target of the vowel of S_3;
- M3L2 is the interval between the lip target and the beginning of the following hand Cued Speech gesture.

All intervals were computed as arithmetic differences, i.e. the second label minus the first. For example, M1A1 = A1 – M1 (ms). For sequences without a consonant in S_2S_3, such as [maaima], mean values of 183 ms were obtained for the M1A1 interval and 84 ms for the A1M2 interval, the A1 instant corresponding to the onset of the glottal stop that the speaker inserted between the production of the two consecutive vowels. The hand target is clearly in advance of the lip area target (M2L2 = 73 ms). The following hand gesture begins after the lip target (M3L2 = –84 ms).

For sequences with consonants, such as [mamamima], a mean value of 239 ms was obtained for the M1A1 interval. This differed significantly from the consonant acoustical beginning. The A1M2 interval reached a mean value of 37 ms. The hand target was therefore reached during the acoustic realization of the consonant in a quasi-synchronization with the acoustic closure event. The lip target was usually reached after the corresponding hand target since a mean value of 256 ms for M2L2 was obtained. Finally the hand movement towards the following syllable placement began, on average 51 ms before the peak of the vowel lip target (M3L2 = 51 ms).

In conclusion, the hand gesture begins before the acoustical onset of the CV syllable (183 ms and 239 ms) and reaches the hand position largely before the lip target, in fact, during the consonant.

6.3.4 *Experiment 2: Hand shape formation*

This experiment examined the association between hand shape formation and consonant information. The corpus was selected so as to have only one finger component per consonant hand shape transition in each sequence. For example, the transition from [p] to [k], i.e., from hand shape N°1 to hand shape N°2 (Figure 6.2), is effected by the extension of the middle finger. Thus the modification of the hand shape required only one main sensor of the data glove. This choice was made to simplify data reading.

6.3.4.1 Corpus Hand shape formation was analysed for two kinds of sequences:

- (i) [mVC_1VC_2V] sequences with the same vowel (V = [a] or [ɛ]) were designed to investigate consonant variation. The C_1 and C_2 consonants were [p] and [k], [s] and [b], or [b] and [m]. This choice resulted in hand

Figure 6.4 Cues for the [mabuma] sequence.

shape modification at fixed hand placement (for example, the [mapaka] sequence is coded at the side position with the appropriate hand shape modifications). Ten repetitions of each sequence were recorded. The analysis focused on the C_1V syllable, resulting in 60 syllables (10 repetitions × 3 consonant groups × 2 vowels).

- (ii) [$mV_1C_1V_2C_2V_1$] sequences varied both vowel and consonant, thus involving both hand shape modification and hand placement transitions. The C_1 and C_2 consonants were [p] and [k], [ʃ] and [g], [s] and [b], or [b] and [m]. The V1 and V2 vowels were [a] and [u], [a] and [e], or [u] and [e]. Thus, for the [mabuma] sequence (see Figure 6.4) coding implicates a transition of the hand from the side position towards the chin and then back to the side position, while the hand shape changes from the N°5 to N° 4 configuration and back to the N°5. The change from 5 to 4 is realized with the thumb facing towards the palm. Five repetitions of each sequence were recorded. The analysis focused on the C_1V_2 syllable, resulting in 60 syllables (5 repetitions × 4 consonant groups × 3 vowel groups). Since an error occurred in the recording for a realization of a [mubemu] sequence, 59 sequences were considered for this corpus.
- In all sequences (with vowel-not-changed and vowel-changed), the beginning of the consonant (A1) is labelled on the acoustic signal. The beginning of the finger gesture is marked at the D1 maximum point of acceleration and the end is marked at the D2 deceleration point of the corresponding raw data trajectory. Similarly for sequences with hand movement from one hand position to another (case of vowel-changed sequences), the hand trajectory was marked by M1 and M2 (Figure 6.5).

6.3.4.2 Results It should be remembered that the analysis focused only on the second syllable. In order to evaluate the coordination between sound, finger, and hand different duration intervals were derived from the events labelled on each signal. For all the sequences:

- D1A1 is the interval between the beginning of the finger gesture and the beginning of the corresponding acoustic consonant;
- A1D2 corresponds to the interval between the beginning of the acoustic consonant and the end of the digit movement.

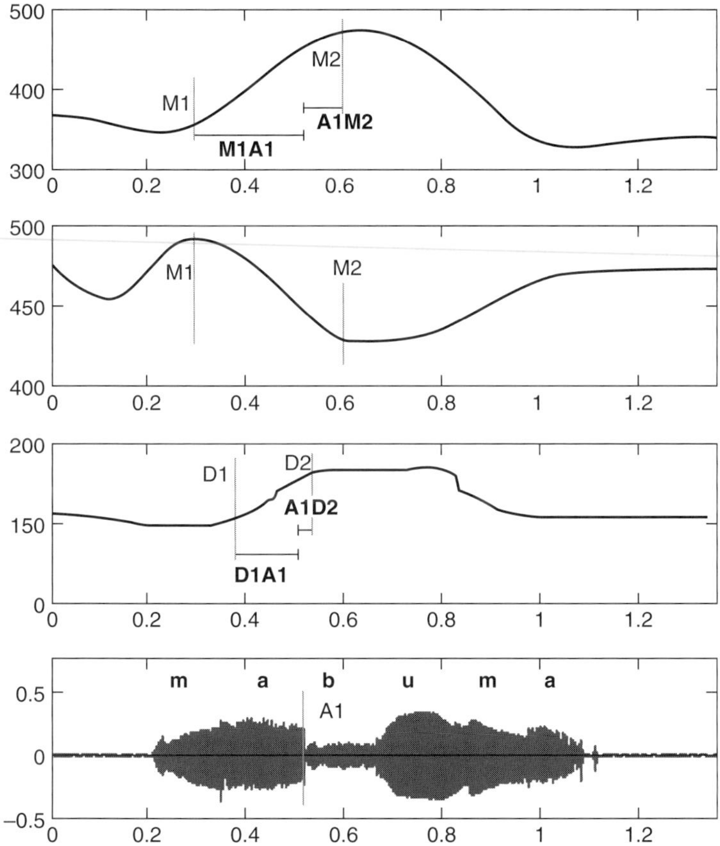

Figure 6.5 Speech vs. lips and hand motion for the [mabuma] sequence. From top to bottom: Horizontal x (cm) and vertical y (cm) hand motion paths are shown in the top two frames (an increase in x means moving the hand from the face to the right side, an increase in y means moving the hand towards the bottom of the face); the bottom two frames contain the temporal deviation of the raw data of the thumb first articulation glove sensor and the corresponding acoustic signal.

In addition, for vowel-changed sequences:

- M1A1 is the interval between the beginning of the hand movement and the beginning of the acoustic consonant;
- A1M2 corresponds to the interval between the acoustic consonantal beginning and the end of the hand gesture.

As in the first experiment, all intervals were computed as arithmetic differences, i.e., the second label minus the first label; for example, D1A1 = A1 – D1 (ms).

For the vowel-not-changed sequences (sequences with only hand shape change, the hand placement being maintained), we obtained mean values of 124 ms for the D1A1 interval and 46.5 ms for the A1D2 interval. Thus the beginning of the finger gesture precedes the acoustic onset of the consonant. The finger finishes its movement just after the beginning of the acoustic realization of the consonant.

For the vowel-changed sequences (both hand shape and hand placement change), mean values of 171 ms for the D1A1 interval and −3 ms for the A1D2 interval were obtained. Thus, for the finger gesture relative to the sound, we observed the same pattern as in the previous result. As regards the hand gesture, mean values of 205 ms for the M1A1 interval and 33 ms for the A1M2 interval were obtained. The hand gesture begins before the finger gesture and consequently well before the onset of the acoustic consonant. The hand target is reached at the beginning of the acoustic realization of the consonant. Finally if we compare duration for hand shape formation in reference to hand transition between two hand placements, we note that the consonant finger gesture is encapsulated in the hand transition.

6.3.5 Summary of the two experiments

There is a noticeable convergence in the results of the two experiments. To summarize, for hand position, it was observed that

- the movement of the hand towards its position begins about 200 ms before the acoustic beginning of the CV syllable. This implies that the gesture begins during the preceding syllable, i.e. during the preceding vowel;
- the hand target is attained at the beginning of the acoustic consonant onset;
- this hand target is therefore reached on average 250 ms before the vowel lip target.

These three results reveal the *anticipatory* gesture of the hand motion relative to the lips as the hand placement gesture covers the duration of the whole syllable, with a temporal advance over the vocalic speech gesture.

Finally, it was observed from the data glove that the hand shape is completely formed at the instant when the hand target position is reached. In addition it was noticed that the hand shape formation gesture uses a large part of the hand transition duration.

6.4 General discussion

6.4.1 Cued Speech co-production

The consideration of the two Cued Speech components within the framework of speech control has a bearing on the future elaboration of a quantitative control model for Cued Speech production. For transmitting consonant information, the control type is figural, i.e., a postural control of the hand configuration (finger configuration). The type of control for transmitting the vowel information is a goal-directed movement performed by the wrist and carried by the arm. These two controls are linked by an in-phase locking. On the other hand, for speech, there are three types of control:

- (i) The mandibular open-close oscillation is the control of a cycle, self-initiated and self-paced (MacNeilage 1998; Abry *et al.* 2002). This is the control of the carrier of speech, the *proximal* control that produces the syllabic rhythm.
- (ii) Following Öhman (1966; see also Vilain *et al.* 2000), the vowel gesture is produced by *global* control of the whole vocal tract – from the glottis to the lips –, i.e., a figural or postural motor control type.
- (iii) The consonant gesture is produced by the control of contact and pressure performed *locally* along the vocal tract.

The carried articulators (tongue and lower lip) together with their coordinated partners (upper lip, velum, and larynx) are involved in these two distal (global and local) controls.

The mandibular and vowel controls are coupled by in-phase locking. Consonantal control is typically in-phase with the vowel for the initial consonant of a CV syllable. But it can be out-of-phase for the coda consonant in a CVC syllable. Finally consonant gestures in clusters within the onset or the coda can be in-phase (e.g., [psa] or [aps]) or out-of-phase ([spa] or [asp]).

As for speech, Cued Speech vowels and consonants depend on the wrist-arm *carrier* gesture, which is analogous to the mandibular rhythm. The control of the vowel *carried* gesture is a goal-directed movement, which aims at local placement of the hand around the face. On the other hand, the consonant *carried* gesture is a postural (figural) one. Thus the two types of control in Cued Speech are inversely distributed in comparison to speech: the configuration of global control of the speech vowel corresponds to a local control in Cued Speech, whereas the local control for the speech consonant corresponds to a global control in Cued Speech.

Once speech rhythm has been converted into Cued Speech rhythm (that is a general CV syllabification with some cluster specificities as in German), the two carriers (mandible and wrist) can be examined with respect to their temporal coordination, i.e., phasing. This CV re-syllabification means that every consonantal Cued Speech gesture will be in phase with its vocalic one, which is not always the case in speech for languages that have more than just CVs. Unlike speech the Cued Speech consonant gesture never hides the beginning of the in-phase vocalic gesture (Öhman's model). As for the phasing of the two carried vowel gestures, our experiments made clear that the Cued Speech vowel gesture did anticipate the speech vowel gesture.

6.4.2 *Towards a topsy-turvy vision of Cued Speech*

The coordination obtained between hand, lips, and sound confirms, in our opinion, the in-principle validity of the advance (lead) of the hand on the sound, programmed as an empirical rule by Duchnowski *et al.* (2000) for their automatic Cued Speech display. Of course the range of this anticipatory behaviour will vary with different speakers, rates, etc., and should be examined by subsequent articulatory studies.

These considerations result in quite a rather upside-down vision of the Cued Speech landscape. The *in-principle* advance of the hand over the lips (and on sound) is crucial for the question of the integration of manual and lip information. Currently Cued Speech has been designed as an augmentation for lip disambiguation. A general pattern seems to appear from our data on the temporal organization of hand and lip gestures in the production of successive CV sequences. The hand attains the vowel placement at the beginning of the CV syllable and moves from that position towards a new one even before the peak acoustic realization of the vowel and before the corresponding vocalic lip target is reached. It seems therefore that production control imposes its temporal organization on the perceptual processing of Cued Speech. This organization leads us to think that the hand placement first gives a set of possibilities for the vowel then the lips determine a unique solution. This hypothesis has been successfully tested within the framework of gating experiments for phoneme identification where recognition of CV syllables has been evaluated across the time course of available online information resulting from the coordination of hand and lip motion (see Cathiard *et al.* 2004; Troille *et al.* 2007; Troille 2009; Troille *et al.* 2010). These studies demonstrated the ability of deaf subjects to recover the anticipatory behaviour of the hand in their Cued Speech perception.

6.5 Acknowledgments

Many thanks to Martine Marthouret, speech therapist at Grenoble Hospital, for helpful discussions; to Mrs G. Brunnel, the Cued Speech speaker, for enduring the recording conditions, and C. Abry and J. L. Schwartz for their stimulating suggestions. This work has been supported by the Remediation Action of the French Research Ministry 'Programme Cognitique', a 'Jeune équipe' project of the CNRS (French National Research Centre) and a BDI grant from CNRS.

7 Bimodal perception within the natural time-course of speech production

M.-A. Cathiard, A. Vilain, R. Laboissière, H. Loevenbruck, C. Savariaux, and J.-L. Schwartz

7.1 Introduction

The purpose of this contribution is to answer a set of questions about the visual perception of speech, given that speech is bimodal. We will claim that, in order to understand the perception of visual speech and its integration to auditory perception, a production and control stance must be adopted. Such a stance leads to the learnability issue of movement control in growing children, i.e. the mastery of speech sound production. These two orientations – the production-control stance and the developmental one – are of course highly disputable. Perception can be conceived as not having any link per se with speech production control and learning. Our bet is that bimodal perceptual processing is given for free by the natural course of speech production. We consider the integration of auditory-visual information to be dependent on the timing coherence of the two dynamic signals. Coherence does not mean simply synchronous acoustic and optic events. It must be emphasized that the articulatory-acoustic temporal organization of speech follows a determined unfolding of action, a time-course that is the basis for perceptual processing. Actually, the possibility that speech can be seen before it is heard, due to anticipatory coarticulation, deserves careful modeling of speech production and its timing in order to be thoroughly understood.

Such a conception of perception based on production timing crucially depends on the model assumed for the structure of speech. Speech is a coarticulated structure. In Öhman's classic model of coarticulation (Öhman 1967a) consonants were superimposed on the vowel-to-vowel (V-to-V) transition. This is somewhat different from related models, as proposed at Haskins Laboratories, where vowel-consonant-vowel gestures simply overlap. In Öhman's model the vowel component has the specific status of a slow-varying signal compared to the relatively fast-varying consonant. In addition, the vowel can be conceived of as a set of features/gestures involving the tongue, the lips, and other articulators, like the velum, including the control of larynx height. Without taking any linguistic-ontological stance about these features/gestures, this is the simplest way we can describe the time-course of the main articulators and identify anticipation and carry-over phenomena in normal dynamic speech, i.e., specify patterns of coarticulation. It should be remembered that, for Öhman, the vowel requires global control of the whole vocal tract, whereas the consonant needs only local control. The coarticulated structure of speech à la Öhman does not imply that the carrier vocalic component will be a primitive. As we demonstrate later this is clearly not the case from a developmental point of view. Moreover, as regards the global vowel command in the basic vowel-to-vowel transition, it will be shown that this is not the only component needed to account for the control of vowel production.

What we propose here is an embedding of different models, which could account for the neural and behavioral development of speech control. We will focus on visible gesture data for the main sound types, ranging from vowels to fricatives, in the vein of our first synthesis on Phonetics and Labiality (Abry *et al.* 1980) dedicated to the *tug-of-war* between rounding in vowels and protrusion in sibilants, the main new topic being the addition of glides. Because of this focus, we will start by integrating a selected set of models and theories of speech production which account precisely for the control of these different types. Our embedding plan starts with MacNeilage's Frame/Content theory, via Öhman's coarticulation model, followed by our 2-Component-Vowel model, which takes into account glide production, and ending with the latest-developing control, the one for sibilants.

Speech movements must be studied within the framework of the theory of biological motion control, integrating the theory of physical motion (biomechanics) and control theory (biocybernetics). When speech movements seem to contradict the well-known laws of motion, one has to search for an explanation within the above-mentioned theories. This is why we will tap into a new control resource for vowel production, our 2-Component-Vowel model. This model deals with a necessary part of the agenda of speech research, namely how to explain why transitional sounds, so-called epentheses, can be produced between voluntary planned sounds, without any specific command. It is of course fundamental to explain why glides emerge in the basic vowel-to-vowel transition that is ubiquitous in speech. Epenthetic sounds are not simply minor physical events. Apart from the fact that they can be recovered in language change by linguistic representations and planned like other sounds, the explanation of epentheses forces us to consider linguistic sounds in the realm of biophysics and biocybernetics. In these domains there is no minor movement that does not have to be explained within a more comprehensive theory.

In movement control, one of the main issues is representation of motion in speech. This issue has direct implications for perception. While it is true that, for consonants, there is no question about the dynamic aspect of at least some phases of these sounds (typically the release phase for plosives), it is not the same for vowels. For vowels, the theory of dynamic specification (Strange and

Bohn 1998) does not seem absolutely necessary to account for production and perception phenomena. The issue of the perception of lip configurations and motion will be discussed when it is relevant to our results.

We present below in three parts the ontogenetic, production, and perception aspects of motion in speech. The V-to-V transition is central to each aspect. The 2-Component-Vowel model, which is designed to incorporate previous V-to-V modeling, and which leads ultimately to the basic VCV temporal organization of speech, is a vital thread linking development to perception. Finally we will obtain a model of speech production in which visual perception can naturally settle, taking into account audiovisual timing. In the concluding section, we propose tests of the global validity of the proposed model, via further audio-visual integration experiments, and increased knowledge of motor control of the inner parts of the vocal tract (which depends at present more crucially on the lips than on accurate data from time-varying area functions).

7.2 The 2-Component-Vowel model

In this section we acknowledge that the priority for our 2-Component-Vowel (2-Comp-V) model is the analysis of the basic vowel-to-vowel transition. We take for granted that on this component Öhman's model is correct. In the V-to-V transitions that display the three major universal dimensions used for vowels, two are highly visible: rounding and height. We will leave aside for the moment one of the main concerns of Öhman's: the timing of the onset of the second vowel with respect to the consonant closure (before and/or during this phase?). We return to this question – specifically in relation to the visibility of the vowel onset through the consonant – in a special section (7.3.1.2) dedicated to further elaboration of the 2-Component-Vowel model. Actually the primary aim of the present section is to show that V-to-V control is not a primitive from a developmental point of view. Our test of Öhman's model uses quantitative articulatory modeling in order to identify the V-to-V component within the intervocalic consonant by using the second vowel's characteristic configuration, and without specifically analyzing the timing of the second vowel onset.

7.2.1 An articulatory modeling test of Öhman's V-to-V

7.2.1.1 An articulatory model built from cineradiographic data Articulatory modeling allows us to test quantitatively different theories of coarticulation. The models used in this study have been designed in such a way that their parameters represent the degrees-of-freedom of the vocal tract of the speaker. This modeling method allows us to study the effects of the action of the degrees-of-freedom, and, at a higher level, to infer motor commands from the observed behaviors.

The data comprise two cineradiographic corpora of two French speakers uttering VCV combinations with C = [b, d, g, ʒ, v], and V = [i, y, u, a]. From these data, two linear anthropomorphic articulatory models have been elaborated. (The present contribution will exemplify only one of these two speaker-based models.) The degrees-of-freedom of the speaker's vocal tract are obtained through an articulatory-driven PCA (Principal Component Analysis) and used as parameters of the model.

The nine parameters: jaw height (JH), tongue body (TB), tongue dorsum (TD), tongue tip (TT), lip height (LH), lip protrusion (LP), lip vertical elevation (LV), larynx height (LH), and tongue advancement (TA), can be assumed to represent the degrees-of-freedom of the articulators of the vocal tract fairly well.

We have developed a method to analyze the coarticulation patterns involved in the production of the VCV sequences in our corpus (described more extensively in Vilain *et al.* 1999). The model affords us a view of global vocal tract contours, as well as insight into the individual actions of each degree-of-freedom of the vocal tract, not only those of the lips and the jaw (which are the most visible), but also those of the tongue namely the body (TB), dorsum (TD), and tip (TT). In other words, we decompose the sagittal function into various activated articulatory parameters and track the evolution in the recruitment of these parameters from the vowel into the consonant.

Figure 7.1 to Figure 7.4 exemplify this method of extracting the actions of the first four articulatory parameters. The midsagittal contours are given in the upper row. In the lower row, the horizontal axis gives the rank order of the lines of the midsagittal grid used to measure and model the vocal tract, from the glottis (line 1) to the apex (line 27). The vertical axis gives the sagittal distance. The upper solid line is the roof contour of the vocal tract, from the pharyngeal wall to the palate and the teeth. The dashed line is the neutral position, to which has been added the variation resulting from the actions of the last five parameters of the model (this is labeled as "raw data"). Two of these five parameters have a small effect on the tongue: namely tongue advance (TA, horizontal displacement of the tip of the tongue), and larynx height (LH). The other three parameters concern the lips: height, protrusion, and vertical elevation. Our analysis does not include the TA and LH parameters, because their effects on the tongue are so small relative to those of the first four tongue parameters.

Among the first four parameters, the "circle" line represents the sagittal configuration of the vocal tract, once the action of the jaw height parameter has been added. Then the action of the tongue body (TB) parameter is added, giving the position of the "plus" line. Adding the tongue dorsum (TD)

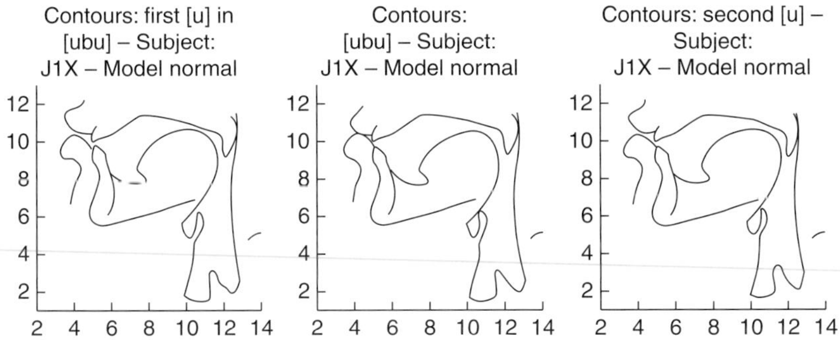

Figure 7.1 Sagittal contours for the three center phases of [u], [b], and [u], in the production of [ubu] (speaker J1X).

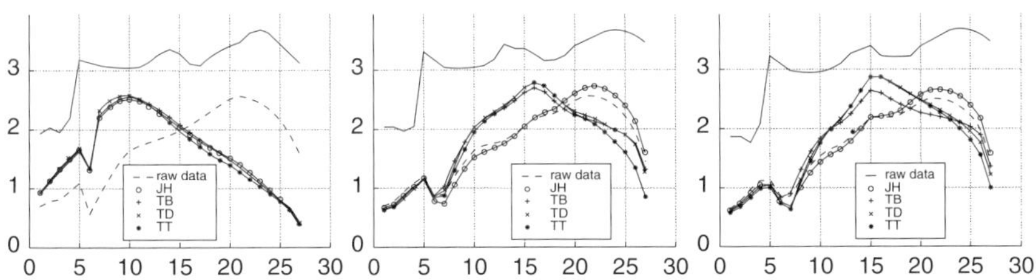

Figure 7.2 Contributions of the four main command parameters for the three center phases of [u], [b], and [u] in the production of [ubu] (speaker J1X).

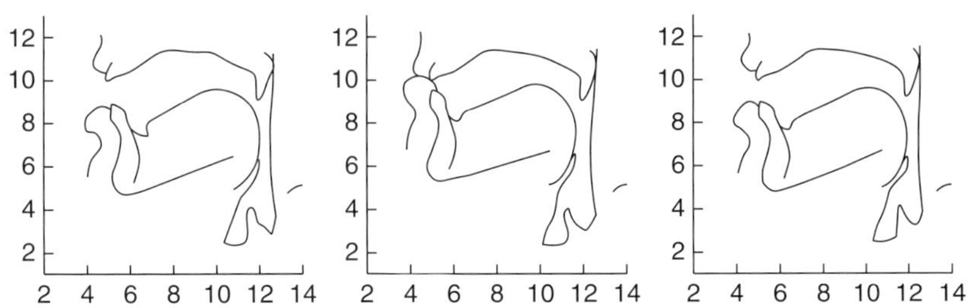

Figure 7.3 Sagittal contours for the three center phases of [a], [b], and [a], in the production of [aba] (speaker J1X).

parameter yields the "x-marked" line. The addition of the tongue tip (TT) action results in the "star" line denoting the final vocal tract configuration, all parameter effects having been computed.

This successive addition of parameter effects is also exemplified when these effects interact (for example, when the action of JH should have lifted up the

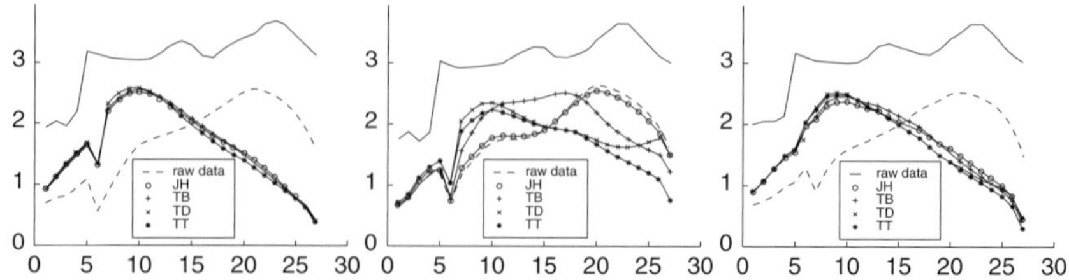

Figure 7.4 Contributions of the four main command parameters (below) for the three center phases for [a], [b], and [a], in the production of [aba] (speaker J1X).

tongue, but TB, TD, and TT bring it back down; see Figure 7.1, Figure 7.2 and discussion in 7.2.1.2), thereby enabling us to highlight the compensation strategies that are implemented during coarticulated speech.

7.2.1.2 A puzzling sequence for coarticulation modeling For all the VCV sequences in the corpus, it proved unproblematic to interpret vocal tract configurations in terms of Öhman's articulatory commands, considering the consonant command as superimposed on the V-to-V command. When we take an [ubu] sequence as an illustration for visible speech of the vocalic rounding dimension, it is obvious that the commands for the vowel are observable throughout the consonant (cf. Figure 7.1); the vocal tract, which is narrowed at the lips and at the velum, is lengthened by lip protrusion and larynx lowering. This is a perfect illustration of the global control of the whole vocal tract for the vowel configuration upon which the lip closure for the consonant is a local perturbation.

Our analysis now focuses on a case that may challenge Öhman's view. In [aba], a developmentally important sequence which displays another effective visible vocalic dimension, height, articulatory modeling revealed, in adult speech, what seemed to be at first examination a lingual compensatory strategy for the vowel: this occurred only during the consonant, not for the vowel and appears paradoxical for Öhman's modeling where the labial consonant must not in principle recruit the tongue for lowering it.

Along the [aba] sequence presented in Figure 7.3, the sagittal contours in the top figures show that the overall open configuration of the vocal tract for the [a] vowel is still fairly present during the labial closure phase. What is this configuration due to? If we now observe Figure 7.4 we can see how the vowel and consonant configurations are achieved by the combination of model parameters. The first [a] is realized by the action of the mandible alone, since the effect of the jaw height parameter (symbolized with the circled line) can be seen to explain almost all of the variation in movement away from the neutral position. The second [a], which comes after the consonant, has exactly the same articulatory components as the first one.

The completion of the consonant is made with quite a different strategy. Jaw height in this case is recruited for another job, i.e., helping the lower lip to reach occlusion with the upper one. Note that it is now the tongue parameters that act to keep the anterior vocal tract open, allowing the posterior tract to be classically constricted. Following Maeda and Honda (1994), we can interpret the tongue body backing as an action of the hyoglossus, pulling the tongue back and down, and the apex positioning can be interpreted as action of the anterior genioglossus, which lowers the anterior part of the tongue. The final tongue configuration is only slightly higher than the preceding and following [a]s. But it is noticeably lower than the position the tongue would have reached if it were simply carried passively by the jaw, as demonstrated below by our simulation data,

As restated above, a bilabial consonant would not be expected to be specified for the action of the tongue, and therefore its production in a context that does not recruit the tongue would be thought to be executed with the jaw and lips only. But strikingly [b] appears here to necessitate a complete recombination of the articulators, aimed at recomposing the open shape of [a]; the very low jaw height parameter necessary for the production of [a] is brought back to zero for the consonant. Yet the body of the tongue is not passively raised by this position of the jaw, as could be supposed. Instead we observe a reorganization of the articulators, whose combined actions recover the vocal tract shape of [a], by compensating for jaw elevation by tongue lowering.

To illustrate the extent of this phenomenon, we have simulated in the articulatory model what would happen if, as we first thought, the consonantal gesture recruiting the jaw and lips were produced with no active tongue shaping as in the previous and following [a] vowel configurations. Figure 7.5 shows the comparison between the modeled contour regenerated from the original [b] configuration (solid line) and a simulated configuration without the compensatory activity of the tongue (dashed line). Rather unexpectedly, the new position of the tongue compensates for the high position of the jaw implied by the lip occlusion. This new combination cannot be considered as a retropropagation of the next [a] configuration, since this second [a] is produced exactly as the first one was, i.e., with the same jaw height parameter value and, again, without any effect of tongue parameters.

Notice that, if this sequence is read in area function terms, Öhman's model of coarticulation is supported, since we have approximately a steady [a] global configuration, just perturbed locally by [b] closure. So it is only at a higher level, that of motor control, that we meet the paradox. In order to support a

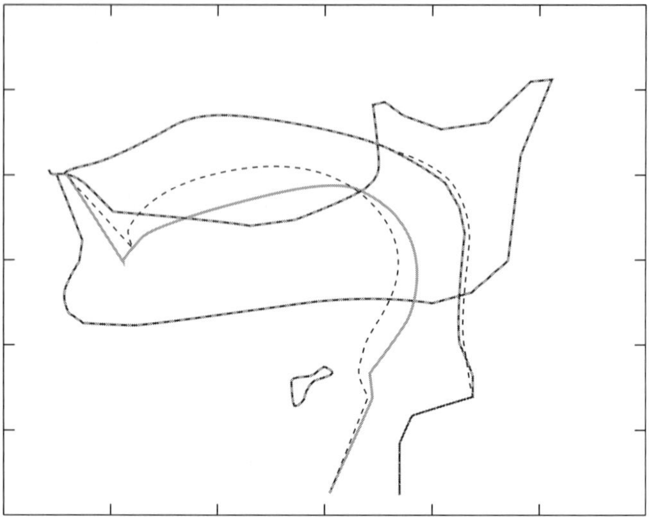

Figure 7.5 Comparison between the modeled contour regenerated from the original [b] configuration (solid) and a simulated configuration without the compensating activity of the tongue (dashed).

dual-channel motor control model of speech, the command parameters of articulatory modeling must be reinterpreted.

7.2.1.3 Questions for Öhman's model at the motor control level This unfolding of events interpreted as commands raises the following questions.

- Is this lingual activity during [b] due to a rapid change in motor commands?
- Does this lingual activity pertain to the vowel? That is, does this contradict the idea of a passive V-V gesture on which the consonant is superimposed, since there exists an active maneuver to keep the vowel stable? If so, the vowel would be controlled through two different articulatory strategies, between which the speaker would have to switch, from the vowel to the vowel within the consonant closure, an abrupt change which seems unlikely.
- Does this lingual activity pertain to the consonant, in which case these different strategies represent the successive activation of vowel and consonant control?

One possibility is that the observed pattern is due to a context-free, phoneme-to-phoneme activation process, such as Joos' overlapping innervation wave theory (Joos 1948), which is very similar to the Haskins model, as disseminated in speech face synthesis via Löfqvist (1990). But the acceptance of such a process implies that the lingual gesture should be considered as a constraint pertaining to the labial consonant, like jaw raising and the labial upward movement. This solution goes against the idea of labials being unspecified for lingual gestures, and cannot be explained by any articulatory or acoustic need.

In the original theory of coarticulation by Öhman (1967a), the dual-channel model is explained by the fact that tongue activity in speech is controlled by sets of muscles with separate neural representations: one for vowels, one for apical consonants, one for dorsals, and one of course for labials. The articulatory commands are therefore transmitted independently of each other, which allows the diphthongal vowel-to-vowel gesture to be carried out while the consonantal gesture is superimposed on it.

What we might propose here is that the configuration for the [a] vowel can be completed with only the action of the jaw, but that actually the lingual muscles are also recruited during the jaw movement. The activation may not result in an effective displacement, since one and the same configuration can correspond to a different set of muscle activations. Nevertheless, activation still exists. In this case, it is the recruitment of the jaw for the production of the consonant that results in tongue activation. The control for the [a] vowel, which was supposed to consist of jaw opening alone, is thus revealed to be more complex, since it involves the tongue as well, through lowering muscles such as the hyoglossus and anterior genioglossus.

This solution is now in line with Öhman's dual-channel model of coarticulation, not only at the level of resulting area functions, but also at the level of motor commands. The vowel command setting is actually constant at the control level for hyoglossus, genioglossus, and jaw muscles for lowering. The consonant command for the labial closure also recruits the jaw muscles, but for an elevating action. The fact that the consonant command is superimposed on the steady vowel command lets the jaw position emerge with different values, lowered for [a], but more elevated for [b] in the [a] context.

A consideration of recently available developmental data – stimulating though limited – will help us rethink Öhman's modeling as embedded within a coherent framework.

7.2.2 *What developmental path for coarticulation control?*

7.2.2.1 Milestones in the development of coarticulation control The applicability of Öhman's model to the issue of speech ontogeny is not unproblematic since there is no evidence that the V-to-V carrier transition is a primitive. Hence it is clear that such a model is basically correct, but must be revised to fit the developmental data. Our approach is to start from the jaw cycles of the 7-month-old canonical babbler (resulting in the common [bababa] or [dadada] types), as a primitive, and to settle the V-to-V transition within the babbling cycle. In other words we will borrow from MacNeilage's (1998) theory before revising Öhman's model.

In a more systematic longitudinal view, recent studies have led us to propose that the unfolding of speech production development could take the following path:

(1) Starting at the so-called canonical babbling stage, we posit a global mastering of the carrier articulator, the mandible alternating closing and opening phases.
(2) Then, what emerges is the independence of the carried articulators, the lower lip and the tongue which allows, during the closing or so-called "closant" phases, the control of local constrictions, together with anatomical parts of the mouth roof (upper lip, hard and soft palate, pharynx wall).
(3) Thereafter we have evidence of the learning, during the opening or so called "vocant" phases, of a global control of the vocal tract.
(4) The stage at which occurs what we will call a local control in vowel production – as accounted for by our 2-Comp-V model – remains uncertain. To our knowledge this question has not yet been addressed by speech developmentalists in these proper terms. But it is rather obvious that glide production precedes mastery of vowel steady states.
(5) There seems to exist a final stage where fricative control of the [ʃ]-type is contrasted with the more precocious [s]; this stage follows the famous *fish/fis* phenomenon (Moskowitz 1970), also worked out by Johnson *et al.* (1981) and cited by Oller and MacNeilage (1983, p. 94). A French child can say "Mathieu sait pas dire *casser* ["to break" instead of *cacher* "to hide"], il dit casser"). The adult mastery of this production corresponds to a rather global "freezing" of at least the tongue blade configuration [as evidenced by, among others, our own observations (Vilain *et al.* 1998); here for [ʃ] in Figure 7.6].

It is important to note that our proposal for an embedding of control schemas is framed in the vein of the development of control for body segments. The parts of the vocal tract that form the core of the "articulatory speech body" are first mastered locally (as the eyes, the head, the trunk, and the hindquarters in locomotor development) before the global mastery of postures (as in locomotion) or figural movements controlling the whole body shape (as in dancing). In this sense we outline here for the first time an integrative developmental model for the control of speech body segments. The alternating succession of global and local controls denotes the integration path in development. In the following section, we will discuss only stages (2) and (3) which are directly relevant in revising Öhman's model.

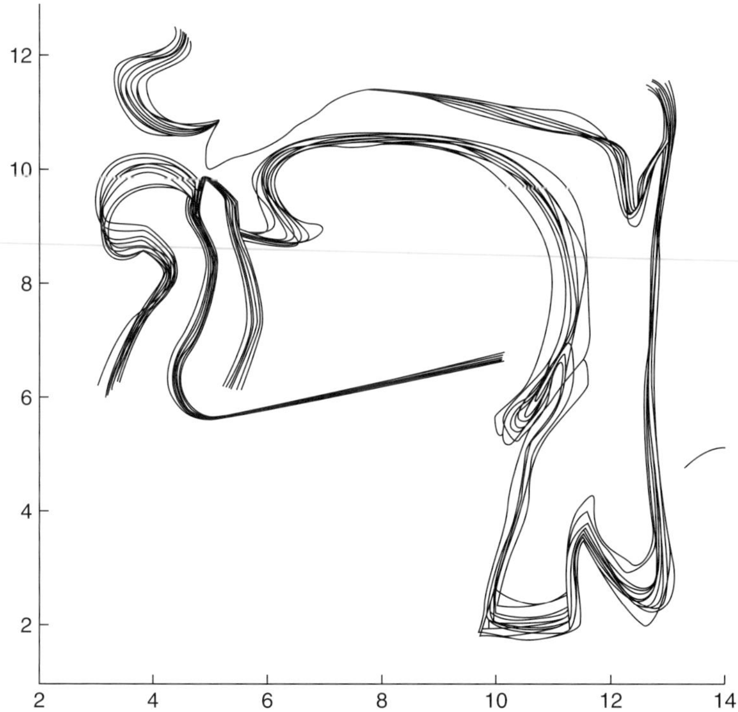

Figure 7.6 Sagittal contours for [ʃ] in all combinations with [i, y, u, a]. Notice the control of a large subpart of the vocal tract: the lips are specifically protruded for this consonant and the tongue blade is specifically stable together with jaw height.

7.2.2.2 Emergence of local constriction control for closants Munhall and Jones (1998) recorded the activities of the lower and upper lips during the production of a [bababa] cycle, by an 8-month-old female baby, and compared this with a [bababa] sequence (with serial order control) produced by an adult (Figure 7.7). The baby pattern shows oscillation, from closed to open configurations, of the lower lip carried by the mandible, but no active movement of the upper lip. "The only upper lip movement occurs in phase with the lower lip motion and is presumably caused by the lower lip forces pushing the upper lip upward after contact . . . This pattern is consistent with [MacNeilage's] proposal that initial babbling primarily involves mandibular motion" (subsequent studies corroborated this interpretation quantitatively, starting with Green *et al.* 2000). At this stage, no control over lip constriction for speech has yet emerged.

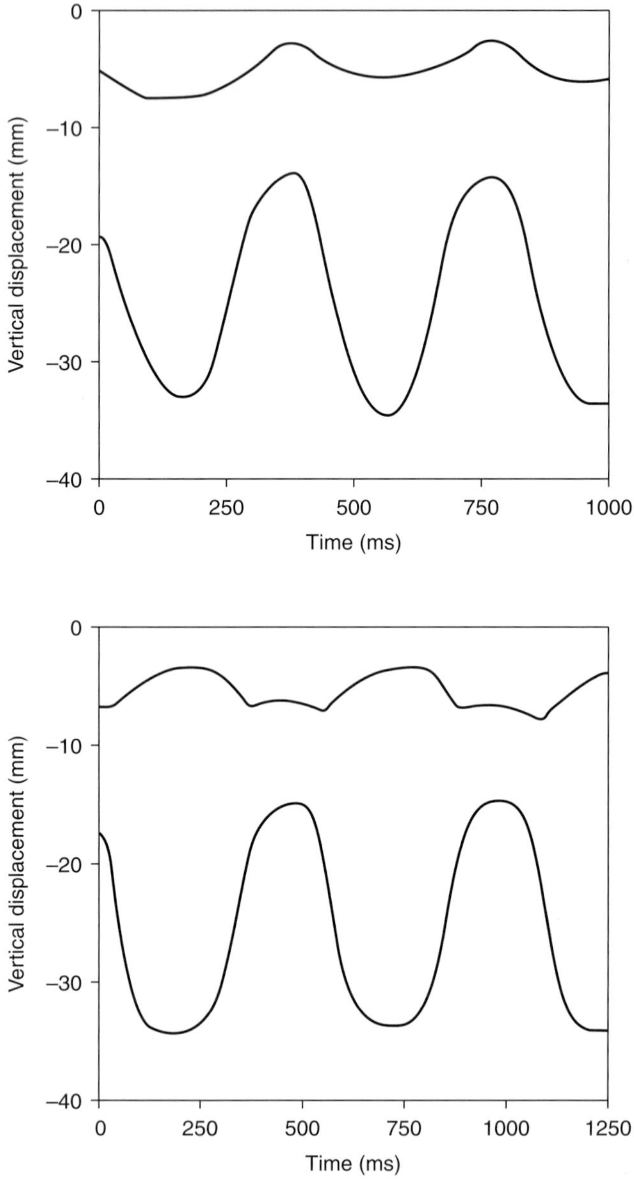

Figure 7.7 Vertical displacement of upper lip (top traces in each figure) and lower lip (bottom traces) as a function of time during repetitive production of [bababa] by (a) an 8-month-old girl and (b) an adult (from Munhall and Jones 1998).

In contrast, the adult pattern shows a similar oscillation of the lower lip together with the jaw, but also an active displacement of the upper lip. The upper lip moves downward to meet the lower lip, and then resists against the pushing of the lower lip (which has proven to be active in current data).

These two patterns exemplify the development of control of the lips for speech. This local control, which assists in completing controlled constrictions, is obviously not yet present in the 8-month-old baby, i.e., by the time of canonical babbling. It becomes available later in development. When? We have at present no information about the date of this emergence. However there is clear evidence that babbling of hearing babies shows more oral [baba] or [dada] than corresponding nasal [mama] or [nana], in the babbling of hearing-impaired infants (Davis and MacNeilage 2000). This calls for an explanation. In addition, the babbling of a baby fitted with hearing aids soon switches towards the production of more oral segments (McCaffrey *et al.* 2001). Could it be that in order to obtain a more effective production (a better effect/effort ratio), the developmental path is to acquire a better control of the closed state of the vocal tract (including nasal port closing and lip contact), a control that could be precociously reinforced through auditory feedback? A relevant example of more effective production in these terms is the greater acoustic intensity found in [baba] than [mama], which would correspond more closely to opening and closing movements induced by jaw articulation.

7.2.2.3 Emergence of global control for vocants What then of the *global* control of the vocal tract that is necessary for the realization of vowels coarticulated with consonants? Sussman *et al.* (1999) have studied the development of CV coarticulation by analyzing the acoustic signal, using locus equations based on formants.[1] In their case study, Sussman and colleagues follow a female baby from age 7 months to age 40 months, from babbling to meaningful speech, and analyze her utterances to obtain F2 at onsets and at vowel midpoints. The locus equations are interpreted as an index of the evolving degree of coarticulation of labial, alveolar, and velar consonants across different vowel contexts from baby to adult patterns. These data are regarded as representative of the way in which segmental independence is progressively acquired with the increasing mastery of coarticulation.

The articulatory paths towards adult-like norms appear to differ across consonant types. For labials, the baby has to learn how vowel tongue position must be integrated with and also independent of lip closure. Locus equations for labials show slow slopes at first. The slopes increase towards adult target slopes around 1 year, at about 14 months, probably indicating that the child is beginning to produce vocalic tongue placements that are quite independent from the consonant.

Coarticulatory effects in alveolars start with a high slope that decreases rapidly in the first months, and then remains below adult slope values until the third year. It can be hypothesized that the child is at first unable to produce independent tongue movements with the two parts of the tongue needed for alveolars and vowels. Then she gains more independent motor control over the different degrees-of-freedom of her tongue, probably guided by the auditory input she receives from her environment. The very low slopes seen during the next months seem to indicate some hyper-resistance to coarticulation, which is a classical phenomenon in the development of new skills. The newly acquired capacity for independent control tends to be over-exploited, before being finely tuned, according to the actual needs of communication.

Velars show the most stable slope values relative to the adult norms; after large fluctuations in the very first months, they retain a high level of coarticulation, even higher than for adults.

It seems easier to produce CVs where both consonant and vowel share the same articulator (as in velar + vowel, where they overlap completely), than to "integrate (labial + vowel), or differentiate (alveolar + vowel) articulatory components in the achievement of CV utterances that meet adult norms" (Sussman *et al.* 1999, p. 1094).

What appears to be going on here is that when the baby acquires the ability to produce differentiated consonant constrictions, she still has to learn global vocal tract control – à la Öhman, that is, from the lips to the larynx, to adapt her production strategies to adult coarticulation norms.

One interesting point is that adult coarticulation values are reached at about the emergence of the first words. This suggests that coarticulation can be used in first word harmony, that is, in continuity with the pre-word stages, preserving frame dominance (Davis and MacNeilage 1995).

7.2.2.4 Öhman revisited in a developmental framework In summary, the development of speech coarticulation seems to proceed as follows:

- The first control is over the mandible, giving rise to syllable-like frames, i.e., global control of the overall carrier component of speech.[2]
- As independence of carried articulators is gained, that is, when the baby begins to control local constrictions (control of the upper and lower lips is obviously not yet mastered at 8 months; it will be available later), here is the very emergence of segmental content.
- The global control of the vocal tract needed to perform adult-like coarticulation patterns coincides in development with control of harmony in first words.

This latter stage is the one in which control of Öhman's V-to-V transition occurs. We can now rephrase our [aba] case. The two [a] vowels, with their tongue lowering actions, do not need any jaw command nor does the [b] consonant, which involves lip actions, but no elevating command on the jaw. These jaw movements are attributed to the carrier component, from which the lip contact control and the lowering of the tongue have, through learning, become independent. The core of the coarticulation phenomenon is that this independence is gained when the lowering action of the vowel can be performed during the closure of the consonant. What seems to be a retro-propagation of the vowel feature/gesture into the consonant is more likely to be a by-product of global control over the whole speech body, which requires a larger time span. This global, slow, control is perhaps the most significant part of Öhman's legacy, the one that we have reinterpreted in terms of postural or figural movement control. Finally Öhman's coarticulation is thus superimposed on the whole babbling cycle, and not the other way round (i.e., not consonants superimposed on V-to-V transitions, as he proposed).

The jaw carrier component is also visible in [ibi], [ubu], and [yby] sequences, though with less or minimal amplitude, depending on the speaker. Unlike for the [a] vowel, the lip and tongue local or global controls have recruited the mandible for these high vowels, as they did for the tongue and/or lip control of fricatives like [s] and [ʃ]. Visible [aba] and [yby], which illustrate height and rounding vowel dimensions, respectively (not to mention the extremely different types of consonant movements such as [b] and [ʃ]), could thus be controlled in a talking face such as conceived (Borel *et al.* 2000; Revéret *et al.* 2000; Badin *et al.* 2002) using learnable control-embedded models.

7.3 The 2-Comp-Vowel model and visible speech

When the V-to-V transition has been mastered, vocalic coarticulation is pervasive in the speech flow, letting vowel dimensions appear more or less auditorily and/or visibly through consonants. In the span of this V-to-V transition, we will claim that glides are as ubiquitous in the speech flow as vowels are. For these glides appear naturally as the transitional portions – say as glide epentheses – between the so-called vowel "steady-state" phases. The question whether these glides are audible and visible during the consonant phase will be addressed later. The main question for the moment will be: Why do they appear within the V-to-V transition? Since the phenomenology of glide epenthesis between vowels has been so poorly established in the motor control literature – although in descriptive phonetics their notation can be traced back at least to Bell and Sweet (Sweet 1880) – we will take time to give an experimental proof of their existence within the different phases of the V-to-V transition: on-gliding, climax (and plateau), off-gliding. Then we will outline the 2-Comp-Vowel model which delivers a more comprehensive account of these different phases of V-to-V transitions including glide epenthesis production and relative timing of V-to-V through C in VCV.

7.3.1 Major visible and audible phases in V-to-V transitions

7.3.1.1 VV transitions As an example, we consider the interpretation of articulatory measurements of lip movement for three French V-to-V phases. Why is this of interest? At present, there is no precise description of the time-course of articulatory constriction inside the vocal tract. In addition, French features an [i]/[y] contrast, which is supported mainly by lip movement. Currently, this analysis is the first direct articulatory evidence available in the world which rests on precise, repeated measurements of lip area sampled at fifty frames per second, using the system developed in our laboratory (Lallouache 1991; Audouy 2000). In our lip motion capture technique, we use blue lips for image preprocessing via chroma-key. This is not a "dirty trick": it is the best non-invasive method to get precise measurements of between-lip area. We will see that this is the only available measurement setup that meets the accuracy requirements for speech, where quite small differences in lip area can produce very different acoustic results, for example, in VV [yi] and VCV [ybi].

From Figure 7.8, we can interpret changes in upper lip protrusion and lip constriction area in a production of a sentence by a male French speaker: "Tu dis (Do you say): 'UHI ise'?" [tydi#yiiz] (where UHI is a "pseudo-Indian" proper name and "ise," third person of pseudo-verb "iser"). For more details see Cathiard (1994). We can identify the following sequence of events:

(1) Constriction and protrusion movement onset for [y] appear to start in phase (note that protrusion starts after a maximum retraction during preceding [i] and a plateau during the pause);
(2) constriction plateau for [y] (but not constriction maximum as discussed further below) is reached first (constriction plateau onset);
(3) then protrusion maximum (indicating vowel climax) together with constriction plateau;
(4) shortly after, protrusion decreases (retraction onset towards the following [i]), a slight constriction area decrease occurs (leading to maximum constriction); this is what we call "off-glide epenthesis," in this case a [ɥ]-glide; this glide is produced by a retraction of the lips together with a narrowing of the lip slit;
(5) and area of constriction increases (constriction offset) finally rejoining protrusion decrease towards the following [i] vowel.

From event (1) to event (2), phase (1)–(2) can be considered as the *on-gliding phase* of the vowel [y]; this phase will be modeled articulatorily and perceptually with reference to our Movement Expansion Model (MEM), which deals essentially with extent of anticipation (Abry *et al.* 1996). Phase (2)–(4) will be labeled as the *climax phase*; it may comprise plateau phases, for example, for [y] an area plateau and even a protrusion plateau; these plateau phases will be

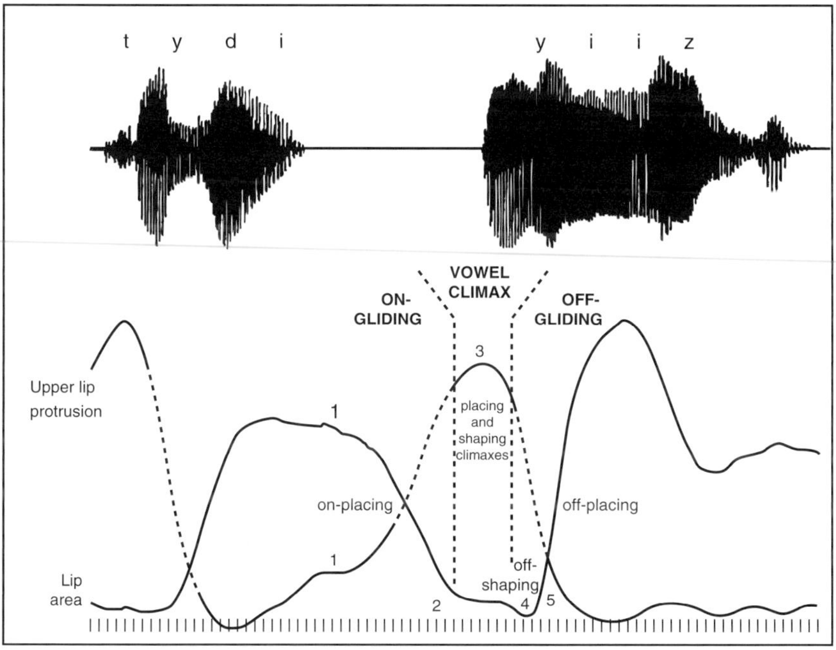

Figure 7.8 Acoustic signal (above) and time-course (below) of upper lip protrusion and lip area for the sentence "Tu dis: UHI ise?" On the horizontal axis, the video frames are indicated by vertical ticks each 20 ms. The following events are indicated. Event (1) corresponds to the constriction and protrusion movement onset for [y] and event (2) to the beginning of the constriction plateau. From event (1) to event (2), phase (1)–(2) can be considered to be the on-gliding phase of the vowel [y]. Event (3) corresponds to the protrusion maximum and index of vowel climax, together with constriction plateau, that is, event (2). Event (4) is a slight constriction area decrease leading to maximum constriction: this is what we call "off-glide epenthesis," in this case a [ɥ]-glide. Event (5) corresponds to an increase in area of constriction together with the protrusion decrease towards the following [i] vowel. Phase (4)–(5) is the off-gliding phase of [y], during which an "off-glide epenthesis" occurs. It is also possible to read events on our time functions in terms of placing and shaping commands, as indicated by labels in lower cases (see text).

explored perceptually. Phase (4)–(5) is the *off-gliding phase* of [y], during which an "*off-glide epenthesis*" occurs; this phase will also be explored perceptually and modeled articulatorily.

Notice that the production can be transcribed more narrowly as [iyɥi], or more precisely as [ijyɥi]. The first [j] glide is produced by the tongue, which is not visible in the lip signal, hence not relevant; in addition, the first glide is produced during the off-setting of the [i] vowel, that is, during the [i] off-gliding phase. "On-glide epentheses," that is, epentheses produced during the on-glide phase of the vowel, will occur for transitions from the [a] vowel to higher vowels (in this case in a [aɥy] transition), as explained below.

Depending on context, some of these phases will be partly audible, partly visible. In this particular production, due to the silent pause, the *on-gliding phase* of the vowel [y] is not audible until the first glottal pulses, at about protrusion maximum. When pause length is varied, this pause context allows V-to-V transition to appear without an intervening consonant; then the influence of the consonant can be added (for pausal contexts, see Cathiard 1994, for visible consonantal types influences, see Troille *et al.* 2010). In other cases the glide could occur during a consonantal closure and be also more visible than audible (see [tydi] description in Section 7.3.1.2).

Let us now focus on this glide epenthesis. For us, the existence of this epenthesis is as evident as other consonantal or vocalic epenthetic by-products like the famous English "Thompson phenomenon" (French *chambre* from Latin *camera*, or svarabhactic vowels, like Russian alternations Lenin*grad* versus Nov*gorod*, etc.). To such examples can be added a well-traced Provençal reflex of Latin *maturu* "ripe" [mavyr], in the Drôme Department (at Mirabel-aux-Baronnies and Nyons, in Duraffour 1969, entry 6446), where after intervocalic [t] spirantization [ð] and deletion, the [v] approximant stemmed from a glide of the [ɥ]-type. We dub this process mnemonically the "*power phenomenon*," with a French-English example, Latin *potere*, Old French *poeir* (Modern French *pouvoir*), giving as a loanword English *power*, through Middle English *poër*, *pouer.*[3]

7.3.1.2 VCV Transitions One of our recent examples is shown in Figure 7.9, where the same speaker, ten years later, utters: "Tu dis 'RUHI ise'?" [tydiRyiiz]. Among his set of variants, the behavior of this glide is quite "hypertrophic." For RUHI, he starts with a plateau constriction, produced during the coarticulated initial rounded [R], which is about 90 mm^2, an area value small enough to contribute quantally to acoustic [y] characteristics (Schwartz *et al.* 1993). Finally, a minimal area constriction of 0.50 mm^2 is reached (20 ms, or 1 image, before = 1.47 mm^2; 2 images before = 10.32 mm^2; and 1 image after = 3.62 mm^2; see Figure 7.10). If one looks backwards at the "Tu dis ..." span, we observe a minimal area constriction of 1.10 mm^2 (1 image before = 2.42 mm^2; 2 images before = 8.92mm^2; and 1 image after = 6.82 mm^2; see Figure 7.11). These values are not observed for vowels but for approximants. The aeroacoustic production of various degrees of frication, in such a small area, depends on pressure values. We did not observe frication into our [yɥi] signals; and into [tydi] the [d] closure prevents any such phenomenon. The crucial point

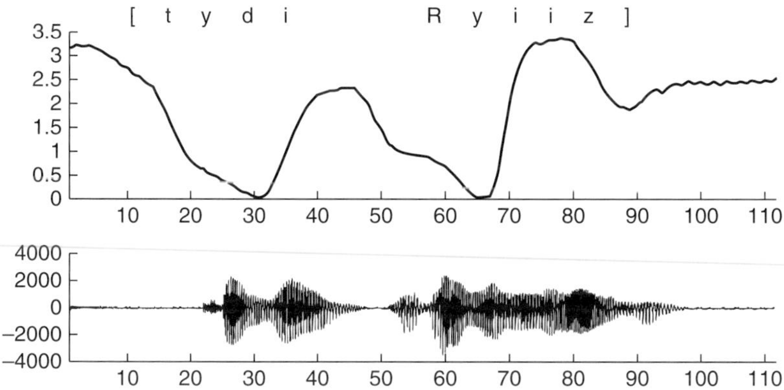

Figure 7.9 Acoustic signal (below; in abscissa: video frame numbers) and time-course of lip area (above; in cm^2) for the sentence "Tu dis RUHI ise?" See Figure 7.10 and Figure 7.11 for area values close to $0\,cm^2$.

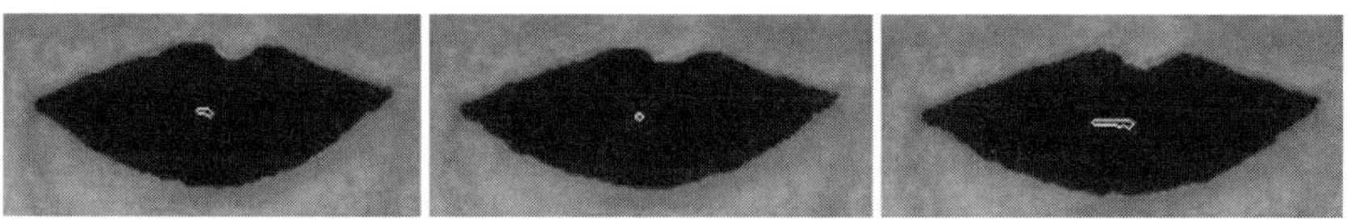

Figure 7.10 Front images extracted from the sequence RUHI in: "Tu dis: RUHI ise?" with lip area measurements. A minimal lip area constriction of $0.5\,mm^2$ is reached between the [y] and the [i] of "RUHI."

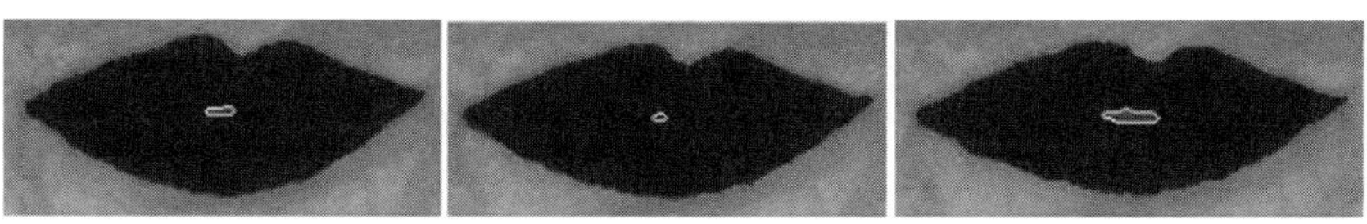

Figure 7.11 Front images extracted from the sequence "Tu dis" in: "Tu dis: RUHI ise?" with lip area measurements. A minimal lip area constriction of $1.1\,mm^2$ is reached between the [y] and the [i] of "tu dis", i.e., during the closure.

here is that, given the accuracy of our measurement system (and we still await the challenge of a similar accuracy from other lip image processing techniques), these sounds with 0.5 or $1\,mm^2$ constriction at the lips do not reach complete closure, with the corresponding acoustic result, as in our [b] examples.[4] Hence RUHI [Ryi], as in *Ruy Blas*, is definitively not [Rybi] "ruby," giving a weird *Ruby Blas*!

The VCV "Tu dis . . ." sequence offers an insight into the disputed issue of the timing of the vowel onset into the V-to-V transition. The minimum constriction area of the [ɥ] approximant occurs about the middle of the [d] closure. Given this, it could be said that the end of the [ɥ] constriction indicates the beginning of the movement toward the following [i]; in other words, this is the onset of the following vowel. In fact, in terms of describing the sequence of movements, and interpreting these movements as consequences of motor control, there is a time delay between the relaxing phase of [y] and the onset phase of [i]. Otherwise the glide would not occur. We will see that the 2-Comp-Vowel model offers such an account of this phenomenon. This represents a different point of view from the classical approach which identifies the onset of the following vowel by using a given criterion such as zero velocity crossing, peak acceleration or 10 percent movement amplitude (see Perkell and Matthies 1992; Abry and Lallouache 1995a; Abry and Lallouache 1995b). For instance, in a C1V1C2V2 sequence like [CyCi], the beginning of movement toward V2 can be seen to occur in the protrusion signal within the *first* consonant (compare Figure 7.9 where protrusion maximum in "Tu dis . . ." occurs during the burst of [t]). The same occurs for [CiCy], where the maximum retraction can occur within the first consonant, and hence be considered as the onset of the movement toward the [y] vowel. The small area value which is quantally efficient for [y] acoustic structure will be reached only within the second consonant: this is classic anticipatory lip-rounding into the preceding consonant. Whereas the maximum area value for [i] in [CyCi] will be reached only within the [i] vowel, even if, taking account of the quantal articulatory-acoustic asymmetry between [i] and [y] regarding their sensitivity to lip area, we set a quantal area value for [i] acoustic structure. Thus this maximum value will definitely not be reached until the acoustic onset of the vowel. Our claim will be that glide epenthesis offers a criterion for indexing the *relaxation* of the preceding vowel posture, hence a cue to the boundary between successive vowels in the V-to-V transition. As we will see in Section 7.3.2.5, the 50 percent perceptual [yi] visual boundary is located at about this glide epenthesis. The simple reason is that in this [yi] transition, one cannot detect the [i] direction of movement until the area increases again. The [ɥ] approximant, the tail of [y] where this vowel is relaxed, which constitutes the first part of the transition towards [i], is actually misleading since it is not indicating a [i] direction, but a closer [y] (cf. *infra*).

More generally glide epenthesis movement can not be attributed to the detour in the transition from one goal to another, qualified as an overshoot in the classical second-order models, where such a detour is due to given stiffness and dampening values (the same for an equilibrium point control). This detour has yet to be explained in biomechanical and biocybernetical terms, if our aim is to keep speech biological movement control within the laws of motion.

7.3.2 *Modeling the "power phenomenon"*

7.3.2.1 Glides under control We will show that glide epentheses are given for free in a 2-Comp-Vowel control model. Consequently do they need a special control status? From a phonological standpoint, it seems that it is only when the transitional glide phase can be manipulated linguistically that there is evidence for a dynamic feature under the control of speakers of a particular language. This is typically the case when the natural transitional consonant [p] in "Thompson" can be lengthened or reduced depending on the linguistic community, Anglo-American or South African (Fourakis and Port 1986). Additionally, since glides (like any other epenthetic phenomenon) can be phonologized, it is not surprising (and not contradictory, as assumed by Ladefoged and Maddieson 1996, pp. 322–324) that, in spite of their transitional origin, they can display a steady-state phase, when they need to be linguistically lengthened or rather geminated (like French nous plions "we fold" [plijɔ̃] *versus* nous pliions "we folded" [plijjɔ̃]).

What is relevant from the control point of view – in production as in perception – is that these transitional glides, like other epentheses, are not *ab initio* programmed per se. They are kinematic by-products of a controlled transition, typically from or onto a high vowel. But initially, as transitional by-products, where do they come from?

7.3.2.2 Glides in the 2-Comp Model: placing and shaping Our production results – together with relevant perception data – are discussed here in the framework of a double-component account of V-to-V transitions. The 2-Comp-Vowel model assumes that in order to control the *geometry* necessary for their aeroacoustic result, all speech sounds can recruit the degrees-of-freedom of the vocal tract in two ways. First, they all have a *placing* component. Second, some of them have an additional *shaping* component, morphing the sagittal and/or coronal geometry, i.e., a control in 2D or 3D vocal tract space.[5]

Placing is the *global* component. For vowels it is achieved mainly by the extrinsic muscles of the tongue, plus the lips. Intrinsic muscles finish the job, *shaping* the tongue groove for [i], bunching the tongue arch for [u]. Other proposals following Öhman's legacy, by Perkell (1969) and Fowler and Smith (1986) converge on the role of this intrinsic-muscle *local* component for consonants, adopted here for glides sometimes considered as "semi-consonants." For the lips the same *shaping* job is done by the two orbicularis muscles as main agonists for [u] and our French [y]. Notice that [a] will not basically display this second component, as we will see below.

When the *placing* and *shaping* components are fairly synchronous, V-to-V transitions without glide epenthesis are produced. Glide epenthesis occurs when *shaping* is relaxed asynchronously with respect to *placing* changes. Such an asynchrony gives rise to glide epenthesis in the transition between vowels.

In summary, during the V-to-V transition there is a change from *placing* to *placing*, i.e., in the targets of the *global* component which determine the vocal tract configurations for the vowel. But, during this transition, there is not a control of *shaping*, i.e., the second, *local* component, which morphs the sagittal and/or coronal vocal tract geometry. Our claim is that glide emergence is a mere consequence of asynchrony between *placing* and *shaping*. Consequently, if such an emergence can be monitored afterwards in order to be linguistically inhibited or enhanced, glides are not a priori controlled.

7.3.2.3 Glides in French syneresis/dieresis French phonology has different timing control of VV sequences in northern *versus* southern dialects. The name of the town of Lyon can be syllabified either [ljɔ̃] or [lijɔ̃]. This is classically described as two trends: northern syneresis *versus* southern dieresis. As an example of this second usage, in the dialect of Savoy, there is no difference between *ciller* "to blink" and *scier* "to saw," both [sije] (instead of standard French [sije] *versus* [sje]); the main phonetic difference between this Francoprovençal usage and the Provençal one is the shortness of the glide in the latter. The same is true for *puer* "to stink" [pyɥe] *versus* [pɥe], the second northern trend being exemplified in backslang *verlan* [ɥep] (not [epy]). Notice that, in spite of these clearly audible transitions, the current practice of French phonologists (Klein 1991) is to transcribe [plije] for *plier* "to fold," but not [pyɥe] for *puer*, [byɥe] for *buée* "condensation," nor [buwe] for *bouée* "buoy."

7.3.2.4 "True" glides and epenthetic glides on the lips As stated previously, there is at present no accurate description of the time-course of articulatory constriction inside the vocal tract that is comparable to what we can obtain at the lips. In order to contrast epenthetic glides *versus* proper glides in French, we used two sequences uttered by the same speaker discussed previously: "T'as dit: 'HUE hisse'?" [tadi#yis] and "T'as dit: 'HUIS'?" [tadi#ɥis] – where HUE and HUIS are real family names and "hisse," third person form of *hisser* "to raise" (see Cathiard *et al.* 1998). As illustrated in Figure 7.12(a), the VV [yi], i.e., [yɥi] data clearly display, after the plateau (here with a mean of 28 mm^2), a 60–80 ms phase of constriction [ɥ] (19 mm^2 for the minimum). Notice that this epenthetic glide occurs when the protrusion begins to decrease. The "true" glide, as realized in the sequence "T'as dit: 'HUIS'?" (Figure 7.12(b)), displays the same swift phase but lacks a preceding plateau. In short, both display a glide constriction phase, the main differences being the absence of protrusion and constriction plateaus in the true glide, and the presence of more constriction (a 7 mm^2 minimum). These [ɥ] constrictions correspond to a lowering of both F2 and F3 in a typical [y] formant convergence (Schwartz *et al.* 1993).

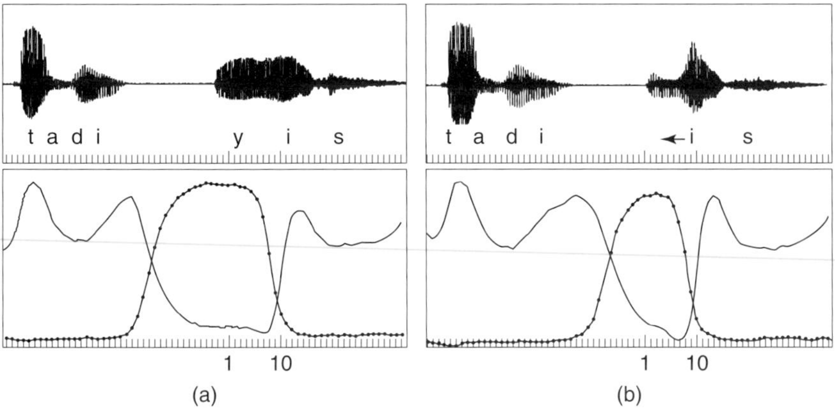

Figure 7.12 Acoustic signal (above) and time-course (below) of upper lip protrusion (line with black boxes) and lip area (continuous line) for the sentence (a) "T'as dit: Hue hisse?" and (b) "T'as dit: Huis?". On the horizontal axis, the frames are indicated by vertical ticks each 20 ms. The numbers from 1 to 10 specify the domain explored, frame by frame, each indicating the last image number of the 10 gated sequences in the corresponding visual perception experiments (see text).

It is now possible to interpret the events numbered on our time functions in Figure 7.8 in terms of *placing* and *shaping* commands:

(1) Constriction and protrusion movements for [y], starting fairly well in phase, are cues of placing initiation (on-placing);
(2) constriction plateau for [y] represents the achievement of placing;
(3) protrusion maximum, index of vowel climax, together with constriction plateau, represents the achievement of shaping (placing and shaping climaxes);
(4) shortly after protrusion decrease, which is an index of placing command towards [i] (in this case, [y] off-placing or unplacing), the [ɥ] glide epenthesis occurs and is an index of [y] off-shaping or unshaping;
(5) and constriction area increase, with protrusion decrease towards the following vowel, is index of [i] *placing*.

Our claim is that glide epenthesis production is explained by command asynchrony. If [i] shaping began synchronously with [i] placing (and coincided with [y] unplacing), [y] unshaping would not be observed so there will be no glide epenthesis. Since [y] unplacing occurs in advance of [i] shaping, [y] unshaping emerges alone, resulting in a glide.

It should also be noted that if epenthetic glides are generally manifested on the area time-course by a dip, they are also detectable by a simple singularity, i.e., an increase in area as sudden as in a plosive release. This [ɥ] offset, as abrupt as a [b] release (except that it does not start from 0 mm^2), means that this singularity in movement time-course is due to peripheral constraints and is not planned as an abrupt movement trajectory. Hence one can infer here also a desynchronization of the shaping command with respect to the placing one.

7.3.2.5 Glide topology in vowel space The glides that emerge during the main V-to-V transitions, from point-vowel to point-vowel, are the following. The transition [iju] corresponds to its asymmetrical counterpart [uwi] as [ijy] corresponds to [yɥi]. This argues decisively in favour of glides as by-products of the *shaping* component release: the lip slit for [u] diminishes (due to *unshaping*, as for [y]), and the same for the tongue groove of [i] (due to *unshaping* of the tongue groove).

Transitions [ija], like [aji], and [uwa], like [awu], involve the low vowel [a] which does not glide. As noted by Ladefoged and Maddieson (1996), non-high [e] and [o] vowels can glide, and we can even exemplify this for a vowel as low as [ɔ] in French *bohémien* "gipsy," [bɔemɛ̃] or [bwemɛ̃]. But [a] does not glide. Maxacali, from Brazil, is not a counterexample, since the low vowel glides only in its "low back variety" (Gudschinsky *et al.* 1970). As far as we know, it could be the same for Marphali, a group of Tibeto-Burman languages in Nepal, where field workers' transcriptions vary between unrounded high-mid [ɤ], low-mid [ʌ̥] and low rounded [ɒ̥] (Mazaudon 1997). So in the case where the transition starts from [a], the glide corresponds to the phase where the final tongue or lip shape is not yet achieved. This is a shaping component setting or "on-glide epenthesis."[6]

7.3.2.6 Glides as by-products due to placing and shaping timing As a first modeling attempt, we will consider for simplicity's sake that observed movement patterns are produced by step commands applied to a second-order system, the actual issue being the timing of such commands.

In [a] with high vowel transitions, on-glide and off-glide epentheses ([awuwa], [ajija], [aɥyɥa] etc.) are produced by the onset and offset shaping commands, respectively, starting from a zero shaping value. As regards shaping/placing asynchrony, in getting from [a] to the higher vowel, the high vowel placing command occurs before the shaping command, and in getting back to [a] the high vowel placing command is carried over into the shaping one. Notice that every shaping onset starting from zero or every shaping offset coming back to this value will produce an epenthetic glide.

In transitions between high vowels command timing can be inferred as follows. Consider as a first simple case, [i]-to-[i] transition, when placing is the same for the two vowels. The fact that a [iji] dieresis is encountered shows that even in the case where the same placing command can be sustained (in tied V-to-V transitions, excluding pauses that are too long), shaping command is reset for each vowel. At the tongue level, shaping command for the first [i] and the shaping for the second [i] are separated by a time gap, sufficient for relaxing shaping towards zero. Hence a [j] epenthetic offglide-onglide is produced.

In [ijy] or [yɥi] ([iju], [uwi]) cases, the shaping functions for the lips are brought into action. We will consider here also that we get the same time gap between shaping functions at the tongue as for [iji], and that the placing commands are overlapping at least during this gap, the overlap being necessary for getting the glide.

Coming back to shaping function at the lips, there is a characteristic asymmetry, already mentioned, between [ijy] and [yɥi].

In [ijy] the lip configuration for [y] is clearly more anticipated than is the case for [i] in [yɥi]. So in [ijy], one can infer a shaping [y] command overlapping with [i] shaping. Since there is no time gap, shaping does not go to zero; so no glide is produced at the lips and no [iɥy] is observed. The [j] glide produced at the tongue during the time gap is perfectly audible, since, in spite of rounding anticipation, the lips are sufficiently open (see [jyjy] perceived as such, not as [ɥyɥy], and this in spite of being rounded throughout; the same is true for [juju]). It should be remembered that, at the tongue, the production of this glide needs the [i] placing command to be active after the shaping one.

In [yɥi], in order to account for the asymmetry just mentioned, there is a gap between the shaping commands at the lips, hence a [ɥ] glide. Notice that the [j] glide, produced simultaneously at the tongue, is not audible as such since the lips are too closed during [ɥ]. We can check in this case that placing commands for the lips are as overlapping as for the tongue since, as noted before, the [i] shaping command is late in its placing, which lets the [ɥ] glide emerge.

In the context of classical issues about coarticulation modeling, this timing organization in the 2-Comp model deserves the following remarks.

The placing component is controlled with overlap whereas the shaping component is not basically overlapping, except for rounding anticipation (cf. the undisputed asymmetry). It should be remembered that non-overlapping commands have not been a creed in speech modeling where overlap can conveniently account for the continuity of movements and evolving dominance of speech units (cf. Haskins' lab view presented by Löfqvist 1990). In our model, when shaping is not overlapping (as in the general case), it could be relevant for the discussion about "troughs" (Gay 1980), provided one considers epenthetic glide to be a concern. In this case, [iji] dieresis could be evidence of two successive vowel-related commands (even in French, at least for Northern dialects; for the difficulty to evidence troughs in French see Perkell 1986). This glide epenthesis movement, a detour in the transition from one vowel goal to another, can then be integrated in a classical second-order model, being explained as a second-order dip-trough, in biomechanical and biocybernetical terms, thus in line with our aim of keeping speech biological movement control within the laws of motion.

When command signals are overlapping, whether for rounding, shaping, or placing in general, the issue about anticipation extent remains. Our MEM model (Abry and Lallouache 1995a; Abry and Lallouache 1995b; Noiray *et al.* 2011) is neither a *time-locked*, nor a *look-ahead* stance, but it accounts for the variable expansion of movement, that depends on the amount of time available to achieve the phonetic goal, more specifically depending on the interval left between two successive phonetic goals (the milliseconds necessary for realizing the consonant(s) within the V-to-V transition or the pausal length between vowels). It is adaptable to individual speaker behavior; this means that the rate of movement expansion is speaker-dependent. The debate is not solved by ad hoc modeling such as in Saltzman (1999), where an arbitrary "side constraint" allows continuous modeling of gestural anticipation from look-ahead to "pure time locking" curves (their Figure 2). In our French data the MEM accounts for the first phase of the V-to-V transition, the so-called on-gliding phase (cf. above).

7.3.2.7 Conclusion In summary, what is relevant from the control point of view is that these transitional glides, like other epentheses, are not programmed per se. They are kinematic by-products of a controlled transition, typically from vowel to vowel, i.e., from *placing* to *placing*. However they do not need a proper control during this transition, i.e., a control of *shaping*, since shaping is set to zero. In the off-gliding phases, like in [iju], [ija], [uwi], [uwa], *shaping* is not initially controlled for the glide; but it is for the preceding vowel. And in the on-gliding phases, like in [aji] and [awu], *shaping* is controlled for the following vowel. To sum up, the 2-Comp-Vowel model can produce epenthetic glides by specifying only the relative timing of its two components, *placing* and *shaping*, in their vowel-to-vowel transitions, whatever the type of control of these transitions, be it dynamic in principle (with step or ramp command signals applied to a second-order system) or even postural in principle (like in the equilibrium point-interpolated shift approach). The gliding movement, which is thus a by-product, can be cancelled if the two transition controls are perfectly synchronous. When the glide is present, its kinematics is in no way the result of a dynamic parameter of control, namely shaping, which is explicitly set to zero.

Consequently, even though glides may be afterwards recovered as *true* controls, in order to be linguistically inhibited or enhanced, they are not *a priori* controlled in order to produce a dynamic perceptual effect, with the proper aim to constrain control recovery in learning.

7.4 The perceptual benefit of the model

Such a dynamic perceptual stance is claimed by the influential Dynamic Specification Theory of vowel perception by Strange and colleagues (Strange and Bohn 1998). Since this theory is not limited to the auditory modality of speech, we will present its basic idea from an auditory-visual perspective. In their chapter in *Hearing by Eye II*, Rosenblum and Saldaña (1998, p. 76) repeatedly claim this idea, "The recent evidence on speechreading, auditory speech and visual event perception – along with a new conception of speech events as gestural – supports time-varying information as primary." After an examination of counterarguments, coming from Cathiard (1994) and Campbell (1996), against their preceding experiment (Rosenblum and Saldaña 1996), they finally put forward the following *visual* issue, "Still, the question remains of where the most salient visual information lies. According to the time-varying information thesis, the most coarticulated portions of the utterance should be the most visually salient. Specific predictions could be made based on the auditory speech findings: for example, dynamic margins around a visible vowel should be more informative than the 'steady-state' portions. Thus, examining the salience of coarticulated portions of visible speech should be a straightforward way to test time-varying information" (Rosenblum and Saldaña 1998, p. 76).

In these "dynamic margins," we easily recognize the *on-gliding* and *off-gliding* phases, and in the "steady-state" portion, the *climax* phase (comprising in fact a culmination, and optional plateaus). We will show where it is in the *off-gliding* phase that the *glide epenthesis* plays its role. In short, our present agenda is to show where, in these visible and/or audible phases, perception settles. Rephrased in terms of our modeling approach: what is the perceptual benefit of the timing organization of the two components of the 2-Comp-Vowel model in the V-to-V transition?

Instead of dividing this part into three sections, corresponding to each of the three phases, we choose a presentation in two phases: perception of on-gliding, then of off-gliding. What about the perception of the climax phase? The reason is not that this "steady-state" phase would be the worse phase for vowel identification (as advocated by Strange's theory). We will show that at the climax, perceptual visual identification is . . . at the climax. So the reason is simply that when taking account of the dynamic issue (when is dynamics needed?), we will always have to compare perceptually this climax phase with the preceding and following phases.

7.4.1 *Why can speech be seen before it is heard?*

7.4.1.1 On-gliding vowel phases in visual perception The answer to Rosenblum and Saldaña (1998) lies explicitly in our perceptual data on the *visual* perception of *anticipation* for the *rounding* gesture (Cathiard 1994; Cathiard *et al.* 1996). It was shown that the "steady-state" portions, corresponding to the articulatory climaxes (or "targets") of the visible vowels, displayed obviously the best identification scores for rounding, whereas the "dynamic margins" gave scores that waxed and waned, like the articulatory gestures did (Cathiard *et al.* 1996, p. 215). Just to deal with the case of anticipation, presentation of frozen images taken in the vicinity of the vowel acoustic onset delivered the same ceiling values (100 percent) as for a time-varying display. The only effect of this moving display concerned the location of the perceptual 50 percent rounding boundary, which occurred during the "dynamic margin" of the vowel; it could occur sometimes 30 ms ahead of the curves recovered from a static presentation. Interestingly, this dynamic benefit was not obtained for an optimal view (which in the case of the rounding gesture we demonstrated to be a profile one); but for front views, where protrusion in-depth can be recovered from *shading* (in frozen views) or *shading-from-motion* (in a movie). To account for this pattern of results, we proposed a *shape-from-shading-from-motion* approach, arguing that the visual vowel shape could be a possible representational format, whereas movement would just be a help for recovering shape, when shape is undersampled (which is typically the case for the point-light displays used by Rosenblum and Saldaña 1996), or not optimally projected (in our case, for the front-viewed waxing rounding gesture).

7.4.1.2 On-gliding phases in auditory-visual vowel timing As concerns specifically the bimodal vowel timing, one of the strongest pieces of natural counterevidence against the claim that "time-varying information is primary" comes from the very temporal organization of visible and audible vowel information in speech (Cathiard *et al.* 1996, p. 219, footnote 1). What we observed in our articulatory-acoustic data was that, in initiating an utterance, after a pause, typically with an initial vowel, the first glottal pulse occurred at or nearly at the point where the articulatory setting of the desired vocalic configuration of the vocal tract was achieved. In the rounding of our French [y], the constriction plateau onset typically occurs first (achievement of placing), and the protrusion component is at its maximum (climax) later, at about the first glottal pulse. It should be remembered that protrusion climax can be an index of the achievement of the *shaping* component of the rounded vowel. This means that it is only when the two components are settled that the acoustics of the vowel is triggered. If the featural/gestural information in the oncoming vowel had to take advantage of the dynamics of the gesture towards its target, the glottal excitation would have to be initiated as soon as possible, that is during the transitional gliding phase, just in order for it to be heard. But this is clearly not what the natural temporal organization of speech reveals. This is why speech can be seen before it is heard (for this now well established view, see our own challenge in Troille *et al.* (2010) demonstrating that in VCVs, speech can also be heard before it is seen, depending on the coordination between the two auditory and visual streams).

The perceptual benefit of this on-gliding phase is predicted by our Movement Expansion Model (which was based primarily on anticipatory rounding data for French) both in the protrusion MEM (Abry and Lallouache 1995a; Abry and Lallouache 1995b) and in the constriction MEM versions (see Abry *et al.* 1996, for a synthesis and a discussion of these perceptual predictions). The perceptual benefit from rounding anticipation, which is predicted by MEM, is clearly due to the achievement of the placing component, a sufficiently small lip area (cf. constriction MEM). This natural configurational and temporal coherence of anticipation has been tested through desynchronization (Cathiard *et al.* 1995; Abry *et al.* 1996). Contrary to global desynchronization results (which show that AV speech is in this respect very robust, see Campbell and Dodd 1980), or to null effects on the sensitivity of vowels to desynchronization (Massaro and Cohen 1993), a categorical switch from [y] to [i] can be obtained when making the acoustic [y] vowel glide ahead of the visual anticipatory [i]/[y] boundary (for a discussion see Abry *et al.* 1994; for AV [i]/[y] integration, see Robert-Ribes *et al.* 1998).

7.4.2 *Perception of the off-gliding phase*

7.4.2.1 The "true" glide versus the vowel with epenthetic glide Our preceding results about the representation of the visual vowel (Cathiard *et al.* 1996) draw attention to the specific case of glides, which could differ from the vowels since they might typically be made of "dynamic margins" only, i.e., basically conceived as intrinsically time-varying in nature. The experiments that we summarize here were designed to address three questions: (1) How many subjects can visually identify the vowel *versus* glide contrast which is possible in their speech community? This question tests the robustness of a contrast that is rather unstable in the world's languages. (2) Do contrasting and non-contrasting subjects process the "steady-state" portion differently? (3) Do the contrasting subjects display a special skill for processing the dynamic portion, i.e., the off-gliding phase with the retraction event and the glide constriction phase? And if so, under what condition?

7.4.2.2 Stimuli and articulatory analysis We used [i#yi] and [i#i] transitions which were embedded in the following carrier sentences which controlled for the pause: "T'as dis: Hue hisse?" [tadi#yis] and "T'as dis: Huis?" [tadi#ɥis]. Ten repetitions of each of these two sentences were recorded audio-visually, at 50 frames/second, by our French talker, with simultaneous front and profile views. After image processing, which delivered, among other parameters, upper lip protrusion and area between the lips, two utterances were selected. Their articulatory time-courses (Figure 7.12) are very similar as concerns the "dynamic margins," i.e., the build-up phase of the rounding gesture and the retraction phase towards [i]. As noted above, they differ essentially in their "steady-state" portion, i.e., the *plateau* phase of protrusion and lip constriction, which is clearly longer for [y] in "T'as dis: Hue hisse?". As mentioned, the "true" glide displays the minimum area constriction, but there is still clearly a glide epenthesis in the "T'as dis: Hue hisse?" realization.

7.4.2.3 Pretest: contrasting [y] and [ɥ] In order to know if the two sequences "T'as dit: Hue hisse" and "T'as dit: Huis" could be identified using *visual* information only, we presented these two sequences in their full time-course, ten times each in a random order, in frontal view. Of the twenty-seven normally hearing French subjects, who had no visual deficit, sixteen obtained an identification score higher than or equal to 60 percent.

Accuracy in identification of the glide *versus* its corresponding vowel, with visual information only, varied by subject. As we noted in our first experiment (Cathiard *et al.* 1998), of twenty-seven subjects, only thirteen succeeded in perceiving the contrast using visual information only.

This corresponds to a phonological dialectal situation in the French-speaking community, where, for example, "muet" ("dumb") can be pronounced [myɥe] or [mɥe], depending on the degree of sensitivity of the subject to realizations with or without a glide. According to Klein's scale for Parisian French (Klein 1991), "Hue hisse" has the lowest probability of being syllabified as [ɥi], whereas "Huis" could hardly give rise to a di-syllabic [yi] ([yɥi] in a more narrow transcription). Consequently we can consider that our experiment corresponds to a kind of maximum possible visual difference.

We decided to test the contribution of the plateau duration and the contribution of the timing of the onset of the retraction phase for all subjects (in Cathiard *et al.* 1998, we tested only subjects who succeeded in the pretest). We hope to specify precisely which articulatory event is differently processed by the subjects who can identify the vowel and the glide on the basis of visual information only (group 1), in comparison with the subjects who cannot (group 2).

7.4.2.4 Variation of the climax phase We first tested the sensitivity of the subjects to *plateau* duration in rounding. We prepared a continuum between "T'as dis: Huis?" and "T'as dis: Hue hisse?". For this aim, we removed from the stimulus "Hue hisse" one full image at the plateau centre, i.e., two frames (interlaced fields), then two and three full images, respectively. So we obtained three intermediate stimuli. Notice that the suppression of a fourth full image of the plateau in "T'as dis: Hue hisse?" would have resulted in a stimulus with a plateau duration as small as the plateau duration of "T'as dis: Huis?."

We presented the five stimuli, in frontal view, ten times each in a random order. Subjects were asked to identify each of them as "Huis" or as "Hue hisse." We separately plotted the mean "Hue hisse" identification percentages for the two groups of subjects (see Figure 7.13). Group 1 comprises subjects who visually distinguished the vowel and the glide contrast (pretest score > 60 percent) and group 2 comprises subjects who did not (pretest score < 60 percent). For the two groups, the identification curves are very similar, with a regular increase of "Hue hisse" identifications from 29 percent to 73 percent

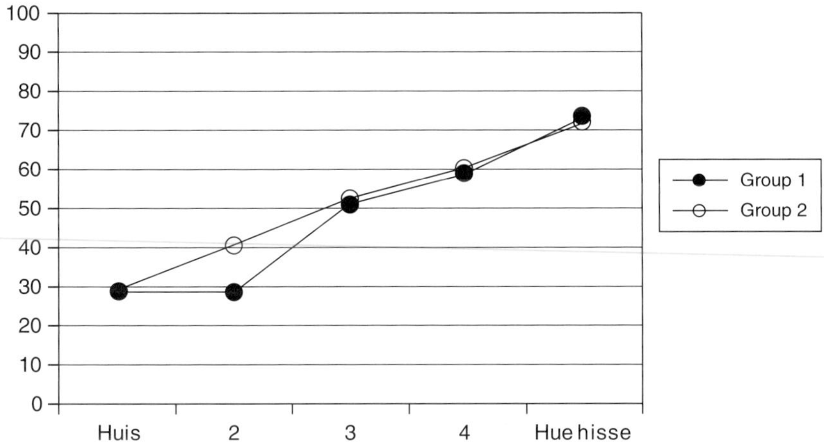

Figure 7.13 "Hue hisse" identification percentages obtained for the continuum (duration of plateau) between "Huis" and "Hue hisse" by the two groups of subjects (see text for explanation).

between "Huis" and "Hue hisse." So all subjects are able to detect the linear increase of the plateau duration, and they do this in a rather psychophysical style, which is not categorical at all. Thus it is not the capacity to process this plateau duration per se that differentiates the two groups of subjects.

7.4.2.5 Perception of the off-glide epenthesis In this second experiment, we explored the timing of the retraction event by a gating technique, in order to obtain the evolution of identification scores step-by-step. For each sequence "T'as dis: Huis?" and "T'as dis: Hue hisse?," we prepared ten gates (each with a duration of 1200 ms), which always included the onset of the sentence and the middle of the rounding plateau. The gates were moved in 20-ms steps, along the retraction gesture. In this display (Figure 7.12) a 20-ms step is achieved by stopping on one of the two fields (or frame, each with an image number) of the video full image (the missing lines being restored by linear interpolation). We tested identification with front and profile angle views. So we have a set of four tests: front "Hue hisse," profile "Hue hisse," front "Huis," and profile "Huis." For each test, the ten gated sequences were presented in random order.

To test whether there could be an effect of perceptual expectancy towards the more dynamic component of the glide (as in our preceding experiment, cf. Cathiard *et al.* 1998), we manipulated the form of the instructions. In one case, a "dynamic" linguistic instruction was given where the subject was asked to identify the gated stimuli as "T'as dit: Hue?" or "T'as dit: Huis?." In the other instruction type, a "static" instruction was given where the subject was asked to identify the gated stimuli as "T'as dit: Hue?" or "T'as dit: Hue hisse?." The motivation behind this instruction manipulation was the following: Does the subject take more advantage of movement when he/she expects a rather dynamic lip configuration (as it is the case for the "dynamic" instruction, with which the subject is prepared to identify a *glide*), than when he/she expects a rather stable lip configuration (with the "static" instruction, with which the subject is prepared to identify a *vowel*)?

Stimulus, instruction order, and angle view were counterbalanced for each subject. As in our preceding experiment, we obtained no significant effect of angle view (see Cathiard *et al.* 1998, for a comment). We therefore mixed the results for front and profile views. The identification curves obtained for each group for the two stimuli and the two instructions are given in Figure 7.14. Notice that the comparison of the two stimuli is made possible because the time-course of the two retraction phases are very similar and closely synchronized respective to the time reference of the last image (10) of the gating procedure. Moreover, the protrusion values for all ten images never differ by more than 6 percent, and the velocity and acceleration profiles are quite similar in both stimuli. We determined the visual boundaries (50 percent) of each curve by probit regression analyses. For the "Hue hisse" stimulus, in both groups, there is no significant difference between the two instructions (dynamic and static). So we pooled their data for further probit comparisons. For group 1, there is a significant difference between the stimuli ("Hue hisse" [Dyn. + Stat.] versus "Huis" [Dyn.]: $\Delta m = 1.0$, i.e., one image number or frame, $p < .05$; "Hue hisse" [Dyn. + Stat.] *versus* "Huis" [Stat.]: $\Delta m = 0.71$, $p < .05$). Moreover, the dynamic instruction gives the most advantage to the glide itself ("Huis" [Dyn.] *versus* "Huis" [Stat.]: $\Delta m = 0.41$, $p < .10$). Group 2 shows also an advantage for the glide, but only for the dynamic instruction ("Hue hisse" [Dyn. + Stat.] *versus* "Huis" [Dyn.]: $\Delta m = 0.75$, $p < .05$).

Figure 7.15 displays the results of our preceding experiment (Cathiard *et al.* 1998) with front and profile views pooled. After probit comparisons, we obtained the following pattern of results. There was no significant difference between the two instructions for the "Hue hisse" stimulus. But there was a significant difference between the two stimuli ("Hue hisse" [Dyn. + Stat.] *versus* "Huis" [Dyn.]: $\Delta m = 1.26$, $p < .05$; "Hue hisse" [Dyn. + Stat.] *versus* "Huis" [Stat.]: $\Delta m = 0.74$, $p < .05$); and a significant difference between the two instructions for the "Huis" stimulus ("Huis" [Dyn.] *versus* "Huis" [Stat.]: $\Delta m = 0.50$, $p < .05$).

In other terms, we can observe a pattern that is globally similar for the subjects in our preceding experiment and group 1 in this experiment, both being contrasting subjects (cf. pretest).

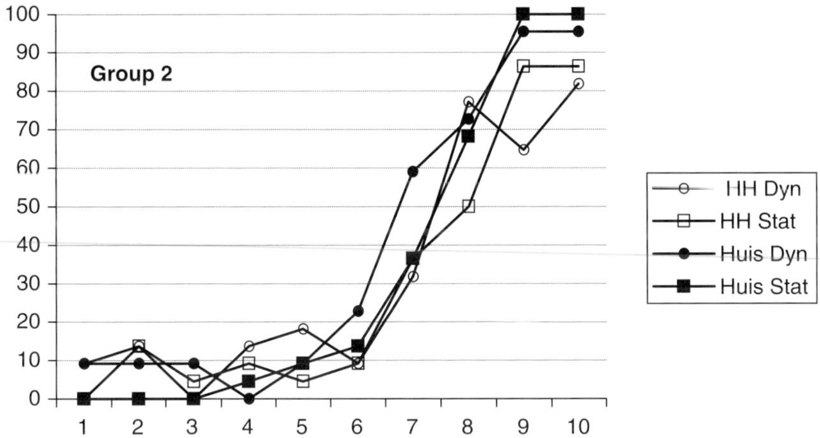

Figure 7.14 Identification curves obtained by contrasting subjects (group 1) compared with non-contrasting subjects (group 2) for "Hue hisse" (HH) and "Huis" (Huis) stimuli, with static (Stat) and dynamic (Dyn) instructions.

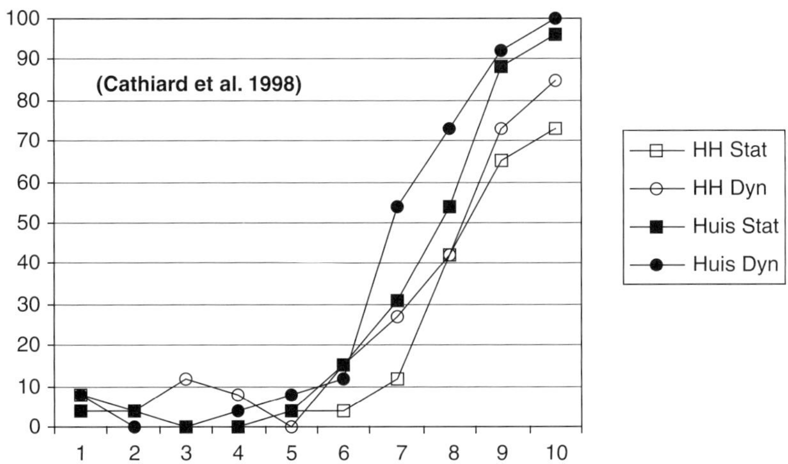

Figure 7.15 Identification curves obtained for "Hue hisse" (HH) and "Huis" (Huis) stimuli, with static (Stat) and dynamic (Dyn) instructions.

7.4.2.6 The glide versus vowel contrast: conclusions The three questions we asked about visual perception were answered as follows. (1) We found that half of our French subjects (sixteen of twenty-seven) were good at identifying the phonological contrast between the vowel [y] versus the glide [ɥ]. This is the same proportion we found previously (thirteen out of twenty-seven subjects in Cathiard *et al.* 1998). This corresponds to the weak linguistic status of the contrast in the French-speaking community. (2) The length of the steady-state portion of the vowel compared to the glide – tested by varying the plateau duration in rounding – was taken into account by all subjects in the present experiment, but it was a psychophysical rather than a categorical processing. (3) When tested on a specific phase, the off-gliding phase, i.e., the retraction event and the glide constriction phase, only the contrasting subjects were able to demonstrate an advantage for the true glide stimulus whatever the attentional linguistic instruction. Moreover, they showed a possible dynamic expectancy advantage for this very stimulus. These contrasting subjects, in this experiment, showed the same pattern as the group we tested in our preceding experiment (Cathiard *et al.* 1998), where we kept only the contrasting subjects. In addition, in the present experiment, we were able to demonstrate that even non-contrasting subjects benefited from dynamic expectation. But in contrast with contrasting subjects, they needed to be oriented by such an expectation in order to take advantage of the gliding nature of the stimulus. So whatever the contrasting skill of the subjects, the off-gliding margin seems to confer an advantage in identifying the vowel/glide contrast; but under a specific perceptual control, that is expectation.

7.4.2.7 Glide boundaries, or why transitions can be misleading Whatever the stimuli and conditions, subjects were able to detect the presence of the following [i] vowel at about the time of glide minimum area, i.e., when constriction area increases again towards the following [i] vowel. This means that the perceptual [y]/[i] boundary is at about the glide constriction phase. The consequence is that there is a fundamental asymmetry between the on-gliding [i]/[y] boundary and the off-gliding [y]/[i] boundary. In this off-gliding phase, the decrease in area constriction is misleading, since even if protrusion decrease (retraction) is an index of [y] unshaping, area decrease cannot be an index of an unrounded vowel such as [i]. So we have a clear case where a dynamic margin is not a monotonic input to information processing about the category of the up-coming vowel (whereas in the [i]/[y] on-gliding phase the visible margin is increasingly informative of [y]).

Such an asymmetry can be accounted for by the 2-Comp-Vowel model and brings constraints to the time-course of perception; it is not possible to explain asymmetrical results in V-to-V perception of the up-coming vowel without taking into account the natural organization of speech events. This is another perceptual benefit from such production modeling.

7.4.2.8 When are visual dynamics needed? From our preceding results we can conclude that dynamic margins cannot be said to be more informative than climaxes unless their temporal and configurational organization is analyzed.

When such a glide epenthesis occurs in a V-to-V transition – this possibility is generally predicted by the 2-Comp-Vowel model – this transition can be misleading for a significant portion of time. And for a true glide for which the dynamic margins are a priori crucial, only half of the subjects are able to visually distinguish this glide versus a vowel at first. So the skill to use current dynamic margin contrasts is still limited to a subset of the linguistic population. The fact that we can, under proper conditioning, i.e., by expectancy pressure, improve this contrast perception (even for unskilled subjects) adds to our understanding of the variability of such a skill. The use of the dynamic margin for the perception of contrasts, at least in visual speech, seems rather marginal, even when this gliding margin – initially a by-product of V-to-V transition in our 2-Comp-Vowel model – can be variably controlled, as in French, for a potential linguistic contrast. More generally such intrinsically variable control seems to be the destiny of epenthetic sounds. As speakers we have of course the potential to detect them, but this does not mean that we use them in linguistic interaction.

This conclusion is in agreement with our previous research stance that not everything in speech is movement. This is precisely what we argued when we proposed to account for our pattern of results in the on-gliding phase of rounding, by suggesting that the visual vowel shape could be a possible representational format, whereas movement would be just a help in recovering shape, when this shape is undersampled, or not optimally viewed. More generally, we argue that not every phase of speech in movement is automatically processed as such (but it remains possible that some movement phases are processed as such, e.g. plosive release movement?). Hence the status of margin does not *ipso facto* confer a perceptual bonus, from the simple fact of being dynamic, and so-called steady-state centers are not de facto less informative for sound identification. This is different from the pervasive Gibsonian time-varying claim, and it is also different from claiming that all is static in speech. It should be remembered that, since a steady-state command can dynamically produce movement (see voicing and trills in Abry *et al.* 1998), we must not neglect the neural mechanisms dedicated to recovering steady shapes from motion, as demonstrated abundantly for vision (e.g. Bradley *et al.* 1998), if not for sound. Until then, one will wonder how babies spontaneously develop audible and visible raspberries . . .

7.5 Conclusion and perspectives

Around 1680–1681, Giovanni Alfonso Borelli published *De motu animalium* (*Romæ, ex typographia Angeli Bernabò*). After having decisively considered – in his *Theoricæ Medicæorum Planetarum ex causis physicis deductæ* (*Florentiæ, ex typographia S.D.M.*, 1666, where he analyzed the motion of the four so-called Medicis' planets of Jove) – that celestial motions and terrestrial ones had to be unified (*pace* the Aristotelian view of a sublunarian disorder without *nomos*), this true heir to Galileo in Pisa applied mechanics to muscle force (as levers) for locomotion, flight, and swimming, in a project to transform Biology into a true branch of Physics and Mathematics.

Since then, Movement Control Science has settled in Biocybernetics as well as in Biorobotics. In this connection, in order to achieve stability in the embedding of multiple non-linear control systems, as proposed above for speech, a very promising property is *contraction* (Slotine and Lohmiller 2001). A non-linear dynamic system is said to be *contractant* if it "forgets" exponentially its initial conditions, and returns quickly to its nominal behavior. This offers a solution to a major problem that could confront our proposal of embedding systems developmentally. For even if our isolated systems were stable, overall stability is not guaranteed when the systems are combined. But if they satisfy the *contraction* property, it can be demonstrated that this property will be maintained in any serial, parallel, or hierarchical combination of such contractant systems. Stability theory clearly addresses the possibility that the intermediate cerebellum (a good candidate for learning internal models) may achieve stability through a *wave variable processor* (Massaquoi and Slotine 1996), in other words a virtual mechanical beam (rod) model transmitting waves with different delays, like the different fast and slow loops of the brain, giving for free the inherent beam stability.

From a related perceptual point of view, biological motion is now a new agenda for the brain. The MT/V5 area has been shown to be active for motion, as well as apparent motion (Stevens *et al.* 2000), illusory motion (Tootell *et al.* 1995), imagined motion (O'Craven *et al.* 1997), and implied motion in static images (Kourtzi and Kanwisher 2000). In a review of the social significance of biological motion, Allison and colleagues (2000, p. 275) pointed to the fact that, in addition to proper motion of bodies or body parts, "the human S[uperior] T[emporal] S[ulcus] region is activated by static views of eyes, mouths [gurning and lipreading, see Campbell, Calvert, and MacSweeney this volume], hands and faces. Thus static views might activate the STS region when they imply motion. However, many of these stimuli do not imply motion in any obvious way." Hence, to quote the Theory-of-Mind approach of Gallagher *et al.* (2000), "this region is sensitive not merely to biological motion but, more generally, to stimuli which signal intentions or intentional activity". At least two other regions that are concerned with the understanding of observation/imitation of intentional actions can be added: in the premotor-Broca region and in the parietal upper and lower lobes. Dubeau and colleagues (2002) added to the somatotopy launched by Rizzolatti and colleagues' "mirror neurons" (Rizzolatti *et al.* 1996b; Rizzolatti *et al.* 2000) for the understanding of intentional action by body parts, and proposed a network. Dubbing their proposal, when observing a mouth action, we will dub STS as answering to "you dig *what* it is?," the parietal cortex to "you feel *how* it is to do that?," and the frontal one to "just do it the *way* you can!," reafferenting to STS for intersensory coordination of self-monitoring.

In our cumulative view of motion in science, the agenda starts from old and new questions. Even the smallest creatures that are visible with the naked eye – as when the seventeenth-century French philosopher, Pascal, exemplified the infinitely small with "cirons," i.e., acarians on Savoy cheese "tomme" – can make us hesitate as to whether we perceive agentive movement of small bugs or aerial movement of dust. And this is still a problem encountered by the Theory of Mind in Cog's robotic agent for leaves in the wind (Scassellati 2001). Let's just quote a series of seminal failures in activating brain regions which detect agentive motion: a bar making the same movement as a hand (no STS: Perrett *et al.* 1989); a virtual hand display, in spite of being driven by a real hand (Decety *et al.* 1994; as criticised by Rizzolatti *et al.* 1996b, p. 249); a mechanical grip instead of a hand (no infant imitation: Meltzoff 1995); mirror neurons non activated for a grooming proposal played on a TV screen, instead of a live performance, for a macaque monkey (Fogassi 2002, pers. comm.) . . . A few years ago the most famous virtual talking head, Baldi, failed to replicate the classic McGurk illusion: no [da] percept for audio [ba] dubbed on visual [ga] (Massaro 1998a). It was in fact a replication of the failure of Summerfield and colleagues (1989), which could have been attributed at the time to the skeletal caricature of the vector-graphic display (no wire + Gouraud). Not the least instructive point of this story is that Summerfield *et al.* finally succeeded with such a poor synthesis, but only after having exposed their subjects to real McGurk displays. Rosenblum and Saldaña (1998) suffered the same mishap with a twenty-eight point-light display. It should not be forgotten that this two-stage procedure – real, then artificial – is the best way of convincing subjects to process sinewave speech as speech. Consequently, embedded benchmark tests (more articulated than simple "believability") for motion processing in speech AV synthesizers could comprise, for both audio and visual motion signals (tactile, say haptic ones in Tadoma), illusion production and/or brain imaging of:

- naïve physical motion;
- naïve biological motion;
- face motion (if specific);
- talking face motion (if specific).
- It is clear that the McGurk illusion is an ultimate challenge for artifacts that would fail to allow the human brain to integrate visual velocity and auditory motion (our proposal in Cathiard *et al.* 2001).

As regards the processing of fine phonetic details for control, detecting very small areas at the lips corresponding to no plosive regime is crucial even for simple computer puppetry. Otherwise your talking head would utter meaninglessly, "Et pubis Rubis Blas subtil marché . . ." (and pubis Ruby Blas subtle trade), instead of the intended, "Et puis Ruy Blas sût-il marcher?" (and then could Ruy Blas walk?). More specifically, as concerns the control and perception of the time-course of V-to-V gestures through C – with a general glide phenomenon "the power effect" (misleading only for those who think that any movement in the transition is the real vowel identity) – our proposals lead us to investigate why, as long as the consonant is there, labial glides are not producing regular McGurk combinations,[7] something like "Tu vdis" or "povtere"?

Visible glides at closures generally give rise to labial consonants only once the plosives have disappeared (for a brief presentation of the experimental test of what we dubbed the "Power McGurk effect," see Cathiard and Abry 2007). The time-course of glides probably counts for something in this trend of "phonological neglect."

These considerations encourage us in our endeavor to explain the main phenomenon which has been of interest in this chapter: how can a ripple in the flow of lip movements give rise to an island in the brain's word memory with such potential power?

7.6 Post-scriptum

The brain imaging agenda we called for just above has begun to be fulfilled. Santi *et al.* (2003) showed that perception of point-light locomotion activated different motor areas from point-light visible speech, which involved, somatotopically, Broca's "mouth" area (see Buccino *et al.* 2001, for a "mirror neuron" account). As regards the static/dynamic issue in visible speech perception we can now take advantage of what seems for us to be the major result in Calvert and Campbell (2003): namely that the network for processing static views (i) is fully included within the dynamic one (which is much larger), and (ii) is left lateralized (unlike the bilateral dynamic one); as in Santi *et al.* (2003) it activates the Broca region. Taken together these results show that a speech – left lateralized – circuit for body parts ("mouth-face") is recruited whenever a linguistic lip shape has to be recognized, i.e. understood; a shape recovered by a structure-from-motion processing in moving point-light displays; whereas full-image motion necessitates a common bilateral processing in order to extract from the flow the shape to be processed by, say, the speech mirror action-understanding system. For a neurocomputational implementation of shape and motion integration, see Giese and Poggio (2003) and for the priority of shape in aperture processing, see Lorenceau and Alais (2001).

7.7 Acknowledgments

Marie-Agnès Cathiard thanks Christian Abry for having led this work with her, since the beginning of the writing of this chapter in 1999, then during its updating from January 2010 until the final corrections in December 2011.

8 Visual and audiovisual synthesis and recognition of speech by computers

N. M. Brooke and S. D. Scott

8.1 Overview

It is now a little while since the authors last worked in this area. One (NMB), has now retired, having entered the field when only a handful of researchers around the world were working in visual speech; the other (SDS), who has now moved into new areas of work, became involved in the field when statistical methods were becoming increasingly powerful and useful. During the period of their research activity, the power, speed, and capabilities of computer systems and computer graphics were increasing very rapidly and their cost was simultaneously falling. There was consequently a shift away from the identification of facial features whose movements could be used to represent and model the visual cues to speech and towards the processing and use of facial images themselves. The increased complexity and volume of data that had to be handled was offset by using statistically based methods to identify and represent those characteristics of the images that might be applied to synthesize and recognize visual speech events. Some of these studies also suggested that a relatively small set of parameters might characterize the dimensionality of the space that separated specific speech events, though their physical and anatomical nature generally remained somewhat obscure. During the same period, the growth of the Internet and of local networks has generated new applications for audiovisual speech synthesis and recognition whilst at the same time eliminating others.

There are many new techniques for exploring human speech production and for developing new approaches to audiovisual processing, including, for example, fMRI. On the other hand, there are other areas that remain relatively unchanged or intractable. Thus, for example, there is still no comprehensive catalogue of facial features or points whose behaviour can fully define, or, alternatively, distinguish the set of visual speech events. Speakers differ greatly in their visible articulatory gestures and this is one of the main obstacles to progress. However, some speakers' visible gestures are known to be easier to understand than others and this may offer a way forward. The paralinguistic gestures, involving the face, head, and body are still incompletely understood, despite the advances that have been made in this area. For example, as this chapter indicates, very simple modelling appears to be very successful in synthesizing the visual effects of speech embodying major head movements. Like the lip gestures themselves, however, many paralinguistic gestures may be small, short-lived, and subtle. The problem in the visual domain is compounded by the partial or intermittent invisibility of some of the visual features, which only complex, intrusive, and expensive methods, like micro-beam X-radiography can reveal fully. Additionally, there may be significant difficulties in relating surface activity on the face to the underlying musculature and its changes. Measurements of the visible movements of particular, identifiable points at the skin surface, for example, around the lips themselves, are unlikely to bear a simple relationship to the underlying muscular changes.

Visual coarticulation effects are known to exist in speech production and the integration of the audio and visual signals, especially in recognition, also remains an interesting area because it is clear that there can be modal asynchronies in the audio and the visual signals which may be complex and temporally extended, certainly beyond phone boundaries and possibly further and both phenomena are likely to be a continuing focus for attention. One of the most successful early models for recognition that takes account of audiovisual asynchrony is described in this chapter. Conversely, the synthesis of facial gestures using an acoustic speech signal as the driver also presents interesting challenges, since it can lead to one-to-many mappings. That is, a single acoustic output may arise from several possible articulatory gestures. In spite of this, it is possible to associate at least some acoustic speech signals with facial measurements. At the same time, the existence of the McGurk effect reinforces the importance of 'getting it right', since mismatched audio and video cues can convey a third, quite different, audiovisual percept.

One major advance for research into visual and audiovisual speech synthesis and recognition is the greatly increased availability of well-defined and agreed corpora of speech data that can be used to compare and assess objectively the performance of synthesizers and recognizers. This marks a very great advance on the situation that pertained when the very early TULIPS corpus appeared. There are, however, still major issues concerning the detailed specification of corpora for particular purposes. For example, the effects of different lighting conditions and angles of view, as well as the controlled construction of multi-speaker corpora, in particular, remain to be fully evolved. Performance measures for synthesis and recognition are also still developing; is it, for example, still appropriate to choose human performance as a measurement baseline, as suggested in this chapter?

The current chapter is concerned to a large extent with the work from the early stages of the field to the point in the new millennium at which significant advances were being made using image data and statistical techniques. It is primarily intended to indicate, therefore, how we got to be where we are now. Some of the issues and problems have now been resolved and others have not. This chapter is therefore intended to complement the other contributions to this volume; it is for the reader to determine which issues remain to be dealt with and which have now been either partially or, indeed, fully resolved. There is still much that needs to be done, including, importantly, continuing analytical experiments in audiovisual speech perception that will support the development of synthesizers and recognizers. It is offered with the hope and wish that our successors will be successful in their endeavours.

8.2 The historical perspective

8.2.1 Visual speech processing and early approaches

One of the prime motivations for the processing of visual speech signals arose from the need to investigate and understand better the nature of speechreading, so that the rehabilitation of the hearing-impaired could be improved. The face is the visible, external termination of the human speech production system, whose articulatory gestures can convey useful cues to production events and, in particular, to the place of articulation of speech sounds. Although the visible gestures by no means uniquely identify individual speech events (Summerfield 1987), the benefits of seeing the face of a speaker, especially where there is noise or hearing-impairment (Sumby and Pollack 1954; Erber 1975), can nonetheless be worthwhile, as the hearing-impaired have of course known for many years. The benefit has been estimated to be equivalent to an increase in the signal-to-noise ratio of about 10–12 dB when identifying words in a sentence uttered against a noise background (MacLeod and Summerfield 1987).

Studying speechreading was severely constrained by the inability to carry out analytical investigations using controlled continua of natural stimuli. Speakers are not able to vary the articulatory gestures of speech in a controllable way and some experiments may even require the presentation of stimuli that cannot be naturally produced by a human speaker. An example of the latter included an experiment to investigate the role of the teeth in the visual identification of the vowel in a range of /bVb/ utterances, using stimuli that were visually identical apart from the presence or absence of the teeth (McGrath *et al.* 1984; Summerfield *et al.* 1989). Animated computer graphics displays of speech movements of the face are in principle capable of overcoming all of these difficulties. One very early attempt at visual speech synthesis used Lissajou's figures displayed on an oscilloscope to simulate lip movements and was probably also the first to be driven by a speech signal (Boston 1973). Controllable syntheses could, however, be achieved more flexibly and easily by using computer graphics simulations of talking faces. The ready availability of relatively cheap, general purpose mini-computers that were powerful enough to create such computer graphics prompted the development of some of the earliest visual speech synthesizers (e.g. Brooke 1982; Montgomery and Hoo 1982; Brooke 1989).

Most of the early visual speech synthesizers were simple vector graphics animated displays of outline diagrams of the main facial articulators, namely, the lips, teeth, and jaw. Very high performance computers were prohibitively expensive for all but the most specialized applications and most general purpose computers were capable only of approximately one million operations per second. The generation of up to ten thousand separate vectors per second, which was the rate needed to create the early visual speech synthesizers, therefore represented a fairly severe requirement. Although it was well known at the time that the teeth and tongue could convey important visual cues, for example, to the identity of vowels, these articulators were difficult to simulate with vector graphics. The teeth posed a problem because they were only intermittently or partially visible and required an effective hidden-line removal algorithm in order to be displayed accurately. The tongue was almost impossible to display because it usually appeared as an indistinct area, rather than as an outline shape. Raster graphics systems were able to generate much more realistic, rendered displays of the human head, but were very expensive (typically ten times the cost of a vector graphics system). In addition, fully rendered animated displays required significantly longer and were significantly more complex to generate than vector graphics displays, which could themselves take over 20 times realtime for the creation of short 'copy' syntheses (syntheses in which the gestures were driven directly from measurements of a human utterance). Nonetheless, a forerunner of the modern visual speech synthesizers had already been developed by the mid 1970s (Parke 1975) and the approach was quickly developed to display facial expressions (e.g. Platt and Badler 1981). The state of visual speech synthesis in the early 1990s has been more fully reviewed elsewhere (Brooke 1992a; Brooke 1992b).

The apparently modest gain that results from seeing a speaker's facial gestures when speech is uttered in a noisy background acquires greater significance when it is realized that changes in the signal-to-noise ratio of a speech signal from −6 dB to +6 dB represent an improvement in word intelligibility from about 20 percent to 80 percent (e.g. MacLeod and Summerfield 1987). Acoustic cues to the place of articulation tend to be easily destroyed by acoustic noise because they are dependent upon phonetic context and upon low intensity, short duration signals usually associated with fine spectral details at the higher frequencies. Acoustic cues to the manner of articulation, however, tend to be associated with relatively slowly changing, spectrally strong features of the acoustic signal at the lower frequencies that are resistant to corruption by noise (Summerfield 1987). The acoustic and visual signals of speech therefore tend to complement each other so that, for example, if both are used together in speech recognition, speech intelligibility in noise should be enhanced. Indeed, human audiovisual speech recognition performance is better than either audio or visual performance in acoustically noisy conditions (Adjoudani and Benoît 1996). This immediately suggests an important potential application for the enhancement of conventional, automatic speech recognition in noisy environments. Automatic visual speech recognition began to develop in the 1980s, when image capture hardware and software capable of capturing the dynamic facial gestures from successive frames of film or video recordings became available. One of the earliest devices was Petajan's visual recognition system, which used special-purpose hardware to capture binary black and white images of the oral region in realtime (Petajan 1984). This device typified many later recognition systems in using image data to extract a relatively small number of time-varying facial features such as the width and height of the lip aperture and the area of the oral cavity. In the 1980s these were used as templates for matching the characteristics of test utterances with libraries of reference templates from the utterances forming the vocabulary of the recognizer (Petajan *et al.* 1988a; Petajan *et al.* 1988b). The main objective of the early prototypical recognition systems was to establish the benefits that were available from the use of visual speech signals. As Section 8.4.4 shows, this issue remains incompletely resolved.

8.2.2 Digital image processing and the data-driven approach

One of the main challenges facing automatic visual speech processing has been to develop the ability to process the quantity of information represented by continuous sequences of moving images within a useable time scale. The synthesis of TV-quality, full-screen colour images, for example, requires the generation of millions of bits of information per second. The data processing rate needed for image capture and analysis was also a problem in early recognition systems and was usually dealt with by extracting feature information from oral images, even when special-purpose hardware began to be available for image capture in realtime (e.g. Petajan 1984). However, it is not always possible to describe all of the important visible information in terms of simple parameters and, despite some early studies (Finn 1986), there is still no comprehensive catalogue describing the facial features that are relevant to speechreading.

By the second half of the 1980s digital image processing equipment was becoming more widely accessible and processor speeds were rapidly increasing through the megahertz range. Fully rendered facial images displayed on raster graphics devices had supplanted the earlier vector graphics and several software packages had been implemented (e.g. Yau and Duffy 1988; Saintourens *et al.* 1990; Terzopoulos and Waters 1990). It also became possible to process images directly. For the first time, data-driven synthesis and, more especially, recognition that did not involve pre-selection of relevant features became a real option. For example, visual speech recognizers were reported that used automatic image processing to follow movements of the lower facial region by detecting the differences between successive images, or by computing optical flows (e.g. Nishida 1986; Pentland and Mase 1989).

One early application of image processing was the use of chroma-key methods to extract lip parameters from video recordings of the face of a speaker, as described in Section 8.3.1 below. Another study from the same period involved the processing of video recordings of the oral region of a speaker enunciating five long vowels in a /hVd/ context. The image sequences were processed to create moving images of the speaker at different spatial and grey-level resolutions (Brooke and Templeton 1990). These were used as visual stimuli in a vowel identification experiment. For this very simple vowel set, the results suggested that images of low resolution (about 16 × 16 pixels and eight grey levels) adequately captured the essential visual cues to vowel identity. The experiment was helpful in setting an approximate lower bound on the amount of data that images had to embody if speechreading was to be possible. To capture even these minimal, low-resolution monochrome video images at the standard 25 frames per second implied the storage of about 20 000 bits per second. For both synthesis and recognition, there is also a lower limit to the frame rate beneath which significant visual information is lost (Pearson and Robinson 1985; Frowein *et al.* 1991). Normal video recording rates (25 frames, or 50 fields per second) are above this lower limit.

The greater computing power of the 1980s also marked the emergence of new, statistically oriented data-processing methods that were proving extremely successful in pattern-recognition tasks, including conventional acoustic speech recognition. The techniques included the so-called Artificial Neural Networks (ANNs) and the class of finite state machines known as hidden Markov models. These have been described elsewhere (e.g. Rabiner 1989b; Beale and Jackson 1990). Both are well suited to data-driven processing as they can build an internal description of images of a speaker's visible gestures without needing a detailed description or understanding either of the nature of the gestures, or how they arise. Images can be treated at the lowest level purely as arrays of pixels.

One form of ANN, the Multi-Layer Perceptron (or MLP), was swiftly applied to visual speech processing. MLPs consist of layers of rather simple processing units. Every unit at each layer generates inputs to all the units of the layer above and the connections can be weighted. These weightings, together with the bias parameters that typically define the properties of each of the processing units, can be adjusted. Given a starting set of random values, the parameters can be successively refined by a training process. In a typical training process, many examples of 'labelled' patterns are presented as input to the first layer of units and the MLP parameters are reiteratively adjusted, using a standard algorithm, until the output units generate the correct labels for each input pattern. The output units usually form an encoder in which, conceptually, one unit produces an output for each specific label and all other units give no output. MLPs can thus 'learn' to generate internal mappings between sets of inputs and outputs during the training process (e.g. Elman and Zipser 1986). One very early use of a three-layer MLP in visual speech processing was to find a mapping between single, 16 × 16 pixel, monochrome images of the oral region of a speaker captured at the nuclei of the three vowels that lie at the corners of the vowel triangle. Once trained, the MLP was used to determine the vowel class labels for previously unseen test images (Peeling *et al.* 1986). Only two processing units were needed in the intermediate layer of the trained MLP. Since this layer is a gateway through which input data passes to the output units, it effectively holds an encoded internal representation of the vowel images and this result suggested that the essential visual cues to vowel identity could be captured by a very small number of parameters. A second MLP-based experiment shortly afterwards (Brooke and Templeton 1990) showed that a machine with just six processing units in the intermediate layer could be trained to identify vowels using 16 × 12 pixel monochrome images of a speaker captured at the nuclei of the eleven non-diphthongal British English vowels in a /bVb/ context. Overall performance was 91 percent correct vowel identification and, for the worst case individual vowel class, 84 percent correct identification. Once again, the real importance of these results was the indication that visual cues to vowel identity could be retained in images of relatively low resolution and, furthermore, that additional significant gains in image compression could be gained by noting that the essential cues could be internally encoded by the MLP with a very small number of parameters.

Whilst MLPs suggested the possibility of further image compression, they were not particularly stable coders; small changes in images could produce large changes in the MLPs' internal representations and vice versa. A well-established statistical technique, Principal Components Analysis, or PCA (Flurry 1988), proved more stable and was potentially at least as efficient in compressing image data as MLPs (Anthony *et al.* 1990). PCA transforms a pattern space into a new space in which as much of the variance of the original data as possible is accounted for by as small a number of axes, or principal components, as possible. Images of the articulatory movements of the face, which is a highly constrained anatomical structure, should show a high degree of structuring. One of the earliest examples of this approach to facial image encoding was reported in 1991 (Turk and Pentland 1991). An independent preliminary experiment also originally reported in 1991 (Brooke and Tomlinson 2000) established the validity of using PCA to compress and encode monochrome oral images of a speaker's gestures. When PCA was performed on approximately 15 000 monochrome oral images of a speaker uttering digit triples, captured at a resolution of 32 × 24 pixels, it was found that about 80 percent of the variance was captured by just

15 principal components (the uncompressed 32 × 24 pixel monochrome images correspond to points in a 768-dimensional space). Given a representative set of training images, it is possible to use the computed principal components to compress similar test images. Results from perceptual tests on the speech readability of monochrome oral images of spoken digit triples reconstructed from a PCA-encoded format showed that the use of more than 15 components did not significantly improve the visual intelligibility of the images (Brooke and Scott 1994b). In one unpublished project (Brooke, Fiske, and Scott), PCA performed on two-dimensional images of the outer lip margins during unrestricted speech production also suggested that two components sufficed to describe their varying contours, a finding consistent with one animated lip model, which uses three parameters to model full three-dimensional movements (Guiard-Marigny *et al.* 1996). A later, multistage variant of PCA was also successfully developed (Brooke and Scott 1998a). It involved dividing images into sub-blocks, PCA encoding each of the sub-blocks and then applying PCA a second time to the coded versions of all of the sub-blocks. This method was used to compress the data from a corpus of sentence utterances video recorded in colour (see Section 8.3.1 below). PCA has been widely used to reduce the dimensionality of data that arises in visual speech processing (e.g. Welsh and Shah 1992; Goldschen *et al.* 1996; Vatikiotis-Bateson *et al.* 1999).

Another technique used to reduce the dimensionality of video image data for audiovisual speech recognition is discrete cosine transforms. In the work carried out by Potamianos *et al.* (Potamianos *et al.* 2001a; Gravier *et al.* 2002b), the size and position of the speaker's mouth in video fields, captured at a rate of 60 Hz, was estimated using face-tracking algorithms. The portions of the video fields containing the mouth were then extracted and size-normalized to 64 × 64 pixels. A two-dimensional, separable discrete cosine transform (DCT) was applied to these normalized mouth images and the twenty-four highest-energy DCT coefficients were stored for each image. Linear interpolation was then applied to the stored features to derive sets of visual coefficients that corresponded to the audio coefficients (100 Hz). Finally, changes in lighting conditions were dealt with by applying feature mean normalization to the sets of linear interpolated coefficients. The reader can find in Potamianos *et al.* (this volume) recognition experiments where this DCT technique is compared to PCA.

Although ANNs can be used to handle time-varying speech patterns (Stork *et al.* 1992; Bregler *et al.* 1993; Lavagetto and Lavagetto 1996; Krone *et al.* 1997), a second type of model, though a very poor representation of the speech production process, has proved to be very successful in speech recognition tasks. It comprises the finite state machines known as hidden Markov models (HMMs). HMMs can embody the time-varying properties of real speech signals and are also able to capture their inherent variability (Rabiner 1989a). HMMs describe each speech event (whether a word, phone or sub-phone element) as a synchronous finite state machine that begins in a starting state then changes state and generates an output pattern for each tick of a clock until it reaches an end state. The properties of the machine are determined by its parameters, which are the set of transition probabilities that govern the likelihood of a particular state succeeding any other, plus a set of state-dependent probability density functions that determine the probability of a particular state generating any one from the set of all possible output patterns. In conventional acoustic speech recognition, each output pattern is a vector that describes the short-term characteristics of the speech signal, for example, as a set of short-term cepstral coefficients. The clock period of HMMs is conventionally equivalent to the frame rate of the short-term observations. The HMM parameters can be computed by presenting the model for each unit in the recognizer's vocabulary with corresponding examples of real speech signals, in the form of sets of pattern vectors. The model parameters are then reiteratively adjusted, using standard algorithms, starting from a set of initial parameter estimates. The recognition process consists in identifying the trained HMM most likely to have generated an unknown test signal. It is possible to build HMMs that represent each phone in the context of its preceding and succeeding phone; these so-called 'triphone' models can help to account for coarticulatory effects. Additionally, since the pattern vectors that HMMs use can be modified very easily, HMMs are well suited to visual speech recognition and to audiovisual recognition simply by replacing or augmenting the conventional, acoustic pattern vectors with a suitable vector to describe the visual features of the speech event. Some pattern vectors use extracted feature values (e.g. Adjoudani and Benoît 1996; Goldschen *et al.* 1996; Jourlin *et al.* 1997; Tamura *et al.* 1998), rather than the image data itself, in a suitably compressed and encoded form, as described earlier in this section and in Section 8.4.4 below.

Both ANNs and HMMs require considerable amounts of training data and a great deal of computational power, especially in the training phase. The resources to deal with these requirements became steadily more abundant during the latter part of the 1980s, which therefore marked a period during which there was an upsurge in visual speech processing. The recognition phase when using trained ANNs and HMMs is relatively light on computing resources. In MLPs, for example, the content and structure of the images presented to a trained machine make no difference to the processing time. Consequently, it became practicable to undertake more demanding applications in audiovisual speech synthesis and recognition as explained in Section 8.4.

8.2.3 *Redefining the goals of visual speech processing*

By the early 1990s, the benefits of visual speech processing were generally recognized and visual speech processing was moving from pilot studies of techniques towards practicable and challenging applications. In speech recognition, work has been focused on capturing, encoding, and integrating visual speech with its audio component to permit robust recognition in noisy environments where, for example, hands-free control of devices is required. In speech synthesis, work has focused on building interactive applications. One such application is the teaching of speechreading by allowing an instructor to generate training material for private use, with the system adapting the training material presented to a learner in response to the learner's progress (Cole *et al.* 1999). Another application is a computer information system controlled by interaction with a complete, computer-generated, virtual humanoid capable of responding to input by the user, via speech and vision (Cassell *et al.* 2000). Given the importance of the head and face to such applications, they have become the prime foci for recent research.

8.3 Heads, faces, and visible speech signals

The head has a complex three-dimensional structure capable of quasi-rotational global movements in three dimensions relative to the rest of the body. These can be informally characterized as head shaking, head nodding, and head tilting, though there is not a simple centre of rotation. In addition, the head is carried on the body, whose movements are therefore superimposed on those of the head itself. The face is also a complex anatomical structure whose tissues possess great mobility and elasticity. In the simplest terms, the surface layers are underlaid by a complex musculature through which they are attached to the rigid bone of the skull. At least thirteen separate groups of muscles are involved in movements of the lips alone (Hardcastle 1976), but many more muscles are involved in the generation of the full range of facial expressions. The latter have been classified and characterized in terms of the actions of the muscle groups in the Facial Action Coding System (Ekman and Friesen 1978).

Not only are the visible gestures of the primary speech articulators therefore complex and subtle, they are normally accompanied by many secondary gestures of the face and indeed of the body, including changes in facial expression and body posture or movements. These are discussed in Section 8.3.2, below. They can all convey important speech cues; often they have less to do with the phonetic content than with the speaker's meaning and intention, that is, they are related more to the understanding of speech than its recognition (see for example, Dittmann 1972; Ekman and Friesen 1978; Ekman 1979; Ekman and Oster 1979). They also play a part in dialogue. Visible, non-verbal cues may even be made in response to a speaker, in order to direct the discourse. An example of this is the quizzical expression that a listener may use to prompt a speaker into giving further information.

However, knowledge about the nature and significance, even of head and body movements, let alone facial expression, during speech production is still far from complete. It is, however, at least conceivable that inappropriate global movements and facial expressions could change the meaning or intention of an utterance in a way similar to that in which mismatched visual and acoustic cues to phonetic content can induce changed percepts (McGurk and MacDonald 1976). This has important implications for automatic visual speech synthesis, as discussed in Sections 8.4.2 and 8.4.4 below.

8.3.1 *Recording and measuring visible speech gestures*

Most of the earliest recordings of speakers' faces were captured on film (e.g. Fujimura 1961). In the 1970s, video recordings were becoming a cheaper alternative, despite having a lower spatial resolution and generally rather long frame exposure times that smeared rapid movements of the oral region (e.g. Brooke and Summerfield 1983). Video recordings were also difficult to handle because of the high cost and limited availability of the equipment that was needed to retrieve the individual fields or frames in sequence so that movements could be tracked. Short time intervals were necessary; 20 to 40 ms intervals were considered only just adequate for capturing the rapid consonantal articulations. Furthermore, the measurement and analysis of speech movements is difficult because the articulatory gestures (a) involve only small movements (the largest excursions rarely if ever exceed 25 mm and are often much smaller); and (b) are superimposed upon the global head and body movements which accompany natural speech. In the experiments conducted to date there has been a trade-off between the accuracy of the data gathered and the range of head and body movements or free facial expressions permitted to the speaker. Recordings have tended to concentrate on the primary visible articulations around the lower face that are most closely related to the phonetic content of an utterance. In some of the very early recordings, the speaker's head was clamped so that any visible movements could be ascribed to articulatory movements of the mouth region alone. This was hardly a way to capture 'natural' speech movements and later experiments allowed the speaker greater freedom of head movement. Where global head movement was permitted, a common strategy has been to track selected points on the head that are not involved in articulation and use their position to compensate for the global movements of the head (Brooke and Summerfield 1983). The tracking of these fixed points has the advantage that it permits the head position and orientation to be quantified so that the global movements and their relation to speech production could in principle be explored. Fixed points of this kind can, however, vary considerably from one individual to another and are not always marked by easily identified anatomical features. It can thus be difficult to establish an accurate reference frame for measurements when speakers are allowed to move freely. Another approach has been to create a 3D model of the speaker's head and then deform the model, through a set of parameters, until it matches the current image of the speaker (Eisert and Girod 1998). A third approach to the elimination of effects due to global head movements is to fix the camera relative to the head, for example, by using a head-mounted boom. Even then, however, there are still small but significant residual head movements relative to the camera. Petajan's 'nostril tracker' is an early example of tracking used in this situation (Petajan 1984). Contemporary recordings of speakers still tend to employ a front facial image and compensate for any global movements by assuming that they are small x and y translations that can be compensated by tracking the position of a few identifiable facial feature points (e.g. Brooke and Scott 1998b).

While many important articulatory gestures can be seen in frontal face images, others, such as lip protrusion, require observation of movements in all three dimensions. Simultaneous recording of movements in all three dimensions is not easy to achieve, especially if the subject is allowed complete freedom of movement. One early method (Brooke and Summerfield 1983) used a mirror angled at 45 degrees to capture simultaneously the front and side views of a speaker in a single recorded image. Usually the recordings involve the marking of points on the face, especially around the lips, lower face, and jaw. These techniques may be acceptable in analytical studies of speech production, but are unlikely ever to be appropriate in a practicable visual speech recognition system, which will probably use a single camera to observe the unmarked faces of speakers with at least a reasonable freedom of movement. Articulators that are only partially or intermittently visible, such as the teeth and the tongue, are known to convey important visual cues also. Their movements can be continuously recorded, but only by the use of very complex, expensive and specialized techniques such as X-ray microbeams, X-ray cineradiography, dynamic MRI, or ultrasound measurements (Perkell 1969; Fujimura 1982; Keller and Ostry 1983; Perkell and Nelson 1985; Echternach *et al.* 2008). These are frequently invasive, and involve the placement of targets at points in the internal vocal tract.

In the 1980s, video recording systems had improved and digital image processing techniques were more widely available. It became possible to collect and analyse facial speech movements using automatic techniques. These included the capture of binary oral images in realtime (Petajan 1984) from which lip contours could be derived, or the extraction of lip parameters from lips that had been painted a cyan colour so that they could be separated from skin tones by chroma-keying (Benoît *et al.* 1992). Large digital frame stores began to make possible the processing and storage of sequences of video-recorded images that could then be retrieved and replayed at normal video frame rates as described in Section 8.2.2 above. Given the increasing capacity of disc storage systems, the greater speed of modern processors, the widespread availability of relatively cheap and efficient digital colour video cameras, and access to very efficient video data compression tools such as MPEG coding, the capture of high-quality moving images of a speaker's face in timescales close to, or even at, realtime is now relatively straightforward. The high capacity of very cheap storage media such as CD-ROM allows large corpora of speech material embodying both video and audio recordings to be created and distributed. For example, 90 minutes of speech material consisting of a single speaker uttering 132 sentences from the SCRIBE corpus has been video recorded in colour at 50 fields (25 frames) per second, complete with audio sampled at 16 KHz. The digitized, 64 × 48-pixel colour images of the oral region were stored and the audio was encoded as the first 24 LPC cepstral coefficients, sampled at 20 ms intervals. All the audiovisual data could be held on just three CD-ROMs (Brooke and Scott 1998b).

Despite the remarkable advances in the technology for data capture, there are still no readily available, general-purpose tools for tracking either the global movements of the head or the topographical features. Automatic feature extraction remains non-trivial. For example, while the most sophisticated real-time tracking systems (e.g. Blake *et al.* 1993; Blake and Isard 1994; Dalton *et al.* 1996) can accurately find and follow changes in shape of the outer lip margins, the inner lip margins, which are known to convey important visual cues to speech (Plant 1980; Montgomery and Jackson 1983), are not so well defined and remain difficult to locate reliably. Also, tracking the variations in lip contours is not necessarily equivalent to tracking the movements of marked points on the face that represent specific locations on the skin surface. Facial surface features are not defined on a contour, except at a few clearly identifiable positions such as the lip corner. Thus, while contours may be an efficient descriptor for lip shapes, they may not be well suited for examining the effects of actions by the facial musculature on changes in configuration of the surface topography.

8.3.2 *Creating visual and audiovisual speech databases*

The main problem in recording speech data for use in audiovisual speech processing applications is agreeing on what kind of material should be captured and under what conditions. Without necessarily attempting to constrain the specific material, a generally-agreed-upon framework is important in order to establish at least the structure and size of a common database that can be used to compare objectively the results obtained, for example, from automatic audiovisual or visual speech recognition using different systems. This has been attempted and to a large extent achieved for conventional audio speech processing. For example, much confusion can be created by simple inconsistencies such as attempting to compare the results from isolated word and continuous audiovisual speech recognition systems (e.g. Brooke *et al.* 1994; Adjoudani and

Benoît 1996; Tomlinson *et al.* 1996). Also, many prototypical audiovisual speech recognition systems used corpora of training and test data, such as the TULIP database and its derivatives, that were really too small to be completely reliable for the assessment of recognition performance (e.g. Movellan and Chadderdon 1996; Matthews *et al.* 1998).

Even now, there is relatively little systematic data available to describe and classify the visible speech articulations, though some work has been done to identify the visemes (e.g. Benoît *et al.* 1992), which are the closest visual equivalent of the abstract sound classes known as phonemes. Just as phoneme sets are language-specific, it seems likely that viseme sets may be language-specific as well; but thus far, there are too few systematic studies available to draw any clear conclusions. It is even possible that the facial gestures for speech events whose production methods are similar may differ among native speakers of different languages. Furthermore, since speech production involves time-varying movements of many articulators that may possess different mechanical properties, like stiffness and inertia, there is not a single, fixed articulatory configuration associated with a particular speech sound. Rather, the vocal tract configurations for a particular speech event are affected by the sounds that precede and follow it. This effect is known as coarticulation and, not surprisingly, manifests itself in the visible, facial gestures as well as in the acoustic outputs of the vocal tract (Benguerel and Pichora-Fuller 1982; Bothe *et al.* 1993). Consequently, a database of speech material must include many samples of each phoneme in different phonetic contexts. An early study (Brooke and Summerfield 1983) employed VCV syllables in the context of the three vowels that lie at the corners of the vowel triangle (see Ladefoged 1975) and a series of /bVb/ and /hVd/ utterances. However, a comprehensive library with multiple samples of all phonemes in the context even of the two adjacent phonemes (in other words, the complete set of triphones) involves a very large database of samples and the coarticulatory effects can in fact extend across a much wider spread of neighbouring phonemes (Ladefoged 1975). Even 90 minutes of recordings of SCRIBE sentences (see Section 8.3.1) can cover only a small proportion of all the possible triphones. Multiple tokens are needed to take account of the natural variations in the productions of even a single speaker. However, recordings of multiple speakers also need to be made to study the inter-speaker variations in articulatory strategies and gestures that are known to exist (Montgomery and Jackson 1983). Until recently, these variations have seriously restricted the application of articulatory synthesis to the creation of acoustic speech signals, despite the potential attractiveness of early accurate and detailed articulatory models (e.g. Mermelstein 1973). Lately, however, there has been a revival in this area with work on fricative constants (Mawass *et al.* 2000; Beautemps *et al.* 2001), and biomechanical modelling of velar stops (Perrier *et al.* 2000).

Recordings of speakers' faces may be treated at one extreme as images whose coded representations define the specific gestures and configurations of the visible articulators. At the other extreme, they can be analysed to find the spatial positions of particular topographical features, such as the corners of the lips, for example. The simplest approach is to make front-facial video recordings under a fixed level of lighting from two sources close to either side of the camera and in the same horizontal plane as the nose, so as to minimize unwanted shadowing and asymmetry. In reality, however, speakers' heads may be presented under a range of lighting conditions and lighting conditions may vary even during short utterances. Similarly, whilst it is possible to make simple x- and y-corrections to measurements taken from different frames to compensate for the small head and body movements made by a speaker in controlled conditions, these corrections do not adequately compensate for the larger variations due to the changes in a speaker's head orientation and position with respect to the observer that can occur in natural speech. While lighting conditions may or may not interfere with techniques that search for and track facial points or features, they can have a large effect on the appearance of the facial image. Consequently, were PCA, for example, to be used to encode facial images (e.g. Brooke and Scott 1998b; Brooke and Tomlinson 2000), it might be expected that codes representing images of identical facial presentations in differing lighting conditions, would vary widely. However, the broadly fixed patterns of articulatory movement for specific utterances might manifest themselves at a deeper level through particular kinds or rates of change in the PCA coefficients, for example. Changes in facial orientation and position would generate additional time-varying changes in the PCA coefficients that would be confounded with the changes due to the visible articulatory gestures.

Recent work has led to the development of an automatic system for facial recognition (Moghaddam *et al.* 1998); it modelled the two mutually exclusive classes of variation in facial images. The first was the class of intra-personal variations due to differences in appearance of the same individual resulting from changes in lighting conditions, facial expression, facial orientation, and position with respect to the camera. The second class, of extra-personal variations, are the differences in facial appearance presented by different individuals. A Bayesian classifier was used to determine whether a pair of images represents the same individual or two different individuals. The technique used an embedded algorithm to isolate, scale, and align the faces from images and was able to deal with changes in head orientation, though the images tested were all essentially front-face presentations and the orientation variations were small. The images also included some lighting changes and variations in facial expression that the recognition system was able to deal with. However, the major objective of the face-recognition task seeks to discount precisely the differences in facial expressions and gestures that are relevant to visual speech processing and, furthermore, seeks to find the extra-personal differences that it would be highly desirable to discount, for example, in visual speech recognition. There currently appear to be no studies that have recorded speakers under controlled ranges of lighting conditions and facial orientations to explore the effects of either on (a) image encoding, in the case of image-based systems; or (b) the effectiveness of tracking algorithms, in the case of feature-oriented systems. Since separate recordings would be needed for each condition, the analysis of the results would need to take account also of the natural variations in articulatory gestures noted earlier. The outcome of the investigations would be directly relevant, for example, to recognition systems, like hidden Markov models, that essentially attempt to account for the variance of the input data.

In addition to the recording of basic visual material as outlined above, account needs to be taken of the differences between gestures that may occur in different kinds of speech activity. For example, spontaneous speech and conversation may not employ the same vocabulary of gestures as reading out loud, or using the telephone. In the very long term, material that reveals the interaction between speakers in a dialogue may be important, but it may perhaps be premature to attempt the specification of corpus material to investigate these aspects of visual speech signals when there is still a dearth of data for exploring more basic questions like the ones outlined above.

One further aspect of visible speech signals is becoming very important, for example, if a synthetic computer agent is to be realized that can simulate realistically a human speaker. It concerns the addition of appropriate facial expressions to the visible articulatory gestures and the interaction between the two. There is currently no analytical information available and no corpus of recorded data, for the following reasons. The simplest view of facial expressions is that the relevant muscular activities concerned with their production, which are well defined (Ekman and Friesen 1978), can be superimposed upon the muscular activities associated with the articulatory gestures. However, it seems more likely that there is a complex coupling between the two. For example, anyone who has attempted to utter speech whilst simultaneously producing a fixed smile or a permanent scowl will be aware that this is unnatural and difficult to do. Not only are the articulatory gestures of speech time varying, the facial expressions themselves are essentially dynamic gestures that vary during speech utterances. A very simple example (Ekman 1979) is provided by the well-known baton gestures of the eyebrows. Furthermore, making a specific facial expression can actually modify the speech production process. Scowling, for example, produces a tightening of the lower facial muscles and a drawing down of the lip corners that dramatically changes the normal articulations and also affects the voice quality of the acoustic output. The empirical investigation of the interaction between facial expressions and speech movements would most naturally start from studies of the articulatory movements in a 'neutral' face, which may be considered the normative baseline. Audiovisual recorded material from natural speech that embodies a range of natural expressions is also required and the time-varying expressions would need to be labelled by hand, much as phonetic transcriptions are created by manual labelling of conventional spoken corpora. It would then be possible to attempt to measure the differences between the expressive and the 'neutral' faces for each class of labelled expressions, in a range of phonetic contexts. This field has yet to be explored in any real depth and the development of an appropriate methodology remains a major challenge. Existing work is centred on the perception of audiovisual speech in the presence of emotions such as amusement, which are easy to activate spontaneously in constrained speech (Aubergé and Lemaître 2000).

A proper understanding of the interaction between the expressive and the articulatory processes demands a far more sophisticated and extensive model of language than we yet possess. Attempts to engineer expressive agents without greater knowledge of this kind may be not only misplaced, but also positively damaging, for reasons that are discussed in Section 8.4.3 below, in relation to purely articulatory gestures.

8.4 Automatic audiovisual speech processing

Additional sources of relevant knowledge should enhance the performance of conventional automatic speech recognition (ASR) systems. This is one of the main reasons for current interest in the visible aspects of speech production. As Section 8.2.1 above argued, visual speech signals tend to complement and therefore augment the acoustic signals. Indeed, the potential relevance and usefulness of visual signals is confirmed by the employment of speechreading, not only by those suffering from hearing-impairment, for whom it is an essential part of successfully managing everyday communication, but also for most normal hearing people, especially when there is a noisy environment. For the reasons given earlier, one of the principal application areas for automatic audiovisual speech recognition is the robust recognition of speech in the presence of background noise in locations such as aircraft cockpits, where hands-free voice control may be required.

The primary requirement in automatic audiovisual speech recognition is therefore to identify the cues from each of the two modalities that are important to the accurate phonetic identification of speech events and to combine those information sources so as to make the best use of both together. This is in fact the second major issue in visual speech processing, along with the management of the volume of information that visual data presents, as noted in Section 8.2.2 above. There is as yet an incomplete understanding of the nature of the visual cues to speech events. Features such as lip separation and lip width are known to be important cues (e.g. McGrath *et al.* 1984), and others have been suggested

(Finn 1986). However, there is still no reliable literature to indicate anything approaching a complete list of visual cues and no established methodology for identifying them. In addition, some of the cues may be very subtle. For example, when some of the identifiable visible features of speech signals were encoded using PCA, some of the higher-order coefficients that contributed very little to the data variance were more important in contributing to successful recognition than lower-order components that accounted for a much greater proportion of the data variance (Goldschen *et al.* 1996). Conventional (acoustic) automatic speech recognition systems can now handle speaker-independent continuous speech with sizeable vocabularies of the order of thousands of words. Variations due, for example, to movements of the speaker relative to the microphone can be fairly readily eliminated (see, for example, Holmes 1988). As the discussion of visual corpora above indicated, there is as yet no adequate body of systematic data to support the construction of speaker-independent audiovisual recognizers and it is much more difficult to compensate for visual variations such as movements of the speaker. Any practicable recognition system will ultimately have to allow the speaker reasonably free movement, at least within a fixed field of view.

Visual speech synthesis, on the contrary, has a wide range of potential applications and the requirements may vary. One possibility is the construction and presentation of material for helping in the teaching, for example, of speech-reading skills. A second is the construction of lifelike computer agents, and a third is the cheap and rapid construction of animated cartoon films. Other, longer-term applications could include automatic film dubbing into a variety of languages by substituting generated facial syntheses for the original actor's face.

In an agent application, high-resolution colour images are required that model very accurately both speech gestures and facial expressions in essentially complete and photographic detail; realism is the primary motivation. For training purposes, the primary requirement for visual speech syntheses is more likely to be that they are speech-readable and embody the essential visual cues to speech events. It may or may not be essential to model the whole head or face. In film cartoon applications, it may be more important to generate animated displays that exaggerate speech and expressive gestures, possibly, in the extreme limit, in a highly formalized or anatomically inappropriate way. This is typical of the animator's art and may rely upon generally accepted conventions that are divorced from reality to achieve a kind of plausibility. A limited ability to exaggerate articulatory movements may also be attractive in training applications when specific gestures may need to be emphasized. One other potentially important application area is the analytical investigation of visual and audiovisual speech perception itself. This could also require the generation of artificial visual stimuli that defy normal articulatory realization, for example, because articulators must be coupled or decoupled in an unnatural way. To illustrate this, consider a hypothetical experiment to determine whether it is the jaw opening or the lip opening that is more important in the perception of the British-English long vowel /a/. One approach might subject observers to a continuum of visual stimuli in which, at one extreme, the mouth opens while the jaw remains stationary and, at the other, the jaw drops while the lips remain closed. In this example, the normally coupled movements of these two articulators must be decoupled.

8.4.1 *Head model architectures for visual speech synthesis*

The development of visual synthesizers basically sprang from early approaches that involved a model of the head, or face, whose conformation could be adjusted to generate a sequence of frames. These could then be displayed in succession sufficiently rapidly to simulate movement. Two-dimensional facial topographies that could be realized through vector graphics were the cheapest and simplest to implement (e.g. Brooke 1982; Montgomery and Hoo 1982; Brooke 1989). One of the earliest raster graphics displays that could be fully rendered to simulate texture and shading was the three-dimensional ‘wire-frame’ model of Parke (1975) in which the polygonal surfaces making up the head could be modified. Indeed, this model was the archetype for its contemporary counterparts, which can also include details of internal features like the teeth and tongue (e.g. Cohen *et al.* 1998). The main challenge underlying the animation of computer graphics displays of this kind remains the derivation and application of control parameters for driving accurately the time-varying movements of the model. They must be simple enough to adjust the time-varying conformation of the wire-frame economically, yet powerful enough to permit a full range of movements and gestures. One way to achieve this is to configure the model for a set of idealized target gestures, for example, a set of phones, then to generate intermediate image frames by interpolating between the target images (Lewis and Parke 1987). There are now techniques for modelling coarticulatory effects, of which the application of a gestural theory of speech production was one important step (Cohen and Massaro 1993). This technique can, however, involve a very great deal of manual tuning to optimize performance. An alternative approach is to attempt to model the head anatomically, including descriptions of the skin, muscle, and bone structures (Platt and Badler 1981; Terzopoulos and Waters 1990; Waters and Terzopoulos 1992). Time-varying muscle-based parameters can then be used to change the shape of the head model. While this is attractive in principle, mechanisms for deriving the muscle parameters are not straightforward. Additionally, the derivation of the control parameters for features that are only partially or intermittently visible may require sophisticated and invasive measurement techniques. Given the greater power of modern processors, it is now also possible to use facial images themselves as the head models for a series of phonetic targets and to ‘morph’ between the target images to simulate movements (e.g. Bregler *et al.* 1997a;

Ezzat and Poggio 1997). Visible coarticulation effects have to be carefully handled in this type of synthesis.

The major advantage of methods based on head models is that they can in principle include facial expressions very easily if suitable modifications can be made to the control parameters to augment the purely articulatory gestures. Attempts have been made to achieve this using a simple catalogue of basic emotions (e.g. Lundeberg and Beskow 1999), but the difficulties of a general solution to the problem have been described earlier. A further advantage of using head models for visual synthesis is that the images can be rendered to any resolution so that it is possible to generate photographically realistic images at only marginally greater computational expense. Modelling of exaggerated or anatomically implausible gestures is potentially straightforward and could in principle be achieved by applying appropriate control parameters.

8.4.2 Data-driven methods for visual speech synthesis

By using HMMs for capturing and describing the statistical properties of image sequences, it is possible to develop visual recognizers, as discussed in Section 8.2.2 above. However, a more unconventional application of trained HMMs (that is, HMMs whose parameters have been established) is to use them to generate outputs. In this way HMMs can become image synthesizers. One of the earliest applications of HMMs for synthesizing oral images (Simons and Cox 1990) used only lip widths and separations as parameters. Parametric representations of a wider range of facial features and their time-varying changes can be used in this way to generate more sophisticated syntheses (e.g. Tamura *et al.* 1998; Okadome *et al.* 1999). It is also possible to create syntheses from HMMs trained on images of a speaker's face without any knowledge of the underlying structure of the images. In order to do this, HMMs are combined with a second statistically based technique, namely, PCA, which can efficiently compress and encode image data as discussed in Section 8.2.2 above. This is the basis of an entirely data-driven approach to visual speech synthesis (Brooke and Scott 1994a; Brooke and Scott 1998a). No modelling of the anatomy or structure of the head and face is required. In effect, the computer can be presented with many sequences of images of a speaker's face, in a PCA-encoded format, from which it can 'learn' how the speaker's facial gestures vary when uttering specific speech sounds. That is, it can use time-varying encoded versions of images to train HMMs to represent each of a set of phones. To synthesize an utterance, the HMMs for the appropriate sequence of sounds are invoked in order and reconstruct what they have 'learned'. In principle, they generate as their outputs a sequence of images, also in a PCA-encoded format. However, since the outputs of HMMs are generated independently, they cannot be used directly to simulate a human speaker's smooth, physiologically constrained outputs. Instead, the HMMs are used to generate PCA-encoded outputs at key points within speech events that are then used to compute a smoothly time-varying sequence of outputs (Brooke and Scott 1998a). Since each HMM is probabilistically driven, the image sequence that any particular HMM generates will vary from one invocation to another. Overall, however, the statistical properties of a large number of invocations will essentially match the variations in production that the HMM encountered during the learning phase. The data-driven methods can therefore model the variations of real speakers' productions. In order to model at least some of the coarticulatory effects, triphone models are employed; the disadvantage of triphone modelling is that a much greater amount of training data is required.

One of the greatest virtues of data-driven modelling is that, because the HMMs are trained on images of real speakers, the images quite naturally embody facial features like the teeth and tongue that are only partially and intermittently visible. There is thus no requirement to estimate and track the position of those features that are most difficult to measure. For the same reason, natural asymmetries of the facial movements and the imperfect skin textures of real faces also arise naturally from the training process. It is thought that some of the shadowing and texturing of the skin surface may provide cues to particular speech events (e.g. Fujimura 1961). In many models, bilateral symmetry of the face is assumed to minimize the volume of control data that is needed to drive the syntheses. In reality, faces are rarely, if ever, entirely symmetrical and one of the advantages of the data-driven approach is that the natural asymmetries are built in. The training phase, although it employs well-defined, standard algorithms (Rabiner 1989b), is computationally expensive. However, the generation of the colour syntheses is rather rapid. Using the prototype synthesizer running on a modest 166 MHz PC, complete sentences could be synthesized at 50 frames per second from a phonetically transcribed input in approximately 6–8 times realtime. At these timescales, it is possible to envisage the interactive construction of visual speech stimuli that can be presented in response to a user. This capability would be important in training applications.

Much of the computational load in synthesis is due to reconstruction of the images from their PCA-encoded format. To reduce this load, codebooks of images together with their PCA codes can be constructed. Image sequences can then be generated entirely by a form of vector quantization that selects the codebook images with PCA codes closest to those computed by the HMM-based synthesizer. These syntheses approach realtime but are less smoothly varying (Brooke and Scott 1998b). In principle it is possible to set a tolerance such that codebook images are selected if their PCA codes lie within the tolerance, but images are reconstructed from the PCA codes otherwise. By adjusting the tolerance, it should be possible to trade off better synthesis timescales against a reduced image quality. The speech-readability of the prototype, non-codebook version of the data-driven synthesizer was estimated in visual perception experiments. These showed that single digit recognition rates in monochrome syntheses of spoken digit triples at a spatial resolution of only 32 × 24 pixels, could reach 63 percent, compared with a rate of 68 percent for monochrome visual displays of real digit triple utterances video-recorded at the same spatial resolution (Scott 1996).

The data-driven approach implies, importantly, that unlike most model-based methods, very little manual tuning or adjustment is needed and a synthesizer can be trained on any speaker if sufficient annotated training data is available. The prototype data-driven visual speech synthesizer described above was constructed to be speech-readable. As a result, it has relatively low spatial resolution. Use of a PCA-based coding scheme with greater image resolution would carry additional computational costs, especially if the whole face were to be generated. It is possible to adjust the transition probabilities of the HMMs to modify the rate of speech production in the syntheses, though this capability is restricted. Similarly, it is not easy to realize significant changes in facial expressions by manipulating the model parameters in the way the head models can be manipulated, though some small adjustments are possible, as described in Section 8.5 below. Data-driven models are thus less convenient if detailed control of the movements of specific facial features is required, for example, to exaggerate particular gestures in a speechreading training application. On the other hand, the increasing power and size of computer systems is such that it may be possible within the fairly near future to consider the creation of sets of trained HMMs that include the variations due to facial expressions. That is, it may be possible to use captured data from real speakers to create HMMs not simply for each triphone, but for each triphone in a number of different facial expressions (see Section 8.3.2 above). At present, however, limited adaptability is one of the major drawbacks of the data-driven approach to synthesis.

8.4.3 Data-driven audiovisual synthesis and synchronization

Visual speech synthesizers, like conventional acoustic speech synthesizers, can be, and frequently were, driven by providing an essentially phonetic description of the utterances to be created, possibly with additional markings to specify their durations. However, for many applications, including the generation of cartoons, or for the film-dubbing application outlined earlier, lip synchronization is vital in order to be able to generate the visual speech syntheses so that they are matched to a pre-existing sound track. One solution might be to generate complete audiovisual syntheses. It is possible to generate an audio speech output using the HMM-based method (from initial proposals by Falaschi *et al.* 1989; Brooke and Scott 1998a; to recent work by Zen *et al.* 2009) in much the same way that the visual output is generated. Feasibility experiments have been carried out using short-term spectral descriptions of acoustic speech, which, although of rather poor quality, were adequate to demonstrate the principles of audiovisual synthesis. Audiovisual syntheses can be created by invoking both the audio and the visual synthesizers and running them independently, but in parallel (Tamura *et al.* 1999; Bailly 2002). Given the natural variations inherent to human articulatory movements, it might not be surprising to encounter complex (and variable) phasing relations between the salient events characterizing the acoustic and the visual consequences of the same articulatory movement. This may have important implications for audiovisual speech recognition, as described in Section 8.4.4 below.

Ideally, however, it would be desirable to drive visual speech synthesizers using acoustic speech signals themselves. This was indeed the way in which one of the earliest data-driven synthesizers was used (Simons and Cox 1990). The same method was developed (Brooke and Scott unpublished) in a pilot experiment that used ergodic (that is, fully connected) HMMs with approximately sixteen states. They were trained on audio and visual data to generate both PCA-encoded image data and cartoon-like syntheses from an acoustic input. Other methods for speech-driven synthesis have also been reported (e.g. Morishima 1998; Agelfors *et al.* 1999). The ability of ANNs to find complex mappings has made them popular tools for both synthesis and recognition. Time-delay neural networks have been used in synthesis for attempting, for example, to map from acoustic speech signals to articulatory parameters (Lavagetto and Lavagetto 1996) and from phones to facial images selected from a pre-determined set (Bothe 1996). A specific acoustic signal may be generated from a number of different articulatory configurations. A rather extreme illustrative example is the production of the /i/ sound. This is usually articulated as a high front vowel with lip spreading, but can also be created with rounded lips if the tongue is moved abnormally far forward and upward (Stevens and House 1955). The inverse problem, namely, the computation of an articulatory configuration given an acoustical or phonetic description of the speech event, is an intractable one-to-many mapping problem (Atal *et al.* 1978). Artificial Neural Networks can present problems if they are used where one-to-many mappings may be encountered. Even if methods exist in which multiple mappings from specific sounds to articulatory gestures can be reliably and successfully found (e.g. Toda *et al.* 2004; Toda *et al.* 2008), the utterance context is likely to be critical in selecting a plausible articulation within a sequence of articulations. One interesting study (Kuratate *et al.* 1998) shows that acoustic speech syntheses, as well as visual syntheses can be achieved using parameters derived from measurements of the facial movements, which indicates a link between the two modalities that might ultimately offer a new route to intrinsic lip synchronization.

It is very important to combine acoustic and visual speech signals accurately. De-synchronization of the acoustic and visual speech signals beyond a critical time window can cause severe perceptual difficulties (see McGrath 1985). However, the naturally occurring time offset between visual and auditory events can provide cues to particular speech events. For example, changes in the categorical perception of sounds in the /ma/, /ba/, and /pa/ continuum can be induced by changing the voice onset timings with respect to visible lip opening (Erber and de Filippo 1978). The McGurk effect (McGurk and MacDonald 1976) is a compelling demonstration of the results of failing to match acoustic and visual data appropriately. For example, a visual /ga/ combined with an acoustic /ba/ produces the percept of a spoken /da/. In other words, not only may a mismatch cause the observer to fail to perceive what was uttered, it may result in an entirely different percept that was neither seen nor heard.

8.4.4 Models for visual and audiovisual automatic speech recognition

One of the earliest approaches to automatic speech recognition used template-matching methods to match test and reference utterances encoded as descriptions of time-varying visible features such as lip width and separation, or oral cavity area and perimeter. Even purely visual recognition was shown to be useful for vocabularies of isolated words such as spoken digits and letters (Petajan 1984; Petajan *et al.* 1988b). Audiovisual recognition at that stage was managed by a heuristic that combined separate audio and visual recognition processes and it was not easy to estimate quantitatively the benefits of using the visual component. Speech intelligibility by humans in all but the very best and quietest of acoustic conditions is always improved if a speaker's face is visible. This is the basis of all attempts to employ visible speech data as an additional source of information, especially in acoustically noisy conditions that severely degrade the performance of most conventional speech recognition systems, even at relatively low levels.

By the mid 1990s, for reasons noted in Section 8.2.2 above, the range of experimental visual and audiovisual recognition systems was already very wide, extending from purely image-based systems at one extreme, to model-based systems at the other. These were reviewed in a contemporary article (Stork *et al.* 1996); it revealed a fundamental division between the feature-based and the image-based views of visual data that persists. What emerged then as a major issue, prompted by investigations of audiovisual speech perception, was the combination of visual and auditory information so as to obtain the maximum benefit from the two together, the importance of which has already been noted. Four models were proposed (Robert-Ribes *et al.* 1993; Robert-Ribes *et al.* 1996). The first is the Direct Identification, or DI, model, in which acoustic and visual data are combined and transmitted directly to a single, bimodal classifier. The second is the Separate Identification, or SI, model that carries out two unimodal classifications. The results from these are then sent forward for fusion and decision-making. The third is the Dominant Recoding, or DR, model. Here, auditory processing is assumed to be dominant and visual data is recoded into the dominant modality. For example, both modalities might be recoded into a tract transfer function. The two estimates are then fed forward for final classification. The fourth model is the Motor-space Recoding, or MR, model. Inputs from both modalities are recoded into an amodal common space, such as the space of articulatory configurations. The two representations are then passed to the classifier.

The DR model was implemented in one early prototype recognition system that attempted to code the visual data into a vocal tract transfer function (Sejnowski *et al.* 1990). However, most of the recognizers to date lie in the continuum between the SI model (e.g. Petajan 1984; Petajan *et al.* 1988a) and the DI model (Brooke *et al.* 1994). Perceptual evidence seems least strong for the SI model and the most general view is that fusion takes place at a level higher than the peripheral system, but prior to categorization (Summerfield 1987; Massaro 1996). The DI model, using a composite audiovisual feature vector, is a particularly straightforward architecture to implement with HMM-based recognition systems. It does not rely on early feature extraction and defers the decision-making process so that as much of the available data as possible can be retained for use. One speaker-dependent system of this kind used continuously spoken digit triple utterances as the vocabulary (Brooke *et al.* 1994; Brooke 1996). The acoustic data, stored at 100 frames per second, consisted of the outputs of a 26-channel filter bank covering the frequency range between 60 Hz and 10 kHz. The visual data was a 10-component PCA-encoded version of 10 × 6 pixel monochrome images of a speaker's oral region. Visual data was captured at 25 frames per second and four replications of each visual frame were used to match the acoustic data rate. The recognizer used the 36-element composite vectors in 3-state triphone HMMs, each state of which was associated with a single multivariate continuous Gaussian distribution and a diagonal covariance matrix. The HMMs were trained on 200 digit triples and tested on 100 digit triples. The visual signals were clean, but spectrally flat noise at various levels was added to the acoustic signal to investigate the performance of the recognition system on speech in noise. The results showed that, although the simple addition of visual data could improve a recognizer's performance, the gain was small, essentially because the contribution from the visual channels was swamped by the errors induced by the noise in the acoustic channels. The gains became more significant when compared to the best available acoustic recognizers that used techniques such as silence tracking and noise masking (Klatt 1976) to counter the effects of acoustic noise. In contrast, other, contemporary approaches to recognition using HMMs tended to compute explicit weighting factors to bias the system in favour of the visual signal when the acoustic noise levels became high (e.g. Adjoudani and Benoît 1996). None of these recognition systems was able to demonstrate a bimodal recognition performance that was consistently better than the unimodal performance in either of the two domains across a wide range of acoustic signal-to-noise ratios. Many of the early systems did not investigate speech in high levels of noise (such as signal-to-noise ratios much below 0 dB).

Conventional HMM-based audiovisual speech recognizers that conform to the DI model, like that described in the previous paragraph, implicitly assume synchrony between the acoustic and the visual data. The HMMs typically consist of three state, left-to-right models without state skipping. It is, however, possible to build HMM-based recognizers that permit a degree of audio and visual asynchrony, at least within phones, though synchrony is re-asserted at the phone boundaries. This approach was tested in a prototypical audiovisual speech recognizer using a technique that was based on single signal decomposition (e.g. Varga and Moore 1990). The operation of this recognizer was similar to that described in the paragraph above, except that the HMMs in this type of architecture were 9-state triphone models arranged as a two-dimensional array of 3×3 states (Tomlinson *et al.* 1996). The rows corresponded to the states of an audio model and the columns to the states of a visual model. The models were entered at the top left-hand state and exited at the bottom right-hand state. Transition between states from top to bottom and left to right, including diagonal transitions, were permitted. Thus, for example, a diagonal path through the HMM would correspond to complete synchrony between the audio and visual signals. The HMMs were trained using separate audio and visual models. This was one of the first experiments on continuous speech recognition to demonstrate a performance that was better in the audiovisual domain than in either of the audio or visual domains separately, throughout a full range of signal-to-noise ratios between +23 dB and –22 dB. In addition, it achieved this performance in a continuous speech recognition task. Despite the novel architecture, this recognizer remains a form of DI model. Work on similar HMM architectures, such as coupled HMMs, is currently being undertaken (Nefian *et al.* 2002). The capability to extend the asynchrony across phone boundaries has not yet been investigated and presents some challenges (see proposals by Saenko and Livescu 2006; Lee and Ebrahimi 2009).

8.5 Assessing and perceiving audiovisual speech

Assessment of the performance of both recognition and synthesis systems is complex, partly because, as Section 8.4 described, there are many possible application areas for these technologies that can have different requirements. In addition, it may be appropriate to distinguish between performance measures based on purely visual speech processing and those based on audiovisual speech processing. For both synthesis and recognition, speech-readability is a central issue, whether it is speech-readability of human signals by machines, as it is in recognition, or speech-readability of machine outputs by humans, as it is in synthesis. More precisely (Kuratate *et al.* 1998), the activity of the vocal tract that generates the acoustic speech signal has time-varying visible correlates that are conveyed by many parts of speakers' faces. The identification of the visual correlates makes them available for automatic speech recognition, whether or not humans actually use them. Conversely, synthesizers that attain a level of 'communicative realism' would minimally embody the audible-visual correlates observed in human oro-facial movement. That is, in a minimal synthesizer, attention should be focused on the visible-acoustic or phonetic aspects of facial movements. Whilst this is a sensible starting point and would be satisfactory for some applications, in others the minimal synthesis would not be adequate. Facial expressions and paralinguistic gestures would also need to be included, as described in Section 8.4 above. In the case of synthesis, most of the guidance in the development of systems is likely to be provided by studies of speech production and speech perception. Conversely, although there is no inherent reason why machines should be bounded by human constraints on operation or performance, it may, however, still be beneficial to understand how (successful) human systems work in order to exploit their known strengths and capabilities when developing artificial processing methods. For both automatic speech synthesis and recognition, human performance is the obvious baseline with which to compare machine performance (e.g. Brooke and Scott 1994a; Brooke *et al.* 1994).

Like the construction of corpora of speech material described in Section 8.3, above, the design of standardized performance assessment material and the precise specification of test conditions is central to the progressive refinement of all automatic systems. The design and application of test material is complex because some speech events are inherently easier to identify in the acoustic domain than in the visual domain and vice versa. In audiovisual testing, it is also necessary to separate the contributions from each of these modalities. No generally agreed-upon methodology appears yet to have emerged.

8.5.1 Automatic audiovisual speech recognition

Some sources of difficulty in comparing results from recognition experiments were indicated in Section 8.3.2 above. A starting point for the comparison of results from different systems would have to include at least specifications to define, for example: whether the recognizer was speaker-dependent, multiple speaker, or speaker-independent; whether the speech was uttered as isolated words, as connected (that is, carefully pronounced) words, or as continuous speech; the acoustic and visual conditions under which the test and training data were acquired; and the nature of the test vocabulary. There is a separate issue concerning the speaker that has to be taken into account. Speakers do not enunciate equally clearly and some speakers produce significantly better results with ASR systems than others. Clarity in the auditory domain has its counterpart in the visual domain also and some speakers are much easier to speechread than others. Without clear specifications of recognition conditions, it is impossible to make a valid comparison of the merits of the various recognizers themselves, let alone of the alternative models for audiovisual speech perception as applied to recognition systems (see Section 8.4.4 above).

It is possible to quote the benefits of using a visual component in recognition systems in a number of different ways. Thus, for example, in early experiments to investigate the benefits of using a visual component when attempting automatic recognition of acoustically noisy speech signals (Brooke *et al.* 1994), one way to express the gain was to indicate, for a fixed level of word accuracy, the change in signal-to-noise ratio of an acoustic speech signal that was equivalent to adding a visual component to the recognizer's input. Alternatively, it was possible to quote the difference in word accuracy for acoustic-only versus acoustic plus visual signal inputs at stated acoustic signal-to-noise ratios. Significant differences in interpretation could result from this choice of presentation. In addition, the conservative use of percentage word accuracy accounted for word insertion errors as well as word deletion and word substitution errors. The commonly used percentage word correct recognition rate accounts only for word substitution and word deletion errors and generally produces an apparently more favourable recognition performance (Tomlinson 1996).

The use of PCA-encoded oral image data to represent the visible aspects of the speech signal showed that it is not the low-order components that always contribute the biggest improvements to audiovisual speech recognition (e.g. Brooke *et al.* 1994; Goldschen *et al.* 1996). This is not necessarily surprising. It may simply imply that, though a particular component contributes a significant variance to the image data, it contributes little to discrimination between different speech events. PCA has nothing to reveal about the way that the phonetic classes are distributed along a particular dimension and linear discriminant analysis (see, e.g. Chatfield and Collins 1991) may offer more useful insights (Brooke *et al.* 1994; Tomlinson *et al.* 1996). Attempting to identify and retain the components that contribute significantly to the speech recognition process, while eliminating those that do not, should improve recognition efficiency. Scatter plots of PCA component values for pairs of phonetic events should reveal which components contribute most to the recognition process for discrimination between particular phonetic pairs. However, no comprehensive study of this kind seems to have been reported yet. A similar approach might also yield information about the usefulness of feature parameters, like lip separation and lip spreading, for the discrimination between different pairs of phonetic events. One objective of such studies might be to compare experimental estimates of the perceptual distances between different speech events with observable visible feature parameters and to seek correlations. Additionally, in order to investigate the value of feature parameters in contrast to pure image data, it might also be possible to perform PCA upon a composite vector of both feature parameters and image pixel intensity data and seek the most significant components for speech recognition.

8.5.2 *Automatic visual and audiovisual speech synthesis*

The production of animated, computer-generated audiovisual speech displays poses a number of perceptual questions. One is whether or not observers treat the syntheses in the same way as normal, human speech productions. In an early vowel identification experiment with a vector graphics synthesizer that displayed only an outline diagram of the facial topography (McGrath *et al.* 1984), errors in vowel identification were similar to those obtained from natural speech recordings. This suggested that the synthetic stimuli were being perceived in a manner analogous to that which is applied to real speech. The ability of the synthesizer to induce the McGurk effect was further confirmation that the syntheses could be perceived as speech-like (see Brooke 1992a). Though it is likely that the more sophisticated syntheses now available are also treated as speech-like, a successful outcome to this test should not necessarily be taken for granted. The test may define one criterion in determining the validity of facial speech syntheses. The literature of human–computer interaction offers guidance on subjective measures for determining the naturalness and acceptability of visual speech syntheses, but more objective tests are difficult to devise. A very simple test for the naturalness of visual speech synthesis, not dissimilar from the well-known Turing test for artificial intelligence, might be to determine whether viewers can discriminate between real and synthesized images of talking faces.

Even now, a very large number of fundamental issues concerning visual and audiovisual speech perception remain to be completely investigated. Some illustrative examples are set out below. Section 8.4 noted the capacity of the data-driven visual speech synthesizers to model bilateral facial asymmetries and real skin textures that could be a possible cue to some speech events. It is not known how important the bilateral asymmetries are, but they are certainly very common in real speakers and their absence might render facial images less natural looking. There is also some anecdotal evidence that fixed frontal views of the oral region of speakers can induce a sense of unease, especially when the viewers are children. The natural global movements of the head, despite not playing a significant part in conveying cues to the phonetic content of speech, may nonetheless also contribute to the acceptability of artificial computer-generated displays.

Some perceptual issues are directly relevant to the synthesis of visual speech gestures. For example, unreported experiments with the data-driven visual speech synthesizer described in Section 8.4.2 above (Brooke and Scott 1998b) indicated that there was no difference in digit recognition rates when otherwise identical syntheses of digit triples were presented in monochrome and in colour. It is, however, not known how colour and monochrome presentations would be likely to affect the results for different vocabularies or the perceived acceptability and naturalness of syntheses. A separate pilot study explored the feasibility of using a simple algorithm to generate facial displays in which the visible articulatory gestures could be accompanied by time-varying global movements of the head. The two-dimensional reconstructed oral images of the visible speech movements were electronically pasted onto a three-dimensional wire-frame model of the lower face in which the oral area was a plausible three-dimensional shape, but did not include the mouth as a feature (Brooke and Scott 1998b). It acted as a shaped screen that could carry the animated display of the visible speech gestures while the wire-frame head model was rotated about the x, y, and z axes. Though no analytical experiments were carried out, the informal response of a number of observers suggested that the syntheses were interpreted as plausible speech-readable gestures even when the head was shown in views that were far from direct frontal presentations. This was unexpected, especially as the three-dimensional information about features like the teeth and tongue that lay within the oral cavity could not be accurately represented in the two-dimensional image projections at large angles of head rotation. However, useful information about visual speech intelligibility might be gained from a programme of analytical experiments. If the results supported the informal observation, it would suggest that there might be a range of applications for a type of talking computer agent (see Section 8.4 above) that could be implemented without the need for detailed three-dimensional head models.

One unresolved issue in visual speech synthesis and its assessment is the need to find objective methods for measuring the differences between the images of a synthesized talking face and the images of a real speaker's facial gestures. One application would be to determine, for example, how accurately a synthesizer is able to simulate specific coarticulatory gestures that may be critical to speech-readability. A simple approach to this problem is possible when using the data-driven method of visual speech synthesis in which the output images are reconstructed from sets of PCA code values generated by HMMs trained on the PCA-encoded images of a real speaker (Scott 1996). Here, it is possible to measure the differences between either the PCA code values or the image pixel values obtained from (a) the synthesized and (b) the recorded images for particular utterances. Optimal time alignment of the real and synthesized utterances can be computed by dynamic time warping. Pilot experiments were carried out with monochrome images of synthesized and real digit triples utterances. A significant correlation was found between the fraction of the total variance accounted for by the PCA coding scheme and both (a) the visual digit recognition rate of synthesized oral images and (b) the root mean squared intensity difference computed from the corresponding sub-blocks of pixels in the reconstructed and raw images. The correlations thus linked subjective and objective performance measures and suggested that the general quality of syntheses could be predicted without necessarily performing complex and expensive perceptual experiments or detailed image analyses.

However, it would be highly desirable to find a generalized method for matching and comparing synthesized images and images of real speakers. This would, minimally, involve scaling and overlaying the image pairs accurately and defining a suitable metric to describe the differences between the image pairs in a way that focused on the visible articulatory gestures. Potentially relevant methods for facial image alignment and comparison have been successfully developed for systems designed to perform facial recognition (Moghaddam *et al.* 1998). As noted in Section 8.3.2, however, facial recognition methods are not designed to focus on the effects of those facial gestures and expressions that are the ones relevant to assessments of the performance of visual speech synthesizers. In the context of visual speech processing, therefore, image comparison appears to remain a largely unresolved problem.

With the development of other facial image alignment and comparison techniques (Moghaddam *et al.* 1998; Hall *et al.* 2000), there has been a move towards generalized methods for matching and comparing synthesized images and images of real speakers (Elisei *et al.* 2001). These methods involve scaling and overlaying image pairs accurately and defining suitable metrics to describe the differences between image pairs in a way that focuses on the visible articulatory gestures.

8.6 Current prospects

The development of powerful, statistically oriented techniques for capturing, analysing, and describing data, together with the availability of large, fast computer systems able to support them, has played a major role in the development of automatic visual and audiovisual speech processing. However, while statistical methods can, for example, find efficient ways to reduce and manage large volumes of data, they are not usually informative about the significance or interpretation of the transformed representations. Spaces like those generated by PCA directly from images as described in Section 8.2.2 illustrate this; the components are unlabelled and even when the effects of variations in individual components are plotted, they rarely suggest simple, equivalent, feature-based facial parameters (e.g. Turk and Pentland 1991); to obtain interpretable movement parameters, it is necessary at least to resort to multistage image analysis (as in Ezzat *et al.* 2002a). The same applies to HMMs, in which the states of the finite state machines relate only weakly, if at all, to the articulatory stages in the production of the speech events that the HMMs model. The properties and behaviour of ANNs like MLPs tend to be expressed by parameters that are distributed throughout the networks. This is one of the characteristics of ANNs that makes them powerful, because they can, for example, continue to function (though not as well) even if part of the network is damaged or destroyed. However, the distribution of the parameters generally makes the behaviour of ANNs difficult to observe and understand. Statistical analyses, including PCA, though powerful and useful techniques, may not be sufficient on their own to reveal the full pattern and structure of the data they themselves generate. This may only emerge through the simultaneous application of sophisticated visualization techniques.

In contrast to the statistically oriented models, speech production processes that involve the muscular control of the configurations of articulatory organs and their time-varying changes are the physical basis of the visible changes that manifest themselves in the gestures and movements of facial features. For this reason, the identification and tracking of the time-varying movements of facial features remains attractive and appropriate. An objective posed by one of the authors (NMB) in 1982 is still relevant, namely, to find the minimal set of facial points whose movements can generate complete and accurate descriptions of a facial speech synthesis that is 'communicatively realistic'. The techniques for achieving this goal are, however, now emerging (Kuratate *et al.* 1998). Notwithstanding this progress, much concerning the speech production process is still not well understood. In particular, there is no convincing account for the inter-speaker differences in the visible articulatory gestures that are known to exist. There are no well-established techniques for seeking the 'deep structures' of speech and there is thus no clear answer, in either the acoustic or visual domains, to questions about what exactly it is that characterizes specific speech events. Similarly, a comprehensive catalogue showing the 'perceptual distance' that separates phones would set a baseline for human recognition performance that could be compared to machine recognition performance. Some studies of this kind have been undertaken (e.g. Summerfield 1987), but the relationship between perceptual distances and the conformation of facial features remains incomplete, as noted in Sections 8.2.2 and 8.5.2 above.

The identity and characteristic properties of phones are among the factors that make the problem of automatic speech recognition difficult and interesting. Perceptual studies suggest numerous mechanisms for visual and audiovisual speech recognition in terms of the categorization of phones. They support the conventional view that the human system operates in a highly parallel way. It seems likely therefore that parallelism could play a major role in automatic visual and audiovisual speech processing systems. The development of highly parallel computing systems is, however, still at a comparatively rudimentary stage. In particular, it is difficult to find useful metalanguages to describe the nature of parallelism and how it can be applied to computational processes. Specifically, appropriate mechanisms are needed for the fusion of information computed by different processes prior to decision making (see also Section 8.4.4).

The success of the modern computational methods has been remarkable. The techniques that have been developed, such as multidimensional morphable models (Ezzat *et al.* 2002a), have made it possible to achieve plausibly realistic visual speech synthesis and to carry out audiovisual speech recognition sufficiently accurately to make some useful applications possible (Brooke *et al.* 1994). It is therefore tempting to concentrate on improving the performance of those techniques and to seek to meet the many demands of the modern world for short-term solutions to specific problems. However, there are risks in doing this without a proper understanding of the nature of visual and audiovisual speech processing. This can be gained only by patient and careful analytical studies, using well-designed and systematic bodies of test data, as this chapter has indicated. For example, even the best of today's visual speech synthesizers would probably be unlikely to pass the 'Turing test' for communicative realism, proposed in Section 8.5.2, let alone a test that included the facial expressions that a computer agent would have to simulate. It is important to understand why they would not.

As Section 8.1 indicated, the early studies of visual speech were generally prompted by interest in the analytical investigation of visual speech processing and the desire to improve the rehabilitation of the hearing-impaired through the better-informed and improved teaching and training of speechreading skills. Speech production studies and perceptual studies of speechreading therefore prompted much of the initial work in the field and, as Section 8.5 suggests, will continue to offer an important contribution to the development of automatic visual and audiovisual speech processing systems. This is likely to be a synergistic collaborative process with the technologists and computer scientists who will in their turn develop the systems that are needed to assist in carrying out those studies.

On a final, more personal note, perhaps the greatest single impetus to the contemporary development of the audiovisual processing of speech was the NATO Advanced Study Institute at Bonas in 1995. For the first time, the whole community of audiovisual speech scientists was brought together, including mathematicians, statisticians, psychologists, linguists, engineers, and computer scientists. This was important because audiovisual speech processing encompasses an unusually wide spectrum of specialist studies and demands a cross-disciplinary approach. The NATO meeting was the catalyst that led to a rapid expansion of the field and also inspired the regular succession of Audiovisual Speech Processing (AVSP) meetings that has followed, largely due to the energy, enthusiasm, and unique leadership of Christian Benoît. The outcomes have now established the field securely and ensured that it will move forward constructively on a suitably broad knowledge base.

9 Audiovisual automatic speech recognition

G. Potamianos, C. Neti, J. Luettin, and I. Matthews

9.1 Introduction

We have made significant progress in *automatic speech recognition* (ASR) for well-defined applications like dictation and medium vocabulary transaction processing tasks in relatively controlled environments (O'Shaughnessy 2003). However, ASR performance has yet to reach the level required for speech to become a truly pervasive user interface. Indeed, even in "clean" acoustic environments, and for a variety of tasks, state-of-the-art ASR system performance lags human speech perception by up to an order of magnitude (Lippmann 1997). In addition, current systems are quite sensitive to channel, environment, and style of speech variation. A number of techniques for improving ASR robustness have met with limited success in severely degraded environments (Ghitza 1986; Nadas *et al.* 1989; Juang 1991; Liu *et al.* 1993; Hermansky and Morgan 1994; Neti 1994; Gales 1997; Jiang *et al.* 2001; De la Torre *et al.* 2005; Droppo and Acero 2008; Benesty *et al.* 2009). Clearly, novel, non-traditional approaches that use sources of information orthogonal to the acoustic input are needed to achieve ASR performance closer to the level of human speech perception, and robust enough to be deployable in field applications. Visual speech is the most promising source of additional speech information, and it is obviously not affected by the acoustic environment and noise.

Human speech perception is bimodal in nature: Humans combine audio and visual information in deciding what has been spoken, especially in noisy environments. The benefit of the visual modality to speech intelligibility in noise has been quantified as far back as in Sumby and Pollack (1954). Furthermore, bimodal fusion of audio and visual stimuli in perceiving speech has been demonstrated in the McGurk effect (McGurk and MacDonald 1976). For example, when the spoken sound /ba/ is superimposed on the video of a person uttering /ga/, most people perceive the speaker as uttering the sound /da/. In addition, visual speech is of particular importance to the hearing-impaired: Mouth movement is known to play an important role in both sign language and simultaneous communication among the deaf (Marschark *et al.* 1998). The hearing-impaired speechread well, possibly better than the general population (Bernstein *et al.* 1998).

There are three key reasons why the availability of visual speech benefits human speech perception (Summerfield 1987): It helps speaker (audio source) localization; it contains speech segmental information that supplements the audio; and it provides complementary information about the place of articulation. The latter is due to the partial or full visibility of articulators such as the tongue, teeth, and lips. Place of articulation information can help disambiguate, for example, the unvoiced consonants /p/ (a bilabial) and /k/ (a velar), the voiced consonant pair /b/ and /d/ (a bilabial and alveolar, respectively), and the nasal /m/ (a bilabial) from the nasal alveolar /n/ (Massaro and Stork 1998). All three pairs are highly confusable on the basis of acoustics alone. In addition, jaw and lower face muscle movement is correlated to the produced acoustics (Yehia *et al.* 1998; Barker and Berthommier 1999), and when this movement is visible, human speech perception has been shown to be enhanced (Summerfield *et al.* 1989; Smeele 1996).

The benefits of visual speech information for speech perception have motivated significant interest in automatic recognition of visual speech, formally known as automatic lipreading, or speechreading (Stork and Hennecke 1996). Work in this field aims at improving ASR by exploiting the visual information from the speaker's mouth region in addition to the traditional audio information, leading to audiovisual automatic speech recognition systems. Not surprisingly, systems that include the visual modality have been shown to outperform audio-only ASR over a wide range of conditions. Such performance gains are particularly impressive in noisy environments, where traditional acoustic-only ASR performs poorly. Improvements have also been demonstrated when speech is degraded due to speech impairment (Potamianos and Neti 2001a) and Lombard effects (Huang and Chen 2001). Coupled with the diminishing cost of quality video capturing systems, these facts make automatic speechreading tractable for achieving robust ASR in certain scenarios (Hennecke *et al.* 1996; Connell *et al.* 2003).

Automatic recognition of audiovisual speech introduces new and challenging tasks when compared to traditional, audio-only ASR. The block diagram of Figure 9.1 highlights these: In addition to the usual audio front end (feature extraction stage), visual features that are informative about speech must be extracted from video of the speaker's face. This requires robust face detection, as well as location estimation and tracking of the speaker's mouth or lips, followed by extraction of suitable visual features. In contrast to audio-only recognizers, there are now two streams of features available for recognition, one for each modality. The combination of the audio and visual streams should ensure that the resulting system performance exceeds the better of the two single-modality recognizers. Both issues, namely the visual front end design and audiovisual fusion, constitute difficult problems, and they have generated significant research work by the scientific community.

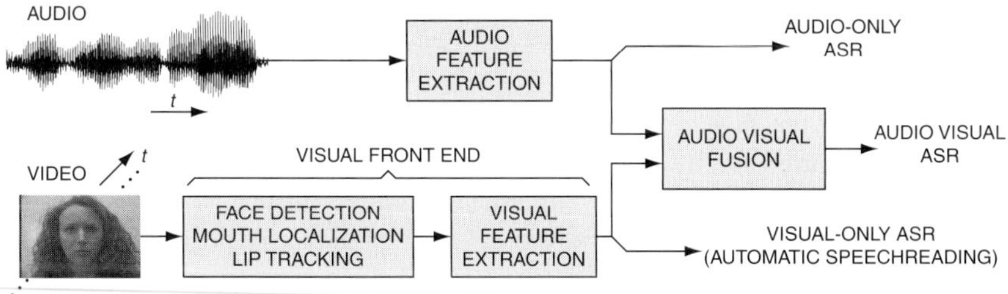

Figure 9.1 The main processing blocks of an audiovisual automatic speech recognizer. The visual front end design and the audiovisual fusion modules introduce additional challenging tasks to automatic recognition of speech, as compared to traditional, audio-only ASR. They are discussed in detail in this chapter.

Indeed, since the mid eighties, numerous articles have concentrated on audio-visual ASR, with the vast majority appearing during the last fifteen years. The first automatic speechreading system was reported by Petajan (1984). Given the video of a speaker's face, and using simple image thresholding, he was able to extract binary (black and white) mouth images, and subsequently, mouth height, width, perimeter, and area, as visual speech features. He then developed a visual-only recognizer based on dynamic time warping (Rabiner and Juang 1993) to rescore the best two choices of the output of the baseline audio-only system. His method improved ASR for a single-speaker, isolated word recognition task on a 100-word vocabulary that included digits and letters. Petajan's work generated significant excitement, and soon various sites established research in audiovisual ASR.

Among the pioneer sites was the group headed by Christian Benoît at the Institute de la Communication Parlée (ICP), in Grenoble, France. For example, Adjoudani and Benoît (1996) investigated the problem of audiovisual fusion for ASR, and compared early and late integration strategies. In the latter area, they considered modality reliability estimation based on the dispersion of the likelihood of the top four recognized words using the audio-only and visual-only inputs. They reported significant ASR gains on a single-speaker corpus of fifty-four French nonsense words. Later, they developed a multimedia platform for audiovisual speech processing, containing a head-mounted camera to robustly capture the speaker's mouth region (Adjoudani *et al.* 1997). Recently, work at ICP has continued in this area, with additional audiovisual corpora collected (French connected letters and English connected digits) and a new audiovisual ASR system reported by Heckmann *et al.* (2001). In addition, the group has been working in related areas, including audiovisual speech enhancement (Girin *et al.* 2001b), speech separation (Girin *et al.* 2001a; Sodoyer *et al.* 2004), coding (Girin 2004), synthesis (Bailly *et al.* 2003), and other aspects of audiovisual speech and face-to-face communication (Dohen *et al.* 2010).

As shown in Figure 9.1, audiovisual ASR systems differ in three main aspects (Hennecke *et al.* 1996; Potamianos and Neti 2003): The visual front end design, the audiovisual integration strategy, and the speech recognition method used. Unfortunately, the diverse algorithms suggested in the literature for automatic speechreading are very difficult to compare, as they are rarely tested on a common audiovisual database. In addition, until the beginnings of this decade (Neti *et al.* 2000; Hazen *et al.* 2004), early audiovisual ASR studies have been conducted on databases of small duration, and, in most cases, limited to a very small number of speakers (mostly less than ten, and often single-subject) and to small vocabulary tasks (Chibelushi *et al.* 1996; Hennecke *et al.* 1996; Chibelushi *et al.* 2002). Such tasks are typically nonsense words (Adjoudani and Benoît 1996; Su and Silsbee 1996), isolated words (Petajan 1984; Matthews *et al.* 1996; Movellan and Chadderdon 1996; Chan *et al.* 1998; Dupont and Luettin 2000; Gurbuz *et al.* 2001; Huang and Chen 2001; Nefian *et al.* 2002), connected letters (Potamianos *et al.* 1998), connected digits (Potamianos *et al.* 1998; Zhang *et al.* 2000; Patterson *et al.* 2002), closed-set sentences (Goldschen *et al.* 1996), or small-vocabulary continuous speech (Chu and Huang 2000). Databases are commonly recorded in English, but other examples are French (Adjoudani and Benoît 1996; Alissali *et al.* 1996; André-Obrecht *et al.* 1997; Teissier *et al.* 1999; Dupont and Luettin 2000), German (Bregler *et al.* 1993; Krone *et al.* 1997), Japanese (Nakamura *et al.* 2000; Fujimura *et al.* 2005), Hungarian (Czap 2000), Spanish (Ortega *et al.* 2004), Czech (Železný and Cisař 2003), and Dutch (Wojdel *et al.* 2002), among others. However, if the visual modality is to become a viable component in real-word ASR systems, research work is required on larger vocabulary tasks, developing speechreading systems on data of sizable duration and of large subject populations. A first attempt towards this goal was the authors' work during the summer 2000 workshop at the Center for Language and Speech Processing at the Johns Hopkins University, in Baltimore, Maryland (Neti *et al.* 2000), where a speaker-independent audiovisual ASR system for Large Vocabulary Continuous Speech Recognition (LVCSR) was developed for the first time. Significant performance gains in both clean and noisy audio conditions were reported.

In this chapter, we present the main techniques for audiovisual speech recognition that have been developed since the mid eighties. We first discuss the visual feature extraction problem, followed by a discussion of audiovisual fusion. In both cases, we provide details of some of the techniques employed during the Johns Hopkins summer 2000 workshop (Neti *et al.* 2000). We also consider the problem of audiovisual speaker adaptation, an issue of significant importance when building speaker-specific models or developing systems across databases. We then discuss the main audiovisual corpora used in the literature for ASR experiments, including the IBM audiovisual LVCSR database. Subsequently, we present experimental results on automatic speechreading and audiovisual ASR. As an application of speaker adaptation, we consider the problem of automatic recognition of impaired speech. Finally, we conclude the chapter with a discussion on the current state of audiovisual ASR, and on what we view as open problems in this area.

9.2 Visual front ends

As was briefly mentioned in the Introduction (see also Figure 9.1), the first main difficulty in the area of audiovisual ASR is the visual front end design. The problem is two-fold: Face, lips, or mouth tracking is first required, followed by visual speech representation in terms of a small number of informative features. Clearly, the two issues are closely related: Employing a lip-tracking algorithm allows one to use visual features such as mouth height or width (Adjoudani and Benoît 1996; Chan *et al.* 1998; Potamianos *et al.* 1998), or parameters of a suitable lip model (Chandramohan and Silsbee 1996; Dalton *et al.* 1996; Luettin *et al.* 1996). On the other hand, a crude detection of the mouth region is sufficient to obtain visual features, using transformations of this region's pixel values that achieve sufficient dimensionality reduction (Bregler *et al.* 1993; Duchnowski *et al.* 1994; Matthews *et al.* 1996; Potamianos *et al.* 2001b). Needless to say, robust tracking of the lips or mouth region is of paramount importance for good performance of automatic speechreading systems (Iyengar *et al.* 2001).

9.2.1 Face detection, mouth, and lip tracking

The problem of face and facial-part detection has attracted significant interest in the literature (Graf *et al.* 1997; Rowley *et al.* 1998; Sung and Poggio 1998; Senior 1999; Li and Zhang 2004; Garcia *et al.* 2007). In addition to automatic speechreading, it has applications to other areas related to audiovisual speech, for example visual text-to-speech (Cohen and Massaro 1994b; Chen *et al.* 1995; Cosatto *et al.* 2000; Bailly *et al.* 2003; Aleksic and Katsaggelos 2004b; Melenchón *et al.* 2009), person identification and verification (Jourlin *et al.* 1997; Wark and Sridharan 1998; Fröba *et al.* 1999; Jain *et al.* 1999; Maison *et al.* 1999; Chibelushi *et al.* 2002; Zhang *et al.* 2002; Sanderson and Paliwal 2004; Aleksic and Katsaggelos 2006), speaker localization (Bub *et al.* 1995; Wang and Brandstein 1999; Zotkin *et al.* 2002), detection of intent to speak (De Cuetos *et al.* 2000) and of speech activity (Libal *et al.* 2007; Rivet *et al.* 2007), face image retrieval (Swets and Weng 1996), and others. In general, robust face and mouth detection is quite difficult, especially in cases where the background, face pose, and lighting are variable (Iyengar and Neti 2001; Jiang *et al.* 2005).

In the audiovisual ASR literature, where issues such as visual feature design, or audiovisual fusion algorithms are typically of more interest, face and mouth detection are often ignored, or at least, the problem is simplified: In some databases for example, the speaker's lips are suitably colored, so that their automatic extraction becomes trivial by chroma-key methods (Adjoudani and Benoît 1996; Heckmann *et al.* 2001). In other works, where audiovisual corpora are shared (for example, the Tulips1, (X)M2VTS, and AMP/CMU databases, discussed later), the mouth regions are extracted once and re-used in subsequent work by other researchers, or sites. Further, there have been efforts in the literature to design wearable audiovisual headsets that, when properly worn, reliably capture the speaker mouth region alone (Huang *et al.* 2004). It should also be noted that in the vast majority of audiovisual databases the faces are frontal with minor face pose and lighting variation. Therefore, in this chapter we focus on frontal pose visual feature extraction. Nevertheless, the approaches and algorithms discussed here carry on to non-frontal head poses as well to a large extent, as demonstrated by the work of Iwano *et al.* (2007), Kumar *et al.* (2007), Kumatani and Stiefelhagen (2007), and Lucey *et al.* (2009).

In general, all audiovisual ASR systems require determining a region-of-interest (ROI) for the visual feature extraction algorithm to proceed. For example, a ROI can be the entire face, in which case a subsequent active appearance model can be used to match to the exact face location (Cootes *et al.* 1998). Alternatively, a ROI can be the mouth-only region, in which case an active shape model of the lips can be used to fit a lip contour (Luettin *et al.* 1996). If appearance-based visual features are to be extracted (see below) the latter is all that is required. Many techniques of varying complexity can be used to locate ROIs. Some use traditional image processing techniques, such as color segmentation, edge detection, image thresholding, template matching, or motion information (Graf *et al.* 1997), whereas other methods use statistical modeling techniques, employing "strong" classifiers like neural networks for example (Rowley *et al.* 1998), or cascades of "weak" classifiers (Viola and Jones 2001). In the following, we describe one such statistical modeling based approach.

9.2.1.1 Face detection and mouth region-of-interest extraction A typical algorithm for face detection and facial feature localization is described in Senior (1999). This technique is used in the visual front end design of Neti *et al.* (2000) and Potamianos *et al.* (2001b), when processing the video of the IBM ViaVoice™ audiovisual database, described later. Given a video frame, face detection is first performed by employing a combination of methods, some of which are also used for subsequent face feature finding. A face template size is first chosen (an 11×11-pixel square, here), and an image pyramid over all permissible face locations and scales (given the video frame and face template sizes) is used to search for possible face candidates. This search is constrained by the minimum and maximum allowed face candidate size with respect to the frame size, the face size increment from one pyramid level to the next, the spatial shift in searching for faces within each pyramid level, and the fact that no candidate face can be of smaller size than the face template. In Potamianos *et al.* (2001b), the face width is restricted to lie within 10% and 75% of the frame width, with a face size increase of 15% across consecutive pyramid levels. Within each pyramid level, a local horizontal and vertical shift of one pixel is used to search for candidate faces.

If the video signal is in color, skin-tone segmentation can be used to quickly narrow the search to face candidates that contain a relatively high proportion of skin-tone pixels. The normalized (red, green, blue) values of each frame pixel are first transformed to the (hue, saturation) color space, where skin tone is known to occupy a range of values largely invariant to most humans and lighting conditions (Graf *et al.* 1997; Senior 1999). In this particular implementation, all face candidates that contain less than 25% of pixels with hue and saturation values that fall within the skin-tone range, are eliminated. This substantially reduces the number of face candidates (depending on the frame background), speeding up computation and reducing spurious face detections. Every remaining face candidate is subsequently size-normalized to the 11×11 face template size, and its grayscale pixel values are placed into a 121-dimensional face candidate vector. Each vector is given a score based on both a two-class (face versus non-face) Fisher linear discriminant and the candidate's distance from face space (DFFS), i.e., the face vector projection error onto a lower, 40-dimensional space, obtained by means of *principal components analysis* (PCA – see below). All candidate regions exceeding a threshold score are considered as faces. Among such faces at neighboring scales and locations, the one achieving the maximum score is returned by the algorithm as a detected face (Senior 1999). An improved version of this algorithm appears in Jiang *et al.* (2005).

Once a face has been detected, an ensemble of facial feature detectors is used to estimate the locations of twenty-six facial features, including the lip corners and centers (twelve such facial features are marked on the frames of Figure 9.2). Each feature location is determined by using a score combination of prior feature location statistics, linear discriminant, and distance from feature space (similar to the DFFS discussed above), based on the chosen feature template size (such as 11×11 pixels).

Before incorporating the described algorithm into our speechreading system, a training step is required to estimate the Fisher discriminant and eigenvectors (PCA) for face detection and facial feature estimation, as well as the facial feature location statistics. Such training requires a number of frames manually annotated with the faces and their visible features. When training the Fisher discriminant, both face and non-face (or facial feature and non-feature) vectors are used, whereas in the case of PCA, face and facial-feature-only vectors are considered (Senior 1999).

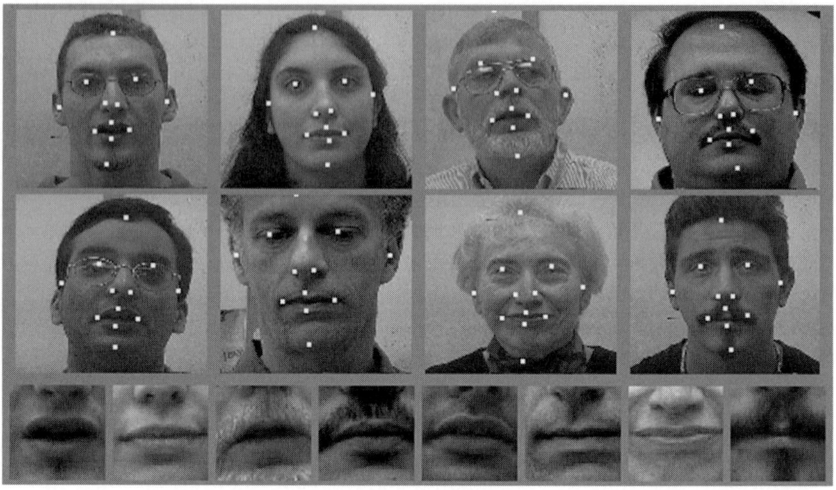

Figure 9.2 Region-of-interest extraction examples. Upper rows: Example video frames of eight subjects from the IBM ViaVoice™ audiovisual database (described below), with superimposed facial features, detected by the algorithm of Senior (1999). Lower row: Corresponding mouth regions-of-interest, extracted as in Potamianos *et al.*(2001b). © 1999 and 2001 IEEE.

Given the output of the face detection and facial feature finding algorithm described above, five located lip contour points are used to estimate the mouth center and its size at every video frame (four such points are marked on the frames of Figure 9.2). To improve ROI extraction robustness to face and mouth detection errors, the mouth center estimates are smoothed over twenty neighboring frames using median filtering to obtain the ROI center, whereas the mouth size estimates are averaged over each utterance. A size-normalized square ROI is then extracted (see Eq. (9.1), below), with sides $M = N = 64$ (see also Figure 9.2). This can contain just the mouth region, or also parts of the lower face (Potamianos and Neti 2001b).

9.2.1.2 Lip contour tracking Once the mouth region is located, a number of algorithms can be used to obtain lip contour estimates. Some popular methods are snakes (Kass *et al.* 1988), templates (Yuille *et al.* 1992; Silsbee 1994), and active shape and appearance models (Cootes *et al.* 1995; Cootes *et al.* 1998).

A snake is an elastic curve represented by a set of control points. The control point coordinates are iteratively updated, by converging towards the local minimum of an energy function, defined on the basis of curve smoothness constraints and a matching criterion with respect to desired features of the

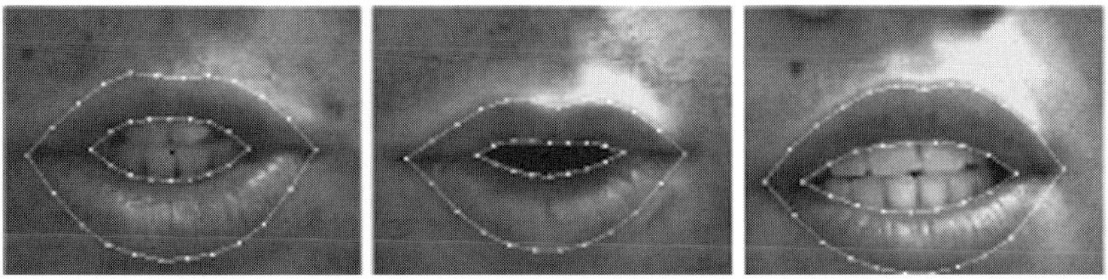

Figure 9.3 Examples of lip contour estimation by means of active shape models (Luettin *et al.* 1996). Depicted mouth regions are from the Tulips1 audiovisual database (Movellan and Chadderdon 1996), and they were extracted preceding lip contour estimation. Reprinted from *Computer Vision and Image Understanding*, 65:2, Luettin and Thacker, Speechreading using probabilistic models, 163–178, © 1997, with permission from Elsevier.

image (Kass *et al.* 1988). Such an algorithm is used for lip contour estimation in the speechreading system of Chiou and Hwang (1997). Another widely used technique for lip tracking is by means of lip templates, employed in the system of Chandramohan and Silsbee (1996) for example. Templates constitute parameterized curves that are fitted to the desired shape by minimizing an energy function, defined similarly to snakes. B-splines, used by Dalton *et al.* (1996), work similarly to the above techniques as well. Combinations of the above have also been used in the literature, as for example by Aleksic *et al.* (2002), where both snakes and templates are employed.

Active shape and appearance models construct a lip shape or ROI appearance statistical model, as discussed in following subsections. These models can be used for tracking lips by means of the algorithm proposed by Cootes *et al.* (1998). This assumes that, given small perturbations from the actual fit of the model to a target image, a linear relationship exists between the difference in the model projection and image, and the required updates to the model parameters. An iterative algorithm is used to fit the model to the image data (Matthews *et al.* 1998). Alternatively, the fitting can be performed by the downhill simplex method (Nelder and Mead 1965), as in Luettin *et al.* (1996). Examples of lip contour estimation by means of active shape models using the latter fitting technique are depicted in Figure 9.3.

9.2.2 *Visual features*

Various sets of visual features for automatic speechreading have been proposed in the literature over the last twenty years. In general, they can be grouped into three categories: (a) Video pixel- (or, appearance) based ones; (b) Lip contour- (or, shape) based features; and (c) Features that are a combination of both appearance and shape (Hennecke *et al.* 1996; Aleksic *et al.* 2005). In the following, we present each category in more detail. Possible post-feature extraction processing is discussed at the end of this section.

9.2.2.1 Appearance-based features In this approach to visual feature extraction, the image part typically containing the speaker's mouth region is considered as informative for lipreading, i.e., the region-of-interest (ROI). This region can be a rectangle containing the mouth, and possibly include larger parts of the lower face, such as the jaw and cheeks (Potamianos and Neti 2001b), or the entire face (Matthews *et al.* 2001). Often, it can be a three-dimensional rectangle, containing adjacent frame rectangular ROIs, in an effort to capture dynamic speech information at this early stage of processing (Li *et al.* 1995; Potamianos *et al.* 1998). Alternatively, the ROI can correspond to a number of image profiles vertical to the lip contour (Dupont and Luettin 2000), or just be a disc around the mouth center (Duchnowski *et al.* 1994). By concatenating the ROI pixel gray-scale (Bregler *et al.* 1993; Duchnowski *et al.* 1994; Potamianos *et al.* 1998; Dupont and Luettin 2000), or color values (Chiou and Hwang 1997), a feature vector is obtained. For example, in the case of an $M \times N$-pixel rectangular ROI, which is centered at location (m_t,n_t) of video frame $V_t(m,n)$ at time t, the resulting feature vector of length $d = M.N$ will be (after a lexicographic ordering)[1]

$$\mathbf{x}_t \leftarrow \left\{ \begin{array}{l} V_t(m,n) : m_t - \lfloor M/2 \rfloor \leq m < m_t + |m/2|, \\ n_t - \lfloor N/2 \rfloor \leq n < n_t + \lceil N/2 \rceil \end{array} \right\} \tag{9.1}$$

This vector is expected to contain most visual speech information. Notice that approaches that use optical flow as visual features (Mase and Pentland 1991; Gray *et al.* 1997) can fit within this framework by replacing in Eq. (9.1) the video frame ROI pixels with optical flow estimates.

Typically, the dimensionality d of vector $\mathbf{x}_t$ in Eq. (9.1) is too large to allow successful statistical modeling (Chatfield and Collins 1991) of speech classes, by means of a hidden Markov model (HMM), for example (Rabiner and Juang 1993). Therefore, appropriate transformations of the ROI pixel values are used as visual features. Movellan and Chadderdon (1996) for example, use low-pass filtering followed by image subsampling and video frame ROI differencing, whereas Matthews *et al.* (1996) propose a non-linear image decomposition using "image sieves" for dimensionality reduction and feature extraction. By far however, the most popular appearance feature representations achieve such reduction by using traditional image transforms (Gonzalez and Wintz 1977). These transforms are typically borrowed from the image compression literature, and the hope is that they will preserve most information relevant to speech-reading. In general, a $D \times d$-dimensional linear transform matrix $\mathbf{P}$ is sought, such that the transformed data vector $\mathbf{y}_t = \mathbf{P}\mathbf{x}_t$ contains most speechreading information in its $D \ll d$ elements. To obtain matrix $\mathbf{P}$, L training examples are given, denoted by $\mathbf{x}_l$, $l = 1, \ldots, L$. A number of possible such matrices are described in the following.

Principal components analysis (PCA) This constitutes the most popular pixel-based feature representation for automatic speechreading (Bregler *et al.* 1993; Bregler and Konig 1994; Duchnowski *et al.* 1994; Li *et al.* 1995; Brooke 1996; Tomlinson *et al.* 1996; Chiou and Hwang 1997; Gray *et al.* 1997; Luettin and Thacker 1997; Potamianos *et al.* 1998; Dupont and Luettin 2000; Hazen *et al.* 2004). The PCA data projection achieves optimal information compression, in the sense of minimum square error between the original vector $\mathbf{x}_t$ and its reconstruction based on its projection $\mathbf{y}_t$; however, appropriate data scaling constitutes a problem in the classification of the resulting vectors (Chatfield and Collins 1991). In the PCA implementation of Potamianos *et al.* (1998), the data are scaled according to their inverse variance, and their correlation matrix $\mathbf{R}$ is computed. Subsequently, $\mathbf{R}$ is diagonalized as $\mathbf{R} = \mathbf{A}\mathbf{\Lambda}\mathbf{A}^T$ (Chatfield and Collins 1991; Press *et al.* 1995), where $\mathbf{A} = [\mathbf{a}_1,..,\mathbf{a}_d]$ has as columns the eigenvectors of $\mathbf{R}$, and $\mathbf{\Lambda}$ is a diagonal matrix containing the eigenvalues of $\mathbf{R}$. Assuming that the D largest such eigenvalues are located at the $j_1, \ldots, j_D$ diagonal positions, the data projection matrix is $\mathbf{P}_{\mathrm{PCA}} = [\mathbf{a}_{j1}, \ldots, \mathbf{a}_{jD}]^T$. Given a data vector $\mathbf{x}_t$, this is first element-wise mean and variance normalized, and subsequently, its feature vector is extracted as $\mathbf{y}_t = \mathbf{P}_{\mathrm{PCA}}\mathbf{x}_t$.

Discrete cosine, wavelet, and other image transforms As an alternative to PCA, a number of popular linear image transforms (Gonzalez and Wintz 1977) have been used in place of $\mathbf{P}$ for obtaining speechreading features. For example, the discrete cosine transform (DCT) has been adopted in several systems (Duchnowski *et al.* 1994; Potamianos *et al.* 1998; Nakamura *et al.* 2000; Neti *et al.* 2000; Scanlon and Reilly 2001; Nefian *et al.* 2002; Barker and Shao 2009); the discrete wavelet transform (DWT – Daubechies 1992) in others (Potamianos *et al.* 1998), and the Hadamard and Haar transforms by Scanlon and Reilly (2001). Most researchers use separable transforms (Gonzalez and Wintz 1977), which allow fast implementations (Press *et al.* 1995) when M and N are powers of 2 (typically, values $M, N = 16, 32$, or 64 are considered). Notice that, in each case, matrix $\mathbf{P}$ can have as rows the image transform matrix rows that maximize the transformed data energy over the training set (Potamianos *et al.* 1998), or alternatively, that correspond to a priori chosen locations (Nefian *et al.* 2002).

Linear discriminant analysis (LDA) The data vector transforms presented above are more suitable for ROI compression than for ROI classification into the set of speech classes of interest. For the latter task, LDA (Rao

1965) is more appropriate, as it maps features to a new space for improved classification. LDA was first proposed for automatic speechreading by Duchnowski *et al.* (1994). There, it was applied directly to the ROI vector. LDA has also been considered in a cascade, following the PCA projection of a single frame ROI vector, or on the concatenation of a number of adjacent PCA projected vectors (Matthews *et al.* 2001).

LDA assumes that a set of classes, C (such as HMM states), is a priori chosen, and, in addition, that the training set data vectors $\mathbf{x}_l$, $l = 1,..,L$ are labeled as $c(l) \in C$. Then, it seeks matrix $\mathbf{P}_{\text{LDA}}$, such that the projected training sample $[\mathbf{P}_{\text{LDA}}\ \mathbf{x}_l$, $l = 1, \ldots, L]$ is "well separated" into the set of classes C, according to a function of the training sample within-class scatter matrix $\mathbf{S}_W$ and its between-class scatter matrix $\mathbf{S}_B$ (Rao 1965). These matrices are given by

$$\mathrm{S}_W = \sum_{c \in C} \Pr(c) \Sigma^{(c)} \text{ and } \mathrm{S}_B = \sum_{c \in C} \Pr(c) (\mathbf{m}^{(c)} - \mathbf{m})(\mathbf{m}^{(c)} - \mathbf{m})^{\mathrm{T}}, \qquad (9.2)$$

respectively. In Eq. (9.2), $\Pr(c) = L_c/L$, $c \in C$, is the class empirical probability mass function, where $L_c = \sum_{l=1}^{L} \delta_{c(l),c}$ and $\delta_{i,j} = 1$, if $i = j$; 0, otherwise; in addition, $\mathbf{m}^{(c)}$ and $\sum^{(c)}$ denote the class sample mean and covariance, respectively; and finally, $\mathbf{m} = \sum_{c \in C} \Pr(c)\ \mathbf{m}^{(c)}$ is the total sample mean. To estimate $\mathbf{P}_{\text{LDA}}$, the generalized eigenvalues and right eigenvectors of the matrix pair $(\mathbf{S}_B, \mathbf{S}_W)$, that satisfy $\mathbf{S}_B\mathbf{F} = \mathbf{S}_W\mathbf{F}\boldsymbol{\Lambda}$, are first computed (Rao 1965; Golub and van Loan 1983). Matrix $\mathbf{F} = [\mathbf{f}_1, \ldots, \mathbf{f}_d]$ has as columns the generalized eigenvectors. Assuming that the D largest eigenvalues are located at the $j_1,..,j_D$ diagonal positions of $\boldsymbol{\Lambda}$, then, $\mathbf{P}_{\text{LDA}} = [\mathbf{f}_{j1}, \ldots, \mathbf{f}_{jD}]^{\mathrm{T}}$. It should be noted that, due to Eq. (9.2), the rank of $\mathbf{S}_B$ is at most $|C| - 1$, where $|C|$ denotes the number of classes (the cardinality of set C); hence $D \leq |C| - 1$ should hold. In addition, the rank of the $d \times d$-dimensional matrix $\mathbf{S}_W$ cannot exceed $L - |C|$; therefore, having insufficient training data with respect to the input feature vector dimension d is a potential problem.

Maximum likelihood data rotation (MLLT) In our speechreading system (Potamianos *et al.* 2001b), LDA is followed by the application of a data *maximum likelihood linear transform* (MLLT). This transform seeks a square, non-singular, data rotation matrix $\mathbf{P}_{\text{MLLT}}$ that maximizes the observation data likelihood in the original feature space, under the assumption of diagonal data covariance in the transformed space (Gopinath 1998). Such a rotation is beneficial, since in most ASR systems diagonal covariances are typically assumed when modeling the observation class conditional probability distribution with Gaussian mixture models. The desired rotation matrix is obtained as

$$\mathbf{P}_{\mathrm{MLLT}} = \arg\max_{\mathrm{P}}\{\det(\mathbf{P})^{L}\prod_{c\in C}(\det(\mathrm{diag}(\mathbf{P}\Sigma^{(c)}\mathbf{P}^{T})))^{-\frac{L_c}{2}}\} \tag{9.3}$$

(Gopinath 1998). This can be solved numerically (Press *et al.* 1995).

Notice that LDA and MLLT are data transforms aiming at improved classification performance and maximum likelihood data modeling. Therefore, their application can be viewed as a feature post-processing stage, and clearly, should not be limited to appearance-only visual data.

9.2.2.2 Shape-based features In contrast to appearance-based features, shape-based feature extraction assumes that most speechreading information is contained in the shape (contours) of the speaker's lips, or more generally (Matthews *et al.* 2001), in the face contours (such as jaw and cheek shape, in addition to the lips). Two types of features fall within this category, geometric features and shape model-based features. In both cases, an algorithm that extracts the inner and/or outer lip contours, or in general, the face shape, is required. A variety of such algorithms were discussed above.

Lip geometric features Given the lip contour, a number of high-level features meaningful to humans can be readily extracted, such as the contour height, width, and perimeter, as well as the area contained within the contour. As demonstrated in Figure 9.4, such features do contain significant speech information. Not surprisingly, a large number of speechreading systems make use of all or a subset of them (Petajan 1984; Adjoudani and Benoît 1996; Alissali *et al.* 1996; Goldschen *et al.* 1996; André-Obrecht *et al.* 1997; Jourlin 1997; Chan *et al.* 1998; Rogozan and Deléglise 1998; Teissier *et al.* 1999; Zhang *et al.* 2000; Gurbuz *et al.* 2001; Heckmann *et al.* 2001; Huang and Chen 2001).

Additional visual features can be derived from the lip contours, such as lip image moments and lip contour Fourier descriptors (see Figure 9.4), that are invariant to affine image transformations. Indeed, a number of central moments of the contour interior binary image, or its normalized moments, as defined in Dougherty and Giardina (1987), have been considered as visual features (Czap 2000). Normalized Fourier series coefficients of a contour parameterization (Dougherty and Giardina 1987) have also been used to augment previously discussed geometric features in some speechreading systems, resulting in improved automatic speechreading (Potamianos *et al.* 1998; Gurbuz *et al.* 2001).

Lip model features A number of parametric models (Basu *et al.* 1998) have been used for lip- or face-shape tracking in the literature, and briefly reviewed

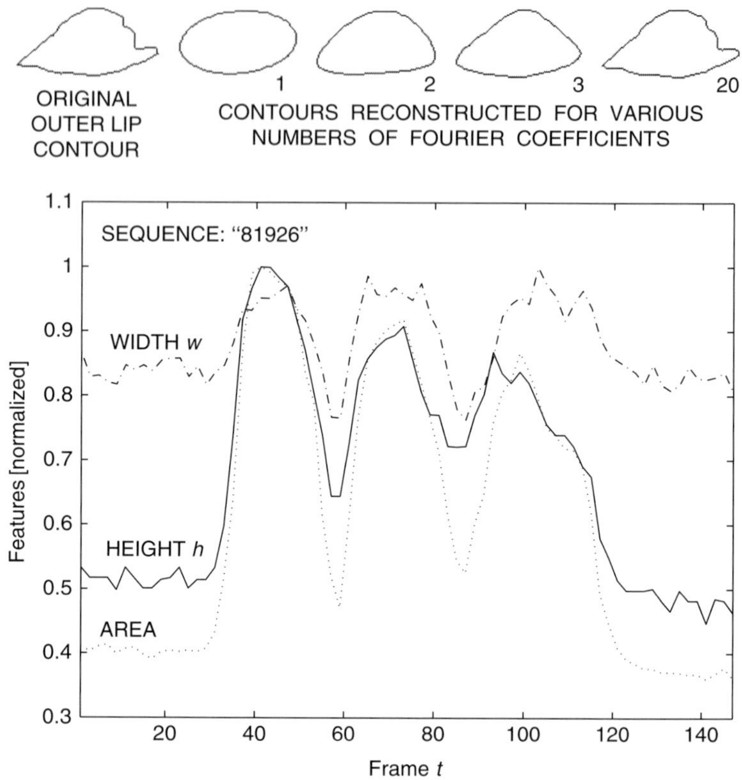

Figure 9.4 Geometric feature approach. Top: Reconstruction of an estimated outer lip contour from 1, 2, 3, and 20 sets of its Fourier coefficients. Bottom: Three geometric visual features, displayed on a normalized scale, tracked over the spoken utterance "81926" of the connected digits database of Potamianos *et al.* (1998). Lip contours are estimated as in Graf *et al.* (1997). © 1997 and 1998 IEEE

in a previous subsection. The parameters of these models can be readily used as visual features. For example, Chiou and Hwang (1997) employ a snake-based algorithm to estimate lip contour, and subsequently use a number of snake radial vectors as visual features. Su and Silsbee (1996), as well as Chandramohan and Silsbee (1996), use lip template parameters instead.

Another popular lip model is the active shape model (ASM). These are flexible statistical models that represent an object with a set of labeled points (Cootes *et al.* 1995; Luettin *et al.* 1996). The object can be the inner and/or outer lip contour (Luettin and Thacker 1997), or the union of various face shape contours as in Matthews *et al.* (2001). To derive an ASM, a number of K contour

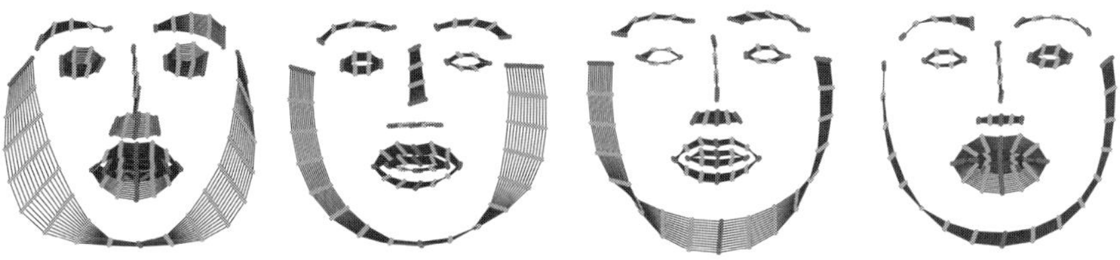

Figure 9.5 Statistical shape model. The top four modes are plotted (left-to-right) at ±3 standard deviations around the mean. These four modes describe 65% of the variance of the training set, which consists of 4072 labeled images from the IBM ViaVoice™ audiovisual database (Neti *et al.* 2000; Matthews *et al.* 2001). © 2000 and 2001 IEEE.

points are first labeled on available training set images, and their coordinates are placed on the $2K$-dimensional shape vectors

$$\mathbf{x}^{(s)} = [x_1, y_1, x_2, y_{2,\ldots,} x_K, y_K]^T. \tag{9.4}$$

Given a set of vectors in Eq. (9.4), PCA can be used to identify the optimal orthogonal linear transform $\mathbf{P}_{\mathrm{PCA}}^{(\mathrm{S})}$ in terms of the variance described along each dimension, resulting in a statistical model of the lip or facial shape (see Figure 9.5). To identify axes of genuine shape variation, each shape in the training set must be aligned. This is achieved using a similarity transform (translation, rotation, and scaling), by means of an iterative Procrustes analysis (Cootes *et al.* 1995; Dryden and Mardia 1998). Given a tracked lip contour, the extracted visual features will be $\mathbf{y}^{(\mathrm{S})} = \mathbf{P}_{\mathrm{PCA}}^{(\mathrm{S})} \mathbf{x}^{(\mathrm{S})}$. Note that vectors in Eq. (9.4) can be the output of a tracking algorithm based on B-splines for example (Dalton *et al.* 1996), or specific "meaningful" points of the lips, appropriately tracked, as the facial animation parameters (Pandzic and Forchheimer 2002; Ekman and Friesen 2003) in Aleksic *et al.* (2002).

9.2.2.3 Joint appearance and shape features Appearance- and shape-based visual features are quite different in nature. In a sense they code low- and high-level information about the speaker's face and lip movements. Not surprisingly, combinations of features from both categories have been employed in a number of automatic speechreading systems.

In most cases, features from each category are just concatenated. For example, Chan (2001) combines geometric lip features with the PCA projection of a subset of pixels contained within the mouth. Luettin *et al.* (1996), as well as Dupont and Luettin (2000), combine ASM features with PCA-based ones, extracted from a ROI that consists of short image profiles around the lip contour. Chiou and Hwang (1997), on the other hand, combine a number of snake lip contour radial vectors with PCA features of the color pixel values of a rectangle mouth ROI.

A different approach to combining the two classes of features is to create a single model of face shape and appearance. An active appearance model (AAM – Cootes *et al.* 1998) provides a framework to statistically combine them. Building an AAM requires three applications of PCA:

- A shape eigenspace calculation that models shape deformations, resulting in PCA matrix $\mathbf{P}^{(\mathrm{S})}_{\mathrm{PCA}}$, computed as above (see Eq. (9.4)).
- An appearance eigenspace calculation to model appearance changes, resulting in a PCA matrix $\mathbf{P}^{(\mathrm{A})}_{\mathrm{PCA}}$, of the ROI appearance vectors. If the color values of the $M \times N$-pixel ROI are considered, such vectors are

$$\mathbf{x}^{(\mathrm{A})} = [r_1, g_1, b_1, r_2, g_2, b_2, \ldots, r_{MN}, g_{MN}, b_{MN}]^T \tag{9.5}$$

similar to vectors of Eq. (9.1).

- Using these, calculation of a combined shape and appearance eigenspace. The latter is a PCA matrix $\mathbf{P}^{(\mathrm{A,S})}_{\mathrm{PCA}}$ on training vectors

$$\mathbf{x}^{(\mathrm{A,S})} = [\mathbf{x}^{(\mathrm{A})^T}\mathbf{W}\mathbf{P}^{(\mathrm{A})^T}_{\mathrm{PCA}},\ \mathbf{x}^{(\mathrm{S})^T}\ \mathbf{P}^{(\mathrm{S})^T}_{\mathrm{PCA}},]^T = [\mathbf{y}^{(\mathrm{A})^T}\mathbf{W}, \mathbf{y}^{(\mathrm{S})^T}]^T, \tag{9.6}$$

where **W** is a suitable diagonal scaling matrix (Matthews *et al.* 2001). The aim of this final PCA is to remove the redundancy due to the shape and appearance correlation and to create a single model that compactly describes shape and the corresponding appearance deformation.

Such a model has been used for speechreading in Neti *et al.* (2000), Matthews *et al.* (2001), and Papandreou *et al.* (2009). An example of the resulting learned joined model is depicted in Figure 9.6. A block diagram of the method, including the dimensionalities of the input shape and appearance vectors (Eq. (9.4) and Eq. (9.5), respectively), their PCA projections $\mathbf{y}^{(\mathrm{S})}$, $\mathbf{y}^{(\mathrm{A})}$, and the final feature vector $\mathbf{y}^{(\mathrm{A,S})}\mathbf{P}^{(\mathrm{AS})}_{\mathrm{PCA}}\mathbf{x}^{(\mathrm{A,S})}$ is depicted in Figure 9.7.

9.2.2.4 Visual feature post-extraction processing In an audiovisual speech recognition system, in addition to the visual features, audio features are also extracted from the acoustic waveform. For example, such features could be mel-frequency cepstral coefficients (MFCCs), or linear prediction coefficients (LPCs), typically extracted at a 100 Hz rate (Deller *et al.* 1993; Rabiner and Juarg 1993; Young *et al.* 1999). In contrast, visual features are generated at the video frame rate, commonly 25 or 30 Hz, or twice that, in the case of interlaced video. Since feature stream synchrony is required in a number of algorithms for audiovisual fusion, as discussed in the next section, the two feature streams must achieve the same rate.

Typically, this is accomplished (whenever required), either after feature extraction, by simple element-wise linear interpolation of the visual features

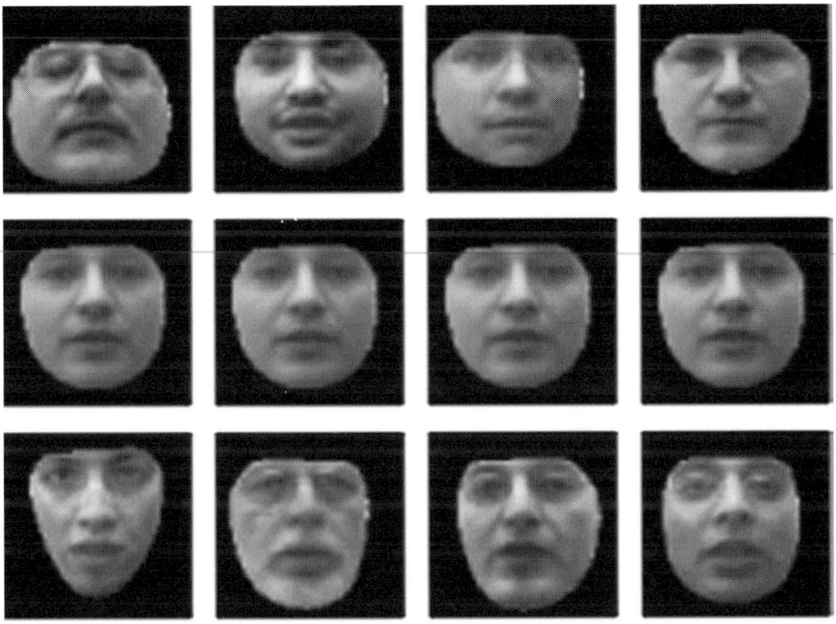

Figure 9.6 Combined shape and appearance statistical model. Center row: Mean shape and appearance. Top row: Mean shape and appearance +3 standard deviations. Bottom row: Mean shape and appearance −3 standard deviations. The top four modes, depicted left-to-right, describe 46% of the combined shape and appearance variance of 4072 labeled images from the IBM ViaVoice™ audiovisual database (Neti *et al.* 2000; Matthews *et al.* 2001).© 2000 and 2001 IEEE.

to the audio frame rate (as in Figure 9.7), or before feature extraction, by frame duplication, to achieve a 100 Hz video input rate to the visual front end. Occasionally, the audio front end processing is performed at a lower video rate.

Another interesting issue in visual feature extraction has to do with feature normalization. In a traditional audio front end, cepstral mean subtraction is often employed to enhance robustness to speaker and environment variations (Liu *et al.* 1993; Young *et al.* 1999). A simple visual feature mean normalization (FMN) by element-wise subtraction of the vector mean over each sentence has been demonstrated to improve appearance feature-based visual-only recognition (Potamianos *et al.* 1998; Potamianos *et al.* 2001b). Alternatively, linear intensity compensation preceding the appearance feature extraction has been investigated by Vanegas *et al.* (1998).

A very important issue in the visual feature design is capturing the dynamics of visual speech. Temporal information, often spanning multiple phone

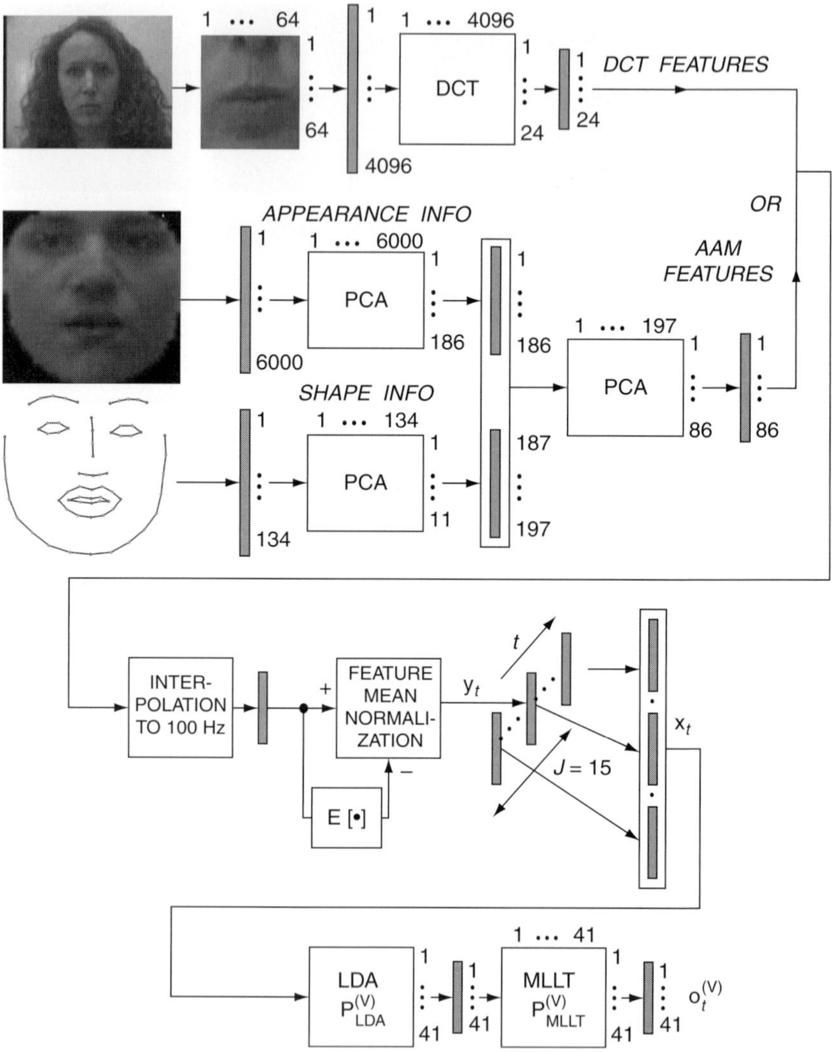

Figure 9.7 DCT- versus AAM-based visual feature extraction for automatic speechreading, followed by visual feature post-extraction processing using linear interpolation, feature mean normalization, adjacent frame feature concatenation, and the application of LDA and MLLT. Vector dimensions as implemented in the system of Neti *et al.* (2000) are depicted.

segments, is known to help human perception of visual speech (Rosenblum and Saldaña 1998). Borrowing again from the ASR literature, dynamic speech information can be captured by augmenting the visual feature vector with its first- and second-order temporal derivatives (Rabiner and Juang 1993; Young *et al.* 1999). Alternatively, LDA can be used, as a means of "learning" a transform that optimally captures the speech dynamics. Such a transform is applied on the concatenation of consecutive feature vectors adjacent to and including the current frame (see also Figure 9.7), i.e., on

$$\mathbf{x}_t = [\mathbf{y}^T_{t-\lfloor J/2 \rfloor}, \ldots, \mathbf{y}^T_t, \ldots, \mathbf{y}^T_{t+\lceil J/2 \rceil - 1}]^T \tag{9.7}$$

with $J = 15$ for example, as in Neti *et al.* (2000) and Potamianos *et al.* (2001b).

Clearly, and as we already mentioned, LDA could be applied to any category of features discussed. The same holds for MLLT, a method that aims to improve maximum likelihood data modeling and, in practice, ASR performance. For example, a number of feature post-processing steps discussed above, including LDA and MLLT, were interchangeably applied to DCT appearance features, as well as to AAM ones, in our visual front end experiments during the Johns Hopkins workshop, as depicted in Figure 9.7 (Neti *et al.* 2000; Matthews *et al.* 2001). Alternate ways of combining feature post-extraction processing steps can easily be envisioned. For example, LDA and MLLT can be applied to obtain within-frame discriminant features (Potamianos and Neti 2001b), which can then be augmented by their first- and second-order derivatives, or followed by LDA and MLLT across frames (see also Figure 9.11). Additional feature transformations can also hold benefit to the system, for example a Gaussianization step, as reported by Huang and Visweswariah (2005).

Finally, an important problem in data classification is the issue of feature selection within a larger pool of candidate features (Jain *et al.* 2000). In the context of speechreading, this matter has been directly addressed in the selection of geometric, lip contour-based features by Goldschen *et al.* (1996) and in the selection of appearance, DCT-based features by Scanlon *et al.* (2004) and Potamianos and Scanlon (2005).

9.2.3 *Summary of visual front end algorithms*

We have presented a summary of the most common visual feature extraction algorithms proposed in the literature for automatic speechreading. Such techniques differ both in their assumptions about where the speechreading information lies, as well as in the requirements that they place on face detection, facial part localization, and tracking. On the one extreme, appearance-based visual features consider a broadly defined ROI and then rely on traditional pattern recognition and image compression techniques to extract relevant speechreading information.

On the other end, shape-based visual features require adequate lip or facial shape tracking and assume that the visual speech information is captured by the shape's form and movement alone. Bridging the two extremes, various combinations of the two types of features have also been used, ranging from simple concatenation to joint modeling.

Comparisons between features within the same class are often reported in the literature (Duchnowski *et al.* 1994; Goldschen *et al.* 1996; Gray *et al.* 1997; Potamianos *et al.* 1998; Matthews *et al.* 2001; Scanlon and Reilly 2001; Seymour *et al.* 2008). Comparisons however across the various types of features are rather limited, as the feature types require quite different sets of algorithms for their implementation. Nevertheless, Matthews *et al.* (1998) demonstrate AAMs to outperform ASMs, and to result in similar visual-only recognition to alternative appearance-based features. Chiou and Hwang (1997) report that their joint features outperform their shape and appearance feature components, whereas Potamianos *et al.* (1998), as well as Scanlon and Reilly (2001), report that DCT-based visual features are superior to a set of lip contour geometric features. Also, Aleksic and Katsaggelos (2004a) compare PCA appearance-based and shape-based features, but with inconclusive results. However, the above are all reported on single-subject data and/or small vocabulary tasks. In a larger experiment, Matthews *et al.* (2001) compare a number of appearance-based features with AAMs on a speaker-independent LVCSR task. All appearance features considered outperformed AAMs. However, it is suspected that the AAM used there was not sufficiently trained.

Although much progress has been made in visual feature extraction, it seems that the identification of the best visual features for automatic speechreading, features that are robust in a variety of visual environments, remains to a large extent unresolved. Of particular importance is that such features should exhibit sufficient speaker, pose, camera, and environment independence. However, it is worth mentioning two arguments in favor of appearance-based features. First, their use is well motivated by human perception studies of visual speech. Indeed, significant information about the place of articulation, such as tongue and teeth visibility, cannot be captured by the lip contours alone. Human speech perception based on the mouth region is superior to perception on the basis of the lips alone and it further improves when the entire lower face is visible (Summerfield *et al.* 1989). Second, the extraction of certain well-performing, appearance-based features such as the DCT is computationally efficient. Indeed, it requires a crude mouth region detection algorithm, which can be applied at a low frame rate, whereas the subsequent pixel vector transform is amenable to fast implementation for suitable ROI sizes (Press *et al.* 1995). These observations are encouraging with regard to work towards the ultimate goal of implementing realtime automatic speechreading systems (Connell *et al.* 2003), operating robustly in realistic visual environments (Potamianos and Neti 2003).

9.3 Audiovisual integration

Audiovisual fusion is an instance of the general classifier combination problem (Jain *et al.* 2000; Sannen *et al.* 2010). In our case, two observation streams are available (audio and visual modalities) and provide information about speech classes, such as context-dependent sub-phonetic units, or at a higher level, word sequences. Each observation stream can be used alone to train single-modality statistical classifiers to recognize such classes. However, one hopes that combining the two streams will give rise to a bimodal classifier with superior performance to both single-modality ones.

Various information fusion algorithms have been considered in the literature for audiovisual ASR (for example, Bregler *et al.* 1993; Adjoudani and Benoît 1996; Hennecke *et al.* 1996; Potamianos and Graf 1998; Rogozan 1999; Teissier *et al.* 1999; Dupont and Luettin 2000; Neti *et al.* 2000; Chen 2001; Chu and Huang 2002; Garg *et al.* 2003; Lewis and Powers 2005; Saenko and Livescu 2006; Marcheret *et al.* 2007; Shao and Barker 2008; Papandreou *et al.* 2009). The proposed techniques differ both in their basic design, and in the adopted terminology. The architecture of some of these methods (Robert-Ribes *et al.* 1996; Teissier *et al.* 1999; Lewis and Powers 2005) is motivated by models of human speech perception (Massaro 1996; Massaro and Stork 1998; Berthommier 2001). In most cases however, research in audiovisual ASR has followed a separate track from work on modeling the human perception of audiovisual speech.

Audiovisual integration techniques can be broadly grouped into feature fusion and decision fusion methods. The first ones are based on training a single classifier (i.e., of the same form as the audio- and visual-only classifiers) on the concatenated vector of audio and visual features, or on any appropriate transformation of it (Adjoudani and Benoît 1996; Teissier *et al.* 1999; Potamianos *et al.* 2001c; Aleksic *et al.* 2005). In contrast, decision fusion algorithms utilize the two single-modality (audio- and visual-only) classifier outputs to recognize audiovisual speech. Typically, this is achieved by linearly combining the class-conditional observation log-likelihoods of the two classifiers into a joint audiovisual classification score, using appropriate weights that capture the reliability of each single-modality classifier, or data stream (Hennecke *et al.* 1996; Rogozan *et al.* 1997; Potamianos and Graf 1998; Dupont and Luettin 2000; Neti *et al.* 2000; Nefian *et al.* 2002; Tamura *et al.* 2005; Marcheret *et al.* 2007; Shao and Barker 2008).

In this section, we provide a detailed description of some popular fusion techniques from each category (see also Table 9.1). In addition, we briefly address two issues relevant to automatic recognition of audiovisual speech. One is the problem of speech modeling for ASR, which poses particular interest in automatic speechreading, and helps establish some background and notation

Table 9.1 *Taxonomy of the audiovisual integration methods considered in this section. Three feature-fusion techniques that differ in the features used for recognition and three decision-fusion methods that differ in the combination stage of the audio and visual classifiers are described in more detail in this chapter.*

Fusion Type	Audiovisual Features	Classification Level
Feature fusion: one classifier chosen	1. **Concatenated** features 2. **Hierarchical discriminant** features 3. **Enhanced** audio features	Sub-phonetic (early)
Decision fusion: two classifiers chosen	Concatenated features	1. Sub-phonetic (**early**) 2. Phone or word (**intermediate**) 3. Utterance (**late**)

for the remainder of the section. We also consider the subject of speaker adaptation, an important element in practical ASR systems.

9.3.1 Audiovisual speech modeling for ASR

Two central aspects in the design of ASR systems are the choice of speech classes that are assumed to generate the observed features, and the statistical modeling of this generation process. In the following, we briefly discuss both issues, since they are often embedded into the design of audiovisual fusion algorithms.

9.3.1.1 Speech classes for audiovisual ASR The basic unit that describes how speech conveys linguistic information is the phoneme. For American English, there exist approximately forty-two such units (Deller *et al.* 1993), generated by specific positions or movements of the vocal tract articulators. Only some of the articulators are visible, however; therefore among these phonemes, the number of visually distinguishable units is much smaller. Such units are called visemes in the audiovisual ASR and human perception literatures (Stork and Hennecke 1996; Campbell *et al.* 1998; Massaro and Stork 1998). In general, phoneme to viseme mappings are derived from human speechreading studies. Alternatively, such mappings can be generated using statistical clustering techniques, as proposed by Goldschen *et al.* (1996) and Rogozan (1999). There is no universal agreement about the exact partitioning of phonemes into visemes, but some visemes are well-defined, such as the bilabial viseme consisting of the phoneme set [/p/, /b/, /m/]. A typical clustering into thirteen visemes is used by Neti *et al.* (2000) to conduct visual speech modeling experiments, and is depicted in Table 9.2.

In traditional audio-only ASR, the set of classes $c \in C$ that needs to be estimated on the basis of the observed feature sequence most often consists of

Table 9.2 *The forty-four phonemes to thirteen visemes mapping considered by Neti* et al. *(2000), using the HTK phone set (Young* et al. *1999).*

Silence	/sil/, /sp/
Lip-rounding based vowels	/ao/, /ah/, /aa/, /er/, /oy/, /aw/, /hh/
	/uw/, /uh/, /ow/
	/ae/, /eh/, /ey/, /ay/
	/ih/, /iy/, /ax/
Alveolar semivowels	/l/, /el/, /r/, /y/
Alveolar fricatives	/s/, /z/
Alveolar	/t/, /d/, /n/, /en/
Palato-alveolar	/sh/, /zh/, /ch/, /jh/
Bilabial	/p/, /b/, /m/
Dental	/th/, /dh/
Labio-dental	/f/, /v/
Velar	/ng/, /k/, /g/, /w/

sub-phonetic units, and occasionally of sub-word units in small vocabulary recognition tasks. For LVCSR, a large number of context-dependent sub-phonetic units are used, obtained by clustering the possible phonetic contexts (tri-phone ones, for example) using a decision tree. In this chapter, such units are exclusively used, defined over tri- or eleven-phone contexts, as described in the Experiments section (Section 9.5).

For automatic speechreading, it seems appropriate, from the human visual speech perception point of view, to use visemic sub-phonetic classes, and their decision tree clustering based on visemic context. Such clustering experiments are reported by Neti *et al.* (2000). In addition, visual-only recognition of visemes is occasionally considered in the literature (Potamianos *et al.* 2001b; Gordan *et al.* 2002). Visemic speech classes are also used for audiovisual ASR at the second stage of a cascade decision fusion architecture proposed by Rogozan (1999), as well as in the dynamic Bayesian network proposed for audiovisual fusion by Terry and Katsaggelos (2008) and a number of experiments reported by Hazen (2006). In general, however, the vast majority of works in the literature employ identical classes and decision trees for both modalities.

9.3.1.2 HMM-based speech recognition The most widely used classifier for audiovisual ASR is the hidden Markov model (HMM), a very popular method for traditional audio-only speech recognition. Additional methods also exist for automatic recognition of speech, and have been employed in audiovisual ASR systems, such as dynamic time warping (DTW), used for example by Petajan (1984), artificial neural networks (ANN), as in Krone *et al.* (1997), hybrid ANN-DTW systems (Bregler *et al.* 1993; Duchnowski *et al.* 1994), hybrid

ANN-HMM ones (Heckmann *et al.* 2001), and support vector machines (SVM, see Gordan *et al.* 2002) – in the latter case for visual-only ASR. Various types of HMMs have also been used for audiovisual ASR, such as HMMs with discrete observations after vector quantization of the feature space (Silsbee and Bovik 1996), or HMMs with non-Gaussian continuous observation probabilities (Su and Silsbee 1996). However, the vast majority of audiovisual ASR systems, to which we restrict our presentation in this chapter, employ HMMs with a continuous observation probability density, modeled as a mixture of Gaussian densities.

Typically in the literature, single-stream HMMs are used to model the generation of a sequence of audio-only or visual-only speech informative features, $\{\mathbf{o}_t^{(s)}\}$, of dimensionality D_s, where $s =$ A,V denotes the audio or visual modality (stream). The HMM emission (class conditional observation) probabilities are modeled by Gaussian mixture densities, given by

$$\Pr(\mathbf{o}_t^{(s)}|c) = \sum_{k=1}^{K_{sc}} w_{sck}\ N_{D_s}(\mathbf{o}_t^{(s)}; \mathbf{m}_{sck}, \mathbf{s}_{sck}) \tag{9.8}$$

for all classes $c \in C$, whereas the HMM transition probabilities between classes are given by $\mathbf{r}_s = [\{\Pr(c'|c''), c'|c'' \in C\}]^T$. The HMM parameter vector is therefore

$$\begin{aligned} \mathbf{a}_s &= \left[\mathbf{r}_s^T, \mathbf{b}_s^T\right]^T, \text{where} \\ \mathbf{b}_s &= \left[\left\{\left[w_{sck}, \mathbf{m}_{sck}^T, \mathbf{s}_{sck}^T,\right]^T, k = 1, \ldots, K_{sc}, c \in C\right\}\right]^T, \end{aligned} \tag{9.9}$$

In Eq. (9.7) and Eq. (9.8), $c \in C$ denote the HMM context-dependent states, whereas mixture weights w_{sck} are positive adding to one; K_{sc} denotes the number of mixtures; and $N_D(\mathbf{o};\mathbf{m},\mathbf{s})$ is the D-variate normal distribution with mean $\mathbf{m}$ and a diagonal covariance matrix, its diagonal being denoted by $\mathbf{s}$.

The *expectation-maximization* (EM) algorithm (Dempster *et al.* 1977) is typically used to obtain *maximum likelihood* estimates of Eq. (9.9). Given a current HMM parameter vector at EM algorithm iteration j, $\mathbf{a}_s^{(j)}$, a re-estimated parameter vector is obtained as

$$\mathbf{a}_s^{(j+1)} = \arg\max_{\mathrm{a}} Q(\mathbf{a}_s^{(j)}, \mathbf{a}|\mathbf{O}^{(s)}). \tag{9.10}$$

In Eq. (9.10), $\mathbf{O}^{(s)}$ denotes training data observations from L utterances $\mathbf{o}_l^{(s)}$, $l = 1, \ldots, L$, and $Q(\bullet,\bullet|\bullet)$ represents the EM algorithm auxiliary function, defined (Rabiner and Juang 1993) as

$$Q(\mathbf{a}',\mathbf{a}''|\mathbf{O}^{(s)}) = \sum_{l=1}^{L} \sum_{\mathrm{c}(l)} \Pr(\mathbf{O}_l^{(s)}, \mathbf{c}(l)|\mathbf{a}') \log(\mathbf{O}_l^{(s)}, \mathbf{c}(l)|\mathbf{a}''). \tag{9.11}$$

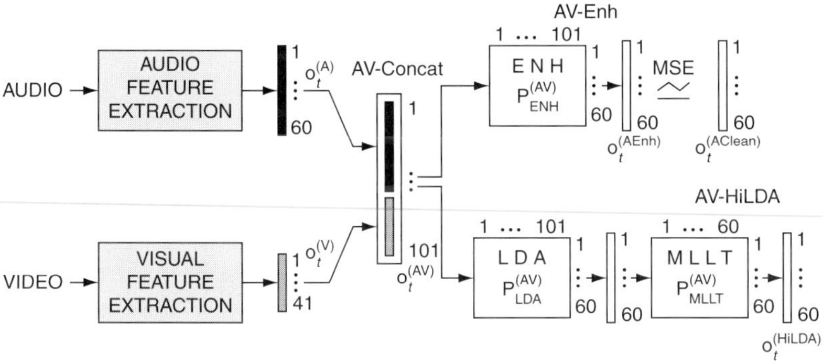

Figure 9.8 Three types of feature fusion considered in this section: Plain audiovisual feature concatenation (AV-Concat), hierarchical discriminant feature extraction (AV-HiLDA), and audiovisual speech enhancement (AV-Enh).

In Eq. (9.11), $c(l)$ denotes any HMM state sequence for utterance l. Replacing it with the best HMM path reduces EM to Viterbi training. As an alternative to maximum likelihood, discriminative training methods can instead be used for HMM parameter estimation (Bahl *et al.* 1986; Chou *et al.* 1994; Woodland and Povey 2002; Huang and Povey 2005).

9.3.2 *Feature fusion techniques for audiovisual ASR*

As already mentioned, feature fusion uses a single classifier to model the concatenated vector of time-synchronous audio and visual features, or appropriate transformations of it. Such methods include plain feature concatenation (Adjoudani and Benoît 1996), feature weighting (Teissier *et al.* 1999; Chen 2001), both also known as direct identification fusion (Teissier *et al.* 1999), and hierarchical linear discriminant feature extraction (Potamianos *et al.* 2001c). The dominant and motor recording fusion models discussed by Teissier *et al.* (1999) also belong to this category, as they seek a data-to-data mapping of either the visual features into the audio space, or of both modality features to a new common space, followed by linear combination of the resulting features. Audio feature enhancement on the basis of either visual input (Girin *et al.* 1995; Barker and Berthommier 1999), or concatenated audiovisual features (Girin *et al.* 2001b; Goecke *et al.* 2002) also falls within this category of fusion, under the general definition adopted above. In this section, we expand on three feature fusion techniques, schematically depicted in Figure 9.8.

9.3.2.1 Concatenative feature fusion Given time-synchronous audio and visual feature vectors $\mathbf{o}_t^{(A)}$ and $\mathbf{o}_t^{(V)}$, with dimensionalities D_A and D_V, respectively, the joint, concatenated audiovisual feature vector at time t becomes

$$\mathbf{o}_t^{(AV)} = [\mathbf{o}_t^{(A)^T}, \ \mathbf{o}_t^{(V)^T}]^T \in R^D, \tag{9.12}$$

where $D = D_A + D_V$. As with all feature fusion methods (i.e., also for vectors in Eq. (9.13) and Eq. (9.14), below), the generation process for a sequence of features in Eq. (9.12) is modeled by a single-stream HMM, with emission probabilities (see also Eq. (9.7))

$$\Pr\left(\mathbf{o}_t^{(AV)} \middle| c\right) = \sum_{k=1}^{K_c} w_{ck} \ N_D(\mathbf{o}_t^{(AV)}; \mathbf{m}_{ck}, \mathbf{s}_{ck})$$

for all classes $c \in C$ (Adjoudani and Benoît 1996). Concatenative feature fusion constitutes a simple approach for audiovisual ASR, implementable in most existing ASR systems with minor changes. However, the vector dimensionality in Eq. (9.12) can be rather high, with the consequent risk of inadequate modeling in Eq. (9.8) due to the curse of dimensionality (Chatfield and Collins 1991). The following fusion technique aims to avoid this, by seeking lower-dimensional representations of Eq. (9.12).

9.3.2.2 Hierarchical discriminant feature fusion Visual features contain less speech classification power than audio features, even in the case of extreme noise in the audio channel (see Table 9.3 in the Experiments section). One would therefore expect that an appropriate lower-dimensional representation of Eq. (9.12) could lead to equal and possibly better HMM performance, given the problem of accurate probabilistic modeling in high-dimensional spaces. Potamianos *et al.* (2001c) have considered LDA as a means of obtaining such a dimensionality reduction. The goal is in fact to obtain the best discrimination among the classes of interest and LDA achieves this on the basis of the data (and their labels) alone, without an a priori bias in favor of either of the two feature streams. LDA is followed by an MLLT-based data rotation (see also Figure 9.8), in order to improve maximum-likelihood data modeling using Eq. (9.8). In the audiovisual ASR system of Potamianos *et al.* (2001c), the proposed method amounts to a two-stage application of LDA and MLLT, first intra-modal on the original audio MFCC and visual DCT features, and then inter-modal on Eq. (9.12), as also depicted in Figure 9.11. It is therefore referred to as HiLDA (hierarchical LDA). The final audiovisual feature vector is (see also Eq. (9.12))

$$\mathbf{o}_t^{(HiLDA)} = \mathbf{P}_{MLLT}^{(AV)} \ \mathbf{P}_{LDA}^{(AV)} \ \mathbf{o}_t^{(AV)}. \tag{9.13}$$

One can set the dimensionality of Eq. (9.13) to be equal to the audio feature vector size, as implemented by Neti *et al.* (2000).

9.3.2.3 Audio feature enhancement Audio and visible speech are correlated since they are constrained to use a common orofacial anatomy. Not surprisingly, a number of techniques have been proposed to obtain estimates of audio features utilizing the visual-only modality (Girin *et al.* 1995; Yehia *et al.* 1998; Barker and Berthommier 1999), or joint audiovisual speech data, in the case where the audio signal is degraded (Girin *et al.* 2001b; Goecke *et al.* 2002). The latter scenario corresponds to the speech enhancement paradigm. Under this approach, the enhanced audio feature vector $\mathbf{o}_t^{(\mathrm{AEnh})}$ can be simply obtained as a linear transformation of the concatenated audiovisual feature vector of Eq. (9.11), namely as

$$\mathbf{o}_t^{(\mathrm{AEnh})} = \mathbf{P}_{\mathrm{ENH}}^{(\mathrm{AV})}\, \mathbf{o}_t^{(\mathrm{AV})} \tag{9.14}$$

where $\mathbf{P}_{\mathrm{ENH}}^{(\mathrm{AV})} = [\mathbf{p}_1^{(\mathrm{AV})}, \mathbf{p}_2^{(\mathrm{AV})}, \ldots, \mathbf{p}_{D_\mathrm{A}}^{(\mathrm{AV})},]^T$ consists of D-dimensional row vectors $\mathbf{p}_i^{(\mathrm{AV})^\mathrm{T}}$ for $i = 1, \ldots, D_\mathrm{A}$, and has dimension $D_\mathrm{A} \times D$ (see also Figure 9.8).

A simple way to estimate matrix $\mathbf{P}_{\mathrm{ENH}}^{(\mathrm{AV})}$ is by considering the approximation $\mathbf{o}_t^{(\mathrm{AEnh})} \approx \mathbf{o}_t^{(\mathrm{AClean})}$ in the Euclidean distance sense, where vector $\mathbf{o}_t^{(\mathrm{AClean})}$ denotes clean audio features available in addition to visual and noisy audio vectors, for a number of time instants t in a training set, T. By Eq. (9.14), this becomes equivalent to solving D_A *mean square error* (MSE) estimations

$$\mathbf{p}_i^{(\mathrm{AV})} = \arg\min_{\mathrm{p}} \sum_{t \in T} [\mathrm{o}_{t,i}^{(\mathrm{AClean})} - \mathbf{p}^T \mathbf{o}_t^{(\mathrm{AV})}]^2 \tag{9.15}$$

for $i = 1, \ldots, D_\mathrm{A}$, i.e., one per row of the matrix $\mathbf{P}_{\mathrm{ENH}}^{(\mathrm{AV})}$. Equation (9.15) results in D_A systems of Yule–Walker equations that can be easily solved using Gauss–Jordan elimination (Press *et al.* 1995). A more sophisticated way of estimating $\mathbf{P}_{\mathrm{ENH}}^{(\mathrm{AV})}$ by using a Mahalanobis type distance instead of Eq. (9.15) is considered by Goecke *et al.* (2002). Non-linear estimation schemes are proposed by Girin *et al.* (2001a) and Deligne *et al.* (2002).

9.3.3 Decision fusion techniques for audiovisual ASR

Although feature fusion techniques (for example, HiLDA) that result in improved ASR over audio-only performance have been documented (Neti *et al.* 2000), they cannot explicitly model the reliability of each modality. Such modeling is extremely important, as speech information content and the discrimination power of the audio and visual streams can vary widely, depending on the spoken utterance, acoustic noise in the environment, visual channel degradation, face tracker inaccuracies, and speaker characteristics. In contrast to feature fusion methods, the decision fusion framework provides a mechanism for capturing the reliability of each modality, by borrowing from classifier combination literature.

Classifier combination based on individual decisions about the classes of interest is an active area of research with many applications (Xu *et al.* 1992; Kittler *et al.* 1998; Jain *et al.* 2000; Sannen *et al.* 2010). Combination strategies differ in various aspects, such as the architecture used (parallel, cascade, or hierarchical combination), possible trainability (static or adaptive), and information level considered at integration: abstract, rank-order, or measurement level, i.e., whether information is available about the best class only, the top n classes (or the ranking of all possible classes), or the likelihood scores. In the audiovisual ASR literature, examples of most of these categories can be found. For example, Petajan (1984) rescores the two best outputs of the audio-only classifier by means of the visual-only classifier, a case of cascade, static, rank-order level decision fusion. Combinations of more than one category, as well as cases where one of the two classifiers of interest corresponds to a feature fusion technique are also possible. For example, Rogozan and Deléglise (1998) use a parallel, adaptive, measurement-level combination of an audiovisual classifier trained on concatenated features (Eq. (9.12)) with a visual-only classifier, whereas Rogozan (1999) considers a cascade, adaptive, rank-order level integration of the two. The lattice rescoring framework used during the Johns Hopkins University workshop (as described in the Experiments section that follows) is an example of a hybrid cascade/parallel fusion architecture (Neti *et al.* 2000; Glotin *et al.* 2001; Luettin *et al.* 2001).

However, by far the most commonly used decision fusion techniques for audiovisual ASR belong to the paradigm of audio- and visual-only classifier integration using a parallel architecture, adaptive combination weights, and class measurement level information. These methods derive the most likely speech class or word sequence by linearly combining the log-likelihoods of the two single-modality HMM classifier decisions, using appropriate weights (Adjoudani and Benoît 1996; Jourlin 1997; Potamianos and Graf 1998; Teissier *et al.* 1999; Dupont and Luettin 2000; Neti *et al.* 2000; Gurbuz *et al.* 2001; Heckmann *et al.* 2001; Nefian *et al.* 2002; Tamura *et al.* 2005; Marcheret *et al.* 2007; Shao and Barker 2008). This corresponds to the adaptive product rule in the likelihood domain (Jain *et al.* 2000), and it is also known as the separate identification model of audiovisual fusion (Rogozan 1999; Teissier *et al.* 1999).

Continuous speech recognition introduces an additional twist to the classifier fusion problem, due to the fact that sequences of classes (HMM states or words) need to be estimated. One can consider three possible temporal levels for combining stream (modality) likelihoods, as depicted in Table 9.1: (a) "Early" integration, i.e., likelihood combination at the HMM state level, which gives rise to the multi-stream HMM classifier (Bourlard and Dupont 1996; Young *et al.* 1999), and forces synchrony between its two single-modality components; (b) "Late" integration, where typically a number of n-best audio and possibly visual-only recognizer hypotheses are rescored by the log-likelihood combination of the two streams, which allows complete asynchrony between the two HMMs; and (c) "Intermediate" integration, typically implemented by means of the product HMM (Varga and Moore 1990), or the coupled HMM (Brand *et al.* 1997), which forces HMM synchrony at the phone, or word, boundaries. Notice that such terminology is not universally agreed upon, and our reference to early or late integration at the temporal level should not be confused with the feature versus decision fusion meaning of these terms in other work (Adjoudani and Benoît 1996).

9.3.3.1 Early integration: state-synchronous multi-stream HMM In its general form, the class conditional observation likelihood of the multi-stream HMM is the product of the observation likelihoods of the HMM single-stream components, raised to appropriate stream exponents that capture the reliability of each modality, or equivalently, the confidence of each single-stream classifier. Such a model has been considered in audio-only ASR where, for example, separate streams are used for the energy audio features and MFCC static features, as well as their first and possibly second-order derivatives, as in Hernando *et al.* (1995) and Young *et al.* (1999), or for band-limited audio features in the multi-band ASR paradigm (Hermansky *et al.* 1996), as in Bourlard and Dupont (1996), Okawa *et al.* (1999), Glotin and Berthommier (2000), among others. In the audiovisual domain, the model becomes a two-stream HMM, with one stream devoted to the audio, and another to the visual modality. As such, it has been extensively used in audiovisual ASR (Jourlin 1997; Potamianos and Graf 1998; Dupont and Luettin 2000; Miyajima *et al.* 2000; Nakamura *et al.* 2000; Neti *et al.* 2000; Tamura *et al.* 2005; Marcheret *et al.* 2007; Shao and Barker 2008; Terry *et al.* 2008). In the system reported by Neti *et al.* (2000) and Luettin *et al.* (2001), the method was applied for the first time to the LVCSR domain.

Given the bimodal (audiovisual) observation vector $\mathbf{o}_t^{(\mathrm{AV})}$, the state emission "score" (it no longer represents a probability distribution) of the multi-stream HMM is (see also Eq. (9.8) and Eq. (9.12))

$$\Pr(\mathbf{o}_t^{(\mathrm{AV})} | c) = \prod_{s \in \{\mathrm{A,V}\}} \left[\sum_{k=1}^{K_{sc}} w_{sck} N_{D_s}(\mathbf{o}_t^{(s)}; \mathbf{m}_{sck}, \mathbf{s}_{sck}) \right]^{\lambda_{sct}} \tag{9.16}$$

Notice that Eq. (9.16) corresponds to a linear combination in the log-likelihood domain. In Eq. (9.16), λ_{sct} denote the stream exponents (weights), that are non-negative, and in general, are a function of the modality s, the

HMM state $c \in C$, and locally, the utterance frame (time) t. Such state- and time-dependence can be used to model the speech class and "local" environment-based reliability of each stream. The exponents are often constrained to $\lambda_{Act} + \lambda_{Vct} = 1$, or 2. In most systems, they are set to global, modality-only dependent values, i.e., $\lambda_s \leftarrow \lambda_{sct}$, for all classes $c \in C$ and time instants t, with the class dependence occasionally being preserved, i.e., $\lambda_{sc} \leftarrow \lambda_{sct}$, for all t. In the latter case, the parameters of the multi-stream HMM (see also Eq. (9.8), Eq. (9.9), and Eq. (9.16))

$$\bar{\mathbf{a}}_{\mathrm{AV}} = [\mathbf{a}_{\mathrm{AV}}^T, \{[\lambda_{\mathrm{A}c}, \lambda_{\mathrm{A}c}]^T, c \in C\}^T], \text{ where } \mathbf{a}_{\mathrm{AV}} = [\mathbf{r}^T, \mathbf{b}_{\mathrm{A}}^T, \mathbf{b}_{\mathrm{V}}^T]^T \tag{9.17}$$

consist of the HMM transition probabilities $\mathbf{r}$ and the emission probability parameters $\mathbf{b}_{\mathrm{A}}$ and $\mathbf{b}_{\mathrm{V}}$ of its single-stream components.

The parameters of $\mathbf{a}_{\mathrm{AV}}$ can be estimated separately for each stream component using the EM algorithm, namely, Eq. (9.10) for $s \in$[A,V] and subsequently, by setting the joint HMM transition probability vector equal to the audio one, i.e., $\mathbf{r} = \mathbf{r}_{\mathrm{A}}$, or alternatively, to the product of the transition probabilities of the two HMMs, i.e., $\mathbf{r} = diag(\mathbf{r}_{\mathrm{A}}\ \mathbf{r}_{\mathrm{V}}^{\mathrm{T}})$ (see also Eq. (9.9)). The latter scheme is referred to in the Experiments section as *AV-MS-Sep*. An obvious drawback of this approach is that the two single-modality HMMs are trained asynchronously (i.e., using different forced alignments), whereas Eq. (9.16) assumes that the HMM stream components are state synchronous. The alternative is to jointly estimate parameters $\mathbf{a}_{\mathrm{AV}}$, in order to enforce state synchrony. Due to the linear combination of stream log-likelihoods in Eq. (9.16), the EM algorithm carries on in the multi-stream HMM case with minor changes (Rabiner and Juang 1993; Young *et al.* 1999). As a result,

$$\mathbf{a}_{\mathrm{AV}}^{(j+1)} = \arg\max_{\mathrm{a}} \left(\bar{a}_{\mathrm{AV}}^{(j)}, \mathbf{a} | \mathbf{O}^{(\mathrm{AV})} \right) \tag{9.18}$$

can be used, a scheme referred to as *AV-MS-Joint*. Notice that the two approaches basically differ in the E-step of the EM algorithm.

In both separate and joint HMM training, the remainder of parameter vector $\bar{\mathbf{a}}_{\mathrm{AV}}$, consisting of the stream exponents, needs to be obtained. Maximum likelihood estimation cannot be used for such parameters, and discriminative training techniques have to be employed instead (Jourlin 1997; Potamianos and Graf 1998; Nakamura 2001; Gravier *et al.* 2002a). This issue is discussed later. Notice that HMM stream parameter and stream exponent training iterations can be alternated in Eq. (9.18).

9.3.3.2 Intermediate integration: product HMM It is well known that visual speech activity can precede the audio signal by as much as 120 ms

(Bregler and Konig 1994; Grant and Greenberg 2001), which is close to the average duration of a phoneme. A generalization of the state-synchronous multi-stream HMM can be used to model such audio and visual stream asynchrony to some extent, by allowing the single modality HMMs to be in asynchrony within a model, but forcing their synchrony at model boundaries instead. Single-stream log-likelihoods are linearly combined at such boundaries using weights, similarly to Eq. (9.16). For LVCSR, a reasonable choice is to force synchrony at the phone boundaries. The resulting phone-synchronous audiovisual HMM is depicted in Figure 9.9, for the typical case of three states used per phone in each modality.

Recognition based on this intermediate integration method requires the computation of the best state sequences for both audio and visual streams. To simplify decoding, the model can be formulated as a product HMM (Varga and Moore 1990). Such a model consists of composite states $\mathbf{c} \in C \times C$, that have audiovisual emission probabilities of a form similar to Eq. (9.16), namely

$$\Pr(\mathbf{o}_t^{(\mathrm{AV})} \,|\, \mathbf{c}) = \prod_{s \in \{\mathrm{A,V}\}} \left[\sum_{k=1}^{K_{sc_s}} w_{sc_s k} N_{D_s}(\mathbf{o}_t^{(s)}; \mathbf{m}_{sc_s k}, \mathbf{s}_{sc_s k}) \right]^{\lambda_{sc_s t}} \qquad (9.19)$$

where $\mathbf{c} = [c_\mathrm{A}, c_\mathrm{V}]^\mathrm{T}$. Notice that in Eq. (9.18), the audio and visual stream components correspond to the emission probabilities of certain audio- and visual-only HMM states, as depicted in Figure 9.9. These single-stream emission probabilities are tied for states along the same row, or column (depending on the modality); therefore the original number of mixture weight, mean, and variance parameters is kept in the new model. However, this is usually not the case with the number of transition probability parameters $\{\Pr(\mathbf{c}'|\mathbf{c}''), \mathbf{c}', \mathbf{c}'' \in C \times C\}$, as additional transitions between the composite states need to be modeled. Such probabilities are often factored as $\Pr(\mathbf{c}'|\mathbf{c}'') = \Pr(c'_\mathrm{A}|\mathbf{c}'')\Pr(c'_\mathrm{V}|\mathbf{c}'')$, in which case the resulting product HMM is typically referred to in the literature as the coupled HMM (Brand *et al.* 1997; Chu and Huang 2000; Chu and Huang 2002; Nefian *et al.* 2002). A further simplification of this factorization can be employed, $\{\Pr(\mathbf{c}'|\mathbf{c}'') = \Pr(c'_\mathrm{A}|\mathrm{c}''_\mathrm{A})\Pr(c'_\mathrm{V}|\mathrm{c}''_\mathrm{V})$, as in Gravier *et al.* (2002a) for example, which results in a product HMM with the same number of parameters as the state synchronous multi-stream HMM.

Given audiovisual training data, product HMM training can be performed similarly to separate, or joint, multi-stream HMM parameter estimation, discussed in the previous subsection. In the first case, the composite model is constructed based on individual single-modality HMMs estimated by Eq. (9.10), and on transition probabilities equal to the product of the audio- and visual-only ones. In the second case, referred to as *AV-MS-PROD* in the experiments reported later, all transition probabilities and HMM stream component parameters are estimated at a single stage using Eq. (9.18) with appropriate

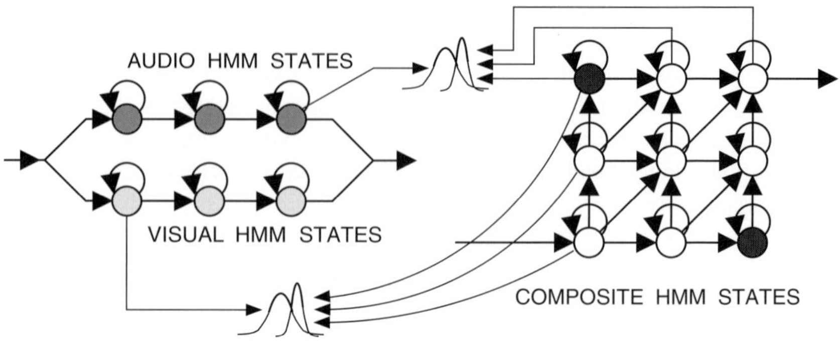

Figure 9.9 Left: Phone-synchronous (state-asynchronous) multi-stream HMM with three states per phone in each modality. Right: Its equivalent product (composite) HMM; black circles denote states that are removed when limiting the degree of within-phone allowed asynchrony to one state. The single-stream emission probabilities are tied for states along the same row (column) to the corresponding audio (visual) state probabilities.

parameter tying. In both schemes, stream exponents need to be estimated separately. In the audiovisual ASR literature, product (or, coupled) HMMs have been considered in some small-vocabulary recognition tasks (Tomlinson *et al.* 1996; Dupont and Luettin 2000; Huang and Chen 2001; Nakamura 2001; Chu and Huang 2002; Nefian *et al.* 2002), where synchronization is sometimes enforced at the word level, and recently for LVCSR (Neti *et al.* 2000; Luettin *et al.* 2001; Gravier *et al.* 2002b).

It is worth mentioning that the product HMM allows the restriction of the degree of asynchrony between the two streams by excluding certain composite states in the model topology. In the extreme case, when only the states that lie in its "diagonal" are kept, the model becomes equivalent to the state-synchronous multi-stream HMM (see also Figure 9.9).

9.3.3.3 Late integration: discriminative model combination A popular stage of combining audio- and visual-only recognition log-likelihoods is at the utterance end, giving rise to late integration. In small-vocabulary, isolated word speech recognition, this can be easily implemented by calculating the combined likelihood for each word model in the vocabulary, given the acoustic and visual observations (Adjoudani and Benoît 1996; Su and Silsbee 1996; Cox *et al.* 1997; Gurbuz *et al.* 2001). However, for connected word recognition, and even more so for LVCSR, the number of possible hypotheses of word sequences becomes prohibitively large. Instead, one has to limit the log-likelihood combination to the top n-best only hypotheses. Such hypotheses can be generated by the audio-only HMM, an alternative audiovisual fusion technique, or can be the union of audio-only and visual-only n-best lists. In this approach, n-best hypotheses for a particular utterance, $[\mathbf{h}_1, \mathbf{h}_2, \ldots, \mathbf{h}_n]$, are first forced-aligned to their corresponding phone sequences $\mathbf{h}_i = [c_{i,1}, c_{i,2}, \ldots, c_{i,Ni}]$ by means of both audio- and visual-only HMMs. Let the resulting phone $c_{i,j}$ boundaries be denoted by $[t^{start}_{i,j,s}, t^{end}_{i,j,s}]$, for $s \in$[A,V], $j = 1, \ldots, N_i$ and $i = 1, \ldots, n$. Then, the audiovisual likelihoods of the n-best hypotheses are computed as

$$\Pr(\mathbf{h}_i) \propto \Pr_{\mathrm{LM}}(\mathbf{h}_i)^{\lambda_{\mathrm{LM}}} \prod_{s\in\{\mathrm{A,V}\}} \prod_{j=1}^{N_i} \Pr\left(\mathbf{o}_t^{(s)}, t \in [t^{\mathrm{start}}_{i,j,s}, t^{\mathrm{end}}_{i,j,s}] \middle| c_{i,j}\right)^{\lambda_{sc_{i,j}}} \tag{9.20}$$

where $\Pr_{\mathrm{LM}}(\mathbf{h}_i)$ denotes the language model (LM) probability of hypothesis $\mathbf{h}_i$. The exponents in Eq. (9.20) can be estimated using discriminative training criteria, as in the discriminative model combination method of Beyerlein (1998) and Vergyri (2000). The method is proposed for audiovisual LVCSR in Neti *et al.* (2000), and it is referred to as *AV-DMC* in the Experiments section.

9.3.3.4 Stream exponent estimation and reliability modeling We now address the issue of estimating stream exponents (weights), when combining likelihoods in the audiovisual decision fusion techniques presented above (see Eq. (9.16), Eq. (9.19), and Eq. (9.20)). As already discussed, such exponents can be set to constant values, computed for a particular audiovisual environment and database. In this case, the audiovisual weights depend on the modality and possibly on the speech class, capturing the confidence of the individual classifiers for the particular database conditions, and are estimated by seeking optimal system performance on matched data. However, in a practical audiovisual ASR system, the quality of captured audio and visual data, and thus of the speech information present in them, can change dramatically over time. To model this variability, utterance-level or even frame-level dependence of the stream exponents is required. This can be achieved by first obtaining an estimate of the local environment conditions and then using pre-computed exponents for this condition, or alternatively, by seeking a direct functional mapping between "environment" estimates and stream exponents. In the following, we expand on these methodologies.

In the first approach, constant exponents are estimated, based on training data, or more often, on so-called held-out data. Such stream exponents cannot be obtained by maximum likelihood estimation (Potamianos and Graf 1998; Nakamura 2001), although approaches based on likelihood normalization have appeared in the literature with moderate success (Hernando 1997; Tamura *et al.* 2005. Typically though discriminative training techniques are used. Some of these methods seek to minimize a smooth function of the minimum classification error (MCE) resulting from the application of the audiovisual model on the data, and employ the generalized probabilistic descent (GPD) algorithm (Chou *et al.* 1994) for stream exponent estimation (Potamianos and Graf 1998; Miyajima *et al.* 2000; Nakamura *et al.* 2000; Gravier *et al.* 2002a). Other techniques use maximum mutual information (MMI) training (Bahl *et al.* 1986), such as the system reported by Jourlin (1997), or the maximum entropy criterion (Gravier *et al.* 2002a). The latter is reported to be faster than MCE-GPD and performs better than it in the case of class-independent exponents. Alternatively, one can seek to directly minimize the word error rate of the resulting audiovisual ASR system on a held-out dataset. In the case of global exponents across all speech classes, constrained to add to a constant, the problem reduces to one-dimensional optimization of a non-smooth function, and can be solved using simple grid search (Miyajima *et al.* 2000; Luettin *et al.* 2001; Gravier *et al.* 2002a). For class-dependent weights, the problem becomes of higher dimension, and the downhill simplex method (Nelder and Mead 1965) can be employed. This technique is used by Neti *et al.* (2000) to estimate exponents for late decision fusion.

In order to capture the effects of varying audio and visual environment conditions on the reliability of each stream, utterance-level, and occasionally frame-level, dependence of the stream weights needs to be considered. In most cases in the literature, exponents are considered as a function of the audio channel signal-to-noise ratio (SNR), and each utterance is decoded based on the fusion model parameters at its SNR (Adjoudani and Benoît 1996; Meier *et al.* 1996; Cox *et al.* 1997; Teissier *et al.* 1999; Gurbuz *et al.* 2001). This SNR value is either assumed known, or estimated from the audio channel (Cox *et al.* 1997). A linear dependence between SNR and audio stream weight has been demonstrated by Meier *et al.* (1996). An alternative technique sets the stream exponents to a linear function of the average conditional entropy of the recognizer output, computed using the confusion matrix at a particular SNR for a small-vocabulary isolated word ASR task (Cox *et al.* 1997). A different approach considers the audio stream exponent as a function of the degree of voicing present in the audio channel, estimated as in Berthommier and Glotin (1999). This method was used at the Johns Hopkins summer 2000 workshop (Neti *et al.* 2000; Glotin *et al.* 2001), and is referred to in the Experiments section as *AV-MS-UTTER*. Finally, Heckmann *et al.* (2002) use a combination of the above-mentioned audio stream indicators to estimate the audio stream exponent.

The above techniques do not allow modeling of possible variations in the visual stream reliability, since they concentrate on the audio stream alone. Modeling such variability in the visual signal domain is challenging, although one could for example consider face detection confidence as one such measure (Connell *et al.* 2003). Typically however this is achieved using confidence measures of the visual-only classifier applied on the extracted visual feature sequence. For example, Adjoudani and Benoît (1996) and Rogozan *et al.* (1997) use the dispersion of both audio-only and visual-only class posterior log-likelihoods to model the single-stream classifier confidences, and then compute the utterance-dependent stream exponents as a closed form function of these dispersions in an unsupervised fashion. Similarly, Potamianos and Neti (2000) consider various confidence measures, such as entropy and dispersion, to capture the reliability of audio- and visual-only classification at the frame level, and they obtain stream exponents using a look-up table over confidence value intervals, estimated on the basis of held-out data. Extensions of this work appear in Garg *et al.* (2003), where a sigmoid function is used instead of the look-up table. This sigmoid is discriminatively trained to map the vector of audiovisual reliability measures to frame-dependent audiovisual exponents. Further, Marcheret *et al.* (2007) employ Gaussian mixture models for this purpose using the above reliability measures, whereas Shao and Barker (2008) use an ANN in a two-step approach to estimating the desired exponents. As input to the ANN, they utilize the entire vector of audio and visual likelihoods of all classes (or an appropriate clustering of them). An alternative approach is followed by Terry *et al.* (2008), where the audio and visual observations are first vector quantized, allowing estimation of the conditional probability of the visual observation centroids given the audio ones. This is subsequently employed (as a measure of audio visual consistency) together with audio-only SNR in stream exponent estimation via an introduced sigmoid function. Finally, Sanchez-Soto *et al.* (2009) propose an entirely unsupervised approach, where stream exponents are estimated as functionals of the inter- and intra-class distances that are computed for each stream observation sequence over the given test utterance.

9.3.4 *Audiovisual speaker adaptation*

Speaker adaptation is traditionally used in practical audio-only ASR systems to improve speaker-independent system performance, when little data from a speaker of interest is available (Gauvain and Lee 1994; Leggetter and Woodland 1995; Neumeyer *et al.* 1995; Anastasakos *et al.* 1997; Gales 1999; Goronzy 2002; Young 2008). Adaptation is also of interest across tasks or environments. In the audiovisual ASR domain, this is of particular importance, since audiovisual corpora are scarce and their collection expensive; therefore adaptation across datasets (in addition to speakers) is also of interest. In general, adaptation can be performed in a supervised or unsupervised fashion, as well as in a batch or incremental mode, depending on the type and availability of the adaptation data (Young 2008).

Given little bimodal adaptation data from a particular speaker, and a baseline speaker-independent HMM, one may wish to estimate adapted HMM parameters that better model the audiovisual observations of the particular speaker. Two popular algorithms for speaker adaptation are maximum likelihood linear regression (MLLR) (Leggetter and Woodland 1995) and maximum a posteriori (MAP) adaptation (Gauvain and Lee 1994). MLLR obtains a maximum likelihood estimate of a linear transformation of the HMM means, while leaving covariance matrices, mixture weights, and transition probabilities unchanged, and it provides successful adaptation with a small amount of adaptation data (rapid adaptation). On the other hand, MAP follows the Bayesian paradigm for estimating the HMM parameters. MAP estimates of HMM parameters slowly converge to their EM-obtained estimates as the amount of adaptation data becomes large; however such a convergence is slow, and therefore, MAP is not suitable for rapid adaptation. In practice, MAP is often used in conjunction with MLLR (Neumeyer *et al.* 1995). Both techniques can be used in the feature fusion (Potamianos and Neti 2001a) and decision fusion models discussed above (Potamianos and Potamianos 1999), in a straightforward manner. One can also consider feature-level (front end) adaptation by adapting, for example, the audio-only and visual-only LDA and MLLT matrices and, if HiLDA fusion is used, the joint audiovisual LDA and MLLT matrices (Potamianos and Neti 2001a). Experiments using these techniques are reported in a later section, all performed in a supervised, batch fashion. Alternative adaptation algorithms also exist, such as speaker adaptive training (Anastasakos *et al.* 1997) and front end MLLR (Gales 1999) that can be used in audiovisual ASR (Vanegas *et al.* 1998; Huang *et al.* 2005; Huang and Visweswariah 2005).

9.3.5 *Summary of audiovisual integration*

We have presented a summary of the most common fusion techniques for audiovisual ASR. We first discussed the choice of speech classes and statistical ASR models that influences the design of some fusion algorithms. Subsequently, we described a number of feature and decision integration techniques suitable for bimodal LVCSR, and finally, briefly touched upon the issue of audiovisual speaker adaptation.

Among the fusion algorithms discussed, decision fusion techniques explicitly model the reliability of each source of speech information, by using stream weights to linearly combine audio- and visual-only classifier log-likelihoods. When properly estimated, the use of weights results in improved ASR over feature fusion techniques, as reported in the literature and demonstrated in the Experiments section. In most systems reported, such weights are set to a constant value over each modality, possibly dependent on the audio-only channel quality (SNR). However, robust estimation of the weights at a finer level (utterance or frame level), based on both audio and visual channel characteristics remains a challenge. Furthermore, the issue of whether speech class dependence of stream weights is desirable has also not been fully investigated. Although such dependence seems to help in late integration schemes (Neti *et al.* 2000), or small-vocabulary tasks (Jourlin 1997; Miyajima *et al.* 2000), the problem remains unresolved for early integration in LVCSR (Gravier *et al.* 2002a).

There are additional open questions relevant to decision fusion. The first concerns the stage of measurement level information integration, i.e., the degree of allowed asynchrony between the audio and visual streams. The second has to do with the functional form of stream log-likelihood combination, as integration by means of Eq. (9.16) is not necessarily optimal and it fails to yield an emission probability distribution. Finally, it is worth mentioning a theoretical shortcoming of the log-likelihood linear combination model used in the decision fusion algorithms considered. In contrast to feature fusion, such combination assumes class conditional independence of the audio and visual stream observations. This appears to be a non-realistic assumption (Yehia *et al.* 1998; Jiang *et al.* 2002).

A number of models are being investigated to overcome some of the above issues (Pan *et al.* 1998; Pavlovic 1998). Most importantly, recent years have seen increasing interest in the use of dynamic Bayesian networks for audiovisual fusion, as a generalization to HMMs (Zweig 1998; Murphy 2002; Bilmes and Bartels 2005). Such examples are the work of Saenko and Livescu (2006), Livescu *et al.* (2007), Lv *et al.* (2007), Terry and Katsaggelos (2008), and Saenko *et al.* (2009).

9.4 Audiovisual databases

A major contributor to the progress achieved in traditional, audio-only ASR has been the availability of a wide variety of large, multi-subject databases on a number of well-defined recognition tasks of different complexities. These corpora have often been collected using funding from US government agencies (for example, the Defense Advanced Research Projects Agency and the National Science Foundation), or through well-organized European activities, such as the Information Society Technologies program funded by the European Commission, or the European Language Resources Association. The resulting databases are made available to interested research groups by the Linguistic Data Consortium (LDC) and the European Language Resources Distribution Agency (ELDA), for example. Benchmarking research progress in audio-only ASR has been possible on such common databases.

In contrast to the abundance of audio-only corpora, there exist only few databases suitable for audiovisual ASR research. This is not only because the field is relatively young, but also due to the fact that audiovisual databases pose additional challenges concerning collection, storage, and distribution not found in the audio-only domain. Most early databases being the result of efforts by a few university groups or individual researchers with limited resources suffer from one or more of the following shortcomings (Chibelushi *et al.* 1996; Hennecke *et al.* 1996; Chibelushi *et al.* 2002; Potamianos *et al.* 2003): They contain a single or small number of subjects, affecting the generalization of developed methods to the wider population; they typically have small duration, often resulting in undertrained statistical models, or non-significant performance differences between various proposed algorithms; they mostly address simple recognition tasks, such as small-vocabulary ASR of isolated or connected words; and finally they mostly consider ideal visual environments with limited variation in head pose (mostly frontal), lighting, and background that do not reflect realistic human–computer interaction scenarios. These limitations have caused a gap in the state of the art between audio-only and audiovisual ASR in terms of recognition task complexity and have hindered practical system deployment. Nevertheless, the past few years have witnessed an effort to address some of these shortcomings; for example, IBM Research has collected a large corpus suitable for speaker-independent audiovisual LVCSR, employed in the experiments during the Johns Hopkins summer 2000 workshop (Neti *et al.* 2000) and discussed further in this section, whereas a number of groups have collected corpora in realistic, visually challenging environments such as automobiles, or data where the recorded subjects appear at a non-frontal head-pose. Details are provided in the next subsections.

9.4.1 Early audiovisual corpora

The first database used for automatic recognition of audiovisual speech was collected by Petajan (1984). Data of a single subject uttering from 2 to 10 repetitions of 100 isolated English words, including letters and digits, were collected under controlled lighting conditions. Since then, several research sites have pursued audiovisual data collection. Some of these early resulting corpora are discussed in this subsection. They cover a number of small-vocabulary recognition tasks and are mostly recorded under ideal visual environment conditions.

Some of these early databases are designed to study audiovisual recognition of consonants (C), vowels (V), or transitions between them. For example, Adjoudani and Benoît (1996) report a single-speaker corpus of 54 $/V_1CV_2CV_1/$ nonsense words (3 French vowels and 6 consonants are considered). Su and Silsbee (1996) recorded a single-speaker corpus of /aCa/ nonsense words for recognition of 22 English consonants. Robert-Ribes *et al.* (1998), as well as Teissier *et al.* (1999) report recognition of 10 French oral vowels uttered by a single subject. Czap (2000) considers a single-subject corpus of $/V_1CV_1/$ and $/C_1VC_1/$ nonsense words for recognition of Hungarian vowels and consonants.

The most popular task for audiovisual ASR is isolated or connected digit recognition. Various corpora allow digit recognition experiments. For example, the Tulips1 database (Movellan and Chadderdon 1996) contains recordings of 12 subjects uttering digits "one" to "four," and has been used for isolated recognition of these four digits in a number of papers (Luettin *et al.* 1996; Movellan and Chadderdon 1996; Gray *et al.* 1997; Vanegas *et al.* 1998; Scanlon and Reilly 2001). The M2VTS database, although tailored to speaker verification applications, also contains digit ("0" to "9") recordings of 37 subjects, mostly in French (Pigeon and Vandendorpe 1997), and it has been used for isolated digit recognition experiments (Dupont and Luettin 2000; Miyajima *et al.* 2000). XM2VTS is an extended version of this database containing 295 subjects in the English language (Messer *et al.* 1999). Additional single-subject digit databases include the NATO RSG10 digit-triples set, used by Tomlinson *et al.* (1996) for isolated digit recognition, and two connected-digits databases reported by Potamianos *et al.* (1998) and Heckmann *et al.* (2001). Finally, three recent databases suitable for multi-subject connected digit recognition are the 36-subject CUAVE dataset, as discussed in Patterson *et al.* (2002), a 100-subject set collected at the University of Illinois at Urbana-Champaign with results reported in Chu and Huang (2000) and Zhang *et al.* (2000), the 97-subject Japanese dataset Aurora-2J-AV (Fujimura *et al.* 2005), and an 11-subject Japanese set reported by Tamura *et al.* (2005). Among these, CUAVE remains the most popular, having been employed by many researchers in their experiments.

Isolated or connected letter recognition constitutes another popular audiovisual ASR task. German connected letter recognition of data of up to six subjects has been reported by Bregler *et al.* (1993), Bregler and Konig (1994), Duchnowski *et al.* (1994), and Meier *et al.* (1996). Krone *et al.* (1997) worked on single-speaker isolated German letter recognition. Single-, or two-subject, connected French letter recognition is considered in Alissali *et al.* (1996), André-Obrecht *et al.* (1997), Jourlin (1997), Rogozan *et al.* (1997), and Rogozan (1999). Finally, for English, a 10-subject isolated letter dataset is used by Matthews *et al.* (1996) and Cox *et al.* (1997), as well as a 49-subject connected letter database by Potamianos *et al.* (1998).

In addition to letter or digit recognition, a number of audiovisual databases have been collected that are suitable for recognition of isolated words. For example, Silsbee and Bovik (1996) have collected a single-subject, isolated word corpus with a vocabulary of 500 words. Recognition of single-subject command words for radio/tape control has been examined by Chiou and Hwang (1997), as well as by Gurbuz *et al.* (2001), and Patterson *et al.* (2001). A 10-subject isolated word database with a vocabulary size of 78 words is considered by Chen (2001) and Huang and Chen (2001). This corpus was collected at Carnegie Mellon University (AMP/CMU database), and has also been used by Chu and Huang (2002), Nefian *et al.* (2002), and Zhang *et al.* (2002), among others. Single-subject, isolated word recognition in Japanese is reported in Nakamura *et al.* (2000) and Nakamura (2001). A single-subject German command word recognition is considered by Kober *et al.* (1997).

Further, a few audiovisual databases are suitable for continuous speech recognition in limited, small-vocabulary domains. Bernstein and Eberhardt (1986a) and Goldschen *et al.* (1996) report small corpora containing TIMIT sentences uttered by up to two subjects. Chan *et al.* (1998) present a dataset of 400 single-subject military command and control utterances. An extended multi-subject version of this database (still with a limited vocabulary of 101 words) is reported in Chu and Huang (2000).

Finally, a number of databases offer a combination of some or all of the above tasks. One example is the AVOZES corpus (Goecke and Millar 2004) that contains 20 subjects uttering connected digits, /VCV/ and /CVC/ words, as well as a small number of sentences, all in Australian English. Another is reported in Wodjel *et al.* (2002) and contains data in Dutch.

9.4.2 Large-vocabulary databases and the IBM ViaVoice™ corpus

Following both technology progress that simplified recording and storage of larger audiovisual sets and research progress in the development of audiovisual speech recognition algorithms, the community started becoming interested in more challenging recognition tasks. In support of such quest, some sites have proceeded with the collection of larger corpora to allow the development of speaker-independent audiovisual LVCSR systems. Two such datasets are the AVTIMIT corpus that contains 4 hrs of phonetically balanced continuous speech utterances by 223 subjects in English (Hazen *et al.* 2004) and the UWB-04-HSCAVC set that contains 40 hrs of data from 100 subjects in Czech (Cisař *et al.* 2005).

A third database suitable for speaker-independent LVCSR is the IBM ViaVoice™ audiovisual database, which remains the largest such corpus to date. It consists of full face frontal video and audio of 290 subjects (see also Figure 9.10), uttering ViaVoice™ training scripts in dictation style, i.e., continuous read speech with mostly verbalized punctuation. The database video is 704 × 480 pixels, interlaced, and captured in color at a rate of 30 Hz (i.e., 60 fields per second are available at a resolution of 240 lines). It is MPEG2 encoded at the relatively high compression ratio of about 50:1. High quality wideband audio is collected synchronously with the video at a rate of 16 kHz and in a relatively clean audio environment (quiet office, with some background computer noise),

Figure 9.10 Example video frames of 10 subjects from the IBM ViaVoice™ audiovisual database. The database contains approximately 50 hrs of continuous, dictation-style audiovisual speech by 290 subjects, collected with minor variations in face pose, lighting, and background (Neti *et al.* 2000).

resulting in a 19.5 dB SNR. The duration of the entire database is approximately 50 hours, and it contains 24 325 transcribed utterances with a 10 403-word vocabulary, from which 21 281 utterances are used in the experiments reported in the next section. In addition to LVCSR, a 50-subject connected digit database has been collected at IBM Research, in order to study the benefit of the visual modality on a popular small-vocabulary ASR task. This DIGITS corpus contains 6689 utterances of 7- and 10-digit strings (both "zero" and "oh" are used) with a total duration of approximately 10 hrs. Furthermore, to allow investigation of automatic speechreading performance for impaired speech (Potamianos and Neti 2001a), both LVCSR and DIGITS audiovisual speech data of a single speech-impaired male subject with profound hearing loss have been collected. In Table 9.3, a summary of the above corpora is given, together with their partitioning as used in the experiments reported in the following section.

9.4.3 *Other recent audiovisual databases*

Another recent direction that has attracted the interest of the research community has been the application of audiovisual ASR in realistic human–computer interaction environments. One such environment is the automobile cabin, where the driver needs to interact with the vehicle voice interface, for example for navigation or other command and control tasks. Not surprisingly, a number of research sites have collected in-vehicle audiovisual databases in support of this scenario. Resulting corpora of such efforts in English are the AVICAR dataset that contains 100 subjects uttering digit strings and TIMIT sentences, recorded using 4 cameras and a microphone array (Lee *et al.* 2004), and a corpus collected by IBM Research containing 87 subjects uttering digit strings, word spellings, and continuous speech geared towards various navigation and other in-vehicle command and control tasks (Potamianos and Neti 2003). Similar, but smaller corpora have also been collected in other languages, for example the

Japanese Aurora 3J-AV dataset containing 58 subjects recorded with 2 cameras and multiple microphones (Fujimura *et al.* 2005), the Czech UWB-03-CIVAVC corpus containing 12 subjects (Železný and Cisař 2003), and the Spanish AV@CAR set of 20 subjects (Ortega *et al.* 2004). Finally, a larger and more recent effort is that of the UTDrive project (Angkititrakul *et al.* 2009).

Yet another interesting aspect of visual and audiovisual speech recognition concerns the head pose of the recorded subject with respect to the camera. In the vast majority of the above mentioned datasets, this is assumed to be mostly frontal. A few researchers though have ventured to investigate how head pose affects speechreading performance. For this purpose, they have collected datasets of mostly small-vocabulary tasks and few subjects, as for example in Iwano *et al.* (2007), Kumar *et al.* (2007), Kumatani and Stiefelhagen (2007), and Lucey *et al.* (2009). Most of these are multi-view databases, i.e. more than one camera (typically, two or three) captures the speaker's face at relatively fixed head-pose view angles.

Finally, a few additional databases exist that can be used for audiovisual ASR, but are most appropriate for other audiovisual speech processing tasks, closely related to ASR. Two such are for example the XM2VTS corpus, already mentioned above (Messer *et al.* 1999), and the VidTIMIT database (Sanderson 2003) that contains data from 43 subjects uttering short sentences. Both are most suitable for speaker recognition experiments. Other interesting datasets are the AVGrid corpus (Cooke *et al.* 2006) that is best suited for audiovisual speaker separation and the MOCHA (Wrench and Hardcastle 2000) and QSMT (Engwall and Beskow 2003) databases that have been used for speech inversion.

9.5 Audiovisual ASR experiments

In this section, we present experimental results on visual-only and audiovisual ASR using mainly the IBM ViaVoice™ database discussed above. Some of these results were obtained during the Johns Hopkins summer 2000 workshop (Neti *et al.* 2000). Experiments conducted later on both these data and the IBM connected digits task (DIGITS) are also reported (Potamianos *et al.* 2001c; Goecke *et al.* 2002; Gravier *et al.* 2002a). In addition, the application of audiovisual speaker adaptation methods to the hearing impaired dataset is also discussed (Potamianos and Neti 2001a). First, however, we briefly describe the basic audiovisual ASR system, as well as the experimental framework used.

9.5.1 The audiovisual ASR system

Our basic audiovisual ASR system utilizes appearance-based visual features that use a discrete cosine transform (DCT) of the mouth region-of-interest (ROI), as described in Potamianos *et al.* (2001b). Given the video of the speaker's face, available at 60 Hz, it first performs face detection and mouth center and size estimation employing the algorithm of Senior (1999). On the basis of these, it extracts a size-normalized, 64×64 greyscale pixel mouth ROI, as discussed in Section 9.2.1 (see also Figure 9.2). Subsequently, a two-dimensional, separable, fast DCT is applied on the ROI, and its 24 highest energy coefficients (over the training data) are retained. A number of post-processing steps are applied on the resulting "static" feature vector, namely: linear interpolation on the audio feature rate (from 60 to 100 Hz); feature mean normalization (FMN) for improved robustness to lighting and other variations; concatenation of 15 adjacent features to capture dynamic speech information (see also Eq. (9.7)); and linear discriminant analysis (LDA) for optimal dimensionality reduction, followed by a maximum likelihood data rotation (MLLT) for improved statistical data modeling. The resulting feature vector $\mathbf{o}_t^{(V)}$ has dimension 41. These steps are described in more detail in the visual front end section of this chapter (see also Figure 9.7). Improvements to this DCT-based visual front end have been proposed in Potamianos and Neti (2001b), including the use of a larger ROI, a within-frame discriminant DCT feature selection, and a longer temporal window (see Figure 9.11). During the Johns Hopkins summer workshop, and in addition to the DCT-based features, joint appearance and shape features from active appearance models (AAMs) have also been employed. In particular, 6000-dimensional appearance vectors containing the normalized face color pixel values and 134-dimensional shape vectors of the face shape coordinates are extracted at 30 Hz and are passed through two stages of principal components analysis (PCA). The resulting "static" AAM feature vector is 86-dimensional, and it is post-processed similarly to the DCT feature vector (see Figure 9.7) resulting in 41-dimensional "dynamic" features.

In parallel to the visual front end, traditional audio features that consist of mel frequency cepstral coefficients (MFCCs) are extracted at a 100 Hz rate. The resulting "static" feature vector is 24-dimensional, and following FMN, LDA on 9 adjacent frames and MLLT, it gives rise to a 60-dimensional dynamic speech vector, $\mathbf{o}_t^{(A)}$, as depicted in Figure 9.11. The audio and visual front ends provide time-synchronous audio and visual feature vectors that can be used in a number of fusion techniques discussed previously in Section 9.3. The derived concatenated audiovisual vector $\mathbf{o}_t^{(AV)}$ has dimension 101, whereas in the HiLDA feature fusion implementation, the bimodal LDA generates features $\mathbf{o}_t^{(HiLDA)}$ with reduced dimensionality 60 (see also Figure 9.11).

In all cases where LDA and MLLT matrices are employed (audio-only, visual-only, and audiovisual feature extraction by means of HiLDA fusion), we consider $|C| = 3367$ context-dependent sub-phonetic classes that coincide with the context-dependent states of an existing audio-only HMM that was previously developed at IBM for LVCSR and trained on a number of audio corpora (Polymenakos *et al.* 1998). The forced alignment (Rabiner and Juang 1993) of the training set audio,

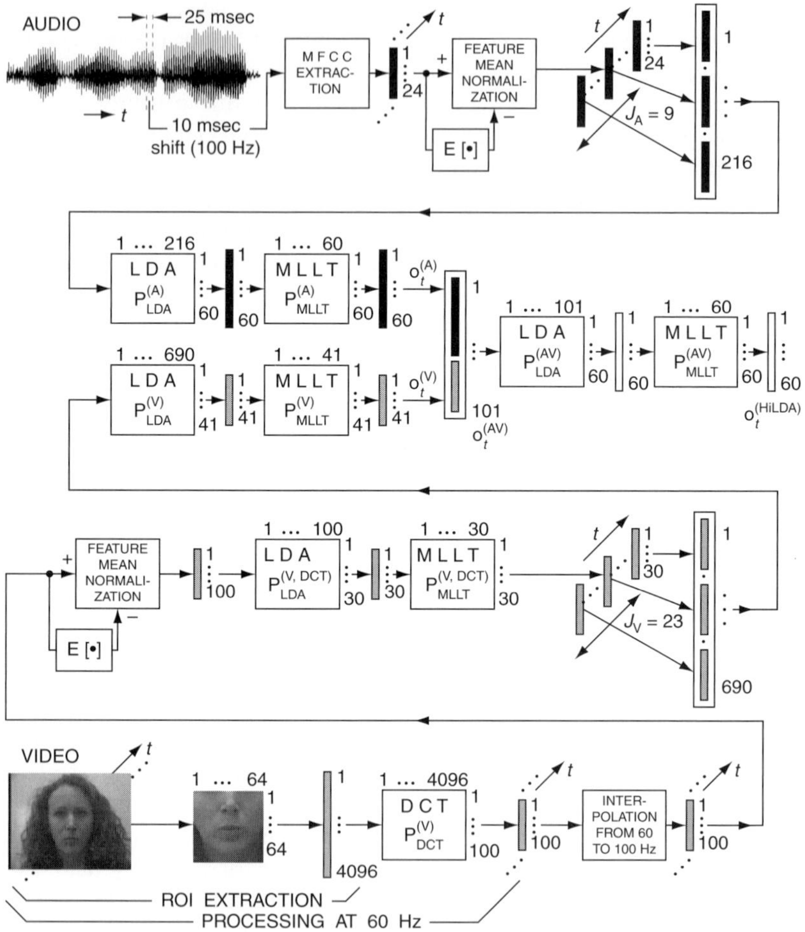

Figure 9.11 The audiovisual ASR system employed in some of the experiments reported in this chapter. In addition to the baseline system used during the Johns Hopkins summer 2000 workshop, a larger mouth ROI is extracted, within-frame discriminant features are used, and a longer temporal window is considered in the visual front end (compare to Figure 9.7). HiLDA feature fusion is employed.

based on this HMM and the data transcriptions, produces labels $c(l) \in C$ for the training set audio-only, visual-only, and audiovisual data vectors $\mathbf{x}_l$, $l = 1, \ldots, L$. Such labeled vectors can then be used to estimate the required matrices $\mathbf{P}_{\mathrm{LDA}}$, $\mathbf{P}_{\mathrm{MLLT}}$, as described in the visual front end section of this chapter.

Table 9.3 *The IBM audiovisual databases discussed and used in the experiments reported in this chapter. Their partitioning into training, held-out, adaptation, and test sets is depicted (duration in hours and number of subjects are shown for each set). Both large-vocabulary continuous speech (LVCSR) and connected digit (DIGITS) recognition are considered for normal, as well as impaired speech. The IBM ViaVoice™ database corresponds to the LVCSR task in the normal speech condition. For the normal speech DIGITS task, the held-out and adaptation sets are identical. For impaired speech, due to the lack of sufficient training data, adaptation of HMMs trained in the normal speech condition is considered.*

Speech condition	Recognition task	Training		Held-out		Adaptation		Test	
		Dur.	Sub.	Dur.	Sub.	Dur	Sub.	Dur.	Sub.
Normal	LVCSR	34:55	239	4:47	25	2:03	26	2:29	26
	DIGITS	8:01	50	0:58	50	0:58	50	0:46	50
Impaired	LVCSR	N/A		N/A		0:11	1	0:11	1
	DIGITS	N/A		N/A		0:08	1	0:06	1

9.5.2 *The experimental framework*

The audiovisual databases discussed above were partitioned into a number of sets in order to train and evaluate models for audiovisual ASR, as detailed in Table 9.3. For both LVCSR and DIGITS speech tasks in the normal speech condition, the corresponding training sets are used to obtain all LDA and MLLT matrices required and the phonetic decision trees that cluster HMM states on the basis of phonetic context, as well as to train all the HMMs reported. The held-out sets are used to tune parameters relevant to audiovisual decision fusion and decoding (such as the multi-stream HMM and language model weights, for example), whereas the test sets are used for evaluating the performance of the trained HMMs. Optionally, the adaptation sets can be employed for tuning the front ends and/or HMMs to the characteristics of the test set subjects. In the LVCSR case, the subject populations of the training, held-out, and test sets are disjoint, thus allowing for speaker-independent recognition, whereas in the DIGITS data partitioning, all sets have data from the same 50 subjects, thus allowing multi-speaker experiments. Consequently, the adaptation and held-out sets for DIGITS are identical. For the impaired speech data, the duration of the collected data is too short to allow HMM training. Therefore, LVCSR HMMs trained on the IBM ViaVoice™ dataset are adapted on the impaired LVCSR and DIGITS adaptation sets (see Table 9.3).

To assess the benefit of the visual modality to ASR in noisy conditions (as well as to the relatively clean audio condition of the database recordings), we artificially corrupt the audio data with additive, non-stationary, speech babble noise at various SNRs. ASR results are then reported at a number of SNRs, within [−1.5,19.5] dB for LVCSR and [−3.5,19.5] dB for DIGITS, with all corresponding front end matrices and HMMs trained in the matched condition. In particular, during the Johns Hopkins summer 2000 workshop, only two audio conditions were considered for LVCSR: the original 19.5 dB SNR audio and a degraded one at 8.5 dB SNR. Notice that, in contrast to the audio, no noise is added to the video channel or features. Many cases of "visual noise" could have been considered, such as additive noise on video frames, blurring, frame rate decimation, and extremely high compression factors, among others. Some studies on the effects of video degradations to visual recognition can be found in the literature (Davoine *et al.* 1997; Williams *et al.* 1997; Potamianos *et al.* 1998; Seymour *et al.* 2008). These studies find automatic speechreading performance to be rather robust to video compression for example, but to degrade rapidly for frame rates below 15 Hz.

The ASR experiments reported next follow two distinct paradigms. The results on the IBM ViaVoice™ data obtained during the Johns Hopkins summer 2000 workshop employ a lattice rescoring paradigm, due to the limitations in large-vocabulary decoding of the early HTK software used there (Young *et al.* 1999). Lattices were first generated prior to the workshop using the IBM Research stack decoder (Hark) with HMMs trained at IBM Research, and subsequently rescored during the workshop, by trained triphone context-dependent HMMs on various feature sets or fusion techniques using HTK. Three sets of lattices were generated for these experiments and were based on clean audio-only (19.5 dB), noisy audio-only, and noisy audiovisual (at the 8.5 dB SNR condition) HiLDA features. In the second experimental paradigm, full decoding results obtained by directly using the IBM Research recognizer are reported. For the LVCSR experiments, 11-phone context-dependent HMMs with 2808 context-dependent states and 47 k Gaussian mixtures are used, whereas for DIGITS recognition in normal speech the corresponding numbers are 159 and 3.2 k (for single-stream models). Decoding using the closed set vocabulary (10 403 words) and a trigram language model is employed for LVCSR (this is the case also for the workshop results), whereas the 11-digit ("zero" to "nine," including "oh") word vocabulary is used for DIGITS (with unknown digit string length).

9.5.3 *Visual-only recognition*

The suitability for LVCSR of a number of appearance-based visual features and AAMs was studied during and after the Johns Hopkins summer workshop (Neti *et al.* 2000; Matthews *et al.* 2001). For this purpose, noisy audio-only lattices were rescored by HMMs trained on the various visual features considered, namely 86-dimensional AAM features, as well as 24-dimensional DCT, PCA

Table 9.4 *Comparisons of recognition performance based on various visual features (three appearance-based features, and one joint shape and appearance feature representation) for speaker-independent LVCSR (Neti* et al. *2000; Matthews* et al. *2001). Word error rate (WER), %, is depicted on a subset of the IBM ViaVoice™ database test set of Table 9.3. Visual performance is obtained after the rescoring of lattices that had been previously generated based on noisy (8.5 dB SNR) audio-only MFCC features. For comparison, characteristic lattice WERs are also depicted (oracle, anti-oracle, and best path based on language model scores alone). Among the visual speech representations considered, the DCT-based features are superior and contain significant speech information.*

Modality	Remarks	WER	Modality	Remarks	WER
Visual	DCT	58.1	Acoustic	MFCC (noisy)	55.0
	DWT	58.8	None	Oracle	31.2
	PCA	59.4		Anti-oracle	102.6
	AAM	64.0		LM best path	62.0

(on 32 × 32 pixel mouth ROIs), and DWT-based features. All features were post-processed as previously discussed to yield 41-dimensional feature vectors (see Figure 9.7). For the DWT features, the Daubechies class wavelet filter of approximating order 3 is used (Daubechies 1992; Press *et al.* 1995). LVCSR recognition results are reported in Table 9.4, depicted in word error rate (WER), %. The DCT outperformed all other features considered. Notice however that these results cannot be interpreted as visual-only recognition, since they correspond to cascade audiovisual fusion of audio-only ASR, followed by visual-only rescoring of a network of recognized hypotheses. For reference, a number of characteristic lattice WERs are also depicted in Table 9.4, including the audio-only result (at 8.5 dB). All feature performances are bounded by the lattice oracle and anti-oracle WERs. It is interesting to note that all appearance-based features considered attain lower WERs (e.g., 58.1% for DCT features) than the WER of the best path through the lattice based on the language model alone (62.0%). Therefore, such visual features do convey significant speech information. AAMs on the other hand did not perform well, possibly due to severe undertraining of the models, resulting in poor fitting to unseen facial data.

As expected, visual-only recognition based on full decoding (instead of lattice rescoring) is rather poor. The LVCSR WER on the speaker-independent test set of Table 9.3, based on per-speaker MLLR adaptation, is reported at 89.2% in Potamianos and Neti (2001b), using the DCT features of the

Table 9.5 *Test set speaker-independent LVCSR audio-only and audiovisual WER (%), for the clean (19.5 dB SNR) and a noisy audio (8.5 dB) condition. Two feature fusion- and five decision fusion-based audiovisual systems are evaluated using the lattice rescoring paradigm (Neti* et al. *2000; Glotin* et al. *2001; Luettin* et al. *2001).*

Audio condition	Clean	Noisy
Audio-only	14.44	48.10
AV-Concat (FF)	16.00	40.00
AV-HiLDA (FF)	13.84	36.99
AV-DMC (DF)	13.65 →12.95	-
AV-MS-Joint (DF)	14.62	36.61
AV-MS-Sep (DF)	14.92	38.38
AV-MS-PROD (DF)	14.19	35.21
AV-MS-UTTER (DF)	13.47	35.27

workshop. Extraction of larger ROIs and the use of within-frame DCT discriminant features and longer temporal windows (as depicted in Figure 9.11) result in the improved WER of 82.3%. In contrast to LVCSR, DIGITS visual-only recognition constitutes a much easier task. Indeed, on the multi-speaker test set of Table 9.3, a 16.8% WER is achieved after per-speaker MLLR adaptation.

9.5.4 Audiovisual ASR

A number of audiovisual integration algorithms presented in the fusion section of this chapter were compared during the Johns Hopkins summer 2000 workshop. As already mentioned, two audio conditions were considered: the original clean database audio (19.5 dB SNR) and a noisy one at 8.5 dB SNR. In the first case, fusion algorithm results were obtained by rescoring pre-generated clean audio-only lattices; in the second condition, HiLDA noisy audiovisual lattices were rescored. The results of these experiments are summarized in Table 9.5. Notice that every fusion method considered outperformed audio-only ASR in the noisy case, reaching up to a 27% relative reduction in WER (from 48.10% noisy audio-only to 35.21% audiovisual). In the clean audio condition, among the two feature fusion techniques considered, HiLDA fusion (Potamianos *et al.* 2001c) improved ASR from a 14.44% audio-only to a 13.84% audiovisual WER. However, concatenative fusion degraded performance to 16.0%. Among the decision fusion algorithms used, the product HMM (AV-MS-PROD) with jointly trained audiovisual components (Luettin *et al.* 2001) improved performance to a 14.19% WER. In addition, utterance-based stream exponents for a jointly trained multi-stream HMM (AV-MS-UTTER), estimated using an average of the voicing present at each utterance, further reduced WER to 13.47%

(Glotin *et al.* 2001), achieving a 7% relative WER reduction over audio-only performance. Finally, a late integration technique based on discriminative model combination (AV-DMC) of audio and visual HMMs (Beyerlein 1998; Vergyri 2000; Glotin *et al.* 2001) produced a WER of 12.95%, amounting to a 5% reduction from the clean audio-only baseline of 13.65% (this differs from the 14.44% audio-only result due to the rescoring of n-best lists instead of lattices). For both clean and noisy audio conditions, the best decision fusion method outperformed the best feature fusion technique considered. In addition, for both conditions, joint multi-stream HMM training outperformed separate training of the HMM stream components, something not surprising, since joint training forces state synchrony between the audio and visual streams.

To further demonstrate the differences between the various fusion algorithms and to quantify the visual modality benefit to ASR, we review a number of full decoding experiments recently conducted for both the LVCSR and DIGITS tasks, at a large number of SNR conditions (Potamianos *et al.* 2001c; Goecke *et al.* 2002; Gravier *et al.* 2002a). All three feature fusion techniques discussed in Section 9.3 are compared to decision fusion by means of a jointly trained multi-stream HMM. The results are depicted in Figure 9.12. Among the feature fusion methods considered, HiLDA feature fusion is superior to both concatenative fusion and the enhancement approach. In the clean audio case for example, HiLDA fusion reduces the audio-only LVCSR WER of 12.37% to 11.56% audiovisual, whereas feature concatenation degrades performance to 12.72% (the enhancement method obviously provides the original audio-only performance in this case). Notice that these results are somewhat different from the ones reported in Table 9.5, due to the different experimental paradigm considered. In the most extreme noisy case considered for LVCSR (−1.5 dB SNR), the audio-only WER of 92.16% is reduced to 48.63% using HiLDA, compared to 50.76% when feature concatenation is employed, and to 63.45% when audio feature enhancement is used. Similar results hold for DIGITS recognition, although the difference between HiLDA and concatenative feature fusion ASR is small, possibly due to the fact that HMMs with significantly fewer Gaussian mixtures are used, and to the availability of sufficient data to train on high-dimensional concatenated audiovisual vectors. The comparison between multi-stream decision fusion and HiLDA fusion reveals that the jointly trained multi-stream HMM performs significantly better. For example, at −1.5 dB SNR, LVCSR WER is reduced to 46.28% (compared to 48.63% for HiLDA). Similarly, for DIGITS recognition at −3.5 dB, the HiLDA WER is 7.51%, whereas the multi-stream HMM WER is significantly lower, namely 6.64%. This is less than one third of the audio-only WER of 23.97%.

A useful indicator when comparing fusion techniques and establishing the visual modality benefit to ASR is the effective SNR gain, measured here with reference to the audio-only WER at 10 dB. To compute this gain, we need to

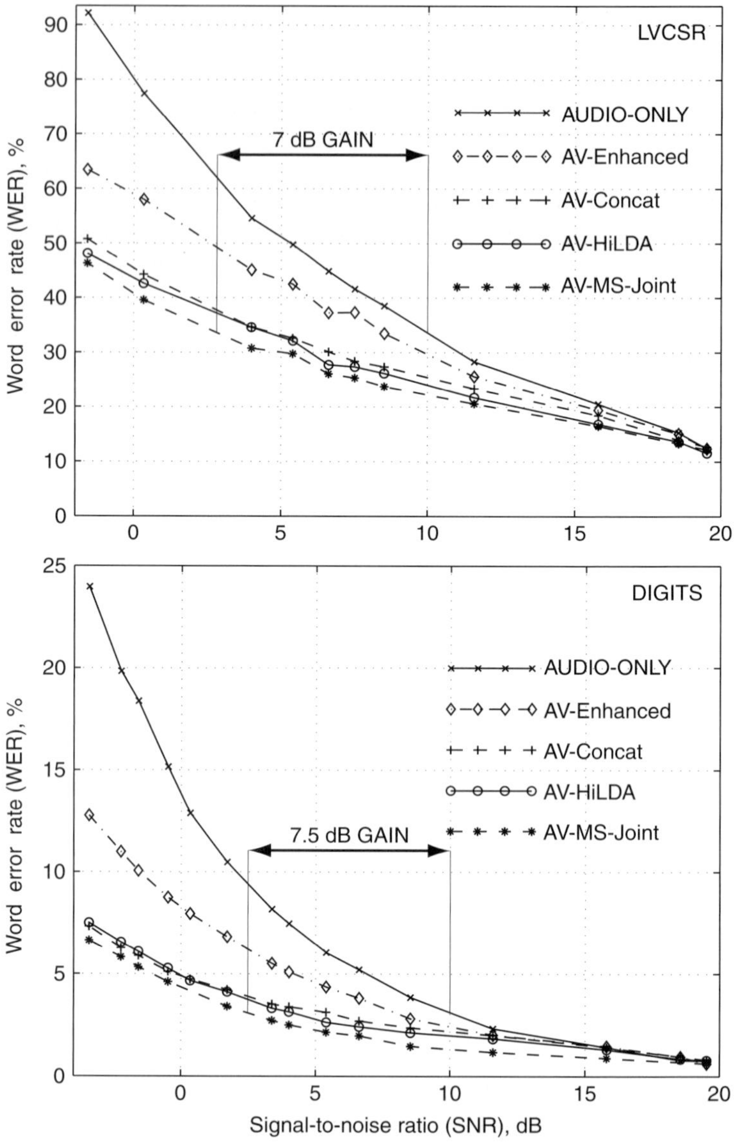

Figure 9.12 Comparison of audio-only and audiovisual ASR by means of three feature fusion (AV-Concat, AV-HiLDA, and AV-Enhanced) algorithms and one decision fusion (AV-MS-Joint) technique, using the full decoding experimental paradigm. WERs vs. audio channel SNR are reported on both the IBM ViaVoice™ test set (speaker-independent LVCSR – top), and on the multi-speaker DIGITS test set (bottom) of Table 9.3. HiLDA feature fusion outperforms alternative feature fusion methods, whereas decision fusion outperforms all three feature fusion approaches, resulting in an effective SNR gain of 7 dB for LVCSR and 7.5 dB for DIGITS, at 10 dB SNR (Potamianos *et al.* 2001c; Goecke *et al.* 2002; Gravier *et al.* 2002a). Notice that the WER ranges in the two graphs differ.

Table 9.6 *Adaptation results on the speech impaired data. WER, %, of the audio-only (AU), visual-only (VI), and audiovisual (AV) modalities, using HiLDA feature fusion, are reported on both the LVCSR (left table part) and DIGITS test sets (right table) of the speech-impaired data using unadapted HMMs (trained in normal speech) as well as a number of HMM adaptation methods. All HMMs are adapted on the joint speech-impaired LVCSR and DIGITS adaptation sets of Table 9.3. For the continuous speech results, decoding using the test set vocabulary of 537 words is reported. MAP followed by MLLR adaptation, and possibly preceded by front end matrix adaptation (Mat), achieves the best results for all modalities and for both tasks considered (Potamianos and Neti 2001a).*

Task		LVCSR			DIGITS	
Method/Modality	AU	VI	AV	AU	VI	AV
Unadapted	116.022	136.359	106.014	52.381	48.016	24.801
MLLR	52.044	110.166	42.873	3.770	16.667	0.992
MAP	52.376	101.215	44.199	3.373	12.103	1.190
MAP+MLLR	47.624	95.027	41.216	2.381	10.516	0.992
Mat+MAP	52.928	98.674	46.519	3.968	8.730	1.190
Mat+MAP+MLLR	50.055	93.812	41.657	2.381	8.531	0.992

consider the SNR value where the audiovisual WER equals the reference audio-only WER (see Figure 9.12). For HiLDA fusion, this gain equals approximately 6 dB for both LVCSR and DIGITS tasks. Jointly trained multi-stream HMMs improve these gains to 7 dB for LVCSR and 7.5 dB for DIGITS, at 10 dB SNR. Full decoding experiments employing additional decision fusion techniques are currently in progress. In particular, intermediate fusion results by means of the product HMM are reported in Gravier *et al.* (2002a).

9.5.5 *Audiovisual adaptation*

We now describe recent experiments on audiovisual adaptation in a case study of single-subject audiovisual ASR of impaired speech (Potamianos and Neti 2001a). As already indicated, the small amount of speech-impaired data collected (see Table 9.3) is not sufficient for HMM training, and call for speaker adaptation techniques instead. A number of such methods, described in a previous section, are used for adapting audio-only, visual-only, and audiovisual HMMs to LVCSR. The results on both speech-impaired LVCSR and DIGITS tasks are depicted in Table 9.6. Due to poor accuracy on impaired speech, decoding on the LVCSR task is performed using the 537-word test set vocabulary of the dataset. Clearly, the mismatch between the normal and impaired-speech data is dramatic, as the "Unadapted" table entries demonstrate. Indeed, the audiovisual WER in the LVCSR task reaches 106.0% (such large numbers occur due to word insertions), whereas the audiovisual WER in the DIGITS task is 24.8% (in comparison, the normal speech, per subject, adapted audiovisual LVCSR WER is 10.2%, and the audiovisual DIGITS WER is only 0.55%, computed on the test sets of Table 9.3).

We first consider MLLR and MAP HMM adaptation using the joint speech-impaired LVCSR and DIGITS adaptation tests. Audio-only, visual-only, and audiovisual performances improve dramatically, as demonstrated in Table 9.6. Due to the rather large adaptation set, MAP performs similarly well to MLLR. Applying MLLR after MAP improves results, and it reduces the audiovisual WER to 41.2% and 0.99% for the LVCSR and DIGITS tasks, respectively, amounting to a 61% and 96% relative WER reduction over the audiovisual unadapted results, and to a 13% and 58% relative WER reduction over the audio-only MAP+MLLR adapted results. Clearly, therefore, the use of the visual modality confers dramatic benefits on the automatic recognition of impaired speech. We also apply front end adaptation, possibly followed by MLLR adaptation, with the results depicted in the Mat+MAP(+MLLR) entries of Table 9.6. Although visual-only recognition improves, the audio-only recognition results fail to do so. As a consequence, audiovisual ASR degrades, possibly due to the fact that, in this experiment, audiovisual matrix adaptation is only applied to the second stage of LDA/MLLT.

9.6 Summary and discussion

In this chapter we provided an overview of the basic techniques for automatic recognition of audiovisual speech proposed in the literature over the past twenty years. The two main issues relevant to the design of audiovisual ASR systems are, first, the visual front end that captures visual speech information, and second, the integration (fusion) of audio and visual features into the automatic speech recognizer used. Both are challenging problems, and significant research effort has been directed towards finding appropriate solutions.

We first discussed extracting visual features from the video of the speaker's face. This process requires first the detection and then tracking of the face, mouth region, and possibly the speaker's lip contours. A number of mostly statistical techniques suitable for the task were reviewed. Various visual features proposed in the literature were then presented. Some are based on the mouth region appearance and employ image transforms or other dimensionality-reduction techniques borrowed from the pattern-recognition literature, in order to extract relevant speech information. Others capture the lip contour and possibly face shape characteristics by means of statistical or geometric models. Combinations of features from these two categories are also possible.

Subsequently, we concentrated on the problem of audiovisual integration. Possible solutions to this problem differ in various aspects, including the classifier and classes used for automatic speech recognition, the combination of single-modality features versus single-modality classification decisions, and in the latter case, the information level provided by each classifier, the temporal level of the integration, and the sequence of the decision combination. We concentrated on HMM-based recognition, based on sub-phonetic classes and assuming time-synchronous audio and visual feature generation. We reviewed a number of feature and decision fusion techniques. Within the first category, we discussed simple feature concatenation, discriminant feature fusion, and a linear audio feature enhancement approach. For decision-based integration, we concentrated on linear log-likelihood combination of parallel, single-modality classifiers at various levels of integration, considering the state-synchronous multi-stream HMM for "early" fusion, the product HMM for "intermediate" fusion, and discriminative model combination for "late" integration. We discussed the training of the resulting models.

Developing and benchmarking feature extraction and fusion algorithms requires available audiovisual data. A limited number of corpora suitable for research in audiovisual ASR have been collected and used in the literature. A brief overview of them was also provided, including a description of the IBM ViaVoice™ database, suitable for speaker-independent audiovisual ASR in the large-vocabulary, continuous speech domain. Subsequently, experimental results were reported using this database, as well as research on additional corpora collected at IBM Research. Some of these experiments were conducted during the summer 2000 workshop at the Johns Hopkins University and compared both visual feature extraction and audiovisual fusion methods for LVCSR. More recent experiments, as well as a case study of speaker adaptation techniques for audiovisual recognition of impaired speech were also presented. These experiments showed that a visual front end can be designed that successfully captures speaker-independent, large-vocabulary continuous speech information. Such a visual front end uses discrete cosine transform coefficients of the detected mouth region of interest, suitably post-processed. Combining the resulting visual features with traditional acoustic ones results in significant improvements over audio-only recognition in both clean and of course degraded acoustic conditions, across small and large vocabulary tasks, as well as for both normal and impaired speech. A successful combination technique is the multi-stream HMM-based decision fusion approach, or the simpler, but inferior, discriminant feature fusion (HiLDA) method.

This chapter clearly demonstrates that, over the past twenty-five years, much progress has been made in capturing and integrating visual speech information into automatic speech recognition. However, the visual modality has yet to become utilized in mainstream ASR systems. This is due to the fact that both practical and research issues remain challenging. On the practical side, the need for high-quality captured visual data, necessary for extracting visual speech information capable of enhancing ASR performance, introduces increased cost, storage, and computer processing requirements. In addition, the lack of common, large audiovisual corpora that address a wide variety of ASR tasks, conditions, and environments, hinders development of audiovisual systems suitable for use in particular applications.

On the research side, the key issues in the design of audiovisual ASR systems remain open and subject to more investigation. In the visual front end design, for example, face detection, facial feature localization, and face shape tracking, robust to speaker, pose, lighting, and environment variation constitute challenging problems. A comprehensive comparison between face appearance- and shape-based features for speaker-dependent versus speaker-independent automatic speechreading is also unavailable. Joint shape and appearance three-dimensional face modeling, used for both tracking and visual feature extraction, has not been considered in the literature, although such an approach could possibly lead to the desired robustness and generality of the visual front end, successfully addressing challenging visual conditions in realistic environments, such as the automobile cabin. In addition, when combining audio and visual information, a number of issues relevant to decision fusion require further study. These include the optimal level of integrating the audio and visual log-likelihoods, the optimal function for this integration, and the inclusion of suitable, local estimates of the reliability of each modality into this function.

Further investigation of these issues is clearly warranted, and it is expected to lead to improved robustness and performance of audiovisual ASR. Progress in addressing some or all of these questions can also benefit other areas where joint audio and visual speech processing is suitable (Chen and Rao 1998; Aleksic *et al.* 2005). Such are for example: speaker identification and verification (Jourlin *et al.* 1997; Wark and Sridharan 1998; Fröba *et al.* 1999; Jain *et al.* 1999; Maison *et al.* 1999; Chibelushi *et al.* 2002; Zhang *et al.* 2002; Aleksic and Katsaggelos 2003; Chaudhari *et al.* 2003; Sanderson and Paliwal 2004; Aleksic and Katsaggelos 2006); visual speech synthesis (Cohen and Massaro 1994b; Chen *et al.* 1995; Yamamoto *et al.* 1998; Cosatto *et al.* 2000; Choi *et al.* 2001; Bailly *et al.* 2003; Aleksic and Katsaggelos 2004b; Fu *et al.* 2005; Melenchón *et al.* 2009; Tao *et al.* 2009); speech intent detection (De Cuetos *et al.* 2000); speech activity detection (Libal *et al.* 2007; Rivet *et al.* 2007); speech synchrony detection (Iyengar *et al.* 2003; Bredin and Chollet 2007; Sargin *et al.* 2007; Kumar *et al.* 2010); speech enhancement (Girin *et al.* 2001b; Deligne *et al.* 2002; Goecke *et al.* 2002); speech coding (Foucher *et al.* 1998; Girin 2004); speech inversion (Yehia *et al.* 1998; Jiang *et al.* 2002; Kjellström *et al.* 2006; Katsamanis *et al.* 2009); speech separation (Girin *et al.* 2001a; Sodoyer *et al.* 2004); speaker localization (Bub *et al.* 1995; Wang and Brandstein 1999;

Zotkin *et al.* 2002); emotion recognition (Cohen *et al.* 2003); and video indexing and retrieval (Huang *et al.* 1999). Improvements in these technologies are expected to result in more robust and natural human–computer interaction.

9.7 Acknowledgments

The authors would like to state that they are solely responsible for the content of this chapter. The views and opinions of the authors expressed herein do not necessarily reflect those of their affiliations.

The authors would like to acknowledge a number of people for particular contributions to this work: Giridharan Iyengar and Andrew Senior (IBM) for their help with face and mouth region detection on the IBM ViaVoice^{TM} and other audiovisual data discussed in this chapter; Rich Wilkins and Eric Helmuth (formerly with IBM) for their efforts in data collection; Guillaume Gravier (currently at IRISA/INRIA Rennes) for the joint multi-stream HMM training and full decoding on the connected digits and LVCSR tasks; Roland Goecke (currently at the Australian National University) for experiments on audiovisual-based enhancement of audio features during a summer internship at IBM; Hervé Glotin (ERSS-CNRS) and Dimitra Vergyri (SRI) for their work during the summer 2000 Johns Hopkins workshop on utterance-dependent multi-stream exponent estimation based on speech voicing, and late audiovisual fusion within the discriminative model combination framework, respectively; and the remaining summer workshop student team members for invaluable help.

Gerasimos Potamianos would also like to acknowledge partial support of the European Commission through FP7-PEOPLE-2009-RG-247948 grant AVISPIRE during the revision of this chapter.

10 Image-based facial synthesis

M. Slaney and C. Bregler

10.1 Facial synthesis approaches

There are many ways to organize a discussion of facial synthesis. Some people highlight quality, or computational efficiency, or particular geometrical representations. In this work we describe a trade-off between smart algorithms and lots of data.

A conventional approach to synthesizing a face is to model it as a three-dimensional computer graphics object. This approach has been used for nearly thirty years and researchers now understand many aspects of the human face. Given an audio signal we know the desired shape of the mouth, how muscles move, how skin stretches, and how light reflects off the skin (Terzopoulos and Waters 1993). Yet with all this knowledge the results using computer graphics approaches are not 100 percent realistic. This observation is not meant as a criticism of previous work, but instead should be considered an indication of the full richness and subtlety of human behavior and perception.

Recently many researchers have advocated an approach based on simple algorithms, but lots of data. This new approach gets its realism from a large collection of image data, reorganizing the images to synthesize new audiovisual utterances. Oversimplifying, an image-based approach knows nothing about how muscles move, or any other properties of a face. Instead the system learns that when the natural face says "pa," the video pixel one inch below the nose changes from pink (lip-colored) to white (teeth). In a sense, we reduce the face synthesis problem to a simple database problem.

In practice, image-based work is not so extreme. A little bit of knowledge about faces goes a long way. We can use this knowledge to reduce the size of the dataset we need to collect and, more importantly, to help synthesize utterances or head poses we have not seen before.

The continuum between knowledge-based and image-based synthesis is shown in Figure 10.1. On the left, the smart algorithms encode knowledge about how faces move and reflect light in computer algorithms. Their advantage is that they can easily generate images of new people, new lighting conditions, or even different animals. On the right, the image-based approaches have the

Figure 10.1 The range of options on the knowledge- to data-based axis of facial synthesis methods.

potential to create super-realistic images. There are uses for both extremes, but practical systems will probably fall somewhere in the middle (Cohen and Massaro 1990).

It is important to note that this dichotomy between knowledge- and data-based algorithms is common in Computer Science. People doing speech recognition used to build a hierarchy of specialized recognizers (Cole *et al.* 1983) but this approach was quickly surpassed by hidden Markov models (HMMs) that learn the probabilities of speech from large collections of speech data (Jelinek 1998). Music synthesis in the 1970s was done using frequency modulation (FM) techniques that synthesize many interesting sounds when given the right parameters. Now musicians use wave tables to synthesize musical sounds – if you want a piano note then record it once and play it back every time you need that note. The polygons of the computer graphics world are often replaced by image-based rendering techniques such as light-fields (Levoy and Hanrahan 1996). Finally the original work on text-to-speech (TTS) calculated the formant frequencies for each phone and synthesized speech by rule (Carlson and Granström 1976; Klatt 1979). The very highest quality results are now generated by collecting hours of speech data, chopping the waveform into collections of phonemes, and rearranging and concatenating them to produce the final results. This approach, known as concatenative synthesis (Hunt and Black 1996), is closest in spirit to our image-based techniques.

While concatenative synthesis systems for speech and music domains were pioneered in the early 1990s (Moulines *et al.* 1990), such example-based techniques were first introduced to animation and video synthesis in 1997 (Bregler *et al.* 1997b) and later refined by Ezzat *et al.* (2002b), and extended to motion capture animation (Arikan and Forsyth 2002; Kovar *et al.* 2002; Pullen and Bregler 2002; Reitsma and Pollard 2007). Another line of research close in spirit to this philosophy has been introduced by Efros and Leung (1999) to image texture synthesis, and by Schoedl *et al.* (2000) to video texture synthesis. More recent research combines acoustic and facial speech with other motion modalities, like facial expression, head motions, and body gestures (Stone *et al.* 2004; Chuang and Bregler 2005; Bregler *et al.* 2009; Williams *et al.* 2010).

Specific to human motion and facial speech synthesis, all of these data-based approaches use a learning/training normalization step to create a database. Most systems do the bulk of the analysis work when building the database so that the synthesis step is as easy as possible. Given a particular task, the synthesis stage finds the appropriate data in the database, warps it to fit the desired scene, and outputs the final pixels.

We will use the Video Rewrite system (Bregler *et al.* 1997b) to demonstrate the basic ideas of image-based facial synthesis. Section 10.2 gives an overview of image-based facial synthesis and Video Rewrite in particular. Section 10.3 describes the analysis stage of Video Rewrite and Section 10.4 describes the synthesis stage of Video Rewrite. Section 10.5 compares and contrasts two other approaches – based on static images and Markov models – for facial synthesis.

10.2 Image-based facial synthesis

Video Rewrite uses a training database of video of a person speaking naturally. To synthesize talking faces it rearranges the contents of the video database to fit the new words. To start, the analysis stage Video Rewrite uses a conventional speech recognition system to segment the speech, and computer vision techniques to find the face and the exact location of the mouth and jaw line. In the synthesis stage, the same speech recognition technology segments the new utterances and then an image-morphing step warps the database images to fit the new words. A separate piece of video, called the *background video* or *background sequence*, provides the rest of the face and the overall head movements. The lip and jaw sequences from the database are inserted into the background sequence. This is shown in Figure 10.2.

In a strict image-based approach we can synthesize only the conditions we have already seen in the training data. Under controlled lighting conditions, we can capture the reflectivity of a simple object from every possible angle (Levoy and Hanrahan 1996) but this is not possible with a talking face. Instead, we look for ways to simplify the problem.

The most important factor when synthesizing talking faces is coarticulation. The shape of the mouth depends primarily on the acoustic phone before and after the current sound. As we are saying one sound our lips are still moving from the shape of the previous sound and starting to move towards the shape of the next sound. It is easier to store a sequence of prototypical phoneme images, but working with triphones is not difficult. In 8 minutes of training video, we

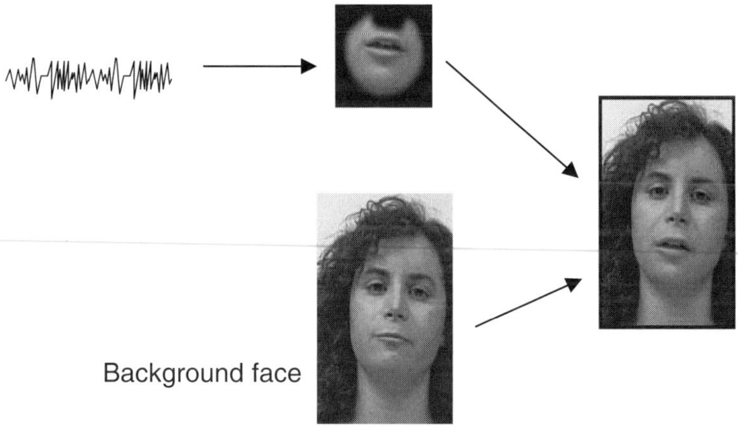

Figure 10.2 The Video Rewrite synthesis system. Speech is recognized and triphone visemes from a database are found. A separate background video is used to provide the head movements and the rest of the face. The database images are transformed and inserted into the background video to form the final video.

found 1700 different triphones, of more than the 19 000 naturally occurring triphone sequences (if we don't have exactly the right triphone, we use the triphone that is closest visually). We found it was important to store the prototypes of many different triphones, and choose the triphone that most closely matched our synthesis needs. Three examples of triphones from a Video Rewrite database are shown in Figure 10.3.

Other factors we need to consider are listed below.

- *Head pose*: We want our subjects to speak and move naturally. But an image of the mouth changes as the head rotates and tilts. Video Rewrite adjusts for small changes in head pose with a planar model. Video Rewrite adjusts for larger changes by modeling the face as an ellipsoid. But even with a sophisticated ellipsoidal model, an image-based approach will never be able to synthesize the profile of a head if all our data is from frontal images. The planar and elliptical model approaches for compensating for head pose are described in Section 10.3.1.
- *Lighting*: We assume without too much error that the reflectivity of skin does not change over the range of allowable head poses. But lighting changes are another matter. Some lighting changes are corrected by fitting a simple illumination model to the data, but if one wants to synthesize a face at a beach and in a nightclub then the training dataset will need images in daylight and in a dark room with the appropriate lights. A lighting-correction technique is described in Section 10.4.3.

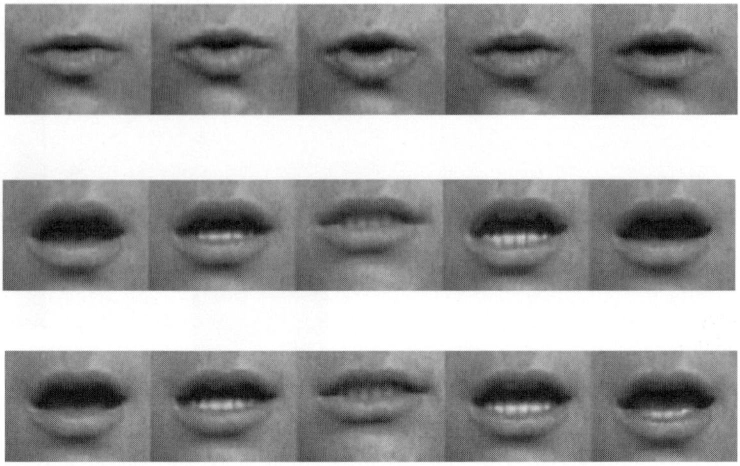

Figure 10.3 The effects of coarticulation. Frames from our training data showing three different triphones show the wide variation in mouth positions, even for the same phones.

- *Emotional content:* There is data indicating that we can hear a smile (Ohala 1994). We can certainly identify a smiling speaker, but we don't have a good model of how the emotional state, as conveyed by an auditory signal, maps into facial positions. It is important that the two signals are consistent since a viewer can identify how much smile is present in both the audio and the visual signals.
- *Utterance length*: The way that we speak changes as we change our rate of speech. Most speakers slur their words as they speak faster. Thus the word "pat" will look different when spoken slowly and carefully, compared to when it is spoken rapidly. We can adjust for this effect by using phone sequences from our database that are close in length to the new audio. Otherwise, we can change the video playback speed to fit the new audio.
- *Eyebrows*: Video Rewrite uses a background face to provide most of the facial image. This includes the eyes and the eyebrows. There is evidence that a speaker's eyebrows are used in concert with their voice to convey a message, but there is no straightforward mapping between acoustics and eyebrow locations. One possible correlation is with the speaker's pitch (Ohala 1994).

In all cases, an image-based solution combines multiple views of the speaker with algorithms that can modify the video to fit the need. Any one image in the training data comes with a coarticulation context, a head pose, a lighting model, and an emotional state. The art in image-based facial synthesis is trading off the different features to choose the best input sequence to modify and concatenate. Fortunately, collecting a large database minimizes all these problems.

The importance of this trade-off was made clear to us when we started working with John F. Kennedy footage from the Cuban missile crisis. This footage was shot before the advent of teleprompters: Kennedy spent half the time looking directly into the camera, and half the time looking down at his notes. Moving from an affine model of the face to an elliptical model helped improve the realism of the Video Rewrite results. But in the end we avoided warping a downward-looking image to a full frontal view unless we really had nothing close to the right viseme sequence in the desired pose. In effect, for any one desired pose we could use only half our training data.

We describe image-based facial synthesis in terms of a video database where images corresponding to small chunks of speech are first normalized so they appear in a standardized form and are stored for easy retrieval. But this is not how we implemented Video Rewrite. Instead, Video Rewrite labels the original video so that it can easily find the appropriate sections of video. There might be ten instances of the word "Cuba" but each will have a slightly different pose, length, and context. We improve the synthesis results by choosing a training example from the original video that has the closest context.

There are two reasons we get better results by leaving the video in its original form. First we improve the image quality by storing just the parameters that normalize each frame. Later when we need to denormalize by a different transform (to insert the mouth pixels into a new background face) we just multiply the transforms. Thus instead of doing two image transforms, each with its own image interpolation stage, we can combine the transforms mathematically and just do one interpolation step. Secondly, by leaving the video in its original form we can more easily choose long sequences of phonemes if they happen to occur in the training set in the right order. The minimum sequence of phones used by Video Rewrite is three phones, or a triphone, but we improve our synthesis quality by using the longest sequence we can find in our database.

10.3 Analyses and normalization

Video Rewrite analyzed the training data to find the location of each segment of speech, and the location and pose of each facial feature. This section describes the analysis Video Rewrite performed on the audio and video data.

Video Rewrite used an HMM speech recognition system (Jelinek 1998) to segment the audio signal. Video Rewrite trained two gender-dependent recognition models using the TIMIT database. If we know the word sequence, segmentation into phonemes is easy. Given the word sequence the recognizer can look up the words in the dictionary and find the expanded phoneme sequence.[1] The recognizer then fits the known phone sequence to the audio data and returns the segment boundaries. This is a comparatively easy task for a speech recognition system.

Video Rewrite knew the approximate location of the head in each video sequence but if this information is not available, a face-finding algorithm (Rowley *et al.* 1998) could be used to get the approximate location. Depending on the amount of out-of-plane motion, Video Rewrite used either an affine transform or an elliptical model to transform each facial image into the canonical pose. Any image can be chosen as the canonical pose, but it is best to use a median pose so that the average pose correction is small.

10.3.1 Pose estimation

For relatively static facial sequences, Video Rewrite used an affine warp to transform each face image in the training set into the canonical form. This transform not only aligns the size, position, and rotation of each facial image, but can also correct some small out-of-plane tilts of the head.

This step is critically important to Video Rewrite's success. Early in the development process the isolated mouth sequences looked realistic, but they looked horrible when inserted into a face. At that point we were inserting the new mouth image into the background at a location determined by the pose estimate, but rounded to the nearest integer pixel location. Our results improved dramatically when we interpolated the mouth images to place the mouth images exactly. Evidently, viewers are so sensitive to the position of the mouth on the face that one pixel jitter was enough to destroy the illusion of a realistic talking face.

Accurately locating the new mouth images on a face is difficult because the true measure of success is how well the teeth are fixed on the skull. We occasionally see the teeth in the training video, but the skull is harder to see. Instead, Video Rewrite looks at portions of the face that are relatively stable and can provide a good estimate of the underlying skull location. These portions of the face are indicated with a mask, which multiplies the facial image. This mask avoids several sections of the face that are unreliable estimates of facial position, including the mouth (it is always moving), the nose (there is specular reflection from the tip, and the nose represents the biggest discrepancy from planar or elliptical models of the face), and eyes (movement). The mask and typical images are shown in Figure 10.4.

Video Rewrite used an affine tracker (Bergen *et al.* 1992) or an elliptical model of the face (Basu *et al.* 1996) to normalize each image in the training data and the background video. The affine warp can exactly compensate for translations and in-plane rotations. The compensation for out-of-plane rotations, such as tilting the head forward, is approximate – compressing the y-axis

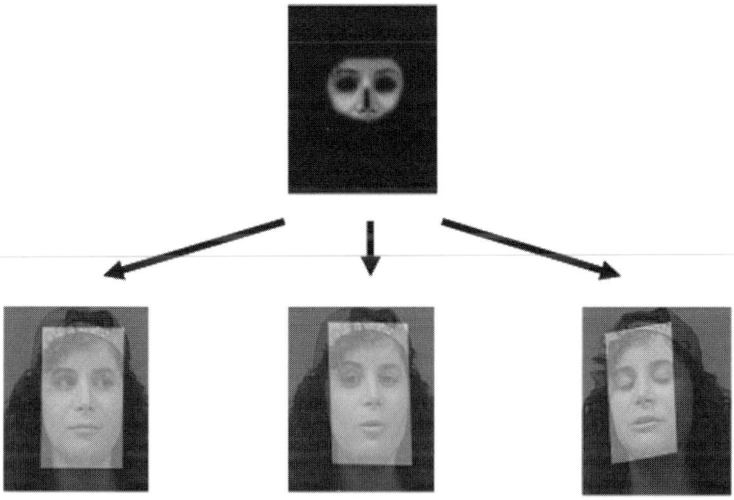

Figure 10.4 The masked portion of the face shown at the top is a reference image used to find the head pose. A white rectangle is superimposed on three facial images to show the estimated affine warp that best matches the reference image.

approximates small amounts of tilt. The affine tracker is less computationally expensive, but does not work as well with out-of-plane rotations of the head. Both algorithms find a transform that warps each image so that it closely matches a reference image.

10.3.1.1 Affine model An affine tracker (Bergen *et al.* 1992) adjusts the parameters of these equations

$$\begin{aligned} u(x,y) &= a_1 + a_2 x + a_3 y \\ v(x,y) &= a_4 + a_5 x + a_6 y \end{aligned}$$

so that a warped image, $I_t(u(x,y),v(x,y))$, at time t matches as closely as possible the reference image $I_0(x,y)$ with the affine warp defined by the a parameters. Using vector notation, this is written

$$U = Xa$$

where $U = [x\ y]^T$, $a = [a_1, a_2, a_3, a_4, a_5, a_6]^T$ and

$$X = \begin{bmatrix} x & y & 0 & 0 & 1 & 0 \\ 0 & 0 & x & y & 0 & 1 \end{bmatrix}.$$

We can use Gauss–Newton to iterate and find a solution for a in terms of small steps δa. The change in a, at each iteration step is given by

$$\left[\sum X^T(\nabla I)(\nabla I)^T X\right]\delta\alpha = -\sum X^T(\nabla I)(\Delta I)$$

Where ∇I is a 2×1 derivative of a pixel location versus x and y, and ΔI is a scalar and describes the difference between the first image and the warped second image using the current estimate of a.

For both computational efficiency and to avoid local minima in the optimization, this optimization step is often combined with hierarchical processing. At the start it is not necessary to work with images at the highest resolution. Instead, the images can be low-pass filtered and subsampled before the iteration described above is performed. Once we converge to a good answer at low resolution we can use this as a starting point on a slightly higher resolution image. An example of the affine model is shown in Figure 10.4.

10.3.1.2 Elliptical model An affine image transformation model is a good fit for planar objects that are rotating by small amounts in space, but a human face is not planar. With large rotations, the 3D structure of the face is apparent and a richer model is needed to capture, and normalize, the motion.

Basu and his colleagues proposed an elliptical model of the face (Basu *et al.* 1996). We would like to find parameters of an elliptical model of the face, $[\alpha,\beta,\gamma,t_x,t_y,t_z]$, where α, β, and γ describe the ellipse's rotations, and t_x, t_y, and t_z describe its position. We would like to recover the best parameters that explain the 2D image data we are considering.

We start with a reference image, usually showing a frontal view of the face, and then hand-fit a 3D ellipse to the image data. (Basu suggests using face-finding software to locate the face in the image and then starting with the closest example from a pre-adjusted set of ellipses.) The optimization step is straightforward. We want to find choices for the six ellipsoidal parameters that best represent the new image in terms of the reference. A set of parameters describes a 3D ellipse, which has a particular projection onto the image plane. We can then take the image points and map them back through the projection transformation to find the brightness of each point on the ellipse. In effect, we color the proposed ellipse with the pixels from the image. When we have the correct transformation parameters, the data for the new image, as mapped onto its ellipse, will agree with the original image's transformation. The multidimensional parameters of this new ellipse can be easily optimized using, for example, the simplex method (Press *et al.* 1995).

10.3.2 Feature tracking

In an image-based rendering system, database entries are chosen and then must be blended. Speech synthesis systems often simply concatenate the database entries to form a new speech signal; listeners are not particularly sensitive to spectral discontinuities at unit boundaries. The same is not true for visual motion. Our eyes are excellent feature trackers and discontinuities in position or velocity are quite evident.

Thus an important step of image-based video synthesis is the ability to track features and blend their positions, velocities, and appearance across synthesis units. This is especially important for Video Rewrite since Video Rewrite combines overlapping triphones using image morphing; the location of the features controls the morphing algorithm.

The tracking problem is simplified once we have used the pose-estimation algorithm described in Section 10.3.1 to normalize the size and the position of the face. There are many ways to track features. Video Rewrite used a technique known as EigenPoints (Covell and Bregler 1996) because it is computationally efficient.

EigenPoints models the connection between an image, I, and the x–y coordinates of the feature we are tracking as a linear relationship. In mathematical terms

$$[x\ y]^T - [\bar{x}\ \bar{y}]^T = M(I - \bar{I}),$$

where M is the matrix that connects the image data, I and its mean, $\bar{I}$, with the location of the features $[x\ y]^T$, with its mean, $[\bar{x}\ \bar{y}]^T$, subtracted.

EigenPoints finds a linear coupling by using a large training set of images and labeled x–y coordinates of the features. The data from one image and its corresponding coordinates are concatenated and form one row of a new matrix. If the image and coordinate data are scaled so they have similar variance, then a singular-value decomposition (SVD) is used to find the vector direction that best characterizes the combined spread of data. Taking into account the effects of noise, the linear mapping, M, is calculated using equation 9 of Covell and Bregler's paper (1996). The result of this processing is shown in Figure 10.5.

The EigenPoints connection is only valid over a limited range of movement. Underlying the EigenPoint theory is the assumption that the image and the coordinate data are linear functions of a single underlying driving process. Thus given an image patch from the face, with the mean removed, we can find the deviation of the control points by a simple matrix multiplication.

But, it is unlikely, for example, that the same process drives the upper lip and the jaw line. In fact they can move relatively independently of each other. Thus

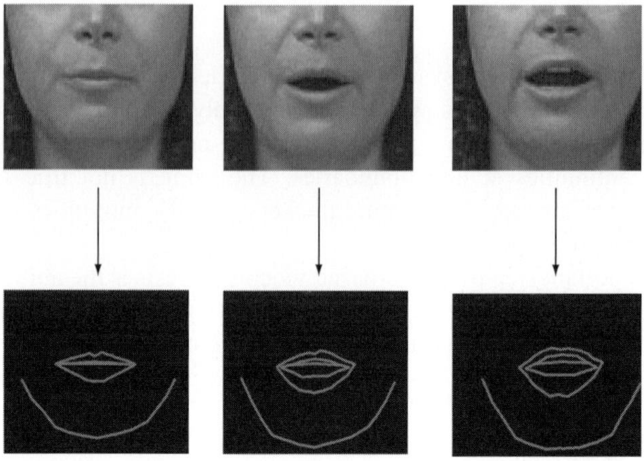

Figure 10.5 EigenPoints is a linear transform that maps image brightness into control point locations. The three images at the bottom show the fiduciary points for the facial images on top.

Video Rewrite uses two different EigenPoints models to capture all the dynamics of the mouth and jaw line.[2]

In Video Rewrite there were two separate EigenPoints analyses. The two EigenPoint models label each image in the training video using a total of 54 EigenPoints: 34 on the mouth (20 on the outer boundary, 12 on the inner boundary, one at the bottom of the upper teeth, and one at the top of the lower teeth) and 20 on the chin and jaw line. The first eigenspace controlled the placement of the 34 fiduciary points on the mouth, using 50×40 pixels around the nominal mouth location, a region that covers the mouth completely. The second eigenspace controlled the placement of the 20 fiduciary points on the chin and jaw line, using 100×75 pixels around the nominal chin location, a region that covers the upper neck and the lower part of the face.

We created the two EigenPoints models for locating the fiduciary points from a small number of images. We hand-annotated 26 images (of 14 218 images total; about 0.2%). We extended the hand-annotated dataset by morphing pairs of annotated images to form intermediate images, expanding the original 26 to 351 annotated images without any additional manual work. We then derived EigenPoints models using this extended dataset.

Video Rewrite used EigenPoints to find the mouth and jaw, and to label their contours. The derived EigenPoints models located the facial features using 6 basis vectors for the mouth and 6 different vectors for the jaw. EigenPoints then placed the fiduciary points around the feature locations: 32 basis vectors place points around the lips and 64 basis vectors place points around the jaw.

10.4 Synthesis

Synthesis in an image-based facial animation system is straightforward. Given a signal, we need to identify the speech sounds, find the best image sequences in our database, and stitch the results together. The synthesis procedure is diagrammed in Figure 10.6.

Video Rewrite uses a speech recognition system to recognize the new speech and translate the audio into a sequence of phonemes (with their durations). In the sections that follow, we will explain how Video Rewrite uses the background image (Section 10.4.1), how the database visemes are selected (Section 10.4.2), and finally how the visemes are morphed and stitched together (Section 10.4.3).

10.4.1 The background video

Video Rewrite uses a background video to set the stage for the new synthesized mouth. The background video provides images of most of the face – especially the eyes – and natural head movements. In the Video Rewrite examples, the background video came from the training video, so the normalization parameters have already been computed. After we selected the new mouth images, the normalizing parameters for each database image are multiplied by the inverse of the background image transform to find the transformation that maps each database image into the background frame.

We chose a background sequence from the training set where the speaker spoke a sentence with roughly the same length as the new utterance. There are undoubtedly important speech cues in the way that we move our head, eyes, and eyebrows as we speak. We do not know what all these cues are. By starting with real facial images and facial movements, we can show some of these cues, without understanding them.

10.4.2 Selecting visemes from the database

The most difficult part of an image-based synthesis method is selecting the right units to combine. There is always a limited database, and many different constraints to satisfy. Video Rewrite chooses the longest possible utterance from the database that has the right visemes, phoneme lengths, and head pose. The design of this trade-off is complicated by the fact that we have information about how some of the factors affect performance (see for example the viseme confusability data in Owens and Blazek 1985), but we have no information about how these factors combine. The problem is more acute because we can partially correct many factors – such as viseme length, head pose, and lighting – but the errors that remain are hard to quantify.

The new speech utterance, as understood by the automatic speech recognition system, determines the target sequence visemes. We would like to find a sequence of triphone videos from our database that matches this new speech utterance. For each triphone in the new utterance, our goal is to find a video example with exactly the transition we need, and with lip shapes that are compatible with the lip shapes in neighboring triphone videos. Since this goal often is not reachable, we compromise by choosing a sequence of clips that approximates the desired transitions and shape continuity. This process is quantified as follows.

Given a triphone in the new speech utterance, Video Rewrite computes a matching distance to each triphone in the video database. The matching metric has two terms: the *phoneme-context distance*, D_p, and the *distance between lip shapes* in overlapping visual triphones, D_s. The total error is

$$\text{Error} = \alpha\ D_p + (1 - \alpha)D_s,$$

where the weight, α, is a constant that trades off the two factors.

The phoneme-context distance, D_p, is based on categorical distances between phoneme categories and between viseme classes. Since Video Rewrite does not need to create a new soundtrack (it needs only a new video track), we can cluster phonemes into viseme classes, based on their visual appearance.

We use twenty-six viseme classes. Ten are consonant classes: (1) /CH/, /JH/, /SH/, /ZH/; (2) /K/, /G/, /N/, /L/; (3) /T/, /D/, /S/, /Z/; (4) /P/, /B/, /M/; (5) /F/, /V/; (6) /TH/, /DH/; (7) /W/, /R/; (8) /HH/; (9) /Y/; and (10) /NG/. Fifteen are vowel classes: one each for /EH/, /EY/, /ER/, /UH/, /AA/, /AO/, /AW/, /AY/, /UW/, /OW/, /OY/, /IY/, /IH, /AE/, /AH/. One class is for silence, /SIL/.

The phoneme-context distance, D_p, is the weighted sum of phoneme distances between the target phonemes and the video-model phonemes within the context of the triphone. This distance is 0 if the phonemic categories are the same (for example, /P/ and /P/). The distance is 1 if they are in different viseme classes (/P/ and /IY/). If they are in different phoneme categories but are in the same viseme class (/P/ and /B/), then the distance is a value between 0 and 1. The intraclass distances are derived from published confusion matrices (Owens and Blazek 1985).

When computing D_p, the center phoneme of the triphone has the largest weight, and the weights drop smoothly from there. Although the video model stores only triphone images, we consider the triphone's original context when picking the best-fitting sequence. In current animations, this context covers the triphone itself, plus one phoneme on either side.

The second error term, D_s, measures how closely the mouth contours match in overlapping segments of adjacent triphone videos. In synthesizing the mouth shapes for "teapot" we want the contours for the /IY/ and /P/ in the lip sequence used for /T-IY-P/ to match the contours for the /IY/ and /P/ in the sequence used for /IY-PP-AA/. Video Rewrite measures this similarity by computing the Euclidean distance, frame by frame, between four-element feature vectors containing the overall lip width, overall lip height, inner lip height, and height of visible teeth.

The lip-shape distance (D_S) between two triphone videos is minimized with the correct time alignment. For example, consider the overlapping contours for the /P/ in /T-IY-P/ and /IY-P-AA/. The /P/ phoneme includes both a silence, when the lips are pressed together, and an audible release, when the lips move rapidly apart. The durations of the initial silence within the /P/ phoneme may be different. The phoneme labels do not provide us with this level of detailed timing. Yet, if the silence durations are different, the lip-shape distance for two otherwise well-matched videos will be large. This problem is exacerbated by imprecision in the HMM phonemic labels.

We want to find the temporal overlap between neighboring triphones that maximizes the similarity between the two lip shapes. Video Rewrite shifts the two triphones relative to each other to find the best temporal offset and duration. Video Rewrite then uses this optimal overlap both in computing the lip-shape distance, D_S, and in cross-fading the triphone videos during the stitching step. The optimal overlap is the one that minimizes D_S while still maintaining a minimum-allowed overlap. Since the fitness measure for each triphone segment depends on that segment's neighbors in both directions, Video Rewrite selects the sequence of triphone segments using dynamic programming over the entire utterance. This procedure ensures the selection of the best segments from the data available.

The experiments performed with Video Rewrite to date have used relatively small databases. We had 8 min of "Ellen" footage, most of which we could easily repurpose. We had 2 min of the "JFK" footage, of which half was useable at any one time due to the extreme poses. Concatenative text-to-speech systems use tens of hours of speech data for their task. The big advantage of data-based approaches for synthesis is that the quality gets better as the database gets larger. Given larger databases, one is more likely to find the exact triphone in the right context, or, in the worst case, to find a segment that needs less modification for the final synthesis.

10.4.3 Morphing and stitching

Video Rewrite produces the final video by stitching together the appropriate entries from the video database. At this point, Video Rewrite has already selected a sequence of triphone videos that most closely matches the target audio. We need to align the overlapping lip images temporally. This internally time-aligned sequence of videos is then time-aligned to the new speech utterance. Finally, the resulting sequences of lip images are spatially aligned and are stitched into the background face. We will describe how Video Rewrite performs each step in turn.

10.4.3.1 Time alignment of triphone videos We combine a sequence of triphone videos to form a new mouth movie. In combining the videos, we want to maintain the dynamics of the phonemes and their transitions. We need to time-align the triphone videos carefully before blending them. If we are not careful in this step, the mouth will appear to flutter open and closed inappropriately.

Video Rewrite aligns the triphone videos by choosing a portion of the overlapping triphones where the two lip shapes are as similar as possible. Video Rewrite makes this choice when we evaluate D_s to choose the sequence of triphone videos (Section 10.4.2). We use the overlap duration and shift that provide the minimum value of D_s for the given videos.

10.4.3.2 Time alignment of the lips to the utterance We now have a self-consistent temporal alignment for the triphone videos. We have the correct articulatory motions, in the correct order to match the target utterance, but these articulations are not yet time-aligned with the target utterance.

Video Rewrite aligns the lip motions with the target utterance by comparing the corresponding phoneme transcripts. The starting time of the center phone in the triphone sequence is aligned with the corresponding label in the target transcript. The triphone videos are then stretched or compressed so that they fit the time needed between the phoneme boundaries in the target utterance.

10.4.3.3 Illumination matching Video Rewrite inserts a series of foreground images into the background video to synthesize new words. Under the best of conditions, the lighting on the face will be consistent and there will not be a noticeable difference at the boundary between the two sets of data. Unfortunately, with the need to collect as large a database as possible, there will often be lighting differences between different portions of the database. This is also likely to happen if we are trying to synthesize audiovisual speech in a large number of lighting conditions.

Video Rewrite uses a planar illumination model to adjust the lighting in the background and foreground images before stitching them together. The edge of the mask image, shown in Figure 10.4, defines a region where we want to be careful to match the lighting conditions. Video Rewrite models the average brightness of the pixels at the edge of the mask with a plane. The foreground image is adjusted by linearly scaling its brightness so that it matches the planar model of the background image. This measurement, in both cases, is only done using the pixels near the edge of the mask so that portions of the face that are moving, such as the mouth, are not included in the matching calculation. A

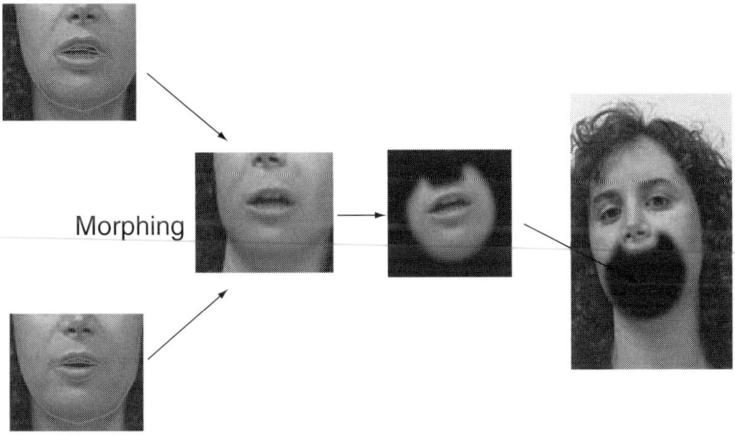

Figure 10.6 The Video Rewrite synthesis process. Two images from the database, with their control points, are combined using morphing. Then this image is transformed to fit into the background image and inserted into the background face.

more sophisticated approach to lighting control and image splining was proposed by Burt and Adelson (1983a).

10.4.3.4 Combining the lips and the background The remaining task is to stitch the triphone videos into the background sequence. The correctness of the facial alignment is critical to the success of the synthesis. The lips and head are constantly moving in the triphone and background footage. Yet, we need to align them so that the new mouth is firmly planted on the face. Any error in spatial alignment causes the mouth to jitter relative to the face – an extremely disturbing effect.

Video Rewrite again uses the mask from Figure 10.4 to find the optimal global transform to register the faces from the triphone videos with the background face. The combined transforms from the mouth and background images to the template face (Section 10.4.2) give a starting estimate in this search. Reestimating the global transform by directly matching the triphone images to the background improves the accuracy of the mapping.

Video Rewrite uses a replacement mask to specify which portions of the final video come from the triphone images and which come from the background video. This replacement mask warps to fit the new mouth shape in the triphone image and to fit the jaw shape in the background image. Figure 10.6 shows an example replacement mask, applied to triphone and background images.

Local deformations are required to stitch the shape of the mouth and jaw line correctly. Video Rewrite handles these two shapes differently. The mouth's shape is completely determined by the triphone images. The only changes made to the mouth shape are imposed to align the mouths within the overlapping triphone images: The lip shapes are linearly cross-faded between the shapes in the overlapping segments of the triphone videos.

The jaw's shape, on the other hand, is a combination of the background jaw line and the two triphone jaw lines. Near the ears, we want to preserve the background video's jaw line. At the center of the jaw line (the chin), the shape and position are determined completely by what the mouth is doing. The final image of the jaw must join smoothly together the motion of the chin with the motion near the ears. To do this, Video Rewrite smoothly varies the weighting of the background and triphone shapes as we move along the jaw line from the chin towards the ears.

The final stitching process is a three-way trade-off in shape and texture among the fade-out lip image, the fade-in lip image, and the background image. As we move from phoneme to phoneme, the relative weights of the mouth shapes associated with the overlapping triphone-video images are changed. Within each frame, the relative weighting of the jaw shapes contributed by the background image and by the triphone-video images is varied spatially.

The derived fiduciary positions are used as control points in morphing. All morphs are done with the Beier–Neely algorithm (Beier and Neely 1992a). For each frame of the output image we need to warp four images: the two triphones, the replacement mask, and the background face. The warping is straightforward since Video Rewrite automatically generates high quality control points using the EigenPoints algorithm.

10.4.3.5 Results The facial animation results for Video Rewrite are documented elsewhere (Bregler *et al.* 1997b). Typical results using John F. Kennedy as a subject are shown in Figure 10.7.

The results are difficult to quantify. Our ultimate goal is lifelike video that is indistinguishable from a real person. We are not at that stage yet, and are often faced with difficult trade-offs, especially when choosing among many different choices in our database.

There are many factors that lead to the overall perception of quality. Most importantly, are the lips and the audio synchronized? This is easiest to judge on plosive sounds and also the hardest to get right since the closure produces little sound.

Are the lip motions smooth? In a sense, the Video Rewrite database is directly capturing motion data. We need to blend the database triphones and preserve the motion information.

Is the border visible between the background and foreground portions of the face? The lighting control described above helps with much of this problem. Yet, with the high-resolution images on a computer screen we could see a slight

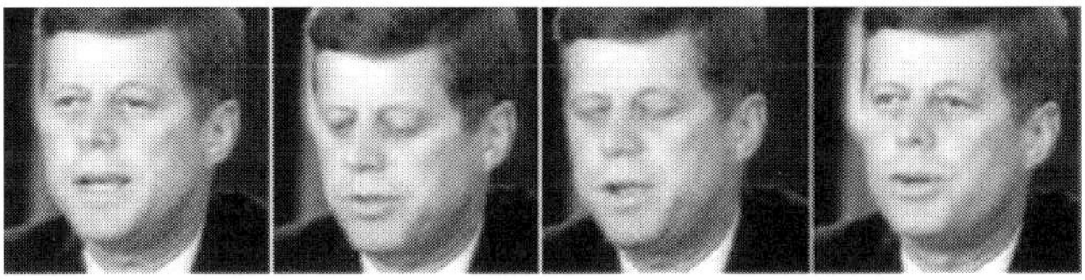

Figure 10.7 Images synthesized by Video Rewrite showing John F. Kennedy speaking (from Bregler *et al.* 1997b).

reduction in resolution in the lip region. We think that our feature tracking was accurate, but not accurate enough to align the individual pores on the face. When neighboring triphones are overlapped, the pores are often averaged out.

Is the jaw line smooth? Does it move in a natural fashion? Does the neck stay fixed? There is a lot happening at the jaw line and its overlap with the neck. It is important that this region of the face look realistic.

10.5 Alternative approaches

There are many ways to use video from real speakers to learn the mapping between audio and facial images – Video Rewrite is just one example. Two other approaches we would like to discuss represent simpler and more complex models of facial animation. In Section 10.5.1 we will describe two systems that represent the face by static images that capture the position of the face at its extreme pose when speaking a viseme. In Section 10.5.2 we describe a system that trains a hidden Markov model to capture the facial motions.

10.5.1 Synthesis with static visemes

Actors (Scott *et al.* 1994) and MikeTalk (Ezzat and Poggio 1998) are systems that synthesize a talking face by morphing between single static exemplar images. For each phoneme, a single prototypical image is captured and represents the target location for the face when saying that particular sound. Thus the /o/ sound is characterized by a single facial image with rounded lips. Image morphing techniques are used to synthesize the intermediate images. MikeTalk uses sixteen static images to synthesize speech – some of these visemes are shown in Figure 10.8.

Systems based on static viseme examples have the same alignment and morphing problems addressed by Video Rewrite. In the Actor system, several dozen fiduciary points on the head and shoulders are manually identified. These provide the alignment information and the control points needed for morphing. In MikeTalk the optic flow procedure described below is used to track facial

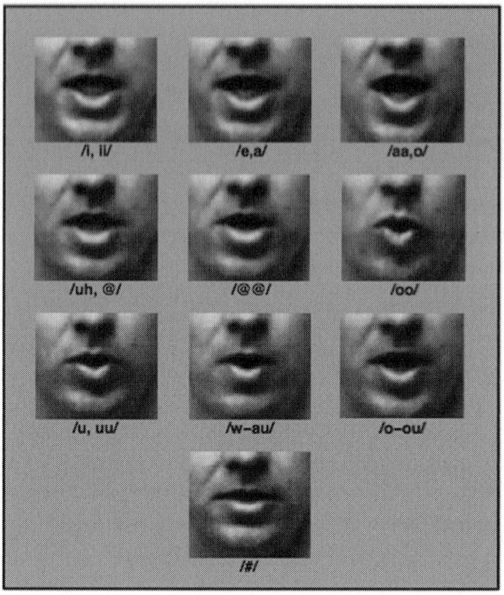

Figure 10.8 Ten of the sixteen static visemes used by the MikeTalk system to synthesize speech (from Ezzat and Poggio 1998).

features, and linear regression on the fixed portions of the face are used to find the global alignment. Optic flow computes the motion between two images by finding a two-dimensional vector field $[d_x\ d_y]^T$ that shows how each pixel in an image moves into the new image. There is little motion between images that are close in time; this makes the optic flow calculation easier. By looking at how each pixel moves every 33 ms, MikeTalk can establish the correspondence between prototype viseme images and morph between visemes.

Synthesizing facial images from prototypical (static) viseme images is straightforward. Using either a TTS system to generate phonemes, as done by MikeTalk, or recognizing the phonemes with ASR, as done by Actor, drives the synthesis process. The correspondence between viseme pixels has already been computed, so synthesis is just a matter of morphing one viseme into the next.

There are two disadvantages of a static viseme system. Most importantly, the detailed motion information that was calculated in the analysis stage is not used. The lips do not move smoothly from one position to the next. Secondly, this type of synthesis does not take into account the effects of coarticulation. When we speak naturally the shape of our mouth and the sounds that we make are dramatically affected by the phonemic context.

We might not, for example, round our lips quite as much when we say the word "boot" at a slower rate as when we say it at a faster rate. Coarticulation has been modeled by filtering the control points, but this approach has not been applied to image-based rendering. Doing so would result in a system that is nearly identical to a system described by Dom Massaro and Mike Cohen based on polygonal models of the face and using texture mapping to provide realistic skin and details.

In contrast, Video Rewrite uses a large database of phonemes in context to capture specific motions and coarticulation. Given a large enough database of examples, this is a simple solution. But it is, perhaps, not as elegant as building a statistical model of visual speech.

10.5.2 Voice puppetry

Matthew Brand (1999) proposed building an HMM to map between an audio signal and the appropriate facial shapes. His system is called Voice Puppetry and it learns a highly constrained model from the data and uses it to drive a conventional polygonal face model or cartoon drawing.

HMMs are a common technique for recognizing speech signals. The HMM model recognizes hidden states – the phoneme sequence the speaker is trying to communicate – based on the observed acoustic signals. The model assumes that the probability of entering any new state depends on a small number of previous states and the observations depend only on the current state.

Voice Puppetry builds a model in four stages. First, the system analyzes the video and builds a spring-constrained model of facial feature positions. These facial features are used to build an entropic Markov model that represents the video signal. Second, the audio corresponding to states determined by the video analysis is noted. Now each stage in the Markov model has both a visual and an auditory observation vector. Third, given new audio, the speech can be decoded and the most likely set of states is determined. Fourth, and finally, the system can traverse the discovered state sequence and generate the most likely set of facial trajectories. These trajectories are used to drive the cartoon character.

An entropic HMM is the key to this method. In a conventional speech recognition system, there are many paths through the model to account for all possible ways of saying any given word. This is unnecessarily complicated for synthesis since we want to produce only the best facial feature locations given any audio signal. Voice Puppetry learns the mapping between audio and video, without converting the speech to a phoneme sequence (and thus avoiding the errors this produces.)

An entropic HMM maximizes the likelihood of a model by adjusting the model parameters. In a Bayesian framework we say

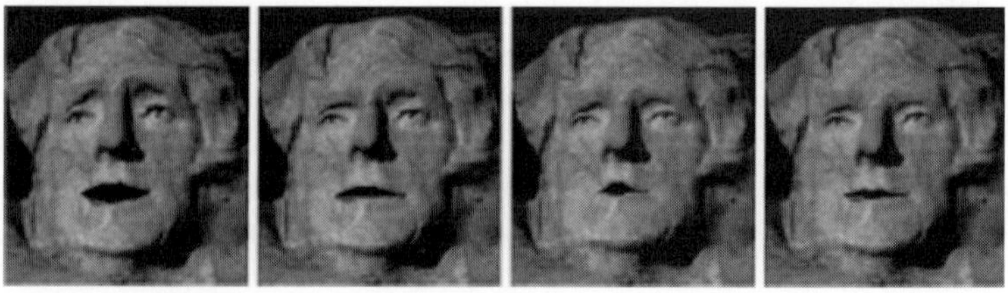

Figure 10.9 Output from the Voice Puppetry system showing how an inanimate object can be made to talk using entropic HMM facial synthesis (from Brand 1999).

$$\theta^* = \arg\max_{\theta}[P(\theta|X) \propto f(X|\theta)P_e(\theta)],$$

where the model parameters are described by θ, and the data is represented by X. The final term in this equation says that we want to maximize the product of (1) the probability of the model as a function of X and a given parameter set, and (2) the probability of seeing that parameter set.

This last term, an entropic prior in Voice Puppetry, says that models that are ambiguous and have less structure are not likely. The entropy of a discrete system is defined as

$$H(\theta) = -\Sigma p_i \log(p_i),$$

and this function is minimized when most of the probabilities are zero. The entropy is turned back into something that looks like a likelihood by exponentiation

$$P_e(\theta) \propto e^{-H(\theta)}.$$

The model is not very specific if any state can follow any other state. Instead we want to drive most of the parameter values to zero so that redundant links in the model are removed. Voice Puppetry starts with a fully connected set of twenty-six states, and prunes this model so that only one of twenty-two states have more than one alternative. This dramatic reduction in model complexity makes it possible for Voice Puppetry to synthesize new facial movements from audio.

Voice Puppetry uses the entropic HMM to drive a conventional 3D polygonal model of a face. The biggest advantage of such an approach is that the model can be built from data collected from one speaker, and applied to any other face – cartoon or otherwise. The face model captures many of the movements, primarily by stretching and shrinking the skin, but does not account for changes

Table 10.1 *Comparing animation systems.*

	MikeTalk	Video Rewrite	Voice Puppetry
Head pose	Average of tracked points	Affine or elliptical	Not needed
Lighting correction	Not needed	Adjust planar model of brightness at mask edges	Not needed
Utterance length	Stretch the interpolation	Choose closest match from database, then linear stretch	Move through model more slowly
Eyebrow movement	No provision	No provision	Some control (but prosody is ignored)
Feature tracking	Optic flow	EigenPoints	Texture-based tracker with spring constraints
Synthesis	Morph between static visemes	Morph overlapping triphones	Drive polygonal graphics model
Coarticulation	No provision	Triphone model	Probabalistic based on training data
Emotion	No provision	No provision	No provision

in appearance due to folding, or even teeth appearing and disappearing (see Figure 10.9).

Some forms of coarticulation are handled well by the entropic HMM that Voice Puppetry has learned. But the very nature of the structure reduction that Voice Puppetry enforces means that there is only one way to say each word. Current work, however, on speech recognition suggests that a different HMM is needed to capture the coarticulation for different speaking rates (Siegler 1995).

10.5.3 Summary of approaches

Table 10.1 summarizes the approaches of each of the three major image-based synthesis systems. The need to handle many of these factors is described in Section 10.2. It should be noted that the extra complexity in Video Rewrite – the need for more robust head-pose and lighting models – is due to the fact that large amounts of data are collected and repurposed to fit new synthesis needs. Since both MikeTalk and Video Puppetry build simple models of how each piece of sound is said, they do not need large databases. This rich database is both a source of complexity and potentially a source of additional randomness that could make the synthesis more lifelike.

10.6 Conclusions

Image-based algorithms are a powerful way to create realistic synthetic images. By starting with real images and rearranging them, we have the potential to create the highest-quality animations, at minimal computational cost and human effort. This chapter has described a wide range of synthesis options: from using static images, to rearranging dynamic segments, to full mathematical models of facial movement. The results so far are not perfect, but they have the potential to do much better, by just adding more data to their databases.

More work is needed in a number of areas. Most importantly, we would like to learn how to capture many more features of the human face, while keeping the database collection effort to a reasonable size.

10.7 Acknowledgments

We appreciate the help from Michele Covell in designing and building Video Rewrite. Matt Brand and Tony Ezzat took time to explain their systems to us. Conversations with Paul Debevec helped us to understand all the ways that data-intensive algorithms have been successful. Finally, we appreciate the efforts of Christian Benoît to help organize and give life to the field of audio–video speech perception.

11 A trainable videorealistic speech animation system

T. Ezzat, G. Geiger, and T. Poggio

11.1 Overview

Is it possible to record a human subject for a few minutes with a video camera, process the recorded data automatically, and then re-animate that subject uttering entirely novel utterances? In this work, we present such a system for achieving videorealistic speech animation.

We choose to focus our efforts in this work on the issues related to the synthesis of novel video, and not novel audio. Thus, novel audio needs to be provided as input to our system. This audio can be either real human audio (from the same subject or a different subject), or synthetic audio produced by a text-to-speech (TTS) system. All that is required by our system is that the audio be phonetically transcribed and aligned. In the case of synthetic audio from TTS systems, this phonetic alignment is readily available from the TTS system itself (Black and Taylor 1997). In the case of real audio, publicly available phonetic alignment systems (Huang *et al.* 1993) may be used.

Our visual speech processing system is composed of two modules. The first module is the multidimensional morphable model (MMM), which is capable of morphing between a small set of prototype mouth images to synthesize new, previously unseen mouth configurations. The second component is a trajectory synthesis module, which uses regularization (Wahba 1990; Girosi *et al.* 1993) to synthesize smooth trajectories in MMM space for any specified utterance. The parameters of the trajectory synthesis module are trained automatically from the recorded corpus using gradient descent learning.

Recording the video corpus takes on the order of 15 minutes. Processing of the corpus may take several weeks, but, apart from the specification of head and eye masks shown in Figure 11.3, is fully automatic, requiring no intervention on the part of the user. The final visual speech synthesis module consists of a small set of prototype images (forty-six images in the case presented here) extracted from the recorded corpus and used to synthesize all novel sequences. Figure 11.1 shows sample images synthesized by the system.

Application scenarios for videorealistic speech animation include: user interface agents for desktops, TVs, or cell phones; digital actors in movies; virtual

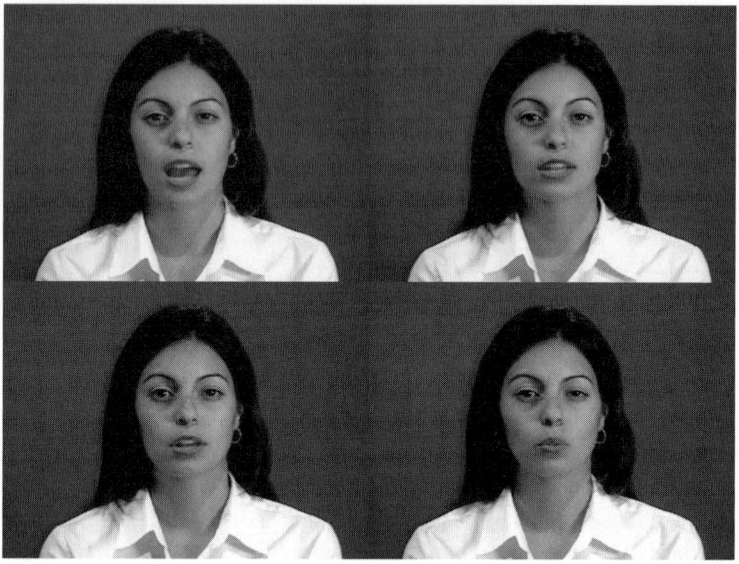

Figure 11.1 Some of the synthetic facial configurations output by the Mary101 system.

avatars in chatrooms; very low bitrate coding schemes (such as MPEG4); and studies of visual speech production and perception.

In the following section, we begin by first reviewing the relevant prior work and motivating our approach.

11.2 Background

11.2.1 Facial modeling

One approach to modeling facial geometry is to use 3D methods. Parke (1974) was one of the earliest to adopt such an approach by creating a polygonal facial model. In current approaches, to increase the visual realism of the underlying facial model, the facial geometry is frequently scanned in using Cyberware laser scanners. Additionally, a texture map of the face extracted by the Cyberware scanner may be mapped onto the 3D geometry (Lee *et al.* 1995b). Guenter *et al.* (1998) demonstrated recent attempts at obtaining 3D face geometry from multiple photographs using photogrammetric techniques. Pighin *et al.* (1998) captured face geometry and textures by fitting a generic face model to a number of photographs. Blanz and Vetter (1999) demonstrated how a large database of Cyberware scans may be morphed to obtain face geometry from a single photograph. More recent 3D methods include Sifakis *et al.* (2005) and Zhang *et al* (2004).

An alternative to the 3D modeling approach is to model the talking face using image-based techniques, where the talking facial model is constructed using a collection of example images captured from the human subject. These methods have the potential of achieving very high levels of videorealism, and are inspired by the recent success of similar sample-based methods for audio speech synthesis (Charpentier and Moulines 1990). We adopt such an approach in this work.

Image-based facial animation techniques need to solve the video generation problem: How does one build a generative model of novel video that is simultaneously photorealistic, videorealistic, and parsimonious? Photorealism means that the novel generated images exhibit the correct visual structure of the lips, teeth, and tongue. Videorealism means that the generated sequences exhibit the correct motion, dynamics, and coarticulation effects (Cohen and Massaro 1993). Parsimony means that the generative model is represented compactly using few parameters.

Bregler *et al.* (1997b) describe an image-based facial animation system called Video Rewrite in which the video generation problem is addressed by breaking down the recorded video corpus into a set of smaller audiovisual basis units. Each one of these short sequences is a triphone segment, and a large database with all the acquired triphones is built. A new audiovisual sentence is constructed by concatenating the appropriate triphone sequences from the database together. Photorealism in Video Rewrite is addressed by using only recorded sequences to generate the novel video. Videorealism is achieved by using triphone contexts to model coarticulation effects. In order to handle all the possible triphone contexts, however, the system requires a library with tens and possibly hundreds of thousands of subsequences, which seems to be an overly redundant and non-parsimonious sampling of human lip configurations. Parsimony is thus sacrificed for videorealism.

Essentially, Video Rewrite adopts a decidedly agnostic approach to animation: since it does not have the capacity to generate novel lip imagery from a few recorded images, it relies on the re-sequencing of a vast amount of original video. Since it does not have the capacity to model how the mouth moves, it relies on sampling the dynamics of the mouth using triphone segments.

This work presents another approach to solving the video generation problem, an approach that has the capacity to generate novel video from a small number of examples as well as the capacity to model how the mouth moves. This approach is based on the use of a multidimensional morphable model (MMM), which is capable of multidimensional morphing between various lip images to synthesize new, previously unseen lip configurations. MMMs have already been introduced in other works (Poggio and Vetter 1992; Beymer and Poggio 1996; Cootes *et al.* 1998; Jones and Poggio 1998; Lee *et al.* 1998; Blanz and Vetter 1999; Black *et al.* 2000). In this work, we develop an MMM variant and demonstrate its utility for facial animation.

MMMs are powerful models of image appearance because they combine the power of vector space representations with the realism of morphing as a generative image technique. Prototype example images of the mouth are decomposed into pixel flow and pixel appearance axes that represent basis vectors of image variation. These basis vectors are combined in a multidimensional fashion to produce novel, realistic, previously unseen lip configurations.

As such, an MMM is more powerful than other vector space representations of images that do not model pixel flow explicitly. Cosatto and Graph (1998), for example, describe an approach that is similar to ours, except that their generative model involved simple pixel blending of images, which fails to produce realistic transitions between mouth configurations.

An MMM is also more powerful than simple one-dimensional morphing between two image endpoints (Beier and Neely 1992a), as well as techniques such as those of Scott *et al.* (1994), Watson *et al.* (1997), and Ezzat and Poggio (2000), which morph between several visemes in a pairwise fashion. By embedding the prototype images in a vector space, an MMM is capable of generating smooth curves through lip space, handling complex speech animation effects in a non-ad hoc manner. The important relationship between MMMs, vector spaces, and regularization networks was pointed out and discussed by Beymer *et al.* (1993; Beymer and Poggio 1996).

11.2.2 Animation

The reader may complete this short state of the art with already published overviews of speech animation methods (Bailly *et al.* 2003; Fagel 2007; Theobald 2007; Fagel *et al.* 2009). Speech animation techniques have traditionally included both key framing methods and physics-based methods, and have been extended more recently to include machine learning methods. In key framing, the animator specifies particular key frames, and the system generates intermediate values (Parke 1974; Pearce *et al.* 1986; Cohen and Massaro 1993; Le Goff *et al.* 1996). In physics-based methods, the animator relies on the laws of physics to determine the mouth movement, given some initial conditions and a set of forces for all time. This technique, which requires modeling the underlying facial muscles and skin, was demonstrated quite effectively by Waters (1987) and Lee *et al.* (1995b). Data-driven methods include the work of Cao *et al.* 2004, who use a motion graph approach similar to that of Bregler *et al.* 1997a. and Cosatto and Graf 1998. Finally, machine learning methods are a new class of animation tools that are trained from recorded data and then used to synthesize new motion. Examples include hidden Markov models (HMMs), which were demonstrated effectively for speech animation by Brooke and Scott

(1994a), Masuko *et al.* (1998) and Brand (1999). More recent methods that are more sophisticated include those of Bailly *et al.* (2008b; 2009).

Speech animation needs to solve several problems simultaneously. Firstly, the animation needs to have the correct motion, in the sense that the appropriate phonemic targets need to be realized by the moving mouth. Secondly, the animation needs to be smooth, not exhibiting any unnecessary jerks. Thirdly, it needs to display the correct dynamics: for example, plosives such as /b/ and /p/ need to occur fast. Finally, speech animation needs to display the correct coarticulation effects, which determine the effects of neighboring phonemes on the current phoneme shape.

In this work, we present a trajectory synthesis module that addresses the issues of synthesizing mouth trajectories with suitable motion, smoothness, dynamics, and coarticulation effects. This module uses a regularization framework (Wahba 1990; Girosi *et al.* 1993) to map from an input stream of phonemes (with their respective frame durations) to a trajectory of MMM shape-appearance parameters. This trajectory is then fed into the MMM to synthesize the final visual stream that represents the talking face.

Unlike Video Rewrite (Bregler *et al.* 1997b), which relies on an exhaustive sampling of triphone segments to model phonetic contexts, coarticulation effects in our system emerge directly from an underlying speech model. Each phoneme in our model is represented as a localized Gaussian target region in MMM space with a particular position and covariance. In the regularization framework that computes the trajectory, the covariance of each phoneme acts as a spring whose tension pulls the trajectory towards each phonetic region with a force proportional to observed coarticulation effects in the data.

However, unlike Cohen and Massaro (1993), who also modeled coarticulation using localized Gaussian-like regions, our model of coarticulation is not hand-tuned, but rather trained from the recorded corpus itself using a gradient descent learning procedure. The training process determines the position and shape of the phonetic regions in MMM space in a manner that optimally reconstructs the recorded corpus data.

11.3 System overview

An overview of our Mary101 system is shown in Figure 11.2. After recording the corpus (Section 11.4), analysis is performed to produce the final visual speech module. Analysis itself consists of three sub-steps. First, the corpus is pre-processed (Section 11.5) to align the audio and normalize the images to remove head movement. Next, the MMM is created from the images in the corpus (Section 11.6.2). Finally, the corpus sequences are analyzed to produce the phonetic models used by the trajectory synthesis module (Sections 11.6.4 and 11.7.2).

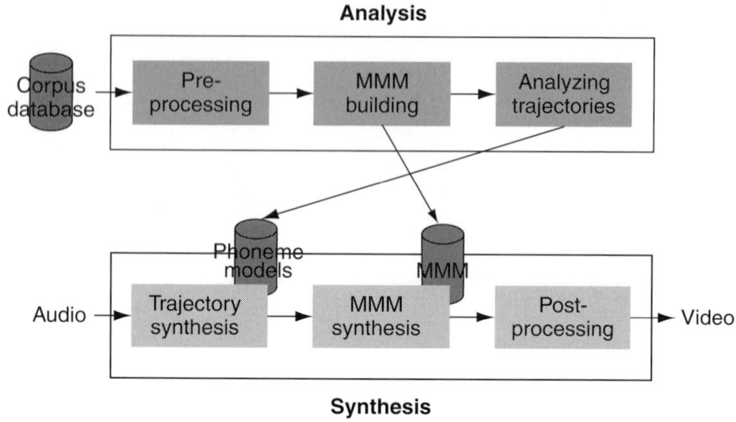

Figure 11.2 An overview of our videorealistic speech animation system.

Given a novel audio stream that is phonetically aligned, synthesis proceeds in three steps. First, the trajectory synthesis module is used to synthesize the trajectory in MMM space using the trained phonetic models (Section 11.6.4). Secondly, the MMM is used to synthesize the novel visual stream from the trajectory parameters (Section 11.7). Finally, the post-processing stage composites the novel mouth movement onto a background sequence containing natural eye and head movements (Section 11.8).

11.4 Corpus

An audiovisual corpus of a human subject uttering various utterances was recorded. Recording was performed at a TV studio against a blue "chroma-key" background with a standard Sony analog TV camera. The data was subsequently digitized at a 29.97 fps NTSC frame rate with an image resolution of 640 by 480 and an audio resolution of 44.1 kHz. The final sequences were stored as Quicktime sequences compressed using a Sorenson coder. The recorded corpus lasts for 15 minutes, and is composed of approximately 30 000 frames.

The recorded corpus consisted of one-syllable and two-syllable words, such as "bed" and "dagger". A total of 152 one-syllable words and 156 two-syllable words were recorded, which comprised about 7 minutes of recorded video. In addition, the corpus included 105 short sentences, such as "The statue was closed to tourists Sunday", which comprised about 7 minutes of recorded video. However, these short sentence utterances were not used in our development of the animation system, but were used only for testing and evaluation purposes.

The subject was asked to utter all sentences in a neutral expression. In addition, the sentences themselves were designed to elicit no emotion from the subject.

11.5 Pre-processing

The recorded corpus data needs to be pre-processed in several ways before it may be processed effectively for re-animation.

First, the audio needs to be phonetically aligned in order to be able to associate a phoneme for each image in the corpus. We perform audio alignment on all the recorded sequences using the CMU Sphinx system (Huang *et al.* 1993), which is publicly available. Given an audio sequence and an associated text transcript of the speech being uttered, alignment systems use forced Viterbi search to find the optimal start and end of phonemes for the given audio sequence. The alignment task is easier than the speech recognition task because the text of the audio being uttered is known a priori.

Second, each image in the corpus needs to be normalized so that the only movement occurring in the entire frame is the mouth movement associated with speech. Although the subject was instructed to keep her head steady during recording, residual head movement nevertheless still exists in the final recorded sequences. Since the head motion is small, we make the simplifying assumption that it can be approximated as the perspective motion of a plane lying on the surface of the face. Planar perspective deformations (Wolberg 1990) have eight degrees of freedom, and can be inferred using four corresponding points between a reference frame and the current frame. We employ optical flow (Horn and Schunck 1981; Bergen *et al.* 1992; Barron *et al.* 1994) to extract correspondences for 640×480 pixels, and use least squares to solve the over-determined system of equations to obtain the eight parameters of the perspective warp. Among the 640×480 correspondences, only those lying within the head mask shown in Figure 11.3 are used. Pixels from the background area are not used because they do not exhibit any motion at all, and those from the mouth area exhibit non-rigid motion associated with speech.

11.6 Multidimensional morphable models

At the heart of our visual speech synthesis approach is the multidimensional morphable model (MMM) representation, which is a generative model of video capable of morphing between various lip images to synthesize new lip configurations.

The basic underlying assumption of the MMM is that the complete set of mouth images associated with human speech lies in a low-dimensional space whose axes represent mouth appearance variation and mouth shape variation. Mouth appearance is represented in the MMM as a set of prototype images extracted from the recorded corpus. Mouth shape is represented in the MMM

Figure 11.3 The head, mouth, eye, and background masks used in the pre-processing and post-processing steps. Specification of these masks is the only manual step required by this system.

as a set of optical flow vectors (Horn and Schunck 1981) computed automatically from the recorded corpus. In the work presented here, 46 images are extracted and 46 optical flow correspondences are computed. The low-dimensional MMM space is parameterized by shape parameters α and appearance parameters β.

The MMM may be viewed as a "black box" capable of performing two tasks: Firstly, given as input a set of parameters (α,β) the MMM is capable of synthesizing an image of the subject's face with that shape-appearance configuration. Synthesis is performed by morphing the various prototype images to produce novel mouth images that correspond to the input parameters (α,β).

Conversely, the MMM can also be used for analysis: given an input lip image, the MMM computes shape and appearance parameters (α,β) that represent the position of that input image in MMM space. In this manner, it is possible to project the entire recorded corpus onto the constructed MMM, and produce a time series of (α_t,β_t) parameters (one set per frame) that represent trajectories of mouth motion in MMM space. We term this operation analyzing the recorded corpus.

In the following sections, we describe how a multidimensional morphable model is defined, how it may be acquired automatically from a recorded video corpus, how it may be used for synthesis, and, finally, how such a morphable model may be used for analysis.

11.6.1 *Definition*

An MMM consists of a set of prototype images $\{I_i,\ i = 1, N\}$ that represent the various lip textures that will be encapsulated by the MMM. One image is designated arbitrarily to be the reference image I_1.

Additionally, the MMM consists of a set of prototype flows $\{C_i,\ i = 1,N\}$ that represent the correspondences between the reference image I_1 and the other prototype images in the MMM. The correspondence from the reference image to itself, C_1, is designated to be an empty, or zero, flow.

In this work, we choose to represent the correspondence maps using relative displacement vectors:

$$C_i(\vec{p}) = \left\{ d_x^i(\vec{p}), d_y^i(\vec{p}) \right\} \tag{11.1}$$

A pixel in image I_l at position $\vec{p} = (x, y)$ corresponds to a pixel in image I_i at position $\left(x + d_x^i(x, y), y + d_y^i(x, y)\right)$.

Previous methods for computing correspondence (Beier and Neely 1992b; Scott *et al.* 1994; Lee *et al.* 1995a) adopted feature-based approaches, in which a set of high-level shape features common to both images is specified. When it is done by hand, however, this feature specification process can become quite tedious and complicated, especially in cases in which a large amount of imagery is involved. In this work, we make use of optical flow (Horn and Schunck 1981; Bergen *et al.* 1992; Barron *et al.* 1994) algorithms to estimate this motion. This motion is captured as a two-dimensional array of displacement vectors, in the same exact format as that shown in Eq. (11.1). In particular, we utilize the coarse-to-fine, gradient-based optical flow algorithms developed by Bergen *et al.* (1992). These algorithms compute the desired flow displacements using the spatial and temporal image derivatives. In addition, they embed the flow estimation procedure in a multiscale pyramidal framework (Burt and Adelson 1983b), where initial displacement estimates are obtained at coarse resolutions, and then propagated to higher resolution levels of the pyramid.

11.6.2 *Building an MMM*

An MMM must be constructed automatically from a recorded corpus of $\{I_j, j = 1,S\}$ images. The two main tasks involved are to choose the image prototypes $\{I_i,\ i = 1,N\}$, and to compute the correspondences $\{C_i, j = 1,N\}$ among them. We discuss the steps to do this briefly below. Note that the following operations are performed on the entire face region, although they need only be performed on the region around the mouth.

11.6.2.1 PCA For the purpose of more efficient processing, principal component analysis (PCA) is first performed on all the images of the recorded video corpus. PCA allows each image in the video corpus to be represented using a set of low-dimensional parameters. This set of low-dimensional parameters may thus be easily loaded into memory and processed efficiently in the subsequent clustering and Dijkstra steps.

Performing PCA using classical autocovariance methods (Bishop 1995) however, usually necessitates loading all the images and computing a very large autocovariance matrix, which requires a lot of memory. To avoid this, we adopt an online PCA method, termed EM-PCA (Roweis 1998; Tipping and Bishop 1999), which allows us to perform PCA on the images in the corpus without loading them all into memory. EM-PCA is iterative, requiring several iterations, but is guaranteed to converge in the limit to the same principal components that would be extracted from the classical autocovariance method. The EM-PCA algorithm is typically run in this work for ten iterations.

Performing EM-PCA produces a set of D 624×472 principal components and a matrix Σ of eigenvalues. In this work, $D = 15$ PCA bases are retained. The images in the video corpus are subsequently projected on the principal components, and each image I_j is represented with a D-dimensional parameter vector p_j.

11.6.2.2 k-means clustering Selection of the prototype images is performed using k-means clustering (Bishop 1995). The algorithm is applied directly on the $\{p_j, j = 1,S\}$ low-dimensional PCA parameters, producing N cluster centers. Typically the cluster centers extracted by k-means clustering do not coincide with actual image data points, so the nearest images in the dataset to the computed cluster centers are chosen to be the final image prototypes $\{I_i, i = 1,N\}$ for use in our MMM.

It should be noted that k-means clustering requires the use of an internal distance metric with which to compare distances between data points and the chosen cluster centers. In our case, since the image parameters are themselves produced by PCA, an appropriate distance metric between two points p_m and p_n is the Mahalanobis distance metric (although other distance metrics may be used):

$$d(p_m, p_n) = (p_m - p_n)^T \Sigma^{-1} (p_m - p_n) \tag{11.2}$$

where $\sum$ is the aforementioned matrix of eigenvalues extracted by the EM-PCA procedure.

We selected $N = 46$ image prototypes in this work, which are partly shown in Figure 11.4. The top left image is the reference image I_1. There is nothing magical about our choice of 46 prototypes; it is simply in keeping with the

Figure 11.4 Twenty-four of the 46 image prototypes included in the MMM. The reference image is the top left frame.

typical number of visemes other researchers have used (Scott *et al.* 1994; Ezzat and Poggio 2000). It should be noted that the 46 prototypes have no explicit relationship to visemes, and instead form a simple basis set of image textures.

11.6.2.3 Dijkstra After the $N = 46$ image prototypes are chosen, the next step in building an MMM is to compute correspondence between the reference image I_1 and all the other prototypes. Although it is in principle possible to compute direct optical flow between the images, we have found that direct application of optical flow is not capable of estimating good correspondence when the underlying lip displacements between images are greater than five pixels.

It is possible to use flow concatenation to overcome this problem. Since the original corpus is digitized at 29.97 fps, there are many intermediate frames that lie between the chosen prototypes. A series of consecutive optical flow vectors between each intermediate image and its successor may be computed and concatenated into one large flow vector that defines the global transformation between the chosen prototypes (see Appendix for details on flow concatenation).

Typically, however, prototype images are very far apart in the recorded visual corpus, so it is not practical to compute concatenated optical flow between them. The repeated concatenation that would be involved across the hundreds or thousands of intermediate frames leads to a considerably degraded final flow.

To compute good correspondence between prototypes, a method is needed to figure out how to compute the path from the reference example I_1 to the chosen image prototypes I_i without repeated concatenation over hundreds or thousands of intermediates frames. We accomplish this by constructing the corpus graph representation of the corpus: A corpus graph is an S-by-S sparse adjacency graph matrix in which each frame in the corpus is represented as a node in a graph connected to k nearest images. The k nearest images are chosen using the k-nearest neighbors algorithm (Bishop 1995), and the distance metric used is the Mahalanobis distance in Eq. 11.2 applied to the PCA parameters p (although other distance metrics are possible). Thus, an image is connected in the graph to the k other images that look most similar to it. The edge weight between a frame and its neighbor is the value of the Mahalanobis distance. We set $k = 20$ in this work.

After the corpus graph is computed, the Dijkstra shortest path algorithm (Cormen *et al.* 1989; Tenenbaum *et al.* 2000) is used to compute the shortest path between the reference example I_1 and the other chosen image prototypes I_i. Each shortest path produced by the Dijkstra algorithm is a list of images from the corpus that cumulatively represent the shortest deformation path from I_1 to I_i as measured by the Mahalanobis distance. Concatenated flow from I_1 to I_i is then computed along the intermediate images produced by the Dijkstra algorithm. Since there are 46 images, $N = 46$ correspondences $\{C_i, i = 1,N\}$ are computed in this fashion from the reference image I_1 to the other image prototypes $\{I_i, i = 1,N\}$.

11.6.3 Synthesis

The goal of synthesis is to map from the multidimensional parameter space (α, β) to an image that lies at that position in MMM space. Since there are 46 correspondences, α is a 46-dimensional parameter vector that controls mouth shape. Similarly, since there are 46 image prototypes, β is a 46-dimensional parameter vector that controls mouth texture. The total dimensionality of (α, β) is 92.

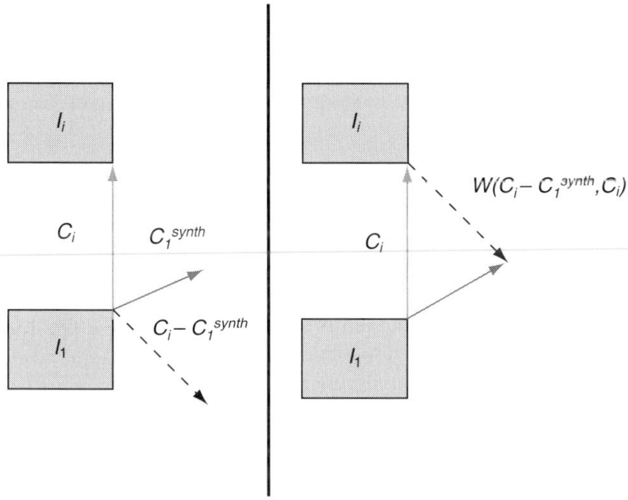

Figure 11.5 The flow reorientation process: First, C_i is subtracted from the synthesized flow $C_{1,s}$. Second, this flow vector is itself forward warped along C_i.

Synthesis first proceeds by synthesizing a new correspondence C^{synth} using linear combination of the prototype flows C_i:

$$C_1^{synth} = \sum_{i=1}^{N} a_i C_i \tag{11.3}$$

The subscript 1 in Eq. (11.3) above is used to emphasize that C_1^{synth} originates from the reference image I_1, since all the prototype flows are taken with I_1 as reference.

Forward warping may be used to push the pixels of the reference image I_1 along the synthesized correspondence vector C_1^{synth}. Notationally, we denote the forward warping operation as an operator $W(I, C)$ that operates on an image I and a correspondence map C (see Appendix for details on forward warping). Also we rewrite C_1^{synth} as $C_{1,s}$ for brevity.

However, a single forward warp will not utilize the image texture from all the examples. In order to take into account all image texture, a correspondence re-orientation procedure first described by Beymer *et al.* (1993) is adopted that re-orients the synthesized correspondence vector $C_{1,s}$ so that it originates from each of the other example images I_i. Reorientation of the synthesized flow $C_{1,s}$ proceeds in two steps, shown figuratively in Figure 11.5. First, C_i is subtracted from the synthesized flow $C_{1,s}$ to yield a flow that contains the correct flow geometry, but which originates from the reference example I_1 rather than the desired example image I_i.

Secondly, to move the flow into the correct reference frame, this flow vector is itself warped along C_i. The entire re-orientation process may be denoted as follows:

$$C_{i,s} = W(C_{1,s} - C_i, C_i) \tag{11.4}$$

Re-orientation is performed for all examples in the example set.

The third step in synthesis is to warp the prototype images I_i along the re-oriented flows $C_{i,s}$ to generate a set of N warped image textures $I_{i,w}$:

$$I_{i,w} = W(I_i, C_{i,s}) \tag{11.5}$$

The fourth and final step is to blend the warped images $I_{i,w}$ using the β parameters to yield the final morphed image:

$$I^{morph} = \sum_{i=1}^{N} \beta_i I_{i,w} \tag{11.6}$$

Combining Eq. (11.1) through Eq. (11.6) together, our MMM synthesis may be written as follows:

$$I^{morph} = \sum_{i=1}^{N} \beta_i W(I_i, W(\sum_{j=1}^{N} \alpha_j C_j - C_i, C_i)). \tag{11.7}$$

Empirically we have found that the MMM synthesis technique is capable of surprisingly realistic re-synthesis of lips, teeth, and tongue. However, the blending of multiple images in the MMM for synthesis tends to blur out some of the finer details in the teeth and tongue (see Appendix C for a discussion of synthesis blur). Shown in Figure 11.6 are some of the synthetic images produced by our system, along with their real counterparts for comparison.

11.6.4 Analysis

The goal of analysis is to project the entire recorded corpus $\{I_j, j=1 \ldots S\}$ onto the constructed MMM, and produce a time series of $\{\alpha_i, \beta_i, j=1 \ldots S\}$ parameters that represent trajectories of the original mouth motion in MMM space.

One possible approach for analysis of images is to perform analysis-by-synthesis. In this approach, used in various forms in Jones and Poggio (1998) and in Blanz and Vetter (1999), the synthesis algorithm is used to synthesize an image $I^{synth}(\alpha, \beta)$ that is then compared to the novel image using an error metric (i.e., the L2 norm). Stochastic gradient descent is then usually performed to change the parameters in order to minimize the error, and the synthesis process

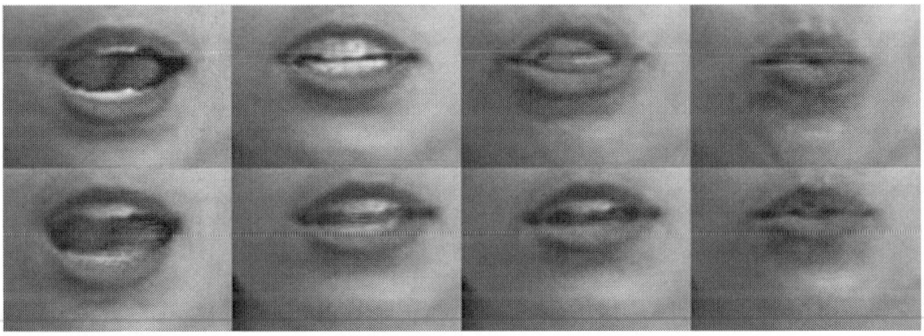

Figure 11.6 Top: Original images from our corpus. Bottom: Corresponding synthetic images generated by our system.

is repeated. The search ends when a local minimum is achieved. Analysis-by-synthesis, however, is very slow in the case when a large number of images are involved.

In this work we choose another method that is capable of extracting parameters $\{\alpha, \beta\}$ in one iteration. In addition to the image I^{novel} to be analyzed, the method requires that the correspondence C^{novel} from the reference image I_1 in the MMM to the novel image I^{novel} be computed beforehand. In our case, most of the novel imagery to be analyzed will be from the recorded video corpus itself, so we employ the Dijkstra approach discussed in Section 11.6.2.3 to compute good quality correspondences between the reference image I_1 and I^{novel}.

Given a novel image I^{novel} and its associated correspondence C^{novel}, the first step of the analysis algorithm is to estimate the parameters α that minimize:

$$\left\| C^{novel} - \sum_{i=1}^{N} \alpha_i C_i \right\|. \tag{11.8}$$

This is solved using the pseudo-inverse:

$$\alpha = (C^T C)^{-1} C^T C^{novel} \tag{11.9}$$

where C above is a matrix containing all the prototype correspondences $\{C_i,\ i = 1,N\}$.

After the parameters α are estimated, N image warps are synthesized in the same manner as described in Section 11.6.3 using flow-reorientation and warping:

$$\mathrm{I}_i^{warp} = W(\mathrm{I}_i, W(\sum_{j=1}^{N} \alpha_j C_j - C_i, C_i)) \tag{11.10}$$

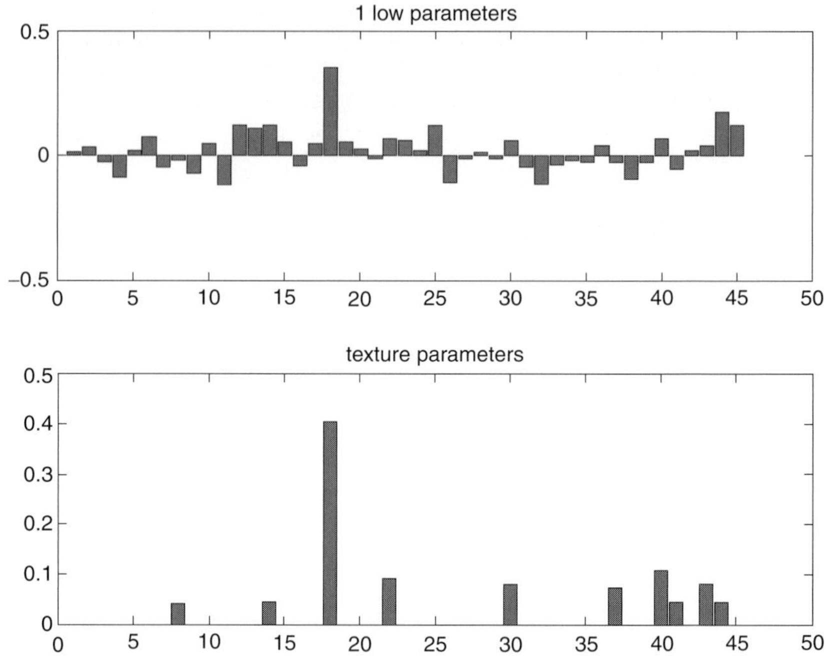

Figure 11.7 Top: Analyzed α_i flow parameters computed for one image. Bottom: The corresponding analyzed β_i texture parameters computed for the same image. The β_i texture parameters are typically zero for all but a few image prototypes.

The final step in analysis is to estimate the values of β as the values that minimize:

$$\left\| \mathrm{I}^{novel} - \sum_{i=1}^{N} \beta_i \mathrm{I}_i \right\| \text{ subject to } \beta_i < 0 \quad \forall i \text{ and } \sum_{i=1}^{N} \beta_i = 1. \qquad (11.11)$$

The non-negativity constraint above on the β_i parameters ensures that pixel values are not negated. The normalization constraint ensures that the β_i parameters are computed in a normalized manner for each frame, which prevents brightness flickering during synthesis. The form of the imposed constraints causes the computed β_i parameters to be sparse (see Figure 11.7), which enables efficient synthesis by requiring only a few image warps (instead of the complete set of 46 warps). Equation (11.11), which involves the minimization of a quadratic cost function subject to constraints, is solved using quadratic programming methods. In this work, we use the Matlab function "`quadprog`".

Each utterance in the corpus is analyzed with respect to the 92-dimensional MMM created in Section 11.6.2, yielding a set of $z_t = (\alpha_t, \beta_t)$ parameters for each utterance. Analysis takes on the order of 15 s per frame on a circa 1998 450 MHz Pentium II machine. Shown in Figure 11.9 in solid lines are examples of analyzed trajectories for α_{12} and β_{28} computed for the word "`tabloid`."

11.7 Trajectory synthesis

11.7.1 Overview

The goal of trajectory synthesis is to map from an input phone stream $\{P_t\}$ to a trajectory $y_t = (\alpha_t, \beta_t)$ of parameters in MMM space. After the parameters are synthesized, Eq. (11.7) from Section 11.6.3 is used to create the final visual stream that represents the talking face.

The phone stream is a stream of phonemes $\{p_t\}$ representing that phonetic transcription of the utterance. For example, the word "one" may be represented by a phone stream $\{p_t, t = 1 \ldots 15\}$ = `(/w/,/w/,/w/,/w/,/uh/,/uh/,/uh/,/uh/,/uh/,/uh/,/n/,/n/,/n/,/n/,/n/)`. Each element in the phone stream represents one image frame. We define T to be the length of the entire utterance in frames.

Since the audio is aligned, it is possible to examine all the flow and texture parameters for any particular phoneme. Shown in Figure 11.8 are histograms for the α_1 parameter for the `/w/`, `/m/`, `/aa/`, and `/ow/` phones. Evaluation of the analyzed parameters from the corpus reveals that parameters representing the same phoneme tend to cluster in MMM space. We represent each phoneme p mathematically as a multidimensional Gaussian with mean μ_p and diagonal covariance Σ_p. Separate means and covariances are estimated for the flow and texture parameters.[1]

The trajectory synthesis problem is framed mathematically as a regularization problem (Wahba 1990; Girosi *et al.* 1993). The goal is to synthesize a trajectory y that minimizes an objective function E consisting of a target term and a smoothness term:

$$E = \underbrace{(y-\mu)^T D^T \Sigma^{-1} D (y-\mu)}_{\text{target term}} + \lambda \underbrace{y^T W^T W y}_{\text{smoothness term}} . \tag{11.12}$$

The desired trajectory y is a vertical concatenation of the individual $y_t = \alpha_t$ terms at each time step (or $y_t = \beta_t$, since we treat flow and texture parameters separately):

$$y = \begin{bmatrix} y_1 \\ \vdots \\ y_T \end{bmatrix} . \tag{11.13}$$

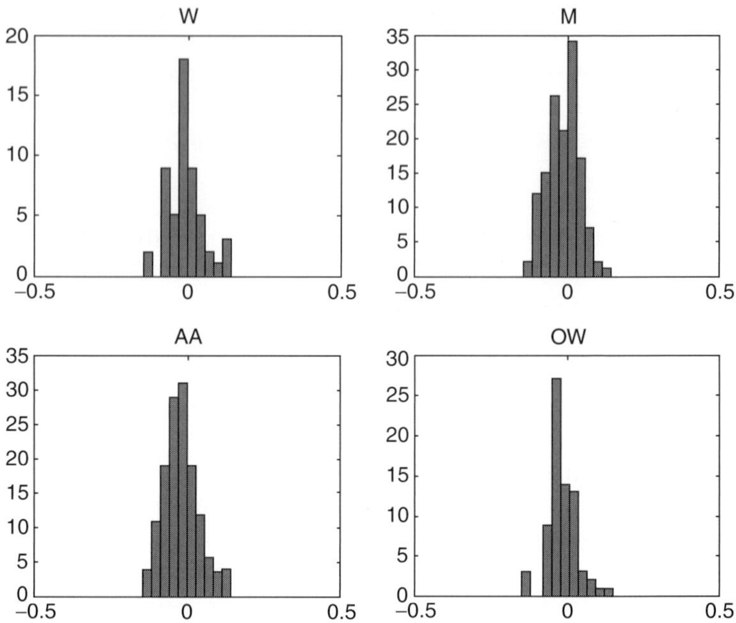

Figure 11.8 Histograms for the α_1 parameter for the /w/, /m/, /aa/, and /ow/ phones.

The target term consists of the relevant means μ and covariances Σ constructed from the phone stream:

$$\mu = \begin{bmatrix} \mu_{P_1} \\ \vdots \\ \mu_{P_T} \end{bmatrix}, \Sigma = \begin{bmatrix} \Sigma_{P_1} & & \\ & \ddots & \\ & & \Sigma_{P_T} \end{bmatrix}. \tag{11.14}$$

The matrix D is a duration-weighting matrix that emphasizes the shorter phonemes and de-emphasizes the longer ones, so that the objective function is not heavily skewed by the phonemes of longer duration:

$$D = \begin{bmatrix} \sqrt{I - \frac{D_{P_1}}{T}} & & \\ & \ddots & \\ & & \sqrt{I = \frac{D_{P_T}}{T}} \end{bmatrix}. \tag{11.15}$$

One possible smoothness term consists of the first-order difference operator:

$$W = \begin{bmatrix} -I & I & & & \\ & -I & I & & \\ & & \ddots & & \\ & & & -I & I \end{bmatrix}. \tag{11.16}$$

Higher orders of smoothness are formed by repeatedly multiplying W with itself: second order $W^T W^T W W$, third order $W^T W^T W^T W W W$, and so on.

Finally, the regularizer λ determines the trade-off between both terms. Taking the derivative of Eq. (11.12) and minimizing yields the following equation for synthesis:

$$(D^T \Sigma^{-1} D + \lambda W^T W) y = D^T \Sigma^{-1} D \mu. \tag{11.17}$$

Given known means μ, covariances Σ, and regularizer λ, synthesis is simply a matter of plugging them into Eq. (11.17) and solving for y using Gaussian elimination. This is done separately for the flow and the texture parameters. In our experiments a regularizer of degree four yielding multivariate additive septic splines (Wahba 1990) gave satisfactory results (see next subsection).

Coarticulation effects in our system are modeled via the magnitude of the variance Σ_p for each phoneme. Small variance means the trajectory must pass through that region in phoneme space, and hence neighboring phonemes have little coarticulatory effect. On the other hand, large variance means the trajectory has a lot of flexibility in choosing a path through a particular phonetic region, and hence it may choose to pass through regions that are closer to a phoneme's neighbors. The phoneme will thus experience large coarticulatory effects.

There is no explicit model of phonetic dynamics in our system. Instead, phonetic dynamics emerge implicitly through the interplay between the magnitude of the variance Σ_p for each phoneme (which determines the phoneme's "spatial" extent), and the input phone stream (which determines the duration in time of each phoneme). Equation (11.12) then determines the speed through a phonetic region in a manner that balances nearness to the phoneme with smoothness of the overall trajectory. In general, we find the trajectories speed up in regions of small duration and small variance (i.e., plosives), while they slow down in regions of large duration and large variance (i.e., silences).

11.7.2 Training

The means μ_p and covariances Σ_p for each phone p are initialized directly from the data using sample means and covariances. However, the sample estimates tend to average out the mouth movement so that it looks under-articulated.

This is particularly problematic in the case of plosives such as /b/ or /p/, where the sample means do not coincide with the complete closure of the lips. As a consequence, there is a need to adjust the means and variances to better reflect the training data.

Gradient descent learning (Bishop 1995) is employed to adjust the mean and covariances. The idea is to use Eq. (11.17) to synthesize a trajectory y for a particular utterance present in the training corpus, and compare it with the actual trajectory of MMM parameters z for that utterance using an error metric. The locations and covariances, μ_p and Σ_p, for the phonemes involved in synthesizing that utterance may then be adjusted using gradient descent to minimize the error between y and z.

We develop this idea as follows. First, the Euclidean error metric is chosen to represent the error between the original utterance z and the synthetic utterance y:

$$E = (z - y)^T (z - y). \tag{11.18}$$

The parameters μ_p, Σ_p need to be changed to minimize this objective function E. The chain rule may be used to derive the relationship between E and the parameters:

$$\frac{\partial E}{\partial \mu_i} = \left(\frac{\partial E}{\partial y}\right)^T \left(\frac{\partial y}{\partial \mu_i}\right) \textbf{ and } \frac{\partial E}{\partial \sigma_{ij}} = \left(\frac{\partial E}{\partial y}\right)^T \left(\frac{\partial y}{\partial \sigma_{ij}}\right). \tag{11.19}$$

The relation, $\frac{\partial E}{\partial y}$, may be obtained from Eq. (11.18)

$$\frac{\partial E}{\partial y} = -2(z - y). \tag{11.20}$$

Since y is defined according to Eq. (11.17), we can take its derivative to compute $\frac{\partial y}{\partial \mu_i}$ and $\frac{\partial y}{\partial \sigma_{ij}}$:

$$\begin{aligned}(D^T\Sigma^{-1}D + \lambda W^T W)\frac{\partial y}{\partial \mu_i} &= D^T\Sigma^{-1}D\frac{\partial \mu}{\partial \mu_i}\\ (D^T\Sigma^{-1}D + \lambda W^T W)\frac{\partial y}{\partial \sigma_{ij}} &= 2D^T\Sigma^{-1}\frac{\partial \Sigma}{\partial \sigma_{ij}}\Sigma^{-1}D(y - \mu).\end{aligned} \tag{11.21}$$

Finally, gradient descent is performed by changing the previous values of the parameters according to the computed gradient:

$$\mu^{new} = \mu^{old} - \eta\frac{\partial E}{\partial \mu} \textbf{ and } \Sigma^{new} = \Sigma^{old} - \eta\frac{\partial E}{\partial \Sigma}. \tag{11.22}$$

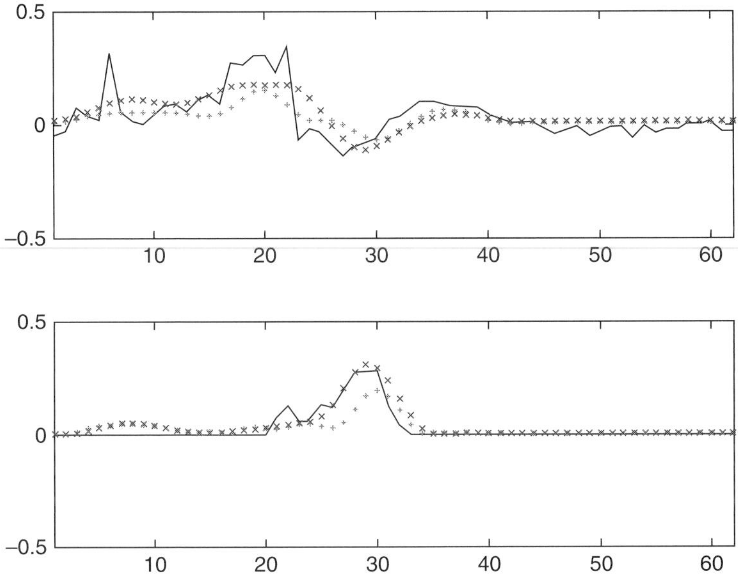

Figure 11.9 Top: The analyzed trajectory for α_{12} (in solid), compared with the synthesized trajectory for α_{12} before training (in dots) and after training (in crosses). Bottom: Same as above, but the trajectory is for β_{28}. Both trajectories are from the word "tabloid."

Cross-validation sessions were performed to evaluate the appropriate value of λ and the correct level of smoothness W to use. The learning rate η was set to 0.001 for all trials, and 15 iterations performed. Comparison between batch and online updates indicated that online updates perform better, so this method was used throughout training. Testing was performed on a set composed of one-syllable words, two-syllable words, and sentences not contained in the training set. The Euclidean norm between the synthesized trajectories and the original trajectories was used to measure error. For flow parameters, the results showed that an adequate smoothness operator is fourth order and an adequate regularizer is $\lambda = 1000$. For texture parameters, the results showed that an adequate smoothness operator is fifth order and an adequate regularizer is $\lambda = 100$. Figure 11.9 depicts synthesized trajectories for the α_{12} and β_{28} parameters before training (in dots) and after training (in crosses) for these optimal values of W and λ.

11.8 Post-processing

Due to the head and eye normalization that was performed during the pre-processing stage, the final animations generated by MMM synthesis exhibit movement only in the mouth region. This leads to an unnerving "zombie"-like quality to the final animations. As in Bregler *et al.* (1997b) and Cosatto and Graf (1998), we address this issue by compositing the synthesized mouth onto a background sequence that contains natural head and eye movement.

The first step in the compositing process is to add Gaussian noise to the synthesized images to regain the camera image sensing noise that is lost as a result of blending multiple image prototypes in the MMM. We estimate means and variances for this noise by computing differences between original images and images synthesized by our system, and averaging over 200 images.

After noise is added, the synthesized sequences are composited onto the chosen background sequence with the help of the masks shown in Figure 11.3. The head mask is first forward-warped using optical flow to fit across the head of each image of the background sequence. Next, optical flow is computed between each background image and its corresponding synthetic image. The synthetic image and the mouth mask from Figure 11.3 are then perspective-warped back onto the background image. The perspective warp is estimated using only the flow vectors lying within the background head mask. The final composite is made by pasting the warped mouth onto the background image using the warped mouth mask. The mouth mask is smoothed at the edges to perform a seamless blend between the background image and the synthesized mouth. The compositing process is depicted in Figure 11.10.

11.9 Computational issues

To use our Mary101 system, an animator first provides phonetically annotated audio. The annotation may be done automatically (Huang *et al.* 1993), semi-automatically using a text transcript (Huang *et al.* 1993), or manually (Sjolander and Beskow 2000).

Trajectory synthesis is performed by Eq. (11.17) using the trained phonetic models. This is done separately for the flow and the texture parameters. After the parameters are synthesized, Eq. (11.7) from Section 11.6.3 is used to create the visual stream with the desired mouth movement. Typically only the image prototypes I_i that are associated with the top 10 values of β_i are warped, which yields a considerable saving in computation time. MMM synthesis takes on the order of about 7 s per frame for an image resolution of 624×472. The background compositing process adds on a few extra seconds of processing time. All times are computed on a single processor 450 MHz Pentium II PC running Linux.

We have synthesized numerous examples using our system, spanning the entire range of one-syllable words, two-syllable words, short sentences, and long sentences. In addition, we have synthesized songs and foreign speech examples.

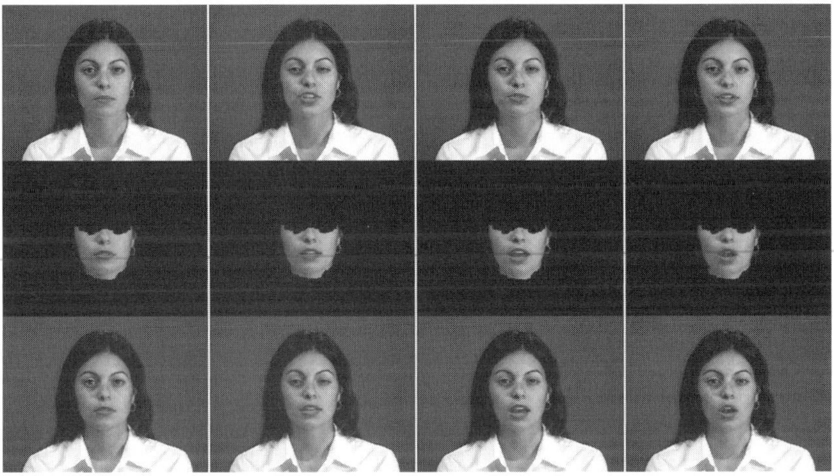

Figure 11.10 The background compositing process. Top: A background sequence with natural head and eye movement. Middle: A sequence generated from our system, with the desired mouth movement and appropriate masking. Bottom: The final composited sequence with the desired mouth movement, but with the natural head and eye movement of the background sequence. The masks from Figure 11.3 are used to guide the compositing process.

Experimentally we have found that reducing the number of prototypes below 30 degrades the quality of the final animations. An open question is whether increasing the number of prototypes significantly beyond 46 will lead to even higher levels of videorealism.

Currently, the time taken to process the entire eight minute recorded corpus to produce the 46-prototype MMM is two to three weeks on a single processor 450 MHz Pentium II PC. In terms of corpus size, it is possible to optimize the spoken corpus so that several words alone elicit the 46 prototypes. This would reduce the duration of the corpus from eight minutes to a few seconds. However, this would degrade the quality of the correspondences computed by the Dijkstra algorithm. In addition, the phonetic training performed by our trajectory synthesis module would degrade as well. Further systematic experiments need to be made in order to evaluate how final performance changes with the size of the corpus.

11.10 Evaluation

The animations produced by the Mary101 system were perceptually evaluated. These animations consisted of synthetic mouth region sequences that were re-composited into real video sequences of Mary101. Evaluation of video-realism of image-based synthesis is currently a very active area of research (Odisio and Bailly 2004; Cosker *et al.* 2005; Theobald *et al.* 2008).

Our evaluation consisted of two sets of experiments. The first set of experiments examined the "realism" of the synthetic animations by estimating a subject's ability to tell the animated images from the real ones. For this purpose, three experiments of visual detection, which can be considered as "Turing tests," were made to gauge if the synthetic image sequences were recognized as such. We named the experiments: single presentation, fast single presentation, and pair presentation. In every experiment we presented each subject with the same number of synthetic and real image sequences and observed the level of correct detection. To the best of our knowledge, to date there has been no systematic perceptual evaluation that uses comparisons between synthetic and real images of the same utterances spoken by the same person, as the Mary101 system has enabled us to do.

The second experiment was an intelligibility experiment, in which subjects were asked to lipread real and synthetic animations of the same utterances. This experiment examined how well one can operate with the animated images as compared with the real ones. The correct recognition of the utterances was measured, and the level of recognition of the synthetic and the real image sequences was compared. The analyses were made for the utterances at the level of whole words, syllables, and phonemes.

In the next few sections we briefly describe the experiments performed and summarize their results. For further details on all experiments, please refer to Geiger *et al.* (2003).

11.10.1 General method

In this section we describe aspects that were common to all the experiments.

Stimuli: The image sequences in all the experiments were run by a computer and presented on a 21″ monitor. The resolution of the image sequences on the monitor was 624 × 472 pixels (15 cm × 11 cm) on which the frontal view of the head and shoulders of Mary101 were presented, in color on a blue background (as in the images of Figure 11.1). The distance of the viewers was set to 50 cm away from the screen. At this distance the display subtended 17 degrees × 12.5 degrees of visual arc for the viewer. The monitor's refresh rate was 60 Hz and the frame rate of the video image sequences was 29.97 frames per second.

In the single and the fast presentation experiments the real audio was part of the stimuli. It was heard from two loudspeakers, one at each side of the monitor. The average audio listening level at the viewers' location was set to 55–65 dB SLP. The audio signals were well-synchronized with the image sequences whether real or synthetic.

A real image sequence of an utterance was taken directly from the digitized video images of Mary101. The synthetic image sequence of an utterance was constructed as discussed in Section 11.8 by re-compositing the synthetic mouth animation into the real image sequence. Consequently only the mouth region was different between the real and synthetic versions, whereas the rest was identical for both. There were minor differences in average luminance and contrast of the mouth region between the real and the synthetic images. The average contrast difference was 4 percent.

One hundred twenty image sequences were prepared as stimuli. They were made of sixty utterances. From each utterance two image sequences were made, one real and one synthetic. A small number of image sequences was randomly selected, from the entire corpus, for presentation in each experiment. The number of presented image sequences varied in each experiment, as will be specified later. The order of the presented image sequences was also randomized. However, in each experiment equal numbers of real and synthetic image sequences were presented to every subject.

The sixty utterances comprised forty single words and twenty sentences. Half of the single words were single-syllable words and half were two-syllable words. Average duration of the single words was about 2 s (range 2–3 s) and about 3 s (range 2–3 s) for sentences. The corpus covered all the phonemes of the English language.

Participants: The participants were recruited by a circulated email message to a large list of addressees. All those who responded and showed up for testing were taken as subjects. In all we had a pool of twenty-four subjects who were assigned to the different experiments. The participants reported themselves to have normal hearing and normal or corrected-to-normal vision. Their ages ranged from 18 to 67 years. They all had college education or were in college at the time of testing. Most were native speakers of American English, as will be specified later for each experiment.

Procedure: The session began with an explanation of the general purpose of the experiment. The subjects were asked "to tell apart animated (synthetic) image sequences from real ones" or in the intelligibility experiment to "tell what was said." The subjects were seated, in a dimly lit room, in front of a computer monitor to be viewed at 50 cm distance. The display of the stimuli was controlled by a computer that was also used to record the subject's responses. The instructions to the subject were different for each experiment, and will be specified accordingly. Before every stimulus presentation, an "X" on a blue background (similar to the background of Mary101), was shown in the middle of the display. The subjects were instructed to fixate their gaze on the X whenever it appeared. The subjects were asked to move their eyes freely after the X disappeared. After a verbal prompt, a stimulus was presented. The subjects were asked to respond according to the instructions. The responses were given orally and were entered into the computer by the experimenter. The options of the responses will be described later for each experiment. However, in all the experiments there was also an option of "don't know (DK)" for the case in which the subject could not choose one of the other options. Thus the experiments were not two-way forced-choice experiments. After the response was entered into the computer, the cycle was repeated until all the stimuli for that experiment had been presented.

After the conclusion of one experiment, the next experiment in the set was performed in a similar manner. There were a total of four experiments, three constituting visual "Turing Test"-like detection tasks, while the fourth was a lipreading/intelligibility task. The order of the experiments presented to each subject was different, but arranged in such a manner so as to yield, at the end of testing, various levels of prior exposure to each experiment. For example, while some subjects performed Experiment 1 with no prior exposure to any other experiment, an equal number of different subjects had one prior exposure to another experiment before performing Experiment 1, while another equal number of different subjects participated in two other experiments prior to Experiment 1. The intelligibility experiment was presented last to most subjects. After all the experiments had been presented to the subject, the results were analyzed and shown (upon request) to the subject. The analyses of the results will be described for each experiment separately.

11.10.2 Experiment 1: Single presentations

In order to establish the level at which the synthetic image sequences were distinguished from the real ones, we presented each image sequence singly, and asked the subjects if it was a real or a synthetic image sequence.

11.10.2.1 Method In addition to the general method described above the particular details for this experiment are described below.

Stimuli: Sixteen image sequences were randomly chosen from the corpus. Half of these were real and half synthetic, not necessarily from the same utterances. In addition, half of the image sequences were of single-word utterances and half of sentences, evenly distributed across real and synthetic image sequences. Every image sequence was accompanied by the real audio of the utterance.

Participants: There were twenty-two subjects (eleven females and eleven males) of whom nineteen were native speakers of American English. For eight of the subjects this experiment was the first in the set of experiments. Another eight subjects had participated in one of the other experiments before this one and the last six subjects had participated in two experiments prior to this one.

Table 11.1 *Results from Experiment 1 "Single presentations." The column measures are means, standard deviation, and significance from chance.*

22 subjects	Mean	SD	p<
All utterances			
% correct	54.26	15.72	0.3
% of DK responses	12.50	16.70	
Single words			
% correct	52.84	16.78	0.5
% of DK responses	12.50	19.29	
Sentences			
% correct	55.68	21.73	0.3
% of DK responses	12.50	17.25	

Procedure: The instructions to the subjects were as follows: "You will be presented with an image sequence of a talking woman; she will say either one word or a sentence. Please indicate if the image sequence you saw was real or synthetic." It was also explained that all the image sequences would be accompanied by the real audio recording of the utterances. As mentioned, the subjects were asked to fix their gaze on the X. After a verbal prompt the utterance was displayed, followed by the reappearance of the X. The subjects were asked to indicate if the image sequence was "real," "synthetic" or, if unable to decide, "don't know." The subjects were allowed to respond without time constraints. The response was entered into the computer by the experimenter, clicking with the mouse on the appropriate field shown in the corner of the monitor. The next cycle followed. There was no mention of the number of image sequences to be presented or the ratio of real to synthetic image sequences (although it is reasonable to assume that the subjects would think it might be half-and-half). At the end of the presention of all sixteen stimuli, a new experiment was prepared and the file with the collected responses was kept for evaluation.

11.10.2.2 Results and discussion **Main results**: A summary of the results from this experiment is shown in Table 11.1. Results from Experiment 1 "Single Presentations." The column measures are means, standard deviation, and significance from chance. The average of the correct identification of the image sequences as either real or synthetic, for all twenty-two subjects on all sixteen image sequences presented, was 54.26%. That number is not significantly different from chance level (50%), as was verified by a t-test. The results are similar when either single-word utterances or sentences were considered separately. (There were three subjects who correctly identified the image sequences at or above 75%, and none below 25%.)

From the real image sequences presented, 74.43% were detected as such, compared with 34.09% of the synthetic image sequences, which means that 65.91% of the synthetic image sequences were detected incorrectly.

These results suggest that when image sequences are presented to the subjects, on average they are unable to tell whether the presented image sequence is synthetic or real.

Additional details: On average, 12.5% of the responses were "DK," where the subjects could not decide if the image sequence was either real or synthetic. These "DK" responses were considered as incorrect responses. This can be justified with relation to the aim of the experiment, which was to gauge the level of positively detecting the animated from the real, and hence the DK responses do not tell them apart.

In addition, a separate analysis was made with regard to subjects who had prior exposure to similar experiments. The results show no significant difference in performance between those who had prior exposure to similar experiments and those who did not (for details see Geiger *et al.* 2003). As there was no significant advantage (or disadvantage) to prior exposure to the other experiments, we regarded the twenty-two subjects as one group.

Regarding particular synthetic utterances, three single-word utterances and one sentence were recognized as synthetic in all cases, suggesting that most synthetic image sequences were evenly distributed with regard to the ability to recognize them as such.

This experiment measures best the impression one gets from a single presented image sequence, whether it is real or animated.

11.10.3 Experiment 2: Fast single presentations

This experiment is basically the same as the previous one, with the difference being that in this experiment the image sequences followed each other with only 1 s intervals between them. Subjects were asked to respond very rapidly, either during the presentation of the image sequence itself or the following 1 s interval. In performing this experiment, we wanted to examine whether the differences between real and synthetic image sequences would be more evident if subjects could compare one to another in rapid succession. The other differences are detailed below.

11.10.3.1 Method **Stimuli**: Eighteen image sequences were randomly chosen from the corpus for each subject, half of which were real and half synthetic, not necessarily from the same utterances. Eight image sequences were of single-word utterances and ten of sentences, in equal numbers of real and synthetic. As in Experiment 1, the real audio accompanied all the image sequences.

Table 11.2 *Results from Experiment 2 "Fast single presentations." The column measures are means, standard deviation, and significance from chance.*

21 subjects	Mean	SD	p<
All utterances			
% correct	52.12	15.66	0.5
% of DK responses	2.65		
Single words			
% correct	50.00	14.79	1
% of DK responses	1.19		
Sentences			
% correct	53.81	20.61	0.2
% of DK responses	4.76		

Participants: Twenty-one subjects participated in this experiment (eleven females and ten males); eighteen were native speakers of American English. For eight subjects this was the first encounter with an experiment; seven had participated in one similar experiment before this one and six had participated in two previous experiments.

Procedure: The procedure was similar to that in Experiment 1. Instead of presenting each image sequence and pausing for the subject's response after each presentation, here the image sequences were presented in blocks of six. In each block the image sequences were presented one after the other with 1 s intervals between them. During the intervals the X was displayed.

11.10.3.2 Results and discussion The results from this experiment are shown in Table 11.2. The average correct identification for the twenty-one subjects was 52.12%, which is not significantly different from chance (50%). (There were no subjects with correct identification rates above 75% or below 25%.) As in Experiment 1, correct identification of the real image sequences (66.67%) was higher than that of the synthetic ones (37.57%).

These results suggest that even when the presentations of the image sequences follow one another rapidly, the subjects, on average, are unable to distinguish the real from the synthetic image sequences. As in Experiment 1, the prior exposure to similar experiments did not affect performance systematically or significantly.

As seen in Table 11.2, the average correct identification for real and synthetic image sequences is 50% for single-word utterances and 58.45% for sentences. Neither is significantly different from chance ($p<1$; $p<0.2$ respectively) and neither is significantly different from the other ($p<0.2$). One possible explanation for this slight difference is that the subjects had a longer time in which to respond when sentences were presented than when single words were presented.

On average, in only 2.6% of the cases did the subjects respond with a DK response. As before, this was considered an incorrect response. The low DK response level suggests that fast presentation makes the experiment more similar to a two-way forced-choice experiment.

11.10.4 Experiment 3: Pair presentations

In this experiment, image sequence *pairs* of the same utterance were presented as stimuli, where one sequence was real and the other was synthetic (but presented in randomized order). The subject's task was to tell the order of the presented real and synthetic image sequences. In the previous experiments the utterances were presented *singly*, making direct comparisons of the real and synthetic image sequences of the same utterance difficult. The following experiment addresses this concern.

11.10.4.1 Method **Stimuli**: Sixteen utterances were randomly chosen from the corpus. This gave thirty-two image sequences, one real and one synthetic from each utterance. Half of the utterances were single words and half sentences. The order of presentation within each pair was also random. There was no audio input in this experiment.

Participants: Participants in this experiment were twenty-two subjects (ten females and twelve males) of whom nineteen were native speakers of American English. For eight subjects this was the first presentation of an experiment; another eight subjects had participated beforehand in one similar experiment and another six subjects had participated before in two similar experiments.

Procedure: The instructions to the subject were: "You will be presented with two image sequences, of the same utterance, one after the other with an interval of 1 s between the end of the first and the beginning of the second. One image sequence is real and the other synthetic appearing in random order. Please indicate the order of the presentation: "real-synthetic," "synthetic-real," or "don't know" (DK). Take your time to answer it." In the interval between the image sequences the X reappeared and the subject was asked to fixate on it.

11.10.4.2 Results and discussion **Main results**: A summary of the results is given in Table 11.3. The average score for correctly identifying the order of the real and the synthetic image sequences, for the twenty-two subjects, was 46.59%, which is not significantly different ($p < 0.5$) from chance level (50%). The correct identification rate was similar for single-word and sentence utterances (45.45% and 47.73% respectively). There were three subjects with above 75% correct identification and one below 25%. These results suggest that even when pairs of real and synthetic image sequences of the same utterances were

Table 11.3 *Results from Experiment 3 "Pair presentations." The column measures are means, standard deviation, and significance from chance.*

22 subjects	Mean	SD	p<
All utterances			
% correct	46.59	21.28	0.5
% of DK responses	28.69		
Single words			
% correct	45.45	27.43	0.5
% of DK responses	28.41		
Sentences			
% correct	47.73	21.70	0.7
% of DK responses	28.98		

presented directly one after the other, subjects are unable to tell the synthetic from the real.

Additional results: The average number of DK responses was 28.68%. As mentioned before, these were considered as incorrect. As in Experiment 1, prior exposure to similar experiments did not affect performance systematically or significantly. On Experiments 1 to 3, which can be thought of as "Turing-like tests," the subjects, on average, were unable to visually distinguish between the animated and the real image sequences.

11.10.5 Experiment 4: Visual speech recognition

In this experiment, subjects were asked to lipread real and synthetic animations of the same utterances when presented without audio. The main difference between this experiment and the ones above was the task: in this experiment the subjects were asked to tell what Mary101 said, reading her lips rather than judging if the image sequences were real or animated.

11.10.5.1 Method **Stimuli**: Each subject was presented with the real and the synthetic image sequences of sixteen utterances, which were randomly chosen from the entire corpus. Eleven utterances were single words and five were sentences. Each utterance was presented twice to each subject, once as a real image sequence and once as synthetic. The image sequences were presented to each subject in random, non-consecutive order to avoid direct priming by the same utterance. On average, the same number of either real or synthetic image sequences were presented first in an utterance.

Participants: Eighteen subjects (eight females and ten males) participated in this experiment, of whom sixteen were native speakers of American English.

Table 11.4 *Numbers of subjects and stimuli, and mean numbers of words, syllables, and phonemes used in Experiment 4, "Visual speech recognition."*

18 subjects	stimuli	words	syllables	phonemes
All utterances	32	65.56	85.89	224.56
Single words	22	22	32.93	90.93
Sentences	10	44.27	53.60	135.60

All had participated in one or more of the experiments above. All were proficient in English.

Procedure: The subject was instructed to "read the lips" of Mary101 and at the end of the stimulus presentation, tell verbally what the utterance, or any part of it, was. As in the previous experiments, at first, the subject was asked to fixate on the X and move the eyes freely once the image sequence appeared. After a verbal prompt of "Ready" by the experimenter, the image sequence was shown. At the end of it, the X reappeared. After the subject's verbal response the experimenter entered the response into the computer by using its keyboard. Thereafter a new cycle started. The subject was encouraged to respond to the whole utterance; however a response to any part of it was also considered valid. When the subject had no idea as to the content of the utterance, an appropriate notation was entered. The evaluations of the correct responses were made separately on three different levels: the number of correct responses to whole words, to syllables, and to phonemes. Once all the subjects were tested, the average responses were calculated.

11.10.5.2 Results and discussion A summary of the results is given in Tables 11.4 and 11.5. The eighteen subjects were presented with thirty-two image sequences each. Due to the different lengths of the sentences and words and due to the random selection of the utterances to be presented to each subject, the total number of words, syllables, and phonemes was different for each subject. However, as seen from Table 11.4, the average number of words presented to each subject was 65.56, which comprised 85.9 syllables or 224.6 phonemes. The subjects responded on average to 81.42% of all the image sequences presented (real and synthetic); most of the responses were incorrect. The high rate of response indicated familiarity with the mode of Mary101's speech whether presented as real or synthetic image sequences.

Average correct recognition of whole words from the real and synthetic image sequences together was 10.74%, that of syllables 12.4%, and that of phonemes, 25.6%, all significantly different from 0 (the significance level is not shown in the table). That level of correct phoneme recognition is similar to the

Table 11.5 *Percentage of responses and percentage correct identification of words, syllables, and phonemes for Experiment 4, "Visual speech recognition."*

18 subjects	responses	words	syllables	phonemes
All utterances				
synthetic and real	81.42	10.74	12.40	25.60
synthetic only (S)	72.92	6.96	8.52	21.19
real only (R)	89.93	14.52	16.29	30.01
t (difference S–R)		–3.595	–4.004	–5.102
p<		0.01	0.001	0.001
Single words				
synthetic and real	83.59	10.35	14.42	33.31
synthetic only (S)	76.26	6.06	9.45	28.07
real only (R)	90.91	14.65	19.40	38.55
t (difference S–R)		–3.308	–3.989	–4.196
p<		0.01	0.001	0.001
Sentences				
synthetic and real	76.67	11.00	11.17	20.45
synthetic only (S)	65.56	7.49	8.04	16.52
real only (R)	87.78	14.51	14.30	24.38
t (difference S–R)		–2.278	–2.496	–3.132
p<		0.05	0.05	0.01

range reported in the literature (Bernstein *et al.* 2000b), but the level is lower for words.

The differential responses to real and synthetic image sequences is what interests us most in this account. For all the utterances presented, the subjects responded on average to 72.92% of the synthetic image sequences as compared with a rate of 89.93% responses to the real. That suggests higher familiarity with the real image sequences than with the synthetic. As seen in Table 11.5, on average, the correct recognition of words, syllables, and phonemes was significantly higher when real image sequences were presented (14.52% correct word, 16.29% correct syllable, 30.01% correct phoneme recognition) than when synthetic ones were presented (6.96%, 8.52%, 21.19% respectively). This relationship holds for the case when all the utterances are considered together (as above), as well as when single words or sentences are considered alone. This indicates that the animated image sequences are not as good for lipreading as the real recordings.

In most cases when the participants tried to figure out what was uttered, they moved their own lips trying to mimic the mouth movements they saw on the screen without uttering any sound. Also, when the participants were casually asked if they could tell if there was any difference between the image sequences, or if they were real or synthetic, they could not. In most cases they thought all the image sequences were real.

11.10.6 General discussion

The Mary101 system has given us the opportunity to compare the perception of real and synthetic image sequences of the same utterances, where only the mouth region was animated and the rest of the talking face was that of the real image sequence. Eye movement and facial expression were identical in both real and synthetic image sequences of an utterance. The advantage is that we were able to perform comparisons using elements of visual speech alone and no other elements of the images. This is different from previous evaluations of animated speech where either entire 3D model faces or comparisons of different types of images were made. As a result, our method also allowed Turing-like tests of visual speech animation.

The first three experiments (Experiments 1–3), each a modified version of the Turing test, were designed to gauge the level of success in recognizing the animated from the real image sequences of the utterances. Each experiment has shown that, on average, the participants could not tell the synthetic from the real. These results held whether the image sequences were presented singly with time for scrutiny (Experiment 1), presented singly with little time to respond (Experiment 2), or presented in pairs, allowing comparison of the real and the synthetic image sequences of the same utterance (Experiment 3).

We refrained from using a simultaneous side-by-side presentation of the image sequences of the same utterances, since the subjects would have shifted their gaze from one image to the other while the utterance was progressing. As a result, we believe the subjects would have compared features instead of focusing on the impression the moving mouth gave throughout the utterances.

In addition, it appears that adding the real audio to the stimuli (Experiments 1 and 2), did not enhance the visual detection of the synthetic from the real, as the detection levels without audio input (Experiment 3) were not significantly different from those from the former ones. In future work, we intend to try Experiment 3 with audio input.

Finally, although the animation of Mary101 achieved the ultimate goal of passing the Turing test, i.e., viewers could not distinguish the animated from the real, it did not satisfactorily pass a more severe scrutiny. Namely, intelligibility of the real image sequences was significantly higher than that of the synthetic (Experiment 4). This was true for recognition of whole words, syllables, and phonemes. This suggests that the animation is not as good as we would like it to be for the purpose of rehabilitation and language learning. Further analysis of the recognition levels of the individual animated phonemes has to be made and compared with those of the real ones.

11.11 Further work

The main limitation of our technique is the difficulty of re-compositing synthesized mouth sequences into background sequences that involve (1) large changes in head pose, (2) changes in lighting conditions, and (3) changes in viewpoint. All these limitations can be alleviated by extending our approach from 2D to 3D. It is possible to envision a realtime 3D scanner that is capable of recording a 3D video corpus of speech. Alternatively, techniques such as those presented by Guenter *et al.* (1998), Pighin *et al.* (1998) or Blanz and Vetter (1999) can be used to map a 2D video corpus into 3D.

The geodesic trajectory synthesis equations described by Brand (1999) and Brand and Hertzmann (2000) are analogous to (and more sophisticated than) the trajectory synthesis techniques we use (Eq. (11.12) and Eq. (11.17)). Although those equations require considerably more training data, it is possible they could lead to higher levels of videorealism.

Clearly the face is used as a conduit to transmit emotion, so one possible avenue to explore is the synthesis of speech under various emotional states. It is possible to record various corpora under different emotional states and create MMMs for each state. During synthesis, the appropriate MMM is selected. An open question to explore is emotional dynamics: how does one transition from a happy MMM to a sad MMM? Additionally, there is also a need to learn generative models of head movement and eye movement tailored for the type of speech being synthesized.

While the coarticulation model proposed in this paper produces synthetic animations that are realistic, it is still necessary to examine the degree with which the model agrees with the recorded data. Does the model predict the coarticulation behavior in real human speech?

Finally, the psychophysics evaluations of our synthetic animations suggest that our animation models are not sophisticated enough yet to achieve speech that is as intelligible as natural speech. Further work needs to be performed to improve intelligibility. In addition, other types of psychophysical evaluations need to be performed, such as evaluating the intelligibility of our system under noisy speech conditions, or evaluating the aesthetic appeal of Mary101 in certain application scenarios.

11.12 Acknowledgments

The authors would like to dedicate this work to the memory of Christian Benoît (Le Goff *et al.* 1996) who was a pioneer in audiovisual speech research.

The authors would like to thank Meredith and Dynasty Models; Craig Milanesi, Dave Konstine, Jay Benoit from MIT Video Productions; Marypat Fitzgerald and Casey Johnson from CBCL; Volker Blanz, Thomas Vetter,

Demetri Terzopoulos, Ryan Rifkin, Pawan Sinha and anonymous reviewers for countless helpful comments on the paper; Luis Pérez-Breva for help with the psychophysics evaluations; David Beymer, Mike Jones, Vinay Kumar, Steve Lines, Roberto Brunelli, and Steve Librande for laying the groundwork; and the numerous subjects who participated in our evaluations.

This work was partially funded by the Association Christian Benoît, NTT Japan, Office of Naval Research, DARPA, and National Science Foundation (Adaptive Man-Machine Interfaces). Additional support was provided by: Central Research Institute of Electric Power Industry, Eastman Kodak Company, DaimlerChrysler AG, Honda R&D Co. Ltd., Komatsu Ltd., Toyota Motor Corporation, and The Whitaker Foundation.

11.13 Appendix

11.13.1 Flow concatenation

Given a series of consecutive images $I_0, I_1 \ldots I_n$, we would like to construct the correspondence map $C_{0(n)}$ relating I_0 to I_n. We focus on the case of the three images I_{i-1}, I_i, I_{i+1} since the concatenation algorithm is simply an iterative application of this three-frame base case. Optical flow is first computed between the consecutive frames to yield C_{i-1}, C_i, C_{i+1}. Note that it is not correct to construct $C_{(i-1)(i+1)}$ as the simple addition of $C_{(i-1)i} + C_{i(i+1)}$ because the two flow fields are calculated with respect to two different reference images. Vector addition needs to be performed with respect to a common origin.

Our concatenation thus proceeds in two steps: to place all vector fields in the same reference frame, the correspondence map $C_{i(i+1)}$ itself is warped *backwards* (Wolberg 1990) along $C_{(i-1)i}$ to create $C^{warped}_{i(i+1)}$. Then $C^{warped}_{i(i+1)}$ and $C_{(i-1)i}$ are both added to produce an approximation to the desired concatenated correspondence:

$$C_{(i-1)(i+1)} = C_{(i-1)i} + C^{warped}_{i(i+1)} \tag{11.23}$$

A procedural version of our backward warp is shown in Figure 11.11. "`BILINEAR`" refers to bilinear interpolation of the four pixel values closest to the point (x,y).

11.13.2 Forward warping

Forward warping may be viewed as "pushing" the pixels of an image I along the computed flow vectors C. We denote the forward warping operation as an operator $W(I,C)$ that operates on an image I and a correspondence map C,

```
for j = 0...height,
 for i = 0...width,
       x = i + dx(i,j);
       y = j + dy(i,j);
       I^warped(i,j) = BILINEAR (I, x, y);
```

Figure 11.11 BACKWARD WARP algorithm.

```
for j = 0height
      for i = 0width,

            x = ROUND (i + α dx(i,j));
            y = ROUND (j + α dy(i,j));
            if (x,y) are within the image
                 I^warped(x,y)= I(i,j);
```

Figure 11.12 FORWARD WARP algorithm.

producing a warped image I^{warped} as final output. A procedural version of our forward warp is shown in Figure 11.12.

It is also possible to forward warp a correspondence map C' along another correspondence C, which we denote as $W(C', C)$. In this scenario, the x and y components of

$$C'(\vec{p}) = \left\{ d'_x(\vec{p}), d'_y(\vec{p}) \right\}$$

are treated as separate images, and warped individually along

C: $W(dx', C)$ and $W(dy', C)$.

11.13.3 Hole-filling

Forward warping produces *black holes* that occur in cases where a destination pixel is not filled in with any source pixel value. This occurs due to inherent non-zero divergence in the optical flow, particularly around the region where the mouth is expanding. To remedy this, a hole-filling algorithm (Chen and Williams 1993) was adopted that pre-fills a destination image with a special reserved background color. After warping, the destination image is traversed in rasterized order and the holes are filled in by interpolating linearly between their non-hole endpoints.

In the context of our synthesis algorithm in Section 11.6.3, hole-filling can be performed *before blending*, or *after blending*. Throughout this chapter, we assume hole-filling is performed before blending, which allows us to subsume the hole-filling procedure into our forward warp operator W and simplify our notation. Consequently (as in Eq. (11.6)), the blending operation becomes a simple linear combination of the hole-filled warped intermediates I_i^{warped}.

In practice, however, we perform hole-filling *after blending*, which reduces the size of the holes that need to be filled, and leads to a considerable reduction in synthesis blur. Post-blending hole-filling requires a more complex blending algorithm than that noted in Eq. (11.6) because the blending algorithm now needs to keep track of holes and non-holes in the warped intermediate images I_i^{warped}:

$$I^{morph}(x, y) = \frac{\sum_{I_i^{warped} \neq hole} \beta_i I_i^{warped}(x, y)}{\sum_{I_i^{warped} \neq hole} \beta_i} \tag{11.24}$$

Typically an accumulator array is used to keep track of the denominator term in Eq. (11.24) above. The synthesized mouth images shown in Figure 11.6 were generated using post-blending hole-filling.

12 Animated speech: research progress and applications

D. W. Massaro, M. M. Cohen, M. Tabain, J. Beskow, and R. Clark

12.1 Background

This chapter is dedicated to Christian Benoît, who almost single-handedly established visible speech as an important domain of research and application. During and after his residence in our laboratory for the academic year 1991–92, Christian and his endearing partner Elisabeth were an important part of our lives. We shared in their marriage and the births of their two children, as well as in many professional challenges and puzzles. We hope that this book provides a legacy for Christian's family and friends, and helps maintain a memory of his personal and professional value.

The human face presents visual information during speech production that is critically important for effective communication. While the voice alone is usually adequate for communication (and can be turned into an engaging instrument by a skilled storyteller), visual information from movements of the lips, tongue, and jaws enhances intelligibility of the message (as is readily apparent with degraded auditory speech). For individuals with severe or profound hearing loss, understanding visible speech can make the difference between communicating effectively with others or a life of relative isolation. Moreover, speech communication is further enriched by the speaker's facial expressions, emotions, and gestures (Massaro 1998b, Chapters 6, 7, 8).

One goal of our research agenda is to create animated agents that produce accurate auditory and visible speech, as well as realistic facial expressions, emotions, and gestures. The invention of such agents has awesome potential to benefit virtually all individuals, but especially those with hearing problems, including the millions of people who acquire age-related hearing loss every year, and for whom visible speech and facial expression take on increasing importance. The animated characters that we are developing can be used to train individuals with hearing loss to "read" visible speech, to improve their processing of limited auditory speech, and to enhance their speech production, and will thereby facilitate access to online information presented orally, and improve face-to-face communication with either real people or lifelike computer characters.

For the past 24 years, we at the Perceptual Science Laboratory at University of California at Santa Cruz (PSL-UCSC) have been improving the accuracy of visible speech produced by Baldi, an animated talking agent (Massaro 1998b, Chapter 13). Baldi has been used effectively to provide curricular instruction and to teach vocabulary to profoundly deaf children at the Tucker Maxon Oral School in Portland Oregon, in a project funded by an NSF Challenge Grant (Massaro, *et al.* 2000; Barker 2003). The Baldi technology in the service of vocabulary learning has been tested in several studies. A detailed review of these tests with deaf and hard-of-hearing students in the learning of speech and language is given in Massaro 2006a, 2006b. Several evaluation experiments showed that both hard-of-hearing and autistic children learned many new words, grammatical constructions, and concepts (Massaro and Bosseler 2003; Massaro and Light 2004a), proving that the application provided an effective learning environment for these children. The research strategy insured that any learning was due to the intervention itself rather than from outside of the lesson environment. Students learned all of the items that they were specifically tutored on and not the items that were only tested. In addition, a delayed test given more than 30 days after the learning sessions took place showed that the children retained over 85 percent of the words that they learned. This learning and retention of new vocabulary, grammar, and language use is a significant accomplishment for these children.

Massaro (2006b) used the same multisensory approach with a computer-animated agent to evaluate the effectiveness of teaching vocabulary to beginning elementary students learning English as a second language. Children, whose native language was Spanish, were tutored by Timo,[1] a new animated character based on Baldi, and tested on English words they did not know. The children learned the words when they were tutored but not words that were simply tested. This result replicates the previous studies carried out on hard-of-hearing and autistic children with Baldi as the animated conversational tutor. In other experiments, we have also observed that Baldi's unique characteristics allow a novel approach to tutoring speech production to both children with hearing loss (Massaro and Light 2004b) and adults learning a new language (Massaro and Light 2003).

Given the success of the tutoring program, it is important to assess whether the facial animation is a significant influence on learning vocabulary. To evaluate this question, an experiment compared to what extent the face facilitated vocabulary learning relative to the voice alone (Massaro and Bosseler 2006). The vocabulary learning consisted of both the receptive identification of pictures and the production of spoken words. Five autistic children were tutored in vocabulary with and without the face. Each child continuously learned to a criterion two sets of words with the face and voice and two sets with just the voice and without the face. The rate of learning was significantly faster and the retention was better with than without the face. Although two of the children did not show a large advantage with the face, the research indicates that at least some autistic children benefit from the face. The better learning and retention with the face was most likely due to the additional information provided by the face but it is still possible that the face was more engaging and motivating which in turn would benefit performance. In either case, it shows the value of animated tutors in the teaching of vocabulary.

The same pedagogy and technology has been employed for language learning with autistic children (Bosseler and Massaro 2004). While Baldi's visible speech and tongue movements probably represent the best of the state of the art in real-time visible speech synthesis by a 3D talking face, speech perception experiments have shown that Baldi's visible speech is still not as effective as video recordings of human faces. Thus, we face the challenge of improving animated speech even more to match that produced by real persons.

12.2 Visible speech synthesis

Visible speech synthesis is a subfield of the more general areas of speech synthesis and computer facial animation. The goal of the visible speech synthesis in the PSL-UCSC has been to obtain a mask with realistic motions, not to duplicate the musculature of the face to control this mask. Our choice is to develop visible speech synthesis in a manner that has proven most successful for audible speech synthesis. We call this technique terminal analogue synthesis because its goal is to simply mimic the final speech product rather than the physiological mechanisms that produce it. Our own current software (Cohen and Massaro 1993, 1994a; Cohen *et al.* 1995; Massaro 1998b) is a descendant of Parke's (1974, 1975, 1982) software and his particular 3D talking head. Our modifications over the last 15 years have included additional and modified control parameters, texture mapping, three generations of a tongue (which was lacking in Parke's model), a new visual speech synthesis coarticulatory control strategy, controls for paralinguistic information and affect in the face, text-to-visible speech synthesis, alignment with natural speech, direct auditory speech to visible speech synthesis, and bimodal (auditory–visual) synthesis (Massaro 1998b; Massaro *et al.* 2000). Most of our current parameters move vertices (and the polygons formed from these vertices) on the face by geometric functions such as rotation of the jaw or translation of the vertices in one or more dimensions (such as lower and upper lip height, or mouth widening). Other parameters work by interpolating between two different face subareas. Many of the face shape parameters such as cheek, neck, and forehead shape, as well as some affect parameters such as smiling use interpolation.

Consisting of about 40 000 lines of C code, the synthesis program runs in realtime on both SGI and PC platforms. Our talking head is available for research purposes to educational and governmental institutions free of charge. When combined with the other modules in the CSLU toolkit,[2] for example, students and researchers can productively explore problems in speech science and computer-animated agents. We have also added to the toolkit additional modules for stimulus manipulation, response recording, and data analyses for psychology experiments in speech and language processing,[3] allowing even more access to and utilization of our technology and research findings.

In our synthesis algorithm, each segment is specified with a target value for each facial control parameter. Coarticulation, defined as changes in the articulation of a speech segment due to the influence of neighboring segments, is based on a model of speech production using rules that describe the relative dominance of the characteristics of the speech segments (Saltzman and Munhall 1989; Löfqvist 1990). For each control parameter of a speech segment, there are also temporal dominance functions dictating the influence of that segment on the control parameter. These dominance functions determine independently for each control parameter how much weight its target value carries against those of neighboring segments, which will in turn decide how the target values are blended. Figure 12.1 illustrates how this approach works for a lip-protrusion control parameter for the word "stew." The dashed curve illustrates a simple ogival interpolation between the segment target values (indicated by circles in the bottom panel), which is at odds with what actually occurs in speech production (Kent and Minifie 1977; Perkell and Chiang 1986). The top panel shows the dominance functions for lip protrusion for each phoneme in the word. Because the functions for /s/ and /t/ are relatively weak compared to that for /uw/, the resulting protrusion (illustrated by the solid curve in the bottom panel) for /uw/ comes earlier in time.

Our coarticulation algorithm also produces realistic speech with changes in speaking rate. When the speaking rate is increased, the durations for segments are decreased but we need not otherwise change dynamic parameters of the dominance functions. By shrinking segment durations, the dominance functions move closer to each other and overlap more. This outcome produces undershooting of the target values, which also occurs when natural speech is articulated more quickly. Thus, the model can handle changes in speaking rate in a natural fashion. The PSL-UCSC coarticulation algorithm has been successfully used in American English and Mexican Spanish (Massaro 1998b, Bands 1.1, 12.5), and French (Le Goff and Benoît 1997). More recently, Baldi now speaks Italian (Cosi *et al.* 2002b) and Arabic (Ouni *et al.* 2003).

Important extensions of our dominance function-based algorithm have been implemented and tested by several researchers (Le Goff 1997; Le Goff and Benoît 1997; Cosi *et al.* 2002a). Rather than use a single exponential-based dominance function form, Le Goff (1997) generalized the shape of that dominance function, yielding several wider functions. In addition, the target values

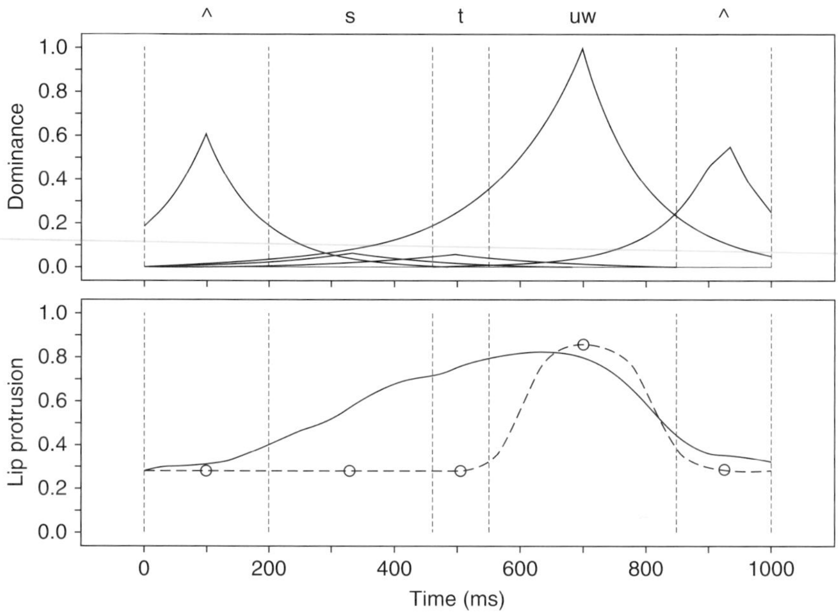

Figure 12.1 Top panel shows dominance functions for lip protrusion for the phonemes in the word "stew." Bottom panel shows the resulting function of the coarticulated control parameter based on these dominance functions (solid line) versus a function based on an ogival interpolated non-coarticulated pattern (dashed line).

and dynamic parameters of the system were automatically trained using facial parametric measurements of a corpus consisting of short French utterances of the form "c'est pas $V_1CV_2CV_1z$?" where V_1 and V_2 were from the set /a,I,y/ and C was from the set /b,d,g,l,R,v,w,z/. Similar explorations were carried out by Cosi *et al.* (2002a), who added some additional terms to the dominance functions to represent temporal resistance of particular segments to the influence of neighbors, and also some further shape variations to the dominance function. This system was trained on six facial parameters measured from a small set of symmetric VCV utterances. Although the fit to these parameters was good, it is uncertain how well the results might generalize to a larger corpus, since in that work a plethora of parameters were highly trained on the small set of utterances.

More parsimonious implementations of coarticulation have also been proposed. In the RULSYS procedure of Gränstrom *et al.* (2002), a control parameter is either defined or undefined for a given segment. If undefined, the control parameter would not be specified for that phoneme and, therefore, it would be free to take on the value of the segment's context. Rounding for /r/ is undefined, for example, because it can be rounded or not depending on context. The undefined parameters take on the values determined by linear interpolation between the closest segments that have defined parameters. We look forward to new solutions to implementing coarticulation and their empirical evaluation.

A central and somewhat unique quality of our work is the empirical evaluation of the visible speech synthesis, which is carried out hand-in-hand with its development. These experiments are aimed at evaluating the realism of our speech synthesis relative to natural speech. Realism of the visible speech is measured in terms of its intelligibility to members of the linguistic community. The goal of this research is to learn how our synthetic visual talker falls short of natural talkers and to modify the synthesis accordingly in order to bring it more in line with natural visible speech. Successive experiments, data analyses of the confusion matrices, and modifications of the synthetic speech based on these analyses have led to a significant improvement in the quality of our visible speech synthesis (Massaro 1998b).

12.3 Illustrative experiment of evaluation testing

Analogous to the evaluation of auditory speech synthesis (Benoît and Pols 1992), evaluation is a critical component of visible speech synthesis. As described in Massaro (1998b), several decisions had to be made about the test items and data analysis. As with most decisions of this type, there are trade-offs and conflicting constraints so that there is no apparently unique solution. In deciding what test items to present to subjects, arguments can be made for the use of speech segments, words, or sentences. Speech segments in the form of nonsense words have the advantage of being purely sensory information with no possible contribution from top-down context. Sentences, in contrast, represent a situation that is more analogous to the use of speech in real-world contexts. In our initial series of evaluations, we chose the intermediate level of single words for a number of reasons. Test words make use of the text-to-speech component of the synthesis and permit the testing of consonant and vowel segments as well as consonant clusters and diphthongs. Test words are also very easy to score if we require that subjects give only single words as responses. Because we want to compare our synthetic talker to a real talker, we use a bimodally recorded test list of one-syllable words in natural speech (Bernstein and Eberhardt 1986b).

Our illustrative study uses the methodology of Cohen *et al.* (1996) and Massaro (1998b) in which a direct comparison is made between people's ability to speechread a natural talker and our synthetic talker. We presented silently for identification monosyllabic English words (such as *sing*, *bin*, *dung*, *dip*, *seethe*) produced either by a natural speaker (Bernstein and Eberhardt 1986b) or our synthetic talker, randomly intermixed. Each evaluation test used a unique set of parameter values and dominance functions for each phoneme as well as our blending function for coarticulation. The AT&T text-to-speech (TtS) module was utilized to provide the phonemic representation for each word and the relative durations of the speech segments, in addition to synthesizing the auditory speech presented as feedback (Sproat 1998). Other characteristics such as speaking rate and average acoustic amplitude were equated for the natural and synthetic talker. The speech on the videodisk was articulated in citation form and thus had a relatively slow speaking rate. The most recent evaluation experiments are presented in Massaro (1998b, Chapter 13). With three successive iterations of modifying Baldi's control parameters, the overall difference in viseme accuracy between the natural talker and Baldi was decreased from .22 to .18 to .10; baseline performance was roughly .74.

In a new modification, we defined two new control parameters for retraction and rounding, which simulate facial muscle actions. For each point involved in the parameter, the parameter value is multiplied by three coefficients for x, y, and z of a vector that is then added to the original point location. Such a mechanism might also be characterized as a patch morph. A change in each of these parameter values modifies the face from one neutral shape (for example, unrounded) to another shape (rounded). These two control parameters allow us to characterize the visible speech in terms of more phonetically based terms, which should allow us to more easily simulate actual speech. The coefficients for these two parameters were derived from physical measurements of one speaker, although we might also derive them from high resolution laser scans of speakers making these particular gestures.

Twelve college students who were native speakers of American English served as subjects, in two 40-minute sessions each day for two days. Up to four at a time were tested in separate sound attenuated rooms under control of the SGI-Crimson computer, with video from the laserdisk (the human talker) or the computer being presented over 13″ color monitors. On each trial they were first presented with a silent word from one of the two faces and then typed in their answer on a terminal keyboard. Only actual monosyllabic English words were accepted as valid answers from a list of about 12 000 derived mainly from the *Oxford English Dictionary*. After all subjects had responded, they received feedback by a second presentation of the word, this time with auditory speech (natural or synthetic depending on whether the face was natural or synthetic) and with the word in written form on the left side of the video monitor.

There were 264 test words, and each word was tested with both synthetic and natural speech, for a total of $2 \times 264 = 528$ test trials. For the counterbalancing of the test words and presentation modes, the subjects were split into two groups. Each group received the same random order of words but with the assignment of the two faces reversed. Five unscored practice trials using additional words preceded each experimental session of 132 test words.

By comparing the overall proportion correct and analyzing the perceptual confusions, we can determine how closely the synthetic visual speech matches the natural visual speech. The questions to be answered are what is the extent of confusions, and how similar are the patterns of confusions for the two talkers. This analysis can be simplified by ignoring confusions that take place between visually similar phonemes. Because of the data-limited property of visible speech in comparison to audible speech, many phonemes are virtually indistinguishable by sight, even from a natural face, and so are expected to be easily confused. To eliminate these likely confusions from consideration, we group visually indistinguishable phonemes into categories called visemes. The concept of viseme has been traditionally used to parallel that of phoneme – in other words, a difference between visemes is significant, informative, and categorical to the perceiver; a difference within a viseme class is not. In general, then, we expect confusions to take place within visemes but not between them. However, some confusion does take place between viseme categories. This is partly because of the difficulty of speechreading. But also, as with most categories, visemes are not sharply defined (they are "fuzzy"), and any sharp definitions imposed are therefore somewhat arbitrary and inaccurate. Even so, it is worthwhile to use some standard viseme groupings in order to assess how well the more meaningful visible speech differences are perceived. As in our previous studies (Massaro 1998b), we grouped the consonants into nine viseme categories. The results were first pooled across experimental sessions and subjects to increase their reliability.

Figure 12.2 presents the word-initial consonant viseme accuracy and confusions for natural (left panel) and synthetic (right panel) speech. The area of

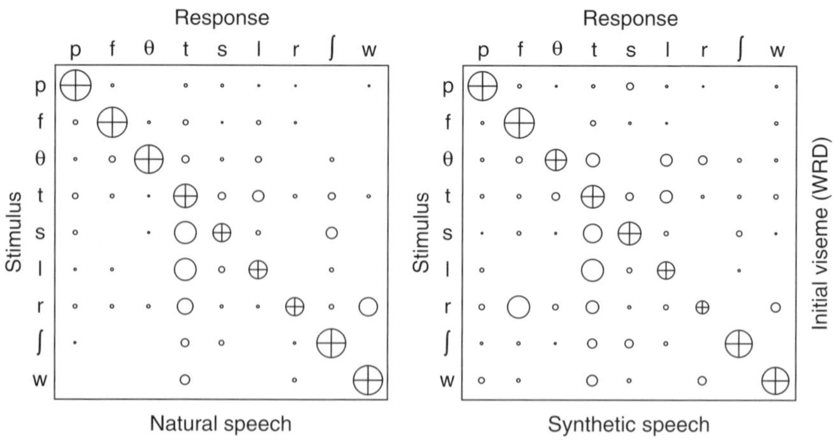

Figure 12.2 Viseme accuracy and confusions for natural and synthetic visual speech.

each circle indicates the proportion of each response to a given stimulus. As can be seen in the figure, the overall level of performance is relatively comparable for the two talkers, except for two major limitations of the synthetic speech. The initial segment /T/ (as in ***thick***) was frequently identified as /t/ or /l/, and initial /r/ was often identified as /f/ or /v/. The overall proportion of correct identification of the initial segment for natural speech (.689) was slightly higher than that for the synthetic talker (.652). The overall difference in viseme accuracy between the natural talker and Baldi was .086, indicating that we achieved a small improvement over our previous set of control parameters. The correlation of the synthetic and natural talker data yielded a correlation of r = .927. The ratio of correct identifications for the synthetic and natural talkers for visemes was 0.946. We turn now to our current work to improve the animated speech.

12.4 The use of synthetic speech and facial animation

In a few instances, individuals have reacted negatively to the use of synthetic auditory speech in our applications. Not only did they claim it sounded relatively robotic (in some cases, people thought there was a resemblance to our California governor in his previous life as a terminator), they were worried that children may learn incorrect pronunciation or intonation patterns from this speech. However, this worry appears to be unnecessary. In agreement with the positive outcomes of direct experimental evaluations described below, Baldi has been used in many different pedagogical applications at the Tucker-Maxon School of Oral Education (www.tmos.org), where Baldi tutored quite successfully with about sixteen hard-of-hearing children who were about 8 to 14 years of age (Barker 2003). The students had either hearing aids or cochlear implants, and were tutored by Baldi an average of about 20 minutes per day. Baldi taught these children receptive vocabulary directly, and also was used in various applications reinforcing the school's curriculum.

As part of the vocabulary tutor, there were recorded speech tasks in which these students imitated and elicited words prompted by Baldi's synthetic speech models. The teachers' impressions were that these children did use Baldi's synthetic speech to produce fairly intelligible words. These students had severe-to-profound hearing losses (90 dB HL or greater) with varying degrees of speech intelligibility and delayed vocabulary skills. Productions of these new words spoken by Baldi seemed to be no better or no worse than their normal articulatory patterns, but the teachers thought these production tasks were beneficial to the students. In addition, the teachers were able to correct the speech synthesizer's pronunciation of a word when it was initially mispronounced by modifying the text input. This was necessary because they noticed that when Baldi mispronounced a word or gave it inappropriate accenting, students were likely to pronounce or intone the word in a similar manner. A number of these students, also described in Barker (2003), who began using Baldi and synthetic speech 7 years ago now have graduated from high school. Obviously, they were still able to achieve academically despite regular exposure to synthetic speech at a fairly young age (Barker 2003). It should be noted that the primary goal was to improve deficit language bases among deaf and hard-of-hearing children, which was believed to be much more critical to academic achievement than perfect pronunciation. For example, a student could read and write quality assignments even though some of the words would be mispronounced. But, in fact, many of the children's receptive vocabulary work with the tutor carried over into intelligible expressive vocabularies.

In addition to these observations, experimental tests demonstrated that hard-of-hearing children improved their pronunciations of words as a direct result of Baldi's tutoring (see Massaro 2006a, for a review). In vocabulary lessons, the children not only improved in their receptive vocabulary but also in their productions of these words (Massaro and Light 2004a). In speech production tutoring on specific speech segments such as /s/, /z/, /t/, and /d/, the application was successful in teaching correct pronunciation of the target words and also generalized to the segments in novel words (Massaro and Light 2004b). This is gratifying because the value of synthetic speech like our animated visible speech tutor is that anything can be said at any time by simply entering the appropriate written text. Natural speech would require that the content be prerecorded by voice talent. This constraint would negate the just-in-time feature of creating lessons. Finally, notwithstanding these justifications, synthetic auditory speech has improved considerably and the synthetic voice of the newer Timo is much more natural sounding than Baldi's original voice.

Analogous arguments exist for facial animation. We have shown that Baldi can be speechread almost as accurately as a real person. In the Jesse *et al.* (2000/01) study described earlier, one of 65 auditory sentences was randomly presented in noise on each trial, and the hearing participants were asked to watch and listen to each sentence and to type in as many words as they could for each sentence. There were three presentation conditions: auditory, auditory paired with the face of the original talker, and auditory paired with the face of Baldi. Pairing the original talker with the auditory speech improved performance by 54% whereas pairing Baldi with the auditory speech gave a 47% improvement. Thus, the large and similar improvement in the two conditions demonstrates that Baldi provides respectable visible speech even though he is synthetic. Although Timo is based on Baldi, research is in progress to test whether Timo's visible speech is as effective as Baldi's. Given this foundation in educational practice, we now turn to the importance of science vocabulary, the unique difficulties it poses, the perceptual and cognitive underpinnings responsible for these difficulties, and how instruction can ameliorate them.

12.5 New structures and their control

We have added internal structures both for improved accuracy and to pedagogically illustrate correct articulation. Although there is a long history of using visible cues in speech training for individuals with hearing loss, these cues have usually been abstract or symbolic rather than direct representations of the vocal tract and articulators. The IBM Speechviewer III application[4] (Mahshie 1998), for example, uses cartoon-like displays to illustrate speech articulation accuracy. Our goal is to create a simulation that is as accurate as possible, and to assess whether this information can guide speech production. We know from children born without sight that the ear can guide language learning. Our question is whether the eye can do the same, or at least the eye supplemented with degraded auditory information.

One immediate motivation for developing a hard palate, velum, teeth, and tongue is their potential utility in language training. Hard-of-hearing children require guided instruction in speech perception and production. Some of the distinctions in spoken language cannot be heard with degraded hearing – even when the hearing loss has been compensated by hearing aids or cochlear implants. To overcome this limitation, one application of our technology is to use visible speech to provide speech targets for the child with hearing loss. Given that many of the subtle distinctions among segments are not visible on the outside of the face, a speech therapist cannot easily illustrate how articulation should occur. The skin of our talking head, on the other hand, can be made transparent or eliminated so that the inside of the vocal tract is visible, or we can present a cutaway view of the head along the sagittal plane. The articulators can also be displayed from different vantage points so that the subtleties of articulation can be optimally visualized. The goal is to instruct the child by revealing the appropriate articulation via the hard palate, velum, teeth, and tongue, in addition to views of the lips and perhaps other aspects of the facial structure.

Visible speech instruction poses many issues that must be resolved before training can be optimized. We are confident that illustration of articulation will be useful in improving the learner's speech, but, of course, this hypothesis must be tested, and it will be important to assess how well learning transfers outside the instructional situation. Another issue is whether instruction should be focused on visible speech or whether it should include auditory input. If speech production mirrors speech perception, then we expect that multimodal training should be beneficial, as suggested by Summerfield (1987). We expect that the child could learn multimodal targets, which would provide more resolution than either modality alone. Another issue concerns whether the visible speech targets should be illustrated in static or dynamic presentations. We plan to evaluate both types of presentation and expect that some combination of modes would be optimal. Finally, the size of the instructional target is an issue. Should

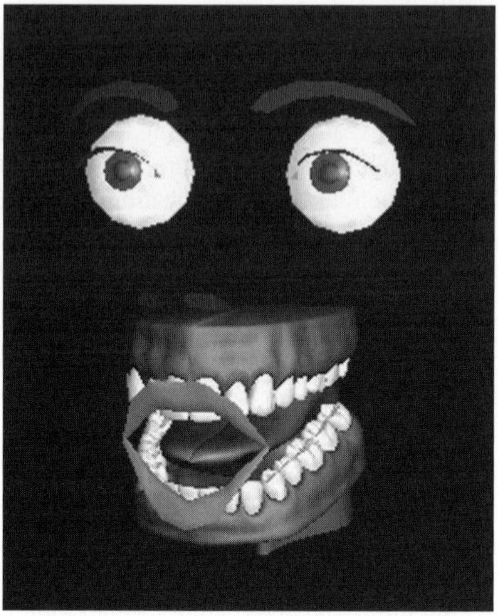

Figure 12.3 New palate and tongue embedded in the talking head.

instruction focus on small phoneme and open syllable targets, or should it be based on larger units of words and phrases? Again, we expect training with several sizes of targets would be ideal.

12.5.1 Tongue, teeth, hard palate, and velum

We have implemented a palate, realistic teeth, and an improved tongue with collision detection in our talking head, Baldi. Figure 12.3 shows our new palate and teeth. A detailed model of the teeth and hard palate was obtained (Viewpoint Datalabs) and adapted to the talking head. To allow realtime display, the polygon count was reduced using a surface simplification algorithm (Cohen *et al.* 1998) from 16 000 to 1600 polygons. This allowed a faster rendering of both the face and articulators. We also plan to implement a moveable velum in the hard palate structure. Figure 12.4 displays the velum in three different states of opening.

12.5.2 Controlling the tongue

Our synthetic tongue is constructed of a polygon surface defined by sagittal and coronal b-spline curves. The control points of these b-spline curves are moved

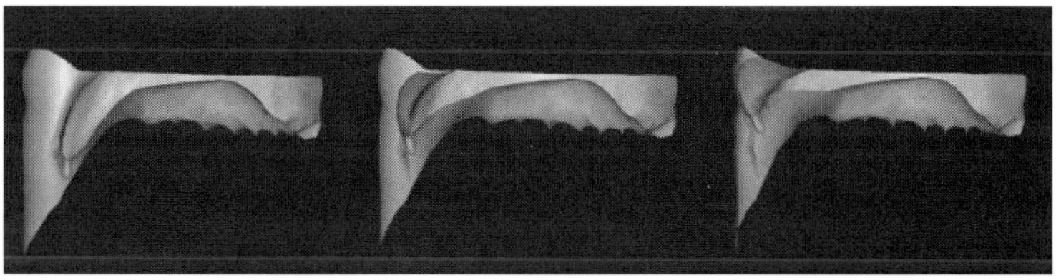

Figure 12.4 Half of palate with velum in three different states of opening.

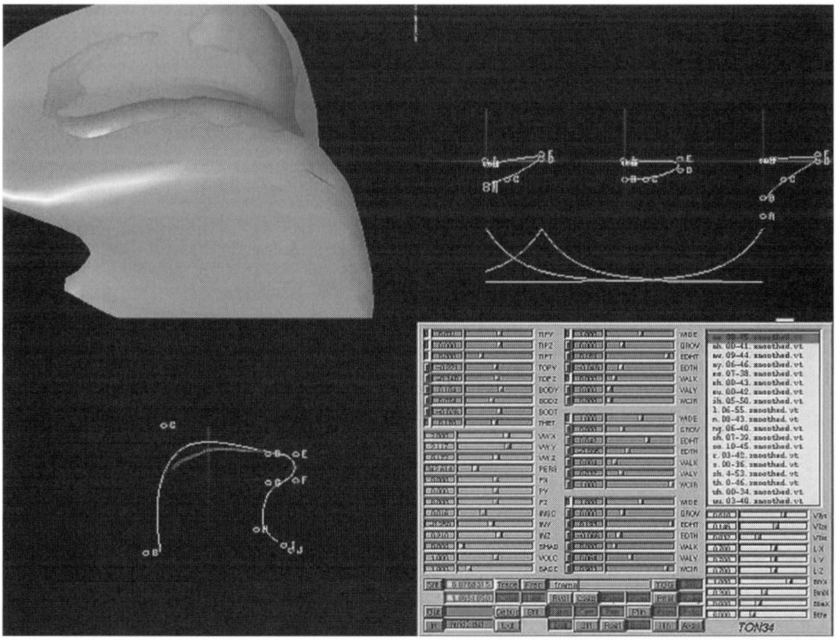

Figure 12.5 Tongue development system (see text for description).

singly and in pairs by speech articulation control parameters. Figure 12.5 illustrates the development system for our third-generation tongue. In this image, taken from the Silicon Graphics computer screen, the tongue is in the upper left quadrant, with the front pointing to the left. The upper right panel shows the front, middle, and back parametric coronal sections (going right to left) along with blending functions just below, which control where front, mid, and back occur. There are nine sagittal and 3×7 coronal parameters, which can be modified with the pink sliders in the lower right panel. The lower left part of Figure 12.5 partially illustrates the sagittal b-spline curve and how it is specified by the control points. For example, to extend the tip of the tongue forward, the pair of points E and F is moved to the right, which then pulls the curve along. To make the tip of the tongue thinner, points E and F can be moved vertically toward each other.

12.5.3 Handling collisions

The tongue, teeth, and palate introduce some geometric complications, since we need to make sure that the tongue hits the teeth and palate appropriately and does not simply travel through them (because they are virtual rather than real). To control the tongue appropriately, we have developed a fast method to detect and correct tongue areas that would intrude into areas of the teeth and palate.

The general principle is that once a point P on the tongue surface is found to be on the wrong side of a boundary (the palate–teeth surface), it is moved back onto that surface. Thus the problem is decomposed into two main parts: detection and correction. Detection is determined by taking the dot product between the surface normal and a vector from P to the surface. The sign of this dot product tells us what side P is on. To correct the point onto the surface, we have examined several strategies with varying computational requirements. One strategy is to compute a parallel projection of the point onto the closest polygon, or onto an edge or a vertex if it does not lie directly above a polygon. This has the drawback that the corrected points will not always be evenly distributed. If the boundary surface is convex, the corrected points could be clustered on vertices and edges of the boundary surface. This approach is also relatively slow (about 40 ms for the entire tongue). A more precise (but even slower) solution takes the vertex normals at the corners of the triangle into account to determine the line of projection, resulting in a better distribution of corrected points. In both of the above methods, a search is required to find the best polygon to correct to.

Collision testing can be performed against the actual polygon surface comprising the palate and teeth, but corrections should only be made to a subset of these polygons, namely the ones that make up the actual boundary of the mouth cavity. To cope with this, we created a liner inside the mouth, which adheres to the inner surface. The liner was created by extending a set of rays from a fixed origin point $\boldsymbol{O}$ inside the mouth cavity at regular longitudes and latitudes, until the rays intersect the closest polygon on the palate or teeth. The intersection points thus form a regular quadrilateral mesh, the liner, illustrated in Figure 12.6. The regular topology of the liner makes collision handling much faster (several ms for the entire tongue), and we can make all corrections along a line towards $\boldsymbol{O}$. With this algorithm, we can omit the polygon search stage, and directly find the correct quadrilateral of the liner by calculating the spherical coordinates of a point which would protrude through the palate relative to $\boldsymbol{O}$.

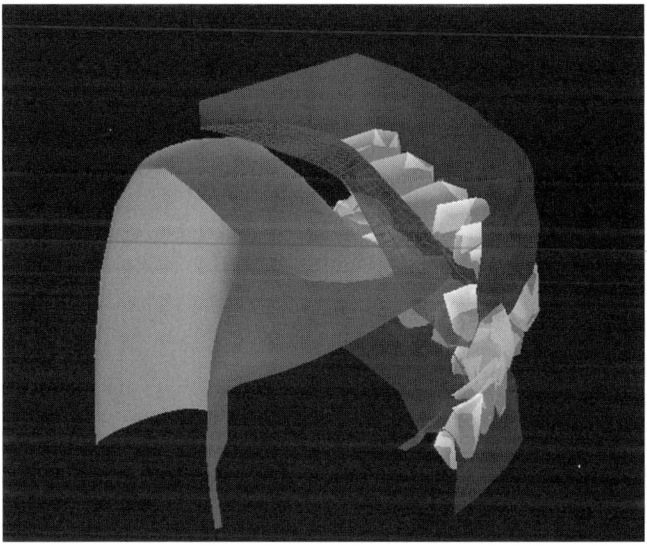

Figure 12.6 Teeth and palate, showing regular quadrilateral mesh liner.

Since the hard palate and the teeth don't change shape over time, we can speed up the collision testing by pre-computing certain information. The space around the internals is divided into a set of 32 × 32 × 32 voxels, which contain information about whether that voxel is *ok*, *not ok*, or *borderline* for tongue points to occupy. This provides a preliminary screening; if a point is in a voxel marked *ok*, no further computation need be done for that point. If the voxel is *borderline*, we need to perform testing and possibly correction, if it is *not ok* we go straight to correction. Figure 12.7 illustrates an example of the screening voxel space. In this set of voxels, the shade of each point indicates the voxel class marking.

12.5.4 Tongue shape training

A minimization approach has been implemented to train our synthetic tongue to correspond to observations from natural talkers. The left panel of Figure 12.8 shows the synthetic b-spline curve along with a contour extracted from an MRI scan in the sagittal plane of a speaker articulating a /d/. The first step in any minimization algorithm is to construct an appropriate error metric between the observed and synthetic data. For the present case, we construct a set of rays from the origin (indicated in Figure 12.8 by the "+" marks interior to the tongue outline) through the observed points and the parametric curve. The error can

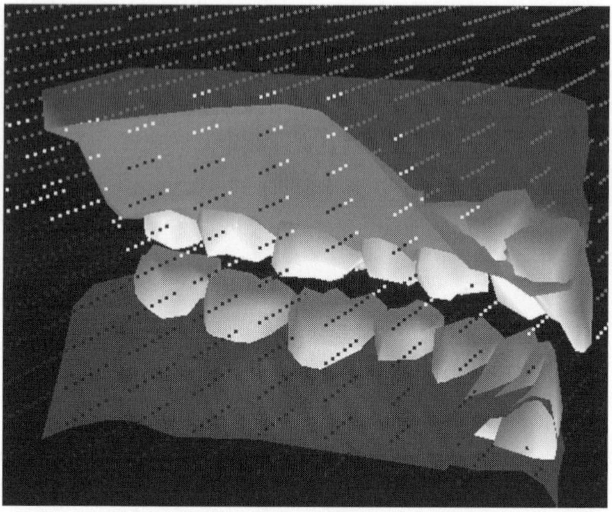

Figure 12.7 Voxel space around the left jaw region, with the anterior end to the right in the picture. Black dots toward the bottom indicate areas where the tongue points are *okay*, gray dots toward the top where the tongue points are *not okay*, and white dots for points that are *borderline* (neither *okay* nor *not okay*).

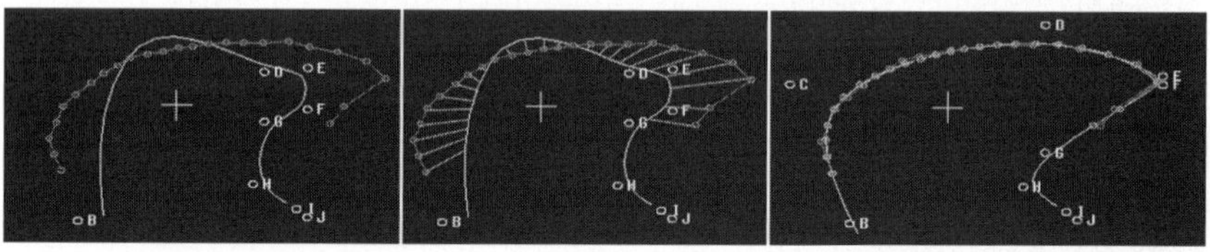

Figure 12.8 Sagittal curve fitting. The left panel shows the sagittal outlines of the synthetic tongue (solid line) and an outline of a /d/ articulation (points connected by line) from an MRI scan. The lettered circles give the locations of the synthetic b-spline curve control points. The center part shows the error vectors between the observed and synthetic curves prior to minimization. The bottom part shows the two curves following the minimization adjustment of control parameters of the synthetic tongue.

then be computed as the sum of the squared lengths of the vectors connecting the two curves. Given this error score, the tongue control parameters (including tip advancement, tip thickness, top advancement) are automatically adjusted using a direct search algorithm (Chandler 1969) so as to minimize the error score. This general approach can be extended to the use of three-dimensional data, although the computation of an error metric is considerably more complex.

12.5.5 *Ultrasound measurements*

In addition to MRI measurements, we are using data from three-dimensional ultrasound measurements to train tongue movements. These data correspond to the upper tongue surfaces for eighteen continuous English sounds (Stone and Lundberg 1996). Four of these ultrasound surfaces are shown in Figure 12.9. These measurements are in the form of quadrilateral meshes assembled from series of 2D slices measured using a rotary ultrasound transducer attached under the chin. It should be noted that the ultrasound technique cannot measure areas such as the tip of the tongue because there is an air cavity between the transducer and the tongue body. We adjust the control parameters of the model to minimize the difference between the observed tongue surface and the surface of the synthetic tongue. To better fit the tongue surface, we have added some additional sagittal and coronal parameters as well as three different coronal sections (for the front, middle and rear sections of the tongue) instead of the prior single

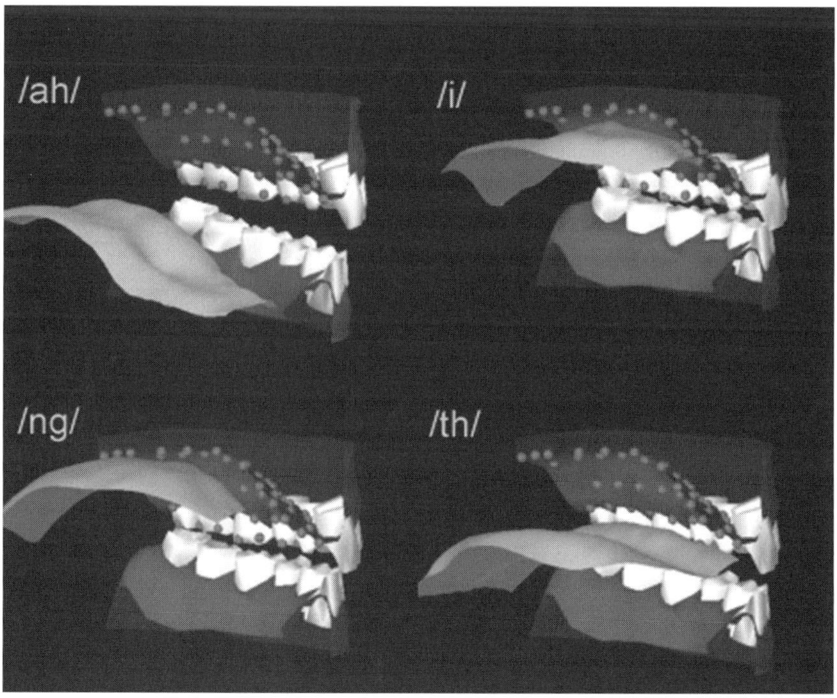

Figure 12.9 Four typical ultrasound-measured tongue surfaces (for segments /a, i, N, T/) with synthetic palate and teeth, and EPG points (data from Stone and Lundberg 1996).

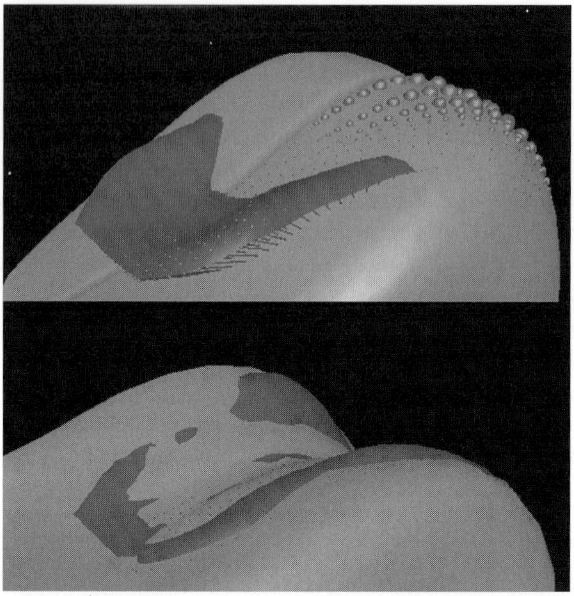

Figure 12.10 3D fit of tongue to ultrasound data. Top and bottom panels show the two surfaces before and after minimization. Error vectors are shown on the right half of the tongue. The size of the sphere on each error vector indicates the distance between the ultrasound and synthetic tongue surfaces.

coronal shape. The control parameters that best fit the observed measurements can then be used to drive visual speech synthesis of the tongue.

A browser in the upper right part of the control panel in Figure 12.5 allows one to select from available ultrasound surface data files. The upper left panel of Figure 12.9 shows the æ ultrasound surface and synthetic tongue simultaneously after some fitting has occurred for the vowel as in b**a**t. Figure 12.10 gives a more detailed view, but part of the ultrasound surface is embedded and cannot be seen. The error (guiding the fitting) is computed as the sum of the squared distances between the tongue and ultrasound along rays going from (0,0,0) to the vertices of the ultrasound quad mesh. A neighboring polygon search method to find tongue surface intersections with the error vectors is used to speed up (~800 ms/cycle) the error calculation after an exhaustive initial search (about 30 s). To prepare for this method the triangular polygon mesh of the tongue is cataloged so that given any triangle we have a map of the attached neighboring triangles. On each iteration of the search process we find which triangle is crossed by an error vector from the ultrasound mesh. Given an initial candidate triangle, we can ascertain whether that triangle intersects the error vector, or if not, in which direction from that triangle the intersecting triangle will occur. We can then use the map of neighboring triangles to get the next triangle to test. Typically, we need to examine only a few such triangles to find which is intersected. We are now also (optionally) constraining the total tongue volume in the fitting process. We compute the volume of the tongue on each iteration, and add some proportion of any change from the original tongue volume to the squared error total controlling the fit. Thus, any parameter changes that would have increased the tongue volume will be compensated for by some other parameters to keep the volume constant.

12.5.6 Synthetic electropalatography

Another source of data for training the tongue is electropalatography (EPG). This type of data is collected from a natural talker using a plastic palate insert that incorporates a grid of about a hundred electrodes that detect contact between the tongue and palate at a fast rate (a full set of measurements 100 times per second). Building on the tongue–palate collision algorithm, we have constructed software for measurement and display of synthetic EPG data. Figure 12.11 shows the synthetic EPG point locations on the palate and teeth. Figure 12.12 shows our synthetic talker with the new teeth and palate along with an EPG display at the left during articulation of /N/ (as in ***sing***). In this display, the contact locations are indicated by points, and those points that are contacted by the synthetic tongue are drawn as larger squares. Comparison of these real EPG data (top left) with synthetic EPG data (bottom left) provides an additional constraint used in training our synthetic tongue. The discrepancy between the number of real and synthetic EPG contacts provides an additional error metric that, together with the ultrasound and volume change error metrics, guide the automatic adjustment of the tongue control parameters to synthesize accurate tongue shapes.

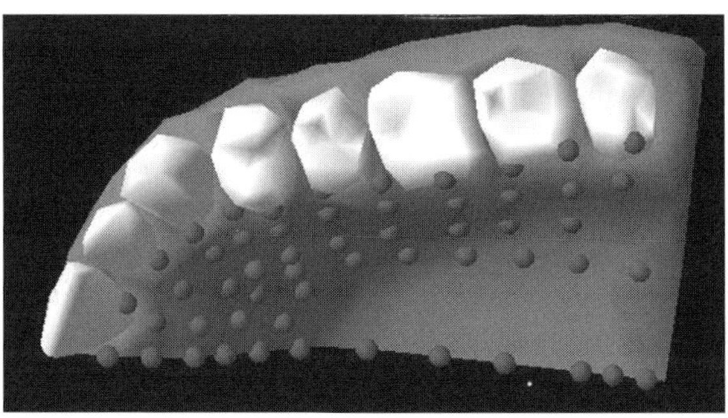

Figure 12.11 EPG points on the synthetic palate.

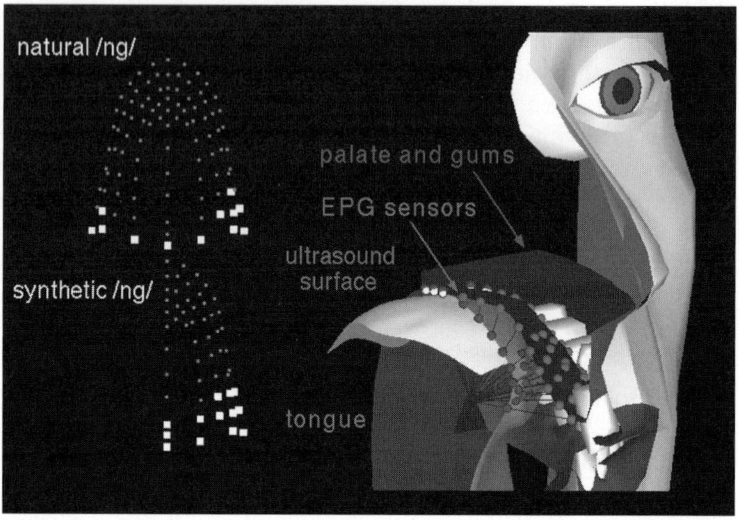

Figure 12.12 Face with new palate and teeth with natural (top left) and synthetic (bottom left) EPG displays for /N/ closure. The smaller dots indicate uncontacted points and the larger squares indicate contacted points. Half of the head is shown cut at the midsagittal plane, except that the full ultrasound target surface shape is displayed.

12.6 Reshaping the canonical head

Our development of visible speech synthesis is based on facial animation of a canonical head, called Baldi. In addition to the original version, which had only the front part of the head, we now have also sculpted a canonical head with somewhat higher resolution that includes the polygons for the back of the head and additional polygons around the mouth. The synthesis, parameter control, coarticulation scheme, and rendering engine are specific to Baldi. It is valuable to be capable of controlling other faces and, therefore, we have developed software to reshape our canonical head to match various target heads. These target heads include both commercial models, such as Viewpoint Data Labs, and 3D Cyberware laser scans. A laser scan of a new target head produces a very high polygon count (hundreds of thousands of polygons) representation. Rather than trying to animate this very high resolution head (which is impossible to do in realtime with current hardware), our software uses these data to reshape our canonical head (the source) to take on the shape of the new target head. In this approach, the facial landmarks on the target head are marked by an operator, and our canonical head is then warped until it assumes as closely as possible the shape of the target head, with the additional constraint that the landmarks of the canonical face move to positions corresponding to those on the target head.

The algorithm used is based on the work of Kent *et al.* (1992), and Shepard (1968). In this approach, all the triangles making up the source and target models are projected on a unit sphere centered at the origin. The models must be convex or star-shaped so that there is at least one point within the model from which all vertices of all triangles are visible. This can be confirmed by a separate vertex visibility test procedure that checks for this requirement. If a model is non-convex or not star-shaped (for example, the shape of the ear, the surface of which crosses a ray from the center of the head several times) then it is necessary to modify these sections of the model in order to meet this requirement, or alternatively, to handle such sections separately.

In our application, the ears, eyes, and lips are handled separately. First, we translate all vertices so that the center point of the model (determined by the vertex visibility test mentioned above) coincides with the coordinate system origin. We then move the vertices so that they are at a unit distance from the origin. At this point, all the vertices of all triangles making up the model are on the surface of the unit sphere. The weighted influence of each landmark is then calculated to determine each source vertex's new position. Then, for each of these source vertices we determine the appropriate location of the projected target model to which a given source vertex projects. This gives us a homeomorphic mapping (one-to-one and onto) between source and target datasets, and we can thereby determine the morph coordinate of each source vertex as a barycentric coordinate of the target triangle to which it maps. This mapping guides the final morph between source and target datasets.

In general, the source and target models may not be in the same coordinate system. In this case, the target model must be transformed to ensure that it lies in the same coordinate space as the source. Even if the models are in the same coordinate spaces, it is unlikely that the respective features (lips, eyes, ears, and nose) are aligned with respect to one another. Shepard (1968) interpolation, a scattered data interpolation technique, is used to help align the two models with respect to one another. A different technique is used to interpolate polygon patches, which were earlier culled out of the target model because they are non-convex. These patches are instead stretched to fit the new boundaries of the culled regions in the morphed head. Because this technique does not capture as much of the target shape's detail as Shepard interpolation, we try to minimize the size of the culled patches. This provides the user with the final complete source model duly morphed to the target model, with all the patches in place. To output the final topology we patch together all the source polygonal patches and then output them in a single topology file. The source connectivity is not disturbed and is the same as the original source connectivity.

The morph itself is a one-to-one correspondence between all points on the source model and unique locations on the target model. We establish absolute coordinate mappings by computing barycentric coordinates and carrying them

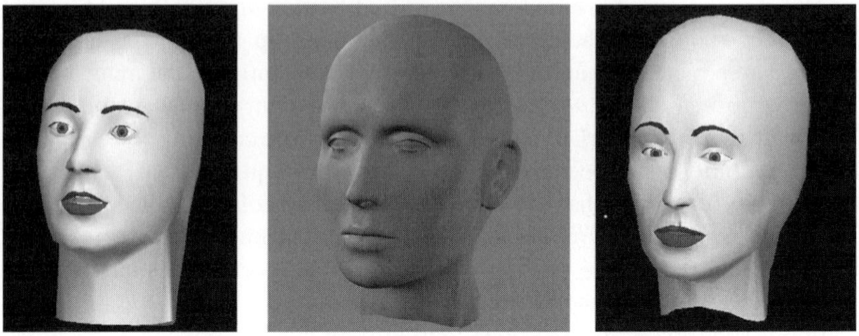

Figure 12.13 Original canonical head (left), a target head (center), and the morphed canonical head (right) derived from our morphing software.

back to the original models to compute the locations to which each point on the source model should morph. The final morphing actually transforms the source model to the required target model in a smooth fashion. Figure 12.13 illustrates the application of our software, morphing our canonical head based on a Viewpoint Data Labs target head.

12.7 Training speech articulation using dynamic 3D measurements

To improve the intelligibility of our talking heads, we have developed software for using dynamic 3D optical measurements (Optotrack) of points on a real face while talking (Cohen *et al.* 2002). At ATR in Kyoto, Japan in April 2001, with the help of Eric Vatikiotis-Bateson and Takaaki Kuratate, we recorded a large speech database with 19 markers affixed to the face of DWM (see Figure 12.14).

Fitting of these dynamic data occurred in several stages. To begin, we assigned points on the surface of the synthetic model that best corresponded to the Optotrack measurement points. There were 19 points on the face in addition to 4 points off the top of the head that were used to remove head motion from these 19 points. Two of the 19 points (on the eyebrows) were not used; the other 17 points were used to train the synthetic face. These correspondences are illustrated in Figure 12.15 with model points (3–4 mm off the synthetic skin surface corresponding to the LED thicknesses) shown as dark spheres, and Optotrack points as white spheres. Before training, the Optotrack data were adjusted in rotation, translation, and scale to best match the corresponding points marked on the synthetic face.

The data collected for the training consisted of 100 CID sentences recorded by DWM speaking in a fairly natural manner. In the first stage fit, for each time

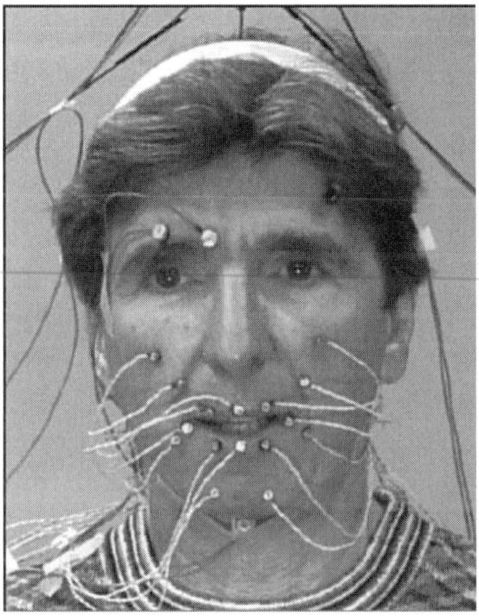

Figure 12.14 Speaker DWM with OPTOTRAK measurement points.

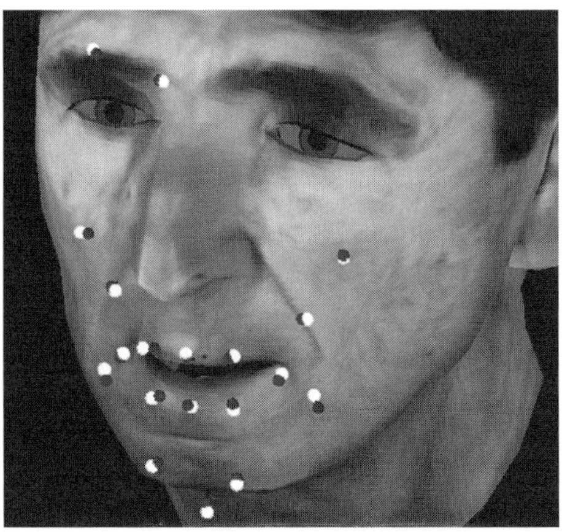

Figure 12.15 Illustrates placement of the points for the new model of WM, which corresponds to Baldi's wireframe morphed into the shape of DWM. These dark points are placed 3mm (4mm for the chin point) off the synthetic surface and the placements of the corresponding measured OPTOTRAK points are given in white.

Table 12.1 *The 10 facial control parameters.*

1	jaw rotation
2	lower lip f-tuck
3	upper lip raising
4	lower lip roll
5	jaw thrust
6	cheek hollow
7	philtrum indent
8	lower lip raising
9	rounding
10	retraction

frame (30 fps) we automatically and iteratively adjusted 10 facial control parameters (shown in Table 12.1) of the face to get the best fit (measured by the root mean square (RMS) of the sum of squared distances) between the Optotrak measurements and the corresponding point locations for the synthetic face. The fit of a given frame was used as the initial values for the next frame. A single jaw rotation parameter was used, but the other 10 parameters were fit independently for the two sides of the face. This yielded 19 best-fitting parameter tracks that could be compared to our standard parametric phoneme synthesis and coarticulation algorithm to synthesize the parameter tracks of the same 100 CID sentences. We used Viterbi alignment on the acoustic speech data of each sentence to obtain the phoneme durations that are required for the synthesis. The difference between the first stage fit and the parametric synthesis with our initial segment definitions gave an RMS error between these curves (normalized for parameter range) of 26 percent.

The 19 best-fitting parameter tracks were then used as the inputs to the second stage fit. In the second stage fit, the goal was to tune the segment definitions (parameter targets, dominance function strengths, attack and decay rates, and peak strength time offsets) used in our coarticulation algorithm (Cohen and Massaro 1993) to get the best fit with the parameter tracks obtained in the first stage fit. The computed parameter tracks of this second stage fit were compared with the parameter tracks obtained from the first stage fit, the error computed, and the parameters (target values and dynamic characteristics) for the 39 phoneme segments adjusted until the best fit was achieved. The RMS for the second stage fit was 12 percent, which shows that the *new* trained parameter targets, dominance function strengths, attack and decay rates, and peak strength time offsets used in our coarticulation algorithm were reasonably accurate in describing the Optotrak data.

In addition to the phoneme definition fit, we have also used phoneme definitions conditional on the following phoneme. In the CID sentences there were 509 such pairs and these context-sensitive phoneme definitions provided an improved match to the parameter tracks of the first stage fit, with an RMS of 6 percent. In summary, we see that using data-driven synthesis can improve the accuracy of our synthesis algorithm. Further work is being carried out to determine how well these trained segment definitions generalize to the synthesis of new sentences by the same speaker, and to speech by other speakers. In addition, intelligibility testing will be carried out as an additional evaluation measure.

12.8 Some applications of electropalatography to speech therapy

As stated earlier, one of our goals is to use visible speech for speech training. This type of training would be similar in some respects to the applied use of electropalatography (EPG). Although initially created as a tool for basic speech research, EPG has been found to be useful in many clinical settings. Research at Queen Margaret College in Edinburgh has shown that many speech disorders can be helped through therapy using EPG (Dent *et al.* 1995; Hardcastle and Gibbon 1997). It has been suggested that although the initial cost of the artificial palate (for the patient) and of the equipment (for the institution or therapist) is relatively high, the savings on clinical time are advantageous both financially and in terms of patient motivation (Nairn *et al.* 1999).

EPG is useful in clinical settings because it provides direct visual feedback (in the form of a computer display) on the contact between the tongue and the palate during speech production. The patient wears a custom-fitted artificial palate embedded with electrodes, and the therapist may wear one as well. The therapist can show a target pattern (perhaps producing the target sound him- or herself), which the patient must try to achieve. For instance, the patient may be presented with a typical contact pattern for /s/: this has much contact at the sides of the palate, with a narrow constriction towards the front of the palate. Certain speech pathologies result in /s/ being produced as a pharyngeal fricative. This would show up on the screen as a lack of contact on the hard palate. The therapist can then instruct the patient as to how to achieve the target pattern. Dent *et al.* (1995) provide a case study where EPG therapy improved the production of lingual stops and fricatives in a patient who had undergone pharyngoplasty.

EPG has also proven useful in clinical assessment by confirming or modifying therapists' intuitions about the nature of the speech pathology presented by a particular speaker (Dent *et al.* 1992). For instance, following the repair of a cleft palate, a patient's speech was still perceived as being nasal during the production of both alveolar and labial stops and fricatives. An EPG examination of the patient's speech showed velar closure during the articulation of all such segments. Once this problem of velar closure was pointed out to the patient, therapy focused on removing the extraneous articulation, and a more natural-sounding production of the alveolar and labial stops and fricatives was achieved.

The production of grooves and affricates can be particularly problematic in many speech pathologies. Dent *et al.* (1995) describe two patients whose productions of /s, ʃ, tʃ/ (as in ***bass***, ***bash***, ***batch***) were perceived as abnormal. In one case, the articulations were perceived as being too dental, and in the other case as being too palatal. An examination of EPG patterns confirmed these perceptions, and therapy focused on achieving correct articulations for these sounds.

Of the twenty-three children examined in the Dent *et al.* (1995) study, EPG therapy was unsuccessful for five of these children. Two of the patients were unable to continue wearing the palate (one lost a tooth to which the palate wire was attached, and the other could not tolerate the palate), and the other three were judged to be less mature emotionally, and less motivated to improve their speech. The authors suggested that given the high cost of obtaining a custom-made artificial palate, therapists and patients must be confident that EPG therapy will succeed and the patient must show sufficient motivation and maturity to proceed with the therapy.

Edwards *et al.* (1997) discuss the usefulness of EPG in examining covert contrasts of alveolar and velar consonants in speech acquisition. Covert contrasts (Hewlett 1988) are phonetic-level contrasts made by a child speaker; these contrasts are not perceptible at the phoneme level by an adult hearer. For instance, a child may produce a significant difference in voice onset time (VOT) for the /p/ and /b/ as in *pet* and *bet* (Macken and Barton 1980; Scobbie *et al.* 1998). However, to the adult hearer, both productions fall into the phoneme category /b/, because in neither utterance is the VOT sufficiently long.

Gibbon *et al.* (1993, 1998) examined two sisters, one of whom had been judged as having acquired the alveolar-velar distinction between /d/ and /g/, and one whose productions of /d/ and /g/ were all judged to be [g]. An EPG study showed that both sisters made an articulatory contrast between /d/ and /g/, and that both had simultaneous velar and alveolar closure during /d/. The difference in perceived phonetic output was found to be due to the sequence of release of the double articulation. If the velar closure was released before the alveolar closure, the stop was perceived as alveolar (as intended). If the alveolar closure was released before the velar closure, the stop was perceived as velar. Moreover, Forrest *et al.* (1990) found that there are spectral differences between a [t] produced for a /t/ and a [t] produced for a /k/. Despite this acoustic contrast, even phonetically trained listeners can disagree on whether a given token is /t/ or /k/ when such double articulations are involved (Gibbon *et al.* 1993). Similar results have been reported for covert contrasts between /s/ and /T/, and for the deletion of /s/ in clusters.

EPG is particularly useful in the treatment of cleft palate speech (Gibbon *et al.* 1998). Cleft palate speech is characterized by double articulations, such as the alveolar-velar double articulation described above; generally weak consonant articulation – for instance, a lack of complete closure for stop consonants as has also been noted in speech affected by acquired dysarthria; abnormally broad or posterior tongue placement; and much lateralization which allows airflow through the sides of the tongue. All of these characteristics can be readily observed in the EPG contact patterns.

EPG is also useful in the description of segments perceived as lateralized fricatives. There is a very wide range of contact patterns for such segments. Some contact patterns show gaps along the sides of the palate where air might escape, and some do not. Most of the contact patterns show complete closure across the palate, although this is not necessarily a characteristic of lateralized fricatives that occur in normal speech (such as those in Welsh). Moreover, the location of the contact varies from speaker to speaker in fricatives, which are perceived as being laterals in disordered speech.

Gibbon *et al.* (1998) studied language-specific effects on cleft palate speech. They showed that overall, the most likely consonants to be affected are coronal and velar obstruents, followed by liquids, and finally bilabial stops. However, there were slight differences within a given language. For instance, Cantonese speakers are more likely to replace the alveolar fricative /s/ with a bilabial fricative and to delete initial consonants than are English speakers. It could be hypothesized that the greater tendency to delete initial consonants is due to the functional load of tone contrasts in Cantonese, since tone contrasts do not exist in English. It is not clear to what extent the size and typology of the consonant phoneme inventory affects the compensatory articulations employed by cleft palate speakers of a given language.

EPG therapy has also proven to be useful in teaching deaf children to produce normal-sounding lingual consonants (Fletcher *et al.* 1991; Dagenais *et al.* 1994; Crawford 1995). The visual feedback from the EPG is deemed to be extremely important to the significant improvement in production. Similarly EPG has been shown to be most successful in teaching older children with functional articulation disorders to produce normal-sounding fricatives, stops, and affricates (Dagenais *et al.* 1994; Dent *et al.* 1995). Children whose /s/ productions were perceived as being lateralized, palatalized, and pharyngalized all showed significant improvement. None of these children could produce the anterior groove configuration necessary for an /s/, so therapy focused on achieving this groove.

Most of the phenomena discussed above can be classified as spatial distortions of speech (see Hardcastle and Gibbon 1997, for an extensive discussion). However, certain speech disorders, such as stuttering (Harrington 1987) or speech affected by acquired apraxia, show temporal distortions. Temporal or serial ordering difficulties occur when the spatial configuration of the EPG pattern looks normal, but there is an error in the duration or sequence of the gesture. At times, a gesture may intrude during speech that is not expected, and is not perceived by the listener or therapist because of its short duration and because it is not expected in the sequence. Hardcastle and Gibbon (1997) give the example of a stutterer's production of the sequence /ɛkstɪ/ (as in *extinct*) transcribed as [ɛkst.ˑ.t.ˑ.ɪ]. The EPG trace shows not only the multiple repetitions of the /t/ together with the long duration of the /s/, but also an intrusive velar closure between the alveolar fricative and the first alveolar stop. This may have been a "carryover" gesture from the velar stop preceding the fricative. At other times, a gesture may intrude during closure for a consonant. For instance, apraxic speakers often have a velar gesture intruding before, during, or after an alveolar gesture; if the intrusive gesture occurs during closure for an alveolar stop, the minimal acoustic energy would result in a lack of audible cues. EPG is particularly useful in these instances.

Other speech difficulties that can be quantified using EPG include transitional difficulties, typical of speakers with acquired apraxia and dysarthria. Transition times between various segments become excessively long; this could result in stop consonants being perceived as released where release is inappropriate, for instance.

Given the success of EPG in speech training, we believe that the visible speech from Baldi could be used for the tutoring of speech production. Although there are both temporal and spatial errors in speech production, the speech tutor developed here focuses only on spatial aspects of speech production, since this is easier to quantify in visual terms.

12.9 Development of a speech tutor

Our speech tutor for deaf children uses Baldi's internal productions, which are based on EPG and ultrasound measurements as described in Section 12.5.5. By making the skin transparent or by showing a sagittal view, Baldi can illustrate pronunciation of sounds that are not normally visible. This section outlines the approach used to develop the tutor. The initial stages of this work required the categorization of a set of "internal visemes." As the name suggests, an internal viseme consists of a group of phonemes that cannot be distinguished from each other, but can be distinguished from all other phonemes, based on an internal view of the oral cavity. It should be stressed that this definition includes only the tongue and the passive articulators in the oral cavity (in other words, the teeth, the alveolar ridge, and the hard palate). The larynx is not included in this scheme, nor is the soft palate (velum). For these reasons, an internal viseme includes both voiced and voiceless cognates, as well as nasals. The scheme is currently limited to consonants.

Ten internal visemes were defined, based primarily on the representation of consonant articulations using EPG data. These internal visemes were interdental, alveolar fricative, post-alveolar fricative, post-alveolar affricate, alveolar stop, velar stop, lateral, rhotic, palatal approximant, and labio-velar approximant. A single phoneme was chosen to represent each viseme. These were, respectively, /θ/ /s/ /ʃ/ /tʃ/ /d/ /g/ /l/ /r/ /j/ /w/. Voiced and voiceless phonemes were included in the same viseme. Thus, the viseme /θ/ also included /ð/ (as in ***th****is*), /s/ also included /z/, /ʃ/ also included /ʒ/ (as in *rou****g****e*), /tʃ/ also included /dʒ/ (as in ***j****u****dg****e*), /d/ also included /t/ and /n/, and /g/ also included /k/ and /ŋ/ (see Table 12.2).

All of the internal visemes can be presented as static targets, with the exception of /tʃ/, which has two phases of production: complete closure in the post-alveolar region, followed by a release into the post-alveolar fricative /ʃ/. The closure portion of /tʃ/ can be presented statically to show that the place of articulation for this consonant is further back than for the alveolar stop /t/.

The second stage of this work involved the development of appropriate views of the oral cavity for the presentation of the internal visemes. Four basic views were developed in the first stages of this work. All views consisted only of the teeth, palate, tongue, and, in some cases, the lips (see below for clarification of when the lips were used). The skin and eyes were removed. The first view was a direct frontal view of the mouth (front view), with 50 percent transparency, and highlighting in yellow of contact between the tongue and the palate. This was intended to partially mimic a typical presentation of the face in lipreading. The second view was of the side of the mouth (side view), again with 50 percent transparency and highlighting of contact between the tongue and the palate. This view was mainly included to contrast /d/ and /l/, since, in principle, the former has contact between the sides of the tongue and the palate, while the latter has no such contact. The third view was called “side cut,” and was similar to side view except that a midsagittal view of the oral cavity was presented (as though the tongue and palate were cut in half). This view was included since it is a typical presentation of consonant and vowel articulations in textbooks of phonetics and speech, and in X-ray drawings of the oral cavity. Tongue highlighting was again present, but transparency was not used (i.e. the representation was solid). The mass of the tongue was presented as bright purple, and contact as a thin yellow line at the top of the tongue. Grooving along the tongue was visible as an earth-colored layer between the mass of the tongue and the contact between the tongue and the palate. The fourth and final view was from the top of the oral cavity (top view). Tongue highlighting was again presented, and transparency was again set at 50 percent. This view was included since it is used to represent tongue–palate contact.

All four views could be presented either with or without the lips. The lips were presented if the viseme involved active rounding of the lips, which included /ʃ/, /tʃ/, /r/, and /w/.

Each internal viseme was then examined in each of the four views, and an attempt was made to determine which views suited which viseme best. A maximum of two views was chosen for a given viseme. The results are

Table 12.2 *The views which best illustrate which views best suit each internal viseme (a category of different phonemes that have very similar internal visible speech). No more than two views were chosen for a given viseme, although their views could also be effective. The top row consists of the internal viseme categories, and the first column lists the different views. A cross indicates that that view gives appropriate and useful information for that viseme. The numbers in each column correspond to the following instructions, which may accompany the presentation of the viseme:*
Make sure the tongue doesn't touch the top front teeth too much. Keep the tongue flat. The air needs to escape between the tongue and the top front teeth.
See where the tongue tip is pointing at the lower teeth. See how there is a deep groove along the tongue.
See how the tongue tip is pointing quite low. See the deep groove along the tongue. See how the tongue is bunched higher up and further back in the mouth than for /s/. Don't forget to round your lips.
The part of your tongue just behind the tip is called the blade. Put the blade where the picture shows you – not right behind the teeth, but a little bit away from the teeth. Keep your tongue bunched up. As you take the blade away from the roof of the mouth, try to keep a deep groove along the tongue, like you practiced for the /sh/.
See how the tongue presses behind the top teeth. See how there is lots of contact between the sides of the tongue all along the mouth.
See how the tongue is pressed against the roof of the mouth at the back.
See how the tip of the tongue is pressing against the teeth, but the sides of the tongue aren't touching anything.
See how the back of the tongue is pushed back in the mouth, towards the throat.
See how the tongue tip curls up in the middle of the mouth, without touching the roof. Don't forget to round your lips.
You need to push the tongue up and back in the mouth, but don't let it press against the roof. Don't forget to round your lips.
See how the tongue is raised in the middle of the mouth. The sides of the tongue touch the teeth and the roof, but not the center part.

	θ	s	·	ṭ	d	g	l	r	w	j
Front view										
Front view with lips										
Side view										
Side view with lips										
Side cut	X	X (2)				X (6)	X			X
Side cut with lips			X (3)	X (4)				X (8)	X (9)	
Top view	X (1)	X			X (5)		X (7)			X (10)
Top view with lips			X	X				X		

presented in Table 12.2. The top row consists of the internal viseme categories, and the first column lists the different views. A cross indicates that that view gives appropriate and useful information for that viseme. The numbers in each column correspond to prototypical instructions, which can accompany the presentation of the viseme. These instructions are also given in Table 12.2. The number is placed next to the view that is deemed to be more useful in the presentation of the viseme.

The purpose of this tutor is to instruct the speaker to produce segments whose internal articulations are not easily viewed by the lipreader. Although the front view was not judged to be useful for any of these internal visemes, it would be useful for the viseme /v/ to show the upper teeth covering the lower lip. The side view was also not judged to be very useful. This was perhaps due to the fact that it repeated much of the information present in the side cut, but without the same level of clarity. (The difference in lateral contact between /d/ and /l/ could be shown clearly using the top view.)

The information presented in Table 12.2 can be used when the viseme is presented in isolation, or as part of a CV sequence. However, when direct comparisons are made between two visemes, it was not always clear what the difference is between them in a given view. For instance, in a top view of /s/ and /ʃ/, there appears to be little difference in contact patterns. However, a side cut view shows that there is a difference, with bunching and raising of the tongue for /ʃ/ but not /s/. For this reason, direct comparisons were made for each possible pair of visemes. Given the results in Table 12.2, only top view and side cut were considered as possible views. These appropriate views are marked by an X in Table 12.3. The view with the lips is presented if either or both of the visemes involve lip rounding. If neither viseme involves lip rounding, it is not presented. It can be seen that for most combinations, both top view and side view can be presented. An X in parentheses, (X), denotes that it is not clear whether this view is useful or not. Testing will be necessary to determine the usefulness of these views in particular, as well as of all the views.

The information in Table 12.3 can also be used in CVC sequences such as the word "sash" or "Seth." The commentaries for the single internal visemes (Table 12.3) can be incorporated for these pairs. For instance, if the word is "Seth," the views would be presented with the following instructions: "For the /s/, see where the tongue tip is pointing at the lower teeth. And see how there is a deep groove along the tongue." Then, "For the /T/, make sure the tongue doesn't touch the top front teeth too much. Keep the tongue flat. The air needs to escape between the tongue and the top front teeth." Although vowels are not explicitly discussed here, for didactic purposes, all vowels would be presented with either the *side cut* or *side cut with lips* view (according to whether rounding is being taught or not).

Table 12.3 *Optimal view to be chosen when direct comparisons are being made between two visemes.*

	Side cut	Side cut + lips	Top view	Top view + lips
T *vs.* g	X		(X)	
T *vs.* l			X	
T *vs.* r		X		(X)
T *vs.* w		X		
T *vs.* j	X			
s *vs.* ʃ		X		
s *vs.* tʃ		X		X
s *vs.* d			X	
s *vs.* g	X		X	
s *vs.* l	X		X	
s *vs.* r		X		(X)
s *vs.* w		X		(X)
s *vs.* j	X			
ʃ *vs.* tʃ		(X)		X
ʃ *vs.* d		X		X
ʃ *vs.* g		X		(X)
ʃ *vs.* l		X		X
ʃ *vs.* r		X		
ʃ *vs.* w		X		(X)
ʃ *vs.* j		(X)		
tʃ *vs.* d		X		X
tʃ *vs.* g		X		X
tʃ *vs.* l		X		X
tʃ *vs.* r		X		X
tʃ *vs.* w		X		X
tʃ *vs.* j		(X)		X
d *vs.* g	X		(X)	
d *vs.* l	X		X	
d *vs.* r		X		X
d *vs.* w		X		(X)
d *vs.* j	X			
g *vs.* l	X		(X)	
g *vs.* r		X		(X)
g *vs.* w		X		(X)
g *vs.* j	X		(X)	
l *vs.* r		X		(X)
l *vs.* w		X		(X)
l *vs.* j	X		(X)	
r *vs.* w		X		
r *vs.* j		X		
w *vs.* j		X		(X)
T *vs.* s	X		X	
T *vs.* ʃ		X		X
T *vs.* tʃ		X		X
T *vs.* d	X		X	

12.10 Empirical Studies

This system was initially developed for the presentation of the internal visemes to deaf children, and the initial application gave very valuable and effective results (Massaro and Light 2004b). It has also been successfully used for native Japanese speakers learning English /r/ and /l/ (Massaro and Light 2003).

More recently, we examined (1) whether speech perception and production of a new language would be more easily learned by ear and eye relative to by ear alone, and (2) whether viewing the tongue, palate, and velum during production is more beneficial for learning than a standard frontal view of the speaker. In addition, we determine whether differences in learning under these conditions are due to enhanced receptive learning from additional visual information, or to more active learning motivated by the visual presentations. Studies were carried out in three different languages: Mandarin, Arabic, and Spanish. Test stimuli were two similar vowels in Mandarin, two similar stop consonants in Arabic, and the two Spanish phonemes absent in English /r/ and /rr/. All of the training and test items were presented in different word contexts. Participants were tested with auditory speech and were either trained (1) unimodally with just auditory speech or bimodally with both auditory and visual speech (Arabic and Spanish studies), and (2) a standard frontal view versus an inside view of the vocal tract (Mandarin study). The visual speech was generated by the appropriate multilingual versions of Baldi, Arabic Badr, Mandarin Bao, and Spanish Baldero. The results test the effectiveness of visible speech for learning a new language. We expected that visible speech would contribute positively to acquiring new speech distinctions and promoting active learning. However, the results did not support that expectation. Rather than forgoing our commitment to visible speech, however, we in retrospect saw many reasons why our short training and testing experiments did not produce positive results. A post mortem analysis produced support for implementing the following embellishments to our training procedure:

1. Tutorial and scrubbing feature on our audiovisual text-to-speech system Bapi (Ouni *et al.* 2005). The animation literature indicates that people learn more from animation when it is demonstrated and explained to them – for example, how it corresponds to what they are supposed to do, what it represents, etc. So with this in mind, we considered ways for participants to learn how the Baldi videos demonstrate what they are supposed to be doing with their articulators. This may be especially relevant with the sagittal view. Suggestions included a brief tutorial at the beginning of the experiment where the experimenter brings attention to relevant features of the video, like where Baldi places his tongue. We could also ask participants to imitate this. An additional possibility is to let participants play with the scrubbing feature on Bapi, which allows the learner to control the time course of the animation by simply moving the mouse.

2. Motivation. Motivation is a potential problem with our experiment: for example, the learning has little context, meaning, or usefulness, and participants are not really accountable for learning, since testing is isolated and no feedback is given regarding pronunciation. One solution that was discussed is to tell participants that they will be tested afterwards by the experimenter. This inter-personal sort of test might motivate participants because they will not want to look ignorant in front of an actual person.
3. Compatibility between training and testing. In the Arabic and Spanish experiments, there is an incompatibility between the training and the testing prompt (training is with the sagittal view, testing is with a frontal view), while this isn't the case in the control condition in which both the training and testing are in a frontal view. Learning is usually optimal when the training and test conditions are equivalent. This discrepancy might hide some of the learning that is potentially gained by experiencing the sagittal view during training.

12.10.1 Baldi on the iPhone and iPad

The Baldi app on the iPhone and the iBaldi app on the iPad transforms any text into Baldi-animated speech. The animation is done locally, which is the only iPhone or iPad application of its kind at this time. Given some text, the user simply presses Play to have Baldi's face and voice communicate the message. One can easily change Baldi's size and orientation using the touch screen interface.

In the Settings view, you can change the audio volume and the speaking rate, as well as show Baldi in a standard Outside View or an Inside View that shows the tongue and inside the mouth (this view is valuable for language learning). You can change Baldi's emotions by varying the sliders for six basic emotions. You can change several at the same time to give a mixture of different emotions.

The text you import can come from Notes, Web pages, RSS feeds, and so on. In all cases, simply select and copy the text from the application, and start Baldi. You can then paste the text. You can also permanently save your favorite texts in your Notes app, and then copy and paste one into the i-Baldi app.

It is possible to show visual cues to help people who are deaf or hard of hearing. The app can show the visual cues alongside of Baldi that would show on the iGlasses we are developing (see the following section). There are two sets of cues: Facial cues on Baldi's face: red nostrils indicate Nasal sounds like m or n; clouds of dots coming out of the mouth indicate Frication sounds like s and sh; and circles indicate Voicing sounds like the sounds of d and v. Disk cues on the side of Baldi's head signal the same Nasal, Frication and Voicing information by lighting up red, white, and blue, respectively.

12.10.2 iGlasses

The need for language aids is pervasive in today's world. There are millions of individuals who have language and speech challenges, and these individuals require additional support for communication and language learning. Currently, however, the needs of these persons, such as limited understanding in face-to-face communication, are not being met. One problem that the people with these disabilities face is that there are not enough skilled teachers, interpreters, and professionals to give them the one-on-one attention that they need. One of our current goals is to develop and implement a pair of eyeglasses (iGlasses) that will facilitate face-to-face communication particularly for hard-of-hearing persons and in difficult hearing situations. The iGlasses project develops technology to supplement the common face-to-face language interaction to enhance intelligibility, understanding, and communication.[5]

Given the limitation of hearing speech for many individuals, the iGlasses will supplement the sound of speech and speechreading with an additional informative visual input. Acoustic characteristics of the speech will be transformed into readily perceivable visual characteristics. The goal is to develop and test the technology required to design a device seamlessly worn by the listener, which will perform continuous real-time acoustic analysis of his or her interlocutor's speech. This device would transform several continuous acoustic features of the talker's speech into continuous visual features, which will be simultaneously displayed on the speechreader's eyeglasses. These acoustic features provide important linguistic information not directly observed on the face and are transformed into visual cues intended to enhance intelligibility and ease of comprehension. This wearable computing device does not require any learning on the part of the talker and is perceptually and linguistically motivated because it is directly based on acoustic and phonetic properties of speech and gives continuous rather than only categorical information.

This work will advance engineering research and speech science by developing a real-time system to automatically detect and track robust characteristics of auditory speech and to transform these continuous acoustic features into continuous supplementary visible features. Previous research and pilot research have demonstrated that neural networks can detect and track robust characteristics of speech. The proposed research extends this work and implements a complete system of transforming continuous acoustic features into continuous supplementary visible features displayed on eyeglasses during face-to-face communication. Pilot research indicates that people can learn to combine these visual cues with the visual information from the face to enhance intelligibility and comprehension. The proposed work will evaluate the learning of several potential visible features in real-world contexts.

The proposed activity will benefit society by providing a research and theoretical foundation for a system that would be naturally available to almost all individuals at a very low cost. It does not require automatic speech recognition, and will always be more accurate regardless of the advances or lack of advances in speech recognition technology. It does not require literate users because no written information is presented as would be the case in a captioning system; it is age-independent in that it might be used by toddlers, adolescents, and throughout the life span; it is functional for all languages because all languages share the corresponding acoustic characteristics; it would provide significant help for people with hearing aids and cochlear implants; and it would be beneficial for many individuals with language challenges and even for children learning to read.

For more information, see www.speechspecs.org/welcome.html

12.11 Additional potential applications

Although our development of a realistic palate, teeth, and tongue is aimed at speech training for persons with hearing loss, several other potential applications are possible. Language training more generally could utilize this technology, as in the learning of non-native languages and in remedial instruction with children with language challenges. Speech therapy during the recovery from brain trauma could also benefit. Finally, we expect that children with reading disabilities could profit from interactions with our talking head.

In face-to-face conversation, of course, the hard palate, the back of the teeth, and much of the tongue are not visible. Thus, we have not had the opportunity to learn the functional validity of these structures in our normal experience with spoken language. We might speculate whether an infant nurtured by our transparent talking head would learn that these ecological cues are functional. If their functional validity was learned, then deaf persons without any hearing at all might be able to completely understand language spoken by a transparent talking head.

Finally, although we have characterized our approach as terminal analogue synthesis, this work brings us closer to articulatory synthesis. The goal of articulatory synthesis is to generate auditory speech via simulation of the physical structures of the vocal tract. It may be that the high degree of accuracy of the internal structures would allow articulatory synthesis based on the synthetic vocal tract shape. Thus we see something of a convergence between the terminal analogue and articulatory-based approaches.

The improvements obtained from measures of real talking faces and documented in the evaluation testing will be codified, incorporated, and implemented in current uses of the visible speech technology. Baldi has achieved an impressive degree of initial success as a language tutor with deaf children

(Massaro *et al.* 2000; Barker 2003). The same pedagogy and technology has been employed for language learning with autistic children (Massaro *et al.* 2003; Bosseler and Massaro 2004; Massaro and Light 2004a). A new Speech Training Tutor is being designed with our colleagues at the Tucker-Maxon Oral School (TMOS) to teach deaf and hearing-impaired children to perceive and produce spoken words, the skills needed for ordinary communication in everyday contexts. One tutor consists of three parts: Same–different discrimination, in which two words are presented and the student decides if they are the same word or two different words; Identification, in which a single word is presented and the student must choose the spoken word from a set of pictures or printed words; and Production, in which the student is presented with a printed word or picture and must pronounce the word. A goal of the Speech Training Tutor is to enable teachers to design specialized applications quickly for individual students. Applications can test a student's ability to discriminate specific sounds in words, to provide training as needed using enhanced auditory and visual features, and continue training and testing until desired performance is achieved with unaltered stimuli. Ultimately, improved visible speech in computer-controlled animated agents will allow all users to extract information from orally delivered presentations. This is especially important for enhanced acquisition of speechreading in newly deafened adults, language acquisition together with word enunciation in children with hearing loss, and those learning a new language.

12.12 Acknowledgments

The research and writing of this chapter were supported by grants from National Science Foundation (Grant No. CDA-9726363, Grant No. BCS-9905176, Grant No. IIS-0086107), Public Health Service (Grant No. PHS R01 DC00236), a Cure Autism Now Foundation Innovative Technology Award, and the University of California, Santa Cruz (Cota-Robles Fellowship). The authors would like to thank Maureen Stone for valuable collaboration on implementing the EPG and Ultrasound measurements, Eric Vatikiotis-Bateson for hosting us for the Optotrak recordings, and Slim Ouni for help on the manuscript.

13 Empirical perceptual-motor linkage of multimodal speech

E. Vatikiotis-Bateson and K. G. Munhall

13.1 Introduction

The view that speech perception and speech production are closely linked is not new and has taken many forms. Stetson (1928) depicted speech as "movements made audible". For Alvin Liberman and colleagues at Haskins Laboratories the production system was integrated with speech perception (Liberman *et al.* 1967). As Liberman (1996) has said:

In all communication, sender and receiver must be bound by a common understanding about what counts; what counts for the sender must count for the receiver, else communication does not occur. Moreover the processes of production and perception must somehow be linked; their representation must, at some point . . . , be the same. (p. 31)

Liberman was wise in his use of "at some point" in the quote above, because the actual relation between perception and production is still largely a mystery. Neither an explicit process nor a neurological mechanism for this linkage in speech has yet been demonstrated; this is despite the discovery of mirror neurons (Rizzolatti *et al.* 1996a), which has created excitement about the action–perception linkage, but has done little to characterize it. In part, brain function studies have glossed over the fact until recently, mainly because production and perception have not been and could not be examined together. Despite their insistence that speech perception is informed by the time-varying characteristics of the vocal tract Liberman and his colleagues (Liberman *et al.* 1967) never examined the link between production data and perception. Indeed they often did not use production-based stimuli for their perception studies, preferring instead to use synthesized speech continua that manipulated formant values, durations, and other parameters useful in determining perceptual category boundaries.

In this chapter, we describe a research paradigm we have developed over the past decade that provides a methodologically sound framework for examining the production and perception of multimodal (auditory and visual) speech together. Briefly, the system entails:

1 the analysis of measured physical structures such as the face and head during speech behavior,

2 an animation system *driven* by both static and time-varying data to produce linguistically realistic talking heads,
3 audiovisual perception experiments whose stimuli consist of synthesized and/or modified natural talking heads.

As we have started to work on these issues, our data-driven animation system was unique in its scope and perceptual validation. Massaro's parameter face model – *Baldi* – predated and indeed inspired our efforts (Massaro and Cohen 1993). *Baldi* was validated perceptually, but was not driven by measured production data. Thankfully, there are now other groups in both the science and entertainment industries that have developed talking head systems that take measured data as input and produce linguistically interpretable output (see Bailly *et al.*, this volume).

13.2 The perception of audiovisual speech

More than fifty years ago, Sumby and Pollack (1954) showed that the intelligibility of speech presented in noisy acoustic conditions was significantly higher when subjects could see the speaker talking. Indeed, this early work underscores most, if not all, of the work presented in this volume. A second critical discovery was reported about 20 years later by McGurk and MacDonald (1976). The so-called McGurk effect, or fusion illusion, occurs when a subject is presented with auditory and visual stimuli corresponding to different speech utterances and perceives something which is neither one. The most consistently tested example is presentation of auditory [bɑ] and visual [gɑ] resulting in perceived /dɑ/ or /ðɑ/.[1]

Sumby and Pollack's work had the important, if now obvious, ramification that speech production must have visual characteristics, though it in no way defined what these characteristics are or what their source might be. As an extreme example of the power of visible events in perceiving audiovisual (AV) speech, the late Christian Benoît's group at the former ICP in Grenoble demonstrated that speech intelligibility is enhanced by the addition of unrealistic visible components such as disembodied lips and/or a skeletal jaw (for overview, see Benoît and Le Goff 1998). Minimally, Benoît's results suggest that speech intelligibility can be enhanced by visible events that have the temporal synchronization and spatial scaling appropriate to the opening and closing of the vocal tract. This line of reasoning has been significantly extended by the work on *cued speech* carried out subsequently by Benoît's colleagues (see Beautemps *et al.*, this volume).

Enhancement to intelligibility can also come from contextualizing events such as the prosodic and paralinguistic structures that help perceivers attend to the degraded acoustic signal and thereby retrieve more of the phonetic content. Indeed, research by Munhall and colleagues (Munhall *et al.* 2004a) has demonstrated how head motion facilitates lexical recovery in audiovisual Speech-in-Noise (SPIN) tasks similar to the paradigm pioneered by Sumby and Pollack in 1954. Unlike the McGurk and MacDonald finding, which implicates visual characteristics at the level of segmental phonetics – e.g., /bɑ/, /gɑ/, /ðɑ/, it is highly unlikely that head motion conveys information about lexical identity. Rather, Munhall *et al.* may have identified a more fundamental role of the head in aligning the perceiver to the signal, a process that must occur in order for a perceiver to parse a signal at finer degrees of spatial and temporal detail.

A third important antecedent to the work described in this chapter was that of Brooke, Summerfield and colleagues who examined many facets of the visual gain to speech intelligibility (Summerfield 1987; Summerfield *et al.* 1989). Their use of quantized image sequences of the lips demonstrated that speech intelligibility may be enhanced when the visual information is severely degraded to just a small number of pixels (Brooke 1996). This work provided the starting point for examining the visual contribution of the entire face. Their attempt to divide auditory and visual speech into complementary modalities – visual information about place and manner of articulation (*ba, fa, da*) vs. auditory information about voicing (*pa, ba*) audiovisual speech perception – showed that

- the auditory and visual modalities may provide complementary information to perceivers (Summerfield 1987), such as visible information about place and manner of articulation (ba, fa, da) as opposed to audible information about voicing (ba vs. pa) (Green and Kuhl 1989; Green and Kuhl 1991);
- the visual gain to speech intelligibility when presented with the speech acoustics degraded by masking noise was estimated at 8–10 dB (Summerfield and Assmann 1989);[2]
- speech intelligibility may be enhanced even when the visual information is severely degraded (e.g., by quantization) to just a small number of pixels (Brooke 1996).

Although subsequent research has refined these early statements (see Grant and Seitz 2000), they set the stage for considering how speech production is related to audiovisual perception. In our work, we have insisted that understanding audiovisual perception requires examining audiovisual stimuli not only for their effects on perception but also in terms of their source characteristics – i.e., production. Note however that we state this only as a methodological necessity for examining the correspondence between production and perception. We do not assume that there is a direct linkage between production and perception for speaker-hearers. This compelling concept, which is fundamental to the *motor theory of speech perception* (Liberman *et al.* 1967) and *theory of direct perception* championed by Carol Fowler and colleagues at Haskins Laboratories (Fowler 1986) and elsewhere (Rosenblum 1994) must be tested empirically. In order to do so, we cannot assume a priori that speaker-hearers make use of the apparent direct linkage between the production and perception processes of audiovisual speech.

13.3 Bringing speech production to the face

Throughout most of its modern history the study of speech production has been impeded by the difficult problem of identifying and measuring relevant events that cannot be observed directly. The production of speech sounds in which the acoustic result is derivative of the production process, entails coordinated action of the respiratory system to generate the air stream conditions needed for vocal fold vibration at the larynx, and complex neuromuscular control of the vocal tract articulators – such as the tongue, lips, jaw, and velum – that shape the vocal tract continuously through time. Indeed, the measurement of the tongue, arguably the most physiologically complex and important vocal tract articulator, has yet to be adequately observed despite the development of numerous X-ray, electromagnetic, and ultrasonic techniques for irradiating soft tissue. In short, speech production has been difficult to visualize directly in anything but a very incomplete and piecemeal fashion.

If direct visualization of vocal tract behavior is not feasible, what indirect means might be attainable by examining the visible and audible outputs of the vocal tract? This question is important both practically and theoretically, and is not new. Alexander Melville Bell's *Visible Speech* of 150 years ago was an early commitment to the belief that hearing-impaired speakers could be trained to use visible information about the vocal tract to improve both their production and perception (Bell 1867). Implicit in his system was the hypothesized three-way linkage between vocal tract behavior, visible motions of the orofacial system, and the speech acoustics that we have exploited in the work described in this chapter.

Bell's system was innovative and brilliant, but it failed to consider the linkage from the side of perception; namely, what information about the vocal tract do perceivers (in Bell's case, speechreaders) need in order to recover speech information from the face? Experiments using the Haskins Pattern Playback (Cooper *et al.* 1952) showed the correspondence between time-varying properties of the speech acoustics and perception, and provided the fundamental insight that speaker-hearers have access to time-varying vocal tract information.[3] This notion serves as the entry point for our work with multimodal speech production and perception.

13.4 Auditory-visual speech production

The rapid development of sophisticated means for physiological data measurement and analysis in recent years has led to a plethora of efforts to examine speech production. Some attempts have been made to model the anatomical and physiological structures necessary to understand the neuromotor and biomechanical mechanisms responsible for the organization and control of observable speech behavior – i.e., articulator motion and/or the acoustic output (Muller and MacLeod 1982; Wilhelms-Tricarico 1995; Payan and Perrier 1997; Sanguineti *et al.* 1998; Dang and Honda 2004; Gerard *et al.* 2006; Buchaillard *et al.* 2009). However, many more have focused on the mapping between specific vocal tract behaviors and the resulting speech acoustics (Mermelstein 1973; Titze *et al.* 1995; Story 2009). In the following sections, we summarize a different approach. Our efforts have been directed at understanding the mappings between the articulator and acoustic motion and secondly to characterize this knowledge in a global model of speech production.

13.5 Correspondences of multimodal speech

Strong correspondences exist between the movements of the face and vocal tract, and the speech acoustics. For the most part, these correspondences are highly linear and are easily characterized with linear and/or simple non-linear estimation techniques (Yehia *et al.* 2000). Figure 13.1 schematizes the correspondences that we and our colleagues have examined between the four domains of physiological and acoustic measurement: vocal tract, face and head, speech acoustics, and orofacial muscle activity (*electromyography* – EMG).

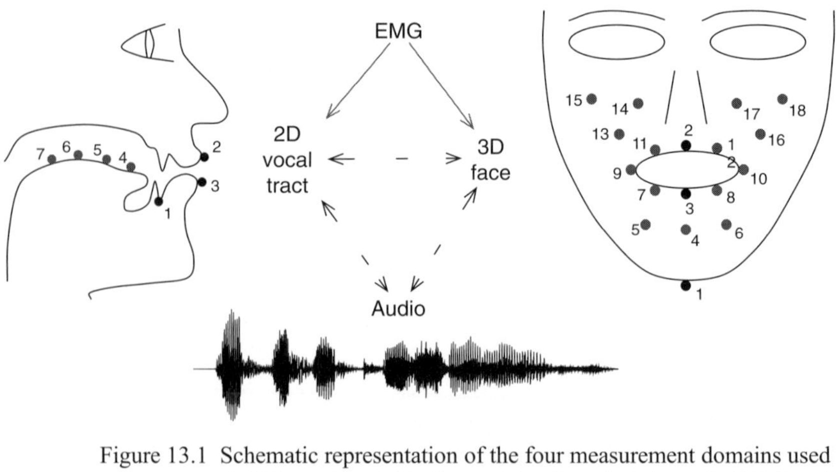

Figure 13.1 Schematic representation of the four measurement domains used in our research: 2D vocal tract, 3D face and head, orofacial muscle EMG, and speech acoustics (adapted from Vatikiotis-Bateson and Yehia 1996).

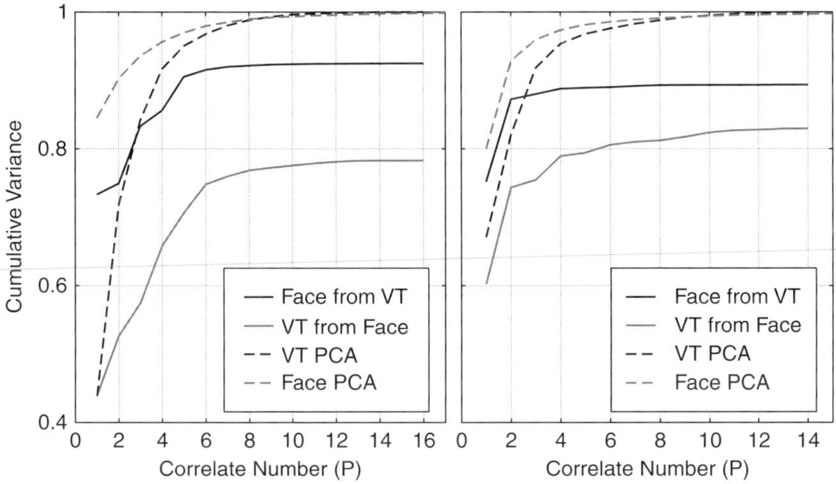

Figure 13.2 Results of within and across domain analysis for a speaker of English (left) and Japanese (right) show the small number of correlates required to characterize multimodal speech data. Dashed lines depict PCA results for recovery of variance within a measurement domain. Solid lines show the extent to which measures in one domain can be estimated from measures of another – e.g., face from vocal tract (adapted from Yehia *et al.* 1998).

Essentially, any signal in one domain can be recovered to a fair extent from signals in any other using multilinear correspondence analyses and simple statistical models such as artificial neural networks. For example, multilinear techniques such as *principal component analysis* (PCA) have been used to estimate face motion reliably from vocal tract articulation and from the speech acoustics and vice versa for speakers of English, French, and Japanese (see Figure 13.2 for speakers of English and Japanese). Thus, motion of vocal tract articulators such as the tongue, lips, and jaw, which we already know can be used to synthesize speech acoustics (Mermelstein 1973), can also be used to estimate face motion at about 95 percent reliability (Yehia *et al.* 1998).

Similarly, intelligible speech acoustics can be recovered from measures of visible motions of the head and face. Using non-linear tools such as an array of simple neural networks, each responsible for estimating a component of the face motion, face motion can be synthesized from the spectral acoustics (Yehia *et al.* 1999). Not surprisingly, the correspondence is strongest for the frequencies in the 2 kHz range, because this is where the second formant (F2) is active, and the second formant is determined by the shape of the front cavity of the vocal tract – in other words that portion of the vocal tract most closely linked to the shape of the visible face. Position and orientation of the head have been shown to be highly correlated with the fundamental frequency (F0) of vocal fold vibration (Yehia *et al.* 2002). In estimating F0 from head motion, orientation is removed and the dimensionality of the 3D position is reduced to one Euclidean path. Finally, moderately accurate estimation of acoustic amplitude requires estimation from both head and face motion. In this way, both the laryngeal source and vocal tract filter components of the acoustics correspond directly to events visible in the motion of the head and face.

Table 13.1 lists the principal findings of the multi-domain analyses that we have examined over the past 15 years. It is important to understand from Table 13.1 that the motion of the face during speech is essentially the inevitable outcome of configuring the vocal tract through time to produce speech acoustics. The jaw, lips, and tongue move continuously producing the necessary vocal tract cavities for vowels and tract constrictions for consonants. Since the face surface is the outer surface of the soft walls of the vocal tract including the lips, it is not surprising that the neuromuscular activity controlling tract configuration has consequences that are inevitably both audible and visible. Thus, from the perspective of speech motor control, the obvious physical and simple statistical connections observed between audible and visible speech suggest that a straightforward linkage exists between the face and vocal tract.

Table 13.1 *Eclectic summary of findings for the analysis of multimodal speech and their causes and/or implications.*

Finding	Cause – Implication
Motions of the lips, cheeks, and chin are highly correlated during speech.	Deformation of the face surface is determined by the time-varying behavior of vocal tract.
Different facial regions are not redundant in their correlation to vocal tract behavior.	The lips alone are not sufficient for specifying the visible correlates of speech production.
Motions of the face, head, and vocal tract are reducible to small numbers of independent correlates.	The dimensionality of the mapping between measurement domains is tractable with simple equations.
Face motion corresponds to the spectral acoustics, head motion to fundamental frequency (F0).	Face and head motion can be synthesized from speech acoustics and vice versa.
Perioral and orofacial muscle EMG corresponds well with both face and vocal tract motion.	Visible speech and vocal tract motions have the same motor source.
Using speech production data to animate realistic talking heads conveys linguistically relevant information to perceivers.	This perceptual evaluation validates a connection between the analysis and perceptibility of visible speech correlates.

13.5.1 Computational model of speech motor control

By the mid 1990s, a number of research groups – e.g., ICP (France), NTT (Japan) – had begun to generate computational models of speech production. At ATR in Japan, Kawato, Vatikiotis-Bateson, and their colleagues made EMG recordings of orofacial muscle activity associated with speech articulation along with measures of articulator motion and the resulting speech acoustics. The muscles recorded were but a small subset of the myriad muscles making up the orofacial system, but they were the muscles typically indicated for

- extrinsic control of tongue position in the oral cavity (e.g., *genioglossus anterior* and *posterior)*,
- opening and closing the jaw (*anterior belly of the digrastic* and *medial pterygoid*),
- combinations of extrinsic (*depressor* and *levator inferiori, mentalis*) and intrinsic (*orbicularis oris inferior* and *superior*) muscles controlling the position and shape of the lips.

Applying a computational paradigm originally developed by Kawato and Uno for the control of arm motion (Uno *et al.* 1989; Kawato 1990), serial strings of phonemes, representative of the cognitive intent to speak, were mapped to intended targets arrayed in vocal tract or articulator space. Artificial neural networks were used to learn the forward dynamics linking recorded muscle activity and articulator acceleration (the second temporal derivative of articulator position). This provided muscle force approximations (in physical systems *Force = Mass x Acceleration)*. When conditioned by an objective function constraining the smoothness of motion trajectories, the muscle force approximation could be used to estimate articulator motion (Hirayama *et al.* 1992). The estimated articulations were then used to estimate vocal tract area functions from which intelligible speech could be synthesized (Hirayama *et al.* 1994); for details and discussion of this approach to speech motor control, see (Munhall *et al.* 2000).

13.5.2 Extending the model to the face

This modeling effort was conceptually promising and mathematically elegant, but it was difficult to make reliable estimates of tongue motion from EMG recordings of two or three extrinsic, but no intrinsic, tongue muscles. Even the measurement of tongue motion was limited to only four or five flesh points on the anterior tongue.[4] The absence of measures of any intrinsic muscles made it impossible to estimate tongue shape, which would have provided the means for specifying relations between the measured flesh points (rather than treating each one independently in the analysis). On the other hand, accurate measures and reliable computational estimates of jaw and lip motion were easily obtained.

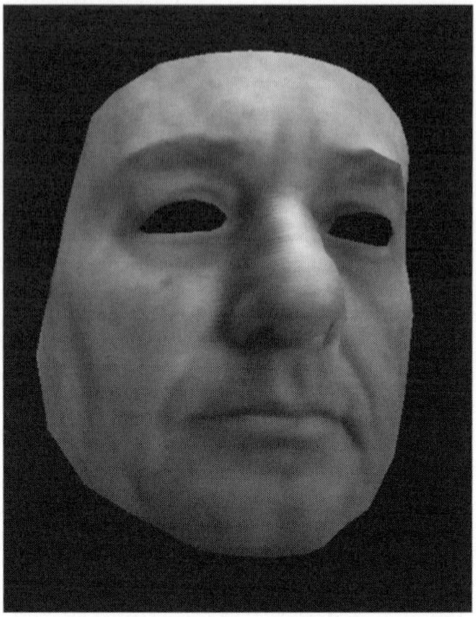

Figure 13.3 A frame taken from EMG-driven animation of the nonsense utterance ['upa] during production of the stressed vowel [u].

Using such measures, it was possible to consider the double role played by the jaw and lips in shaping the vocal tract and deforming the face surface.

Specifically, the same orofacial muscle activity and motion data that were used previously to model the vocal tract were now applied to modeling facial motion. Two approaches to modeling audiovisual speech production using the physiological data measured at ATR were attempted: one was a biomechanical model incorporating stylized skeletal and tissue structures and dynamics; the other was a functional model based on the statistical manipulation of static face shapes and time-varying measures of visible, acoustic, and articulatory events.

The biomechanical model was a modification of the muscle-based face model developed by Terzopoulos and Waters (Waters 1987; Terzopoulos and Waters 1990), initially for synthesizing facial motion from anatomical and physiological data (Terzopoulos and Waters 1993) and later for text-to-audiovisual synthesis (Lee *et al.* 1995b). As of 1995, the model contained twenty-two muscles including the perioral muscles which were added to accommodate our muscle EMG for speech production (see Figure 13.3). However, the model's muscle dynamics had to be completely restructured before the model could synthesize facial motion from muscle EMG input (Vatikiotis-Bateson *et al.* 1996). This was achieved by Lucero and Munhall in Canada (Lucero and Munhall 1999; Pitermann and Munhall 2001), resulting in the best *data driven* animations we have seen to date.

A major difficulty for this approach, as with any *first principles* approach, is the high degree of structural and computational complexity required to create realistic animations. This problem is exacerbated when one must rely on recorded muscle EMG to *drive* the model because it is difficult to obtain and interpret.[5] Therefore, we undertook a statistical approach to characterizing the visual characteristics of speech production that did not rely on complex non-linear estimation techniques and did not require difficult muscle EMG data.

13.6 Talking head animation

In the preceding discussion of the analysis of measured data for facial motion and vocal tract behavior, we focused on the strong correspondence that exists between measurements made in the vocal tract and facial motion domains. During the course of our research, we have also ascertained that phonetically relevant facial motions are slow moving, highly linearized, distributed over large portions of the lower face, and not so difficult to recover from either vocal tract behavior or acoustic signals.

This last point is important because, while the face motion may be the most accessible to measurement and recording, it is the most informationally impoverished of the three domains of speech measurement discussed in this chapter. The signals of both the midsagittal vocal tract and the speech acoustics are both richer than the face motion. Note however, this does not mean that the full richness is easily accessed using our current measurement tools. A small number of flesh point measures of the midsagittal tongue, lips, and jaw provide about the same quality signal as that recovered from the 3D face (Yehia *et al.* 1998).

It is critical therefore to evaluate the quality of the linkage computed between the various measurement domains. Our approach to this has been to synthesize faces from vocal tract and/or acoustic signals and test whether or not the resulting talking head animations contain the same linguistic information as natural talking faces. To this end, a facial animation system was developed whose control parameters are measured data (Kuratate *et al.* 1998; Kuratate *et al.* 2005). The system combines time-varying measures of facial motion and facial deformation parameters extracted from static scans of 3D faces as schematized in Figure 13.4.

Animations created with this system based on recordings of face and head motion and speech acoustics have been evaluated by Munhall and colleagues for intelligibility under conditions of auditory degradation (Munhall *et al.* 2003). Despite many cosmetic deficiencies in the animations such as lack of teeth, visible tongue, and eyes (masked by digital sunglasses), Figure 13.5 shows that the same order of intelligibility gain is obtained for the animations as for natural audiovisual stimuli of the sort originally published by Sumby and Pollack (1954). In addition, these animations demonstrate the importance of the head in lexical recovery.

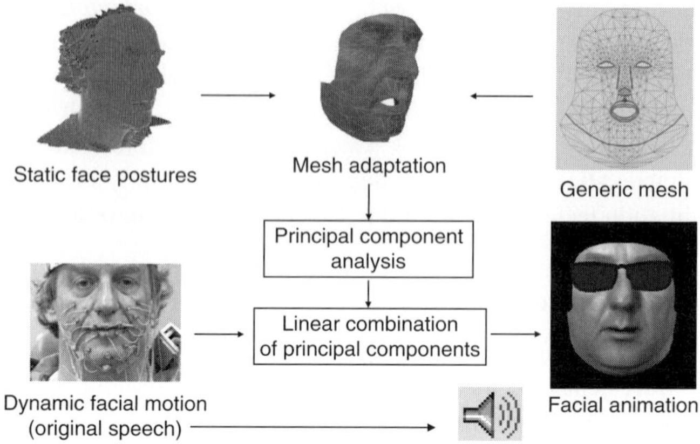

Figure 13.4 Schematic overview of kinematics-based animation. Static 3D head scans for nine expressive postures (top left) are fit with a generic face mesh (top right) in order to compute a small set of geometric deformation parameters for a speaker's face using principal component analysis (PCA). The resulting mean face (middle) is then parameterized frame by frame by the time-varying position of face markers recorded during speech production (bottom left). The video texture map is attached to the deformed mesh for each frame (lower right) and animated along with the speech signal (original or modified).

Parallel studies of brain function during audiovisual perception are being conducted by Callan and colleagues at ATR using fMRI and the same or similar stimuli. Natural and synthetic talking-head stimuli have been examined under various auditory and visual conditions (Callan *et al.* 2003; Callan *et al.* 2004).

13.7 The importance of physical structure

In recent years, much emphasis has been placed on demonstrating the value of time-varying events in modeling the processes of production and perception. In visual perception, the recovery of structure from motion has been demonstrated using random dot stereograms (Julesz and Payne 1968). In the perception of speech acoustics, the same point has been made by Remez and colleagues for spectrally degraded *sinewave synthesis* (Remez *et al.* 1994, see also this volume). As discussed in more detail below, this has been demonstrated elegantly for multimodal speech perception by Rosenblum and colleagues who have used point light displays to demonstrate the sufficiency of time-varying information

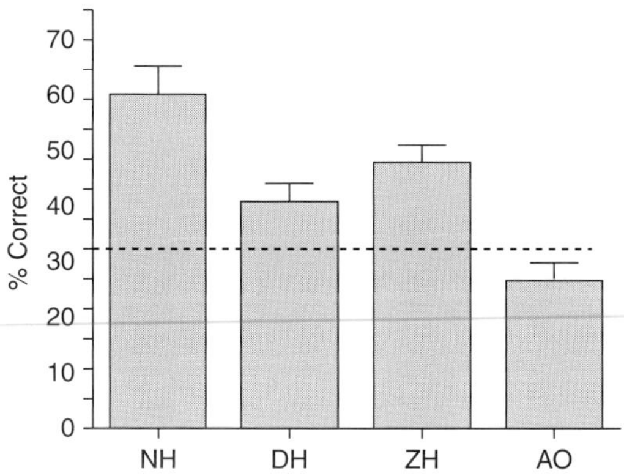

Figure 13.5 Percentages of correctly identified Hiragana (syllabic) characters for Japanese sentences presented under three *degraded audio plus synthetic talking head* conditions – normal head motion (NH), double head motion (DH), and zero head motion (ZH) – and one *degraded audio only* condition (AO). Intelligibility of all multimodal conditions was significantly better than AO (adapted from Munhall *et al.* 2004b). The dashed line is a visual aid for differentiating the audiovisual and audio-only conditions.

in producing the McGurk effect (McGurk and MacDonald 1976, see also chapters by Burnham and Sekiyama and others in this volume). By contrast, the role of the static properties of an object such as shape and texture in conveying linguistically relevant speech information has received relatively little attention only recently (Jordan *et al.* 2000; McCotter and Jordan 2003).

In our work we have championed the importance of time-varying information in characterizing and understanding spoken communication. Now that the validity of dynamic information is no longer in dispute, we have begun to consider what role the physical attributes of speakers play in multimodal speech processing. Ironically, we must first partial out the contribution of the dynamic attributes. Figure 13.6 shows two non-contiguous frames excerpted from a video sequence. Superimposed on the video frames (top row) and shown independently (bottom) are the image motion vectors, computed at 1 cm intervals using *optical flow* (Horn and Schunck 1981). Comparing the motion vector (lower) frames in the figure, it is clear that shape information for the head emerges during motion. What cannot be so easily discerned from the motion, even when viewing the video is that in addition to moving his head, the subject (Christian Benoît) is also speaking.

Is this just a matter of resolution? That is, if motion vectors were computed for each pixel of the image, would viewers then be able to discern the motion of

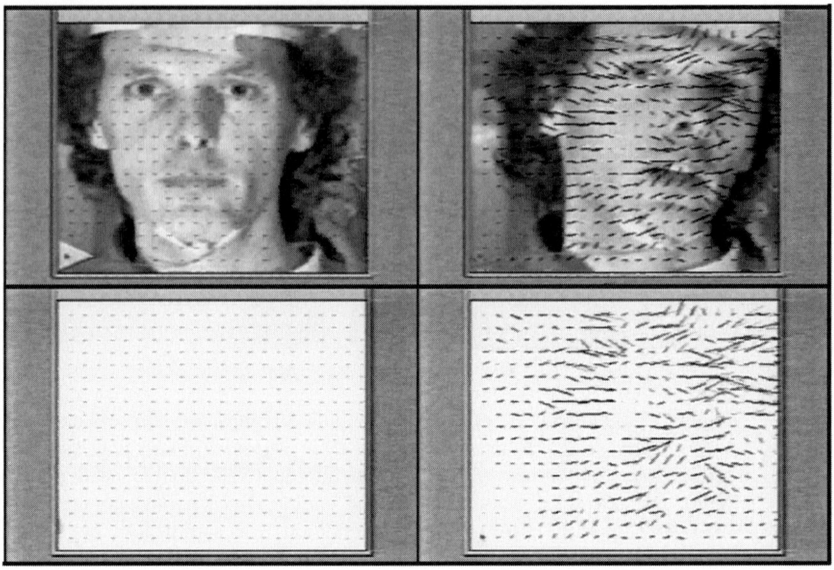

Figure 13.6 Simple depiction using optical flow (velocity vectors scaled) of the importance of structure in motion (top) and motion to recover structure (bottom).

the lips and jaw on the moving head? This is essentially what has been demonstrated by Rosenblum and colleagues using point light displays (Rosenblum *et al.* 1996). With a large number (about 40) of markers placed on the head, around the mouth, on the chin, and even on the teeth, the visual information was sufficient to induce the McGurk effect in viewing listeners. Similar efforts by us using point light displays corresponding to the much smaller sets of markers (11 or 18) used to drive our animations have also shown enhanced intelligibility. This would suggest that resolution is not critical. However, we have so far been unable to replicate the pattern of enhancement effects for face and face-plus-head motion seen by Rosenblum *et al.* for point lights and by us for animated talking heads driven by the same sparse motion data (Munhall *et al.* 2004b).

As discussed in the next section, data resolution per se is probably not the issue, but it may be confounded by the necessity for point light displays to be perceived as face objects in order to obtain the same visual enhancement pattern seen for animations and natural faces. There may be some minimum point density required for point light arrays to be perceived as faces. This is what we believe underlies the Rosenblum *et al.* results. If true, then both motion and structure are necessary to inform speech perception.

13.7.1 The effects of spatial and temporal filtering on perception

An implication of the previous discussion is that it is the motion of structures (rather than the motion of points) that is key to visual perception of speech, and that the resolution of the motion of those structures need not be very high. Our first indication that high spatial resolution might not be necessary for audio-visual perception came when we examined perceiver eye motion (Vatikiotis-Bateson *et al.* 1998). Perceivers continued to foveate on the speaker's eyes for substantial periods of time across a range of degraded auditory (speech in noise) and visual (image size) conditions.

At that time, we surmised that perceivers may exploit fine-grained temporal information instead of fine-grained spatial information. However, recent studies conducted by us and our students suggest that neither the spatial nor the temporal resolution needs to be fine-grained for perceivers to recover the visual speech information. In one study (Munhall *et al.* 2004c), video image sequences were spatially filtered using band-pass (one octave in width) and low-pass filters, and presented with noise-degraded audio. Band-pass filtering demonstrated that linguistic information exists at a range of spatial frequencies, peaking between 5.5 and 11 cycles per face (c/f), but continuing into the higher frequencies. No frequency band afforded full recovery of the visual information, so we could not know to what extent the information at any given frequency was complementary or redundant to any other. Use of low-pass filters, whose cut offs corresponded to the upper boundary of each band-pass filter, demonstrated that perceivers could recover all of the visual speech information from video low-pass filtered at 7.3 c/f, which is the upper bound of the 5.5 c/f band-pass filter shown in Figure 13.7.

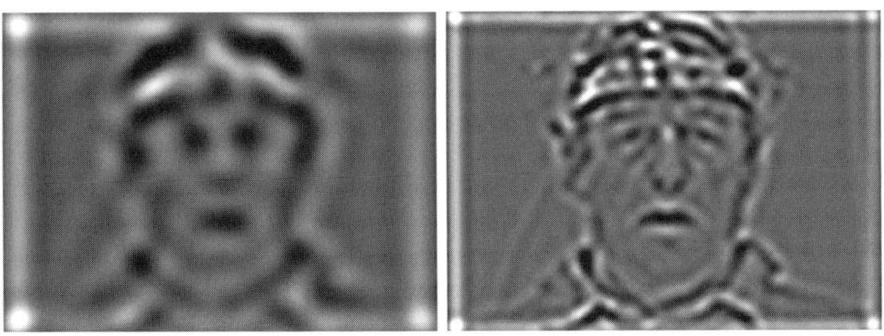

Figure 13.7 Shown are images band-pass filtered at the two lowest spatial resolutions. At 2.7 c/f, no information is recovered by perceivers, and for the 5.5 c/f face less than full recovery is attained. When these two center frequencies are combined into one low-pass filtered image sequence, full recovery of the speech information is achieved.

The Munhall *et al.* findings for spatial frequency in English have been replicated for Japanese and Portuguese and extended to the temporal domain by de Paula *et al.* (2006). Earlier work by Vitkovich and Barber (1994) had suggested that visual speech information becomes degraded at frame rates lower than about 15 frames per second (fps). However, in that study, lower frame rates were obtained by frame decimation. It is a well-known legacy of the film industry that frame rates below 16 fps flicker and look choppy because of the transport time between frames during which the image is black. Therefore, in constructing the stimuli for de Paula's studies, temporal information was removed without reducing the frame rate.

De Paula's results confirmed our suspicion that frame decimation introduces a confound. When there is no flicker, the degradation of speech information begins between 9 and 12 fps, a substantially slower frame rate than the 16 fps observed by Vitkovich and Barber (1994). Note that this lower rate matches the 9 Hz cut-off frequency found to provide the strongest correspondences between the speech acoustics and motions of the vocal tract, face, and head (Yehia *et al.* 2002). We believe both phenomena to be related to the fact that is also the event rate for opening and closing the vocal tract (corresponding to syllable rates of 4.5–6 Hz).

13.7.2 Non-face faces: the case of talking cuboids

Another indication of the importance of structure in processing visual speech information is provided by Harold Hill's work at ATR with *cuboids*. Cuboids are animations of cubical heads incorporating the same kinematic data for motion of the head, lips, and jaw that was used to animate the linguistically informative Talking Heads discussed earlier. Perceivers were shown cuboids animated with every possible combination of motion data components (e.g., head + lips, jaw alone) and presented with noise-degraded audio (cf. Figure 13.8).

Using the same Japanese sentences that Munhall *et al.* used to study head motion effects (Munhall *et al.* 2004b), a fundamentally different result was obtained for the cuboids. Across all conditions, only the lips enhanced intelligibility (by about 10 percent). It is also interesting that the jaw, which is the strongest contributor to facial deformation for this speaker (Kuratate *et al.* 1998), makes no contribution when implemented in the cuboid animation. It may be that the jaw's contribution to perception is quite different than its contribution to face deformation. What is needed is a similarly systematic test of the contributing kinematic components using the talking head animation system; but it is clear, at least, that the difference in structure between a face and a cuboid does influence the recovery and perhaps the visibility of visual speech information.

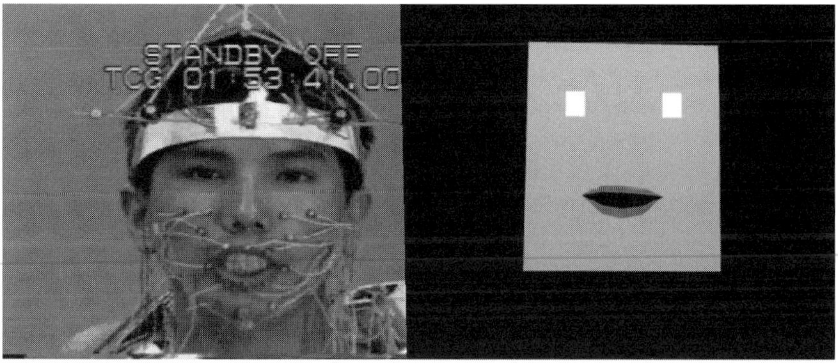

Figure 13.8 The original 3D position data were recorded using OPTOTRAK. Markers on the head rig, the chin, and around the border of the lips (left) were used to animate the cuboid (right).

13.7.3 The role of constant features in speech perception

The results of auditory and audiovisual studies examining speaker characteristics such as age, gender, and familiarity have been highly variable.[6] Examinations of language and ethnicity differences have also proved controversial. For example, Sekiyama and Tohkura (1993) proposed a language effect on audiovisual perception by showing that Japanese perceivers do not make as much use of visual speech information when perceiving Japanese as they do when listening to other languages such as English. On the other hand, Massaro and colleagues found audiovisual performance for perceivers of the two languages to be about equal (Massaro *et al.* 1993; Sekiyama and Tohkura 1993).

Part of the problem may be due to confusion about where to look for and how to classify linguistic and constant, non-linguistic features. Much has been made of the dynamism of speech behavior for both production and perception (Remez *et al.* 1994). It is clear that many non-linguistic features are also inherently dynamic. Expressive gestures such as smile, discourse-related eye-blinks, and emphatic use of the eyebrows are all dynamic. But there are more subtle links as well. For example, perceivers can extract identity information from time-varying speech behavior in one modality and apply it to speech behavior in another modality (Kamachi *et al.* 2003; Lachs and Pisoni 2004; Rosenblum *et al.* 2006). Crucial to the cross-modal identification is not the content of the speech, but rather the manner in which it is produced (Lander *et al.* 2007); identification succeeds only when the manner (e.g., casual vs. careful speech) of the two productions is the same.[7]

Although little more than speculation at this stage, we want to emphasize that time-varying behavior is produced by physical structures that have static properties that shape both the range and time-course of possible deformations. We tend to forget this because important static properties such as the age, ethnicity, and gender of a person, which can be readily discerned from a photograph, are assumed to have either constant influence on speech behavior (age, gender) or none at all (ethnicity). This assumption may stem from the tradition of considering only the auditory modality, perhaps non-trivially reinforced in recent years by ethics review boards that steer science away from such classifications. The status of static properties becomes less clear when multimodal perception is considered. For example, as a physical account for the Sekiyama and Tohkura (1993) result, it has been argued that the broader, flatter, and smoother surface of Japanese faces provides fewer contrasts and therefore conveys less visual speech information (Hiki and Fukuda 1996).

In order to begin assessing the integration of visible structural properties of the face and head with time-varying audiovisual speech behavior, a large database of 3D full-head scans was constructed at ATR International beginning in 1999 (Vatikiotis-Bateson *et al.* 1999). The database now consists of scan sets for more than 500 subjects: ethnic Caucasian and Japanese males and females (Kuratate and Vatikiotis-Bateson 2004). Each subject's scan set consists of nine orofacial postures represented as a facial mesh containing approximately 500 nodes and several reference features (e.g., eyes, lips, hairline). These are the postures used for generating the facial deformation parameters of the talking head animation system (Kuratate *et al.* 2005), and are the result of differences in both the structural morphology and the interpretation of instructions such as "smile with your mouth closed."

Just as PCA reduces the dimensionality of the postural data to a mere handful of principal components for generation of linguistically realistic animations, gender and ethnicity can also be distinguished (Figure 13.9), but not with the same degree of independence (orthogonality) of components (Vignali *et al.* 2003). Furthermore, perceivers have difficulty correctly identifying the gender and ethnicity of faces re-synthesized from the reduced set of components. In order to match the structural decomposition to perceiver judgments, more sophisticated decomposition of the database is required. In particular, *linear discriminant analysis* (LDA) recovers about 70 percent of the variability in gender and ethnicity with two non-orthogonal components. As shown in Figure 13.10, *multiple discriminant analysis* gives even better results, recovering about 95 percent of the postural variability using two components, and corresponds better to perceiver judgments (Vignali *et al.* 2003).

Mining the database for structural features corresponding to ethnicity, gender, and facial postures is only a small, preliminary part of its usefulness. These can now be used to create both naturalistic and systematically distorted

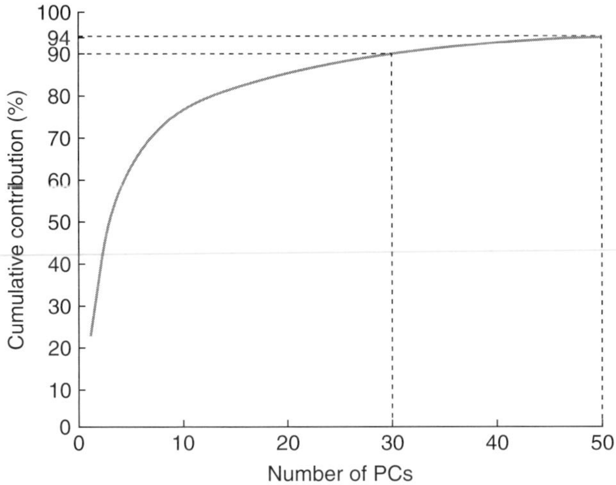

Figure 13.9 The cumulative contribution of ranked components (PCA) to the variance of 2700 3D face scans (300 subjects × 9 postures)

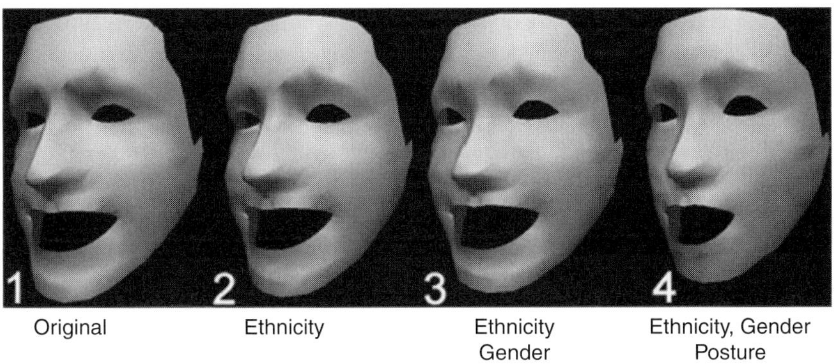

Figure 13.10 *Multiple discriminant analysis* (MDA) computed for the entire 3D face database recovers 95 percent of the variability for any posture of any subject (1, 4) using two components corresponding to ethnicity (2) and gender (3).

animations from time-varying input of audiovisual behavior (Kuratate *et al.* 2005). Talking head stimuli can be generated that mix the motion data for one speaker and the facial deformation parameters of another. Just as easily, the structural parameters can be distorted along individual dimensions (e.g., smiling, gender) or in combination in producing talking head stimuli for perceptual evaluation. It is our hope that systematic examination of the controllable parameters of the facial structure will provide at least a partial answer to how speech behavior, expressive gesture, and physical structure contribute to the production and perception of multimodal communicative behavior.

13.8 Communicative versus cosmetic realism

Substantial advances have been made by the entertainment industry to meet the challenges posed by naturalistic animation of humans and other animals, realistic or imaginary. Interestingly, there has been less success with realistic animation of speaking characters. There is a trade-off between the acceptability of the animated speech and the realism of the speaker. Cartoon characters can talk all they want and we are amused. Yet, when a video realistic character is synthesized, the speech becomes jarring if viewed for more than a few seconds at a time. This conundrum, undoubtedly related to the *uncanny valley* phenomenon coined by Masahiro Mori in describing human responses to realistic humanoid robots, continues to plague filmmakers even today in generating video realistic humans using computer graphics. Even a decade ago, perceptual evaluations of talking heads, when conducted at all, went no further than "How does it look?" Such sacrifice of communicative realism in favor of cosmetic realism received a positive response so long as shots were kept very short (1–2 seconds). In recent years, however, Hollywood has shifted its focus back to communicative realism, as *computer graphics imagery* (CGI) has become the cost-effective way to generate special effects in an ever-widening sphere of physically impossible realities. Now, entire films are animated using high-quality 3D motion capture of body motion, facial expressions, and even speech. It is no longer acceptable for characters to speak away from the camera or for very short periods of time. Now, the sacrifice has been reversed as video realism of the actors is replaced by increasing degrees of communicative realism. The realism of the speech in films such as *Avatar*, released in 2009, is at least as good as anything we have done in the speech science community, but the characters doing the speech are no longer video realistic representations of the actors doing the talking.

In this chapter, we have described work that addresses the question, "How can linguistically relevant speech information be characterized and transmitted auditorily and visually?" In fine-tuning our animation system to produce linguistically veridical talking heads, we have focused on correcting mapping errors between physical measures and model parameters such as the nodes of the face mesh. We have also optimized our data collection to provide maximum range with minimum additional computation – not to save computation time, but to reduce the error inevitably introduced by additional computation. So, for example, we reduced the set of scanned 3D faces used to estimate the facial deformation parameters from 28 to 9 postures. Finally, we have avoided attempting to model anything that we cannot model properly and that is not essential. Teeth and eyes are extremely difficult to do even with a team of CGI experts, and it is not clear that parameter models can get them right without hand tuning.

Thus, our animations are linguistically informative and we avoid the uncanny valley by sparse representation of the finer details of the face. One of the greatest challenges has been the modeling of the lips, which are critical cosmetically and communicatively. The position data used to animate the lips typically are recorded at the vermilion borders that separate the lips from the rest of the face. Unfortunately, measures made at these borders are almost uncorrelated with the inner dimensions of the lips, and especially the size and shape of the oral aperture (Munhall *et al.* 1994). In order to specify the shape of the inner lip surfaces, either an internal structure model or some indirect means of estimating lip shape over time is needed. Without either, the lips tend to be more rigid than they should be, and their range of motions smaller than in reality.

In order to examine the hypothesized trade-off between cosmetic quality and intelligibility, we attempted to "improve" lip behavior in the animations by adding texture and kinematic constraints on velocity and acceleration to lip shape. The resulting lips "looked better" both statically and when animated. However, when these new animations were presented to perceivers in a preliminary *Speech-In-Noise* (SPIN) task, the intelligibility results were not impressive.[8] Figure 13.11 is presented for illustration only. Since the experimental conditions (e.g., number of stimulus categories) and the posture sets used to compute the static deformation parameters of the face are different for the two studies, we cannot say for certain at this time that the cosmetically improved animations on the right are less intelligible than the unimproved ones on the left. We believe that a proper test will show this to be the case, because of relatively small enhancement of the NH (normal head motion) condition compared to the AO (audio alone) condition. In previous studies, we have shown 9-posture deformation sets to generate more accurate animations than the 28-posture set shown (Vatikiotis-Bateson *et al.* 1999) and the enhancement of intelligibility for normal head motion to be at least as good or better than the NH condition shown for the 28-posture set here (Munhall *et al.* 2004c).

One obvious reason why adding kinematic constraints might reduce the relevant speech information in the modified animations is that the kinematic constraints distort the motion capture data for the lips, smoothing and reducing the range of motion of any given mesh node. It may also be that the contribution of the recorded lip motion to speech perception is already close to threshold for having any effect at all. Five years ago, we could barely obtain perceptual validation of any animation. Enough progress has been made since then that we (and many others) can now consider more elaborate questions. It is unlikely that

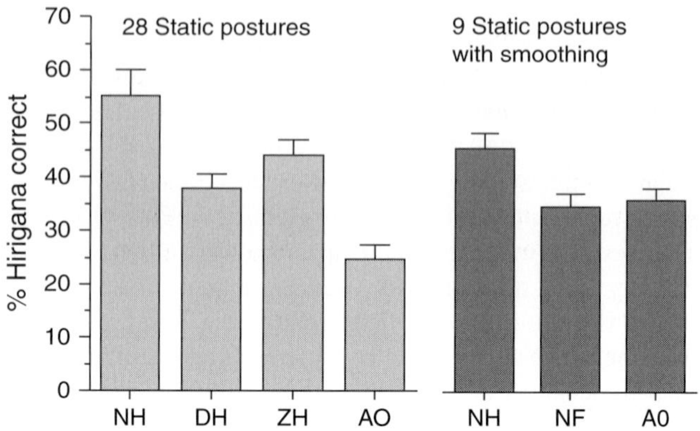

Figure 13.11 Intelligibility results for Japanese sentences animated from the same motion data, but with different sets of postures defining the facial deformation space and with kinematic constraints added to the lips for the set on the right. These sets should not be compared (see text).

communicative and cosmetic realism are simply orthogonal to each other. In all likelihood, it is just the reverse; namely, cosmetic and communicative features reinforce or blend into one another. Clearly, these two domains need to be examined together, but to do so will require the collaboration of the entertainment industry, whose resources span a much broader range of science and art than most academic and even industrial research settings can afford. If achieved, such collaboration would serve the entire spectrum of research and commercial applications, including a major one in the entertainment industry – the animation of talking faces that incorporate the dynamic and static characteristics of specific actors *and* convey linguistically relevant information.

13.9 Summary

In this chapter, we have described our approach to examining the production and perception of multimodal speech. The key feature of the approach has been to forge an empirical link between production and perception by using the data of production in a controlled manner as stimuli for perceptual evaluation. Our aim has been to keep things as simple as possible so that we can understand them and so that we can progress in an orderly fashion. That is, by using multilinear processes to the greatest extent possible, rather than more opaque non-linear estimations such as those provided by artificial neural networks, we have made modest sense of our observations of structure, function, and behavior across a wide range of measurement domains, including brain function (fMRI), neuromotor activity (EMG), vocal tract, orofacial, and head motions, and the speech acoustics. In the time it has taken to prepare this volume for publication, other research groups have made significant strides in extending this approach or in developing their own approaches. There are now myriad commercial applications for facial animation from motion capture data or more abstract inputs such as text that enable different and often more elaborate questions to be asked such as how orofacial speech behavior and other components of communicative expression are integrated in production and processed in perception.

13.10 Acknowledgments

Both authors acknowledge the generous support of ATR throughout development of this research. In particular, we thank S. Yano, Y. Tohkura, K. Shimohara, M. Kawato for their intellectual humor and support. We also are indebted to all the researchers and students we have had the good fortune to work with at ATR, Queen's University, and Haskins Laboratories. These include Takaaki Kuratate, Hani Yehia, Daniel Callan, Jeffrey Jones, Christian Kroos, Greg Jozan, Hugo de Paula, Guillaume Vignali, and Inge-Marie Eigsti. Grant support was provided by NSERC (Canada), NIH (USA), and TAO/NICT (Japan).

14 Sensorimotor characteristics of speech production

G. Bailly, P. Badin, L. Revéret, and A. Ben Youssef

14.1 Introduction

The production of speech sounds, in which the acoustics results from the production process, entails coordinated action of the respiratory system to generate the air stream conditions needed for vocal fold vibration at the larynx, and complex neuromuscular control of the vocal tract articulators – such as the tongue, lips, jaw, and velum – that shape the vocal tract continuously through time. When we speak, we have access to a large variety of signals that inform us about the current state variables of the production process. These somesthetic signals include motor commands available as copies of efferent[1] motorneural commands, proprioceptive signals that for example give access to muscular elongation or acoustic structure via tissue vibration and haptic signals delivered by surface tissues, as well as exteroceptive acoustic information delivered by the ears. When we speak, the interlocutor has access to exteroceptive acoustic and visual information about our articulation. Thus both speakers and listeners have access to a great variety of redundant and complementary information associated with speech movements.

In this chapter, we describe and discuss approaches to examining the visible characteristics of speech production and their link with other sensory information, in particular articulation and acoustics.

14.2 Speech maps

A sensorimotor representation of speech movements that links causes and effects, somesthetic and exteroceptive signals, in a coherent and comprehensive quantitative mapping, is a prerequisite for language learning. These predictive *speech maps* (Abry *et al.* 1994; Abry and Badin 1996; Bailly 1997) are central to language acquisition, articulatory planning, and multimodal perception; they enable the comparison of sensory requirements with motor plans, the adjustment of motor plans to sensory requirements or environmental conditions, as well as the fusion of partial multimodal components using a priori information.

The articulatory-to-acoustic map The most studied speech map is the *articulatory-to-acoustic* mapping. This articulatory-to-acoustic map is central to the controversy on the nature of speech representation. *Motor* theories (Mattingly and Studdert-Kennedy 1991) suppose that the objective of speech perception is to recover the underlying organization of articulatory gestures. As a result these theories are confronted with the problem of acoustic-to-articulatory inversion (Bailly *et al.* 1991). *Direct* theories (Fowler 1996) suppose also that we do have access to the "objects" producing the sounds but via a direct association between each object and its sensitive properties that requires neither a priori experience nor understanding of the production process. *Auditory* theories (Stevens 1989a) suppose that in their acoustic forms sounds are sufficiently distinguishable (Sussman *et al.* 1991) and that the objective of speech perception is to extract robust acoustic features. However auditory theories should also propose a framework for learning articulatory control that ought at some stage to include the acquisition of an articulatory-to-acoustic map. Being able to recover articulation from its audible consequences seems thus essential for language acquisition and motor control.

The articulatory-to-visual map It is also clear that vision can help this recovery. Neither motor nor auditory theories incorporate, however, the visual dimension in their framework. Perception experiments and developmental studies have nevertheless shown that speech is clearly multimodal. While hearing-impaired people can supplement the impoverished auditory signal with lipread information, listeners with good hearing also integrate visual speech information in a noisy environment (Sumby and Pollack 1954; Erber 1975). Even with a clear auditory source, this integration can help comprehension, especially when listening to a foreign language or a passage with difficult semantic content (Reisberg *et al.* 1987). The McGurk illusion (McGurk and MacDonald 1976) shows that we simply cannot avoid this innate audiovisual integration. Language acquisition studies also show that speech development is significantly affected by a visual impairment; whereas bilabials are clearly predominant in early speech (Vihman *et al.* 1985) and reinforced in hearing-impaired children (Stoel-Gammon 1988), they are less predominant in the first words of the blind child (Mulford 1988). Moreover, audiovisual integration is crucial for localization and attention; both children and adults are very sensitive to audiovisual discrepancies (Dodd 1979; Rosenblum *et al.* 1997).

14.3 Degrees-of-freedom in a speech task

The causal chain of audiovisual speech production is relatively complex and seems highly non-linear. First, motor neurons set a minimal length of the muscle above which the muscle generates force (Feldman 1986; Leedham and Dowling 1995). The force/length relationship is almost linear for small movements, but saturates for a higher stretching of the muscle. Displacements of insertion points of the muscles and muscle tissues properties such as volume conservation produce changes of the vocal tract shape and the facial geometry. The relationship between muscle activations and lengths and geometric changes is again highly non-linear, due to the nature of both the coupling between muscle tissue and skin, and the viscoelastic properties of soft tissue. Additional sources of non-linearity are contact between visible organs (such as those involved in bilabials) or between deeper organs (such as contact between the teeth, the cheeks, the lips, or the tongue). Furthermore, the movements can be audible and visible, partially or completely inaudible or invisible, or both.

We will show in the following that, despite both this expected highly non-linear mapping between muscular activations and their audible/visible consequences, and the huge dimensionality of the state variables that describe the speech production system, (1) statistical analysis of the experimental data can uncover systematic sources of variation that can be identified and accounted for by a small number of basic gestures, and (2) all movements of the biomechanical system can be approximated as a linear combination of such basic gestures.

14.3.1 Degrees-of-freedom

Statisticians use the expression "degrees-of-freedom" (*dof*) to describe the number of variables in the final calculation of a statistics that are free to vary. The lack of a priori knowledge about the observed phenomenon is often compensated for by a statistically strong but often physically plausible assumption of independence between these variables. As regards the sensorimotor maps that organize state variables of the production process within causal relations, one may ask whether the "natural" variables within a map (for example, efferent motor commands of every muscle of the speech apparatus) can be considered as *dof*. This is certainly not the case: first of all because of physical constraints such as the limited elasticity and the relative incompressibility of human tissue; secondly because structural arrangements of the musculoskeletal system impose biomechanical coupling between muscles and organs. Finally, as emphasized by Kelso and colleagues (Kugler *et al.* 1980; Kelso *et al.* 1986), the speech production apparatus is made of a large number of neuromuscular components that offer a potentially huge dimensionality and which must be functionally coupled in order to produce relatively simple gestures. Maeda (1991) refers to a similar concept in terms of elementary articulators.

One *independent dof* may be more precisely defined for a given speech articulator as one variable that can control completely a specific variation of shape and position of this articulator, and that is statistically independent of the other *dof* over a set of tasks. The *dof* are thus highly dependent on the tasks considered. Here we will focus on *dof* of articulatory and facial movement related to speech.

14.3.2 Degrees-of-freedom and speech maps

We can identify the *dof* of most state variables of the speech production system including motor commands, vocal tract geometry, facial deformation, and acoustic structure using statistical analysis. Once the proper *dof* have been identified in each map, the speech production system is characterized by independent state variables in each map, and statistical models of sensorimotor links between the maps can be built (see for example the currently popular Bayesian framework in Ruiz *et al.* 1998; Thrun 1998). These mappings treat the speech production system as a black box fed by motor commands that act on the system and its environment, and which receives sensory input of the consequences of these actions. When sensory inputs are direct consequences of the motor commands, the mapping constitutes a *forward model* that is supposed to be an abstract representation of the underlying physical system – or physical *plant* in terms of robotics (Jordan and Rumelhart 1991). When some characteristics of the plant are known, it seems reasonable to drive this forward mapping with explicit causal relations inferred from the plant. Obvious examples for speech are bilabial or tongue-tip trills that a naive interpretation would identify as being controlled by individual voluntary lip contractions and releases, while they are actually controlled by only one gesture involving an adequate equilibrium between lip contraction and intraoral pressure (McGowan 1992; Abry *et al.* 1998). Another example is the intrinsic ability of the jaw to control the global shape of the vocal tract and organize speech rhythm (MacNeilage and Davis 1990; Studdert-Kennedy 1991). Jaw movement is a major determinant of facial deformation, and the *dof* of such underlying articulators should not be forgotten when analyzing movements of speech organs and/or facial deformations.

We describe below models of underlying speech organs and facial deformation and identify their *dof* for speech. The taxonomy of models adopted here is common to both internal and external models. We distinguish three sorts of models: (1) *geometric models*, where geometric parameters are identified as *dof* of elementary points of the mesh describing the surface of the articulators and produce ad hoc deformations of a certain number of neighboring vertices, (2) *biomechanical models* where the musculoskeletal system underlying the movements is clearly identified, and (3) *functional models* where the *dof* emerge from the analysis of corpora of data associated with task-specific mesh deformations.

14.4 Models of the underlying speech organs

Despite numerous studies on 3D models of the face and lips, work on 3D models of the underlying speech organs is scarce and rarely covers the deformation of the 3D vocal tract.

14.4.1 Geometric models

Most geometrical models of the tongue shape have been determined using midsagittal contours of the tongue obtained by X-ray technology. The first 2D articulatory models of the underlying speech organs were geometrical; the degrees of freedom of the articulatory plant were decided a priori and fitted to the data a posteriori (Coker 1968; Liljencrants 1971; Mermelstein 1973). The very few 3D geometrical models of the tongue built so far follow this two-step procedure. Based on Stone *et al.*'s ultrasonic tongue surface data (1990; 1996), Cohen *et al.* (1998) developed a 3D tongue model made of a polygon surface defined by sagittal and coronal b-spline curves. The dimensionality of the control parameters is very high (9 sagittal and 21 coronal parameters). A functional model was then further developed (see Section 14.4.3 below); a minimization algorithm was thus used to fit parts of the synthetic 3D tongue geometry to 3D ultrasound measurements of tongue surfaces for 18 sustained vocalizations of English vowels and consonants (Stone and Lundberg 1996) and high-level speech articulation control parameters have been identified and further linked to the original b-spline control parameters (see Massaro *et al.*, this volume).

14.4.2 Biomechanical models

Following Perkell's development (1974) of a midsagittal biomechanical model of the tongue, Kiritani and colleagues (1976) developed what appears to be the first 3D biomechanical tongue model. This simple model is constructed of 14 hexaedra defined by 24 nodes; *finite element modeling* (FEM) is used to implement simple linear isotropic elastic properties of muscles as well as volume conservation. In this simple model, the number of potential control parameters (contraction of each vertex) is of the same order of magnitude as the number of nodes. Hashimoto and Suga (1986) also use a 3D tongue model made of 170 nodes and where 13 independent muscles can be controlled to fit X-ray contours of vowels. More recently Wilhelms-Tricarico (1995) designed a 3D model of the tongue with more sophisticated tissue simulation, including 8 independent muscles and 42 elements.

Dang and Honda (1998; 2004) also developed a quasi-3D physiologically based articulatory model of tongue, jaw, and vocal tract wall, based on

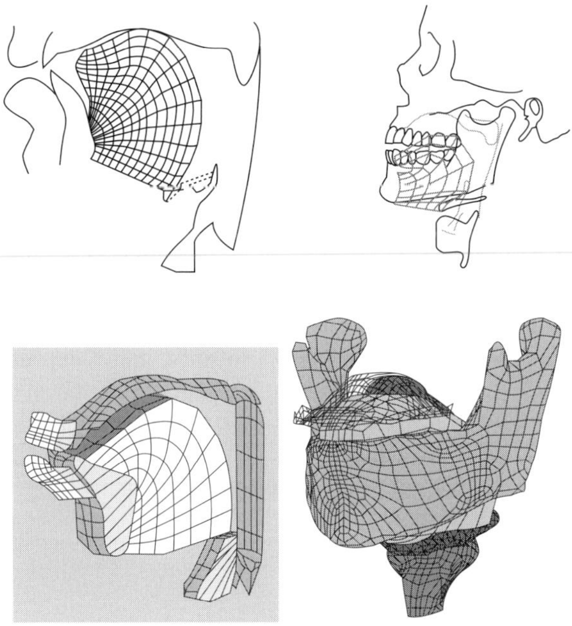

Figure 14.1 2D and 3D biomechanical models of the tongue. From left to right: Payan and Perrier's sagittal tongue model (1997), Sanguinetti *et al.*'s jaw, tongue, and hyoid midsagittal model (1998), Dang and Honda's vocal tract model (2004), and the latest version of GIPSA-lab's 3D tongue model (Gérard *et al.* 2003; Gérard *et al.* 2004; Buchaillard *et al.* 2009) placed in the neighboring bony structures.

volumetric *magnetic resonance images* (MRI) from one male Japanese speaker. The tongue is represented by a 2 cm-thick layer defined by nodes in three sagittal planes, delimiting 120 polyhedrons. The 11 muscles of the tongue model are simulated based on a mass-spring approach that allows large tissue deformation and tongue-wall contact. The model includes also a *mandible-hyoid* bone complex that is controlled by 8 muscles. Another line of biomechanical models initiated by Wilhelms-Tricarico (1995) and pursued at the former Institut de la Communication Parlée (ICP, now part of GIPSA-Lab) by Payan, Perrier and colleagues (Gérard *et al.* 2006; Buchaillard *et al.* 2009; Nazari *et al.* 2010) focuses on a better understanding of tongue and lips movement as a result of the arrangement of muscular fibers and the properties of the muscles. Note that at present other speech organs – larynx and velum – are not simulated or controlled in any of these models. Figure 14.1 illustrates their structures.

This biomechanical approach has the advantage of always producing plausible tongue or lips geometry due to muscular and tissue reactions. However, the price for this is that the controller is also in charge of the complex coordination of a high number of parameters controlling the muscular activity for producing a given vocal tract geometry or a given sound (Bailly *et al.* 1997). In fact, the *dof* of these complex 3D biomechanical systems are not task-specific; for instance, jaw models (Laboissière *et al.* 1996) can be employed indifferently for studying speech or chewing (Ostry and Munhall 1994). When such complex biomechanical systems are fitted to the anatomy of a specific speaker, the *dof* identified are very close to those of functional models below. Using a fairly complete biomechanical model of the tongue, jaw, and hyoid controlled by 17 muscles (3 intrinsic and 4 extrinsic tongue muscles, 7 muscles attached to the jaw and 3 attached to the hyoid bone), Sanguineti *et al.* (1998) showed, for example, that systematic sources of variation in an X-ray database can be accounted for with only six independent commands: two for controlling jaw rotation and protrusion, one for larynx height, and three for the tongue.

14.4.3 Functional models

Unlike geometric and biomechanical models that are fitted to data a posteriori, functional models are based on articulatory data measured on one or several subjects, and the *dof* of the plant emerge from the data by statistical analysis. Such models have been initially applied to midsagittal data (see for example Lindblom and Sundberg 1971; Maeda 1990). We also analyzed 1200 X-ray images of cineradiography where a French male speaker utters VCV sequences (Beautemps *et al.* 2001). Degrees-of-freedom extracted from the 51 target vocalic and consonantal configurations collected in the corpus (see Figure 14.2) are identical to the ones extracted from the 1200 X-ray images. As can be seen below, extensive 3D data of the vocal tract in action are currently unavailable, and we have to rely on the generalization capabilities of our modeling procedures and on the appropriate choice of representative configurations for validating models learned from restricted training material.

Most studies identify at least two *dof* for the tongue: *tongue body* and *tongue dorsum* components which describe, respectively, the *front-back* and *flattening-arching* movements of the tongue. The tongue tip clearly possesses two additional independent degrees of freedom that describe, respectively, its vertical and longitudinal movements. Additional movements of the tongue root are observed in languages such as Akan which exploits vowel pairs contrasting the value of the *advanced tongue root* (±ATR) feature (Lindau 1979). The tongue root is also involved in less systematic phonological contrasts such as the English tense/lax contrast (Ladefoged *et al.* 1972). Note that the statistical

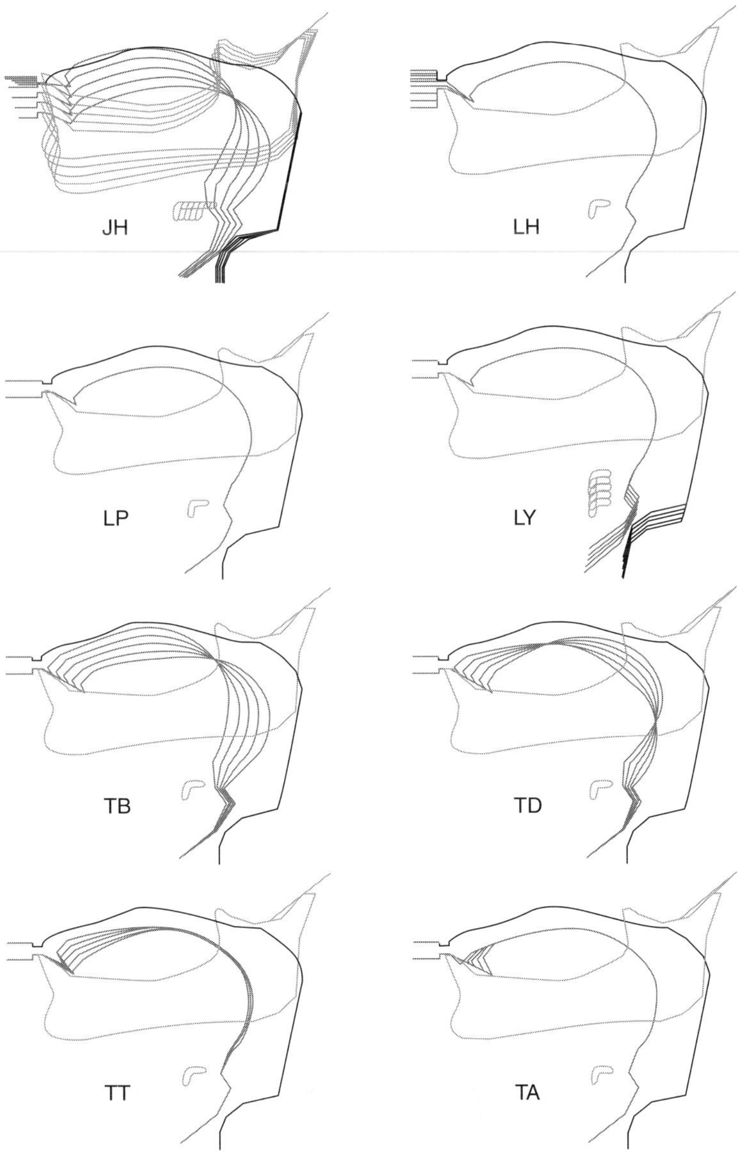

Figure 14.2 Independent movements of the four articulators shaping the vocal tract geometry: jaw, lips, tongue, and larynx. From left to right, bottom to top: jaw rotation; lip aperture, protrusion; laryngeal vertical movement, tongue body, dorsum, and apex (vertical and longitudinal) movements (from Beautemps *et al.* 2001). Note the movements of the hyoid bone strongly correlated with jaw rotation and vertical placement of the larynx. Some degrees-of-freedom (velum, jaw advance, lip raising) are not shown.

models built using these data differ in the way this tongue root movement is taken into account. Harshman *et al.* (1977) showed that tongue root movement for English tense/lax pairs can be ascribed to the sole *tongue dorsum* movement – tense vowels generally being articulated with an advanced tongue root and a higher tongue height, both resulting from the synergetic activity of the *posterior* and *anterior genioglossus* (Baer *et al.* 1998). Jackson (1988), on the other hand, found that three independent tongue parameters were necessary to describe Lindau's data, that is, independent control of tongue root advance and tongue height that could be explained by decoupled activities of the *anterior* and *posterior genioglossus* (Tiede 1996). In an MRI study, Tiede (1996) confirms the different implementations of the tongue root contrast in both languages. Once again, it is shown that muscles can be used in different ways in order to act as either *agonist* or *antagonist* muscles for different movements.

Even though 3D data have been used extensively for the last 10 years to complement midsagittal studies, almost no 3D functional tongue models have been developed from real data. Stone and Lundberg (1996) reconstructed and described the 3D tongue surface of 18 sustained vocalizations of American English sounds using ultrasound data, but did not develop a full 3D model (1990; 1997). Models of the *vocal tract*, i.e. the tract resulting from the connection of the various speech articulators but without explicit reference to any specific articulator, were developed by Yehia and Tiede (1997) based on MR images of sustained Brazilian Portuguese vowels, and also by Badin *et al.* (1998), based on a more extensive set of sustained French vowels and consonants. More recently, Badin *et al.* (2000; 2002; 2006) extracted from the same MR images the volume surface of the tongue; instead of the simpler extraction of the supraglottal airways in MR images, they aimed to identify the deformations of speech organs that shape the airways that constitute the vocal tract (see Figure 14.3).

14.4.4 Discussion

Badin and Serrurier's (2006) study shows that the articulatory *dof* of the tongue, (see Figure 14.3) identified using the midsagittal contours (Beautemps *et al.* 2001), predict most of the variance of the 3D data. They found that 87 percent of the variance of the MRI data is explained by the set of six parameters identified on the midsagittal contours. The residual variance may be explained primarily by the non-linear effects of compression of the tongue against hard surfaces (such as the tongue tip against the hard palate) occulted by the pure statistical representation of such observations in the 2D data. Interestingly, it was observed that the lateral consonant [l] seems mainly to be obtained by a depression of the tongue body achieved through a combination of jaw lowering, tongue body backing, and tongue tip elevating. These movements, which can be observed in the midsagittal plane, appear to be capable of creating the lateral

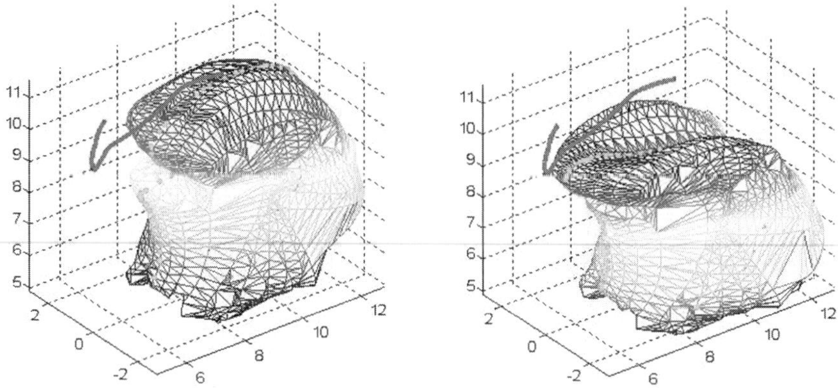

Figure 14.3 Illustration of a functional 3D model of the tongue (from Badin and Serrurier 2006). Postures for extreme tongue dorsum positions are displayed in this example.

channels characteristic of [l] without further transversal control of the coronal section. These findings seem to support the view that most of the information about tongue movement is available in the midsagittal contour and that 3D tongue models can supply the lateral dimension missing in experimental settings that deliver real-time information about tongue movements in the midsagittal plane. The findings have also been reproduced more recently by Engwall (2000) for a Swedish speaker using a quasi-identical experimental setting and modeling procedure. Comparing MRI, *electropalatography* (EPG), *electromagnetic articulography* (EMA) and dynamic MRI (Engwall 2004), Engwall concludes that statistical MRI is indeed representative of dynamic speech.

14.5 Models of facial deformation

Because they have wider potential applications, 3D lip and face models are by far more numerous than 3D tongue models. All true 3D models are made of meshes of nodes that are connected together, usually by triangles, in order to form surfaces. The various models that can be found in the literature differ in the number of nodes, their arrangement, and the principles underlying their control.

14.5.1 Geometrical models

Parke (1982; 1996) was among the first researchers to develop a model of face/lips with a relatively low number of facial nodes and a relatively high number of control parameters; his approach involves the blending of two complementary strategies (Parke 1982, p. 62): (1) "to observe the surface properties of faces and develop *ad hoc* sets that allow these observed characteristics to be specified parametrically," and (2) to "deal directly with the underlying structures that cause facial expression," referring to a more physiologically oriented approach. Parke's model, that led to a number of implementations (Cohen *et al.* 1998; Eisert and Girod 1998; Kulju *et al.* 1998), is made of approximately 400 vertices (Parke and Waters 1996, p. 195) among which the mouth region is controlled by 10 parameters; it can produce a wide range of facial expressions, but as it was not specifically developed for speech, it needs the coordination of many control parameters to obtain typical speech gestures (this coordination has moreover to be established in an ad hoc manner). In addition, these control parameters are heterogeneous, as some can be each of the 3D coordinates of a single point such as the mouth corner, while others can drive complex articulatory gestures such as the tuck for labiodentals.

A similar approach has become a standard in the context of the industrial *ISO/IEC MPEG-4* norm (Pockaj *et al.* 1999); the 3D coordinates of the 84 feature points are controlled by a set of 68 FAP (facial action parameters) that "are responsible for describing the movements of the face, both at low level (i.e. displacement of a specific single point of the face) or at high level (i.e. reproduction of a facial expression)" (Pockaj *et al.* 1999, p. 33). This type of face/lip model aims at being general, which may constitute an interesting feature, though at the cost of a disproportion between the number of control parameters versus the number of nodes: (1) they are developed without strong reference to specific subjects' data and in particular they are not speech-specific, (2) they are controlled by a rather high number of control parameters, transferring the responsibility of the coherence of movements to the controller, and (3) they sometimes lack spatial resolution for small details (such as wrinkles) that can be useful for speech or expressions such as smiling.

14.5.2 Biomechanical models

Biomechanical models constitute another type of approach to face/lip modeling; namely, this approach aims at describing not only the geometry of the face in terms of a mesh of nodes, but also the biophysics underlying the associated movements. One of the very first biomechanical models was developed by Platt and Badler (1981). They simulated face muscles using fibers of springs connecting the skull and jaw bones, and nodes, both defining the face mesh and muscle interconnections. The organization of control of these muscles is based on the *facial action coding system* (FACS) developed by Ekman and Friesen (1978). The FACS constitutes a set of all possible basic actions performable on a human face; each basic action, called an *action unit* (AU), is a minimal action in the sense that it cannot be broken down into smaller actions. As Platt and Badler designed the AUs to be closely connected with the anatomy of the face, each AU is controlled by either a single muscle or a small set of closely related muscles. This allows a wide range of facial gestures to be realized, but rests on a high number of parameters (about 40 to 50 AUs are used). Waters (1987) developed a similar anatomically based model, where about 20 muscle actuators are taken into account. Terzopoulos and Waters (1993) extended this work to incorporate a physics-based synthetic tissue model. They defined 44 action units (AU) involving one or more muscles and associated activation levels to implement facial expressions. More recently, Lucero and Munhall (1999) followed up Terzopoulos and Waters' work by implementing an EMG control applied to seven perioral muscles, and driving the model from EMG data recorded on one subject.

Note finally that more realistic models of skin deformation using *finite element* techniques (see for example Larrabee 1986; Chabanas and Payan 2000) may solve the intrinsic limitations of mass-springs models in terms of dynamic stability (Pitermann 2004) and strain/stress relations. The biomechanical model recently developed by Nazari *et al* (2010) consists notably of three layers of full and degenerated hexahedral elements (see Figure 14.4). Muscle fibres are modeled by macrofibres and cable (tension only) elements. The model accounts for non-linear elastic properties of face tissues, contacts between upper and lower lip and between lips and teeth.

14.5.3 Functional models

A third approach to face/lip modeling involves collecting 3D coordinates of fleshpoints of a real speaking face and trying to explain motion variance by a

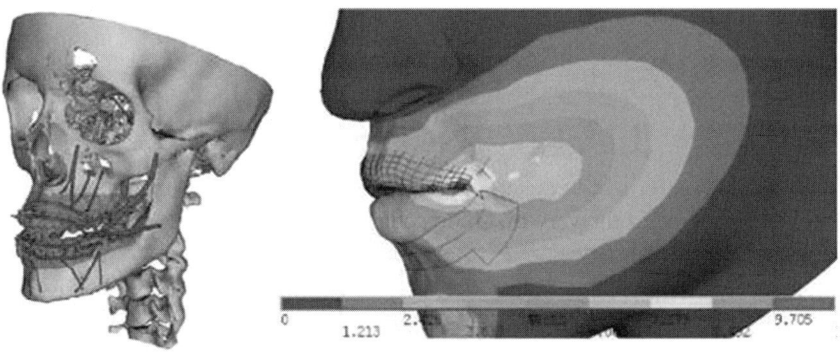

Figure 14.4 The biomechanical model of the face developed by Nazari *et al.* (2010). Left: insertions of the lip muscles. Right: effect of the coordinate action of the Mentalis and Orbicularis Oris Peripheralis.

small number of independent parameters. Unlike the tongue where a fixed or adaptive grid is used to intersect the moving organ and provides a constant number of artificial fleshpoints, video- or magnetic-based motion capture devices can directly provide the positions of a few dozen real fleshpoints at high frame rate. Geometric models should, however, complement such a pure data-driven approach for capturing movements of organs that either are too small or for which attaching markers is impossible (such as lips and eyes).

We show below that simple and robust linear models can be built from these data. Note that, reciprocally, these models can be used for regularizing motion capture data. Users of most commercial products still spend hours in manually cleaning and labeling raw data. This lengthy and costly task can be substantially reduced by using analysis-by-synthesis techniques that estimate the *dof* of a model built from a few carefully chosen clean data: noisy and incomplete raw data can then be cleaned and complemented by fitting them with the model, taking advantage of the smoothing (and regularizing) capabilities related to the model low dimensionality.

Lips Guiard-Marigny *et al.* (1996) have worked out a 3D model of the lips from the geometrical analysis of the lips of one French speaker. The lip shape is generated in two steps: (1) an articulatory model generates 3D coordinates of 30 feature points organized in three contours (Revéret and Benoît 1998); (2) a geometric model interpolates between these 30 feature points to generate the final lip mesh of continuously defined curves. This geometric model has been adapted to lip morphologies of different speakers. For three French subjects studied by Revéret and Benoît (1998), the lip geometry could be controlled by three independent parameters emerging clearly from *principal component analysis* (PCA); a massive lip protrusion/rounding gesture (lips1), a lower lip opening/closure gesture (lips2), and an upper lip opening/closure gesture (lips3) as needed for subjects to produce labio-dentals and the rounded open fricative [ʃ]. We will show that this ranking is conserved when considering also the jaw contribution to lip movement (see below).

Face A similar two-step procedure can be followed for the face. Model-based video analysis (Cootes *et al.* 1995) consists first in adapting a 2D or 3D generic geometric model to sample images (Pighin *et al.* 1999; Pighin *et al.* 2002), identifying independent parameters for the shape and appearance, eventually connecting the two of them (Cootes *et al.* 1998; Odisio *et al.* 2004) and then using a simple analysis-by-synthesis framework to adapt automatically the predicted appearance of the model to the series of observed appearances of the speaker. Instead of positioning the control parameters of the generic model manually, 3D-to-3D matching procedures (Szeliski and Lavallée 1996; Couteau *et al.* 2000) can be used to adjust the generic mesh to the raw facial surface

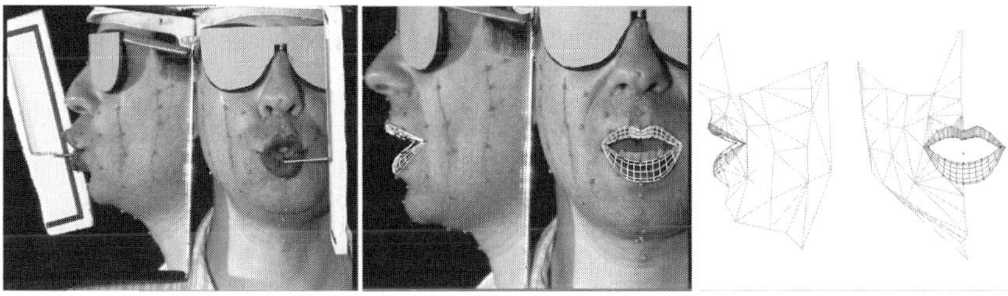

Figure 14.5 Example of video image for /a/: Subject fitted with the jaw splint (left); subject with the lip mesh superimposed (middle); complete mesh whose 3D vertices are determined by the measured articulatory data (right).

obtained by a laser range finder (Vatikiotis-Bateson *et al.* 1999) or motion capture data (Bérar *et al.* 2003; 2006).

A one-step procedure that uses directly labeled motion-capture data confirms that facial *dof* used for speech are less than a dozen. On a corpus of 34 sustained articulations (French vowels and consonants), Badin *et al.* (2000; 2002) supplemented the 30 feature points of the lip model described previously with 34 fleshpoints obtained by sticking beads on the right-hand side of the subject's face and with the 3D jaw position obtained by a jaw splint (see Figure 14.5). In addition to a jaw height (jaw1) parameter that explains 57 percent of the lip data variance, they found that the remaining lip geometry is effectively controlled by the three independent parameters mentioned above, plus a marginal contribution of the jaw advance necessary to complement lips3 with a jaw retraction (jaw2) in labio-dentals in order to enable the labio-dental contact. These five parameters (jaw1, lips1, lips2, lips3, jaw2) explain respectively 16.2, 74.4, 3.7, 2.2, and 0.3 percent of the variance, amounting to a total of about 96.9 percent of the 65 3D facial data points (see Figure 14.6). An additional parameter extracted as the first PCA mode of the data residual of the entire face (skin1), connected to clear vertical movements of the throat, explains an additional 0.8 percent of the facial data points, amounting to a total of about 97.7 percent of the variance. Note that this last parameter could provide a visible trace of the movement of underlying articulators such as the larynx, the tongue, or the hyoid bone. This parameter effectively contributes to the recovery of underlying *dof*, especially larynx height (see Section 14.6.2 and Table 14.1).

Further analysis (Bailly *et al.* 2003) of the position of 168 beads stuck on both sides of the subject's face revealed no additional *dof* (see Figure 14.7). Note also that these speech-specific facial *dof*s are expected to be language- and speaker-independent. For the eight speakers (Arabic male, French male and females, German male, English female, Australian-English male, Japanese male) we have studied so far, the semantics of these parameters is robust, given the

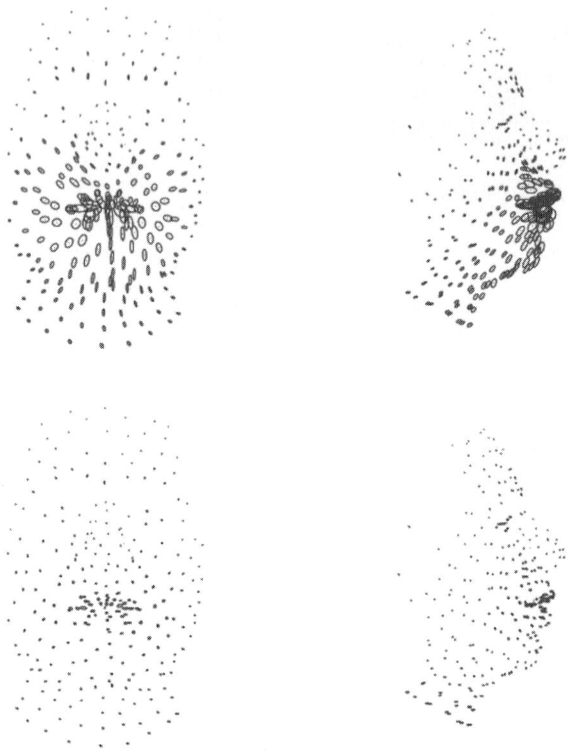

Figure 14.6 Dispersion ellipses for each original (left) and residual (right) facial and lip point (± 1 standard deviation). The RMS residual error is less than 0.4 mm.

fact that the same "guided" linear modeling is used (Elisei *et al.* 2001b; Fagel *et al.* 2008; Bailly *et al.* 2009; Tran *et al.* 2010).

Analysis of extensive motion capture data (230 meaningful utterances) collected on a speech cuer (Gibert *et al.* 2004b; Gibert *et al.* 2005) also revealed no difference between *dof* estimated from a few dozen visemes and from 200 000 frames. Again, the careful choice of representative configurations may compensate for small amounts of training material.

14.5.4 Discussion

From the description of the underlying articulators, it seems that muscle synergies underlying facial motions are based on a small set of "basic motions."

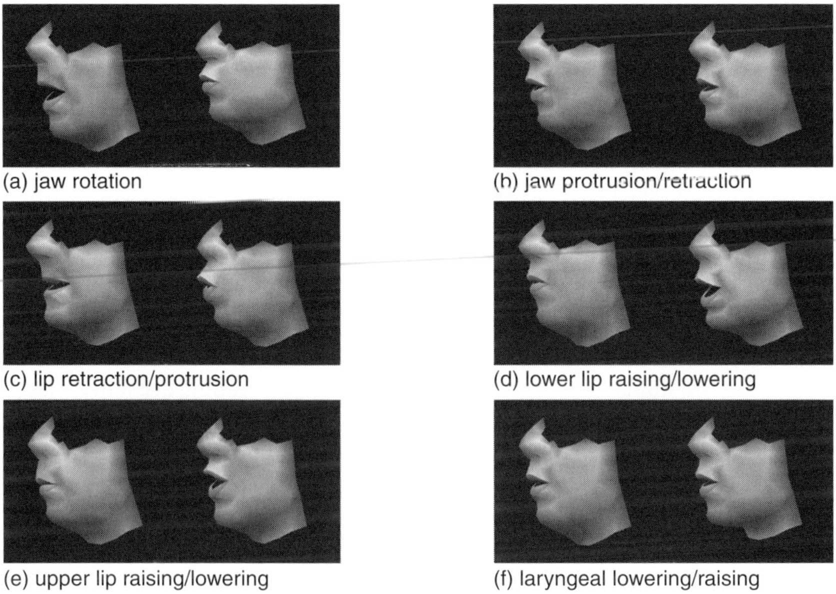

Figure 14.7 Articulatory *dof* of facial speech movements (from Revéret *et al.* 2000). We show here the deformation produced from the neutral face by (very) extreme values of each articulatory parameter (±2 standard deviations).

Individual movements and sequences of movements can be accounted for by a simple additive control model. For speech, less than 10 basic facial motions have been identified (6 in Badin *et al.* 2000) that should be compared to the 68 MPEG4 FAP. Of course these FAP are actually mostly low level, and do not take into account speech specific gestures, which led Vignoli and Braccini (1999) to add another layer of control parameters, called AP (articulatory parameters), corresponding to mouth height, mouth width, protrusion, and jaw rotation, that control the FAP. Indeed, the implementation of the FAP is never explained clearly; Pockaj *et al.* (1999) mention that "the *intelligence* of the decoder [the face/lip model] . . . resides in its ability of extrapolating the movement of tens of vertices starting from the displacement of a single feature point," and give some hints towards ad hoc definitions of FAP. Eisert and Girod (1998) indicate that their "generic face model contains a table describing how the control points of the mesh are translated or rotated for each [of the 46] FAP [that they implemented]." No indication is given about how to produce this table. They finally use their face model for facial motion estimation. However, such a model-based image analysis, now widely used for head movement and facial motion tracking, is very sensitive to the dimensionality of the search space. Using Parke's

(1982) terminology, "the quality of the [articulatory control] parameters set [that] refers to the appropriateness and efficiency of the parameters." Low dimension articulatory parameters acting independently on the whole shape regularize favorably the optimization method that should match the projection of the 3D face with the analyzed image. Using AP instead of FAP is thus quite efficient. It is also appropriate since the optimization always converges to a plausible facial shape, and incomplete FAP specification – always possible within MPEG4/SNHC – can be regularized via their redundancy (Elisei *et al.* 2001a).

14.6 Linking articulatory degrees-of-freedom

We have established that both vocal tract and facial shape can be represented in maps with few dimensions, and that these dimensions combine in a fairly simple way to control the corresponding shapes. A given speech gesture may be represented as a multidimensional trajectory in these maps. In this section we examine the complexity of the links between maps, and question the possibility of using both forward and inverse links between maps to predict the trajectory in one map from the trajectory observed in another.

14.6.1 Complementarity, redundancy, and synergy

Psychologists have happily investigated the perception of audiovisual speech (e. g. Sumby and Pollack 1954) for the past five decades. It is undeniable that useful knowledge has been produced about the extent to which the visibility of a speaker's face enhances intelligibility of audible speech and under what conditions. For example, we know that visual enhancement of intelligibility amounts to about a 10 dB improvement in signal (MacLeod and Summerfield 1987). It is also clear that – *ceteris paribus* – the auditory modality takes precedence over the visual, though the visual modality can provide information essential to auditory localization, which in turn influences intelligibility (Driver 1996). More phonetically oriented research carried out by Green and colleagues (1991; 1996) has shown the sensitivity of visual information to differences in vocal tract configuration, such as place (for example, labial /b/ versus alveolar /d/, or velar /g/) and manner (for example, plosive /p/ versus fricative /f/) of articulation.

The basic question investigated in this section was addressed by Summerfield (1979; 1987); namely, how is the phonetically relevant information distributed across the visual and auditory modalities? Are the two modalities complementary, providing mode-specific "cues" to phonetic identity? There is some evidence that speech features mainly concerned with manner of articulation are best transmitted by the audio channel, while some other features mostly related to place of articulation are best transmitted by the visual channel (McGurk and MacDonald 1976; Robert-Ribes *et al.* 1998).

Concerning features related to place of articulation, cues provided by the lips such as rounding are more robust in the visual channel than in the audio channel, whereas cues provided by the tongue such as backness are most robust in the audio channel. But complementarity does not account for all the distribution of auditory and visual phonetic cues; in fact phonetic information seems to be specified *redundantly* as well. From perception experiments on the auditory, visual, and audiovisual identification of vowels in noise, Robert-Ribes and colleagues showed also that all individual phonetic features are better transmitted in the audiovisual mode than by each modality separately. Moreover, vision does increase intelligibility of noisy acoustic stimuli even when it does not convey discriminant phonetic information per se, just because of temporal cueing (Schwartz *et al.* 2003) and attentional phenomena. In the following sections we examine quantitatively the articulatory, visual, and acoustic dimensions during speech production.

14.6.2 Seeing the vocal tract

Imaging techniques such as X-ray and more recently MRI provide unique experimental setups for collecting complete midsagittal vocal tract contours as well as profiles of the lower face at a reasonable frame rate. In our research group, we used the 3D functional model of the lower face (see Section 14.5.3) and of the tongue (see Section 14.4.3) to analyze the profiles extracted from cineradio-films and used to develop a midsagittal, functional vocal tract model for the same speaker. An analysis-by-synthesis procedure was performed on 51 target configurations, as illustrated in Figure 14.8 for two of them. Since both sets of data have been aligned onto the same coordinate system linked to the upper incisor and the bite plane, no head movement correction was necessary, and only parameters of facial deformation were optimized. The RMS fitting error for the entire dataset is less than one mm. It is of the same order of magnitude as the usual modeling error for soft tissue reconstruction by functional models.

Table 14.1 relates the correlation coefficients between the six facial parameters obtained by the analysis-by-synthesis procedure and the ten individual vocal tract parameters that describe each X-ray midsagittal image. We also give the correlation coefficients between the six facial parameters estimated by a multi linear regression from all visible *dof* and the ten individual vocal tract parameters. While lip and jaw parameters common to both models are almost perfectly reconstructed (LH, LP, LV, and JH) – thus assessing the relevance of the mapping procedure – a large part of the variance of some tongue parameters (TB, TT) as well as the larynx height (LY) may be also quite well reconstructed from facial (visible) movements. However, tongue advance (TA), velum height (VH), and tongue dorsum (TD) cannot be faithfully recovered from facial deformation.

Table 14.1 *Mapping visible* dof *to underlying articulatory* dof. *Correlation coefficients between individual articulatory and facial* dof *are computed for 51 target configurations. The last column shows the correlation coefficients between each articulatory parameter and its estimation by a linear regression using all facial* dof. *Correlation coefficients above 0.8 are in bold type. Except for jaw rotation, no parameter that has an effect on tongue position reaches this level of correlation.*

Xray\Face	jaw1	lips1	lips2	lips3	jaw2	Skin1	linear mapping
LH	0.50	–	**0.84**	0.83	–	0.11	**0.99**
LP	0.13	**0.96**	0.34	–	–	0.33	**0.98**
JH	**-1.00**	-0.19	-0.44	-0.40	–	-0.15	**1.00**
TB	0.24	–	-0.24	–	0.35	-0.24	0.71
TD	-0.11	0.20	0.22	0.18	-0.50	-0.12	0.64
TT	0.33	0.34	0.39	0.37	–	-0.24	0.74
TA	–	–	–	-0.18	-0.17	–	0.37
LY	–	0.57	-0.26	-0.46	-0.13	0.25	**0.84**
VH	-0.13	0.22	-0.16	-0.16	0.29	0.22	0.47
LV			-0.47	0.55	-0.26	-0.50	**0.99**

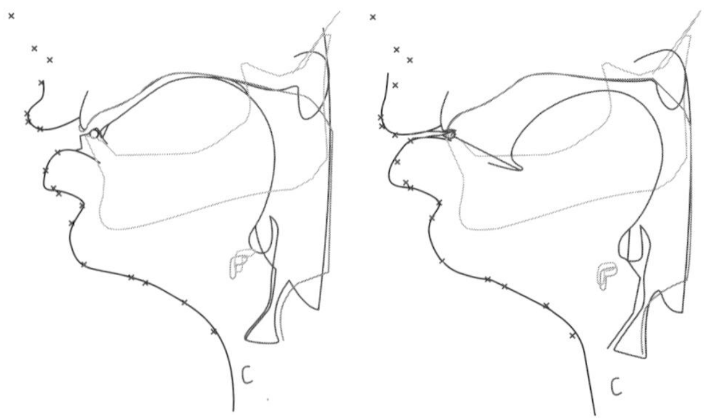

Figure 14.8 Comparison of midsagittal profiles extracted from X-ray images and fitted with the midsagittal vocal tract model (Beautemps *et al.* 2001), for two articulations (the center of the occlusion in an [igy] sequence, left, and the center of a sustained [u], right); original X-ray profiles used to derive the model (thick lines); profiles predicted by the X-ray model, including a schematic contour of the jaw and the hyoid bone (thin lines); and midsagittal 3D fleshpoints (crosses) of the 3D model of the lower part of the face developed for the same speaker using photogrammetry (Badin *et al.* 2000). The RMS fitting error between the facial contour and the midsagittal 3D fleshpoints is here 0.86 mm.

The fact that such a high amount of the variance of the tongue posture may be recovered from the face seems quite surprising, and may partially explain why good lipreaders can reach high intelligibility scores. However, we should not deduce from these results that visible movements and articulation are correlated to such a degree that we do not need to complement visual information! Other linguistic and non-linguistic dimensions provided by phonotactic constraints of the language, syntax, and topic certainly help lipreaders.

As illustrated in Figure 14.9, labial (facial) doubles cannot actually be disambiguated; the linear model does not recover vocal tract shapes that have the same facial correlates but differ in lingual articulation. This is also true for tongue/palate constriction as exemplified in Figure 14.10; the higher jaw

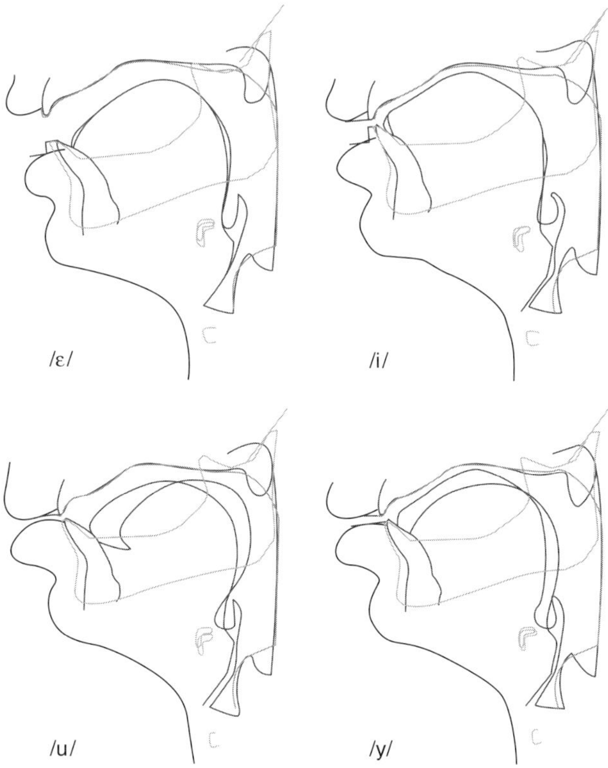

Figure 14.9 Predicting vocalic vocal tract configurations from the face. Top: two successful examples for vowels [ɛ] and [i], which follow the general synergy open/back and closed/front. Bottom: for the two labial doubles [u] and [y], the inverse model predicts quasi-identical tongue shapes. Same conventions as for Figure 14.8.

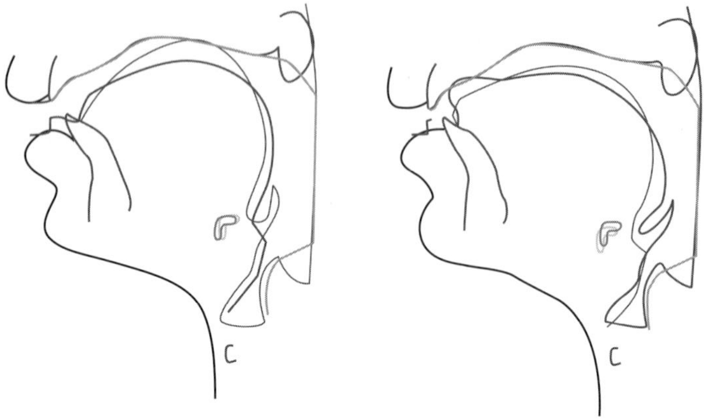

Figure 14.10 Failing to predict consonantal vocal tract constriction from the face. Left: the centre of the occlusion in an [aga] sequence; right: same for [ada]. Same conventions as for Figure 14.8.

posture in [ada] results in a more front position of the tongue, but that is quite insufficient for predicting and correctly generating the adequate alveolar constriction. Globally, the optimal mapping between face and lingual articulation captures the general tendency, appropriate to most languages – here French – to associate closed lips with a frontal posture of the tongue and open lips with a back articulation (see Figure 14.11): finer details of the lingual articulation that are fairly important for sound characterization – notably formation of constrictions – cannot be recovered from facial movement only (Bailly and Badin 2002). Based on the computation of the acoustic transfer functions, we have shown that the resulting acoustic space shrinks drastically towards its center (Bailly and Badin 2002). These results have been confirmed by Engwall and Beskow (2003) using simultaneous dynamic EMA and facial motion capture recordings of a Swedish male speaker.

More complex, non-linear, and contextual mappings (see for example voice transformation techniques applied to the articulatory-to-acoustic mapping in Shiga and King 2004) could possibly enhance the crude multilinear mapping considered here. We notably compared multilinear, GMM- and HMM-based mapping techniques on EMA data (Ben Youssef *et al.* 2010). The aim was to recover the *xy* coordinates of three coils placed on the tongue from the three coils placed on the lips and lower incisors. The speech dataset was here much larger (17 minutes of speech excluding silence) and consisted of short sentences. The results show that contextual information crucially improves the

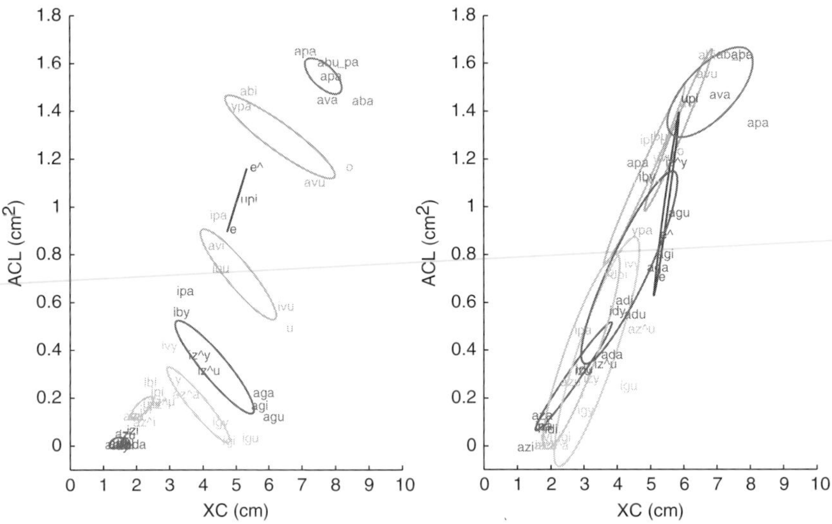

Figure 14.11 Original (left) compared to recovered (right) lingual constriction in a tentative face-to-vocal tract inversion procedure; XC is the distance from the upper incisors to the main constriction along the vocal tract midline, while ACL is the cross-sectional area of the constriction. The mapping does not recover the constrictions occurring (mainly for [g], see filled dispersion ellipsis) in the velo-palatal region and broadens the place of articulation of original front articulations. Globally the face-to-tongue mapping tends to correlate ACL with XC.

mapping. GMM-based mapping techniques (Toda *et al.* 2008; Ben Youssef *et al.* 2009) using medium-sized windows (110 ms) to characterize the input facial movements outperform the other techniques, in particular HMM-based techniques that use a phonetic alignment (Hiroya and Honda 2004; Nakamura *et al.* 2006). The best parameterization results in a mean prediction error of 2.9 mm and a correlation of 0.8. This should be compared with the 3.64 mm and 3.88 mm obtained respectively by the HMM-based mapping and the multilinear model. However, the detailed analysis of predicted tongue shapes evidences the same undershooting and centralization problems commented above: non-front vowels and unrounded consonants are still highly confused (see Figure 14.12).

We have shown here that neither RMS results nor raw correlations are sufficient to assess the performance of the mapping, and that geometric, acoustic, and phonetic consequences of the predicted movements should be examined.

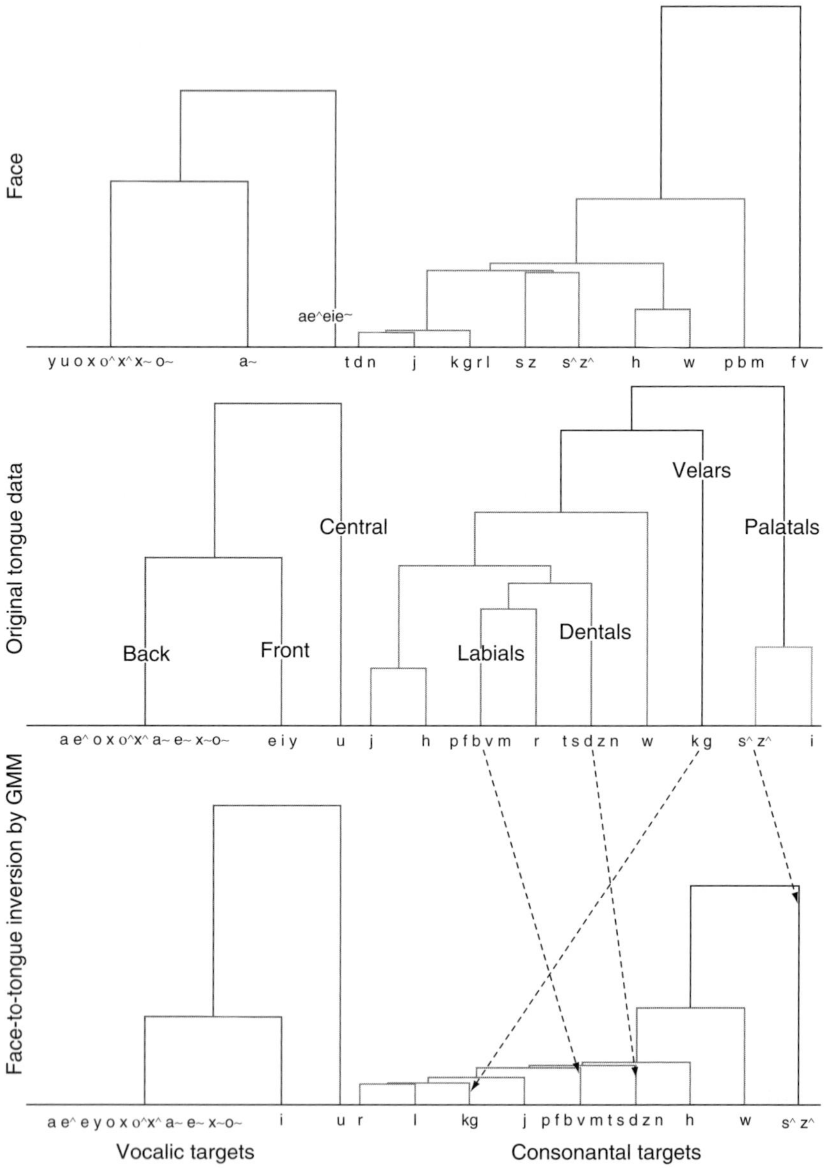

Figure 14.12 Comparing confusion trees for vowels (left) and consonants (right). The most significant three groups for vowels and nine groups for consonantal targets are shown. From top to bottom: original face data, original tongue data, and tongue recovered from face by the best GMM-mapping. If the recovery of places of articulation for vowels is rather good (particularly for [i] and [u]), consonantal contrasts are strongly degraded, with the exception of rounded palatal fricatives.

These mappings should also be subjectively evaluated. Despite a few experiments showing that unrealistic visible components such as disembodied lips, skeletal jaws (Benoît and Le Goff 1998), or virtual tongues (Massaro and Light 2003; Engwall and Bälter 2007; Badin *et al.* 2008; Badin *et al.* 2010) may enhance speech intelligibility and language-learning abilities, it is quite difficult to determine whether speech intelligibility is enhanced only by visible events that have the temporal synchronization and spatial scaling appropriate to the opening and closing of the vocal tract, or whether these visible components really bring additional comprehensive phonetic features.

14.6.3 Driving facial animation from acoustics

The best-conditioned speech mapping is certainly the acoustics-to-facial motion mapping. Most facial movements described in Section 14.5.3 – when made audible – have acoustic consequences. For example, Yehia *et al.* (1998) report that "80 percent . . . of the variance observed in the RMS amplitude and LSP parametric representation of the spectral envelope [are explained by linear estimators relating facial movement to acoustics]." Reliable, complete, and precise characterizations of acoustics and facial motion are easily accessible and up-to-date context-sensitive mapping techniques such as mentioned above – GMM- or HMM-based – are very efficient (Hiroya and Honda 2004; Toda *et al.* 2004; Toda *et al.* 2008; Ben Youssef *et al.* 2009). This is not the case for vocal tract motion.

An obvious application of acoustics-to-facial motion mapping is audiovisual synthesis; current text-to-speech synthesis systems may be easily coupled with facial animation if articulatory movements of the avatar can be directly predicted from the synthetic speech output. However, most audiovisual synthesizers synchronize facial animation with synthetic speech output by minimally imposing on facial animation the phonemic boundaries computed by the text-to-speech system – or extracted from natural utterances (Cohen and Massaro 1993; see also Slaney, this volume, Ezzat, this volume). The prediction of facial movement via acoustics-to-facial motion mapping has the obvious advantage of potentially preserving finer cinematic coherence between the two modalities. We evaluate below different control models proposed in studies for predicting facial animation using the same training material for all models.

14.6.4 Movement generation and rendering

A system able to produce audiovisual speech from phonetic input generally consists of three modules: (1) a movement generation system that plans articulatory movements according to the phonological task, (2) a shape model that specifies how the geometry of the face is affected by these movements, and

(3) an appearance model that specifies how the skin texture – or more generally the face appearance – renders this shape deformation. Not all facial animation systems distinguish between these steps or identify these intermediary representation spaces (articulatory, shape, and appearance) for building synthetic animations. For example, image-based techniques that overlay facial regions (Bregler *et al.* 1997b; Slaney, this volume) or morph between target images extracted from real videos (Ezzat and Poggio 1998, this volume) do not impose a priori a distinction between shape and appearance. Similarly, systems using visemes as elementary units (Ezzat and Poggio 1998) do not always distinguish between a "high-level" parametric control and a finer "low-level" shape deformation model. For a more extensive presentation of models and modules currently used, the reader is referred to recent reviews (Bailly 2002; Bailly *et al.* 2003).

The systematic evaluation performed by Pandzic *et al.* (1999) on 190 subjects showed in fact that although offering quite acceptable intelligibility gains, synthetic faces seem to require more cognitive effort and more mental resources than natural speech. They noted that "*some synthetic faces require more than others*." If incoherent or impoverished audiovisual stimuli require more processing time and result in increased cognitive load, it seems interesting to separate out the contributions of the different generation modules to the overall quality. Moreover evaluation procedures should distinguish between the adequacy of the movement generation system, the shape, and the appearance models in replicating the underlying motor control and biophysics of natural faces.

14.6.5 Comparing "pure motion" stimuli

In our experiment, a point-light display was used to get rid of any possible improper rendering of movements due to a specific appearance model (Rosenblum and Saldaña 1996; 1998). Despite the fact that, compared to full-face stimuli, the point-light display tends to decrease intelligibility gains, subjects proved to be quite sensitive to the degree of coherence between acoustics and the proposed facial motion (Odisio and Bailly 2004).

Both natural ground-truth motion capture data and synthetic articulatory trajectories pilot the same data-driven speaker-specific linear shape model built using the procedure described in Section 14.5.3. Subjects were asked to rate on a five-point scale (incoherent, unsatisfactory, average, satisfactory, and excellent) the degree of coherence between the audio signal and the proposed facial motion. No head motion was added and the face was viewed from the front.

We compared three different synthesis methods: (1) acoustic-to-articulatory mapping where low-pass filtered (10 Hz) LSP spectral trajectories are mapped with articulatory movements using MLR; (2) audiovisual concatenation where multimodal segments of the training material – here diphones – are stretched/compressed to fit phonemic boundaries (Hällgren and Lyberg 1998; Minnis and Breen 1998; Gibert *et al.* 2005, for an extension to text-to-cued speech synthesis); and (3) coarticulation modeling that computes context-dependent articulatory targets and transition functions from the phonemic string (see also a similar approach in Cohen and Massaro 1993; Elisei *et al.* 2001b).

Again, crude multilinear acoustic-to-articulatory mapping is quite unsatisfactory despite a high coefficient of correlation between observed and predicted articulatory trajectories (> 0.9 using the training material). We also showed that an audiovisual concatenative synthesis scheme that intrinsically preserves coherence between acoustic structure and facial motion has the potential to generate high-quality movements. Other data-driven coarticulation modeling techniques (Brooke and Scott 1998b; HMM-based as in Tamura *et al.* 1998; or based on more complex context-dependent targets and transition functions such as in Okadome *et al.* 1999; Hiroya and Honda 2004; Govokhina *et al.* 2006) should also be tested.

14.7 Discussion

Underlying speech organs have clear visible and audible consequences. We have shown that it is possible to build functional facial models that successfully associate the movements of these organs with articulatory control parameters that drive facial deformations. This could guarantee that the movement of partially visible articulators can be recovered simultaneously from their direct visible trace (teeth, tongue, or velum are sometimes partially visible) and from their indirect visible or acoustical consequences.

We have considered in our mappings only quasi-static mapping information. Dynamic information (see Lander and Bruce, this volume) may provide additional cues that may help listeners – and thus automatic systems – to recover underlying gestures (for example, the articulation of [l] vs. [d] in a back context requires a less ample jaw closing gesture and may reveal the strong recruitment of the tongue tip versus the tongue body). The possibility that *shape-from-motion* recovery schemes (Johansson 1973) may provide crucial information requires further investigation.

Although functional models can simulate the links between articulation and audiovisual state variables, the scarcity, the heterogeneity, and the amount of experimental data available reduce drastically the choice of statistical models that could be used to describe the links. Precise interactions between speech organs such as collisions producing compressions, passive slips, or active trills cannot be easily taken into account by standard statistical models. On the other hand, physical models will be sufficiently mature in the near future to incorporate most of these precise interactions but should be *scaled* to conform to speaker-specific control strategies and anatomy. This conformation problem has been in most cases poorly addressed. Although we know that anatomy and control strategies are far from being orthogonal dimensions (see for example the links between tongue articulation and palate shape in Hashi et al. 1998), most models only scale prototypical behavior to some specific anatomy such as that promoted by the interaction between FAP and FDP in the MPEG4/SNHC face model, where both are expressed according to basic measures such as mean nose or mouth length. Few studies attempt to alter articulation when scaling anatomy (Harshman 1976). Note that a similar challenge consists in coproducing speech movements and facial expressions, particularly those altering the lower face (Bailly *et al.* 2008a).

Another main challenge of the sensorimotor mapping concerns timing constraints and their physical dynamical correlates. In fact, orofacial movements in speech must satisfy precise timing constraints. For instance, the distinction between voiced and voiceless stops is controlled by the simple coordination of glottal opening and release of occlusion. On the perception side, the effect of presentation frame rate of visual speech stimuli on lipreading performance (Vitkovich and Barber 1994) shows that more visual information becomes available when temporal resolution of the stimuli is increased. Data on the sensitivity of perceivers to the phasing relation between audio and visual stimuli is quite controversial; perceivers seem quite tolerant to asynchronous bimodal stimuli (Massaro and Cohen 1993), but they are also highly perturbed by the desynchronization between audio and visual events that are crucial for the identification of phonetic features. In particular, Breeuwer and Plomp (1986) show that the perception of the voicing contrast between /p/ and /b/ in English is greatly affected by desynchronization that artificially manipulates the phasing between the onset of vocal fold vibration and bilabial occlusion release. Similarly, Cathiard *et al.* (1995) show that desynchronization affects perception as soon as a configurational incoherence is detected. These results suggest that perceivers may compensate for a certain time delay between coherent audio and visual information but are very sensitive to phasing incoherence or errors in stimuli alignment. This too requires further research. The TD-HMM lipsync model proposed by Govokhina *et al.* (Govokhina *et al.* 2007; Bailly *et al.* 2009) aims to capture such phone-dependent phasing relations.

Finally the poor performance of the direct sensorimotor mappings tested in Section 14.6 does not obviate the ability of these mappings to provide audiovisual enhancement. Audiovisual binding results from both early and late integration processes (Bernstein *et al.* 2004). Early "pre-phonetic" integration processes notably exploit audiovisual synchronization patterns that explain reduced but significant intelligibility gains in spite of neutral (Schwartz *et al.* 2003) or impoverished visual information (Berthommier 2003).

14.8 Conclusions

In spoken language production and perception, multiple sources of information are available to support the encoding and the identification of speech. The identification process uses the signal-dependent information as well as general knowledge such as linguistic and phonological structure of the language, the topic, and the situation. Priming experiments show for example that we have expectations concerning the internal structure of input signals (Grosjean 1983), and that cognitive load is increased when input signals are impoverished. We thus may expect that impoverished coherence between audio and video signals may still improve intelligibility – notably by preserving speech detection – but should have a major effect on the cognitive load.

The data we have shown here suggest that the visible characteristics of speech production provide both redundant and complementary information on the sounds actually produced. Given the phonological structure of the language, visible movements have been shown to provide some information on the place of articulation of underlying speech organs. This information appears insufficient to recover the proper lingual constriction, which confirms a posteriori the importance of the information provided by manual cued speech (Cornett and Daisey 1992; Beautemps *et al.*, this volume) or gathered by the hand placement on the face in Tadoma (Reed *et al.* 1992).

The amount of a priori information that our interlocutor possesses about our idiosyncrasies, the topic, and the situation, varies continuously. Communication is thus adaptive: we adapt our articulation to communication needs and environmental conditions (Junqua 1993). These strategies are multimodal; we can favor visible or audible contrasts (Beautemps *et al.* 1999) depending on environmental conditions (Schulman 1988; Summer *et al.* 1988) or communication constraints that, for example, force us to whisper (Matsuda and Kasuya 1999). It is understandable that speakers use both visible and audible articulators and that the phonological systems exploit contrasts in both modalities resulting in a *synergy* between the auditory and visual channels. This perception-oriented model of communication should take into account our articulatory possibilities and the production–perception links to elaborate optimal and ecological communication strategies.

Motor – as well as auditory – theories of speech perception should thus be able to manipulate intersensory relations and lead to models of phonetic variability within a consistent framework (Abry and Badin 1996; Yehia *et al.* 1998). We have presented here some preliminary comprehensive models of speech articulation that could constitute a kernel of such intersensory maps. These mappings should also benefit audiovisual speech technology including synthesis, speech, language and face recognition, and audiovisual compression and speech enhancement by exploiting the a priori information about the intrinsic cohesion of audiovisual stimuli (Bailly *et al.* 2010).

14.9 Acknowledgments

The work conducted at ICP and GIPSA-Lab within the Talking Machines team and described in this chapter owes a lot to the initial pioneering work conducted by the late Christian Benoît until his untimely death in 1998. We are also indebted to Jean-Luc Schwartz and Pascal Perrier for the fruitful comments made on earlier versions of this chapter. Frédéric Elisei and Matthias Odisio have provided the most recent virtual clone of Pierre Badin. We thank very sincerely Alain Arnal and Christophe Savariaux (ICP) for their help with the video recordings. This work has been partially supported by the Agence Rhône-Alpes en Sciences Sociales et Humaines (ARASSH; project: "A Virtual Talking Head"), by France Telecom R&D ("3D models of talking faces"), by the French National Network for Telecom Research (RNRT, TempoValse project), and by the French National Agency for Research (ANR-08-EMER-001–02, *ARTIS*).

Notes

Chapter 2. Visual speech perception

1. Unless otherwise stated, discussion of deaf individuals refers to individuals with profound hearing impairments (bilateral impairments of at least 90 dB HL across the frequencies 500, 1000, and 2000 Hz). The term "congenitally deaf" refers to profound hearing impairment at birth, although identification of the condition may have occurred later, within the first six months. Finally, the deaf individuals discussed here have hearing parents, English as a first and primary language, and eight or more years in oral or mainstream education. Generalizations about this group of individuals likely vary from generalizations concerning the group with congenital, profound hearing impairments, deaf parents, and sign language as a first and primary language. In any event, the similarities and/or differences between the groups have not been adequately studied, and the remarks in this chapter are not intended to extend to the latter group.
2. In the literature, not every phoneme in a stimulus set may get assigned to a viseme class, because at the level defined for visemes one or more phonemes is not within a cluster that comprises the criterion number of responses. For purposes here, it was necessary to assign every phoneme to some equivalence class for each level of equivalence classes.
3. The analyses with arcsine transformed scores are reported here (figures show untransformed results).

Chapter 3. Dynamic information for face perception

1. The term dynamic (also see Benoît *et al.* 1995a, Christie and Bruce 1998) has been used to describe the informational form sometimes known as kinematic (Rosenblum, Johnson, and Saldaña 1996) or time-varying (Rosenblum and Saldaña 1998). It must be noted that formally, visual information cannot be truly 'dynamic' as it does not contain the relevant mass component (see Runeson and Frykholm 1981). We use the term dynamic to refer to the changes that occur in information over the time course of an event.
2. It should be emphasized that the sampling technique used in this study to produce the different presentation rates also varied the selection and number of frames displayed in each condition. Hence the effect of presentation rate may simply be a reflection of these differences rather than dependent on the temporal dynamic aspects of the observed motion.

Chapter 4 Investigating auditory-visual speech perception development

1. The role of attentional resources in this process becomes apparent a little later in development; 14-month-olds discriminate a phonetically close contrast, in a simple discrimination task but not in a word learning task that requires these nonsense words be associated with objects. On the other hand 8-month-olds show discrimination of the 'bih-dih' contrast in both tasks (Stager and Werker 1997). Thus, while 14-month-olds can perceive the difference between 'bih' and 'dih', they do not demonstrate this discrimination when attention is directed elsewhere (to word learning).

Chapter 5. Brain bases for seeing speech: fMRI studies of speechreading

1. See 5.9 for a glossary of all the acronyms and neuroanatomical terms used in this chapter.
2. Inhibitory (i.e. subadditive) activation for audiovisual compared with unimodal input can be observed in other parts of the superior temporal gyrus (e.g. Wright *et al.* 2003), while incongruent or desynchronized audiovisual pairings can show graded activation in STS correlated with their relative coherence (e.g. Stevenson *et al.* 2010). While the findings are variable, they are generally consistent with the idea that STSp is a primary binding site for congruent, coherent audiovisual speech processing. Current research using dynamic methods is likely to moderate this picture, since subadditive (i.e. negative) interactions between audition and vision can also be observed over superior temporal regions in EEG responses (Besle *et al.* 2008; Pilling 2009).
3. Influences of vision on audition may be coordinated via subcortical (thalamic) systems, which "set" and maintain oscillatory brain activity (whole brain rhythms), which could tune such activity to the time-varying characteristics of an utterance. This could provide a further mechanism for early influences of one primary sensory modality on the other (Schroeder *et al.* 2008). Such phase-reset amplification systems can apply to interactions between people, as well as to intra-individual processes (see Scott *et al.* 2009, for a similar notion from the perspective of motor systems in speech processing). Under this proposal, early influences of vision on audition within primary sensory regions may reflect synchronized co-activation of those regions via thalamo-cortical routes, rather than direct visual cortex to auditory cortex routes.
4. The Capek *et al.* (2008a) findings appear to be at odds with an earlier study (MacSweeney, Calvert *et al.* 2002a, following MacSweeney *et al.* 2001), which found meager evidence of activation in superior temporal regions in deaf compared with hearing participants. While similar analysis techniques were used, participants and task differed in the 2008 and 2002/2001 studies. In the earlier studies, only six deaf people took part, and their language background was more variable than that of the native signers in the Capek *et al.* (2008a) study. The more recent study required participants to assess each (unpredictable) word that they saw being spoken – while the earlier study used well-learned digit sequences for silent rehearsal (as in Calvert *et al.* 1997). It is plausible that together these task differences elicited the observed differences.
5. It's plausible that the apparent anatomical distinction between the Sadato *et al.* and the Capek *et al.* studies reflects different analysis procedures, and hence different labels

for these parts of the lateral superior temporal lobe, rather than distinct neuroanatomical differences. At all events, posterior parts of the early (auditory) speech processing system appear to be implicated in both sets of studies.

Chapter 6. Temporal organization of Cued Speech production

1. In memory of Orin Cornett who invented the Cued Speech method at Gallaudet University and to Christian Benoît who initiated Cued Speech synthesis at the ICP laboratory (France).
2. The first studies on Cued Speech production were conducted at the ICP laboratory by Attina and colleagues from 2001 (Attina *et al.* 2002c; Attina *et al.* 2002b; Attina *et al.* 2002a; Attina *et al.* 2002d; Attina *et al.* 2003a; Attina *et al.* 2003b; Cathiard *et al.* 2003; Attina *et al.* 2004a; Attina *et al.* 2004b) in the framework of a 'Jeune Equipe' project of the French CNRS and a Cognitive program of the French Research Ministry. A first prototype of an image-based Cued Speech synthesizer integrating temporal rules has also been realized (Attina *et al.* 2003b; Attina *et al.* 2004a). A 3D model of Cued Speech gestures followed (Gibert *et al.* 2004a; Gibert *et al.* 2004c; Gibert *et al.* 2004b; Gibert *et al.* 2005).
3. 'When two consonants precede a vowel, as in the word *steep*, the first consonant is cued in the base [side] position and the hand moves quickly to the vowel position while the second consonant cue is formed, in synchronization with the lip movements. The lips should assume the position for the first consonant as it is cued, but one should not begin making the sound until the hand is approaching the position in which the contiguous consonant and the following vowel are to be cued. This makes it possible to pronounce the syllable naturally.' This instruction clearly means that the cuer should wait until the covering [i] vowel gesture has settled before beginning to utter the [s], which is artificially coded with a schwa instead of its natural [i] covering.
4. Velocity and acceleration profiles are derived at each instant from first- and second-order development of the 4 Hz low-pass filtered position, respectively.

Chapter 7. Bimodal perception within the natural time-course of speech production

1. For recent use and caveat about locus equations, see respectively Tabain and Butcher (1999), and Löfqvist (1999). Such equation slopes are obviously also dependent on the rate of opening of the consonantal articulators; in the most clear case, that of bilabials, even if the overall vocal tract shape for the vowel were fully anticipated into the closure phase, the rate of opening of the lips obviously could not be as fast as required theoretically for producing the same second formant values at the onset and target phases of the vowel (slope 1, intercept 0). Anyway, we have to use provisionally the only longitudinal study which addresses specifically this issue of the emergence of coarticulation.
2. Neurophysiological data give evidence that this control could originate in the medial premotor system, with the supplementary motor area (SMA) as pacer and initiator. See work by Abry *et al.* (2002), who meta-analyzed a collection of more than fifty

cases of a specific CVCV aphasia. They coined the term "frame aphasia," in support of MacNeilage's frame/content theory of speech production, ontogeny, and evolution, in agreement (1) with the aphasiologist Chris Code, pioneer of corpora of non-meaningful recurring utterances (see Code 2005) and (2) with MacNeilage's theory (see Davis and MacNeilage 2000).

3. We know the *power* story is more complicated than the French *pouvoir* one. Interpretation of *w* as a glide avoiding a hiatus, as in French, cannot account for parallels like *tower*, *flower*, or *flour*, *hour* (from Romance), *sour* (from Germanic), etc. Due to a change of stress in *poër*, from *ë* to *o*, this *o* changed to *u*, which diphthongized in *au*. Since there is actually a glide phenomenon in both languages (a *w* off-glide in the realization of the *au* diphthong), instead of the "*pouvoir phenomenon*" we will continue to dub it the "*power phenomenon.*"
4. This is the same precision as that required inside the vocal tract where one must be able to generate the different regimes resulting from a "lingual traverse across a few millimetres" as in *east* (Studdert-Kennedy 1989).
5. The necessity to analyze the vocal tract tube in 3D is obvious from the description of nineteenth-century phoneticians – with terms like "pursed lips," "grooved tongue," etc. – up to recent aeroacoustic modeling (Motoki *et al.* 2000). Using ultrasound or MRI, vocal tract imaging has greatly improved our knowledge of sound production. See PCA on 3D images by Badin *et al.* (2002), and for ultrasound, a simplified classification of configurations in two factors, openness degree and coronal shape type (crescent and ellipse) by Stone and Vatikiotis-Bateson (1995) (see also Stone *et al.* 2000).
6. Note that our current account of glides in a control model for the vowel is not reminiscent of any of the "particle/element/prime" phonologies, in which the combinatorial devices (for references see Kenstowicz 1994, p. 451) are not grounded in such an articulatory control model. For a recent comeback of phonological discussions on the representation of glides (after the longstanding post-SPE proposal by Kaye and Lowenstamm (1984), that they were simply a consequence of syllabic *position*), see the contributions to the Workshop *Towards a Phonetic and Phonological Typology of Glides*, Albuquerque, New Mexico, US, 2006, published by Chitoran et Nevins (2008). Contrary to the emphasis put by Padgett (2008) on the control of the *constriction feature*, the solution given by our 2-Comp model is a *relaxation* of the precision control for constriction (*shaping*), which produces a "consonantalization" of the type *jocu*, jeu "play" (via [d]).
7. This may have been the case in some languages, like in Albanian where [f] (a reflex of [v] before an unvoiced consonant) appears after a rounded vowel: *trofte* "trout" (cf. Latin *tructa*) *versus dreite* "right" (cf. Lat. *d(i)rectu*). But Rumanian [p] is found in *noapte* "night" (Lat. *nocte*) as in *drept* "right," that is, also without an original rounded vowel (Rosetti 1968).

Chapter 9. Audiovisual automatic speech recognition

1. Throughout this work, boldface lowercase symbols denote column vectors, and boldface capital symbols denote matrices. In addition, $\bullet^T$ denotes vector or matrix transpose, and *diag*(•), *det*(•) denote matrix diagonal and determinant, respectively.

Chapter 10. Image-based facial synthesis

1. We had to add many pronunciation variations to the dictionary to describe how Kennedy pronounced words in his Boston accent.
2. A better solution is to use a Wiener filter, or canonical correlation, to find the optimum linear mapping between the two spaces (Slaney and Covell 2000).

Chapter 11. A trainable videorealistic speech animation system

1. Technically, since the texture parameters are non-negative, they are best modeled using Gamma distributions not Gaussians. In that case, Eq. (11.12) needs to be re-written for Gamma distributions. In practice, however, we have found Gaussians to work well enough for texture parameters.

Chapter 12. Animated speech: research progress and applications

1. http://animatedspeech.com/
2. http://cslu.cse.ogi.edu/toolkit/
3. http://mambo.ucsc.edu/psl/tools/
4. http://www-3.ibm.com/able/snsspv3.html.
5. http://www.speechspecs.org/

Chapter 13. Empirical perceptual-motor linkage of multimodal speech

1. The McGurk effect has captivated the attention of numerous researchers and is discussed further in the chapters by Remez and Burnham *et al.*
2. Such quantification of the visual gain is of limited value since it depends on so many things. In particular the gain is affected by the signal-to-noise (S/N) level, the type of noise (e.g., white, pink, multi-talker babble), the alertness of subject, and probably myriad other factors.
3. The Haskins Pattern Playback synthesizes consonant-vowel sequences such as *ba, da, ga* by optically tracking representations of formants painted onto a plastic sheet. Changes in shape of the formant trajectory correspond to changes of frequency over time.
4. Given that the anterior tongue shapes the front cavity, its effect on the acoustics will be strongest for the second formant (F2). This could explain why the results obtained (Yehia *et al.* 1998) for the mapping between vocal tract shape (based on anterior tongue measures) and the speech acoustics were strongest in the 2–3 kHz range.
5. The model muscle dynamics specify forces for each muscle. Although muscle force can be computed from EMG signals and the corresponding kinematics (acceleration which is proportional to force), the interrelation of force, EMG, and acceleration is uniquely dependent on conditions of the EMG that will change even over the course of a single recording session for one individual (Loeb and Gans 1986).
6. We focus here on how constant perceptual features arise from *amodal* aspects of speech production and do not consider their connection to non-linguistic, expressive

gestures produced concurrently and often *mode-dependently* during interpersonal and human–computer interaction (HCI – e.g. Cassell *et al.* 2000; Cassell and Tartaro 2007).

7. Manner and style of speaking are highly discernible in static presentations as well, although attempts to account for such *static dynamism* seem to be limited largely to gestalt approaches to phenomenology.
8. This work was carried out by Marcia Riley at ATR, while preparing her PhD in Computer Science at Georgia Technical University (USA).

Chapter 14 Sensorimotor characteristics of speech production

1. Efferent signals represent the feed forward control necessary to initiate movement by forcing the contraction of a muscle.

References

Abry, C. and P. Badin (1996). *Speech mapping as a framework for an integrated approach to the sensori-motor foundations of language.* ETRW on Speech Production Modelling: from Control Strategies to Acoustics. Autrans, France.

Abry, C., P. Badin, K. Mawass and X. Pelorson (1998). "The Equilibrium Point Hypothesis and control space for relaxation movements or 'When is movement actually needed to control movement?'" *Les Cahiers de l'ICP, Bulletin de la Communication Parlée*. Grenoble. **4**: 27–33.

Abry, C., P. Badin and C. Scully (1994). Sound-to-gesture inversion in speech: the Speech Maps approach. *Advanced speech applications*. K. Varghese, S. Pfleger and J. P. Lefèvre. Berlin, Springer: 182–196.

Abry, C. and L.-J. Boë (1986). "Laws for lips." *Speech Communication* **5**: 97–104.

Abry, C., L.-J. Boë, P. Corsi, R. Descout, M. Gentil and P. Graillot (1980). Labialité et phonétique. Données fondamentales et études expérimentales sur la géométrie et la motricité labiales. Grenoble, Université des Langues et Lettres.

Abry, C., M.-A. Cathiard, J. Robert-Ribès and J.-L. Schwartz (1994). "The coherence of speech in audio-visual integration." *Cahiers de Psychologie Cognitive/Current Psychology of Cognition* **13**(1): 52–59.

Abry, C. and M.-T. Lallouache (1995a). "Pour un modèle d'anticipation dépendant du locuteur. Données sur l'arrondissement en français." *Bulletin de la Communication Parlée*. **3**: 85–99.

Abry, C., M.-T. Lallouache and M.-A. Cathiard (1996). How can coarticulation models account for speech sensitivity to audio-visual desynchronization? *Speechreading by Humans and Machines*. D. G. Stork and M. E. Hennecke. Berlin, Springer: 247–255.

Abry, C. and T. Lallouache (1995b). *Modeling lip constriction anticipatory behaviour for rounding in French with the MEM (Movement Expansion Model)*. Proceedings of the International Congress of Phonetic Sciences. Stockholm, Sweden, pp. 152–155.

Abry, C., M. Stefanuto, A. Vilain and R. Laboissière (2002). What can the utterance "tan, tan" of Broca's patient Leborgne tell us about the hypothesis of an emergent "babble-syllable" downloaded by SMA? *Phonetics, Phonology and Cognition*. J. Durand and B. Laks. Oxford University Press: 226–243.

Abry, C., A. Vilain and J.-L. Schwartz (2009). *Vocalize to Localize*. Amsterdam, Benjamins Current Topics 13.

Adjoudani, A. and C. Benoît (1996). On the integration of auditory and visual parameters in an HMM-based ASR. *Speechreading by Humans and Machines*. D. G. Stork and M. E. Hennecke. Berlin, Springer: 461–472.

Adjoudani, A., T. Guiard-Marigny, B. Le Goff, L. Revéret and C. Benoît (1997). *A multimedia platform for audio-visual speech processing*. European Conference on Speech Communication and Technology. Rhodes, Greece, pp. 1671–1674.

Agelfors, E., J. Beskow, B. Granström, M. Lundeberg, G. Salvi, K.-E. Spens and T. Öhman (1999). *Synthetic visual speech driven from auditory speech*. Auditory-visual Speech Processing Workshop. Santa Cruz, CA, pp. 123–127.

Aldridge, J. and G. Knupfer (1994). "Public safety: improving the effectiveness of CCTV security systems." *Journal of Forensic Science Society* **34**(4): 257–263.

Alégria, J., J. Leybaert, B. Charlier and C. Hage (1992). On the origin of phonological representations in the deaf: Hearing lips and hands. *Analytic Approaches to Human Cognition*. J. Alégria, D. Holender, J. Junça de Morais and M. Radeu. Amsterdam, Elsevier: 107–132.

Aleksic, P. S. and A. K. Katsaggelos (2003). An audio-visual person identification and verification system using FAPs as visual features. Workshop on Multimedia User Authentication. Santa Barbara, CA, pp. 80–84.

(2004a). *Comparison of low- and high-level visual features for audio-visual continuous automatic speech recognition*. International Conference on Acoustics, Speech and Signal Processing. Montreal, Canada, pp. 917–920.

(2004b). "Speech-to-video synthesis using MPEG-4 compliant visual features." *IEEE Transactions on Circuits and Systems for Video Technology* **14**(5): 682–692.

(2006). "Audio-visual biometrics." *Proceedings of the IEEE* **94**(11): 2025–2044.

Aleksic, P. S., G. Potamianos and A. K. Katsaggelos (2005). Exploiting visual information in automatic speech processing. *Handbook of Image and Video Processing*. A. Bovic. Burlington, MA, Elsevier: 1263–1289.

Aleksic, P. S., J. J. Williams, Z. Wu and A. K. Katsaggelos (2002). "Audio-visual speech recognition using MPEG-4 compliant visual features." *EURASIP Journal on Applied Signal Processing* **1**: 1213–1227.

Alissali, M., P. Deléglise and A. Rogozan (1996). *Asynchronous integration of visual information in an automatic speech recognition system*. International Conference on Spoken Language Processing. Philadelphia, PA, pp. 34–37.

Alley, T. R. (1999). *Perception of static and dynamic computer displays of facial appearance in applied settings*. International Conference on Perception and Action. Edinburgh.

Allison, T., A. Puce and G. McCarthy (2000). "Social Perception from visual cues: role of STS region." *Trends in Cognitive Science* **4**: 267–278.

Anastasakos, T., J. McDonough and J. Makhoul (1997). *Speaker adaptive training: A maximum likelihood approach to speaker normalization*. International Conference on Acoustics, Speech and Signal Processing. Munich, Germany, pp. 1043–1046.

Andersson, U. and B. Lidestam (2005). "Bottom-up driven speechreading in a speechreading expert: the case of AA." *Ear and Hearing* **26**: 214–224.

André-Obrecht, R., B. Jacob and N. Parlangeau (1997). *Audiovisual speech recognition and segmental master slave HMM*. European Tutorial Workshop on Audio-Visual Speech Processing. Rhodes, Greece, pp. 49–52.

Andruski, J. E., S. E. Blumstein and M. Burton (1994). "The effect of subphonetic differences on lexical access." *Cognition* **52**: 163–187.

Angkititrakul, P., J. H. L. Hansen, S. Choi, T. Creek, J. Hayes, J. Kim, D. Kwak, L. T. Noecker and A. Phan (2009). UT Drive: The smart vehicle project. *In-Vehicle*

Corpus and Signal Processing for Driver Behavior. K. Takeda, J. H. L. Hansen, H. Erdoggan and H. Abut. New York, Springer: 55–67.

Anthony, D., E. Hines, J. Barham and D. Taylor (1990). *A comparison of image compression by neural networks and principal component analysis*. IEEE International Joint Conference on Neural Networks. San Diego, CA, pp. 339–344.

Arikan, O. and D. Forsyth (2002). *Interactive motion generation from examples*. SIGGRAPH. San Antonio, TX, pp. 483–490.

Arnal, L. H., B. Morillon, C. A. Kell and A. L. Giraud (2009). "Dual neural routing of visual facilitation in speech processing." *Journal of Neurosciences* **29**(43): 13445–13453.

Atal, B. S., J. J. Chang, M. V. Mathews and J. W. Tukey (1978). "Inversion of articulatory-to-acoustic transformation in the vocal tract by a computer sorting technique." *Journal of the Acoustical Society of America* **63**: 1535–1555.

Attina, V., D. Beautemps and M.-A. Cathiard (2002a). *Contrôle de l'anticipation vocalique d'arrondissement en Langage Parlé Complété*. Journées d'Etudes sur la Parole. Nancy, France.

(2002b). *Coordination of hand and orofacial movements for CV sequences in French cued speech*. International Conference on Speech and Language Processing. Boulder, USA, pp. 1945–1948.

(2002c). *Organisation spatio-temporelle main–lèvres–son de séquences CV en Langage Parlé Complété*. Journées d'Etudes sur la Parole. Nancy, France.

(2003a). *Temporal organization of French cued speech production*. International Conference of Phonetic Sciences. Barcelona, Spain, pp. 1935–1938.

(2004a). *Cued Speech production: giving a hand to speech acoustics*. CFA/DAGA'04. Strasbourg, France, pp. 1143–1144.

Attina, V., D. Beautemps, M.-A. Cathiard and M. Odisio (2003b). *Towards an audiovisual synthesizer for Cued Speech: rules for CV French syllables*. Auditory-Visual Speech Processing. St-Jorioz, France, pp. 227–232.

(2004b). "A pilot study of temporal organization in cued speech production of French syllables: rules for a cued speech synthesizer." *Speech Communication* **44**: 197–214.

Attina, V., M.-A. Cathiard and D. Beautemps (2002d). *Controlling anticipatory behavior for rounding in French cued speech*. Proceedings of ICSLP. Denver, Colorado, pp. 1949–1952.

Aubergé, V. and L. Lemaître (2000). *The prosody of smile*. ISCA Workshop on Speech and Emotion. Newcastle, Ireland, pp. 122–126.

Audouy, M. (2000). Logiciel de traitement d'images vidéo pour la détermination de mouvements des lèvres. Grenoble, ENSIMAG, Projet de fin d'études, option génie logiciel.

Auer, E. T. and L. E. Bernstein (1997). "Speechreading and the structure of the lexicon: Computationally modeling the effects of reduced phonetic distinctiveness on lexical uniqueness." *Journal of the Acoustical Society of America* **102**: 3704–3710.

Auer, E. T., L. E. Bernstein, R. S. Waldstein and P. E. Tucker (1997). *Effects of phonetic variation and the structure of the lexicon on the uniqueness of words*. ESCA Workshop on Audio-visual Speech Processing: Cognitive and Computational Approaches. Rhodes, Greece, pp. 21–24.

Auer, E. T., Jr., (2002). "The influence of the lexicon on speechread word recognition: contrasting segmental and lexical distinctiveness." *Psychonomic Bulletin & Review* **9**(2): 341–347.

Auer, E. T., Jr. and L. E. Bernstein (2007). "Enhanced visual speech perception in individuals with early onset hearing impairment." *Journal of Speech, Language, and Hearing Research* **50**(5): 1157–1165.

Auer, E. T., Jr., L. E. Bernstein and P. E. Tucker (2000). "Is subjective word familiarity a meter of ambient language? A natural experiment on effects of perceptual experience." *Memory and Cognition* **28**: 789–797.

Badin, P., G. Bailly, M. Raybaudi and C. Segebarth (1998). *A three-dimensional linear articulatory model based on MRI data*. International Conference on Speech and Language Processing. Sydney, Australia, pp. 417–420.

Badin, P., G. Bailly, L. Revéret, M. Baciu, C. Segebarth and C. Savariaux (2002). "Three-dimensional linear articulatory modeling of tongue, lips and face based on MRI and video images." *Journal of Phonetics* **30**(3): 533–553.

Badin, P., P. Borel, G. Bailly, L. Revéret, M. Baciu and C. Segebarth (2000). *Towards an audiovisual virtual talking head: 3D articulatory modeling of tongue, lips and face based on MRI and video images*. Proceedings of the 5th Speech Production Seminar. Kloster Seeon, Germany, pp. 261–264.

Badin, P. and A. Serrurier (2006). *Three-dimensional linear modeling of tongue: Articulatory data and models*. International Seminar on Speech Production (ISSP). Ubatuba, SP, Brazil, pp. 395–402.

Badin, P., Y. Tarabalka, F. Elisei and G. Bailly (2008). *Can you "read tongue movements"*? Interspeech. Brisbane, Australia, pp. 2635–2637.

Badin, P., Y. Tarabalka, F. Elisei and G. Bailly (2010). "Can you 'read tongue movements'? Evaluation of the contribution of tongue display to speech understanding." *Speech Communication* **52**(4): 493–503.

Baer, T., P. Alfonso and K. Honda (1998). "Electromyography of the tongue muscles during vowels in /@pVp/ environment." *Annual Bulletin of the Research Institute for Logopedics and Phoniatrics* **22**: 7–19.

Bahl, L. R., P. F. Brown, P. V. DeSouza and L. R. Mercer (1986). *Maximum mutual information estimation of hidden Markov model parameters for speech recognition*. International Conference on Acoustics, Speech and Signal Processing. Tokyo, Japan, pp. 49–52.

Bailly, G. (1997). "Learning to speak. Sensori-motor control of speech movements." *Speech Communication* **22**(2–3): 251–267.

Bailly, G. (2002). *Audiovisual speech synthesis. From ground truth to models*. International Conference on Speech and Language Processing. Boulder, Colorado, pp. 1453–1456.

Bailly, G. and P. Badin (2002). *Seeing tongue movements from outside*. International Conference on Speech and Language Processing. Boulder, Colorado, pp. 1913–1916.

Bailly, G., P. Badin, D. Beautemps and F. Elisei (2010). Speech technologies for augmented communication. *Computer Synthesized Speech Technologies: Tools for Aiding Impairment*. J. Mullennix and S. Stern. Hershey, PA, IGI Global: 116–128.

Bailly, G., A. Bégault, F. Elisei and P. Badin (2008a). *Speaking with smile or disgust: data and models*. Auditory-Visual Speech Processing Workshop (AVSP). Tangalooma, Australia, pp. 111–116.

Bailly, G., M. Bérar, F. Elisei and M. Odisio (2003). "Audiovisual speech synthesis." *International Journal of Speech Technology* **6**: 331–346.

Bailly, G., O. Govokhina, G. Breton, F. Elisei and C. Savariaux (2008b). *The trainable trajectory formation model TD-HMM parameterized for the LIPS 2008 challenge.* Interspeech. Brisbane, Australia, pp. 2318–2321.

Bailly, G., O. Govokhina, F. Elisei and G. Breton (2009). "Lip-synching using speaker-specific articulation, shape and appearance models." *Journal of Acoustics, Speech and Music Processing. Special issue on "Animating Virtual Speakers or Singers from Audio: Lip-Synching Facial Animation"* ID 769494: 11 pages.

Bailly, G., R. Laboissière and A. Galván (1997). Learning to speak: Speech production and sensori-motor representations. *Self-Organization, Computational Maps and Motor Control*. P. Morasso and V. Sanguineti. Amsterdam, Elsevier: 593–615.

Bailly, G., R. Laboissière and J.-L. Schwartz (1991). "Formant trajectories as audible gestures: An alternative for speech synthesis." *Journal of Phonetics* **19**(1): 9–23.

Banesty, J., J. Chen, Y. Huang and I. Cohen (2009). *Noise Reduction in Speech Processing*. Berlin, Springer.

Barker, J. and X. Shao (2009). "Energetic and informational masking effects in an audiovisual speech recognition system." *IEEE Transactions on Audio, Speech, and Language Processing* **17**(3): 446–458.

Barker, J. P. and F. Berthommier (1999). *Estimation of speech acoustics from visual speech features: A comparison of linear and non-linear models*. International Conference on Auditory-Visual Speech Processing. Santa Cruz, CA, pp. 112–117.

Barker, L. J. (2003). "Computer-assisted vocabulary acquisition: The CSLU vocabulary tutor in oral-deaf education." *Journal of Deaf Studies and Deaf Education* **8**: 187–198.

Barron, J. L., D. J. Fleet and S. Beauchemin (1994). "Performance of optical flow techniques." *International Journal of Computer Vision* **12**(1): 43–77.

Bartlett, J. C., S. Hurry and W. Thorley (1984). "Typicality and familiarity of faces." *Memory & Cognition* **12**: 219–228.

Bassili, J. N. (1978). "Facial motion in the perception of faces and of emotional expressions." *Journal of Experimental Psychology: Human Perception and Performance* **4**: 373–379.

Basu, S., I. Essa and A. Pentland (1996). *Motion regularization for model-based head tracking*. International Conference on Pattern Recognition (ICPR). Vienna, Austria, pp. 611–616.

Basu, S., N. Oliver and A. Pentland (1998). *3D modeling and tracking of human lip motions*. International Conference on Computer Vision. Mumbai, India, pp. 337–343.

Baudouin, J. Y., S. Sansone and G. Tiberghien (2000). "Recognizing expression from familiar and unfamiliar faces." *Pragmatics & Cognition* **8**(1): 123–147.

Bavelier, D. and H. J. Neville (2002). "Cross-modal plasticity: where and how?" *Nature Reviews Neuroscience* **3**(6): 443–452.

Beale, R. and T. Jackson (1990). *Neural Computing: An Introduction*. Bristol, Institute of Physics Publishing.

Beautemps, D., P. Badin and G. Bailly (2001). "Degrees of freedom in speech production: analysis of cineradio- and labio-films data for a reference subject, and articulatory-acoustic modeling." *Journal of the Acoustical Society of America* **109** (5): 2165–2180.

Beautemps, D., P. Borel and S. Manolios (1999). *Hyper-articulated speech: auditory and visual intelligibility*. EuroSpeech. Budapest, Hungary, pp. 109–112.

Beier, T. and S. Neely (1992a). "Feature-based image metamorphosis." *Computer Graphics* **26**(2): 35–42.

Beier, T. and S. Neely (1992b). Feature-based image metamorphosis. Computer Graphics (Proc. ACM SIGGRAPH), ACM, pp. 35–42.

Bell, A. M. (1867). *Visible Speech: The Science of Universal Alphabetics*. London, Simkin, Marshall & Co.

Ben Youssef, A., P. Badin and G. Bailly (2010). *Can tongue be recovered from face? The answer of data-driven statistical models*. Interspeech. Tokyo, pp. 2002–2005.

Ben Youssef, A., P. Badin, G. Bailly and P. Heracleous (2009). *Acoustic-to-articulatory inversion using speech recognition and trajectory formation based on phoneme hidden Markov models*. Interspeech. Brighton, pp. 2255–2258.

Benguerel, A.-P. and M. K. Pichora-Fuller (1982). "Coarticulation effects in lipreading." *Journal of Speech and Hearing Research* **25**: 600–607.

Benoît, C. (2000). *Bimodal speech: Cognitive and computational approaches*. International Conference on Human and Machine Processing of Language and Speech. Bangkok, Chulalongkorn University Press, pp. 314–328.

Benoît, C., C. Abry, M.-A. Cathiard, T. Guiard-Marigny and M.-T. Lallouache (1995a). *Read my lips: Where? How? When? And so . . . What*? 8th International Congress on Event Perception & Action. Marseille, France, pp. 423–426.

Benoît, C., T. Guiard-Marigny, B. Le Goff and A. Adjoudani (1995b). Which components of the face do humans and machines best speechread? *Speechreading by Humans and Machines*. D. G. Stork and M. E. Hennecke. Berlin, Springer: 315–328.

Benoît, C., T. Lallouache, T. Mohamadi and C. Abry (1992). A set of French visemes for visual speech synthesis. *Talking Machines: Theories, Models and Designs*. G. Bailly and C. Benoît. Amsterdam, Elsevier: 485–501.

Benoît, C. and B. Le Goff (1998). "Audio-visual speech synthesis from French text: Eight years of models, designs and evaluation at the ICP." *Speech Communication* **26**: 117–129.

Benoît, C. and L. C. W. Pols (1992). On the assessment of synthetic speech. *Talking Machines: Theories, Models and Designs*. G. Bailly, C. Benoît and T. R. Sawallis. Amsterdam, Elsevier: 435–441.

Benoit, M. M., T. Raij, F. H. Lin, I. P. Jääskeläinen and S. Stufflebeam (2010). "Primary and multisensory cortical activity is correlated with audiovisual percepts." *Human Brain Mapping* **31**(4): 526–538.

Bérar, M., G. Bailly, M. Chabanas, M. Desvignes, F. Elisei, M. Odisio and Y. Pahan (2006). Towards a generic talking head. *Towards a better understanding of speech production processes*. J. Harrington and M. Tabain. New York, Psychology Press: 341–362.

Bérar, M., G. Bailly, M. Chabanas, F. Elisei, M. Odisio and Y. Pahan (2003). *Towards a generic talking head*. 6th International Seminar on Speech Production. Sydney, Australia, pp. 7–12.

Bergen, J. R., P. Anandan, K. J. Hanna and R. Hingorani (1992). *Hierarchical model-based motion estimation*. European Conference on Computer Vision. Santa Margherita, Italy, pp. 237–252.

Berger, K. W. (1972). "Visemes and homophenous words." *Teacher of the Deaf* **70**: 396–399.

Bernstein, L. E., E. T. Auer, J. K. Moore, C. W. Ponton, M. Don and M. Singh (2000a). *Does Auditory Cortex Listen to Visible Speech*? San Francisco, CA, Cognitive Neuroscience Society.

(2002). "Visual speech perception without primary auditory cortex activation." *Neuroreport* **13**(3): 311–315.

Bernstein, L. E., E. T. Auer Jr. and J. K. Moore (2004). Audiovisual speech binding: Convergence or association? *Handbook of Multisensory Processing*. G. A. Calvert, C. Spence and B. E. Stein. Cambridge, MA, MIT Press: 203–223.

Bernstein, L. E., E. T. Auer Jr., M. Wagner and C. W. Ponton (2008). "Spatiotemporal dynamics of audiovisual speech processing." *Neuroimage* **39**(1): 423–435.

Bernstein, L. E., D. C. Coulter, M. P. O'Connell, S. P. Eberhardt and M. E. Demorest (1993). *Vibrotactile and haptic speech codes*. International Conference on Tactile Aids, Hearing Aids, and Cochlear Implants. Stockholm, Sweden.

Bernstein, L. E., M. E. Demorest and P. E. Tucker (1998). What makes a good speechreader? First you have to find one. *Hearing by Eye II*. R. Campbell, B. Dodd and D. Burnham. Hove, UK, Psychology Press: 211–227.

(2000b). "Speech perception without hearing." *Perception & Psychophysics* **62**: 233–252.

Bernstein, L. E. and S. P. Eberhardt (1986a). Johns Hopkins Lipreading Corpus I-II: Disc 1. Baltimore, MD, Johns Hopkins University.

(1986b). Johns Hopkins Lipreading Corpus Videodisk Set. Baltimore, MD, Johns Hopkins University.

Bernstein, L. E., P. Iverson and E. T. Auer Jr. (1997). *Elucidating the complex relationships between phonetic perception and word recognition in audiovisual speech perception*. Workshop on Auditory-Visual Speech Processing. Rhodes, Greece, pp. 89–92.

Bernstein, L. E., J. Jiang, A. Alwan and E. T. Auer Jr. (2001). *Similarity structure in visual phonetic perception and optical phonetics*. Workshop on Auditory-Visual Speech Processing. Ąalborg, Denmark, pp. 50–55.

Bertelson, P., J. Vroomen and B. de Gelder (1997). *Auditory-visual interaction in voice localization and in bimodal speech recognition: The effects of desynchronization*. ESCA Workshop on Audio-Visual Speech Processing: Cognitive and Computational Approaches. Rhodes, Greece, pp. 97–100.

Berthommier, F. (2001). *Audio-visual recognition of spectrally reduced speech*. International Conference on Auditory-Visual Speech Processing. Aalborg, Denmark, pp. 183–189.

(2003). *A phonetically neutral model of the low-level audiovisual interaction*. Auditory-Visual Speech Processing. St-Jorioz, France, pp. 89–94.

Berthommier, F. and H. Glotin (1999). *A new SNR-feature mapping for robust multi-stream speech recognition*. International Congress on Phonetic Sciences. San Francisco, CA, pp. 711–715.

Besle, J., C. Fischer, A. Bidet-Caulet, F. Lecaignard, O. Bertrand and M. H. Giard (2008). "Visual activation and audiovisual interactions in the auditory cortex during speech perception: intracranial recordings in humans." *Journal of Neurosciences* **28** (52): 14301–14310.

Besle, J., A. Fort, C. Delpuech and M. H. Giard (2004). "Bimodal speech: early suppressive visual effects in human auditory cortex." *European Journal of Neuroscience* **20**: 2225–2234.

Beyerlein, P. (1998). *Discriminative model combination*. International Conference on Acoustics, Speech and Signal Processing. Seattle, WA, pp. 481–484.

Beymer, D. and T. Poggio (1996). "Image representations for visual learning." *Science* **272**: 1905–1909.

Beymer, D., A. Shashua and T. Poggio (1993). Example based image analysis and synthesis. Boston, MA, MIT AI Lab., Tech. Rep. no. 1431.

Bilmes, J. and C. Bartels (2005). "Graphical model architectures for speech recognition." *IEEE Signal Processing Magazine* **22**(5): 89–100.

Binder, J. R., J. A. Frost, T. A. Hammeke, P. S. Bellgowan, J. A. Springer, J. N. Kaufman and E. T. Possing (2000). "Human temporal lobe activation by speech and non-speech sounds." *Cerebral Cortex* **10**: 512–528.

Binder, J. R., S. M. Rao, T. A. Hammeke, F. Z. Yetkin, A. Jesmanowicz, P. A. Bandettini, E. C. Wong, L. D. Estkowski, M. D. Goldstein and V. M. Haughton (2004). "Functional magnetic resonance imaging of human auditory cortex." *Annals of Neurology* **35**(6): 662–672.

Bingham, G. P. (1987). "Kinematic form and scaling – Further investigations on the visual perception of lifted weight." *Journal of Experimental Psychology: Human Perception and Performance* **13**(2): 155–177.

Bishop, C. M. (1995). *Neural Networks for Pattern Recognition*. Oxford, Clarendon Press.

Black, A. and P. Taylor (1997). The Festival speech synthesis system. University of Edinburgh.

Black, M., D. Fleet and Y. Yaccob (2000). "Robustly estimating changes in image appearance." *Computer Vision and Image Understanding, Special Issue on Robust Statistical Techniques in Image Understanding* **78**(1): 8–31.

Blake, A., R. Curwen and A. Zisserman (1993). "A framework for spatiotemporal control in the tracking of visual contours." *International Journal of Computer Vision* **11**: 127–145.

Blake, A. and M. Isard (1994). "3D position, attitude and shape input using video tracking of hands and lips." *Computer Graphics Proceedings* (Annual Conference Series (ACM)): 185–192.

Blanz, V. and T. Vetter (1999). *A morphable model for the synthesis of 3D faces*. SIGGRAPH. Los Angeles, CA, pp. 187–194.

Borel, P., P. Badin, L. Revéret and G. Bailly (2000). *Modélisation articulatoire linéaire 3D d'un visage pour une tête parlante virtuelle*. Actes des 23èmes Journées d'Etude de la Parole. Aussois, France, pp. 121–124.

Bosseler, A. and D. W. Massaro (2004). "Development and evaluation of a computer-animated tutor for vocabulary and language learning in children with autism." *Journal of Autism and Developmental Disorders* **33**: 653–672.

Boston, D. W. (1973). "Synthetic facial communication." *British Journal of Audiology* **7**: 95–101.

Bothe, H.-H. (1996). Relations of audio and visual speech signals in a physical feature space: implications for the hearing-impaired. *Speechreading by Humans and Machines*. D. G. Stork and M. E. Hennecke. Berlin, Springer: 445–460.

Bothe, H.-H., F. Rieger and R. Tackmann (1993). Visual speech and co-articulation effects. IEEE International Conference on Acoustics, Speech, and Signal Processing, pp. E634–E637.

Bould, E., N. Morris and B. Wink (2008). "Recognising subtle emotional expressions: the role of facial movements." *Cognition & Emotion* **22**: 1569–1587.
Bourlard, H. and S. Dupont (1996). *A new ASR approach based on independent processing and recombination of partial frequency bands*. International Conference on Spoken Language Processing. Philadelphia, PA, pp. 426–429.
Bradley, D. C., G. C. Chang and R. A. Andersen (1998). "Encoding of three-dimensional structure-from-motion by primate area MT neurons." *Nature* **392**: 714–717.
Brancazio, L. and J. L. Miller (2005). "Use of visual information in speech perception: Evidence for a visual rate effect both with and without a McGurk effect." *Perception & Psychophysics* **67**: 759–769.
Brand, M. (1999). *Voice puppetry*. SIGGRAPH'99. Los Angeles, CA, pp. 21–28.
Brand, M. and A. Hertzmann (2000). *Style machines*. SIGGRAPH. New Orleans, LO, pp. 183–192.
Brand, M., N. Oliver and A. Pentland (1997). *Coupled hidden Markov models for complex action recognition*. Conference on Computer Vision and Pattern Recognition. San Juan, Puerto Rico, pp. 994–999.
Bredin, H. and G. Chollet (2007). "Audiovisual speech synchrony measure: Application to biometrics." *EURASIP Journal on Advances in Signal Processing* **1**: 179–190.
Breeuwer, M. and R. Plomp (1986). "Speechreading supplemented with auditorily presented speech parameters." *Journal of the Acoustical Society of America* **79** (2): 481–499.
Bregler, C., M. Covell and M. Slaney (1997a). *Video rewrite: visual speech synthesis from video*. International Conference on Auditory-Visual Speech Processing. Rhodes, Greece, pp. 153–156.
(1997b). *VideoRewrite: driving visual speech with audio*. SIGGRAPH'97. Los Angeles, CA, pp. 353–360.
Bregler, C., H. Hild, S. Manke and A. Waibel (1993). *Improving connected letter recognition by lipreading*. International Conference on Acoustics, Speech and Signal Processing. Minneapolis, MN, pp. 557–560.
Bregler, C. and Y. Konig (1994). *"Eigenlips" for robust speech recognition*. International Conference on Acoustics, Speech and Signal Processing. Adelaide, Australia, pp. 669–672.
Bregler, C., G. Williams, S. Rosenthal and I. McDowall (2009). *Improving acoustic speaker verification with visual body-language features*. ICASSP. Taipei, Taiwan, pp. 1909–1912.
Bregman, A. S. (1990). *Auditory Scene Analysis: The Perceptual Organization of Sound*. Cambridge, MA, MIT Press.
Bristow, D., G. Dehaene-Lambertz, J. Mattout, C. Soares, T. Gliga, S. Baillet and J.-F. Mangin (2008). "Hearing faces: How the infant brain matches the face it sees with the speech it hears." *Journal of Cognitive Neuroscience* **21**: 905–921.
Brooke, N. M. (1982). "Visual speech synthesis for speech perception experiments." *Journal of the Acoustical Society of America* **71**(S77).
(1989). Visible speech signals: investigating their analysis, synthesis and perception. *The Structure of Multimodal Dialogue*. M. M. Taylor, F. Néel and D. G. Bouwhuis. Amsterdam, North-Holland: 249–258.
(1992a). Computer graphics animations of speech production. *Advances in Speech, Hearing and Language Processing*. W. A. Ainsworth. London, JAI Press: 87–134.

(1992b). Computer graphics synthesis of talking faces. *Talking Machines: Theories, Models and Designs*. G. Bailly and C. Benoît. Amsterdam, Elsevier: 505–522.

(1996). Talking heads and speech recognisers that can see: the computer processing of visual speech signals. *Speechreading by Humans and Machines*. D. G. Stork and M. E. Hennecke. Berlin, Springer: 351–371.

Brooke, N. M. and S. D. Scott (1994a). *Computer graphics animations of talking faces based on stochastic models*. International Symposium on Speech, Image-processing and Neural Networks. Hong Kong, pp. 73–76.

(1994b). *PCA image coding schemes and visual speech intelligibility*. Proceedings of the Institute of Acoustics, Autumn Meeting. Windermere, England, pp. 123–129.

(1998a). *An audio-visual speech synthesiser*. ETRW on Speech Technology in Language Learning. Marhölmen, Sweden, pp. 147–150.

(1998b). *Two- and three-dimensional audio-visual speech synthesis*. Auditory-Visual Speech Processing Workshop (AVSP). Terrigal, Australia, pp. 213–218.

Brooke, N. M. and A. Q. Summerfield (1983). "Analysis, synthesis and perception of visible articulatory movements." *Journal of Phonetics* **11**: 63–76.

Brooke, N. M. and P. D. Templeton (1990). *Visual speech intelligibility of digitally processed facial images*. Proceedings of the Institute of Acoustics, Autumn Meeting. Windermere, England, pp. 483–490.

Brooke, N. M. and M. J. Tomlinson (2000). Processing facial images to enhance speech communications. *The Structure of Multimodal Dialogue II*. M. M. Taylor, F. Néel and D. G. Bouwhuis. Philadelphia, John Benjamins Publishing Company: 465–484.

Brooke, N. M., M. J. Tomlinson and R. K. Moore (1994). *Automatic speech recognition that includes visual speech cues*. Proceedings of the Institute of Acoustics, Autumn Meeting. Windermere, England, pp. 15–22.

Brothers, L. (1990). "The social brain: a project for integrating primate behavior and neurophysiology in a new domain." *Concepts in Neuroscience* **1**: 27–51.

Bruce, V. (1994). "Stability from variation: The case of face recognition. The M.D. Vernon memorial lecture." *Quarterly Journal of Experimental Psychology* **47A**: 5–28.

Bruce, V., D. Carson, M. A. Burton and A. W. Ellis (2000). "Perceptual priming is not a necessary consequence of semantic classification of pictures." *Quarterly Journal of Experimental Psychology* (**53A**): 239–323.

Bruce, V. and S. Langton (1994). "The use of pigmentation and shading information in recognising the sex and identities of faces." *Perception* **23**: 803–822.

Bruce, V. and T. Valentine (1985). "Identity priming in face recognition." *British Journal of Psychology* **76**: 373–383.

(1988). When a nod's as good as a wink. The role of dynamic information in facial recognition. *Practical Aspects of Memory: Current Research and Issues*. M. M. Gruneberg and E. Morris. Hillsdale, NJ, Erlbaum.

Bruce, V. and A. W. Young (1986). "Understanding face recognition." *British Journal of Psychology* **77**: 305–327.

Bruner, J. S. and R. Tagiuri (1954). The perception of people. *Handbook of Social Psychology, Vol 2. Reading*. G. Lindzey. Boston, MA, Addison-Wesley: 634–654.

Bruyer, R., C. Laterre, X. Seron, P. Feyereisen, E. Strypstein, E. Pierrard and D. Rectem (1983). "A case of prosopagnosia with some preserved covert remembrance of familiar faces." *Brain and Cognition* **2**: 257–284.

Bub, U., M. Hunke and A. Waibel (1995). *Knowing who to listen to in speech recognition: Visually guided beamforming*. International Conference on Acoustics, Speech and Signal Processing. Detroit, MI, pp. 848–851.

Buccino, G., F. Binkofski, G. R. Fink, L. Fadiga, L. Fogassi, V. Gallese, R. J. Seitz, K. Zilles, G. Rizzolatti and H. J. Freund (2001). "Action observation activates premotor and parietal areas in a somatotopic manner: A fMRI study." *European Journal of of Neuroscience* **13**: 400–404.

Buchaillard, S., P. Perrier and Y. Payan (2009). "A biomechanical model of cardinal vowel production: muscle activations and the impact of gravity on tongue positioning." *Journal of the Acoustical Society of America* **126**(4): 2033–2051.

Burnham, D. (1986). "Developmental loss of speech perception: Exposure to and experience with a first language." *Applied Psycholinguistics* **7**: 206–240.

(1998). Language specificity in the development of auditory-visual speech perception. *Hearing by Eye II: Advances in the Psychology of Speechreading and Auditory-visual Speech*. R. Campbell, B. Dodd and D. Burnham. Hove, UK, Psychology Press: 27–60.

(2000). *Excavations in language development: Cross-linguistic studies of consonant and tone perception*. International Conference on Human and Machine Processing of Language and Speech. Bangkok, Thailand, Chulalongkorn University Press.

(2003). "Language specific speech perception and the onset of reading." *Reading and Writing: An Interdisciplinary Journal* **16**: 573–609.

Burnham, D., V. Ciocca, C. Lauw, S. Lau and S. Stokes (2000). *Perception of visual information for Cantonese tones*. Australian International Conference on Speech Science and Technology. Canberra, Australian Speech Science and Technology Association, pp. 86–91.

Burnham, D. and B. Dodd (1996). Auditory-visual speech perception as a direct process: The McGurk effect in infants and across languages. *Speechreading by Humans and Machines*. D. G. Stork and M. E. Hennecke. Berlin, Springer: 103–114.

(1998). "Familiarity and novelty in infant cross-language studies: Factors, problems, and a possible solution." *Advances in Infancy Research* **12**: 170–187.

(2004). "Auditory-visual speech integration by pre-linguistic infants: Perception of an emergent consonant in the McGurk effect." *Developmental Psychobiology* **44**: 204–220.

Burnham, D., E. Francis, D. Webster, S. Luksaneeyanawin, C. Attapaiboon, F. Lacerda and P. Keller (1996). *Perception of lexical tone across languages: Evidence for a linguistic mode of processing*. International Conference on Spoken Language Processing, pp. 2514–2517.

Burnham, D. and S. Lau (1998). *The effect of tonal information on auditory reliance in the McGurk effect*. International Conference on Auditory-Visual Speech Processing. Terrigal, Australia, pp. 37–42.

(1999). *The integration of auditory and visual speech information with foreign speakers: the role of expectancy*. AVSP. Santa Cruz, CA, pp. 80–85.

Burnham, D., S. Lau, H. Tam and C. Schoknecht (2001). *Visual discrimination of Cantonese tone by tonal but non-Cantonese speakers, and by non-tonal language speakers*. International Conference on Auditory-Visual Speech Processing. Aalborg, Denmark, pp. 155–160.

Burnham, D. and K. Mattock (2010). Auditory Development. *Handbook of Infant Development: 2nd Edition. Volume I: Basic Research.* G. Bremner and T. D. Wachs. Blackwood, NJ, Wiley-Blackwell.

Burnham, D., M. Tyler and S. Horlyck (2002). Periods of speech perception development and their vestiges in adulthood. *An Integrated View of Language Development: Papers in Honor of Henning Wode*. P. Burmeister, T. Piske and A. Rohde. Trier, Germany, Wissenschaftlicher Verlag Trier.

Burt, P. and E. H. Adelson (1983a). "A multiresolution spline with application to image mosaics." *ACM Transactions on Graphics* **2**(4): 217–236.

(1983b). "The Laplacian pyramid as a compact image code." *IEEE Transactions on Communications* **31**(4): 532–540.

Burton, A. M., V. Bruce and P. J. B. Hancock (1999). "From pixels to people: a model of familiar face recognition." *Cognitive Science* **23**: 1–31.

Burton, A. M., V. Bruce and R. A. Johnston (1990). "Understanding face recognition with an interactive activation model." *British Journal of Psychology* **81**: 361–380.

Burton, A. M., S. Wilson, M. Cowan and V. Bruce (1999). "Face recognition in poor quality video: evidence from security surveillance." *Psychological Sciences* **10**: 243–248.

Butcher, N. (2009). Investigating the dynamic advantage for same and other-race faces. Unpublished PhD Thesis, University of Manchester.

Cabeza, R. and A. Kingstone (2006). *Handbook of Functional Neuroimaging of Cognition*. Cambridge, MA, MIT Press

Callan, D. E., A. Callan, E. Kroos and E. Vatikiotis-Bateson (2001). "Multimodal contributions to speech perception revealed by independent component analysis: a single sweep EEG study." *Cognitive Brain Research* **10**: 349–353.

Callan, D. E., J. A. Jones, K. Munhall, A. M. Callan, C. Kroos and E. Vatikiotis-Bateson (2003). "Neural processes underlying perceptual enhancement by visual speech gestures." *Neuroreport* **14**(17): 2213–2218.

Callan, D. E., J. A. Jones, K. G. Munhall, C. Kroos, A. Callan and E. Vatikiotis-Bateson (2004). "Multisensory-integration sites identified by perception of spatial wavelet filtered visual speech gesture information." *Journal of Cognitive Neuroscience* **16**: 805–816.

Calvert, G. A., M. J. Brammer, E. T. Bullmore, R. Campbell, S. D. Iversen and A. S. David (1999). "Response amplification in sensory-specific cortices during cross-modal binding." *Neuroreport* **10**: 2619–2623.

Calvert, G. A., E. T. Bullmore, M. J. Brammer, R. Campbell, S. C. Williams, P. K. McGuire, P. W. Woodruff, S. D. Iversen and A. S. David (1997). "Activation of auditory cortex during silent lipreading." *Science* **276**: 593–596.

Calvert, G. A. and R. Campbell (2003). "Reading speech from still and moving faces: The neural substrates of visible speech." *Journal of Cognitive Neuroscience* **15**: 57–70.

Calvert, G. A., R. Campbell and M. J. Brammer (2000). "Evidence from functional magnetic resonance imaging of crossmodal binding in the human heteromodal cortex." *Current Biology* **10**: 649–657.

Calvert, G. A., C. Spence and B. E. Stein (2004). *The Handbook of Multisensory Processes*. Cambridge, MA, MIT Press.

Calvert, G. A. and T. Thesen (2004). "Multisensory Integration: methodological approaches and emerging principles in the human brain." *Journal of Physiology* **98**(1–3): 191–205.

Campbell, R. (1986). "The lateralisation of lip-reading: A first look." *Brain and Cognition* **5**: 1–21.

(1996). Seeing brains reading speech: A review and speculations. *Speechreading by Humans and Machines*. D. Stork and M. Hennecke. Berlin, Springer: 115–133.

(2008). "The processing of audiovisual speech." *Philosophical Transactions of the Royal Society of London B* **363**: 1001–1010.

(2011). Speechreading: what's missing? *The Oxford Handbook of Face Processing*. A. Calder, G. Rhodes and J. Haxby. Oxford University Press: 605–630

Campbell, R., B. Brooks, E. H. F. De Haan and T. Roberts (1996). "Dissociating face processing skills – decisions about lip-read speech, expression and identity." *Quarterly Journal of Experimental Psychology, Section A: Human Experimental Psychology* **49**(2): 295–314.

Campbell, R. and B. Dodd (1980). "Hearing by eye." *Quarterly Journal of Experimental Psychology* **32**: 85–99.

Campbell, R., B. Dodd and D. Burnham (1998). *Hearing by Eye II. The Psychology of Speechreading and Auditory-Visual Speech*. Hove, UK, Psychology Press Ltd.

Campbell, R., T. Landis and M. Regard (1986). "Face recognition and lipreading: a neurological dissociation." *Brain* **109**: 509–521.

Campbell, R., M. MacSweeney, S. Surguladze, G. Calvert, P. K. McGuire, J. Suckling, M. J. Brammer and A. S. David (2001). "Cortical substrates for the perception of face actions: An fMRI study of the specificity of activation for seen speech and for meaningless lower face acts." *Cognitive Brain Research* **12**: 233–243.

Campbell, R., J. Zihl, D. Massaro, K. Munhall and M. M. Cohen (1997). "Speechreading in the akinetopsic patient, L.M." *Brain* **120**: 1793–1803.

Cao, Y., P. Faloutsos, E. Kohler and F. Pighin (2004). *Real-time speech motion Synthesis from recorded motions*. ACM Siggraph/Eurographics Symposium on Computer Animation. Grenoble, France, pp. 345–353.

Capek, C. M., D. Bavelier, D. Corina, A. J. Newman, P. Jezzard and H. J. Neville (2004). "The cortical organization of audio-visual sentence comprehension: an fMRI study at 4 Tesla." *Brain Research: Cognitive Brain Research* **20**: 111–119.

Capek, C. M., R. Campbell, M. MacSweeney, B. Woll, M. Seal, D. Waters, A. S. Davis, P. K. McGuire and M. J. Brammer (2005). The organization of speechreading as a function of attention. Cognitive Neuroscience Society Annual Meeting, poster presentation.

Capek, C. M., M. Macsweeney, B. Woll, D. Waters, P. K. McGuire, A. S. David, M. J. Brammer and R. Campbell (2008a). "Cortical circuits for silent speechreading in deaf and hearing people." *Neuropsychologia* **46**(5): 1233–1241.

Capek, C. M., D. Waters, B. Woll, M. MacSweeney, M. J. Brammer, P. K. McGuire, A. S. David and R. Campbell (2008b). "Hand and mouth: cortical correlates of lexical processing in British Sign Language and speechreading English." *Journal of Cognitive Neuroscience* **20**(7): 1220–1234.

Capek, C. M., B. Woll, M. MacSweeney, D. Waters, P. K. McGuire, A. S. David, M. J. Brammer and R. Campbell (2010). "Superior temporal activation as a function of linguistic knowledge: insights from deaf native signers who speechread." *Brain and Language* **112**(2): 129–134.

Carlson, R. and B. Granström (1976). "A text-to-speech system based entirely on rules." *IEEE International Conference on Acoustics, Speech, and Signal Processing*: 686–688.

Cassell, J., J. Sullivan, S. Prevost and E. Churchill (2000). *Embodied Conversational Agents*. Cambridge, MA, MIT Press.

Cassell, J. and A. Tartaro (2007). "Intersubjectivity in human-agent interaction." *Interaction Studies* **8**(3): 391–410.

Catford, J. C. (1977). *Fundamental Problems in Phonetics*. Indiana University Press.

Cathiard, M.-A. (1994). La perception visuelle de l'anticipation des gestes vocaliques: cohérence des évènements audibles et visibles dans le flux de la parole. Doctorat de Psychologie Cognitive, Université Pierre Mendès France, Grenoble.

Cathiard, M.-A. and C. Abry (2007). *Speech structure decisions from speech motion coordinations*. International Congress of Phonetic Sciences. Saarbrücken, Germany, pp. 291–296.

Cathiard, M.-A., C. Abry and M.-T. Lallouache (1996). Does movement on the lips mean movement in the mind? *Speechreading by Humans and Machines*. D. G. Stork and M. E. Hennecke. Berlin, Springer: 211–219.

Cathiard, M.-A., C. Abry and J.-L. Schwartz (1998). *Visual perception of glides versus vowels*. International Conference on Auditory-visual Speech Processing. Terrigal, Australia, pp. 115–120.

Cathiard, M.-A., V. Attina and D. Alloatti (2003). *Labial anticipation behavior during speech with and without Cued Speech*. International Conference of Phonetic Sciences. Barcelona, Spain, pp. 1939–1942.

Cathiard, M.-A., F. Bouaouni, V. Attina and D. Beautemps (2004). *Etude perceptive du décours de l'information manuo-faciale en Langue Française Parlée Complétée*. Journées d'Etudes de la Parole. Fez, Morocco, pp. 113–116.

Cathiard, M.-A., T. Lallouache, T. Mohamadi and C. Abry (1995). *Configurational vs. temporal coherence in audiovisual speech perception*. International Congress of Phonetic Sciences. Stockholm, Sweden, pp. 218–221.

Cathiard, M.-A., J.-L. Schwartz and C. Abry (2001). *Asking a naive question to the McGurk effect : why does audio [b] give more [d] percepts with visual [g] than with visual [d]?* International Auditory-Visual Speech Processing Workshop. Scheelsminde, Denmark, pp. 138–142.

Chabanas, M. and Y. Payan (2000). *A 3D Finite Element model of the face for simulation in plastic and maxillo-facial surgery*. International Conference on Medical Image Computing and Computer-Assisted Interventions. Pittsburgh, USA, pp. 1068–1075.

Chan, M. T. (2001). *HMM based audio-visual speech recognition integrating geometric- and appearance-based visual features*. Workshop on Multimedia Signal Processing. Cannes, France, pp. 9–14.

Chan, M. T., Y. Zhang and T. S. Huang (1998). *Real-time lip tracking and bimodal continuous speech recognition*. Workshop on Multimedia Signal Processing. Redondo Beach, CA, pp. 65–70.

Chandler, J. P. (1969). "Subroutine STEPIT – Finds local minima of a smooth function of several parameters." *Behavioral Science* **14**: 81–82.

Chandramohan, D. and P. L. Silsbee (1996). *A multiple deformable template approach for visual speech recognition*. International Conference on Spoken Language Processing. Philadelphia, PA, pp. 50–53.

Chandrasekaran, C., A. Trubanova, S. Stillittano, A. Caplier and A. A. Ghazanfar (2009). "The natural statistics of audiovisual speech." *PLoS Computational Biology* **5**(7): e1000436.

Charlier, B. L. and J. Leybaert (2000). "The rhyming skill of children educated with phonetically augmented speechreading." *Quarterly Journal of Experimental Psychology A*, **53**: 349–375.

Charpentier, F. and E. Moulines (1990). "Pitch-synchronous waveform processing techniques for text-to-speech using diphones." *Speech Communication* **9**(5–6): 453–467.

Chatfield, C. and A. J. Collins (1991). *Introduction to Multivariate Analysis*. London, Chapman and Hall.

Chaudhari, U. V., G. N. Ramaswamy, G. Potamianos and C. Neti (2003). *Information fusion and decision cascading for audio-visual speaker recognition based on time-varying stream reliability prediction*. International Conference on Multimedia and Expo. Baltimore, MD, pp. 9–12.

Chen, S. E. and L. Williams (1993). *View interpolation for image synthesis*. SIGGRAPH. Anaheim, CA, pp. 279–288.

Chen, T. (2001). "Audiovisual speech processing. Lip reading and lip synchronization." *IEEE Signal Processing Magazine* **18**(1): 9–21.

Chen, T., H. P. Graf and K. Wang (1995). "Lip synchronization using speech-assisted video processing." *IEEE Signal Processing Letters* **2**(4): 57–59.

Chen, T. and D. W. Massaro (2004). "Mandarin speech perception by ear and eye follows a universal principle." *Perception & Psychophysics* **66**: 820–836.

Chen, T. and R. R. Rao (1998). "Audio-visual integration in multimodal communication." *Proceedings of the IEEE* **86**(5): 837–851.

Chibelushi, C. C., F. Deravi and J. S. D. Mason (1996). Survey of audio visual speech databases. Swansea, United Kingdom, Department of Electrical and Electronic Engineering, University of Wales.

(2002). "A review of speech-based bimodal recognition." *IEEE Transactions on Multimedia* **4**(1): 23–37.

Chiou, G. and J.-N. Hwang (1997). "Lipreading from color video." *IEEE Transactions on Image Processing* **6**(8): 1192–1195.

Chitoran, I. and A. Nevins (2008). "Studies on the phonetics and phonology of glides." *Lingua: Special issue* **118**(12).

Choi, K. H., Y. Luo and J.-N. Hwang (2001). "Hidden Markov model inversion for audio-to-visual conversion in an MPEG-4 facial animation system." *Journal of VLSI Signal Processing – Systems for Signal, Image, and Video Technology* **29**(1–2): 51–62.

Chou, W., B.-H. Juang, C.-H. Lee and F. Soong (1994). "A minimum error rate pattern recognition approach to speech recognition." *International Journal of Pattern Recognition and Artificial Intelligence* **8**(1): 5–31.

Christie, F. and V. Bruce (1998). "The role of dynamic information in the recognition of unfamiliar faces." *Memory and Cognition* **26**(4): 780–790.

Chu, S. and T. Huang (2000). *Bimodal speech recognition using coupled hidden Markov models*. International Conference on Spoken Language Processing. Beijing, China, pp. 747–750.

(2002). *Audio-visual speech modeling using coupled hidden Markov models*. International Conference on Acoustics, Speech and Signal Processing. Orlando, FL, pp. 2009–2012.

Chuang, E. and C. Bregler (2005). "Mood swings: expressive speech animations." *ACM Transactions on Graphics* **24**(2): 331–347.

Cisař, P., M. Železný, Z. Krňoul, J. Kanis, J. Zelinka and L. Müller (2005). *Design and recording of Czech speech corpus for audio-visual continuous speech recognition*.

International Conference on Auditory-Visual Speech Processing. Vancouver Island, Canada, pp. 93–96.

Code, C. (2005). Syllables in the brain: evidence from brain damage. *Phonological Encoding and Monitoring in Normal and Pathological Speech.* R. J. Hartsuiker, R. Bastiaanse, A. Postma and F. N. K. Wijnen. Hove, Sussex, Psychology Press.

Cohen, I., N. Sebe, A. Garg, L. S. Chen and T. S. Huang (2003). "Facial expression recognition from video sequences: temporal and static modeling." *Computer Vision and Image Understanding* **91**(1–2): 160–187.

Cohen, M. M., J. Beskow and D. W. Massaro (1998). *Recent developments in facial animation: an inside view.* Auditory-Visual Speech Processing Workshop (AVSP). Terrigal, Sydney, Australia, pp. 201–206.

Cohen, M. M. and D. W. Massaro (1990). "Synthesis of visible speech." *Behavior Research Methods: Instruments & Computers* **22**: 260–263.

(1993). Modeling coarticulation in synthetic visual speech. *Models and Techniques in Computer Animation*. D. Thalmann and N. Magnenat-Thalmann. Tokyo, Springer: 141–155.

(1994a). "Development and experimentation with synthetic visible speech." *Behavioral Research Methods and Instrumentation* **26**: 260–265.

(1994b). *What can visual speech synthesis tell visual speech recognition*? Asilomar Conference on Signals, Systems, and Computers. Pacific Grove, CA.

Cohen, M. M., D. W. Massaro and R. Clark (2002). *Training a talking head*. Fourth International Conference on Multimodal Interfaces. Pittsburgh, Pennsylvania.

Cohen, M. M., R. L. Walker and D. W. Massaro (1995). *Perception of synthetic visual speech*. Speechreading by Man and Machine: Models, Systems and Applications. Chateau de Bonas, France, NATO Advanced Study Institute 940584.

(1996). Perception of synthetic visual speech. *Speechreading by Humans and Machines*. D. G. Stork and M. E. Hennecke. New York, Springer: 153–168.

Coker, C. H. (1968). Speech synthesis with a parametric articulatory model. Reprinted in *Speech Synthesis*. J. L. Flanagan and L. R. Rabiner. Stroudsburg, PA, Dowden, Hutchinson and Ross: 135–139.

Cole, R., D. W. Massaro, J. de Villiers, B. Rundle, K. Shobaki, J. Wouters, M. Cohen, J. Beskow, P. Stone, P. Connors, A. Tarachow and D. Solcher (1999). *New tools for interactive speech and language training: Using animated conversational agents in the classrooms of profoundly deaf children*. ESCA/SOCRATES Workshop on Method and Tool Innovations for Speech Science Education. London, UK.

Cole, R. A., R. Stern, M. S. Phillips, S. M. Brill, P. A. P. and P. Specker (1983). *Feature-based speaker independent recognition of English letters*. International Conference on Acoustics, Speech, and Signal Processing, pp. 731–734.

Colin, C., M. Radeau, A. Soquet, D. Demolin, F. Colin and P. Deltenre (2002). "Mismatch negativity evoked by the McGurk-MacDonald effect: a phonetic representation within short-term memory." *Clinical Neurophysiology* **113**: 495–506.

Connell, J. H., N. Haas, E. Marcheret, C. Neti, G. Potamianos and S. Velipasalar (2003). *A real-time prototype for small-vocabulary audio-visual ASR*. International Conference on Multimedia and Expo. Baltimore, MD, pp. 469–472.

Connine, C. M., D. G. Blasko and J. Wang (1994). "Vertical similarity in spoken word recognition: Multiple lexical activation, individual differences, and the role of sentence context." *Perception & Psychophysics* **56**: 624–636.

Cooke, M., J. Barker, S. Cunningham and X. Shao (2006). "An audio-visual corpus for speech perception and automatic speech recognition." *Journal of the Acoustical Society of America* **120**(5): 2421–2424.

Cooper, F. S., P. C. Delattre, A. M. Liberman, J. M. Borst and L. J. Gerstman (1952). "Some experiments on the perception of synthetic speech sounds." *Journal of the Acoustical Society of America* **24**: 597–606.

Cootes, T. F., G. J. Edwards and C. J. Taylor (1998). *Active appearance models*. European Conference on Computer Vision. Freiburg, Germany, pp. 484–498.

Cootes, T. F., C. J. Taylor, D. H. Cooper and J. Graham (1995). "Active shape models – their training and application." *Computer Vision and Image Understanding* **61**(1): 38–59.

Cormen, T. H., C. E. Leiserson, R. L. Rivest and C. Stein (1989). *Introduction to Algorithms*. Boston, MA, The MIT Press and McGraw-Hill Book Company.

Cornett, R. O. (1967). "Cued Speech." *American Annals of the Deaf* **112**: 3–13.

(1982). Le Cued Speech. *Aides manuelles à la lecture labiale et perspectives d'aides automatiques*. F. Destombes. Paris, Centre scientifique IBM-France.

(1988). "Cued Speech, manual complement to lipreading, for visual reception of spoken language." *Principles, practice and prospects for automation. Acta Oto-Rhino-Laryngologica Belgica* **42**(3): 375–384.

Cornett, R. O. and M. E. Daisey (1992). *The cued speech resource book for parents of deaf children*. Raleigh, NC, The National Cued Speech Association, Inc.

Cosatto, E. and H. P. Graf (1998). *Sample-based synthesis of photo-realistic talking heads*. Computer Animation. Philadelphia, PA, pp. 103–110.

Cosatto, E., G. Potamianos and H. P. Graf (2000). *Audio-visual unit selection for the synthesis of photo-realistic talking-heads*. International Conference on Multimedia and Expo. New York, NY, pp. 1097–1100.

Cosi, P., E. Caldognetto, G. Perin and C. Zmarich (2002a). *Labial coarticulation modeling for realistic facial animation*. IEEE International Conference on Multimodal Interfaces. Pittsburgh, PA.

Cosi, P., M. M. Cohen and D. W. Massaro (2002b). *Baldini: Baldi speaks Italian*. International Conference on Spoken Language Processing. Denver, CO, pp. 2349–2352.

Cosker, D., D. Marshall, P. Rosin, S. Paddock and S. Rushton (2005). "Towards perceptually realistic talking heads: models, metrics and McGurk." *ACM Transactions on Applied Perception (TAP)* **2**(3): 270–285.

Couteau, B., Y. Payan and S. Lavallée (2000). "The Mesh-Matching algorithm : an automatic 3D mesh generator for finite element structures." *Journal of Biomechanics* **33**(8): 1005–1009.

Covell, M. and C. Bregler (1996). *Eigenpoints*. International Conference on Image Processing. Lausanne, Switzerland, pp. 471–474.

Cox, S., I. Matthews and A. Bangham (1997). *Combining noise compensation with visual information in speech recognition*. European Tutorial Workshop on Audio-Visual Speech Processing. Rhodes, Greece, pp. 53–56.

Crawford, R. (1995). "Teaching voiced velar stops to profoundly deaf children using EPG, two case studies." *Clinical Linguistics and Phonetics* **9**: 255–270.

Czap, L. (2000). *Lip representation by image ellipse*. International Conference on Spoken Language Processing. Beijing, China, pp. 93–96.

Dagenais, P. A., P. Critz-Crosby, S. G. Fletcher and M. J. McCutcheon (1994). "Comparing abilities of children with profound hearing impairments to learn consonants using electropalatography or traditional aural-oral techniques." *Journal of Speech and Hearing Research* **37**: 687–699.

Dalton, B., R. Kaucic and A. Blake (1996). Automatic speechreading using dynamic contours. *Speechreading by Humans and Machines*. D. G. Stork and M. E. Hennecke. Berlin, Springer: 373–382.

Damasio, A. R., D. Tranel and H. Damasio (1990). "Varieties of face agnosia – Different neuropsychological profiles and neural substrates." *Journal of Clinical and Experimental Neuropsychology* **12**(1): 675–687.

Damasio, H. and A. R. Damasio (1989). *Lesion Analysis in Neuropsychology*. Oxford University Press.

Dang, J. and K. Honda (1998). *Speech production of vowel sequences using a physiological articulatory model*. International Conference on Spoken Language Processing. Sydney, Australia, pp. 1767–1770.

(2004). "Construction and control of a physiological articulatory model." *Journal of Acoustical Society of America* **115**(2): 853–870.

Daubechies, I. (1992). *Wavelets*. Philadelphia, PA, S.I.A.M.

Davis, B. L. and P. F. MacNeilage (1995). "The articulatory basis of babbling." *Journal of Speech and Hearing Research* **38**: 1199–1211.

(2000). "An embodiment perspective on the acquisition of speech perception." *Phonetica* **57**(2–4): 229–241.

Davoine, F., H. Li and R. Forchheimer (1997). Video compression and person authentication. *Audio-and Video-based Biometric Person Authentication*. J. Bigün, G. Chollet and G. Borgefors. Berlin, Springer: 353–360.

De Cuetos, P., C. Neti and A. Senior (2000). *Audio-visual intent to speak detection for human computer interaction*. International Conference on Acoustics, Speech and Signal Processing. Istanbul, Turkey, pp. 1325–1328.

de Gelder, B., P. Bertelson, J. Vroomen and H. C. Chen (1995). *Interlanguage differences in the McGurk effect for Dutch and Cantonese listeners*. European Conference on Speech Communication and Technology. Madrid, Spain, pp. 1699–1702.

de Gelder, B. and J. Vroomen (1992). Auditory and visual speech perception in alphabetic and nonalphabetic Chinese/Dutch bilinguals. *Cognitive Processing in Bilinguals*. R. J. Harris. Amsterdam, Elsevier: 413–426.

de Gelder, B., J. Vroomen and L. van der Heide (1991). "Face recognition and lipreading in autism." *European Journal of Cognitive Psychology* **3**: 69–86.

de Haan, E. H. F., A. Young and F. Newcombe (1987). "Face recognition without awareness." *Cognitive Neuropsychology* **4**: 385–415.

De la Torre, A., A. M. Peinado, J. C. Segura, J. L. Perez-Cordoba, M. C. Benítez and A. J. Rubio (2005). "Histogram equalization of speech representation for robust speech recognition." *IEEE Transactions on Speech and Audio Processing* **13**(3): 355–366.

Decety, J., D. Perani, M. Jeannerod, V. Bettinardi, B. Tadary, R. Woods, J. C. Mazziotta and F. Fazio (1994). "Mapping motor representations with positron emission tomography." *Nature* **371**: 600–602.

Delattre, P. C., A. M. Liberman and F. S. Cooper (1955). "Acoustic loci and transitional cues for consonants." *Journal of the Acoustical Society of America* **27**: 769–773.

Deligne, S., G. Potamianos and C. Neti (2002). *Audio-visual speech enhancement with AVCDCN (audio-visual codebook dependent cepstral normalization)*. International Conference on Spoken Language Processing. Denver, CO, pp. 1449–1452.

Deller Jr., J. R., J. G. Proakis and J. H. L. Hansen (1993) *Discrete-Time Processing of Speech Signals*. Englewood Cliffs, NJ, Macmillan Publishing Company.

Demorest, M. E., L. E. Bernstein and G. P. DeHaven (1996). "Generalizability of speech-reading performance on nonsense syllables, words, and sentences: Subjects with normal hearing." *Journal of Speech and Hearing Research* **39**(4): 697–713.

Dempster, A. P., N. M. Laird and D. B. Rubin (1977). "Maximum likelihood from incomplete data via the EM algorithm." *Journal of the Royal Statistical Society* **39**(1): 1–38.

Dent, H., F. Gibbon and W. Hardcastle (1992). Inhibiting an abnormal lingual pattern in a cleft palate child using electropalatography (EPG). *Interdisciplinary Perspectives in Speech and Language Pathology*. M. M. Leahy and J. L. Kallen. Dublin, Trinity College: 211–221.

(1995). "The application of electropalatography (EPG) to the remediation of speech disorders in school-aged children and young adults." *European Journal of Disorders of Communication* **30**: 264–277.

dePaula, H., H. C. Yehia, D. Shiller, G. Jozan, K. G. Munhall and E. Vatikiotis-Bateson (2006). Analysis of audiovisual speech intelligibility based on spatial and temporal filtering of visible speech information. *Speech Production: Models, Phonetic Processes, and Techniques*. J. Harrington and M. Tabain. Hove, Psychology Press: 135–147.

Desjardins, R. N., J. Rogers and J. F. Werker (1997). "An exploration of why pre-schoolers perform differently than do adults in audiovisual speech perception tasks." *Journal of Experimental Child Psychology* **66**: 85–110.

Desjardins, R. N. and J. F. Werker (1996). *4-month-old female infants are influenced by visible speech*. International Conference of Infant Studies. Providence, RI.

(2004). "Is the integration of heard and seen speech mandatory for infants?" *Developmental Psychobiology* **45**: 187–203.

Dittmann, A. T. (1972). "Developmental factors in conversational behaviour." *Journal of Communication* **22**: 404–423.

Dittrich, W. H., T. Troscianko, S. E. G. Lea and D. Morgan (1996). "Perception of emotion from dynamic point-light displays represented in dance." *Perception* **25**: 727–738.

Dodd, B. (1979). "Lipreading in infants: Attention to speech presented in and out of synchrony." *Cognitive Psychology* **11**: 478–484.

Dodd, B. and D. K. Burnham (1988). "Processing speechread information." *The Volta Review: New Reflections on Speechreading* **90**: 45–60.

Dodd, B. and R. Campbell (1987). *Hearing by Eye: The Psychology of Lipreading*. London, Erlbaum.

Dodd, B., B. McIntosh and L. Woodhouse (1998). Early lipreading ability and speech and language development of hearing-impaired pre-schoolers. *Hearing by Eye II: Advances in the Psychology of Speechreading and Auditory-visual Speech*. R. Campbell, B. Dodd and D. Burnham. Hove, UK, Psychology Press: 229–242.

Dohen, M., J.-L. Schwartz and G. Bailly (2010). "Speech and Face-to-face Communication – An Introduction." *Speech Communication* **52**: 477–480.

Dougherty, E. R. and C. R. Giardina (1987). *Image Processing – Continuous to Discrete. Vol. I: Geometric, Transform, and Statistical Methods*. Englewood Cliffs, NJ, Prentice Hall.

Driver, J. (1996). "Enhancement of selected listening by illusory mislocation of speech sounds due to lip-reading." *Nature* **381**: 66–68.

Droppo, J. and A. Acero (2008). Environmental robustness. *Springer Handbook of Speech Processing*. J. Banesty, M. M. Sondhi and Y. Huang. Berlin, Springer: 653–679.

Dryden, I. L. and K. V. Mardia (1998). *Statistical Shape Analysis*. London, John Wiley and Sons.

Dubeau, M. C., M. Iacoboni, L. Koski, J. Markovac and J. C. Mazziotta (2002). Topography for body-parts motion in the posterior STS region. Perspectives on Imitation: from cognitive neuroscience to social venue. Royaumont Abbey, France.

Duchenne, G. B. (1990). *The Mechanism of Human Facial Expression*. Cambridge University Press.

Duchnowski, P., D. S. Lum, J. C. Krause, M. G. Sexton, M. S. Bratakos and L. D. Braida (2000). "Development of speechreading supplements based on automatic speech recognition." *IEEE Transactions on Biomedical Engineering* **47**(4): 487–496.

Duchnowski, P., U. Meier and A. Waibel (1994). *See me, hear me: Integrating automatic speech recognition and lip-reading*. International Conference on Spoken Language Processing. Yokohama, Japan, pp. 547–550.

Dupont, S. and J. Luettin (2000). "Audio-visual speech modeling for continuous speech recognition." *IEEE Transactions on Multimedia* **2**(3): 141–151.

Duraffour, A. (1969). *Glossaire des patois franco-provençaux*. Paris, Editions du CNRS.

Echternach, M., J. Sundberg, S. Arndt, T. Breyer, M. Markl, M. Schumacher and B. Richter (2008). "Vocal tract and register changes analysed by real-time MRI in male professional singers – a pilot study." *Logopedics Phoniatrics Vocology* **33**(2): 67–73.

Edwards, J., F. Gibbon and M. Fourakis (1997). "On discrete changes in the acquisition of the alveolar/velar stop contrast." *Language and Speech* **40**.

Edwards, K. (1998). "The face of time: Temporal cues in facial expression of emotion." *Psychological Sciences* **9**(4): 270–276.

Efros, A. A. and T. K. Leung (1999). *Texture synthesis by non-parametric sampling*. IEEE International Conference on Computer Vision, pp. 1033–1038.

Eisert, P. and B. Girod (1998). "Analyzing facial expressions for virtual conferencing." *IEEE Computer Graphics & Applications: Special Issue: Computer Animation for Virtual Humans* **18**(5): 70–78.

Ekman, P. (1979). About brows: emotional and conversational signals. *Human Ethology*. M. von Cranach, K. Foppa, W. Lepenies and D. Ploog. Cambridge University Press: 169–249.

(1982). *Emotion and the Human Face*. Cambridge University Press

Ekman, P. and W. Friesen (1978). *Facial Action Coding System (FACS): A technique for the measurement of facial action*. Palo Alto, CA, Consulting Psychologists Press.

(2003). *Facial Action Coding System*. Palo Alto, CA, Consulting Psychologists Press Inc.

(1982). "Felt, false, and miserable smiles." *Journal of Nonverbal Behavior* **6**(4): 238–252.

Ekman, P., W. V. Friesen and R. C. Simons (1985). "Is the startle reaction an emotion." *Journal of Personality and Social Psychology* **49**(5): 1416–1426.

Ekman, P. and H. Oster (1979). "Facial expressions of emotion." *Annual Reviews of Psychology* **30**: 527–554.

Elisei, F., G. Bailly, M. Odisio and P. Badin (2001a). *Clones parlants vidéo-réalistes: application à l'interprétation de FAP-MPEG4*. CORESA. Dijon, France, pp. 145–148.

Elisei, F., M. Odisio, G. Bailly and P. Badin (2001b). *Creating and controlling video-realistic talking heads*. Auditory-Visual Speech Processing Workshop (AVSP). Scheelsminde, Denmark, pp. 90–97.

Elliott, T. M. and F. E. Theunissen (2009). "The modulation transfer function for speech intelligibility." *PLoS Computational Biology* **5.3**: e1000302.

Ellis, A. W., A. M. Burton, A. W. Young and B. M. Flude (1997). "Repetition priming between parts and wholes: Tests of a computational model of familiar face recognition." *British Journal of Psychology* **88**: 579–608.

Ellis, A. W., B. M. Flude, A. Young and A. M. Burton (1996). "Two loci of repetition priming in the recognition of familiar faces." *Journal of Experimental Psychology – Learning, Memory, and Cognition* **22**: 295–308.

Elman, J. L. and D. Zipser (1986). "Learning the hidden structure of speech." *Journal of the Acoustical Society of America* **83**: 1615–1626.

Engwall, O. (2000). *A 3D tongue model based on MRI data*. International Conference on Speech and Language Processing. Beijing, China, pp. 901–904.

(2004). *From real-time MRI to 3D tongue movements*. International Conference on Speech and Language Processing. Jeju, Korea, pp. 1109–1112.

Engwall, O. and O. Bälter (2007). "Pronunciation feedback from real and virtual language teachers." *Journal of Computer Assisted Language Learning* **20**(3): 235–262.

Engwall, O. and J. Beskow (2003). *Resynthesis of 3D tongue movements from facial data*. EuroSpeech. Geneva, pp. 2261–2264.

Erber, N. P. (1975). "Auditory-visual perception of speech." *Journal of Speech and Hearing Disorders* **40**: 481–482.

Erber, N. P. and C. L. de Filippo (1978). "Voice/mouth synthesis and tactile/visual perception of /pa, ba, ma/." *Journal of the Acoustical Society of America* **64**: 1015–1019.

Erdener, D. and D. Burnham (under review). "Auditory-visual speech perception development in English-speaking children."

Etcoff, N. L. (1984). "Selective attention to facial attention and facial emotion." *Neuropsychologia* **22**: 281–295.

Ezzat, T., G. Geiger and T. Poggio (2002a). "Trainable videorealistic speech animation." *ACM Transactions on Graphics* **21**(3): 388–398.

(2002b). *Trainable videorealistic speech animation*. SIGGRAPH. San Antonio, TX, pp. 388–398.

Ezzat, T. and T. Poggio (1997). *Videorealistic talking faces: a morphing approach*. International Conference on Auditory-Visual Speech Processing. Rhodes, Greece, pp. 141–144.

(1998). *MikeTalk: a talking facial display based on morphing visemes*. Computer Animation. Philadelphia, PA, pp. 96–102.

(2000). "Visual speech synthesis by morphing visemes." *International Journal of Computer Vision* **38**: 45–57.

Fagel, S. (2007). *Audiovisual speech: analysis, synthesis, perception and recognition*. International Congress of Phonetic Sciences. Saarbrücken, Germany, pp. 275–278.

Fagel, S., G. Bailly and B.-J. Theobald (2009). "Animating virtual speakers or singers from audio: lip-synching facial animation." *EURASIP Journal on Audio, Speech, and Music Processing* **2009**(ID 826091): 2 pages.

Fagel, S., F. Elisei and G. Bailly (2008). *From 3-D speaker cloning to text-to-audiovisual-speech*. Interspeech. Brisbane, Australia, pp. 2325–2328.

Falaschi, A., M. Giusiniani and M. Verola (1989). *A hidden Markov model approach to speech synthesis*. Eurospeech. Paris, pp. 187–190.

Fant, C. G. M. (1966). A note on vocal tract size factors and non-uniform F-pattern scalings. *Quarterly Progress and Status Report*. Stockholm, Sweden, Speech Transmission Laboratory, Royal Institute of Technology: 21–38.

Feldman, A. G. (1986). "Once more on the equilibrium-point hypothesis (lambda model) for motor control." *Journal of Motor Behavior* **18**: 17–54.

Finn, K. I. (1986). An investigation of visible lip information to be used in automatic speech recognition. Georgetown University, Washington, DC.

Fisher, C. G. (1968). "Confusions among visually perceived consonants." *Journal of Speech and Hearing Research* **11**: 796–804.

Fleetwood, E. and M. Metzger (1998). *Cued Language Structure. An analysis of Cued American English Based on Linguistic Principles*. Silver Spring, MD, Calliope Press.

Fletcher, S. G., P. A. Dagenais and P. Critz-Crosby (1991). "Teaching consonants to profoundly hearing-impaired speakers using palatometry." *Journal of Speech and Hearing Research* **34**: 929–942.

Flurry, B. (1988). *Common Principal Components and Related Multivariate Models*. New York, Wiley.

Forrest, K., G. Weismer, M. Hodge, D. A. Dinnsen and M. Elbert (1990). "Statistical analysis of word-initial /k/ and /t/ produced by normal and phonologically disordered children." *Clinical Linguistics and Phonetics* **4**: 327–340.

Forster, K. I. (1979). Levels of processing and the structure of the language processor. *Sentence Processing: Psycholinguistic Studies Presented to Merrill Garret*. W. E. Cooper and E. C. T. Walker. Hillsdale, NJ, Erlbaum.

Foucher, E., L. Girin and G. Feng (1998). *Audiovisual speech coder: Using vector quantization to exploit the audio/video correlation*. Workshop on Audio Visual Speech Processing. Terrigal, Australia, pp. 67–71.

Fourakis, M. and R. Port (1986). "Stop epenthesis in English." *Journal of Phonetics* **14**: 197–221.

Fowler, C. A. (1986). "An event approach to the study of speech perception from a direct-realist perspective." *Journal of Phonetics* **14**(1): 3–28.

(1996). "Listeners do hear sounds, not tongues." *Journal of the Acoustical Society of America* **99**(3): 1730–1741.

Fowler, C. A. and M. R. Smith (1986). Speech perception as "Vector Analysis": An approach to the problem of invariance and segregation. *Invariance and Variability in Speech Processes*. J. S. Perkell and D. H. Klatt. Hillsdale, NJ, Erlbaum: 123–139.

Francis, P. L. and G. McCroy (1983). *Infants' bimodal recognition of human stimulus configurations*. Biennial meeting of the Society for Research in Child Development. Detroit, USA.

Freyd, J. J. (1987). "Dynamic mental representations." *Psychological Review* **94**: 427–438.

(1993). Five hunches about perceptual processes and dynamic representations. *Attention and Performance, XIV: Synergies in Experimental Psychology, Artificial Intelligence and Cognitive Neuroscience – A Silver Jubilee*. D. Meyer and S. Kornblum. Cambridge, MA, MIT Press: 99–120.

Freyd, J. J. and T. M. Pantzer (1995). Static patterns moving in the mind. *Creative Cognition Approaches*. S. Smith, T. B. Ward and R. A. Finke. Cambridge, MA, MIT Press: 181–204.

Fridriksson, J., D. Moser, J. Ryalls, L. Bonilha, C. Rorden and G. Baylis (2008). "Modulation of frontal lobe speech areas associated with the production and perception of speech movements." *Journal of Speech and Language, Hearing Research* **52**: 812–819.

Friston, K. J., C. D. Frith, P. F. Liddle and R. S. J. Frackowiak (1993). "Functional connectivity: the principal component analysis of large (PET) Data sets." *Journal of Cerebral Blood Flow and Metabolism* **13**: 5–14.

Fröba, B., C. Küblbeck, C. Rothe and P. Plankensteiner (1999). *Multi-sensor biometric person recognition in an access control system*. International Conference on Audio and Video-based Biometric Person Authentication. Washington, DC, pp. 55–59.

Frowein, H. W., G. F. Smoorenburg, L. Pyters and D. Schinkel (1991). "Improved speech recognition through videotelephony: experiments with the hard of hearing." *IEEE Journal on Selected Areas in Communications* **9**: 611–616.

Fu, S., R. Gutierrez-Osuna, A. Esposito, P. K. Kakumanu and O. N. Garcia (2005). "Audio/visual mapping with cross-modal hidden Markov models." *IEEE Transactions on Multimedia* **7**(2): 243–252.

Fujimura, H., C. Miyajima, K. Itou, K. Takeda and F. Itakura (2005). *Analysis of a large in-car speech corpus and its application to multimodal ASR*. International Conference on Acoustics, Speech and Signal Processing. Philadelphia, PA, pp. 445–448.

Fujimura, O. (1961). "Bilabial stop and nasal consonants: a motion picture study and its anatomical implications." *Journal of Speech and Hearing Research* **4**: 233–247.

(1982). "Computer-controlled X-ray microbeam – method, history and sample results." *Journal of the Acoustical Society of America* **71**: S31.

Fuster-Duran, A. (1996). Perception of conflicting Audio-Visual Speech: An Examination across Spanish and German. *Speechreading by Humans and Machines*. D. G. Stork and M. E. Hennecke. Berlin, Springer: 135–143.

Gales, M. J. F. (1997). *"Nice" model based compensation schemes for robust speech recognition*. ESCA-NATO Workshop on Robust Speech Recognition for Unknown Communication Channels. Pont-à-Mousson, France, pp. 55–59.

(1999). Maximum likelihood multiple projection schemes for hidden Markov models. Cambridge University.

Gallagher, H. L., F. Happé, N. Brunswick, P. C. Fletcher, U. Frith and C. D. Frith (2000). "Reading the mind in cartoons and stories: An fMRI study of 'theory of mind' in verbal and nonverbal tasks." *Neuropsychologia* **38**: 11–21.

Garcia, C., J. Ostermann and T. Cootes (2007). "Facial image processing." *EURASIP Journal on Image and Video Processing* **1**.

Garg, A., G. Potamianos, C. Neti and T. S. Huang (2003). *Frame-dependent multi-stream reliability indicators for audio-visual speech recognition*. International Conference on Acoustics, Speech, and Signal Processing. Hong Kong, China, pp. 24–27.

Garner, W. R. (1974). *The Processing of Information and Structure*. Potomac, MD, Erlbaum.

Gauvain, J.-L. and C.-H. Lee (1994). "Maximum a posteriori estimation for multivariate Gaussian mixture observations of Markov chains." *IEEE Transactions on Speech and Audio Processing* **2**(2): 291–298.

Gay, T. (1980). *Dynamic properties of lip movement in speech*. International Seminar on Labiality. Lannion, France.

Geiger, G., T. Ezzat and T. Poggio (2003). Perceptual evaluation of video-realistic speech. Cambridge, MA, Massachusetts Institute of Technology: 224.

Gérard, J.-M., P. Perrier, Y. Payan and R. Wilhelms-Tricarico (2004). "A new 3D dynamical biomechanical tongue model." *Journal of the Acoustical Society of America* **115**(5): 2431.

Gérard, J.-M., R. Wilhelms-Tricarico, P. Perrier and Y. Payan (2003). "A 3D dynamical biomechanical tongue model to study speech motor control." *Recent Research Developments in Biomechanics* **1**: 49–64.

Gérard, J.-M., P. Perrier and Y. Payan (2006). 3D biomechanical tongue modelling to study speech production. *Speech Production: Models, Phonetic Processes, and Techniques*. J. Harrington and M. Tabain. New York, Psychology Press: 85–102.

Ghazanfar, A. A. (2009). "The multisensory roles for auditory cortex in primate vocal communication." *Hearing Research* **258**(1–2): 113–120.

Ghazanfar, A. A., J. X. Maier, K. L. Hoffman and N. K. Logothetis (2005). "Multisensory integration of dynamic faces and voices in rhesus monkey auditory cortex." *Journal of Neurosciences* **25**(20): 5004–5012.

Ghazanfar, A. A. and C. E. Schroeder (2006). "Is neocortex essentially multisensory?" *Trends in Cognitive Science* **10**(6): 278–285.

Ghitza, O. (1986). "Auditory nerve representation as a front end for speech recognition in noisy environments." *Computer, Speech and Language* **1**: 109–130.

Gibbon, F., H. Dent and W. Hardcastle (1993). "Diagnosis and therapy of abnormal alveolar stops in a speech-disordered child using EPG." *Clinical Linguistics and Phonetics* **7**: 247–268.

Gibbon, F., T. Whitehill, W. J. Hardcastle, S. Stokes and M. Nairn (1998). Cross-language (Cantonese/English) study of articulatory error patterns in cleft palate speech using electropalatography (EPG). *Clinical Phonetics and Linguistics*. W. Ziegler and K. Deger. London, Whurr: 165–176.

Gibert, G., G. Bailly, D. Beautemps, F. Elisei and R. Brun (2005). "Analysis and synthesis of the 3D movements of the head, face and hand of a speaker using cued speech." *Journal of the Acoustical Society of America* **118**(2): 1144–1153.

Gibert, G., G. Bailly and F. Elisei (2004a). *Audiovisual text-to-cued speech synthesis*. 5th Speech Synthesis Workshop. Pittsburgh, PA, pp. 85–90.

Gibert, G., G. Bailly, F. Elisei, D. Beautemps and R. Brun (2004b). *Audiovisual text-to-cued speech synthesis*. Eusipco. Vienna, Austria, pp. 1007–1010.

Gibert, G., G. Bailly, F. Elisei, D. Beautemps and R. Brun (2004c). *Evaluation of a speech cuer: from motion capture to a concatenative text-to-cued speech system*. Language Resources and Evaluation Conference. Lisbon, Portugal, pp. 2123–2126.

Giese, M. A. and T. Poggio (2003). "Neural mechanisms for the recognition of biological movements." *Neuroscience Letters* **4**: 179–192.

Giraud, A. L. and E. Truy (2002). "The contribution of visual areas to speech comprehension: a PET study in cochlear implants patients and normal-hearing subjects." *Neuropsychologia* **40**(9): 1562–1569.

Girin, L. (2004). "Joint matrix quantization of face parameters and LPC coefficients for low bit rate audiovisual speech coding." *IEEE Transactions on Speech and Audio Processing* **12**(3): 265–276.

Girin, L., A. Allard and J.-L. Schwartz (2001a). *Speech signals separation: A new approach exploiting the coherence of audio and visual speech*. Workshop on Multimedia Signal Processing. Cannes, France, pp. 631–636.

Girin, L., G. Feng and J.-L. Schwartz (1995). *Noisy speech enhancement with filters estimated from the speaker's lips*. European Conference on Speech Communication and Technology. Madrid, Spain, pp. 1559–1562.

Girin, L., J.-L. Schwartz and G. Feng (2001b). "Audio-visual enhancement of speech in noise." *Journal of the Acoustical Society of America* **109**(6): 3007–3020.

Girosi, F., M. Jones and T. Poggio (1993). "Regularization Theory and Neural Network Architectures." *Neural Computation* **7**(2): 219–269.

Gleason, H. A. (1961). *An Introduction to Descriptive Linguistics. Revised Edition*. Holt, NY, Rinehart, & Winston.

Glotin, H. and F. Berthommier (2000). *Test of several external posterior weighting functions for multiband full combination ASR*. International Conference on Spoken Language Processing. Beijing, China, pp. 333–336.

Glotin, H., D. Vergyri, C. Neti, G. Potamianos and J. Luettin (2001). *Weighting schemes for audio-visual fusion in speech recognition*. International Conference on Acoustics, Speech and Signal Processing. Salt Lake City, UT, pp. 173–176.

Goecke, R. and J. B. Millar (2004). *The audio-video Australian English speech data corpus AVOZES*. International Conference on Spoken Language Processing. Jeju Island, South Korea, pp. 2525–2528.

Goecke, R., G. Potamianos and C. Neti (2002). *Noisy audio feature enhancement using audio-visual speech data*. International Conference on Acoustics, Speech and Signal Processing. Orlando, FL, pp. 2025–2028.

Goh, W. D., D. B. Pisoni, K. I. Kirk and R. E. Remez (2001). "Audio-visual perception of sinewave speech in an adult cochlear implant user: A case study." *Ear and Hearing* **22**: 412–419.

Goldschen, A. J., O. N. Garcia and E. D. Petajan (1996). Rationale for phoneme-viseme mapping and feature selection in visual speech recognition. *Speechreading by Humans and Machines*. D. G. Stork and M. E. Hennecke. Berlin, Springer: 505–515.

Golub, G. H. and C. F. van Loan (1983). *Matrix Computations*. Baltimore, MD, The Johns Hopkins University Press.

Gonzalez, R. C. and P. Wintz (1977). *Digital Image Processing*. Reading, MA, Addison-Wesley Publishing Company.

Gopinath, R. A. (1998). *Maximum likelihood modeling with Gaussian distributions for classification*. International Conference on Acoustics, Speech and Signal Processing. Seattle, WA, pp. 661–664.

Gordan, M., C. Kotropoulos and I. Pitas (2002). "A support vector machine-based dynamic network for visual speech recognition applications." *EURASIP Journal on Applied Signal Processing*: 1248–1259.

Goronzy, S. (2002). *Robust Adaptation to Non-Native Accents in Automatic Speech Recognition*. Berlin, Springer.

Govokhina, O., G. Bailly and G. Breton (2007). *Learning optimal audiovisual phasing for a HMM-based control model for facial animation*. ISCA Speech Synthesis Workshop. Bonn, Germany.

Govokhina, O., G. Bailly, G. Breton and P. Bagshaw (2006). *TDA: A new trainable trajectory formation system for facial animation*. InterSpeech. Pittsburgh, PA, pp. 2474–2477.

Graf, H. P., E. Cosatto and G. Potamianos (1997). *Robust recognition of faces and facial features with a multi-modal system*. International Conference on Systems, Man, and Cybernetics. Orlando, FL, pp. 2034–2039.

Granström, B., D. House and I. Karlsson (2002). *Multimodality in language and speech systems*. Dordrecht, Kluwer Academic Publishers

Grant, K. W. and S. Greenberg (2001). *Speech intelligibility derived from asynchronous processing of auditory-visual information*. International Conference on Auditory-Visual Speech Processing. Aalborg, Denmark, pp. 132–137.

Grant, K. W. and P. F. Seitz (2000). "The use of visible speech cues for improving auditory detection of spoken sentences." *Journal of the Acoustical Society of America* **108**: 1197–1208.

Grassegger, H. (1995). *McGurk Effect in German and Hungarian listeners*. International Congress of Phonetic Sciences. Stockholm, Sweden, pp. 210–213.

Gravier, G., S. Axelrod, G. Potamianos and C. Neti (2002a). *Maximum entropy and MCE based HMM stream weight estimation for audio-visual ASR*. International Conference on Acoustics, Speech and Signal Processing. Orlando, FL, pp. 853–856.

Gravier, G., G. Potamianos and C. Neti (2002b). *Asynchrony modeling for audio-visual speech recognition*. Human Language Technology Conference. San Diego, CA, pp. 853–856.

Gray, M. S., J. R. Movellan and T. J. Sejnowski (1997). Dynamic features for visual speech-reading: A systematic comparison. *Advances in Neural Information Processing Systems*. M. C. Mozer, M. I. Jordan and T. Petsche. Cambridge, MA, MIT Press. **9**: 751–757.

Green, J. R., C. A. Moore, M. Higashikawa and R. W. Steeve (2000). "The physiologic development of speech motor control: Lip and jaw coordination." *Journal of Speech, Language and Hearing Research* **43**: 239–255.

Green, K. P. (1996). The use of auditory and visual information in phonetic perception. *Speechreading by Humans and Machines*. D. G. Stork and M. E. Hennecke. Berlin, Springer: 55–77.

(1998). The use of auditory and visual information during phonetic processing: Implications for theories of speech perception. *Hearing by Eye II: Advances in the Psychology of Speechreading and Auditory-visual Speech*. R. Campbell, B. Dodd and D. Burnham. Hove, UK, Psychology Press: 3–25.

Green, K. P. and P. K. Kuhl (1989). "The role of visual information in the processing of place and manner features in speech perception." *Perception & Psychophysics* **45** (1): 34–41.

(1991). "Integral processing of visual place and auditory voicing information during phonetic perception." *Journal of Experimental Psychology: Human Perception and Performance* **17**: 278–288.

Green, K. P., P. K. Kuhl, A. N. Meltzoff and K. N. Stevens (1991). "Integrating speech information across talkers, gender, and sensory modality: Female faces and male voices in the McGurk effect." *Perception & Psychophysics* **50**: 524–536.

Grosjean, F. (1983). "How long is the sentence? Prediction and prosody in the on-line processing of language." *Linguistica* **21**: 501–529.

Gudschinsky, S. C., H. Popovich and F. Popovich (1970). "Native reaction and phonetic similarity in Maxakali phonology." *Language* **46**(1): 77–88.

Guenter, B., C. Grimm, D. Wood, H. Malvar and F. Pighin (1998). *Making faces*. SIGGRAPH. Orlando, USA, pp. 55–67.

Guiard-Marigny, T., A. Adjoudani and C. Benoît (1996). 3D models of the lips and jaw for visual speech synthesis. *Progress in Speech Synthesis*. J. P. H. van Santen, R. W. Sproat, J. P. Olive and J. Hirschberg. Berlin, Springer: 247–258.

Gurbuz, S., Z. Tufekci, E. Patterson and J. N. Gowdy (2001). *Application of affine-invariant Fourier descriptors to lipreading for audio-visual speech recognition*. International Conference on Acoustics, Speech and Signal Processing. Salt Lake City, UT, pp. 177–180.

Hackett, T. A. (2003). The comparative anatomy of the primate auditory cortex. *Primate Audition: Ethology and Neurobiology*. A. A. Ghazanfar. Boca Raton, FL, CRC Press: 199–219.

Haist, F., A. W. Song, K. Wild, T. L. Faber, C. A. Popp and R. D. Morris (2001). "Linking sight and sound: fMRI evidence of primary cortex activation during visual word recognition." *Brain & Language* **76**: 340–350.

Hall, D., J. L. Crowley and V. Colin de Verdière (2000). "View invariant object recognition using coloured receptive fields." *Machine Graphics & Vision* **9**(2): 341–352.

Hall, D. A., C. Fussell and A. Q. Summerfield (2005). "Reading fluent speech from talking faces: typical brain networks and individual differences." *Journal of Cognitive Neuroscience* **17**(6): 939–953.

Hällgren, Å. and B. Lyberg (1998). *Visual speech synthesis with concatenative speech*. Auditory-Visual Speech Processing Workshop (AVSP). Terrigal, Sydney, Australia, pp. 181–183.

Hamilton, R. H., J. T. Shenton and H. Branch Coslett (2006). "An acquired deficit of audiovisual speech processing." *Brain & Language* **98**: 66–73.

Hardcastle, W. J. (1976). *Physiology of Speech Production*. London, Academic Press.

Hardcastle, W. J. and F. Gibbon (1997). Electropalatography and its clinical applications. *Instrumental Clinical Phonetics*. M. J. Ball and C. Code. London, Whurr: 149–193.

Harrington, J. (1987). Coarticulation and stuttering: an acoustic and electropalatographic study. *Speech Motor Dynamics in Stuttering*. H. Peters and W. Hulstijn. New York, Springer: 381–392.

Harshman, R. (1976). PARAFAC: Methods of three-way factor analysis and multi-dimensional scaling according to the principle of proportional profiles, UCLA.

Harshman, R., P. Ladefoged and L. Goldstein (1977). "Factor analysis of tongue shapes." *Journal of the Acoustical Society of America* **62**: 693–707.

Hashi, M., J. R. Westbury and K. Honda (1998). "Vowel posture normalization." *Journal of the Acoustical Society of America* **104**(4): 2426–2437.

Hashimoto, K. and S. Suga (1986). "Estimation of the muscular tensions of the human tongue by using a three-dimensional model of the tongue." *Journal of the Acoustical Society of Japan* **7**: 39–46.

Haxby, J. V., E. A. Hoffman and M. I. Gobbini (2002). "Human neural systems for face recognition and social communication." *Biological Psychiatry* **51**: 59–67.

Hazen, T. J. (2006). "Visual model structures and synchrony constraints for audio-visual speech recognition." *IEEE Transactions on Speech and Audio Processing* **14**(3): 1082–1089.

Hazen, T. J., K. Saenko, C.-H. La and J. R. Glass (2004). *A segment-based audio-visual speech recognizer: Data collection, development, and initial experiments*. International Conference on Multimodal Interfaces. State College, PA, pp. 235–242.

Heckmann, M., F. Berthommier and K. Kroschel (2001). *A hybrid ANN/HMM audio-visual speech recognition system*. International Conference on Auditory-Visual Speech Processing. Aalborg, Denmark, pp. 190–195.

Heckmann, M., F. Berthommier and K. Kroschel (2002). "Noise adaptive stream weighting in audio-visual speech recognition." *EURASIP Journal on Applied Signal Processing*: 1260–1273.

Hennecke, M. E., D. G. Stork and K. V. Prasad (1996). Visionary speech: Looking ahead to practical speechreading systems. *Speechreading by Humans and Machines*. D. G. Stork and M. E. Hennecke. Berlin, Springer: 331–349.

Hermansky, H. and N. Morgan (1994). "RASTA processing of speech." *IEEE Transactions on Speech and Audio Processing* **2**(4): 578–589.

Hermansky, H., S. Tibrewala and M. Pavel (1996). *Towards ASR on partially corrupted speech*. International Conference on Spoken Language Processing. Philadelphia, PA, pp. 462–465.

Hernando, J. (1997). *Maximum likelihood weighting of dynamic speech features for CDHMM speech recognition*. International Conference on Acoustics, Speech and Signal Processing. Munich, Germany, pp. 1267–1270.

Hernando, J., J. Ayarte and E. Monte (1995). *Optimization of speech parameter weighting for CDHMM word recognition*. European Conference on Speech Communication and Technology. Madrid, Spain, pp. 105–108.

Hertrich, I., S. Dietrich and H. Ackermann (2010). "Cross-modal interactions during perception of audiovisual speech and nonspeech signals: An fMRI study." *Journal of Cognitive Neuroscience*: [Epub ahead of print: PMID: 20044895].

Hertrich, I., K. Mathiak, W. Lutzenberger and H. Ackermann (2009). "Time course of early audiovisual interactions during speech and nonspeech central auditory processing: a magnetoencephalography study." *Journal of Cognitive Neuroscience* **21** (2): 259–274.

Hertrich, I., K. Mathiak, W. Lutzenberger, H. Menning and H. Ackermann (2007). "Sequential audiovisual interactions during speech perception: a whole-head MEG study." *Neuropsychologia* **45**(6): 1342–1354.

Hess, U. and R. E. Kleck (1990). "Differentiating emotion elicited and deliberate facial expressions." *European Journal of Social Psychology* **20**: 369–385.

(1994). "The cues decoders use in attempting to differentiate emotion-elicited and posed facial expressions." *European Journal of Social Psychology* **24**: 367–381.

Hewlett, N. (1988). "Acoustic properties of /k/ and /t/ in normal and phonologically disordered speech." *Clinical Linguistics and Phonetics* **2**: 29–45.

Hickok, G. and D. Poeppel (2004). "Dorsal and ventral streams: a framework for understanding aspects of the functional anatomy of language." *Cognition* **92**: 67–99.

(2007). "The cortical organization of speech processing." *Nature Reviews: Neuroscience Letters* **8**: 393–402.

Hiki, S. and Y. Fukuda (1996). Multiphasic analysis of the basic nature of speechreading. *Speechreading by Man and Machine*. D. G. Stork and M. E. Hennecke. Berlin, Springer: 239–246.

Hirayama, M., E. Vatikiotis-Bateson and M. Kawato (1994). Inverse dynamics of speech motor control. *Advances in Neural Information Processing Systems 6*. S. J. Hanson, J. D. Cowan and C. L. Giles. San Mateo, CA, Morgan Kaufmann: 1043–1050.

Hirayama, M., E. Vatikiotis-Bateson, M. Kawato and K. Honda (1992). *Neural network modeling of speech motor control*. International Conference on Spoken Language Processing. Banff, Alberta, pp. 883–886.

Hiroya, S. and M. Honda (2004). "Estimation of articulatory movements from speech acoustics using an HMM-based speech production model." *IEEE Transactions on Speech and Audio Processing* **12**(2): 175–185.

Hirsh, I. J. and C. E. Sherrick (1961). "Perceived order in different sense modalities." *Journal of Experimental Psychology* **62**: 423–432.

Hisanaga, S., K. Sekiyama, T. Igasaki and N. Murayama (2009). *Audiovisual speech perception in Japanese and English: Inter-language differences examined by event-related potentials*. International Conference on Auditory-Visual Speech Processing. Norwich, UK, pp. 38–42.

Hockley, N. S. and L. Polka (1994). *A developmental study of audiovisual speech perception using the McGurk paradigm*. Poster presented at the 12th Meeting of the Acoustical Society of America. Austin, Texas. See abstract in *Journal of the Acoustical Society of America*, 1994, 1996, 3309.

Holmes, J. N. (1988). *Speech Synthesis and Recognition*. Wokingham, UK, Van Nostrand Rheinhold.

Horlyck, S., A. Reid and D. Burnham (2010). "The relationship between learning to read and language specific speech perception: Maturation vs experience." *Journal for the Scientific Study of Reading* DOI: 10.1080/10888438.2010.546460.

Horn, B. K. P. and B. G. Schunck (1981). "Determining optical flow." *Artificial Intelligence Review* **17**: 185–203.

Huang, F. J. and T. Chen (2001). *Consideration of Lombard effect for speechreading*. Workshop on Multimedia Signal Processing. Cannes, France, pp. 613–618.

Huang, J., Z. Liu, Y. Wang, Y. Chen and E. K. Wong (1999). *Integration of multimodal features for video scene classification based on HMM*. Workshop on Multimedia Signal Processing. Copenhagen, Denmark, pp. 53–58.

Huang, J., E. Marcheret and K. Visweswariah (2005). *Rapid feature space speaker adaptation for multi-stream HMM-based audio-visual speech recognition*. International Conference on Multimedia and Expo. Amsterdam, The Netherlands, pp. 338–341.

Huang, J., G. Potamianos, J. Connell and C. Neti (2004). "Audio-visual speech recognition using an infrared headset." *Speech Communication* **44**(4): 83–96.

Huang, J. and D. Povey (2005). *Discriminatively trained features using fMPE for multi-stream audio-visual speech recognition*. European Conference on Speech Communication Technology. Lisbon, Portugal, pp. 777–780.

Huang, J. and K. Visweswariah (2005). *Improving lip-reading with feature space transforms for multi-stream audio-visual speech recognition*. European Conference on Speech Communication Technology. Lisbon, Portugal, pp. 1221–1224.

Huang, X., F. Alleva, H. W. Hon, M. Y. Hwang, K. F. Lee and R. Rosenfeld (1993). "The SPHINX-II speech recognition system: an overview." *Computer Speech and Language* **7**(2): 137–148.

Humphreys, G. W., N. Donnelly and M. J. Riddoch (1993). "Expression is computed separately from facial identity, and it is computed separately for moving and static faces. Neuropsychological evidence." *Neuropsychologia* **31**(2): 173–181.

Hunt, A. J. and A. W. Black (1996). Unit selection in a concatenative Speech synthesis system using a large speech database. International Conference on Acoustics, Speech and Signal Processing. Atlanta, GA, pp. 373–376.

Iverson, P., L. E. Bernstein and E. T. Auer, Jr. (1998). "Phonetic perception and word recognition." *Speech Communication* **26**: 23–43.

Iwano, K., T. Yoshinaga, S. Tamura and S. Furui (2007). "Audiovisual speech recognition using lip information extracted from side-face images." *EURASIP Journal on Audio, Speech, and Music Processing* **ID 64506**: 9 pages.

Iyengar, G. and C. Neti (2001). *Detection of faces under shadows and lighting variations.* Workshop on Multimedia Signal Processing. Cannes, France, pp. 15–20.

Iyengar, G., H. J. Nock and C. Neti (2003). *Audio-visual synchrony for detection of monologues in video archives*. International Conference on Acoustics, Speech and Signal Processing. Hong Kong, China, pp. 772–775.

Iyengar, G., G. Potamianos, C. Neti, T. Faruquie and A. Verma (2001). *Robust detection of visual ROI for automatic speechreading.* Workshop on Multimedia Signal Processing. Cannes, France, pp. 79–84.

Jackson, A. and J. Morton (1984). "Facilitation of auditory word recognition." *Memory & Cognition* **12**: 568–574.

Jackson, M. T. T. (1988). "Analysis of tongue positions: Language-specific and cross-linguistic models." *Journal of the Acoustical Society of America* **84**: 124–143.

Jain, A., R. Bolle and S. Pankanti (1999). Introduction to Biometrics. *Biometrics. Personal Identification in Networked Society.* A. Jain, R. Bolle and S. Pankanti. Norwell, MA, Kluwer Academic Publishers: 1–41.

Jain, A. K., R. P. W. Duin and J. Mao (2000). "Statistical pattern recognition: A review." *IEEE Transactions on Pattern Analysis and Machine Intelligence* **22**(1): 4–37.

Jakobson, R., G. Fant and M. Halle (1969). *Preliminaries to Speech Analysis.* Cambridge, MA, MIT Press

Jeffers, J. and M. Barley (1971). *Speechreading (Lipreading).* Springfield, IL, Charles C. Thomas.

Jelinek, F. (1998). *Statistical Methods for Speech Recognition*. Cambridge, MA, MIT Press.

Jesse, A., N. Vrignaud, M. Cohen and D. W. Massaro (2000/01). "The processing of information from multiple sources in simultaneous interpreting." *Interpreting* **5**: 95–115.

Jiang, H., F. Soong and C. Lee (2001). *Hierarchical stochastic feature matching for robust speech recognition.* International Conference on Acoustics, Speech and Signal Processing. Salt Lake City, UT, pp. 217–220.

Jiang, J., A. Alwan, L. Bernstein, P. Keating and E. Auer (2000). *On the correlation between facial movements, tongue movements and speech acoustics.* International Conference on Speech and Language Processing. Beijing, China, pp. 42–45.

Jiang, J., A. Alwan, P.A. Keating, E.T. Auer and L.E. Bernstein (2002). "On the relationship between face movements, tongue movements and speech acoustics." *Journal of Applied Signal Processing* **11**: 1174–1188.

Jiang, J., E. T. Auer, Jr., A. Alwan, P. A. Keating and L. E. Bernstein (2007). "Similarity structure in visual speech perception and optical phonetics." *Perception & Psychophysics* **69**(7): 1070–1083.

Jiang, J., G. Potamianos and G. Iyengar (2005). *Improved face finding in visually challenging environments*. International Conference on Multimedia and Expo. Amsterdam, The Netherlands, pp. 1078–1081.

Johansson, G. (1973). "Visual perception of biological motion and a model for its analysis." *Perception & Psychophysics* **14**: 201–211.

Johnson, C.J., W.P. Hardee and S.W. Long (1981). Perceptual basis for phonological simplification of the fricative class. Paper presented for the American Speech, Language and Hearing Association.

Johnson, J.A., L.D. Rosenblum and M.A. Schmuckler (1995). "The McGurk effect in infants." *Journal of the Acoustical Society of America* **97**(2aSC7): 3286.

Johnson, K., E.A. Strand and M. D'Imperio (1999). "Auditory-visual integration of talker gender in vowel perception." *Journal of Phonetics* **27**: 359–384.

Jones, D.K. (2011). *Diffusion MRI: Theory, Methods and Applications*. Oxford University Press

Jones, M. and T. Poggio (1998). *Multidimensional morphable models: A framework for representing and matching object classes*. International Conference on Computer Vision. Bombay, India, pp. 683–688.

Joos, M. (1948). "Acoustic Phonetics." *Language* **24**(Supplement): 1–137.

Jordan, M.I. and D.E. Rumelhart (1991). *Forward models: Supervised learning with a distal teacher*. Cambridge, MA, MIT, Center for Cognitive Sciences.

Jordan, T.R., M.V. McCotter and S.M. Thomas (2000). "Visual and audiovisual speech perception with color and gray-scale facial images." *Perception & Psychophysics* **62**(7): 1394–1404.

Jordan, T.R. and S.M. Thomas (2001). "Effects of horizontal viewing angle on visual and audiovisual speech recognition." *Journal of Experimental Psychology: Human Perception and Performance* **27**(6): 1386–1403.

Jourlin, P. (1997). *Word-dependent acoustic-labial weights in HMM-based speech recognition*. Auditory-Visual Speech Processing Conference. Rhodes, Greece, pp. 69–72.

Jourlin, P., J. Luettin, D. Genoud and H. Wassner (1997). "Acoustic-labial speaker verification." *Pattern Recognition Letters* **18**(9): 853–858.

Juang, B.H. (1991). "Speech recognition in adverse environments." *Computer, Speech and Language* **5**: 275–294.

Julesz, B. and R.A. Payne (1968). "Differences between monocular and binocular stroboscopic movement perception." *Vision Research* **8**: 433–444.

Junqua, J.-C. (1993). "The Lombard Reflex and its role on human listeners and automatic speech recognizers." *Journal of the Acoustical Society of America* **93**(1): 510–524.

Kamachi, M., V. Bruce, S. Mukaida, J. Gyoba, S. Yoshikawa and S. Akamatsu (2001). "Dynamic properties influence the perception of facial expressions." *Perception* **30**: 875–887.

Kamachi, M., H. Hill, K. Lander and E. Vatikiotis-Bateson (2003). "'Putting the face to the voice': matching identity across modality." *Current Biology* **13**: 1709–1714.

Kass, M., A. Witkin and D. Terzopoulos (1988). "Snakes: Active contour models." *International Journal of Computer Vision* **1**(4): 321–331.

Katsamanis, A., G. Papandreou and P. Maragos (2009). "Face active appearance modeling and speech acoustic information to recover articulation." *IEEE Transactions on Audio, Speech, and Language Processing* **17**(3): 411–422.

Kawato, M. (1990). Computational schemas and neural network models for formation and control of multijoint arm trajectory. *Neural Networks for Control.* I. W. T. Miller, R. S. Suton and P. J. Werbos. Cambridge, MA, MIT Press: 197–228.

Kaye, J. and J. Lowenstamm (1984). De la syllabicité. *La forme sonore du langage.* F. Dell. Paris, Hermann: 123–159.

Keller, E. and D. J. Ostry (1983). "Computerised measurement of tongue dorsum movements with pulsed-echo ultrasound." *Journal of the Acoustical Society of America* **73**: 1309–1315.

Kelso, J. A. S., E. L. Saltzman and B. Tuller (1986). "The dynamical theory of speech production: Data and theory." *Journal of Phonetics* **14**: 29–60.

Kemp, R., G. Pike, P. White and A. Musselman (1996). "Perception and recognition of normal and negative faces: the role of shape from shading and pigmentation cues." *Perception* **25**: 37–52.

Kendon, A. (1967). "Some functions of gaze-direction in social interaction." *Acta Psychologica* **26**: 22–63.

Kenstowicz, M. (1994). *Phonology in Generative Grammar.* Oxford, Blackwell.

Kent, J. R., R. E. Parent and W. E. Carlson (1992). "Shape Transformation of Polyhedral Objects." *Computer Graphics* **26**(2): 47–54.

Kent, R. D. and F. D. Minifie (1977). "Coarticulation in recent speech production models." *Journal of Phonetics* **5**: 115–133.

Kiritani, S., K. Miyawaki, O. Fujimura and J. E. Miller (1976). "A computational model of the tongue." *Annual Bulletin of the Research Institute of Logopedics and Phoniatrics, University of Tokyo* **10**: 243–252.

Kittler, J., M. Hatef, R. P. W. Duin and J. Matas (1998). "On combining classifiers." *IEEE Transactions on Pattern Analysis and Machine Intelligence* **20**(3): 226–239.

Kjellström, H., O. Engwall and O. Bälter (2006). *Reconstructing tongue movements from audio and video.* International Conference on Spoken Language Processing. Pittsburgh, PA, pp. 2238–2241.

Klatt, D. H. (1976). *A digital filterbank for spectral masking.* IEEE International Conference on Acoustics, Speech, and Signal Processing. Philadelphia, USA, pp. 573–576.

(1979). "Synthesis by rule of consonant-vowel syllables." *Working papers of the Speech Communication Group, MIT, Cambridge* **3**: 93–104.

Klein, M. (1991). Vers une approche substantielle et dynamique de la constituance syllabique. Le cas des semi-voyelles et des voyelles hautes dans les usages parisiens. Thèse de Doctorat de Linguistique: Paris.

Kleinke, C. L. (1986). "Gaze and eye contact: a research review." *Psychological Bulletin* **100**(1): 78–100.

Knappmeyer, B., I. M. Thornton and H. H. Bülthoff (2003). "Facial motion can bias the perception of facial identity." *Vision Research* **43**: 1921–1936.

Knight, B. and A. Johnston (1997). "The role of movement in face recognition." *Visual Cognition* **4**(3): 265–273.

Kober, R., U. Harz and J. Schiffers (1997). *Fusion of visual and acoustic signals for command-word recognition. International Conference on Acoustics, Speech and Signal Processing*. Munich, Germany, pp. 1495–1497.

Kourtzi, Z. and N. Kanwisher (2000). "Activation in human MT/MST by static images with implied motion." *Journal of Cognitive Neuroscience* **12**: 48–55.

Kovar, L., M. Gleicher and F. Pighin (2002). *Motion graphs*. SIGGRAPH. San Antonio, TX, pp. 501–508.

Kozlowski, L. T. and J. E. Cutting (1977). "Recognizing the sex of a walker from a dynamic point light display." *Perception & Psychophysics* **21**: 575–580.

Krone, G., B. Talle, A. Wichert and G. Palm (1997). *Neural architectures for sensorfusion in speech recognition*. Auditory-Visual Speech Processing Conference. Rhodes, Greece, pp. 57–60.

Kugler, P. N., J. A. S. Kelso and M. T. Turvey (1980). On the concept of coordinative structures as dissipative systems: I. Theoretical lines of convergence. *Tutorials in Motor Behavior*. G. E. Stelmach and J. Requin. New York, North-Holland: 3–47.

Kuhl, P. K. and A. N. Meltzoff (1982). "The bimodal perception of speech in infancy." *Science* **218**: 1138–1141.

(1984). "The intermodal representation of speech in infants." *Infant Behavior & Development* **7**: 361–381.

(1988). Speech as an intermodal object of perception. *Perceptual development in infancy: The Minnesota Symposia on Child Psychology*. A. Yonas. Hillsdale, NJ, Erlbaum. **20**: 235–266.

Kuhl, P. K., M. Tsuzaki, Y. Tohkura and A. Meltzoff (1994). *Human processing of auditory-visual information in speech perception: Potential for multimodal human-machine interfaces*. International Conference on Spoken Language Processing. Tokyo, pp. S11–14.11.

Kulju, J., M. Sams and K. Kaski (1998). "A Finnish-Talking Head." *Linguistica Uralica* **3**: 329–333.

Kumar, K., T. Chen and R. M. Stern (2007). *Profile view lip reading*. International Conference on Acoustics, Speech and Signal Processing. Honolulu, HI, pp. 429–432.

Kumar, K., G. Potamianos, J. Navratil, E. Marcheret and V. Libal (2010). Audio-visual speech synchrony detection by a family of bimodal linear prediction models. *Multibiometrics for Human Identification*. B. Bhanu and V. Govindaraju. Cambridge University Press.

Kumatani, K. and R. Stiefelhagen (2007). *State synchronous modeling on phone boundary for audio visual speech recognition and application to multi-view face images*. International Conference on Acoustics, Speech and Signal Processing. Honolulu, HI, pp. 417–420.

Kuratate, T. and E. Vatikiotis-Bateson (2004). *Estimating 3d face expression postures for animation from photographs using a 3d face database*. SIGGRAPH/Eurographics Symposium on Computer Animation. Grenoble, France, pp. 22–23.

Kuratate, T., E. Vatikiotis-Bateson and H. Yehia (2005). Estimation and animation of faces using facial motion mapping and a 3D face database. *Computer-graphic facial reconstruction*. J. Clement and M. Marks. Burlington, MA, Elsevier: 325–346.

Kuratate, T., H. Yehia and E. Vatikiotis-Bateson (1998). *Kinematics-based synthesis of realistic talking faces*. Auditory-Visual Speech Processing Conference. Terrigal, Sydney, Australia, pp. 185–190.

Kurucz, J., G. Feldmar and W. Werner (1979). "Proso-affective agnosia associated with chronic organic brain syndrome." *Journal of the American Geriatrics Society* **27**: 91–95.

Kushnerenko, E., T. Teinonen, A. Volein and G. Csibra (2008). "Electrophysiological evidence of illusory audiovisual speech percept in human infants." *Proceedings of the National Academy of Science, USA* **105**: 11442–11445.

Kushnerenko, E., P. Tamalski, H. Ribeiro, A. Potton, E. Axelsson, and D. G. Moore (2010). Audiovisual speech integration: Visual attention to articulation affects brain responses in 6-9-month-old infants. First Joint Conference of EPS/SEPEX 15–17 April, 2010, Granada, Spain.

Laboissière, R., D. J. Ostry and A. G. Feldman (1996). "Control of multi-muscle systems: Human jaw and hyoid movements." *Biological Cybernetics* **74**(3): 373–384.

Lachs, L. and D. B. Pisoni (2004). "Specification of crossmodal source information in isolated kinematic displays of speech." *Journal of the Acoustical Society of America* **116**(1): 507–518.

Lachs, L., D. B. Pisoni and K. I. Kirk (2001). "Use of audiovisual information in speech perception by prelingually deaf children with cochlear implants: A first report." *Ear and Hearing* **22**: 236–249.

Ladefoged, P. (1975). *A Course in Phonetics*. New York, Harcourt-Brace-Jovanovich.

Ladefoged, P., J. DeClerk, M. Lindau and G. Papcun (1972). An auditory-motor theory of speech production. *Working papers in Phonetics*. Los Angeles, University of California. **22**: 48–75.

Ladefoged, P. and I. Maddieson (1996). *The Sounds of the World's Languages*. Oxford, Blackwell Publishers.

Lallouache, M.-T. (1991). Un poste Visage-Parole couleur. Acquisition et traitement automatique des contours des lèvres. PhD Thesis; Institut National Polytechnique: Grenoble, France.

Lander, K. and V. Bruce (2001). "Recognizing famous faces: exploring the benefits of facial motion." *Ecological Psychology* **12**(4): 259–272.

(2003). "The role of motion in learning new faces." *Visual Cognition* **10**: 897–912.

(2004). "Repetition priming of moving faces." *Memory & Cognition* **32**: 640–647.

Lander, K., V. Bruce, P. J. Hancock and E. Smith (2009). "Multiple repetition priming of faces: Massed and spaced presentations." *Visual Cognition* **17**: 598–616.

Lander, K., V. Bruce and H. Hill (2001). "Evaluating the effectiveness of pixelation and blurring on masking the identity of familiar faces." *Applied Cognitive Psychology* **15**(1): 101–116.

Lander, K., F. Christie and V. Bruce (1999). "The role of movement in the recognition of famous faces." *Memory and Cognition* **27**(6): 974–985.

Lander, K. and L. Chuang (2005). "Why are moving faces easier to recognize?" *Visual Cognition* **12**: 429–442.

Lander, K., L. Chuang and L. H. V. Wickham (2006). "Recognizing identity from natural and morphed smiles." *Quarterly Journal of Experimental Psychology, Section A: Human Experimental Psychology* **59**: 801–808.

Lander, K. and R. Davies (2007). "Exploring the role of characteristic motion when learning new faces." *Quarterly Journal of Experimental Psychology* **60**: 519–526.

Lander, K. and R. Davies (2008). "Does face familiarity influence speechreadability?" *Quarterly Journal of Experimental Psychology* **61**: 961–967.

Lander, K., H. Hill, M. Kamachi and E. Vatikiotis-Bateson (2007). "It's not what you say but the way you say it: Matching faces and voices." *Journal of Experimental Psychology: Human Perception and Performance* **33**: 905–914.

Lander, K., G. W. Humphreys and V. Bruce (2004). "Exploring the role of motion in prosopagnosia: Recognizing, learning and matching faces." *Neurocase* **10**: 462–470.

Larrabee, W. (1986). "A Finite Element Model of skin deformation, I. Biomechanics of skin and soft tissue: a review." *Laryngoscope* **96**: 399–405.

Lavagetto, F. and P. Lavagetto (1996). Time delay neural networks for articulatory estimation from speech: suitable subjective evaluation protocols. *Speechreading by Humans and Machines*. D. G. Stork and M. E. Hennecke. Berlin, Springer: 437–444.

Lazard, D. S., H. J. Lee, M. Gaebler, C. A. Kell, E. Truy and A. L. Giraud (2010). "Phonological processing in post-lingual deafness and cochlear implant outcome." *Neuroimage* **49**(4): 3443–3451.

Le Goff, B. (1997). Synthèse à partir du texte de visage 3D parlant français. PhD dissertation. Institut de la Communication Parlée; Institut National Polytechnique: Grenoble, France.

Le Goff, B. and C. Benoît (1997). *A French-speaking synthetic head*. ESCA/ESCOP workshop on Audio-Visual Speech Processing. Rhodes, Greece, pp. 145–148.

Le Goff, B., T. Guiard-Marigny and C. Benoît (1996). Analysis-synthesis and intelligibility of a talking face. *Progress in Speech Synthesis*. J. P. H. van Santen, R. W. Sproat, J. P. Olive and J. Hirschberg. Berlin, Springer Verlag: 235–246.

Lee, B., M. Hasegawa-Johnson, C. Goudeseune, S. Kamdar, S. Borys, M. Liu and T. Huang (2004). *AVICAR: Audio-visual speech corpus in a car environment*. International Conference on Spoken Language Processing. Jeju Island, Korea, pp. 2489–2492.

Lee, H. J., E. Truy, G. Mamou, D. Sappey-Marinier and A. L. Giraud (2007). "Visual speech circuits in profound acquired deafness: a possible role for latent multimodal connectivity." *Brain* **130**(11): 2929–2941.

Lee, J.-S. and T. Ebrahimi (2009). *Two-level bimodal association for audiovisual speech recognition*. Advanced Concepts for Intelligent Vision Systems. Bordeaux, France, pp. 133–144.

Lee, S. Y., K. Y. Chwa and Y. S. Sung (1995a). *Image metamorphosis using snakes and free-form deformations*. SIGGRAPH. Los Angeles, CA, pp. 439–448.

Lee, S. Y., G. Wolberg and S. Y. Shin (1998). "Polymorph: An algorithm for morphing among multiple images." *IEEE Computer Graphics Applications* **18**(1): 58–71.

Lee, Y., D. Terzopoulos and K. Waters (1995b). *Realistic modeling for facial animation*. SIGGRAPH. Los Angeles, CA, pp. 55–62.

Leedham, J. S. and J. J. Dowling (1995). "Force-length, torque-angle and EMG-joint angle relationships of the human in vivo biceps brachii." *European Journal of Applied Physiology* **70**(5): 421–426.

Leggetter, C. J. and P. C. Woodland (1995). "Maximum likelihood linear regression for speaker adaptation of continuous density hidden Markov models." *Computer Speech and Language* **9**(2): 171–185.

Lesner, S. A. and P. B. Kricos (1981). "Visual vowel and diphthong perception across speakers." *Journal of the Academy of Rehabilitative Audiology* **14**: 252–258.

Levänen, S. (1999). "Neuromagnetic studies of human auditory cortex function and reorganization." *Scandinavian Audiology* **27**(49): 2–6.

Levoy, M. and P. Hanrahan (1996). *Light field rendering*. Annual Conference on Computer Graphics (SIGGRAPH). New Orleans, LA, USA, pp. 31–42.

Lewis, J. P. and F. I. Parke (1987). *Automated lip-synch and speech synthesis for character animation*. ACM Conference on Computer-Human Interaction and Computer Graphics. Toronto, Canada, pp. 143–147.

Lewis, M. B. and H. D. Ellis (1999). "Repeated repetition priming in face recognition." *Quarterly Journal of Experimental Psychology* **52**: 927–955.

Lewis, T. W. and D. M. W. Powers (2005). *Distinctive feature fusion for improved audio-visual phoneme recognition*. International Symposium on Signal Processing and its Applications. Sydney, Australia, pp. 62–65.

Lewkowicz, D. J. (2000). "The development of intersensory temporal perception: An epigenetic systems/limitations view." *Psychological Bulletin* **126**: 281–308.

Leybaert, J. (1996). "La lecture chez l'enfant sourd : l'apport du Langage Parlé Complété." *Revue Française de Linguistique Appliquée, Paris, AFLA* **1**: 81–94.

(2000). "Phonology acquired through the eyes and spelling in deaf children." *Journal of Experimental Child Psychology* **75**: 291–318.

Leybaert, J. and J. Lechat (2001). "Phonological similarity effects in memory for serial order of cued speech." *Journal of Speech, Language and Hearing Research* **44**: 949–963.

Li, N., S. Dettmer and M. Shah (1995). *Lipreading using eigensequences*. International Workshop on Automatic Face- and Gesture-Recognition. Zurich, Switzerland, pp. 30–34.

Li, S. Z. and Z. Zhang (2004). "FloatBoost learning and statistical face detection." *IEEE Transactions on Pattern Analysis and Machine Intelligence* **26**(9): 1112–1123.

Libal, V., J. Connell, G. Potamianos and E. Marcheret (2007). *An embedded system for in-vehicle visual speech activity detection*. International Workshop on Multimedia Signal Processing. Chania, Greece, pp. 255–258.

Liberman, A. M. (1979). "How abstract must a motor theory of speech perception be?" *Revue de Phonetique Appliquée* **49/50**: 41–58.

(1982). "On finding that speech is special." *American Psychologist* **37**(2): 148–167.

(1996). *Speech: A Special Code*. Cambridge, MA, MIT Press.

Liberman, A. M. and F. S. Cooper (1972). In search of the acoustic cues. *Papers in Linguistics and Phonetics to the Memory of Pierre Delattre*. A. Valdman. The Hague, Mouton: 329–338.

Liberman, A. M., F. S. Cooper, D. P. Schankweiler and M. Studdert-Kennedy (1967). "Perception of the speech code." *Psychological Review* **74**: 431–461.

Liberman, A. M. and I. G. Mattingly (1985). "The motor theory of speech perception revisited." *Cognition* **21**: 1–36.

(1989). "A specialization for speech perception." *Science* **243**: 489–494.

Liberman, A. M. and D. H. Whalen (2000). "On the relation of speech to language." *Trends in Cognitive Sciences* **4**: 187–196.

Light, L. L., F. Kayra-Stuart and S. Hollander (1979). "Recognition memory for typical and unusual faces." *Journal of Experimental Psychology: Human Learning and Memory* **5**: 212–228.

Liljencrants, J. (1971). "A Fourier series description of the tongue profile." *Speech Transmission Laboratory – Quarterly Progress Status Report* **4**: 9–18.

Lindau, M. (1979). "The feature Expanded." *Journal of Phonetics* **7**: 163–176.

Lindblom, B. and J. Sundberg (1971). "Acoustic consequences of lip, tongue, jaw, and larynx movement." *Journal of the Acoustical Society of America* **50**: 1166–1179.

Lippmann, R. P. (1997). "Speech recognition by machines and humans." *Speech Communication* **22**(1): 1–15.

Lisker, L. (1978). "Rapid vs. rabid: A catalogue of acoustic features that may cue the distinction." *Haskins Laboratories: Status Report on Speech Research* **SR-54**: 127–132.

Liu, F., R. Stern, X. Huang and A. Acero (1993). *Efficient cepstral normalization for robust speech recognition*. ARPA Workshop on Human Language Technology. Princeton, NJ.

Livescu, K., Ö. Çetin, M. Hasegawa-Johnson, S. King, C. Bartels, N. Borges, A. Kantor, P. Lal, L. Yung, A. Bezman, S. Dawson-Haggerty, B. Woods, J. Frankel, M. Magimai-Doss and K. Saenko (2007). *Articulatory feature-based methods for acoustic and audio-visual speech recognition: Summary from the 2006 JHU Summer Workshop*. International Conference on Acoustics, Speech and Signal Processing. Honolulu, HI, pp. 621–624.

Loeb, G. E. and C. Gans (1986). *Electromyography for experimentalists*. University of Chicago Press.

Löfqvist, A. (1999). "Interarticulator phasing, locus equations, and degree of coarticulation." *Journal of the Acoustical Society of America* **106**(4): 2022–2030.

(1990). Speech as audible gestures. *Speech Production and Speech Modeling*. W. J. Hardcastle and A. Marchal. Dordrecht, Kluwer Academic Publishers: 289–322.

Loh, M., G. Schmid, G. Deco and W. Ziegler (2010). "Audiovisual matching in speech and nonspeech sounds: a neurodynamical model." *Journal of Cognitive Neuroscience* **22**: 240–247.

Lorenceau, J. and D. Alais (2001). "Form constraints in motion binding." *Nature Neuroscience* **4**(7): 745–751.

Luce, P. (1986). Neighborhoods of words in the mental lexicon. Research on Speech Perception Tech. Rep. No. 6. Bloomington, IN, Speech Research Laboratory, Department of Psychology, Indiana University.

Luce, P. A., S. D. Goldinger, E. T. Auer, Jr. and M. S. Vitevitch (2000). "Phonetic priming, neighborhood activation, and PARSYN." *Perception & Psychophysics* **62**: 615–625.

Luce, P. A. and D. B. Pisoni (1998). "Recognizing spoken words: The neighborhood activation model." *Ear & Hearing* **19**: 1–36.

Lucero, J. C. and K. G. Munhall (1999). "A model of facial biomechanics for speech production." *Journal of the Acoustical Society of America* **106**: 2834–2848.

Lucey, P., G. Potamianos and S. Sridharan (2009). Visual speech recognition across multiple views. *Visual Speech Recognition: Lip Segmentation and Mapping*. A. W. -C. Liew and S. Wang. Hershey, PA, IGI Global: 294–325.

Ludman, C. N., A. Q. Summerfield, D. Hall, M. Elliott, J. Foster, J. L. Hykin, R. Bowtell and R. G. Morris (2000). "Lipreading ability and patterns of cortical localisation studied using fMRI." *British Journal of Audiology* **34**: 225–230.

Luettin, J., G. Potamianos and C. Neti (2001). *Asynchronous stream modeling for large vocabulary audio-visual speech recognition*. International Conference on Acoustics, Speech and Signal Processing. Salt Lake City, UT, pp. 169–172.

Luettin, J. and N. A. Thacker (1997). "Speechreading using probabilistic models." *Computer Vision and Image Understanding* **65**(2): 163–178.

Luettin, J., N. A. Thacker and S. W. Beet (1996). *Speechreading using shape and intensity information*. International Conference on Spoken Language Processing. Philadelphia, PA, pp. 58–61.

Lundeberg, M. and J. Beskow (1999). *Developing a 3-D agent for the August dialogue system*. Auditory-Visual Speech Processing Conference. Santa Cruz, CA, pp. 151–156.

Luria, A. R. (1973). *The Working Brain*. London, Penguin Books.

Lv, G., D. Jiang, R. Zhao and Y. Hou (2007). *Multi-stream asynchrony modeling for audio-visual speech recognition*. International Symposium on Multimedia. Washington, DC, pp. 37–44.

MacKain, K., M. Studdert-Kennedy, S. Spieker and D. Stern (1983). "Infant intermodal speech perception is a left-hemisphere function." *Science* **219**: 1347–1348.

Macken, M. and D. Barton (1980). "The acquisition of the voicing contrast in Spanish: A phonetic and phonological study of word-initial stop consonants." *Journal of Child Language* **7**: 433–458.

MacLeod, A. and Q. Summerfield (1987). "Quantifying the contribution of vision to speech perception in noise." *British Journal of Audiology* **21**: 131–141.

MacNeilage, P. (1998). "The frame/content theory of evolution of speech production." *Behavioral and Brain Sciences* **21**(4): 499–548.

MacNeilage, P. F. and B. Davis (1990). Acquisition of speech production: The achievement of segmental independence. *Speech Production and Speech Modelling*. W. J. Hardcastle and A. Marschal. Dordrecht, Kluwer Academic Publishers: 55–68.

MacSweeney, M., E. Amaro, G. A. Calvert, R. Campbell, A. S. David, P. K. McGuire, S. C. R. Williams, B. Woll and M. J. Brammer (2000). "Activation of auditory cortex by silent speechreading in the absence of scanner noise: An event-related fMRI study." *Neuroreport* **11**: 1729–1734.

MacSweeney, M., M. J. Brammer, D. Waters and U. Goswami (2009). "Enhanced activation of the left inferior frontal gyrus in deaf and dyslexic adults during rhyming." *Brain* **132**: 1928–1940.

MacSweeney, M., G. A. Calvert, R. Campbell, P. K. McGuire, A. S. David, S. C. R. Williams, B. Woll and M. J. Brammer (2002a). "Speechreading circuits in people born deaf." *Neuropsychologia* **40**(7): 801–807.

MacSweeney, M., R. Campbell, G. A. Calvert, P. K. McGuire, A. S. David, J. Suckling, C. Andrew, B. Woll and M. J. Brammer (2001). "Activation of auditory cortex by speechreading in congenitally deaf people." *Proceedings of the Royal Society of London* **B.268**: 451–457.

MacSweeney, M., R. Campbell, B. Woll, M. J. Brammer, V. Giampietro, A. S. David, G. A. Calvert and P. K. McGuire (2006). "Lexical and sentential processing in British Sign Language." *Human Brain Mapping* **27**(1): 63–76.

MacSweeney, M., R. Campbell, B. Woll, V. Giampietro, A. S. David, P. K. McGuire, G. A. Calvert and M. J. Brammer (2004). "Dissociating linguistic and nonlinguistic gestural communication in the brain." *Neuroimage* **22**(4): 1605–1618.

MacSweeney, M., B. Woll, R. Campbell, P. K. McGuire, A. S. David, S. C. Williams, J. Suckling, G. A. Calvert and M. J. Brammer (2002b). "Neural systems underlying British Sign Language and audio-visual English processing in native users." *Brain* **125**: 1583–1593.

Maeda, S. (1990). Compensatory articulation during speech: Evidence from the analysis and synthesis of vocal-tract shapes using an articulatory model. *Speech Production and Speech Modelling*. W. J. Hardcastle and A. Marchal. Dordrecht, Kluwer Academic Publishers.

(1991). "On articulatory and acoustic variabilities." *Journal of Phonetics* **19**: 321–331.

Maeda, S. and K. Honda (1994). "From EMG to formant patterns of vowels: the implication of vowel systems spaces." *Phonetica* **51**: 17–29.

Mahshie, J. J. (1998). "Balloons, penguins, and visual displays SpeechViewer III: solid tool for specialists." *Perspectives in Education and Deafness* **16**(4).

Maison, B., C. Neti and A. Senior (1999). *Audio-visual speaker recognition for broadcast news: some fusion techniques*. Workshop on Multimedia Signal Processing. Copenhagen, Denmark, pp. 161–167.

Marcheret, E., V. Libal and G. Potamianos (2007). *Dynamic stream weight modeling for audio-visual speech recognition*. International Conference on Acoustics, Speech and Signal Processing. Honolulu, HI, pp. 945–948.

Marschark, M., D. LePoutre and L. Bement (1998). Mouth movement and signed communication. *Hearing by Eye II*. R. Campbell, B. Dodd and D. Burnham. Hove, UK, Psychology Press: 245–266.

Marslen-Wilson, W. D. (1987). "Functional parallelism in spoken word recognition." *Cognition* **25**: 71–102.

(1989). Access and integration: Projecting sound onto meaning. *Lexical Access and Representation*. W. D. Marslen-Wilson. Cambridge, MA, Bradford.

(1990). Activation, competition, and frequency in lexical access. *Cognitive Models of Speech Processing*. G. T. M. Altmann. Cambridge, MA, MIT Press: 148–172.

(1993). Issues of process and representation in lexical access. *Cognitive Models of Speech Processing: The Second Sperlonga Meeting*. G. T. Altmann and R. Shillcock. Hillsdale, NJ, Erlbaum: 187–210.

Marslen-Wilson, W. D. and P. Warren (1994). "Levels of perceptual representation and process in lexical access: Words, phonemes, and features." *Psychological Review* **101**: 653–675.

Mase, K. and A. Pentland (1991). "Automatic lipreading by optical flow analysis." *Systems and Computers in Japan* **22**(6): 67–75.

Massaquoi, S. G. and J. -J. E. Slotine (1996). "The intermediate cerebellum may function as a wave-variable processor." *Neuroscience Letters* **215**: 60–64.

Massaro, D. W. (1987). *Speech Perception by Ear and Eye: A Paradigm for Psychological Inquiry*. Hillsdale, NJ, USA, Erlbaum.

(1996). Bimodal speech perception: a progress report. *Speechreading by Humans and Machines*. D. G. Stork and M. E. Hennecke. Berlin, Springer: 79–102.

(1998a). *Illusions and issues in bimodal speech perception*. Auditory-Visual Speech Processing Conference. Terrigal, Sydney, Australia, pp. 21–26.

(1998b). *Perceiving Talking Faces: From Speech Perception to a Behavioral Principle*. Cambridge, MA, MIT Press.

(2006a). A computer-animated tutor for language learning: Research and applications. *Advances in the Spoken Language Development of Deaf and Hard-of-hearing Children*. P. E. Spencer and M. Marshark. New York, Oxford University Press: 212–243.

(2006b). The psychology and technology of talking heads: Applications in Language Learning. *Natural, Intelligent and Effective Interaction in Multimodal Dialogue*

Systems O. Bernsen, L. Dybkjaer and J. van Kuppevelt. Dordrecht, Kluwer Academic Publishers: 183–214.

Massaro, D. W. and A. Bosseler (2003). "Perceiving speech by ear and eye: multimodal integration by children with autism." *Journal of Developmental and Learning Disorders* **7**: 111–146.

(2006). "Read my lips: The importance of the face in a computer-animated tutor for autistic children learning language." *Autism: The International Journal of Research and Practice* **10**(5): 495–510.

Massaro, D. W., A. Bosseler and J. Light (2003). *Development and evaluation of a computer-animated tutor for language and vocabulary learning*. International Congress of Phonetic Sciences. Barcelona, pp. 143–146.

Massaro, D. W. and M. M. Cohen (1993). "Perceiving asynchronous bimodal speech in consonant-vowel and vowel syllables." *Speech Communication*(**13**): 127–134.

Massaro, D. W., M. M. Cohen and J. Beskow (2000). Developing and evaluating conversational agents. *Embodied Conversational Agents*. J. Cassell, J. Sullivan, S. Prevost and E. Churchill. Cambridge, MA, MIT Press: 287–318.

Massaro, D. W. and J. Light (2003). *Read my tongue movements: bimodal learning to perceive and produce non-native speech /r/ and /l/*. European Conference on Speech Communication and Technology. Geneva, Switzerland, pp. 2249–2252.

(2004a). "Improving the vocabulary of children with hearing loss." *Volta Review* **104** (3): 141–174.

(2004b). "Using visible speech for training perception and production of speech for hard of hearing individuals." *Journal of Speech, Language, and Hearing Research* **47**(2): 304–320.

Massaro, D. W. and D. G. Stork (1998). "Speech recognition and sensory integration." *American Scientist* **86**(3): 236–244.

Massaro, D. W., B. B. Thompson and E. Laren (1986). "Developmental changes in visual and auditory contributions to speech perception." *Journal of Experimental Child Psychology* **41**: 93–113.

Massaro, D. W., M. Tsuzaki, M. M. Cohen, A. Gesi and R. Heredia (1993). "Bimodal speech perception: An examination across languages." *Journal of Phonetics* **21**: 445–478.

Masuko, T., T. Kobayashi, M. Tamura, J. Masubuchi and K. Tokuda (1998). *Text-to-visual speech synthesis based on parameter generation from HMM*. International Conference on Acoustics, Speech and Signal Processing. Seattle, WA, pp. 3745–3748.

Matsuda, M. and H. Kasuya (1999). *Acoustic nature of the whisper*. EuroSpeech. Budapest, Hungary, pp. 133–136.

Matsuzaki, N. and T. Sato (2008). "The perception of facial expressions using two-frame apparent motion." *Perception* **37**: 1560–1568.

Matthews, I., J. A. Bangham and S. Cox (1996). *Audio-visual speech recognition using multiscale nonlinear image decomposition*. International Conference on Spoken Language Processing. Philadelphia, PA, pp. 38–41.

Matthews, I., T. Cootes, S. Cox, R. Harvey and J. A. Bangham (1998). *Lipreading using shape, shade and scale*. Auditory-visual Speech Processing Workshop. Terrigal, Sydney, Australia, pp. 73–78.

Matthews, I., G. Potamianos, C. Neti and J. Luettin (2001). *A comparison of model and transform-based visual features for audio-visual LVCSR*. International Conference on Multimedia and Expo. Tokyo, Japan.

Mattingly, I. G. and M. Studdert-Kennedy (1991). *Modularity and the Motor Theory of Speech Perception*. Hillsdale, NJ, Erlbaum.

Mattys, S., L. E. Bernstein and E. T. Auer, Jr. (2002). "Stimulus-based lexical distinctiveness as a general word recognition mechanism." *Perception & Psychophysics* **64**: 667–679.

Mawass, K., P. Badin and G. Bailly (2000). "Articulatory synthesis of French fricative consonants." *Acta Acoustica* **86**: 136–146.

Mazaudon, M. (1997). */a/ glide in Sino-Tibetan*. International Conference of Linguists. Paris.

McCaffrey, H. A., B. Davis, P. F. MacNeilage and D. von Hapsburg (2001). "Effects of multichannel cochlear implantation on the organization of early speech." *The Volta Review: New Reflections on Speechreading* **101**(1): 5–29.

McClelland, J. L. and J. L. Elman (1986). "The TRACE model of speech perception." *Cognitive Psychology* **18**: 1–86.

McClelland, J. L. and D. E. Rumelhart (1981). "An interactive activation model of context effects in letter perception: Part 1. An account of basic findings." *Psychological Review* **88**: 375–407.

McCotter, M. V. and T. R. Jordan (2003). "The role of facial colour and luminance in visual and audiovisual speech perception." *Perception* **32**(8): 921–936.

McDonald, J. and H. McGurk (1978). "Visual influences on speech perception processes." *Perception & Psychophysics* **24**: 253–257.

McGowan, R. S. (1992). "Tongue-tip trills and vocal-tract wall compliance." *Journal of the Acoustical Society of America* **91**: 2903–2910.

McGrath, M. (1985). An examination of cues for visual and audio-visual speech perceptions using natural and computer-generated faces. University of Nottingham.

McGrath, M. and Q. Summerfield (1983). "Intermodal timing relations and audio-visual speech recognition by normal-hearing adults." *Journal of the Acoustical Society of America* **77**: 678–685.

McGrath, M., Q. Summerfield and M. Brooke (1984). *Roles of lips and teeth in lipreading vowels*. Proceedings of the Institute of Acoustics. Windermere, England, pp. 401–408.

McGurk, H. and L. Buchanan (1981). Bimodal speech perception: Vision and hearing. Unpublished manuscript, Department of Psychology, University of Surrey.

McGurk, H. and J. MacDonald (1976). "Hearing lips and seeing voices." *Nature* **264**: 746–748.

McLeod, P., W. Dittrich, J. Driver, D. Perrett and J. Zihl (1996). "Preserved and impaired detection of structure from motion by a 'motion-blind' patient." *Visual Cognition* **3** (4): 363–391.

Meier, U., W. Hürst and P. Duchnowski (1996). *Adaptive bimodal sensor fusion for automatic speechreading*. International Conference on Acoustics, Speech and Signal Processing. Atlanta, GA, pp. 833–836.

Melenchón, J., E. Martínez, F. De La Torre and J. A. Montero (2009). "Emphatic visual speech synthesis." *IEEE Transactions on Audio, Speech, and Language Processing* **17**(3): 459–468.

Meltzoff, A. N. (1995). "Understanding the intention of others: re-enactment of intended acts by 18-month-old children." *Developmental Psychology* **31**: 838–850.

Mermelstein, P. (1973). "An articulatory model for the study of speech production." *Journal of the Acoustical Society of America* **53**: 1070–1082.

Messer, K., J. Matas, J. Kittler, J. Luettin and G. Maitre (1999). *XM2VTS: The extended M2VTS database*. International Conference on Audio and Video-based Biometric Person Authentication. Washington, DC, pp. 72–76.

Miller, L. M. and M. D'Esposito (2005). "Perceptual fusion and stimulus coincidence in the cross-modal integration of speech." *Journal of Neuroscience* **25**(25): 5884–5893.

Minnis, S. and A. P. Breen (1998). *Modeling visual coarticulation in synthetic talking heads using a lip motion unit inventory with concatenative synthesis*. International Conference on Speech and Language Processing. Beijing, China, pp. 759–762.

Mitchell, R. E. and M. A. Karchmer (2004). "When parents are deaf versus hard of hearing: Patterns of sign use and school placement of deaf and hard-of-hearing children." *Journal of Deaf Studies and Deaf Education* **9**(2): 133–152.

Miyajima, C., K. Tokuda and T. Kitamura (2000). *Audio-visual speech recognition using MCE-based HMMs and model-dependent stream weights*. International Conference on Spoken Language Processing. Beijing, China, pp. 1023–1026.

Moghaddam, B., W. Wahid and A. Pentland (1998). Beyond eigenfaces: probabilistic matching for face recognition. Boston, USA, MIT. Media Laboratory, Perceptual Computing Section.

Mohammed, T., R. Campbell, M. MacSweeney, F. Barry and M. Coleman (2006). "Speechreading and its association with reading among deaf, hearing and dyslexic individuals." *Clinical Linguistics and Phonetics* **20**(7–8): 621–630.

Mohammed, T., R. Campbell, M. MacSweeney, E. Milne, P. Hansen and M. Coleman (2005). "Speechreading skill and visual movement sensitivity are related in deaf speechreaders." *Perception* **34**(2): 205–216.

Montgomery, A. A. and G. S. Hoo (1982). "ANIMAT: a set of programs to generate, edit and display sequences of vector-based images." *Behavioural Research Methods and Instrumentation* **14**: 39–40.

Montgomery, A. A. and P. L. Jackson (1983). "Physical characteristics of the lips underlying vowel lipreading performance." *Journal of the Acoustical Society of America* **73**: 2134–2144.

Montgomery, A. A., B. E. Walden and R. A. Prosek (1987). "Effects of consonantal context on vowel lipreading." *Journal of Speech and Hearing Research* **30**: 50–59.

Morishima, S. (1998). *Real-time talking head driven by voice and its application to communication and entertainment*. International Conference on Auditory-visual Speech Processing. Terrigal, Sydney, Australia, pp. 195–200.

Morton, J. (1979). Word recognition. *Psycholinguistics 2: Structures and Processes*. J. Morton and J. D. Marshall. London, Paul Elek.

Moskowitz, A. (1970). "The two-year-old stage in the acquisition of English phonology." *Language* **46**: 426–441.

Motoki, K., P. Badin, X. Pelorson and H. Matsuzaki (2000). *A modal parametric method for computing acoustic characteristics of three-dimensional vocal tract models*. 5th Seminar on Speech Production: Models and Data & CREST Workshop on Models of Speech Production: Motor Planning and Articulatory Modelling. Kloster Seeon, Bavaria, pp. 325–328.

Möttönen, R., G. A. Calvert, I. P. Jääskeläinen, P. M. Matthews, T. Thesen, J. Tuomainen and M. Sams (2006). "Perceiving identical sounds as speech or non-speech modulates activity in the left posterior superior temporal sulcus." *Neuroimage* **30**(2): 563–569.

Möttönen, R., J. Järveläinen, M. Sams and R. Hari (2005). "Viewing speech modulates activity in the left SI mouth cortex." *Neuroimage* **24**(3): 731–737.

Möttönen, R., M. Schürmann and M. Sams (2004). "Time course of multisensory interactions during audiovisual speech perception in humans: a magnetoencephalographic study." *Neuroscience Letters* **363**(2): 112–115.

Moulines, E., P. Emerard, D. Larreur, J. L. Le Saint Milon, L. Le Faucheur, F. Marty, F. Charpentier and C. Sorin (1990). *A real-time French text-to-speech system generating high-quality synthetic speech*. ICASSP. Albuquerque, NM, pp. 309–312.

Movellan, J. R. and G. Chadderdon (1996). Channel separability in the audio-visual integration of speech: a Bayesian approach. *Speechreading by Humans and Machines*. D. G. Stork and M. E. Hennecke. Berlin, Springer: 473–487.

Mugitani, R., T. Kobayashi and K. Hiraki (2008). "Japanese infants show language-specific development in audiovisual integration of vowels." *Transactions on Technical Committee of Psychological and Physiological Acoustics, The Acoustical Society of Japan* **38**: 615–619. (In Japanese with English abstract.)

Mulford, R. (1988). First words of the blind child. *The Emergent Lexicon: The Child's Development of a Linguistic Vocabulary*. M. D. Smith and J. L. Locke. New York, Academic Press: 293–338.

Muller, E. M. and G. M. MacLeod (1982). "Perioral biomechanics and its relation to labial control." *Journal of the Acoustical Society of America* **71**: S33.

Munhall, K., J. A. Jones, D. E. Callan, T. Kuratate and E. Vatikiotis-Bateson (2004a). "Visual prosody and speech intelligibility." *Psychological Science* **15**(2): 133–137.

Munhall, K. G., P. Gribble, L. Sacco and M. Ward (1996). "Temporal constraints on the McGurk effect." *Perception & Psychophysics* **58**: 351–362.

Munhall, K. G. and J. A. Jones (1998). "Articulatory evidence for syllabic structure." *Behavioural and Brain Sciences* **21**(4): 524–525.

Munhall, K. G., J. A. Jones, D. Callan, T. Kuratate and E. Vatikiotis-Bateson (2003). "Visual prosody and speech intelligibility: Head movement improves auditory speech perception." *Psychological Sciences* **15**(2): 133–137.

Munhall, K. G., J. A. Jones, D. Callan, T. Kuratate and E. Vatikiotis-Bateson (2004b). "Visual prosody and speech intelligibility: Head movement improves auditory speech perception." *Psychological Sciences* **15**(2): 133–137.

Munhall, K. G., M. Kawato and E. Vatikiotis-Bateson (2000). Coarticulation and physical models of speech production. *Papers in Laboratory Phonology V. Acquisition and the Lexicon*. M. Broe and J. Pierrehumbert. Cambridge University Press: 9–28.

Munhall, K. G., C. Kroos, G. Jozan and E. Vatikiotis-Bateson (2004c). "Spatial frequency requirements for audiovisual speech perception." *Perception & Psychophysics* **66**: 574–583.

Munhall, K. G., P. Servos, A. Santi and M. A. Goodale (2002). "Dynamic visual speech perception in a patient with visual form agnosia." *Neuroreport* **13**: 1793–1796.

Munhall, K. G., M. K. Tiede and E. Vatikiotis-Bateson (1994). "Looking at lips: Methods of extracting facial movement parameters." *Journal of the Acoustical Society of Japan*: 365–366.

Munhall, K. G. and E. Vatikiotis-Bateson (1998). The moving face during speech communication. *Hearing by Eye II: Advances in the Psychology of Speechreading and Auditory-visual Speech*. R. Campbell, B. Dodd and D. Burnham. Hillsdale, NJ, Erlbaum: 123–139.

Murphy, K. P. (2002). Dynamic Bayesian networks: Representation, inference, and learning. PhD Thesis. Computer Science Division, University of California.

Musacchia, G., M. Sams, T. Nicol and N. Kraus (2006). "Seeing speech affects acoustic information processing in the human brainstem." *Experimental Brain Research* **168** (1–2): 1–10.

Musacchia, G., M. Sams, E. Skoe and N. Kraus (2007). "Musicians have enhanced subcortical auditory and audiovisual processing of speech and music." *Proceedings of the National Academy of Sciences, USA* **104**(40): 15894–15898.

Nadas, A., D. Nahamoo and M. Picheny (1989). "Speech recognition using noise adaptive prototypes." *IEEE Transactions on Acoustics, Speech, and Signal Processing* **37**: 1495–1503.

Nairn, M. J., W. J. Hardcastle, F. Gibbon, R. Razzell, L. Crampin, L. Harvey and B. Reynolds (1999). CLEFTNET Scotland: Applications of new technology to the investigation and treatment of speech disorders associated with cleft palate within a Scottish context. *Pathologies of Speech and Language: Advances in Clinical Phonetics and Linguistics*. B. Massen and P. Groenen. London, Whurr: 307–314.

Nakamura, K., T. Toda, Y. Nankaku and K. Tokuda (2006). *On the use of phonetic information for mapping from articulatory movements to vocal tract spectrum*. ICASSP. Toulouse, France, pp. 93–96.

Nakamura, S. (2001). Fusion of audio-visual information for integrated speech processing. *Audio- and Video-based Biometric Person Authentication*. J. Bigun and F. Smeraldi. Berlin, Springer: 127–143.

Nakamura, S., H. Ito and K. Shikano (2000). *Stream weight optimization of speech and lip image sequence for audio-visual speech recognition*. International Conference on Spoken Language Processing. Beijing, China, pp. 20–23.

Nazari, M. A., P. Perrier, M. Chabanas and Y. Payan (2010). "Simulation of dynamic orofacial movements using a constitutive law varying with muscle activation." *Computer Methods in Biomechanics & Biomedical Engineering* **13**(4): 469–482.

Nearey, T. M. (1997). "Speech perception as pattern recognition." *Journal of the Acoustical Society of America* **101**: 3241–3254.

Nefian, A. V., L. Liang, X. Pi, X. Liu and K. Murphy (2002). "Dynamic Bayesian networks for audio-visual speech recognition." *EURASIP Journal on Applied Signal Processing*: 1274–1288.

Nelder, J. A. and R. Mead (1965). "A simplex method for function minimisation." *Computing Journal* **7**(4): 308–313.

Neti, C. (1994). *Neuromorphic speech processing for noisy environments*. International Conference on Neural Networks. Orlando, FL, pp. 4425–4430.

Neti, C., G. Potamianos, J. Luettin, I. Matthews, H. Glotin, D. Vergyri, J. Sison, A. Mashari and J. Zhou (2000). Audio-Visual Speech Recognition. Final Workshop 2000 Report. Baltimore, MD, Center for Language and Speech Processing, The Johns Hopkins University.

Neumeyer, L., A. Sankar and V. Digalakis (1995). *A comparative study of speaker adaptation techniques*. European Conference on Speech Communication and Technology. Madrid, Spain, pp. 1127–1130.

Newman, A. J., T. Supalla, P. Hauser, E. L. Newport and D. Bavelier (2010). "Prosodic and narrative processing in American Sign Language: An fMRI study." *Neuroimage*: [Epub ahead of print] PMID: 20347996.

Nicholls, G. (1979). *Cued Speech and the Reception of Spoken Language*. McGill University, Montreal.
Nicholls, G. and D. Ling (1982). "Cued Speech and the reception of spoken language." *Journal of Speech and Hearing Research* **25**: 262–269.
Nishida, S. (1986). *Speech recognition enhancement by lip information*. CHI Conference – Human Factors in Computing Systems. New York, pp. 198–204.
Nitchie, E. B. (1916). "The use of homophenous words." *Volta Review* **18**: 83–85.
Noiray, A., M.-A. Cathiard, L. Ménard and C. Abry (2011). "Test of the Movement Expansion Model: Anticipatory vowel lip protrusion and constriction in French and English speakers." *Journal of the Acoustical Society of America* **129**(1): 340–349.
Norris, D. (1994). "SHORTLIST: a connectionist model of continuous speech recognition." *Cognition* **52**: 189–234.
Nygaard, L. C. and D. B. Pisoni (1995). Speech perception: New directions in research and theory. *Speech, Language, and Communication. Handbook of Perception and Cognition*. J. L. Miller and P. Eimas. San Diego, CA, Academic Press: 63–96.
Nygaard, L. C., M. S. Sommers and D. B. Pisoni (1994). "Speech perception as a talker-contingent process." *Psychological Sciences* **5**: 42–46.
O'Craven, K. M., B. R. Rosen, K. K. Kwong, A. Treisman and R. L. Savoy (1997). "Voluntary attention modulates fMRI activity in human MT-MST." *Neuron* **18**: 591–598.
O'Shaughnessy, D. (2003). "Interacting with computers by voice: Automatic speech recognition and synthesis." *Proceedings of the IEEE on Neural Networks* **91**(9): 1272–1305.
O'Toole, A. J., D. A. Roark and H. Abdi (2002). "Recognizing moving faces: a psychological and neural synthesis." *Trends in Cognitive Sciences* **6**: 261–266.
Odisio, M. and G. Bailly (2004). *Audiovisual perceptual evaluation of resynthesised speech movements*. International Conference on Speech and Language Processing. Jeju, Korea, pp. 2029–2032.
Odisio, M., G. Bailly and F. Elisei (2004). "Tracking talking faces with shape and appearance models." *Speech Communication* **44**(1–4): 63–82.
Oerlemans, M. and P. Blamey (1998). Touch and auditory-visual speech perception. *Hearing by Eye: Part 2, The Psychology of Speechreading and Auditory-visual Speech*. R. Campbell, B. Dodd and D. Burnham. Hillsdale, NJ, Erlbaum: 245–281.
Ohala, J. J. (1992). The segment: Primitive or derived? *Papers in Laboratory Phonology II: Gesture, Segment, Prosody*. G. J. Docherty and D. R. Ladd. Cambridge University Press: 166–183.
(1994). The frequency code underlies the sound symbolic use of voice pitch. *Sound Symbolism*. L. Hinton, J. Nichols and J. J. Ohala. Cambridge University Press: 325–347.
Öhman, S. E. G. (1966). "Coarticulation in VCV utterances: Spectrographic measurements." *Journal of the Acoustical Society of America* **39**: 224–230.
(1967a). "Numerical model of coarticulation." *Journal of the Acoustical Society of America* **41**: 310–320.
(1967b). Word and sentence intonation: a quantitative model. Stockholm, Sweden, Speech Transmission Laboratory – Department of Speech Communication and Music Acoustics – KTH: 20–54.

Ojanen, V. (2005). Neurocognitive mechanisms of audiovisual speech perception. Dissertation for the degree of Doctor of Science in Technology, Helsinki University of Technology. Laboratory of Computational Science and Engineering.

Okada, K. and G. Hickok (2009). "Two cortical mechanisms support the integration of visual and auditory speech: a hypothesis and preliminary data." *Neuroscience Letters* **452**(3): 219–223.

Okadome, T., T. Kaburagi and M. Honda (1999). *Articulatory movement formation by kinematic triphone model*. IEEE International Conference on Systems, Man, and Cybernetics. Tokyo, Japan, pp. 469–474.

Okawa, S., T. Nakajima and K. Shirai (1999). *A recombination strategy for multi-band speech recognition based on mutual information criterion*. European Conference on Speech Communication and Technology. Budapest, Hungary, pp. 603–606.

Okazawa, H., Y. Naito, Y. Yonekura, N. Sadato, S. Hirano, S. Nishizawa, Y. Magata, K. Ishizu, N. Tamaki, I. Honjo and J. Konishi (1996). "Cochlear implant efficiency in pre- and post-lingually deaf subjects: a study with H2(15)0 and PET." *Brain* **119**: 1297–1306.

Oller, D. K. and P. F. MacNeilage (1983). Development of speech production: Perspectives from natural and perturbed speech. *The Production of Speech*. P. F. MacNeilage. New York, Heidelberg, Berlin, Springer: 91–108.

Ortega, A., F. Sukno, E. Lleida, A. Frangi, A. Miguel, L. Buera and E. Zacur (2004). *AV@CAR: A Spanish multichannel multimodal corpus for in-vehicle automatic audio-visual speech recognition*. Language Resources and Evaluation Conference. Lisbon, Portugal, pp. 763–766.

Ostry, D. J. and K. G. Munhall (1994). "Control of jaw orientation and position in mastication and speech." *Journal of Neurophysiology* **71**: 1528–1545.

Ouni, S., M. M. Cohen and D. W. Massaro (2005). "Training Baldi to be Multilingual: A case study for an Arabic Badr." *Speech Communication* **45**: 115–137.

Ouni, S., D. W. Massaro, M. M. Cohen, K. Young and A. Jesse (2003). *Internationalization of a talking head*. International Congress of Phonetic Sciences. Barcelona, Spain, pp. 2569–2572.

Owens, E. and B. Blazek (1985). "Visemes observed by hearing-impaired and normal-hearing adult viewers." *Journal of Speech and Hearing Research* **28**: 381–393.

Padgett, J. (2008). "Glides, vowels, and features." *Lingua. Special Section: Studies on the Phonetics and Phonology of Glides, I. Chitoran and A. Nevins* **118**(12): 1937–1955.

Pan, H., Z.-P. Liang, T. J. Anastasio and T. S. Huang (1998). *A hybrid NN-Bayesian architecture for information fusion*. International Conference on Image Processing. Chicago, IL, pp. 368–371.

Pandzic, I., J. Ostermann and D. Millen (1999). "Users evaluation: synthetic talking faces for interactive services." *The Visual Computer* **15**: 330–340.

Pandzic, I. S. and R. Forchheimer (2002). *MPEG-4 Facial Animation. The Standard, Implementation and Applications*. Chichester, John Wiley & Sons

Papandreou, G., A. Katsamanis, V. Pitsikalis and P. Maragos (2009). "Adaptive multi-modal fusion by uncertainty compensation with application to audiovisual speech recognition." *IEEE Transactions on Audio, Speech, and Language Processing* **17**(3): 423–435.

Pardo, J. S. and R. E. Remez (2006). The perception of speech. *The Handbook of Psycholinguistics*, 2nd edn. M. Traxler and M. A. Gernsbacher. New York, Academic Press: 201–248.

Parke, F. I. (1974). *A parametric model for human faces*. Salt Lake City, University of Utah.

(1975). "A model for human faces that allows speech synchronized animation." *Journal of Computers and Graphics* **1**(1): 1–4.

(1982). "A parametrized model for facial animation." *IEEE Computer Graphics and Applications* **2**(9): 61–70.

Parke, F. I. and K. Waters (1996). *Computer Facial Animation*. Wellesley, MA, A.K. Peters.

Parry, F. M., A. W. Young, J. S. Saul and A. Moss (1991). "Dissociable face processing impairments after brain injury." *Journal of Clinical and Experimental Neuropsychology* **13**: 545–558.

Patterson, E. K., S. Gurbuz, Z. Tufekci and J. N. Gowdy (2001). *Noise-based audio-visual fusion for robust speech recognition*. International Conference on Auditory-Visual Speech Processing. Aalborg, Denmark, pp. 196–199.

(2002). *CUAVE: A new audio-visual database for multimodal human-computer interface research*. International Conference on Acoustics, Speech and Signal Processing. Orlando, FL, pp. 2017–2020.

Patterson, M. and J. Werker (1999). "Matching phonetic information in lips and voice is robust in 4.5-month-old infants." *Infant Behavior & Development* **22**(2): 237–247.

(2002). "Infants' ability to match dynamic information in the face and voice." *Journal of Experimental Child Psychology* **81**: 93–115.

(2003). "Two-month-old infants match phonetic information in lips and voice." *Developmental Science* **6**(2): 191–196.

Paulesu, E., D. Perani, V. Blasi, G. Silani, N. A. Borghese, U. De Giovanni, S. Sensolo and F. Fazio (2003). "A functional-anatomical model of lipreading." *Journal of Neurophysiology* **90**: 2005–2013.

Pavlovic, V. (1998). *Multimodal tracking and classification of audio-visual features*. International Conference on Image Processing. Chicago, IL, pp. 343–347.

Payan, Y. and P. Perrier (1997). "Synthesis of V-V sequences with a 2D biomechanical tongue model controlled by the Equilibrium Point Hypothesis." *Speech Communication* **22**: 185–205.

Pearce, A., B. L. M. Wyvill, G. Wyvill and D. R. Hill (1986). *Speech and expression: A computer solution to face animation*. Graphics Interface. Calgary, Canada, pp. 136–140.

Pearson, D. E. and J. A. Robinson (1985). "Visual communication at very low data rates." *Proceedings of the IEEE* **73**: 795–811.

Peeling, S. M., R. K. Moore and M. J. Tomlinson (1986). *The multilayer perceptron as a tool for speech pattern processing research*. Proceedings of the Institute of Acoustics, Autumn Meeting. Windermere, England, pp. 307–314.

Pegg, J. E. and J. F. Werker (1997). "Adult and infant perception of two English phones." *Journal of the Acoustical Society of America* **102**(6): 3742–3753.

Pekkola, J., V. Ojanen, T. Autti, I. P. Jaaskelainen, R. Möttönen, A. Tarkiainen and M. Sams (2005). "Primary auditory cortex activation by visual speech: an fMRI study at 3 Tesla." *NeuroReport* **16**: 125–128.

Pelphrey, K. A., J. P. Morris, C. R. Michelich, T. Allison and G. McCarthy (2005). "Functional anatomy of biological motion perception in posterior temporal cortex: An FMRI study of eye, mouth and hand movements." *Cerebral Cortex* **15**: 1866–1876.

Pentland, A. and K. Mase (1989). *Lipreading: automatic visual recognition of spoken words*. Boston, MIT Media Lab Vision Science.

Perkell, J. S. (1969). *Physiology of Speech Production: Results and Implications of a Quantitative Cineradiographic Study*. Cambridge, MA, MIT Press.

(1974). A physiologically-oriented model of tongue activity during speech production, MIT.

(1986). Coarticulation strategies: "Preliminary implications of a detailed analysis of lower lip protrusion movements." *Speech Communication* **5**: 47–68.

(1990). Testing theories of speech production: Implications of some detailed analyses of variable articulatory data. *Speech Production and Speech Modelling*. W. J. Hardcastle and A. Marchal. London, Kluwer Academic Publishers: 263–288.

Perkell J. S. and C. Chiang (1986). Preliminary support for a "hybrid model" of anticipatory coarticulation. International Conference on Acoustics. Toronto, Canada, pp. A3–6.

Perkell, J. S. and M. L. Matthies (1992). "Temporal measures of anticipatory labial coarticulation for the vowel [u]: Within- and cross-subject variability." *Journal of the Acoustical Society of America* **91**: 2911–2925.

Perkell, J. S. and W. L. Nelson (1985). "Variability in the production of the vowels /i/ and /a/." *Journal of the Acoustical Society of America* **77**: 1889–1895.

Perrett, D. I., M. H. Harries, R. Bevan, S. Thomas, P. J. Benson, A. J. Mistlin, A. J. Chitty, J. K. Hietanen and J. E. Ortega (1989). "Frameworks of analysis for the neural representation of animate objects and actions." *Journal of Experimental Biology* **146**: 87–113.

Perrier, P., Y. Payan, J. S. Perkell, M. Zandipour, X. Pelorson, V. Coisy and M. L. Matthies (2000). *An attempt to simulate fluid-walls interactions during velar stops*. Seminar on Speech Production: Models and Data. Munich, Germany, pp. 149–152.

Petajan, E. D. (1984). *Automatic lipreading to enhance speech recognition*. Global Telecommunications Conference. Atlanta, GA, pp. 265–272.

Petajan, E. D., B. Bischoff, D. Bodoff and N. M. Brooke (1988a). *An improved automatic lipreading system to enhance speech recognition*. CHI 88 Conference Proceedings: Human Factors in Computing Systems. Washington, DC, pp. 19–25.

Petajan, E. D., N. M. Brooke, B. J. Bischoff and D. A. Bodoff (1988b). *Experiments in automatic visual speech recognition*. Symposium of the Federation of Acoustical Societies of Europe (FASE). Edinburgh, pp. 1163–1170.

Pettito, L., R. J. Zatorre, K. Gauna, E. J. Nikelski, D. Dostie and A. C. Evans (2000). "Speech-like cerebral activity in profoundly deaf people processing signed languages: Implications for the neural basis of human language." *National Academy of Sciences* **97**(25): 13961–13966.

Pigeon, S. and L. Vandendorpe (1997). The M2VTS multimodal face database. *Audio and Video-based Biometric Person Authentication*. J. Bigün, G. Chollet and G. Borgefors. Berlin, Springer: 403–409.

Pighin, F., J. Hecker, D. Lischinski, R. Szeliski and D. H. Salesin (1998). *Synthesizing realistic facial expressions from photographs*. Proceedings of SIGGRAPH. Orlando, FL, USA, pp. 75–84.

Pighin, F., R. Szeliski and D. H. Salesin (1999). "Resynthesizing facial animation through 3D model-based tracking." *International Conference on Computer Vision* **1**: 143–150.

(2002). "Modeling and animating realistic faces from images." *International Journal of Computer Vision* **50**(2): 143–169.

Pike, G. E., R. I. Kemp, N. A. Towell and K. C. Phillips (1997). "Recognising moving faces: The relative contribution of motion and perspective view information." *Visual Cognition* **4**(4): 409–437.

Pilling, M. (2009). "Auditory event-related potentials (ERPs) in audiovisual speech perception." *Journal of Speech, Language and Hearing Research* **52**(4): 1073–1081.

Pisoni, D. B. and R. E. Remez (2004). *Handbook of Speech Perception*. Cambridge, MA, MIT Press.

Pitermann, M. (2004). *Chaos dans la modélisation des tissus mous*. Journées d'Etude sur la Parole. Fez, Morocco, pp. 401–404.

Pitermann, M. and K. G. Munhall (2001). "An inverse dynamics approach to facial animation." *Journal of the Acoustical Society of America* **110**: 1570–1580.

Plant, G. L. (1980). "Visual identification of Australian vowels and diphthongs." *Australian Journal of Audiology* **2**: 83–91.

Platt, S. M. and N. I. Badler (1981). "Animating facial expressions." *Computer Graphics* **15**(3): 245–252.

Pockaj, R., M. Costa, F. Lavagetto and C. Braccini (1999). *MPEG-4 facial animation: an implementation*. International Workshop on Synthetic–Natural Hybrid Coding and Three Dimensional Imaging. Santorini, Greece, pp. 33–36.

Poggio, T. and T. Vetter (1992). Recognition and structure from one 2D model view: observations on prototypes, object classes and symmetries. Boston, MA, MIT AI Lab., Tech. Rep. 1347.

Pollick, F. E., H. Hill, A. Calder and H. Paterson (2003). "Recognising facial expression from spatially and temporally modified movements." *Perception* **32**: 813–826.

Polymenakos, L., P. Olsen, D. Kanevsky, R. A. Gopinath, P. S. Gopalakrishnan and S. Chen (1998). *Transcription of broadcast news – some recent improvements to IBM's LVCSR system*. International Conference on Acoustics, Speech, and Signal Processing. Seattle, WA, pp. 901–904.

Potamianos, G. and H. P. Graf (1998). *Discriminative training of HMM stream exponents for audio-visual speech recognition*. International Conference on Acoustics, Speech and Signal Processing. Seattle, WA, pp. 3733–3736.

Potamianos, G., H. P. Graf and E. Cosatto (1998). *An image transform approach for HMM based automatic lipreading*. International Conference on Image Processing. Chicago, IL, pp. 173–177.

Potamianos, G., J. Luettin and C. Neti (2001c). *Hierarchical discriminant features for audio-visual LVCSR*. International Conference on Acoustics, Speech and Signal Processing. Salt Lake City, UT, pp. 165–168.

Potamianos, G. and C. Neti (2000). *Stream confidence estimation for audio-visual speech recognition*. International Conference on Spoken Language Processing. Beijing, China, pp. 746–749.

Potamianos, G. and C. Neti (2001a). *Automatic speechreading of impaired speech*. International Conference on Auditory-Visual Speech Processing. Aalborg, Denmark, pp. 177–182.

Potamianos, G. and C. Neti (2001b). *Improved ROI and within frame discriminant features for lipreading*. International Conference on Image Processing. Thessaloniki, Greece, pp. 250–253.

Potamianos, G. and C. Neti (2003). *Audio-visual speech recognition in challenging environments*. European Conference on Speech Communication Technology. Geneva, Switzerland, pp. 1293–1296.

Potamianos, G., C. Neti, G. Gravier, A. Garg and A. W. Senior (2003). "Recent advances in the automatic recognition of audiovisual speech." *Proceedings of the IEEE* **91**(9): 1306–1326.

Potamianos, G., C. Neti, G. Iyengar and E. Helmuth (2001a). *Large-vocabulary audio-visual speech recognition by machines and humans*. EuroSpeech. Aalborg, Denmark.

Potamianos, G., C. Neti, G. Iyengar, A. W. Senior and A. Verma (2001b). "A cascade visual front end for speaker independent automatic speechreading." *International Journal of Speech Technology* **4**(3–4): 193–208.

Potamianos, G. and A. Potamianos (1999). *Speaker adaptation for audio-visual speech recognition*. European Conference on Speech Communication and Technology. Budapest, Hungary, pp. 1291–1294.

Potamianos, G. and P. Scanlon (2005). *Exploiting lower face symmetry in appearance-based automatic speechreading*. Workshop on Audio-Visual Speech Processing. Vancouver Island, Canada, pp. 79–84.

Preminger, J. E., H.-B. Lin, M. Payen and H. Levitt (1998). "Selective visual masking in speechreading." *Journal of Speech, Language, and Hearing Research* **41**: 564–575.

Press, W. H., B. P. Flannery, S. A. Teukolsky and W. T. Vetterling (1995). *Numerical Recipes in C. The Art of Scientific Computing*. Cambridge University Press.

Puce, A., T. Allison, S. Bentin, J. C. Gore and G. McCarthy (1998). "Temporal cortex activation in humans viewing eye and mouth movements." *Journal of Neurosciences* **18**: 2188–2199.

Pullen, K. and C. Bregler (2002). *Motion capture assisted animation: texturing and synthesis*. SIGGRAPH. San Antonio, TX, pp. 501–508.

Rabiner, L. R. (1989a). "A tutorial on hidden Markov models and selected applications in speech recognition." *IEEE Transactions on Audio, Speech, and Language Processing* **77**: 257–286.

(1989b). "A tutorial on hidden Markov models and selected applications in speech recognition." *Proceedings of the IEEE* **77**: 257–286.

Rabiner, L. R. and B.-H. Juang (1993). *Fundamentals of Speech Recognition*. Englewood Cliffs, NJ, Prentice Hall.

Rao, C. R. (1965). *Linear Statistical Inference and Its Applications*. New York, John Wiley and Sons.

Raphael, L. J. (1971). "Preceding vowel duration as a cue to the perception of the voicing characteristic of word final consonants in American English." *Journal of the Acoustical Society of America* **51**: 1296–1303.

Rauschecker, J. P. and S. K. Scott (2009). "Maps and streams in the auditory cortex: nonhuman primates illuminate human speech processing." *Nature Neuroscience Reviews* **12**(6): 718–724.

Reale, R. A., G. A. Calvert, T. Thesen, R. L. Jenison, H. Kawasaki, H. Oya, M. A. Howard and J. F. Brugge (2007). "Auditory-visual processing represented in the human superior temporal gyrus." *Neuroscience* **145**(1): 162–184.

Reed, C. M., W. M. Rabinowitz, N. I. Durlach and L. D. Braida (1985). "Research on the Tadoma method of speech communication." *Journal of the Acoustical Society of America* **77**(1): 247–256.
Reed, C. M., W. M. Rabinowitz, N. I. Durlach, L. A. Delhorne, L. D. Braida, J. C. Pemberton, B. D. Mulcahey and D. L. Washington (1992). "Analytic study of the Tadoma method: improving performance through the use of supplementary tactual displays." *Journal of Speech and Hearing Research* **35**: 450–465.
Reisberg, D., J. McLean and A. Goldfield (1987). Easy to hear but hard to understand: a lipreading advantage with intact auditory stimuli. *Hearing by Eye: The Psychology of LipReading*. B. Dodd and R. Campbell. Hillsdale, NJ, Erlbaum: 97–113.
Reitsma, P. S. A. and N. S. Pollard (2007). "Evaluating motion graphs for character animation." *ACM Transactions on Graphics* **26**(4): 18-es.
Remez, R. E. (1994). A guide to research on the perception of speech. *Handbook of Psycholinguistics*. M. A. Gernsbacher. New York, Academic Press: 145–172.
(1996). "Auditory form and gestural topology in the perception of speech." *Journal of the Acoustical Society of America* **99**: 1695–1698.
Remez, R. E., J. M. Fellowes, D. B. Pisoni, W. D. Goh and P. E. Rubin (1998). "Multimodal perceptual organization of speech: Evidence from tone analogs of spoken utterances." *Speech Communication* **26**: 65–73.
Remez, R. E., J. M. Fellowes and P. E. Rubin (1997). "Talker identification based on phonetic information." *Journal of Experimental Psychology: Human Perception and Performance* **23**: 651–666.
Remez, R. E., P. E. Rubin, S. M. Berns, J. S. Pardo and J. M. Lang (1994). "On the perceptual organization of speech." *Psychological Review* **101**(1): 129–156.
Remez, R. E., P. E. Rubin, D. B. Pisoni and T. D. Carrell (1981). "Speech perception without traditional speech cues." *Science* **212**: 947–950.
Revéret, L., G. Bailly and P. Badin (2000). *MOTHER: a new generation of talking heads providing a flexible articulatory control for video-realistic speech animation*. International Conference on Speech and Language Processing. Beijing, China, pp. 755–758.
Revéret, L. and C. Benoît (1998). *A new 3D lip model for analysis and synthesis of lip motion in speech production*. Auditory-Visual Speech Processing Workshop (AVSP). Terrigal, Australia, pp. 207–212.
Rivet, B., L. Girin and C. Jutten (2007). "Visual voice activity detection as a help for speech source separation from convolutive mixtures." *Speech Communication* **49** (7–8): 667–677.
Rizzolatti, G. and M. A. Arbib (1998). "Language within our grasp." *Trends In Neurosciences* **21**: 188–194.
Rizzolatti, G. and L. Craighero (2004). "The mirror-neuron system." *Annual Review of Neuroscience* **27**: 169–192.
Rizzolatti, G., L. Fadiga, V. Gallese and L. Fogassi (1996a). "Premotor cortex and the recognition of motor actions." *Cognitive Brain Research* **3**: 131–141.
Rizzolatti, G., L. Fadiga, M. Matelli, V. Bettinardi, E. Paulesu, D. Perani and F. Fazio (1996b). "Localization of grasp representations in humans by PET: I. Observation versus execution." *Experimental Brain Research* **111**: 246–252.
Rizzolatti, G., L. Fogassi and V. Gallese (2000). "Mirror neurons: Intentionality detectors?" *International Journal of Psychology* **35**: 205–205.

Robert-Ribes, J., T. Lallouache, P. Escudier and J.-L. Schwartz (1993). *Integrating auditory and visual representations for audiovisual vowel recognition*. Eurospeech. Berlin, pp. 1753–1756.

Robert-Ribes, J., M. Piquemal, J.-L. Schwartz and P. Escudier (1996). Exploiting sensor fusion architectures and stimuli complementarity in AV speech recognition. *Speechreading by Humans and Machines*. D. G. Stork and M. E. Hennecke. Berlin, Springer: 193–210.

Robert-Ribes, J., J.-L. Schwartz, T. Lallouache and P. Escudier (1998). "Complementarity and synergy in bimodal speech: Auditory, visual and audio-visual identification of French oral vowels in noise." *Journal of the Acoustical Society of America* **103**(6): 3677–3689.

Roberts, B., R. J. Summers and P. J. Bailey (2010). "The perceptual organization of sine-wave speech under competitive conditions." *Journal of the Acoustical Society of America* **128**: 804–817.

Rogozan, A. (1999). "Discriminative learning of visual data for audiovisual speech recognition." *International Journal on Artificial Intelligence Tools* **8**(1): 43–52.

Rogozan, A. and P. Deléglise (1998). "Adaptive fusion of acoustic and visual sources for automatic speech recognition." *Speech Communication* **26**(1–2): 149–161.

Rogozan, A., P. Deléglise and M. Alissali (1997). *Adaptive determination of audio and visual weights for automatic speech recognition*. European Tutorial Workshop on Audio-Visual Speech Processing. Rhodes, Greece, pp. 61–64.

Rönnberg, J. (1995). Perceptual compensation in the deaf and blind: Myth or reality? *Compensating for Psychological Deficits and Declines*. R. A. Dixon and L. Bäckman. Mahwah, NJ, Erlbaum: 251–274.

Rönnberg, J., J. Andersson, S. Samuelsson, B. Soderfeldt, B. Lyxell and J. Risberg (1999). "A speechreading expert: The case of MM." *Journal of Speech Language and Hearing Research* **42**: 5–20.

Rönnberg, J., S. Samuelsson and B. Lyxell (1998). Conceptual constraints in sentence-based lipreading in the hearing-impaired. *Hearing by Eye (II): The Psychology of Speechreading and Auditory-visual Speech*. R. Campbell, B. Dodd and D. Burnham. Hove, UK, Psychology Press: 143–153.

Rose, S. A., A. W. Gottfried and W. H. Bridger (1981). "Cross-modal transfer in 6-month-old infants." *Developmental Psychology* **17**: 661–669.

Rosenblum, L. D. (1994). "How special is audiovisual speech integration?" *Current Psychology of Cognition* **13**(1): 110–116.

Rosenblum, L. D., J. A. Johnson and H. M. Saldaña (1996). "Point-light facial displays enhance comprehension of speech in noise." *Journal of Speech and Hearing Research* **39**(6): 1159–1170.

Rosenblum, L. D. and H. M. Saldaña (1996). "An audiovisual test of kinematic primitives for visual speech perception." *Journal of Experimental Psychology: Human Perception and Performance* **22**(2): 318–331.

(1998). Time-varying information for visual speech perception. *Hearing by Eye: Part 2, The Psychology of Speechreading and Audiovisual Speech*. R. Campbell, B. Dodd and D. Burnham. Hillsdale, NJ, Erlbaum: 61–81.

Rosenblum, L. D., M. A. Schmuckler and J. A. Johnson (1997). "The McGurk effect in infants." *Perception & Psychophysics* **59**(3): 347–357.

Rosenblum, L. D., N. M. Smith, S. Nichols, J. Lee and S. Hale (2006). "Hearing a face: Cross-modal speaker matching using isolated visible speech." *Perception & Psychophysics* **68**: 84–93.
Rosetti, A. L. (1968). *Istoria limbii române*. Bucureßti, Editura Pentru Literatura.
Rosner, B. S. and J. B. Pickering (1994). *Vowel Perception and Production*. New York, Oxford University Press.
Roweis, S. (1998). EM algorithms for PCA and SPCA. *Advances in Neural Information Processing Systems 10*. M. I. Jordan, M. J. Kearns and S. A. Solla. Boston, MA, MIT Press: 626–632.
Rowley, H. A., S. Baluja and T. Kanade (1998). "Neural network-based face detection." *IEEE Transactions on Pattern Analysis and Machine Intelligence* **20**(1): 23–38.
Ruiz, A., P. E. Lopez-de-Teruel and M. C. Garrido (1998). "Probabilistic inference from arbitrary uncertainty using mixtures of factorized generalized Gaussians." *Journal of Artificial Intelligence Research* **9**: 167–217.
Runeson, S. and G. Frykholm (1981). "Visual perception of lifted weight." *Journal of Experimental Psychology: Human Perception and Performance* **7**: 733–740.
Sadato, N., T. Okada, M. Honda, K. I. Matsuki, M. Yoshida, K. Kashikura, W. Takei, T. Sato, T. Kochiyama and Y. Yonekura (2005). "Cross modal integration and changes revealed in lip movement, random-dot motion and sign languages in the hearing and deaf." *Cerebral Cortex* **15**: 1113–1122.
Saenko, K. and K. Livescu (2006). *An asynchronous DBN for audiovisual speech recognition*. IEEE Workshop on Spoken Language Technology (SLT). Palm Beach, Aruba.
Saenko, K., K. Livescu, J. Glass and T. Darrell (2009). "Multistream articulatory feature-based models for visual speech recognition." *IEEE Transactions on Pattern Analysis and Machine Intelligence* **31**(9): 1700–1707.
Saffran, J. R., R. N. Aslin and E. L. Newport (1996). "Statistical learning by 8-month-old infants." *Science* **274**: 1926–1928.
Saintourens, M., M.-H. Tramus, H. Huitric and M. Nahas (1990). *Creation of a synthetic face speaking in real time with a synthetic voice*. ETRW on Speech Synthesis. Autrans, France, pp. 249–252.
Saldaña, H. M. and L. D. Rosenblum (1993). "Visual influences on auditory pluck and bow judgments." *Perception & Psychophysics* **54**: 406–416.
(1994). "Selective adaptation in speech perception using a compelling audiovisual adaptor." *Journal of the Acoustical Society of America* **95**: 3658–3661.
Saltzman, E. (1999). *Nonlinear dynamics of temporal patterning in speech*. International symposium on dynamics of the production and perception of speech. Berkeley, CA, pp. 59–65.
Saltzman, E. L. and K. G. Munhall (1989). "A dynamical approach to gestural patterning in speech production." *Ecological Psychology* **1**(4): 1615–1623.
Sams, M., R. Aulanko, M. Hamalainen, R. Hari, O. V. Lounasmaa, S.-T. Lu and J. Simola (1991). "Seeing speech: visual information from lip movements modifies activity in the human auditory cortex." *Neuroscience Letters* **127**: 141–145.
Sams, M. and S. Levänen (1996). Where and when are the heard and seen speech integrated: magnetoencephalographical (MEG) studies. *Speechreading by Humans and Machines*. D. G. Stork and M. E. Hennecke. Berlin, Springer: 233–238.

Sánchez-Soto, E., A. Potamianos and K. Daoudi (2009). "Unsupervised stream-weights computation in classification and recognition tasks." *IEEE Transactions on Audio, Speech, and Language Processing* **17**(3): 436–445.

Sanderson, C. (2003). Automatic person verification using speech and face information. PhD Thesis. School of Microelectronic Engineering; Griffith University: Brisbane, Australia.

Sanderson, C. and K. K. Paliwal (2004). "Identity verification using speech and face information." *Digital Signal Processing* **14**(5): 449–480.

Sanguineti, V., R. Laboissière and D. J. Ostry (1998). "A dynamic biomechanical model for neural control of speech production." *Journal of the Acoustical Society of America* **103**(3): 1615–1627.

Sannen, D., E. Lughofer and H. Van Brussel (2010). "Towards incremental classifier fusion." *Intelligent Data Analysis* **14**(1): 3–30.

Santi, A., P. Servos, E. Vatikiotis-Bateson, T. Kuratate and K. Munhall (2003). "Perceiving biological motion: Dissociating talking from walking." *Journal of Cognitive Neuroscience Letters* **15**(6): 800–809.

Sargin, M. E., Y. Yemez, E. Erzin and A. M. Tekalp (2007). "Audiovisual synchronization and fusion using canonical correlation analysis." *IEEE Transactions on Multimedia* **9**(7): 1396–1403.

Sato, M., G. Buccino, M. Gentilucci and L. Cattaneo (2010). "On the tip of the tongue: modulation of the primary motor cortex during audiovisual speech perception." *Speech Communication* **52**(6): 533–541.

Saxe, R. and N. Kanwisher (2003). "People thinking about thinking people. The role of the temporo-parietal junction in 'theory of mind'." *Neuroimage* **19**: 1835–1842.

Scanlon, P., G. Potamianos, V. Libal and S. M. Chu (2004). *Mutual information based visual feature selection for lipreading*. International Conference on Spoken Language Processing. Jeju Island, Korea.

Scanlon, P. and R. Reilly (2001). *Feature analysis for automatic speechreading*. Workshop on Multimedia Signal Processing. Cannes, France, pp. 625–630.

Scassellati, B. (2001). Foundations for a theory of mind for a humanoid robot. Department of Computer Science and Electrical Engineering; MIT: Boston, MA.

Schiff, W., L. Banka and G. De Bordes Galdi (1986). "Recognising people seen in events via dynamic 'mugshots'." *American Journal of Psychology* **99**: 219–231.

Schmidt, R. A. (1988). *Motor Control and Learning: A Behavioral Emphasis*. Champaign, IL, Human Kinetics Publishers.

Schoedl, A., R. Szeliski, D. H. Salesin and I. Essa (2000). *Video textures*. SIGGRAPH. New Orleans, LA, pp. 489–498.

Schroeder, C. E., P. Lakatos, Y. Kajikawa, S. Partan and A. Puce (2008). "Neuronal oscillations and visual amplification of speech." *Trends in Cognitive Science* **12**(3): 106–113.

Schulman, R. (1988). "Articulatory dynamics of loud and normal speech." *Journal of the Acoustical Society of America* **85**(1): 295–312.

Schultz, J. and K. Pilz (2009). "Natural facial motion enhances cortical responses to faces." *Experimental Brain Research* **194**: 465–475.

Schwartz, J.-L., D. Beautemps, C. Abry and P. Escudier (1993). "Inter-individual and cross-linguistic strategies for the production of the [i] vs [y] contrast." *Journal of Phonetics* **21**: 411–425.

Schwartz, J.-L., F. Berthommier and C. Savariaux (2003). *Auditory syllabic identification enhanced by non-informative visible speech.* Auditory-visual Speech Processing Workshop. St-Jorioz, France, pp. 19–24.

Schweinberger, S. R., A. M. Burton and S. W. Kelly (1999). "Asymmetric dependencies in perceiving identity and emotion: experiments with morphed faces." *Perception & Psychophysics* **61**(6): 1102–1115.

Schweinberger, S. R., T. Klos and W. Sommer (1995). "Covert face recognition in prosopagnosia: A dissociable function?" *Cortex* **31**: 521–536.

Schweinberger, S. R. and G. R. Soukup (1998). "Asymmetric relationships among perceptions of facial identity, emotion, and facial speech." *Journal of Experimental Psychology: Human Perception and Performance* **24**(6): 1748–1765.

Schwippert, C. and C. Benoît (1997). *Audiovisual intelligibility of an androgynous speaker.* ESCA Workshop on Audio-visual Speech Processing: Cognitive and Computational Approaches. Rhodes, Greece, pp. 81–84.

Scobbie, J. M., F. Gibbon, W. J. Hardcastle and P. Fletcher (1998). Covert contrasts and the acquisition of phonetics and phonology. *Clinical Phonetics and Linguistics*. W. Ziegler and K. Deger. London, Whurr: 147–156.

Scott, K. C., D. S. Kagels, S. H. Watson, H. Rom, J. R. Wright, M. Lee and K. J. Hussey (1994). *Synthesis of speaker facial movement to match selected speech sequences.* Australian Conference on Speech Science and Technology. Perth, Australia, pp. 620–625.

Scott, S. D. (1996). A data-driven approach to visual speech synthesis. PhD Thesis, University of Bath.

Scott, S. K. and I. S. Johnsrude (2003). "The neuroanatomical and functional organization of speech perception." *Trends in Neurosciences* **26**: 100–107.

Scott, S. K., C. McGettigan and F. Eisner (2009). "A little more conversation, a little less action. Candidate roles for the motor cortex in speech perception." *Nature Reviews Neuroscience* **10**: 295–302.

Scott, S. K., S. Rosen, H. Lang and R. J. Wise (2006). "Neural correlates of intelligibility in speech investigated with noise vocoded speech – a positron emission tomography study." *Journal of the Acoustical Society of America* **120**: 1075–1083.

Seitz, P. F., L. E. Bernstein and E. T. Auer, Jr. (1995). PhLex (Phonologically Transformable Lexicon): A 35,000-word computer readable pronouncing American English lexicon on structural principles, with accompanying phonological transformation software scripts, and word frequencies. Washington, DC, Gallaudet Research Institute.

Sejnowski, T. J., B. P. Yuhas, M. H. Goldstein and R. E. Jenkins (1990). Combining visual and acoustic speech signals with a neural network improves intelligibility. *Advances in Neural Information Processing Systems*. D. S. Touretzky. San Mateo, CA, Morgan-Kaufman Publishers: 232–239.

Sekiyama, K. (1994). "Differences in auditory-visual speech perception between Japanese and Americans: McGurk effect as a function of incompatibility." *Journal of the Acoustical Society of Japan* **15**: 143–158.

(1997). "Cultural and linguistic factors in audiovisual speech processing: The McGurk effect in Chinese subjects." *Perception & Psychophysics* **59**: 73–80.

Sekiyama, K. and D. Burnham (2008). "Impact of language on development of auditory-visual speech perception." *Developmental Science* **11**(2): 306–320.

Sekiyama, K., I. Kanno, S. Miura and Y. Sugita (2003). "Audiovisual speech perception examined by fMRI and PET." *Neuroscience Reearch* **47**: 277–287.

Sekiyama, K. and Y. Tohkura (1991). "McGurk effect in non-English listeners: Few visual effects for Japanese subjects hearing Japanese syllables of high auditory intelligibility." *Journal of the Acoustical Society of America* **90**: 1797–1805.

(1993). "Inter-language differences in the influence of visual cues in speech perception." *Journal of Phonetics* **21**: 427–444.

Sekular, R., A. B. Sekular and R. Lau (1997). "Sound alters visual motion perception." *Nature* **385**: 308.

Senior, A. W. (1999). *Face and feature finding for a face recognition system.* International Conference on Audio and Video-based Biometric Person Authentication. Washington, DC, pp. 154–159.

Seymour, R., D. Stewart and J. Ming (2008). "Comparison of image transform-based features for visual speech recognition in clean and corrupted video." *EURASIP Journal on Image and Video Processing* **ID 810362**: 9 pages.

Shams, L., Y. Kamitani and S. Shimojo (2000). "What you see is what you hear." *Nature* **408**: 788.

Shao, X. and J. Barker (2008). "Stream weight estimation for multistream audio-visual speech recognition in a multispeaker environment." *Speech Communication* **50**(4): 337–353.

Sheffert, S. M., D. B. Pisoni, J. M. Fellowes and R. E. Remez (2002). "Learning to recognize talkers from natural, sinewave and reversed speech samples." *Journal of Experimental Psychology: Human Perception and Performance* **28**(6): 1447–1469.

Shepard, D. (1968). *A two-dimensional function for irregularly spaced data.* Proceedings ACM National Conference, pp. 517–524.

Shepard, R. N. and S. Chipman (1970). "Second-order isomorphism of internal representations: Shapes of states." *Cognitive Psychology* **1**: 1–17.

Shiga, Y. and S. King (2004). *Source-filter separation for articulation-to-speech synthesis*. International Conference on Speech and Language Processing. Jeju, Korea, pp. 1913–1916.

Shuttleworth, E. C. J., V. Syring and N. Allen (1982). "Further observations on the nature of prosopagnosia." *Brain and Cognition* **1**: 752–765.

Siegler, M. A. (1995). Measuring and compensating for the effects of speech rate in large vocabulary continuous speech recognition. PhD Thesis, Carnegie Mellon University, Pittsburgh, PA.

Sifakis, E., I. Neverov and R. Fedkiw (2005). "Automatic determination of facial muscle activations from sparse motion capture marker data." *ACM Transactions on Graphics (SIGGRAPH Proceedings)* **24**: 417–425.

Silsbee, P. L. (1994). *Motion in deformable templates*. International Conference on Image Processing. Austin, TX, pp. 323–327.

Silsbee, P. L. and A. C. Bovik (1996). "Computer lipreading for improved accuracy in automatic speech recognition." *IEEE Transactions on Speech and Audio Processing* **4**(5): 337–351.

Simons, A. D. and S. J. Cox (1990). *Generation of mouthshapes for a synthetic talking head.* Proceedings of the Institute of Acoustics, Autumn Meeting. Windermere, England, pp. 475–482.

Singer, G. and R. H. Day (1969). "Visual capture of haptically-judged depth." *Perception & Psychophysics* **5**: 315–316.
Siva, N. (1995). The effects of motor inexperience on perception of the auditory-visual illusion in speech perception. Unpublished MSc Thesis, University of Washington.
Siva, N., E. B. Stevens, P. K. Kuhl and A. N. Meltzoff (1995). "A comparison between cerebral-palsied and normal adults in the perception of auditory-visual illusions." *Journal of the Acoustical Society of America* **98**: 2983.
Sjolander, K. and J. Beskow (2000). *Wavesurfer – an open source speech tool.* International Conference on Speech and Language Processing. Beijing, China, pp. 464–467.
Skipper, J. I., H. C. Nusbaum and S. L. Small (2005). "Listening to talking faces: motor cortical activation during speech perception." *Neuroimage* **25**: 76–89.
Skipper, J. I., V. van Wassenhove, H. C. Nusbaum and S. L. Small (2007). "Hearing lips and seeing voices: how cortical areas supporting speech production mediate audio-visual speech perception." *Cerebral Cortex* **17**(10): 2387–2399.
Slaney, M. and M. Covell (2000). *FaceSync: a linear operator for measuring synchronization of video facial images and audio tracks.* Neural Information Processing Systems (NIPS). Denver, CO, pp. 814–820.
Slotine, J.-J. E. and W. Lohmiller (2001). "Modularity, evolution, and the binding problem: a view from stability theory." *Neural Networks* **14**: 137–145.
Smeele, P. M. T. (1996). Psychology of human speechreading. *Speechreading by Humans and Machines*. D. G. Stork and M. E. Hennecke. Berlin, Springer: 3–15.
Smith, Z. M., B. Delgutte and A. J. Oxenham (2002). "Chimaeric sounds reveal dichotomies in auditory perception." *Nature* **416**: 87–90.
Söderfeldt, B., M. Ingvar, J. Ronnberg, L. Eriksson, M. Serrander and S. Stone-Elander (1997). "Signed and spoken language perception studied by positron emission tomography." *Neurology* **49**: 82–87.
Sodoyer, D., L. Girin, C. Jutten and J.-L. Schwartz (2004). "Developing an audio-visual speech source separation algorithm." *Speech Communication* **44**(1–4): 113–125.
Sproat, R. (1998). *Multilingual Text-to-Speech Synthesis: The Bell Labs Approach*. Boston, MA, Kluwer.
Stager, C. L. and J. F. Werker (1997). "Infants listen for more phonetic detail in speech perception than in word-learning tasks." *Nature* **388**: 381–382.
(1998). Methodological issues in studying the link between speech-perception and word learning. *Advances in Infancy Research*. C. Rovee-Collier, L. Lipsitt and H. Hayne. Stamford, CT, Ablex.
Steede, L. L., J. J. Tree and G. J. Hole (2007). "I can't recognize your face but I can recognize it's movement." *Cognitive Neuropsychology* **24**: 451–466.
Stein, B. E. and M. A. Meredith (1993). *The Merging of the Senses*. Cambridge, MA, MIT Press.
Stetson, R. H. (1928). *Motor Phonetics*. Amsterdam, North-Holland.
Stevens, J. A., P. Fonlupt, M. Shiffrar and J. Decety (2000). "New aspects of motion perception: Selective neural encoding of apparent human movements." *Neuroreport* **11**: 109–115.
Stevens, K. N. (1981). Constraints imposed by the auditory system on the properties used to classify speech sounds: Data from phonology, acoustics, and psychoacoustics.

The Cognitive Representation of Speech. T. Myers, J. Laver and J. Anderson. Amsterdam, North-Holland.
(1989a). "On the quantal nature of speech." *Journal of Phonetics* **17**(1/2): 3–45.
(1989b). "Primary features and their enhancement in consonants." *Language* **65**: 81–106.
(1998). *Acoustic Phonetics*. Cambridge, MA, MIT Press.
and A. S. House (1955). "Development of quantitative description of vowel articulation." *Journal of the Acoustical Society of America* **27**: 484–493.
Stevenson, R. A., N. A. Altieri, S. Kim, D. B. Pisoni and T. W. James (2010). "Neural processing of asynchronous audiovisual speech perception." *Neuroimage* **49**(4): 3308–3318.
Stoel-Gammon, C. (1988). "Prelinguistic vocalizations of hearing-impaired and normally hearing subjects: A comparison of consonantal inventories." *Journal of Speech Hearing Disorders* **53**: 302–315.
Stone, M. (1990). "A three dimensional model of tongue movement based on ultrasound and x-ray microbeam data." *Journal of the Acoustical Society of America* **87**: 2207–2217.
Stone, M., D. DeCarlo, I. Oh, C. Rodriguez, A. Stere, A. Lees and C. Bregler (2004). "Speaking with hands: creating animated conversational characters from recordings of human performance." *ACM Transactions on Graphics* **23**(3): 506–513.
Stone, M., D. Dick, A. S. Douglas, E. P. Davis and C. Ozturk (2000). *Modelling the internal tongue using principal strains*. 5th Seminar on Speech Production: Models and Data & CREST Workshop on Models of Speech Production: Motor Planning and Articulatory Modelling. Kloster Seeon, Germany, pp. 133–136.
Stone, M., M. H. Goldstein and Y. Zhang (1997). "Principal component analysis of cross sections of tongue shapes in vowel production." *Speech Communication* **22**: 173–184.
Stone, M. and A. Lundberg (1996). "Three-dimensional tongue surface shapes of English consonants and vowels." *Journal of the Acoustical Society of America* **99** (6): 3728–3737.
Stone, M. and E. Vatikiotis-Bateson (1995). "Trade-offs in tongue, jaw, and palate contributions to speech production." *Journal of Phonetics* **23**: 81–100.
Stork, D. G. and M. E. Hennecke (1996). *Speechreading by Humans and Machines*. Berlin, Springer.
Stork, D. G., M. E. Hennecke and K. V. Prasad (1996). Visionary speech: looking ahead to practical speechreading systems. *Speechreading by Humans and Machines*. D. G. Stork and M. E. Hennecke. Berlin, Springer: 331–350.
Stork, D. G., G. Wolff and E. Levine (1992). *Neural network lipreading system for improved speech recognition*. IEEE International Joint Conference on Neural Networks. Baltimore, MD, pp. 285–295.
Story, B. H. (2009). "Vocal tract modes based on multiple area function sets from one speaker." *Journal of the Acoustical Society of America* **125**(4): 141–147.
Strange, W. and O.-S. Bohn (1998). "Dynamic specification of coarticulated German vowels." *Journal of the Acoustical Society of America* **104**(1): 488–504.
Strelnikov, K., J. Rouger, J. F. Demonet, S. Lagleyre, B. Fraysse, O. Deguine and P. Barone (2010). "Does brain activity at rest reflect adaptive strategies? Evidence from speech processing after cochlear implantation." *Cerebral Cortex* **10**: 1217–1222.

Studdert-Kennedy, M. (1986). Development of the speech perceptuo-motor system. *Precursors of Early Speech*. B. Lindblom and R. Zetterstrom. New York, Stockton Press: 206–217.

(1989). Visual perception of phonetic gestures. *Handbook of Research on Face Processing*. A. W. Young and H. D. Ellis. Amsterdam, Elsevier: 217–222.

(1991). Language development from an evolutionary perspective. *Biological and Behavioral Determinants of Language Development*. N. A. Krasnegor, D. M. Rumbaugh, R. L. Schiefelbusch and M. Studdert-Kennedy. Hillsdale, NJ, Erlbaum: 5–28.

Su, Q. and P. L. Silsbee (1996). *Robust audiovisual integration using semicontinuous hidden Markov models*. International Conference on Spoken Language Processing. Philadelphia, PA, pp. 42–45.

Suh, M.-W., H.-J. Lee, J. S. Kim, C. K. Chung and S. A. Oh (2009). "Speech experience shapes the speechreading network and subsequent deafness facilitates it." *Brain* **132**: 2761–2771.

Sumby, W. H. and I. Pollack (1954). "Visual contribution to speech intelligibility in noise." *Journal of the Acoustical Society of America* **26**: 212–215.

Summer, W. V., D. B. Pisoni, R. H. Bernacki, R. I. Pedlow and M. A. Stokes (1988). "Effects of noise on speech production: acoustic and perceptual analyses." *Journal of the Acoustical Society of America* **84**(3): 917–928.

Summerfield, A., A. MacLeod, M. McGrath and M. Brooke (1989). Lips, teeth, and the benefits of lipreading. *Handbook of Research on Face Processing*. A. W. Young and H. D. Ellis. Amsterdam, Elsevier: 223–233.

Summerfield, Q. (1979). "Use of visual information for phonetic perception." *Phonetica* **36**: 314–331.

(1987). Some preliminaries to a comprehensive account of audio-visual speech perception. *Hearing by Eye: The Psychology of Lipreading*. B. Dodd and R. Campbell. Hillsdale, NJ, Erlbaum: 3–51.

(1991). Visual perception of phonetic gestures. *Modularity and the Motor Theory of Speech Perception*. I. G. Mattingly and M. Studdert-Kennedy. Hillsdale, NJ, Erlbaum: 117–138.

Summerfield, Q. and P. F. Assmann (1989). "Auditory enhancement and the perception of concurrent vowels." *Perception & Psychophysics* **45**: 529–536.

Summerfield, Q. and M. McGrath (1984). "Detection and resolution of audio-visual incompatibility in the perception of vowels." *Quarterly Journal of Experimental Psychology* **36A**: 51–74.

Sung, K. and T. Poggio (1998). "Example-based learning for view-based human face detection." *IEEE Transactions on Pattern Analysis and Machine Intelligence* **20**(1): 39–51.

Sussman, H., C. Duder, E. Dalston and A. Cacciatore (1999). "Acoustic analysis of the development of CV coarticulation: a case study." *Journal of Speech, Language, and Hearing Research* **42**: 1080–1096.

Sussman, H. M., H. A. McCaffrey and S. A. Matthews (1991). "An investigation of locus equations as a source of relational invariance for stop place categorization." *Journal of the Acoustical Society of America* **90**(3): 1309–1325.

Sweet, H. (1880). "Sound notation." *Transactions of the Philological Society*: 177–235.

Swets, D. L. and J. Weng (1996). "Using discriminant eigenfaces for image retrieval." *IEEE Transactions on Pattern Analysis and Machine Intelligence* **18**(8): 831–836.

Szeliski, R. and S. Lavallée (1996). "Matching 3-D anatomical surfaces with non-rigid deformations using octree-splines." *International Journal of Computer Vision* **18** (2): 171–186.

Szycik, G. R., H. Jansma and T. F. Münte (2009). "Audiovisual integration during speech comprehension: an fMRI study comparing ROI-based and whole brain analyses." *Human Brain Mapping* **30**(7): 1990–1999.

Tabain, M. and A. Butcher (1999). "Stop consonants in Yanyuwa and Yindjibarndi: locus equation data." *Journal of Phonetics* **27**: 333–357.

Tamura, M., S. Kondo, T. Masuko and T. Kobayashi (1999). *Text-to-audio-visual speech synthesis based on parameter generation from HMM*. EUROSPEECH. Budapest, Hungary, pp. 959–962.

Tamura, M., T. Masuko, T. Kobayashi and K. Tokuda (1998). *Visual speech synthesis based on parameter generation from HMM: speech-driven and text-and-speech-driven approaches*. Auditory-visual Speech Processing Workshop. Terrigal, Sydney, Australia, pp. 219–224.

Tamura, S., K. Iwano and S. Furui (2005). *A stream-weight optimization method for multi-stream HMMs based on likelihood value normalization*. International Conference on Acoustics, Speech and Signal Processing. Philadelphia, PA, pp. 469–472.

Tanaka, J. W. and M. J. Farah (1993). "Parts and wholes in face recognition." *Quarterly Journal of Experimental Psychology: Human Experimental Psychology* **46**(2): 225–245.

Tao, J., L. Xin and P. Yin (2009). "Realistic visual speech synthesis based on hybrid concatenation method." *IEEE Transactions on Audio, Speech, and Language Processing* **17**(3): 469–477.

Teissier, P., J. Robert-Ribes and J.-L. Schwartz (1999). "Comparing models for audio-visual fusion in a noisy-vowel recognition task." *IEEE Transactions on Speech and Audio Processing* **7**(6): 629–642.

Tenenbaum, J. B., V. de Silva and J. C. Langford (2000). "A global geometric framework for nonlinear dimensionality reduction." *Science* **290**: 2319–2323.

Terry, L. H. and A. K. Katsaggelos (2008). *A phone-viseme dynamic Bayesian network for audio-visual automatic speech recognition*. International Conference on Pattern Recognition. Tampa, FL, pp. 1–4.

Terry, L. H., D. J. Shiell and A. K. Katsaggelos (2008). *Feature space video stream consistency estimation for dynamic stream weighting in audio-visual speech recognition*. International Conference on Image Processing. San Diego, CA, pp. 1316–1319.

Terzopoulos, D. and K. Waters (1990). "Physically-based facial modeling, analysis and animation." *Journal of Visual and Computer Animation* **1**: 73–80.

(1993). "Analysis and synthesis of facial image sequences using physical and anatomical models." *IEEE Transactions on Pattern Analysis and Machine Intelligence* **15**: 569–579.

Theobald, B.-J. (2007). *Audiovisual speech synthesis*. International Congress of Phonetic Sciences. Saarbrücken, Germany, pp. 285–290.

Theobald, B.-J., S. Fagel, G. Bailly and F. Elisei (2008). *LIPS2008: Visual speech synthesis challenge*. Interspeech. Brisbane, Australia, pp. 2310–2313.

Thomas, S. M. and T. R. Jordan (2004). "Contributions of oral and extraoral facial movement to visual and audiovisual speech perception." *Journal of Experimental Psychology: Human Perception and Performance* **20**(5): 873–888.

Thompson-Schill, S. L. (2005). Dissecting the language organ: a new look at the role of Broca's area in language processing. *Twenty-first Century Psycholinguistics: Four Cornerstones*. A. Cutler. Hillsdale, NJ, Erlbaum: 173–189.

Thrun, S. (1998). "Bayesian landmark learning for mobile robot localization." *Machine Learning* **33**(1): 41–76.

Tiede, M. K. (1996). "An MRI-based study of pharyngeal volume contrasts in Akan and English." *Journal of Phonetics* **24**: 399–421.

Tipping, M. E. and C. M. Bishop (1999). "Mixtures of probabilistic principal component analyzers." *Neural Computation* **11**(2): 443–482.

Titze, I. R., S. S. Schmidt and M. R. Titze (1995). "Phonation threshold pressure in a physical model of the vocal fold mucosa." *Journal of the Acoustical Society of America* **97**(5): 3080–3084.

Toda, T., A. W. Black and K. Tokuda (2004). *Acoustic-to-articulatory inversion mapping with Gaussian mixture model*. ICSLP. Jeju, South Korea, pp. 1129–1132.

(2008). "Statistical mapping between articulatory movements and acoustic spectrum using a Gaussian mixture model." *Speech Communication* **50**(3): 215–227.

Tomlinson, M. J. (1996). A study into the audio and visual integration of speech for automatic recognition. University of Bath.

Tomlinson, M. J., M. J. Russell and N. M. Brooke (1996). *Integrating audio and visual information to provide highly robust speech recognition*. IEEE International Conference on Acoustics, Speech, and Signal Processing. Atlanta, GA, pp. 821–824.

Tootell, R. B. H., J. B. Reppas, A. M. Dale, R. B. Look, M. I. Sereno, R. Malach, T. J. Brady and B. R. Rosen (1995). "Visual motion aftereffect in human cortical area MT revealed by functional magnetic resonance imaging." *Nature* **375**: 139–141.

Tran, V.-A., G. Bailly and H. Loevenbruck (2010). "Improvement to a NAM-captured whisper-to-speech system." *Speech Communication – special issue on Silent Speech Interfaces* **52**(4): 314–326.

Trautmann, S. A., T. Fehr and M. Herrmann (2009). "Emotions in motion: dynamic compared to static facial expressions of disgust and happiness reveal more wide-spread emotion-specific activations." *Brain Research* **1284**: 100–115.

Triesman, A. (1993). The perception of features and objects. *Attention: Selection, Awareness, and Control. A tribute to Donald Broadbent*. A. Baddely and L. Weiskrantz. Oxford, Clarendon Press: 5–35.

Troille, E. (2009). De la perception audiovisuelle des flux oro-faciaux en parole à la perception des flux manuo-faciaux en Langue française Parlée Complétée. Adultes et Enfants: Entendants, Aveugles et Sourds. PhD Thesis. GIPSA-Lab; Stendhal University: Grenoble, France: 250 pages.

Troille, E., M.-A. Cathiard and C. Abry (2007). *A perceptual desynchronization study of manual and facial information in French Cued Speech*. ICPhS. Saarbrücken, Germany, pp. 291–296.

(2010). "Speech face perception is locked to anticipation in speech production." *Speech Communication, Special Issue: Speech and Face-to-Face Communication* **52**(6): 513–524.

Trout, J. D. (2001). "The biological basis of speech: What to infer from talking to the animals." *Psychological Review* **108**: 523–549.

Turk, M. and A. Pentland (1991). "Eigenfaces for recognition." *Journal of Cognitive Neuroscience* **3**(1): 71–86.

Tyler, L. K and U. H. Frauenfelder (1987). The process of spoken word recognition: An introduction. *Spoken Word Recognition*. Cambridge, MA, MIT Press.

Uchanski, R., L. Delhorne, A. Dix, L. Braida, C. Reed and N. Durlach (1994). "Automatic speech recognition to aid the hearing impaired: Prospects for the automatic generation of cued speech." *Journal of Rehabilitation Research and Development* **31**: 20–41.

Uno, Y., M. Kawato and R. Suzuki (1989). "Formation and control of optimal trajectory in human multijoint arm movement." *Biological Cybernetics* **61**: 89–101.

Valentine, T. (1991). "A unified account of the effects of distinctiveness, inversion and race in face recognition." *Quarterly Journal of Experimental Psychology* **43A**: 161–204.

Valentine, T. and V. Bruce (1986). "The effects of distinctiveness in recognising and classifying faces." *Perception* **15**: 525–535.

Valentine, T. and A. Ferrara (1991). "Typicality in categorization, recognition and identification: Evidence from face recognition." *British Journal of Psychology* **82**: 87–102.

Valli, C. and C. Lucas (1992). *A Resource Text for ASL Users: Linguistics of American Sign Language*. Washington, DC, Gallaudet University Press.

Van Atteveldt, N. M., V. C. Blau, L. Blomert and R. Goebel (2010). "fMR-adaptation indicates selectivity to audiovisual content congruency in distributed clusters in human superior temporal cortex." *BMC Neuroscience* **11**(11): doi: 10.1186/1471-2202-1111-1111.

van Wassenhove, V., K. W. Grant and D. Peoppel (2005). "Visual speech speeds up the neural processing of auditory speech." *Proceedings of the National Academy of Science, USA* **102**: 1181–1186.

Vanegas, O., A. Tanaka, K. Tokuda and T. Kitamura (1998). *HMM-based visual speech recognition using intensity and location normalization*. International Conference on Spoken Language Processing. Sydney, Australia, pp. 289–292.

Varga, A. P. and R. K. Moore (1990). *Hidden Markov model decomposition of speech and noise*. IEEE International Conference on Acoustics, Speech, and Signal Processing. Albuquerque, New Mexico, pp. 845–848.

Vatikiotis-Bateson, E., I.-M. Eigsti, S. Yano and K. G. Munhall (1998). "Eye movement of perceivers during audiovisual speech perception." *Perception & Psychophysics* **60**: 926–940.

Vatikiotis-Bateson, E., T. Kuratate, M. Kamachi and H. Yehia (1999). *Facial deformation parameters for audiovisual synthesis*. Auditory-Visual Speech Processing Workshop (AVSP). Santa Cruz, CA, University of California, pp. 118–122.

Vatikiotis-Bateson, E., K. G. Munhall, M. Hirayama, Y. C. Lee and D. Terzopoulos (1996). The dynamics of audiovisual behavior in speech. *Speechreading by Humans and Machines*. D. G. Stork and M. E. Hennecke. Berlin, Springer: 221–232.

Vatikiotis-Bateson, E. and H. Yehia (1996). "Physiological modeling of facial motion during speech." *ASJ Transactions of the Technical Committee on Psychological and Physiological Acoustics* **H-96**: 1–8.

Vergyri, D. (2000). Integration of multiple knowledge sources in speech recognition using minimum error training. PhD Thesis, Center for Speech and Language Processing, The Johns Hopkins University.

Vignali, G., H. Hill, T. Kuratate and E. Vatikiotis-Bateson (2003). *Linking the structure and perception of 3D faces: gender, ethnicity, and expressive posture*. Auditory-visual Speech Processing Workshop. St-Jorioz, France, pp. 193–198.

Vignoli, F. and C. Braccini (1999). *A text-speech synchronization technique with applications to talking heads*. Auditory-Visual Speech Processing Conference. Santa Cruz, California, USA, pp. 128–132.

Vihman, M. M., M. A. Macken, R. Miller, H. Simmons and J. Miller (1985). "From babbling to speech: A re-assessment of the continuity issue." *Language* **61**: 397–445.

Vilain, A., C. Abry and P. Badin (1998). *Coarticulation and degrees of freedom in the elaboration of a new articulatory plant: Gentiane*. International Congress on Spoken Language Processing. Sydney, Australia, pp. 3147–3150.

(1999). *Motor equivalence evidenced by articulatory modelling*. European Conference on Speech Communication and technology. Budapest, Hungary, pp. 169–172.

(2000). *Coproduction strategies in French VCVs: confronting Öhman's model with adult and developmental articulatory data*. 5th Seminar on Speech Production: Models and Data & CREST Workshop on Models of Speech Production: Motor Planning and Articulatory Modelling. Kloster Seeon, Germany, pp. 81–84.

Viola, P. and M. Jones (2001). *Rapid object detection using a boosted cascade of simple features*. Computer Vision and Pattern Recognition Conference. Kauai, HI, pp. 511–518.

Vitkovich, M. and P. Barber (1994). "Effects of video frame rate on subjects' ability to shadow one of two competing verbal passages." *Journal of Speech and Hearing Research* **37**: 1204–1210.

Vokey, J. R. and J. D. Read (1992). "Familiarity, memorability, and the effect of typicality on the recognition of faces." *Memory & Cognition* **20**: 291–302.

von Kriegstein, K., O. Dogan, M. Grüter, A. L. Giraud, C. A. Kell, T. Grüter, A. Kleinschmidt and S. J. Kiebel (2008). "Simulation of talking faces in the human brain improves auditory speech recognition." *Proceedings of the National Academy of Sciences of the United States of America* **105**(18): 6747–6752.

Wahba, G. (1990). *Spline Models for Observational Data*. Philadelphia, PA, SIAM Press.

Walden, B. E., S. A. Erdman, A. A. Montgomery, D. M. Schwartz and R. A. Prosek (1981). "Some effects of training on speech recognition by hearing-impaired adults." *Journal of Speech and Hearing Research* **24**: 207–216.

Walden, B. E., R. A. Prosek, A. A. Mongomery, C. K. Scherr and C. J. Jones (1977). "Effects of training on the visual recognition of consonants." *Journal of Speech and Hearing Research* **20**: 130–145.

Walker-Andrews, A. S., L. E. Bahrick, S. S. Raglioni and I. Diaz (1991). "Infants' bimodal perception of gender." *Ecological Psychology* **3**: 55–75.

Walker, S., V. Bruce and C. O'Malley (1995). "Facial identity and facial speech processing: Familiar faces and voices in the McGurk effect." *Perception & Psychophysics* **57**(8): 1124–1133.

Wang, C. and M. S. Brandstein (1999). *Multi-source face tracking with audio and visual data*. Workshop on Multimedia Signal Processing. Copenhagen, Denmark, pp. 475–481.

Wark, T. S. and S. Sridharan (1998). *A syntactic approach to automatic lip feature extraction for speaker identification*. International Conference on Acoustics, Speech and Signal Processing. Seattle, WA, pp. 3693–3696.

Warren, C. and J. Morton (1982). "The effects of priming on picture recognition." *British Journal of Psychology* **73**: 117–130.

Warren, J. D., S. K. Scott, C. J. Price and T. D. Griffiths (2006). "Human brain mechanisms for the early analysis of voices." *Neuroimage* **31**: 1389–1397.

Waters, K. (1987). "A muscle model for animating three-dimensional facial expression." *Computer Graphics* **21**(4): 17–24.

Waters, K. and D. Terzopoulos (1992). "The computer synthesis of expressive faces." *Philosophical Transactions of the Royal Society of London (B)* **335**: 87–93.

Watkins, K. E., A. P. Strafella and T. Paus (2003). "Seeing and hearing speech excites the motor system involved in speech production." *Neuropsychologia* **41**: 989–994.

Watson, S., J. Wright, K. C. Scott, D. S. Kagels, D. Freda and K. J. Hussey (1997). An advanced morphing algorithm for interpolating phoneme images to simulate speech. Jet Propulsion Laboratory, California Institute of Technology.

Weikum, W. M., A. Vouloumanos, J. Navarra, S. Soto-Faraco, N. Sebastian-Galles and J. F. Werker (2007). "Visual language discrimination in infancy." *Science & Consciousness Review* **316**: 1159.

Weiss, F., G. S. Blum and L. Gleberman (1987). "Anatomically based measurement of facial expressions in simulated versus hypnotically induced affect." *Motivation and Emotion* **11**: 67–81.

Welsh, W. J. and D. Shah (1992). "Facial feature image coding using principal components." *Electronics Letters* **28**: 2066–2067.

Werker, J. F. and J. S. Logan (1985). "Cross-language evidence for three factors in speech perception." *Perception & Psychophysics* **37**: 35–44.

Werker, J. F. and R. C. Tees (1984a). "Cross language speech perception: Evidence for perceptual reorganization during the first year of life." *Infant Behavior and Development* **7**: 49–63.

(1984b). "Phonemic and phonetic factors in adult cross-language speech perception." *Journal of the Acoustical Society of America* **75**: 1866–1878.

(1999). "Influences on infant speech processing: Toward a new synthesis." *Annual Review of Psychology* **50**: 509–535.

Wertheimer, M. (1938). Laws of organization in perceptual forms. *Sourcebook of Gestalt Psychology*. W. D. Ellis. London, Routledge & Kegan Paul: 71–88.

Wilhelms-Tricarico, R. (1995). "Physiological modeling of speech production: Methods for modeling soft-tissue articulators." *Journal of the Acoustical Society of America* **5**: 3085–3098.

Williams, G., G. Taylor, K. Smolskiy and C. Bregler (2010). *Body motion analysis for multimodal identity verification*. IEEE International Conference on Pattern Recognition. Istanbul, Turkey.

Williams, J. J., J. C. Rutledge, D. C. Garstecki and A. K. Katsaggelos (1997). *Frame rate and viseme analysis for multimedia applications*. Workshop on Multimedia Signal Processing. Princeton, NJ, pp. 13–18.

Wise, R. J. S., S. K. Scott, S. C. Blank, C. J. Mummery, K. Murphy and E. A. Warburton (2001). "Separate neural subsystems within 'Wernicke's' area." *Brain* **124**: 83–95.

Wojdel, J. C., P. Wiggers and L. J. M. Rothkrantz (2002). *An audio-visual corpus for multimodal speech recognition in Dutch language*. International Conference on Spoken Language Processing. Denver, CO, pp. 1917–1920.

Wolberg, G. (1990). *Digital Image Warping*. Los Alamitos, CA, IEEE Computer Society Press.

Woodhouse, L., L. Hickson and B. Dodd (2009). "Review of visual speech perception by hearing and hearing-impaired people: clinical implications." *International Journal of Language and Communication Disorders* **44**(3): 253–270.

Woodland, P. and D. Povey (2002). *Minimum phone error and I-smoothing for improved discriminative training*. International Conference on Acoustics, Speech, and Signal Processing. Orlando, FL, pp. 105–108.

Woodward, M. F. and C. G. Barber (1960). "Phoneme perception in lipreading." *Journal of Speech and Hearing Research* **3**(3): 212–222.

Wozniak, V. D. and P. L. Jackson (1979). "Visual vowel and diphthong perception from two horizontal viewing angles." *Journal of Speech and Hearing Research* **22**: 355–365.

Wrench, A. A. and W. J. Hardcastle (2000). *A multichannel articulatory speech database and its application for automatic speech recognition*. Seminar on Speech Production. Kloster Seeon, Germany, pp. 305–308.

Wright, T. M., K. A. Pelphrey, T. Allison, M. J. McKeown and G. McCarthy (2003). "Polysensory interactions along lateral temporal regions evoked by audiovisual speech." *Cerebral Cortex* **13**: 1034–1043.

Xu, L., A. Krzyzak and C. Y. Suen (1992). "Methods of combining multiple classifiers and their applications in handwritten character recognition." *IEEE Transactions on Systems, Man, and Cybernetics* **22**(3): 418–435.

Yakel, D. A., L. D. Rosenblum and M. A. Fortier (2000). "Effects of talker variability on speechreading." *Perception & Psychophysics* **62**: 1405–1412.

Yamamoto, E., S. Nakamura and K. Shikano (1998). "Lip movement synthesis from speech based on hidden Markov models." *Speech Communication* **26**(1–2): 105–115.

Yau, J. F. S. and A. D. Duffy (1988). "A texture mapping approach to 3-D facial image synthesis." *Computer Graphics Forum* **17**: 129–143.

Yehia, H., T. Kuratate and E. Vatikiotis-Bateson (1999). *Using speech acoustics to drive facial motion*. International Congress of Phonetic Sciences. San Francisco, pp. 631–634.

(2000). *Facial animation and head motion driven by speech acoustics*. 5th Seminar on Speech Production: Models and Data & CREST Workshop on Models of Speech Production: Motor Planning and Articulatory Modelling. Kloster Seeon, Germany, pp. 265–268.

(2002). "Linking facial animation, head motion and speech acoustics." *Journal of Phonetics* **30**(3): 555–568.

Yehia, H. and M. K. Tiede (1997). *A parametric three-dimensional model of the vocal-tract based on MRI data*. IEEE International Conference on Acoustics, Speech and Signal Processing, pp. 1619–1622.

Yehia, H. C., P. E. Rubin and E. Vatikiotis-Bateson (1998). "Quantitative association of vocal-tract and facial behavior." *Speech Communication* **26**: 23–43.

Young, A. W., K. H. McWeeny, D. C. Hay and A. W. Ellis (1986). "Matching familiar and unfamiliar faces on identity and expression." *Psychological Research* **48**: 63–68.

Young, A. W., F. Newcombe, E. H. F. De Haan, M. Small and D. C. Hay (1993). "Face perception after brain injury – Selective impairments affecting identity and expression." *Brain* **166**(4): 941–959.

Young, S. (2008). HMMs and related speech recognition technologies. *Springer Handbook of Speech Processing*. J. Banesty, M. M. Sondhi and Y. Huang. Berlin, Springer: 539–557.

Young, S., D. Kershaw, J. Odell, D. Ollason, V. Valtchev and P. Woodland (1999). *The HTK Book*. Cambridge, Entropic Ltd.

Yuille, A. L., P. W. Hallinan and D. S. Cohen (1992). "Feature extraction from faces using deformable templates." *International Journal of Computer Vision* **8**(2): 99–111.

Železný, M. and P. Cisař (2003). *Czech audio-visual speech corpus of a car driver for in-vehicle audio-visual speech recognition*. International Conference on Audio-Visual Speech Processing, St-Jorioz, France, pp. 169–173.

Zen, H., K. Tokuda and A. W. Black (2009). "Statistical paarametric speech synthesis." *Speech Communication* **51**: 1039–1064.

Zhang, L., N. Snavely, B. Curless and S. M. Seitz (2004). "Spacetime faces: High resolution capture for modeling and animation." *ACM Transactions on Graphics* **23**(3): 548–558.

Zhang, X., C. C. Broun, R. M. Mersereau and M. Clements (2002). "Automatic speech-reading with applications to human–computer interfaces." *EURASIP Journal on Applied Signal Processing*: 1228–1247.

Zhang, Y., S. Levinson and T. Huang (2000). *Speaker independent audio-visual speech recognition*. International Conference on Multimedia and Expo. New York, NY, pp. 1073–1076.

Zotkin, D. N., R. Duraiswami and L. S. Davis (2002). "Joint audio-visual tracking using particle filters." *EURASIP Journal on Applied Signal Processing* **11**: 1154–1164.

Zweig, G. G. (1998). Speech recognition with dynamic Bayesian networks. PhD Thesis. Computer Science Division, University of California: Berkeley, CA.

Index